CORRECTIONS: PAST, PRESENT, AND FUTURE

Jeanne B. Stinchcomb, Ph.D.

Associate Professor, Department of Criminology and Criminal Justice
Florida Atlantic University
Ft. Lauderdale, Florida

Mission of the American Correctional Association

The American Correctional Association provides a professional organization for all individuals and groups, both public and private, that share a common goal of improving the justice system.

American Correctional Association Staff

Gwendolyn Chunn, President
James A. Gondles, Jr., CAE, Executive Director
Gabriella M. Klatt, Director, Communications and Publications
Harry Wilhelm, Marketing Manager
Alice Heiserman, Manager of Publications and Research
Michael Kelly, Associate Editor
Dana M. Murray, Graphics and Production Manager
Michael Selby, Graphics and Production Associate

Cover designed by Joseph Fuller, II

Printed in the United States of America by Versa Press, East Peoria, IL.

ISBN: 1-56991-218-1

This publication may be ordered from:

American Correctional Association
4380 Forbes Boulevard
Lanham, Maryland 20706-4322
1-800-222-5646

For information on publications and videos available from ACA, contact our worldwide web home page at: www.aca.org

Library of Congress Cataloging in Publication Data

Stinchcomb, Jeanne B.
    Corrections: past, present, and future / Jeanne B. Stinchcomb.
      p. cm.
    Includes bibliographical references and index.
    ISBN 1-56991-218-1 (pbk)
Corrections—United States. 2. Corrections—United States—History. I. American Correctional Association. II. Title.

HV9471.S834 2005
364.6'0973—dc22   2004062333

CONTENTS

Part 4: Special Populations, Legal Issues, and the Future

DEDICATION

. . . . . Reflecting the past. . . . . Describing the present. . . . . Building the future

To everyone who has offered inspiration to someone without a dream . . . leadership to someone without direction . . . encouragement to someone without hope. For without you, there would be no change. And without change, there can be no correction.

—Jeanne B. Stinchcomb

PREFACE

Remember when our biggest worry was Y2K? Back then, the prevailing thought was that January 1, 2000, would be the major dividing line in our life. We thought that time would be reckoned according to a before-and-after demarcation of the turn of the century. Some even catastrophically predicted that widespread disaster would accompany our transition into the twenty-first century, but despite our fears, the new century unfolded uneventfully.

Just months later, however, anxieties over international terrorism quickly replaced—and far outpaced—apprehensions about computer crashes. Time is now divided into before and after that fateful moment on September 11, 2001. The date when the twin Trade Towers crumbled truly will live in infamy. New Yorkers, no longer able to focus visually on these familiar landmarks, lost their sense of direction. And for a brief moment, so did we as a nation, but we recovered.

Before September 11, parts of our national well-being had wandered astray. In the aftermath, they were compassionately rediscovered. A complacent population was suddenly more vigilant. Flag-waving came back into style. A nation that had been fragmented by everything from presidential politics to ethnic diversity suddenly found itself united by the threat of a common enemy. We readily shared blood with unknown victims. We generously offered money. Some served in a war abroad. Others stayed alert at home. Patriotism ran rampant. Compassion replaced complacency—at least briefly.

Then, the economy took a nosedive. People sought the safety and security of home. Airlines suffered near-bankruptcy. Tourists disappeared. Unemployment skyrocketed. Businesses laid off employees. Colleges and universities slashed budgets. Retirees who thought their "nest egg" was secure desperately searched for work. Even some prisons closed their doors in a number of states—and not for lack of inmates.

In times like these, we are all reminded that each of us is just a few paychecks away from being destitute, but those who are already over the brink of desperation are affected the most. Many of these individuals are correctional clients: the same clients who have experienced the impact of our "lock-'em-up-and-throw-away-the key" approach to public policy.

In our intensity to remove anyone who offends us from free society, we have created crowded correctional facilities, confronted legal impediments, and encountered fiscal dilemmas. As a result, corrections has suffered from the repercussions of unplanned releases, "no frills" rebellions, and scaled-back programming. Since it is one of the largest components of most state budgets, corrections was an obvious target when tax revenues plummeted following 9/11. As the director of corrections in a state with a deficit in the billions of dollars put it, "You don't save that kind of money by cutting back on toilet paper!" But how much are we really saving by curtailing everything from drug treatment to vocational training? Surely, this is a prime example of how short-term cutbacks incur long-term costs.

Nevertheless, a textbook is not the place for taking sides on such issues. Whatever the topic, readers deserve to have an objective discussion of all points of view to analyze the facts and make informed decisions. Thus, in these upcoming chapters, you will find comprehensive coverage of:

- The need for custody as well as treatment
- The emergence of restorative as well as retributive justice
- The impact of jails as well as prisons
- The development of private as well as public correctional facilities
- The use of community-based alternatives as well as custodial confinement
- The rights as well as restrictions of those behind bars
- The current trends as well as future challenges facing corrections

Balancing the pros and cons, this book tackles controversial issues from capital punishment and three-strikes legislation to inmate amenities, truth-in-sentencing, speculative prisons, electronic monitoring, boot camps, home furloughs, even the use of condoms behind bars. Additionally, this text discusses twenty-first century challenges that are transforming the field today, such as:

- High-tech innovations—from ground-penetrating radar to telemedicine, smart cards, retinal image scanning, satellite surveillance, and variable threat lasers
- Proactive approaches for reducing crowding, controlling inmates, and managing stress
- What works in correctional treatment—from cognitive restructuring to therapeutic communities
- Current trends in staff certification, workforce diversity, vicarious liability, and employee drug testing
- Contemporary approaches to correctional administration, with special emphasis on quality management and visionary leadership

As the title of this book reflects, it seeks to *reflect the past, report the present, and build the future*. In that regard, it is marked by an upbeat optimism that is not generally characteristic of corrections. In a field that society often identifies with past failures, it is difficult to keep focused on a more promising future.

Like the victims of 9/11, the human disasters of corrections can become front-page headlines. The difference is that they do not rate presidential visits.

They do not qualify for federal assistance. They do not arouse heartfelt public compassion. To the contrary, they are more likely to harden a public already convinced that corrections itself is a misnomer—more concerned with how long-term offenders can be segregated than with how well they can be reassimilated.

Working in such an adverse environment, correctional staff face the monumental challenge of maintaining a positive outlook in the face of overwhelming odds against them. In that respect, they share much in common with their clients. Both have a long-term stake in the direction that public policy is heading in the twenty-first century—but then, so do we all.

—Jeanne B. Stinchcomb

ACKNOWLEDGMENTS

Writing a book is never a solitary venture, and this is no exception. From brief insights to boundless efforts, many people contributed to preparing the final product. At the risk of overlooking some, special appreciation is extended to:

- Staff of the *American Correctional Association*—especially *Gabriella Klatt, Alice Heiserman, Michael Kelly, Marc Fisher, Michael Selby, Jack Greene* (formerly of ACA), *Bob Levinson, and Diane Geiman* for their resourceful assistance and productive comments.

- *Caroline Harlow* and *Allen Beck* at the Bureau of Justice Statistics, along with *Howard Snyder* at the Office of Juvenile Justice and Delinquency Prevention (U.S. Department of Justice), whose timely, accurate, and detailed responses to requests for documentation restore one's faith in government's responsiveness.

- Staff of the *National Institute of Corrections' Information Center* and the *National Criminal Justice Reference Center*, whose ongoing help with locating relevant resources was invaluable.

- The *American Jail Association*—particularly *Ken Kerle*, for always "being there" whenever his dependable advice, capable assistance, or networking contacts were needed.

- All of the anonymous reviewers, whose positive feedback provided encouraging support, and whose constructive criticism offered guiding visions for improvement.

- *Kim Ciccarelli, Mark Greenwald, Keisha Woodstock,* and *Wendy Wagner,* former research assistants (now graduates of Florida Atlantic University's master's program in Justice Policy and Management), whose tenacious research capabilities, commitment to excellence, and ongoing perseverance will sorely be missed during the next revision of this book.

- And most importantly—*Jim Stinchcomb*—my professional mentor, personal partner, and perpetual supporter

While responsibility for the contents of this book is mine, recognition for everything from the inspiration to write it to the ability to research it belongs to them. Without some of you, it would not have evolved as well. Without others, it would not have emerged at all.

With admiration for your capabilities, and appreciation for applying them to this project,

—Jeanne B. Stinchcomb

FOREWORD

With the publication of this textbook, the American Correctional Association (ACA) has taken a major step into the academic marketplace. We want to provide students with the most comprehensive up-to-date information that is available—but also to make it readable and interesting. This combination creates a unique textbook. It is accompanied by an instructor's guide that contains learning objectives, discussion questions, website references, test items, and a complete bibliography.

The author, Dr. Jeanne Stinchcomb, is well respected in academic circles. Her prior textbook, *Introduction to Corrections*, was published by Prentice Hall. This book is its worthy successor. Dr. Stinchcomb serves on ACA's Research Council and the Council on Professional Education. She served as chair of the National Commission on Correctional Certification from 2000-2005, so not only is she a qualified academic and writer, she also is involved in the practice of corrections and therefore is well aware of both correctional research and real-world issues.

Since 1870 the American Correctional Association has promoted the education and professional development of correctional practitioners, volunteers and students. We strive to provide the resources professionals working in all facets of the corrections field need to succeed. ACA accomplishes this through our numerous periodicals and publications, online courses, professional certification, national workshops, and member networking. Recently, ACA developed a student chapter program, in which criminal-justice student organizations at colleges and universities can become a chapter of ACA. This enables students to learn more about potential careers in corrections, access ACA resources, and network with practitioners from across the country. Our website, www.aca.org, contains information on all of these programs and resources as well as research information and links to hundreds of organizations dealing with criminal justice issues.

In the meantime, whether you are a practitioner, a student, or both, you will find this book true to its title as it explores the past, describes the present, and looks toward the future. It is comprehensive and reader friendly. But perhaps most importantly, it is realistic.

I wish you much success with your academic studies and professional endeavors.

James A. Gondles, Jr., CAE
Executive Director
American Correctional Association

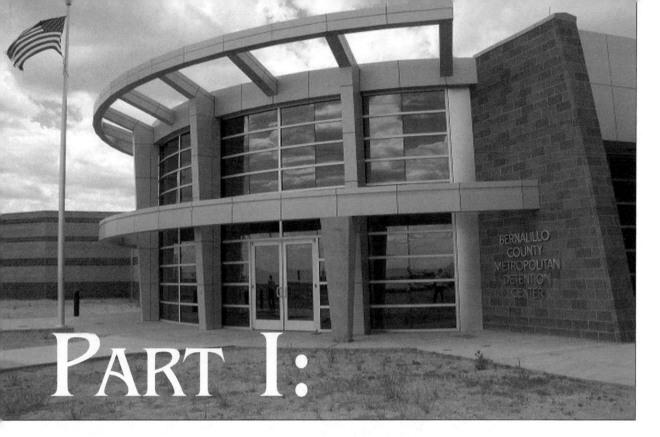

PART I:

THE NATURE, SCOPE, AND FUNCTION OF CORRECTIONS

66 Justice in a democracy demands fair treatment of all citizens, neither ignoring victims nor degrading prisoners.[1] 99

—American Correctional Association

Corrections is both fascinating and frustrating. Changing the direction of an offender's life can be an exciting challenge. Helping a juvenile get back on the right track, guiding an ex-offender toward a law-abiding lifestyle, offering treatment to an alcoholic, or simply making time in a correctional facility more tolerable for an inmate all can be very personally rewarding experiences. Corrections offers unlimited opportunities for such meaningful social contributions—for work that has a purpose and makes a difference.

At the same time, when corrections does not function effectively, it can be a frustrating experience. When the same offenders keep reappearing in the correctional system, when needed resources are unavailable, when there is controversy over what corrections should be accomplishing, when the public is unconcerned and unsupportive, when even other agencies in the criminal justice system do not work cooperatively together, much of the fascination is

Photo, Above: After arrest, most inmates begin their correctional journey at a local jail. Here is the 2,200-bed direct supervision facility of the Bernalillo County Metropolitan Detention Center in New Mexico. Courtesy of Mark Goldman and Associates, project architect/engineers, joint venture of CBL/DCSW (Custer-Basarich, Ltd. and Design Collaborative of the Southwest) with the Durrant Group.

diminished. Facing such obstacles can create confusion and conflict. It also can provide the potential for change—if obstacles are seen as opportunities.

Certainly, there is considerable opportunity for change in corrections. But before exploring where corrections might be tomorrow, it is essential to determine where this field is today and how it got there. Only with an understanding of the past and the present can we begin to shape the future. Thus, Part I of this book focuses on an overview of the nature, scope, and function of corrections.

The framework is set in Chapter 1 with a description of what is included in this vast collection of facilities, programs, and services called "corrections." After providing a better understanding of the correctional conglomerate, Chapter 1 then addresses the fragmented functions and separate jurisdictions, which have emerged from our democratic system of local government control. The public's role in shaping correctional practices is illustrated further by considering the impact of two conflicting models of policymaking—the medical model with its treatment emphasis, and the justice model with its focus on constraining and punishing criminal behavior through incarceration. Pursuing these issues, we realize how correctional practices have changed over time as social opinion has fluctuated.

Based on that foundation, Chapter 2 explores the impact of sentencing policies on corrections. As sentencing practices have shifted from indeterminate (wide-ranging) to determinate (fixed), we see how the nature of structured sentencing guidelines, truth-in-sentencing, and similar approaches fulfill crime-related public policies and generate correctional caseloads and institutional populations. Since it is society's response to crime that is of greatest concern to corrections, Chapter 2 concludes with a review of the various perspectives that have guided public opinion—from retribution, deterrence, and incapacitation to rehabilitation and reintegration.

With this background, Chapter 3 takes a step back in time to see how corrections has evolved. Although we would find it difficult to imagine living in a society without prisons or jails, these have been relatively recent "inventions." The harshness of past punishment practices is described in vivid detail—in contrast to the more humanitarian forces that eventually resulted in the evolution of correctional institutions, the reform movement, and the rehabilitative era. Historical developments are viewed in the context of changing public opinion to explore the relationship between corrections and social policy. This section concludes with a consideration of how the past has shaped the present, along with a challenge for the future—accommodating demands for punishment without abandoning directions toward positive change. In corrections, it is easy to resign oneself to the frustrations. The challenge is to rekindle the fascinations.

Endnote

1.   American Correctional Association, *The American Prison: From the Beginning . . . A Pictorial History*, Lanham, Maryland: American Correctional Association, 1983, p. 253.

CHAPTER 1

THE CORRECTIONAL FRAMEWORK

66 Corrections remains a world almost unknown to law-abiding citizens, and even those within it often know only their own particular corner.[1] **99**

—President's Commission on Law Enforcement
and Administration of Justice

Chapter Overview

Much of the confusion surrounding corrections and what it should be accomplishing is related to the wide variety of institutions, programs, and services provided within what is broadly viewed as "corrections." This chapter therefore begins by considering just what is included within this vast correctional conglomerate—what exactly is corrections? But even understanding the nature of corrections reveals only part of its complexity, for corrections does not operate in isolation. As a component of the criminal justice system, corrections interacts with—and is affected by—both law enforcement and the courts. The criminal justice system, in turn, is part of a broader network of government. As an agency of government, corrections is related to the executive, legislative, and judicial functions of government in general, along with the criminal justice system in particular.

Government, in turn, is influenced by the values, opinions, and interests of society. As a public service ultimately responsive to the community, corrections also is subject to various political and social pressures. At times, these have created conflicting expectations of corrections. When society demands public policies that emphasize goals ranging from retribution and punishment

3

to treatment and rehabilitation, it is sometimes difficult to determine exactly what corrections is supposed to be accomplishing. The question, therefore, becomes not just what corrections is, but what it is expected to do. As a member of society, you not only have a personal stake in the answers, but also a role in shaping them.

✹ Learning Goals

Do you know:

1. Why corrections can be considered a "conglomerate"?
2. The three levels of government at which corrections functions?
3. The differences between prisons and jails?
4. The percentage of inmates under correctional supervision who are confined in custodial institutions, as compared with those under community supervision?
5. The differences between probation and parole?
6. How to define "corrections"?

The Correctional Conglomerate

In private enterprise, a massive business corporation with far-reaching markets, numerous customers, and a vast array of different products and services would be called a "conglomerate." Similarly, a government service composed of as many employees, clients, and diverse activities as corrections also can be considered a conglomerate. The difference between a business conglomerate and corrections is that in corrections you have a personal stake in the "profits" or "losses" of corrections—it is your tax dollars that support it, citizens in your community who are its "customers" or "consumers," and your safety that is involved in its success or failure. Moreover, it is through your elected and appointed government officials that the policies, procedures, and future directions of corrections are established. It is, therefore, in your interest to take a closer look at this correctional conglomerate.

As with any conglomerate, operating the correctional system requires a massive amount of fiscal and human resources. How much does corrections cost? The answer is almost $57 billion annually.[2] As indicated in Figure 1.1, corrections has been receiving a steadily increasing share of total criminal justice resources.

Likewise, Figure 1.2 clearly shows the skyrocketing pace of growth in correctional costs during recent years. As a result, corrections has been consuming an increasing share of tax dollars—far outpacing the growth in educational spending in many states.[3] Already correctional expenditures have overtaken Medicaid as the fastest growing item in state budgets across the country.[4] From 1977 to 2001, state and local expenditures for corrections increased by more than 1,100 percent.[5] Experts are expressing concern that this spending pattern may continue until it hits "critical mass"—the point at which "there are few (or no) resources available for anything else."[6]

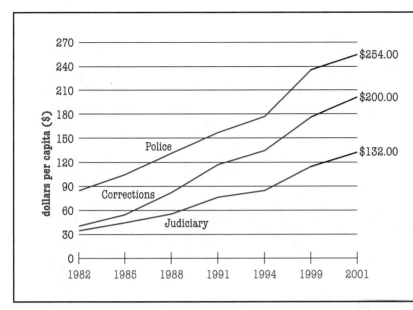

figure 1.1

Per capita expenditures for the justice system.

Source: *Sourcebook of Criminal Justice Statistics*, 2002, Washington, DC: U.S. Department of Justice, 2003, p. 11; and Lynn Bauer and Steven D. Owens, "Justice Expenditure and Employment in the U.S., 2001," *Bureau of Justice Statistics Bulletin*, Washington, DC: U.S. Department of Justice, 2004, p. 8.

How many people does all of that money employ? The more than 747,000 correctional employees throughout the country[7] would populate a large city with people in positions ranging from correctional officers to administrators, social workers, psychologists, psychiatrists, doctors, nurses, lawyers, teachers, counselors, secretaries, and maintenance personnel. In fact, just about every professional and support occupation probably is employed somewhere in the correctional conglomerate. Where do all of these employees work? Four percent work in the federal government, 63 percent work in the fifty states, and 32 percent are in the thousands of localities throughout the United States.[8]

How many clients does this conglomerate serve? Picture the combined populations of Baltimore, Dallas, and San Diego. On any given day, an estimated 6.7 million adults were under some form of correctional supervision.[9] Statistically, of every thirty-two adults, one is currently a correctional client. Of course, you would need to visit a prison or jail to encounter many of them, but do not mistakenly assume that the majority are confined to secure institutions. Most are not.

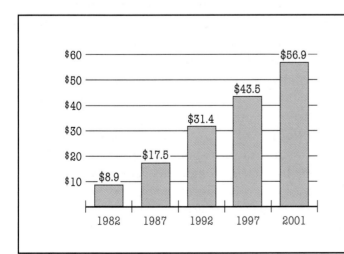

figure 1.2

The cost of corrections (in billions).

Source: Lynn Bauer and Steven D. Owens, "Justice Expenditure and Employment in the U.S., 2001," *Bureau of Justice Statistics Bulletin*, Washington, DC: U.S. Department of Justice, 2004, p. 2.

Jail and prison crowding is not a new phenomenon. Here are jail inmates at the beginning of the last century. Courtesy of the American Correctional Association.

Custodial Institutions

Corrections is easily stereotyped by its most visible physical structures—custodial institutions. For adults, these are prisons and jails. For juveniles, there are training schools, detention centers, and boot camps. In fact, what do you picture when you hear the word "corrections"? Often, your first thought is of a forbidding-looking gray fortress surrounded by thick concrete walls with rifles protruding from guard towers, where expressionless inmates move in dull routines under the constant supervision of uniformed officers. That is generally the image of corrections portrayed in movies and on television. But of all adult inmates housed in correctional institutions throughout the United States, only about 20 percent are serving time in such maximum-security prisons.[10] Far more inmates are confined to *medium-security* institutions—where wire fencing replaces concrete walls, armed towers are nonexistent, and inmate supervision is less intense. The lowest-risk offenders, who can be trusted with more freedom, are serving their sentences or preparing for parole in minimum-security facilities such as halfway houses, which bear no more resemblance to a prison than does a college dormitory or an apartment building.

In addition to being distinguished by their level of security, correctional institutions function within all three levels of government: local, state, and federal. The private sector also provides correctional services and now operates a sizable number of custodial institutions. But in practice, corrections is primarily a function of state government. States are responsible for the operation of prisons, where inmates serving time in excess of one year generally are confined. Those convicted of federal crimes who are sentenced to a year or more serve their time in federal prisons. There are far fewer federal (84) than state (1,320) prisons in the United States.[11]

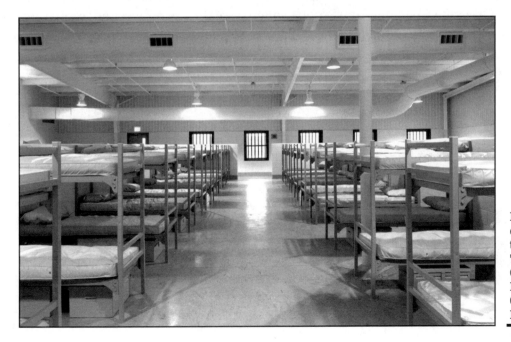

In contrast to prisons, local jails traditionally hold those serving sentences of less than one year and unconvicted persons awaiting trial who either cannot make bail or are determined to be a potential threat to the community if released. The courts later may establish eligibility for some other type of pretrial release program, such as electronic monitoring or release on one's own recognizance. If not, the suspect—who is still innocent in the eyes of the law—remains confined pending trial.

Such unconvicted offenders make up about 60 percent of the population of local jails.[12] This means that almost 400,000 technically innocent people are incarcerated throughout the country, and the longer their trials are delayed,

Dormitory housing, while cost effective, is not appropriate for those needing greater security. This is the dormitory at North Central Correctional Institution, Marion, Ohio. Courtesy of NBBJ, Columbus, Ohio. Photo by Randall Lee Schieber.

the longer they remain incarcerated. That is not meant to imply that many such inmates are not of a sufficient potential threat to the community to justify their confinement. But it does point out that a sizable number of correctional clients at the local level enter the correctional system after arrest by the police but before a formal finding of guilt or innocence by the courts.

While the federal government also incarcerates those serving short sentences or awaiting trial, federal jails are usually called Metropolitan Correctional Centers. There are considerably more local jails (3,365)[13] than state prisons (1,320), but, ironically, there are fewer inmates confined in local jails (665,475) than in state or federal prisons (1,367,856).[14] Although jails are more numerous, they generally are smaller facilities designed to hold fewer offenders.

Noncustodial Alternatives

Most clients in the correctional conglomerate, however, are not serving time in either of these correctional institutions. Of all adults who are under some form of correctional supervision, almost three out of four are not confined in prison or jail.[15] As Figure 1.3 illustrates, the vast majority (70 percent) are actually serving their sentence in the community through such noncustodial alternatives as probation or parole. This certainly dispels any notion that corrections exclusively—or even typically—involves those serving time in secure confinement.

Clients under community supervision are predominately either on probation or parole. As the largest consumers of correctional services, probation and parole can be thought of as the "bookends" of corrections,[16] since they occur on either end of incarceration. That is, probation is usually a community-based sentence provided as an alternative to going to an institution, whereas parole is early release provided as an alternative to remaining in an institution. Both enable the offender to serve time in the community rather than in a correctional facility. But probation is a sentencing alternative used by the courts instead of incarceration, whereas parole is an administrative decision to conditionally release an inmate from prison following a period of confinement.

Despite the fact that such noncustodial alternatives as probation and parole are not the most visible part of corrections, they represent the largest

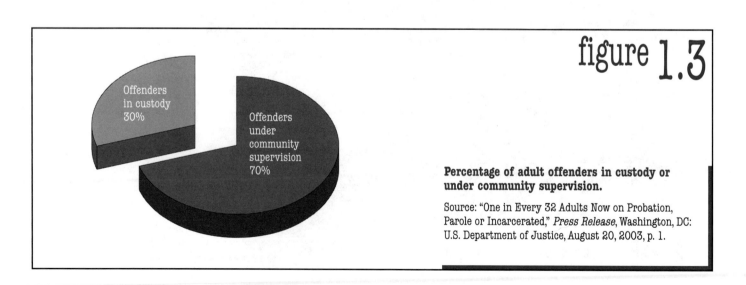

figure 1.3

Percentage of adult offenders in custody or under community supervision.

Source: "One in Every 32 Adults Now on Probation, Parole or Incarcerated," *Press Release*, Washington, DC: U.S. Department of Justice, August 20, 2003, p. 1.

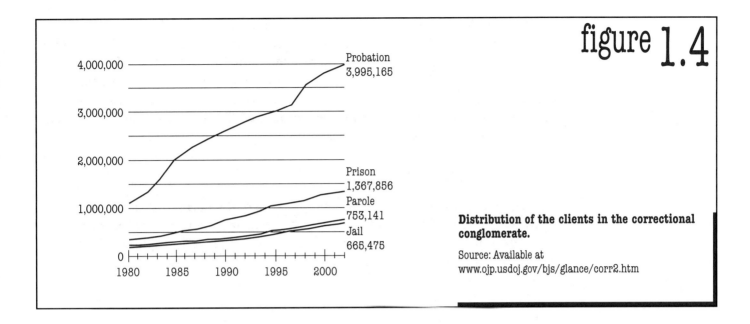

figure 1.4

Distribution of the clients in the correctional conglomerate.

Source: Available at
www.ojp.usdoj.gov/bjs/glance/corr2.htm

component of the correctional conglomerate. Probationers are by far the largest population served by corrections, as shown in Figure 1.4. And even though several states have abolished it, more than 753,000 adults are still on parole.[17] Additionally, noncustodial alternatives are not limited to probation and parole. Some offenders are paying fines, making restitution, or performing community service in lieu of incarceration.

Corrections likewise encompasses criminal suspects who are released from jail after arrest on their "promise to appear" at trial. Growing numbers of these pretrial releasees are being electronically monitored while under "house arrest." That is, they are confined to their home for specified curfew hours, with their presence monitored by electronic devices. Although such alternatives to incarceration are sometimes criticized for being too lenient, they generally are reserved for less serious offenders, and anyone who thinks that one's home cannot be "confining" should read a judge's account of his voluntary experiment with electronic monitoring.[18]

Juvenile Programs and Facilities

The correctional conglomerate is not limited to physical structures and noncustodial alternatives for adults. Also included are juveniles housed in detention or participating in many residential and nonresidential treatment programs. Juvenile correctional services are provided at the local and state levels of government, along with considerable involvement of the private sector.

Like their adult counterparts, most youths are not confined primarily in secure institutions. There are considerably fewer juveniles in locked-down custodial institutions and detention centers than there are on probation or in alternative community-based facilities, group homes, or other programs.[19]

This does not mean that many children are not dealt with as severely as adults, and in some cases, perhaps more severely. Unlike its adult counterpart, the juvenile correctional system embraces a wider clientele. It includes both delinquents (whose offenses would be considered crimes if they were older) and status offenders (whose activities are considered illegal only because of their age), as well as children voluntarily admitted by their parents, and in some cases, even can extend to those who are dependent or neglected. Although corrections does not have jurisdiction over what dispositions juveniles receive by the courts, there is a widespread movement toward dealing more harshly with serious delinquents involved in violent crime, while removing from secure confinement those whose behavior poses no obvious threat to society.

Corrections Defined

Figure 1.5 illustrates the basic components of the correctional conglomerate. Although the specific functions for which this conglomerate is responsible vary in different parts of the country, in general, corrections encompasses the following custodial institutions and noncustodial, community-based alternatives:

Custodial Institutions

- Jails: local correctional institutions for those awaiting trial or serving short sentences (usually medium security)
- Prisons: state or federal correctional institutions for those serving sentences longer than one year (usually, medium or maximum/close security)
- Other (less secure) facilities: local, state, or federal facilities for low-risk offenders serving sentences or preparing for parole, such as halfway houses
- Juvenile detention centers: local or state facilities confining juvenile defendants prior to adjudication
- Training schools and secure institutions: local, state, or private custodial facilities confining adjudicated juvenile offenders

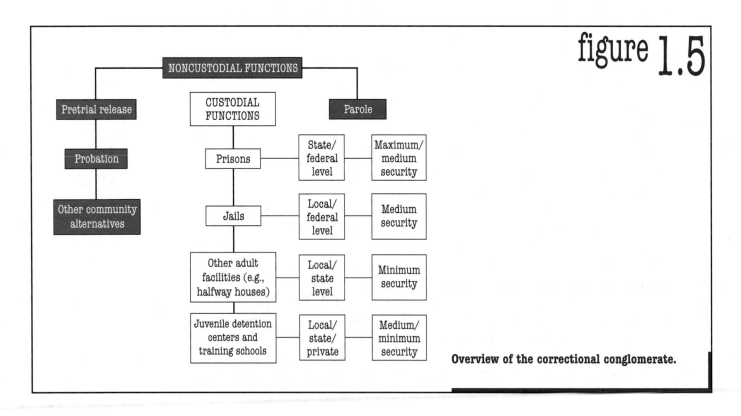

figure 1.5

Overview of the correctional conglomerate.

Noncustodial Alternatives

- Pretrial release programs: alternatives to incarceration for those awaiting trial
- Probation: a conditional sentence that is served under supervision in the community
- Parole (or similarly, mandatory supervised release): conditional release after serving time in prison
- Other community-based programs: restorative justice, restitution, community service, community treatment programs, electronic monitoring, and other noncustodial alternatives
- Group homes and juvenile treatment programs: residential and nonresidential alternatives to secure confinement for juveniles

As the prior listing illustrates, responsibilities of the correctional conglomerate extend from violent criminals in maximum security to far less serious offenders serving time in community-based facilities; from unconvicted suspects awaiting trial in jail to convicted offenders on probation or home confinement; from offenders on parole to children in juvenile detention. From these diverse, wide-ranging functions, it becomes apparent that corrections is essentially accountable for the care, custody, and control of offenders through either confinement or noninstitutional alternatives. In this context, control is meant to encompass not only discipline and incapacitation, but also the multitude of activities involved in treatment, rehabilitation, or otherwise changing behavior while under correctional jurisdiction. Ideally, the outcome of such efforts is to replace correctional control with self-control.

Thus, corrections can be defined as *the combination of public and private services with legal authority to provide for the care, custody, and control of those accused or convicted of a crime or status offense.* How effectively is that authority used? How well are care, custody, and control provided? Who are those accused or convicted of an offense? As in any human endeavor, there are no simple answers, but all of these topics will be addressed as we explore the correctional conglomerate in greater detail, discovering its fascinations as well as its frustrations.

Learning Goals

Do you know:

1. The difference between the criminal justice functions of the legislative, judicial, and executive branches of government?
2. What is meant by "jurisdictional separation" and "functional fragmentation" within the criminal justice system?
3. How the effectiveness of the justice system could be improved with a criminal justice impact assessment policy?

Government, Society, and Corrections

The workload of corrections is determined by other components of the justice system, as well as by government practices and social values in general. The police can decide whether or not to make an arrest. Judges can decide whether to incarcerate an offender, and if so, for what period of time. Corrections cannot decide which clients to accept and has limited influence over how long they will remain under correctional supervision. The policies, procedures, and practices of the entire justice system have a significant impact on corrections. Like the assembly line that produces an inferior product when something goes wrong along the way, much of the success or failure of corrections is dependent on the entire criminal justice system, and the governmental structure within which it operates and the citizens who determine its policies.

The social and civic foundations on which corrections is built date back to the origins of this country. Seeking freedom from the strong arm of central government control that they had experienced in their homelands, early settlers brought with them fierce sentiments favoring local government autonomy. The democratic form of government that they established through the U.S. Constitution reserves specific, limited powers for the federal level of government. All other governing authority is allocated to states and localities. By separating jurisdictions in this manner, local autonomy was created.

To further assure that no one branch became so powerful as to endanger the rights and freedoms guaranteed by the Constitution, government was further divided into legislative, judicial, and executive functions.

Legislative. Legislative branches of government operating at the local, state, and federal level have the power to make laws solely within their own jurisdiction. Local ordinances created by county or city commissions therefore apply only within that county or city. Laws enacted by state legislatures apply statewide. Federal legislation passed by the U.S. Congress applies nationwide.

Judicial. Again within their jurisdiction, courts decide the guilt or innocence of defendants and the constitutionality of the law. When a local law is violated, a trial court of limited jurisdiction hears the case. If the violation involves a state law, the case is processed in a general trial court (sometimes called superior, district, or circuit court), with appeals made to the state supreme court. When a federal law is violated, the matter is referred to a federal district court. Cases involving a substantial constitutional issue may be appealed to the U.S. Supreme Court, which is the only court whose rulings apply throughout the country.

Executive. Law enforcement and corrections are part of the executive branch of government. Just as an executive in private enterprise manages the operations of a company, police and correctional officials manage the day-to-day operations of government that are related to crime and corrections. The police are entrusted with enforcing the laws created by the legislature. Corrections is charged primarily with implementing the sanctions decreed by the courts (although the jail also confines some suspects prior to trial). County sheriffs combine both functions, since they have authority to enforce laws as well as administer the county jail. Like their legislative and judicial counterparts, police and corrections operate only within their specific jurisdiction. Local municipal police and county sheriffs can enforce laws within their

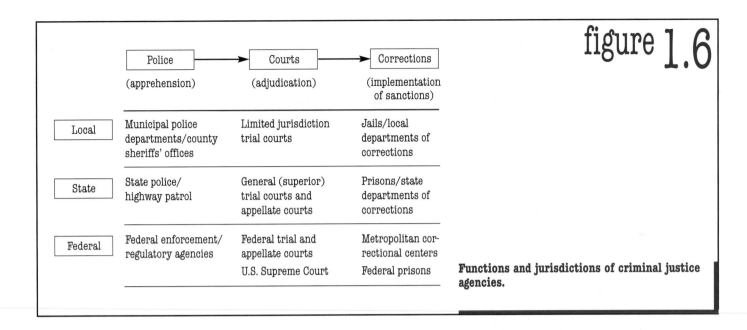

figure 1.6

	Police (apprehension)	Courts (adjudication)	Corrections (implementation of sanctions)
Local	Municipal police departments/county sheriffs' offices	Limited jurisdiction trial courts	Jails/local departments of corrections
State	State police/ highway patrol	General (superior) trial courts and appellate courts	Prisons/state departments of corrections
Federal	Federal enforcement/ regulatory agencies	Federal trial and appellate courts U.S. Supreme Court	Metropolitan cor- rectional centers Federal prisons

Functions and jurisdictions of criminal justice agencies.

employing city, county, or town. State police or highway patrol officers have statewide jurisdiction. Federal agents enforce federal criminal statutes throughout the country. Similarly, jails represent the local branch of corrections; prisons operate at the state level; and the federal government maintains both jails (usually called "metropolitan correctional centers") and prisons for federal offenders (*see* Figure 1.6).

Jurisdictional Separation and Functional Fragmentation

As might be expected, these divisions of government by function and jurisdiction have both benefits and drawbacks. On the one hand, they bring government closer to the people and provide checks and balances to assure that no one agency becomes too powerful. On the other hand, they foster jurisdictional separation and functional fragmentation—that is, lack of cooperation, insufficient coordination, and even territorial rivalries. Like the loyal employee of one company who views outside firms and competitors as rivals, employees of criminal justice agencies may tend to view others in the system with suspicion and mistrust.

Law enforcement officers are understandably frustrated when, practically before they have completed their paperwork, they see the offenders they arrest out on bail. Similarly, prosecutors are upset when inappropriate police procedures require them to reduce charges, omit evidence, or even lose cases. Corrections is equally frustrated when the police and the courts keep delivering clients who are in greater need of jobs, shelter, medical care, psychiatric treatment, or substance abuse programs than of confinement in secure institutions. And everyone is disillusioned when corrections fails to "correct." When the same people continue recycling through the system, it is apparent that the system is not working.

Fragmentation of the criminal justice system is not unlike the fragmentation that can occur within a family as parents and children pursue conflicting activities—when everyone is operating on different schedules; when no one takes time to listen to the others; when each believes that his or her interests are most important; when no one works to keep everyone together as a unit. Similarly, a system becomes fragmented when its parts function independently, becoming isolated from each other. In criminal justice, each component serves different clients, performs different functions, and pursues different directions, often working at cross-purposes. Yet, like a dysfunctional family, the actions of each affect those of the others.

In large part, this lack of coordination results from the autonomy that was purposely built into each component of criminal justice. The police, courts, and corrections have separate and distinct missions, which are at times almost contradictory. Each has separate budgets, personnel, physical facilities, missions, and policies. They often must compete with each other for scarce fiscal

 # Close-up On Corrections

UNANTICIPATED CONSEQUENCES

The citizens of Pleasantville were concerned about rising crime rates and no longer felt safe in their community. Demands for more police protection resulted in the city commission authorizing additional funds for the hiring of twenty-five more police officers. Dissatisfaction with what the public felt was lenient sentencing resulted in the election of judges who campaigned on the promise to "get tough" with criminals. To the public's surprise, crime did not decline, but in fact increased, and convicted offenders actually spent less time incarcerated. Why?

Perhaps more crime was being committed. More likely, more crimes were being detected by the newly authorized recruits. Although their average arrest rate remained about the same, the total number of arrests increased with the additional officers.

No extra funds were authorized for jail personnel, but bookings and admissions increased proportionately with the added arrests. Nor were more funds allocated for the prosecutor's office or public defender, both of whom worked under the burden of increasing caseloads. Everyone had less time to prepare for more cases, and prosecutors felt pressured to negotiate pleas to avoid further trial delays. Judges kept their promise to increase the length of sentences, but the state prison, operating under a court-mandated population limit, simply could not admit any more offenders. Those sentenced to prison therefore backed up in the already crowded jail, where exhausted staff—burned-out, overworked, and seeing no end in sight—began resigning. To make room for more inmates, prison officials were authorized by the state legislature to initiate an early-release program. Previously, offenders served an average of two-thirds of their court-imposed sentence before being eligible for release. The average dropped to one-third with early release measures.

One of the offenders released through the program returned to Pleasantville and engaged in a spree of robberies that resulted in the death of a prominent citizen. The community was outraged and once again called for more police protection and stiffer sentences.

and human resources. Yet, the actions of each have ripple effects throughout the "system," as illustrated in the prior "Close-up On Corrections." Although Pleasantville is a fictitious community, the scenario illustrates the all-too-real domino effect of one component of the system on the others. Communities throughout the country are experiencing similar results today.

Criminal Justice Impact Assessment

When plans are made to construct a public building, it is mandatory to conduct an impact study to assess the potential damage to the environment. But few states require a similar system-impact assessment to determine the potential systemwide disruption of new public policies.

Whenever police departments are expanded, new laws are created, sentencing practices are altered, or any other crime-related action is taken, the change will create a ripple effect throughout the criminal justice system. In many cases, the impact can be so severe that unanticipated consequences will result. In fact, as described in the last close-up, the long-term outcome may be completely contradictory to the initial intent. If no one anticipates how crowded jails and prisons will become with more punitive sentences, if no one provides the resources to expand the capacity of corrections to deal with more offenders, then no one will be satisfied when "longer" sentences actually translate into less time served.

The legislative branch of government has a tendency to increase prison sentences with great public fanfare. But when it becomes apparent that correctional facilities cannot accommodate the influx, lawmakers much more quietly authorize speeded-up formulas whereby inmates can amass credits toward early release. Such measures are short-term, shortsighted reactions to crisis conditions. If we truly wish to change and improve corrections, it must be done in a proactive, long-term manner.

Using statistical-projection techniques, decision makers can estimate the impact of new policies on future correctional populations and project associated costs. Some might argue that prison capacity or financial limitations should not determine criminal justice practices. But criminal justice policy does not operate in a vacuum and "must be held accountable for its effect on the allocation of human and fiscal resources. At some point, we must ask whether we can afford to lock up everyone who offends us."[20]

In that respect, the American Bar Association's Criminal Justice Committee has called for a "rational sentencing policy" in response to the nation's drug crisis, which, among other things, recommends that "all legislative actions affecting sentencing should be accompanied by a prison impact statement."[21] Additionally, a National Institute of Justice report suggests that a "funding plan" be included in mandatory sentencing legislation to "ensure awareness of and responsibility for long-term costs."[22] With the foresight of a systemwide impact assessment, new policies and programs could be implemented more sensibly. Citizens and elected officials would know in advance what effect would be created on the system, what staffing and physical facilities would be needed for effective implementation, and what the ultimate cost would be. The quick-fix, shortsighted "solutions" and fads that have characterized so much of the management of criminal justice agencies could be replaced by long-term analysis.

Independent decisions could be replaced by systemwide planning. Reacting to change could be replaced by proactively addressing challenges. Without such foresight, criminal justice agencies will continue to compete for limited resources, trying to do more with less, but in fact, doing more less effectively.

✸ Learning Goals

Do you know:

1. How the democratic process influences correctional practices?
2. The difference between the medical model, the justice model, and the balanced and restorative model of public policy?
3. How corrections has been affected by society's change from the medical model to the justice model?

Conflicting Correctional Goals

Systemwide planning through an impact assessment of criminal justice policy would better coordinate the efforts of police, courts, and corrections, but it is not a panacea for resolving their differences. To function effectively, a system requires goals upon which all components mutually agree.

Even within criminal justice agencies themselves, goals can be contradictory. Some police administrators, for example, place greater emphasis on crime prevention and community partnerships; others focus on "by-the-book" enforcement and criminal apprehension. Some judges stress holding offenders fully accountable for their crimes; others are more likely to consider extenuating circumstances. Some correctional officials see their mission as incapacitation; others believe that corrections has a responsibility to promote behavioral change. In fact, within the correctional system itself, there are a wide variety of opinions about what constitutes "success." Correctional officers think it is no escapes. Teachers think it is a GED or an educated person. Social workers think it is a rehabilitated person. Administrators think it is someone who has successfully done his or her time.[23]

Although these are admittedly broad generalizations based on narrow occupational perspectives, they do illustrate the conflicting views reflected by differing community sentiments. In that regard, it must be acknowledged that criminal justice decision makers do not function in isolation. They are responsible to elected officials, who, in turn, are responsible to the public.

The Public's Role in Policymaking

Elected officials carry out the mandate of the public through the administrators they appoint. For example, politicians elected on a strong law-and-order platform are likely to express public opinion through the appointment of police chiefs and correctional administrators who share their philosophy. In fact, the office of the sheriff—responsible for both law enforcement and the jail—presents a direct expression of public attitudes, since it is typically an elected position. If the public is dissatisfied with the outcome, the next election may find incumbents facing strong opposition from politicians with a different perspective. Thus, our democratic system of government assures that the opinions of the majority will be influential in the establishment of public policies. The difficulty for the criminal justice system is continuing to operate efficiently in the midst of such political pressures and policy changes.

Changing Public Policies

In the past several decades, criminal justice agencies have been required to adjust to dramatic shifts in public policies concerning crime. The public has changed its perspective about what causes people to commit crime, what types of sentences offenders should receive, and what corrections should be accomplishing.[24] Such changes are reflected in what has come to be known as the medical model and the justice model of criminal justice policymaking.

Before exploring these policy models in greater detail, however, it is important to note that they do not necessarily represent clearly defined, distinct phases or an overnight transition from one to the other. Rather, each emerged gradually over time, and in fact, the "medical" and "justice" labels attached to them were coined in retrospect. It is only through the analysis of hindsight that their philosophies and resulting practices appear to be so unique and even contradictory today. The shift from the medical model to the justice model was an evolutionary change driven by prevailing social opinion as expressed in the political arena, and ultimately reflected in public policy. Nor are the concepts of these approaches completely mutually exclusive. As we will see later, elements of both can be combined into an integrated justice/treatment model. But first, let us review the ingredients of each.

The Medical Model. When you are ill, you see a doctor. You trust the doctor to diagnose your problem and prescribe medication to cure your illness. You do not expect the doctor to punish you for being sick. Similarly, the medical model of criminal justice (prevalent from the 1930s through the mid-1970s), views offenders as engaging in crime because of forces beyond their control. The forces shaping criminal behavior might be psychological (for example, mental illness), sociological (for example, disruptive family environment), economic (for example, unemployment), or even physiological (for example, improper diet). The point is that offenders are not held strictly accountable for their actions any more than a patient suffering from an illness would be.

Because much of the burden for crime causation is placed on society in this line of reasoning, it is society that the medical model holds responsible for "diagnosing" the offender's "illness" and prescribing a "cure." This view translated into corrections being accountable for converting clients into law-abiding citizens and successfully returning them to the community—that is, rehabilitating and reintegrating them.

It is not surprising that the medical model emerged in the 1930s, when exciting advances in psychology, psychiatry, and social work were demonstrating the potential for successful treatment of personal and social problems. It was also during this era that a worldwide economic depression changed our outlook. Many who had previously believed that success and stability were solely the products of one's own initiative began to realize that external forces that we cannot control also shape our destiny. The principles of the medical model clearly reflected public opinion at the time.

If offenders were to be effectively treated according to the medical model, it was essential that sentencing address their individual needs. Yet social and psychological sciences are somewhat imprecise, making it difficult to determine how long a client would require treatment before being "cured." The object of sentencing under this model was therefore to "determine the conditions most conducive to rehabilitation,"[25] which translated into indeterminate sentences.

Under indeterminate sentencing practices, convicted offenders receive flexible terms, which can range anywhere from one year (or less) to life. Indeterminate sentencing was designed to enable a specific treatment plan to be prepared in which the offender participated for an indefinite period of time until rehabilitated. When correctional officials, in conjunction with treatment personnel, determined that rehabilitation had occurred, the inmate was released on parole.

But while the medical model was so named because of its resemblance to the medical profession, it did not apply quite so precisely to corrections. Criminals convicted of the same offenses ended up serving widely differing lengths of time in correctional institutions, creating sentencing disparities.

Some inmates learned to manipulate the system to their advantage, essentially faking behavioral changes. Others were able to adjust their behavior while confined, but—unable to cope with freedom—reverted to criminal activities (in other words, recidivated) upon release. Nor did taxpayers provide the full array of resources needed to adequately address the wide-ranging needs of correctional clientele, even assuming that their needs could be accurately identified.

Corrections may have been faced with an impossible mandate. But few took this into consideration as escalating crime rates, more conservative public attitudes, and high rates of recidivism created "get-tough-on-crime" demands by the mid-1970s. Perhaps the most devastating blow to the medical model came with the 1974 "Martinson report,"[26] which often has been cited to demonstrate the ineffectiveness of various forms of treatment programs: "Although the report merely confirmed the reality which correctional workers had been facing for years—namely, that some approaches work with some offenders under certain conditions and that nothing works with all offenders under all conditions—it had profound political and policy effects on corrections."[27]

Combined with other social forces that were challenging the assumptions of the medical model, the Martinson report was interpreted as evidence that the model was not working. As the public lost confidence in the ability of corrections to truly "rehabilitate," their faith in the principles of the medical model also eroded.

The Justice Model. By the mid-1970s, society had become increasingly frustrated with the system's inability to deal effectively with crime. No longer were people as eager to "excuse" criminal behavior as the product of forces outside of the offender's control. A renewed emphasis on personal responsibility emerged, which eventually became known as the justice (or crime control) model, since its focus was on controlling crime and seeing justice served.

Under this new philosophy, people are viewed as capable of making rational choices—of deciding through their own free will whether or not to engage in

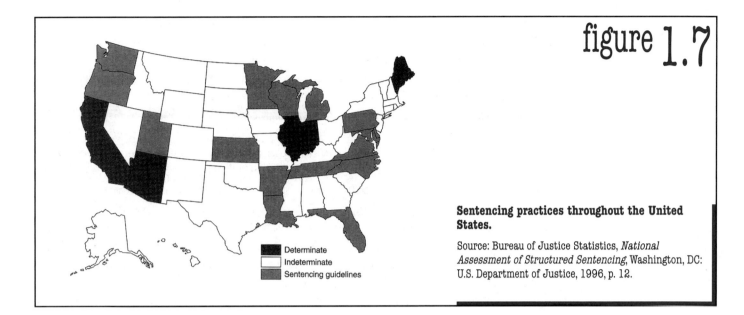

figure 1.7

Sentencing practices throughout the United States.

Source: Bureau of Justice Statistics, *National Assessment of Structured Sentencing*, Washington, DC: U.S. Department of Justice, 1996, p. 12.

■ Determinate
□ Indeterminate
▨ Sentencing guidelines

crime. It therefore stands to reason that if one freely elects to commit a crime, punishment should follow to deter other potential criminals, achieve justice, and hold the person accountable for his or her actions.

Unlike the indeterminate sentencing practices of the medical model, determinate sentences of "flat" or "fixed" length are the hallmark of the justice model. States embracing the justice model often employ sentencing guidelines that are either presumptive (required) or advisory, as shown in Figure 1.7.

With such guidelines, sanctions are designed to be clear-cut and predictable. The theory is that this way, criminals know what punishment will be imposed for their actions, similar crimes will receive similar sentences, and projected release dates will not be subject to manipulation. With sentences that are proportional to the seriousness of the crime, the justice model maintains that offenders receive their "just deserts," society obtains retribution for their criminal acts, and the community is protected during the period of their incarceration. Since this model is not based on the goal of rehabilitation, the length of the sentence is not determined by treatment effectiveness. Punishment is seen as being for the "good of society; treatment for the good of the offender."[28]

The justice model incorporates treatment only on a voluntary basis, in keeping with the belief that changing one's behavior cannot be forced, but rather, requires voluntary consent. As with the commission of crime, it holds that one must freely elect whether to seek personal change. Under the medical model, involvement in treatment was virtually required to become eligible for parole. However, the justice model would not penalize inmates who do not choose to participate in treatment, and in fact, advocates the abolishment of parole discretion to assure more uniformity in sentencing.

Implications for Corrections

As every correctional official knows all too well, the theory underlying public policy has not necessarily reflected the reality of operational practices. While a conservative society enthusiastically embraced the punitive sentencing, free will, and just-deserts principles of the justice model, corrections has not escaped blame for the failures of its clients. When ex-offenders recidivate, the public still wants to know why corrections is not doing its job, while many correctional employees wonder just what that job is supposed to be.

Whether implicitly or explicitly responsible for crime prevention, corrections often becomes the scapegoat when the crimes of ex-offenders are not prevented. Public policies notwithstanding, it is corrections that remains accountable for its former clients. The fact that this situation is not officially recognized and endorsed by society only makes the mission of corrections all the more difficult and ambiguous. It is like telling a football coach to win games, then restricting the game plan and the equipment (not to mention the draft choices). Corrections was never well equipped to fulfill its rehabilitative function, and when that function became submerged with the justice model, it created a situation of accountability without authority. Although corrections remains inherently "responsible" for its clients, it has neither the scope of authority nor sufficiency of resources to fulfill that responsibility successfully.

In contrast to the rehabilitation and reintegration goals of the medical model, the mission of corrections has changed to a greater emphasis on incapacitation under the justice model. In recent years, this approach intensified as the public became increasingly frustrated with the crime problem. Today, all states have mandatory sentencing laws covering everything from the use of a firearm during the commission of a crime to drunk driving and drug-related offenses. Moreover, as rhetoric took on fever pitch during the 1990s, states virtually jockeyed to surpass each other's punitive responses to crime. This atmosphere created the era of "three strikes" laws that mandate lengthy (sometimes life) terms for a third felony conviction. In part, the logic behind such legislation was to selectively incapacitate those identified as a danger to the community because of the seriousness of their crimes and potential for recidivism. However, at least one study has found that "more than one-third of all federal prisoners incarcerated under mandatory laws for drug offenses were considered low-level offenders."[29] Other research has reported little or no deterrent effects of mandatory sentencing laws.[30]

Nevertheless, with mandatory treatment no longer required, the justice model defines the role of corrections as "legally and humanely" controlling the offender (either through community supervision or incarceration) and providing "voluntary treatment services."[31] In theory, corrections is therefore not accountable for changing behavior, but only for safe and secure control during the period in which the offender is under correctional supervision. (*See* Figure 1.8 for a summary of the differences between the medical model, the justice model, and the balanced/restorative justice model).

Balanced and Restorative Justice. In the meantime, an alternative to both the medical model and the justice model is emerging. Known as the balanced and restorative justice model, this approach attempts to balance or reconcile the interests of the offender, the victim, and the community. Under this new perspective, the justice process focuses on:

- Offender accountability: restoring victim's losses

- Community protection: matching risk with intervention strategy

- Competency development: improving the offender's ability to function in a productive way [32]

figure 1.8

	Medical Model	Justice Model	Balanced and Restorative Justice Model
Crime is a result of...	Forces in society over which the offender has little or no control	The free will of the offender, who elects to engage in crime over law-abiding alternatives	Interpersonal conflict involving one person's violation of another
Crime is best prevented by...	Changing the motivations that shape one's behavior	The deterrent effect of swift and certain punishment	Changing the offender's perspective to accept accountability for harmful actions and building positive social relationships
Sentencing should be designed to...	Cure the offender through treatment, rehabilitation, and reintegration into the community	Punish the offender, protect society, and hold criminals accountable for their behavior through incarceration	Repair the harm caused by crime, with sentencing input by victim and community
The sentence should be...	Indeterminate (flexible)	Determinate (fixed)	A balanced response addressing the victim, offender, and community needs
Inmates should be released from confinement...	Through parole, when they are rehabilitated	Through mandatory release, after they have served their full term	After being provided with opportunities to make reparation [Note: Incarceration is minimized; used for public-safety threats only]

Comparison of the medical, justice, and balanced/restorative justice models.

Since this model is becoming the framework for shaping new directions in the juvenile justice system, it is explained in greater detail in Chapter 12, but its potential for application to the adult criminal justice system may well begin to capture the attention of policymakers anxious for an alternative with meaningful consequences that holds offenders responsible for their behavior without overreliance on costly incarceration. In that regard, balanced and restorative justice can provide a more productive option for both victims and offenders as well as protection for the community.[33]

If for no other reason than economic self-interest, the burgeoning prison and jail population that is anticipated well into the next decades may stimulate rethinking about the nature of society's response to crime. In any event, as long as there is crime, there will be a need for corrections—regardless of what specific ideologies and public policies guide its practices.

Summary

Developing a framework for the study of corrections is no easy task, given the complexity of its services, the nature of its relationships with the rest of the criminal justice system, and the impact of public policies on its operations. At a cost of some $57 billion, more than 747,000 workers service the needs of 6.7 million clients in the correctional conglomerate. This conglomerate includes both custodial institutions and community-based alternatives. It assists adults as well as juveniles. It operates maximum-, medium-, and minimum-security facilities and programs. It functions at the federal, state, and local level of government, and even within the private sector. In short, it provides care, custody, and control to those accused or convicted of a criminal offense, but it does not do so in a vacuum.

Every action taken, every policy formulated, every priority established by the criminal justice system has a potential impact on corrections. It is the product of a system burdened by functional fragmentation and jurisdictional separation. It is affected by the laws created by the legislature, appointments made by elected officials, and decisions rendered by the judiciary. Yet, perhaps above all, it is a reflection of the changing values, beliefs, and attitudes of society—which has variously directed corrections to treat, rehabilitate, and reintegrate offenders through the medical model, and more recently, simply to control those confined under the justice model. It is a complex, diverse, and often frustrating field of endeavor—which is exactly what makes it such a challenging, dynamic, and fascinating subject of study.

Endnotes

1.   President's Commission on Law Enforcement and Administration of Justice, *Task Force Report: Corrections*, Washington, D.C.: U.S. Government Printing Office, 1967, p. 1.

2.   Lynn Bauer and Steven D. Owens, "Justice Expenditure and Employment in the United States, 2001," *Bureau of Justice Statistics Bulletin*, Washington, D.C.: U.S. Department of Justice, May 2004, p. 4.

3.   "Prison Spending Up; Funds for Education Down," *Community Corrections Report*, Vol. 2, No. 5, July/August 1995, p. 11.

4.   William M. DiMascio, *Seeking Justice: Crime and Punishment in America*, New York: Edna McConnell Clark Foundation, 1997, p. 8.

5.   Bauer and Owens, "Justice Expenditure and Employment," p. 4.

6.   "Behind the Numbers: Analyzing Growth in Corrections," *Corrections Alert*, Vol. 3, No. 3, May 6,1996, p.1, quoting Larry Solomon of the National Institute of Corrections.

7.   Bauer and Owens, "Justice Expenditure and Employment," p. 5.

8.   *Ibid.*

9.   "Adult correctional populations," available at http://www.ojp.usdoj.gov/bjs/correct.htm, citation is as of August 2004.

10.   James J. Stephan and Jennifer C. Karberg, *Census of State and Federal Correctional Facilities*, 2000, Washington, D.C.: U.S. Department of Justice, August 2003, p. 7.

11.   *Ibid.*, p. iv. There are also 264 privately operated prisons.

12.   Paige M. Harrison and Jennifer C. Karberg, "Prison and Jail Inmates at Midyear 2002," *Bureau of Justice Statistics Bulletin*, Washington, D.C.: U.S. Department of Justice, April 2003, p. 8.

13.   James J. Stephan, *Census of Jails, 1999*, Washington, D.C.: U.S. Department of Justice, August, 2001, p. iii.

14.   Press Release, "One in Every 32 Adults Now on Probation, Parole, or Incarcerated," U.S. Department of Justice, Office of Justice Programs, August 20, 2003, p. 1.

15. *Ibid.*

16. Lawrence F. Travis, *Introduction to Criminal Justice*, Cincinnati, Ohio: Anderson Publishing Company, 1990, pp. 384-385.

17. Press Release, "One in Every 32 Adults," p. 1.

18. Alan Abrahamson, "Home Unpleasant during House Arrest, Judge Learns," *Corrections Today*, Vol. 53, No. 4, July 1991, p. 76.

19. Howard Snyder and Melissa Sickmund, *Juvenile Offenders and Victims: 1999 Report*, Washington, D.C.: Office of Juvenile Justice and Delinquency Prevention, 1999, pp. 160 and 186.

20. Nola M. Joyce, "A View of the Future: The Effect of Policy on Prison Population Growth," *Crime and Delinquency*, Vol. 38, No. 3, July 1992, p. 368.

21. *Responding to the Problem of Drug Abuse: Strategies for the Criminal Justice System*, Washington, D.C.: Draft Report of Ad Hoc Committee, Criminal Justice Section, American Bar Association, 1992, p. 60. *See also* Judith Greene, "Controlling Prison Crowding," *Corrections Today*, Vol. 59, No. 1, February 1997, pp. 50-65.

22. Dale Parent *et al.*, "Key Legislative Issues in Criminal Justice: Mandatory Sentencing," *National Institute of Justice: Research in Action*, January 1997, p. 2.

23. Klaus P Hilgers, "What Is Our Product? A New Perspective on Corrections," unpublished paper, Clearwater, Florida: Epoch Consultants, 1991, p. 3.

24. Much of this section is summarized from William G. Archambeault and Betty J. Archambeault, *Correctional Supervisory Management*, Englewood Cliffs, New Jersey: Prentice Hall, 1982, pp.164-168.

25. *Ibid.*, p. 165.

26. Robert Martinson, "What Works—Questions and Answers about Prison Reform," *The Public Interest*, Vol. 35, Spring 1975, pp. 22-54.

27. Archambeault and Archambeault, *Correctional Supervisory Management*, p. 3.

28. *Ibid.*, p 165.

29. *An Analysis of Non-Violent Drug Offenders with Minimal Criminal Histories*, Washington, D.C.: U.S. Department of Justice, 1994.

30. John P. O'Connell, Jr., "Throwing Away the Key (and State Money)," *Spectrum*, Winter 1995. *See also Why "3 Strikes and You're Out" Won't Reduce Crime*, Washington, D.C.: The Sentencing Project, 1994.

31. Archambeault and Archambeault, *Correctional Supervisory Management*, p. 166.

32. Gordon Bazemore, *Balanced and Restorative Justice: Program Summary*, Washington, D.C.: U.S. Department of Justice, Office of Juvenile Justice and Delinquency Prevention, 1994, p.2.

33. Leena Kurki, "Incorporating Restorative and Community Justice into American Sentencing and Corrections," *Sentencing and Corrections: Issues for the 21st Century*, No. 3, September 1999.

CHAPTER 2

THE IMPACT OF SENTENCING POLICIES ON CORRECTIONS

> **"** Right now, we think that the imposition of a sentence is our way of saying to the offender, "We're done with you." In the future, we should look at this moment as an opportunity to say, "We're just beginning to deal with you."[1] **"**
>
> —Jeremy Travis

Chapter Overview

Criminal activity is portrayed in fiction as an exciting lifestyle, but, in reality, many "criminals" are rather inconspicuous people whose involvement in crime is more an inability to cope with life than a search for excitement. These include the alcoholics, the drug addicts, and social "misfits" who often can be more harmful to themselves than to others.

The primary types of offenders arrested are not murders, armed robbers, or rapists. They are drunk drivers (1.4 million), thieves (1.1 million), and drug sellers or users (1.5 million).[2] Perhaps you know some of them as friends, coworkers, classmates, neighbors, or even family members. The typical criminal is not a bizarre monster with grotesque features. Crime is largely a feature of seemingly ordinary people. Some of them do very extraordinary things, but most do not. Anyone who has ever driven home after having too much to drink, taken something of value from a store or office, or used illegal drugs has committed a crime for which many Americans are arrested every day.

It is such ordinary people who compose a large portion of the clientele of corrections. They have violated the criminal law and, therefore, have damaged the social order by their failure to conform to expected behavior. In addition, of course, they are the ones who got caught.

Ultimately, it is the manner in which society responds to criminal behavior that determines the essence of corrections. That response is initiated by legislative action, which designates certain behaviors as "criminal" and therefore punishable by law. It then is guided by police officers on the street as they make day-to-day decisions about what laws to enforce, against whom, and under what circumstances. Additionally, it is shaped by prosecutorial and judicial discretion as selected cases proceed further into the justice system. All of these preliminary activities, interventions, and discretionary decisions are influenced by the public opinions and political pressures that formulate social policy choices. As we saw in Chapter 1, such policies during recent years have fluctuated between a rehabilitative (medical model) and a retributive (justice model) orientation toward crime. However, the impact of such policy choices is most apparent in the nature of sentencing, which, in turn, shapes correctional practices.

Learning Goals

Do you know:

1. How crime statistics affect corrections?
2. The percentage of felony suspects ultimately convicted in the criminal justice system?
3. What range of sentencing options is available to the courts?

Corrections and the Criminal Justice System

The crime statistics generated by police intervention are of concern to corrections for two reasons. First, they influence social policy. Crime data often fuel the fear and outrage that result in public demands for more punitive responses to criminal behavior. The public's perception of crime influences voting behavior—and subsequently, justice system policies and practices. Secondly, crime statistics concern corrections because they generate the correctional caseload. This does not mean that those represented in crime data immediately become correctional clients. Many crimes are not solved, and even when arrests are made, hundreds of thousands of cases are settled or dropped before penetrating further into the system. As shown in Figure 2.1, offenders will have been through a long screening process by the time they arrive on a caseload or in a correctional institution. In fact, Figure 2.1 points out that only a slight majority (54 percent) of felony suspects are ultimately convicted and become correctional clients.

As the justice process moves from arrest to arraignment and, potentially, adjudication, prosecutors and judges enter the picture—both of whom are either elected or politically appointed officials. Thus, they are also well-grounded in decision making that is responsive to prevailing public opinion.

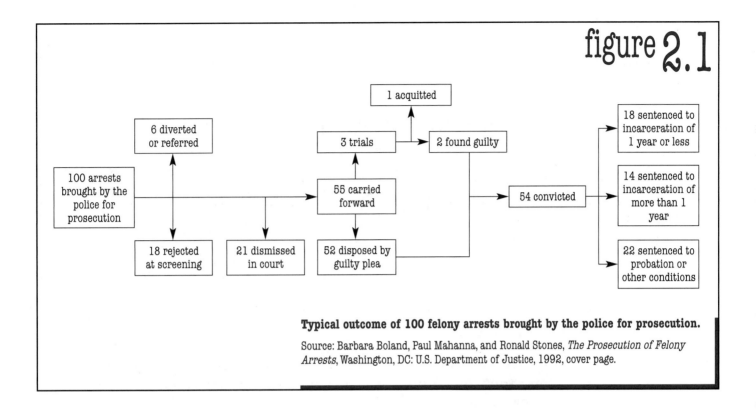

Typical outcome of 100 felony arrests brought by the police for prosecution.

Source: Barbara Boland, Paul Mahanna, and Ronald Stones, *The Prosecution of Felony Arrests*, Washington, DC: U.S. Department of Justice, 1992, cover page.

Prosecutors play a key role in deciding whether to press charges, how vigorously to pursue a case, and what penalty to advocate. But it is the sentencing judge who most clearly and directly reflects the mandates of the public, and affects the functions of the correctional system. For it is judges who determine what form of punishment the offender will receive and how long this punishment will endure. Although we will see how judicial decision making has been curtailed by legislative mandates in recent years, judges, nevertheless, are critical gatekeepers at the termination point of the criminal-justice filtering process.

The definition of corrections in Chapter 1 noted that responsibility for correctional care, custody, and control extends to adult criminals and juvenile delinquents who either are *accused* or *convicted* of violating the law. Corrections does not have the authority to intervene until a person is at least formally charged with a crime by the police, although in practice, most correctional services are provided after the accused offender is convicted and sentenced by the courts. As cases penetrate further and further into the criminal justice system, the number of offenders who remain in the system diminishes. As a result, corrections in general—and custodial institutions in particular—become the repository for those who were not able to "escape" at any prior stage. It is primarily those who pass through this ultimate screening process who become clients of the correctional conglomerate—and it is the sanctions imposed on that clientele which largely shape the nature of correctional practices.

Sentencing Options

Some would point out that sentencing is not the business of corrections— that corrections is responsible only for the implementation of sanctions imposed by the courts. Technically, that is true, but as a former official of the American

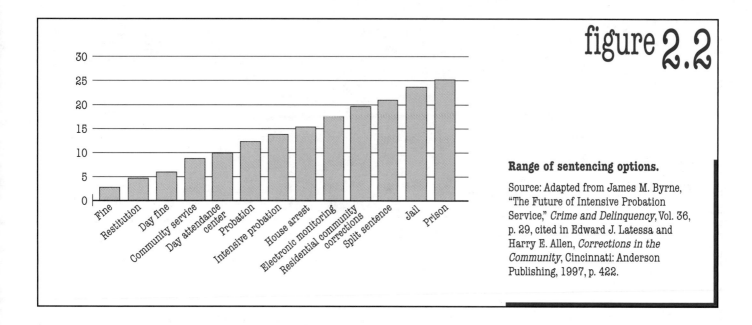

Range of sentencing options.

Source: Adapted from James M. Byrne, "The Future of Intensive Probation Service," *Crime and Delinquency*, Vol. 36, p. 29, cited in Edward J. Latessa and Harry E. Allen, *Corrections in the Community*, Cincinnati: Anderson Publishing, 1997, p. 422.

Correctional Association has noted, "Sentencing defines the very nature of our work. To the extent that sentences are unjust, we who must carry them out become agents of injustice."[3]

It is, of course, the decisions of judges that ultimately determine how just or unjust the sentencing process is. As detailed in Figure 2.2, judges can elect to impose sentences ranging from a fine, restitution, or community service, to probation, electronic monitoring, incarceration, or even capital punishment. Sentences which fall in the mid-range of severity—between probation and incarceration—are known as *intermediate sanctions*, and include options such as intensive supervision probation, house arrest, or electronic monitoring.

As we have seen in terms of the number of correctional clients under community supervision rather than institutional confinement, judges are most likely to select *noncustodial* sentencing alternatives. Certainly, the sentencing of a felon who has committed a serious violent crime is likely to result in incarceration, but particularly in less serious property cases, probation is the sentencing option used most frequently.[4] Although probation, fines, and other community-based programs are sometimes viewed as being too lenient by "letting offenders off" without "real punishment," they do impose conditions and intrusions on a person's life that can appear quite punishing from the perspective of the offender. In fact, it is not unheard of for someone to opt for incarceration in the face of a highly restrictive community alternative. However, community-based correctional approaches generally are preferable for both the public and the nondangerous offender, since they offer a number of advantages by:

- allowing the offender to remain employed, thereby enabling family support, payment of fines, or victim compensation

- avoiding the negative and stigmatizing effects of imprisonment

- providing some supervision without breaking ties to the community

- reducing costs to the public, since community-based approaches are far less expensive than incarceration

In deciding what disposition to impose, judges often rely on probation officers to prepare a *presentence investigation* (PSI). This report outlines the offender's prior record (if any), family stability, employment, education, problems in such areas as substance abuse, and other relevant factors, along with a sentencing recommendation. While the PSI report has been very influential over the years in determining case disposition, its influence is more restricted today in states with mandatory-sentencing guidelines. That is because in a number of jurisdictions, the sanction the offender receives is no longer primarily a function of judicial discretion.[5]

 # Learning Goals

Do you know:

1. The differences between determinate and indeterminate sentences?
2. What sentencing guidelines have been designed to achieve?
3. How mandatory-minimum provisions have curtailed judicial discretion?
4. What is meant by truth in sentencing and how it has been influenced by federal funding?
5. How restorative justice potentially conflicts with current sentencing trends?

Indeterminate and Determinate (Structured) Sentencing

The sentencing options available to judges are established by legal statutes. This means that judicial discretion is bound by limits imposed by the law. Traditionally, such boundaries have been quite flexible. From the 1930s to the mid-1970s, virtually every jurisdiction in the United States maintained *indeterminate sentencing* practices.[6] Under this approach to sentencing, the intent was to tailor dispositions to the specific needs of individual offenders, along

Many prisons have expanded their capacity to accommodate increasing numbers of offenders incarcerated under determinate sentencing. Courtesy of the Federal Bureau of Prisons, Butner, North Carolina Medical Center.

with the safety risks they posed.[7] Thus, judges had extensive discretion, an offender's prison term could range widely (for example, ten to twenty years), two offenders convicted of similar crimes could be sentenced to significantly different terms, and release from confinement was determined by the state's parole board.

Many states still retain either full-blown indeterminate sentencing or some form of it.[8] But dissatisfaction with unequal punishment for similar offenses—as well as public demands to "toughen up" on serious crime—had begun to stimulate a significant change by the mid-1970s, when Maine and California became the first states to enact *determinate sentencing*. Also called *structured* sentencing because it more closely limits and controls judicial discretion, determinate sentencing uses legislatively established *sentencing guidelines*.

Sentencing Guidelines

Along with the federal government, twenty-two states have enacted some form of sentencing guidelines, and another seven are studying proposals to establish them.[9] In some states, these guidelines are legislatively mandated, while in others they are considered "advisory," and compliance with them is voluntary. In some jurisdictions, they are accompanied by the abolishment of parole, but in others, early supervised release from a correctional institution is still an option.

Contrary to popular belief, sentencing guidelines were not necessarily designed to be more punitive by imposing longer prison terms. In fact, only half of the states that have implemented sentencing guidelines report that their primary reason was a desire for harsher penalties,[10] nor were they designed to create strict uniformity in sentencing by, for example, imposing the same sentence on all armed robbers. Given differences in the nature of the offense, the level of harm inflicted, and the offender's past criminal record, that would be just as unfair as more subjective sentencing. Rather, the majority of states

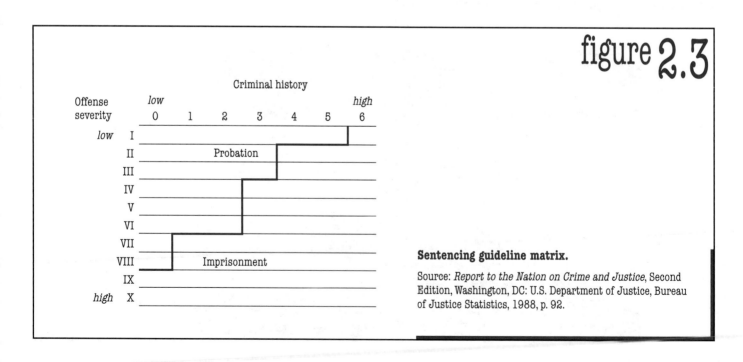

Sentencing guideline matrix.

Source: *Report to the Nation on Crime and Justice*, Second Edition, Washington, DC: U.S. Department of Justice, Bureau of Justice Statistics, 1988, p. 92.

indicate that their guidelines were enacted to achieve greater equality in sentencing.[11] Objective guidelines were meant to produce a more equitable and rational approach to arriving at a sentence—one that would allow for some variation within a consistently applied framework. As the matrix in Figure 2.3 shows, the guidelines generally take into account both the severity of the offense and the offender's prior criminal record.

In most states, judges still have some discretion to deviate from sentencing guidelines through "upward" or "downward" departures, particularly when aggravating or mitigating circumstances are involved. Aggravating circumstances—such as an especially heinous crime or complete lack of remorse by the offender—could justify a more severe penalty. On the other hand, mitigating circumstances—youthfulness or prior abuse of the offender—might call for a less serious penalty, resulting in a downward departure from the guidelines. Even where exceptions are permitted, however, such decisions must be justified in writing, with the judge's rationale subject to review to prevent abuse of judicial discretion. Moreover, both guideline departures and judicial discretion become obsolete concepts when mandatory-minimum terms are specified by law.

Mandatory Minimums

Perhaps the most prevalent form of *mandatory-minimum* legislation in recent years has been "three-strikes" statutes that require substantial sentences—up to life-imprisonment without parole—for a third-felony offense.

 # Close-up On Corrections

THE REALITIES OF MANDATORY-MINIMUM SENTENCING

- A man with no criminal record accepted $5 to give an acquaintance a lift to a fast food restaurant, where the acquaintance was arrested for selling 100 grams of crack to an undercover drug agent. The judge who imposed the mandatory ten-year sentence on the driver was moved to tears and called the sentence "a grave miscarriage of justice."

- A man convicted of first-offense simple possession of a pound and a half of cocaine was sentenced to mandatory life-imprisonment. When arrested, he voluntarily surrendered a concealed, registered handgun, perhaps not realizing that this would make the penalty for his drug offense the same as the penalty for murdering a police officer.

- A secretary was sentenced to a five-year mandatory-minimum term because her drug-dealing son hid 120 grams of crack in her attic.

Source: Henry Scott Wallace, "Mandatory Minimums and the Betrayal of Sentencing Reform: A Legislative Dr. Jekyll and Mr. Hyde," *Federal Probation*, Vol. 57, No. 3, September 1993, p. 13.

Because mandatory statutes direct judges to impose fixed sentences in a "machine-like manner," the wisdom of giving so much power to the legislature in a democratic form of government has come into question.[12]

Beyond the issue of properly balancing power between the legislative and judicial branches of government, some have questioned the equity of such sentences. After studying mandatory-minimum sentences for drug-related crimes, the American Bar Association criticized these penalties as being unfair and distorted, as well as requiring expenditures that are "disproportionate to any deterrent or rehabilitative effect they might have."[13]

Since such mandates essentially "tie the hands" of the sentencing judge, they have been denounced as "worse than useless . . . counterproductive."[14] In a protest very uncharacteristic of federal judges, all twelve federal judicial circuits have issued statements opposing mandatory sentencing, and several prominent judges have either resigned or refused to hear cases involving mandatory drug charges.[15] Some of the reasons for these drastic actions are illustrated in the prior "Close-up On Corrections," which describes bizarre but true examples of the unjust and disproportionate sentences that can result from the rigid uniformity of three-strikes sentencing practices.

Fiscal Impact of Mandated Sentencing

In addition to dramatically reducing judicial discretion, mandatory-minimum sentencing statutes have had a tremendous impact on corrections. As they have been applied to drug offenses, for example, these mandates have had two primary effects—first, an increase in the proportion of arrested drug offenders who are sentenced to prison; and second, an increase in the length of time that these offenders serve.[16] With more offenses drawing longer and more compulsory prison terms, overcrowded correctional institutions have become a burdensome byproduct of changes in sentencing practices.

Given the more punitive emphasis on drug involvement that has characterized this public policy shift, it is not surprising that much of the growth among institutional populations can be attributed to drug-related offenses. Between 1985 and 1995, for example, the population of drug offenders in state prisons increased by 478 percent—more than double the increase for any other offense category.[17] One comparison study of two groups of low-level drug traffickers sentenced before and after the adoption of mandatory minimums and sentencing guidelines concluded that the additional time spent in prison for the second group would cost taxpayers approximately $515 million.[18]

As ever-less-serious offenders find themselves drawn into the ever-wider net cast by mandated-sentencing policies, the result can become an issue of diminishing returns for the resources expended. In terms of cost-effectiveness, for instance, analysts report that spending tax dollars on reducing drug consumption through treatment would reduce serious crimes fifteen times more effectively than incapacitating offenders by funding mandatory prison terms.[19] Likewise, another study concludes that interventions with high-risk families have considerably greater long-term benefit than three-strikes policies.[20] But as high-cost cellblocks take priority over proactive social programs on the fiscal agenda, opportunities for early intervention are lost, thereby reinforcing a

reactive cycle that continually heightens the cost of crime at the expense of preventive efforts that could begin to break the cycle.

Racial Impact of Mandated Sentencing

Even more troublesome than lost fiscal opportunities is the potential for racial discrimination in the process of implementing mandatory-minimum sanctions. It has already been noted that much of the sentencing enhancements and mandates accompanying the justice model have been directed toward drug-related offenses. In practical terms, this means that such policies have disproportionately affected minority groups, particularly African Americans. Between 1990 and 1997, for example, the number of black inmates serving time for drug offenses increased by 60 percent (compared to 46 percent for white inmates).[21]

Moreover, reports have surfaced of racial disparities among the steps involved in administratively implementing mandatory-minimum sanctions (such as how charges are pursued, prior records are calculated, plea bargains are negotiated, and so on).[22] One report, for example, found that in comparison to whites, blacks were 21 percent more likely (and Hispanics 28 percent more likely) to receive a mandatory-prison term for offenses that fall under three-strikes legislation.[23] While some may question these findings, the overall picture is clear—of all sentenced inmates in 1999, almost half (43 percent) were black males. Calculating incarceration rates by age shows that 11 percent of black males in their twenties or early thirties were in prison or jail in 1999 (compared to 3 percent of Hispanic males and 1.5 percent of white males in the same age group).[24] When the analysis is expanded to include everyone under some form of correctional supervision, almost one of every three black males between twenty and twenty-nine years of age was either incarcerated or on probation or parole in 1995.[25] Nor is this dismal picture projected to improve. As shown in Fig. 2.4, projection of the lifetime likelihood of imprisonment for

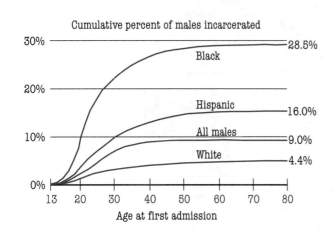

figure 2.4

Cumulative percent of males incarcerated

Lifetime likelihood of imprisonment for males.

Source: Thomas P. Bonczar and Allen J. Beck, "Lifetime Likelihood of Going to State or Federal Prison," *Bureau of Justice Statistics Bulletin*, Washington, DC: U.S. Department of Justice, 1997, p. 1 (based on constant 1991 rates of first incarceration).

black males is almost double that of Hispanics and nearly seven times the percentage for white males.

In response to these figures, it might be argued that the African-American population has become more likely to engage in crime. However, contrary evidence shows that more than half (51.4 percent) of the increase in the number of inmates between 1980 and 1996 can be explained by the greater likelihood of receiving a prison sentence (with only 11.5 percent attributable to higher offense rates).[26] Why have minorities been so disproportionately affected by justice-model sentencing practices? The next "Close-up On Corrections" provides some insights into this troubling question.

Sentencing Alternatives

By the beginning of the twenty-first century, however, several states were beginning to recognize the devastating economic, social, and human impact of mandatory drug laws. Just as California was in the forefront of the "three-strikes" movement, it again took the lead in sentencing reform. With the approval in November 2000 of Proposition 36, the Substance Abuse and Crime Prevention Act, California voters have dramatically changed the battle plan in the "war on drugs." Now, certain nonviolent adult offenders who use or possess illegal drugs receive treatment in the community rather than incarceration, in an effort to:

- preserve jail and prison space for serious violent offenders
- enhance public safety by reducing drug-related crime
- improve public health by reducing drug abuse through treatment

Since California's pioneering effort, a number of states have passed similar reforms, with more appearing on ballots throughout the country each year. In states that have advanced such public-policy alternatives, the challenge now

Close-up On Corrections

is to assure that adequate resources are available to meet additional treatment demands.[27]

Truth in Sentencing

But adequate resources historically have not been associated with public-policy transitions. This is the primary reason that, even with the greater certainty of being incarcerated for a longer time under determinate policies, the sentence received has not always been the one served. It is one thing to sentence an offender to a particular amount of time behind bars, but assuring that the sentence imposed actually matches the time served can be quite a different matter.

As harsher sentencing practices produced widespread prison crowding, a number of states began to discover that the pace of new construction could not keep up with the demand for more bed space. Facing court-imposed mandates to reduce crowding, states resorted to measures ranging from sentence reductions through generous "good time" credits to wholesale release of large groups of offenders to make room for incoming inmates. Whatever the remedy, the result was the early release of many offenders who had originally been sentenced to considerably longer terms. Inevitably, some of them continued a life of crime, and their involvement in several high-profile incidents generated a public outcry for "truth in sentencing."

Congress responded to the crowding crisis in 1994 by making hundreds of millions of dollars in grants available to help states build or expand prisons—with one major catch. To be eligible for these federal funds, states had to pass laws or adopt guidelines that require violent offenders to serve at least 85 percent of the sentence imposed. Thus, parole eligibility and good-time credits had to be restricted or eliminated. By 1997, all fifty states had received funding under this program by documenting that violent offenders now serve a substantial portion of their sentences.[28] As shown in Figure 2.5, violent offenders released in 1996 were serving an average of forty-five months, or about half of their average eighty-five-month sentence. Under truth-in-sentencing laws mandating 85 percent, they would serve an average of eighty-eight months in prison, based on the average sentence of 104 months for violent offenders in 1996. More recently, however, some states are expressing concerns that the truth-in-sentencing grants are too small to offset the construction and operating costs that would be required to adhere to the 85 percent requirement. Vermont, for example, estimated that it would cost several million dollars to comply with the federal requirements to be eligible for $80,000 in grant funding.[29]

Restorative Sentencing

While various forms of indeterminate and determinate sentencing tend to characterize the criminal justice process in most states, there is yet another alternative that has been developing for the past several decades, beginning in the juvenile justice system—restorative justice.[30] Also called the "balanced approach," it differs from traditional sentencing practices by involving the

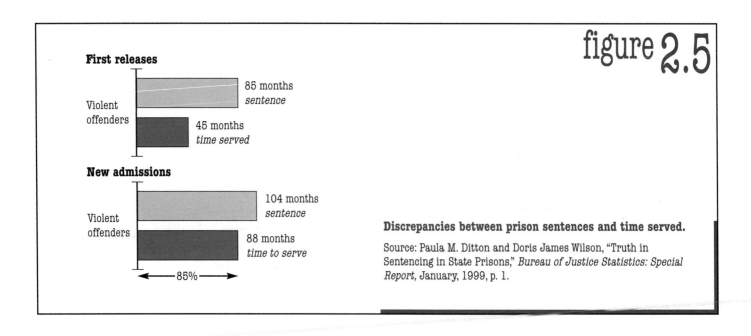

figure 2.5

First releases

Violent offenders

85 months *sentence*

45 months *time served*

New admissions

Violent offenders

104 months *sentence*

88 months *time to serve*

←—— 85% ——→

Discrepancies between prison sentences and time served.

Source: Paula M. Ditton and Doris James Wilson, "Truth in Sentencing in State Prisons," *Bureau of Justice Statistics: Special Report*, January, 1999, p. 1.

figure 2.6

Restorative justice model.

Source: Office of Juvenile Justice and Delinquency Prevention, U.S. Department of Justice.

interests of all relevant stakeholders in the sentencing process—the victim, the offender, and the community (as illustrated in Figure 2.6).

Rather than simply punishing the offender, restorative justice seeks to repair the harm that occurred and "restore" community well-being. It therefore assumes a broad-based, problem-solving approach that attempts to individualize justice by emphasizing accountability, while providing help to the offender, protecting the community, and compensating victims for their losses. But doing so calls for an unstructured, unstandardized approach that is based on the unique circumstances of each case—quite the opposite of the uniformity required under structured sentencing guidelines. As a result, restorative goals of achieving relevant, individualized dispositions come into conflict with contemporary trends toward certainty and consistency in sentencing.[31] Until this discrepancy is resolved—or the public opinion that is fueling it changes direction—it is uncertain whether the balanced and restorative approach ever will exert as much influence on adult sentencing as it has within the juvenile justice system.

Fragmented Sentencing

As is apparent by now, there is no unified approach to sentencing in the United States. To the contrary, public policies governing sentencing range from the flexibility of indeterminate and restorative approaches to the fixed nature of determinate practices that are further structured by mandatory minimum-sentencing guidelines. The result has been a fragmentation of sentencing throughout the country. No longer is there anything that can be called "the American system" of sentencing.[32] In large part, that is a reflection of the lack of a general consensus about what sentencing is designed to accomplish, as illustrated in the next "Close-up On Corrections." And if we are uncertain about just what it is that we hope to accomplish through the sentencing process, we are even more unsure about what those who implement the sanctions of the courts should be striving to achieve. For although public policy sets the broad parameters within which corrections functions, as we will see shortly, it does not always provide very clear-cut guidance or direction for correctional operations.

Close-up On Corrections

 Learning Goals

Do you know:

1. What forms of retribution are used today?
2. The difference between specific and general deterrence?
3. What selective incapacitation is and what issues it raises?
4. Why rehabilitation is associated with indeterminate-sentencing practices?
5. Why reintegration is necessary following release from correctional custody?
6. Which correctional goals are reflected in the justice model and which are represented by the medical model?

Crime-Related Public Policy

Despite the current popularity of a more punitive approach to criminal punishment, some people question why their tax dollars have to support "criminals" at all. The answer involves public policy, which is often a tradeoff between economic goals and social values—a balance between what is *economically feasible* and what is *humanely desirable*. In fact, as the next "Close-up On Corrections" describes, during ancient and medieval times, society kept neither its serious offenders nor those who consumed more than they produced.

Public policy is a reflection of the prevailing views of society, which can differ widely when it comes to dealing with criminal behavior. Public opinion concerning the appropriate response to crime forms the basis for identifying the purpose of corrections—that is, what corrections is supposed to be

Close-up On Corrections

EVOLUTION OF MORAL VALUES

An Indian tribe in Labrador maintained a custom that the eldest son would kill his parents in a respectful and ritualistic manner when they began to consume more than they produced. Early Eskimo cultures had a practice in which the aging parents would kiss their families good-bye, go sit on the ice, and wait to die. Similarly, ancient Romans threw themselves into the Tiber River during times of famine.

Primitive, ancient, and medieval people often did not have enough to eat and simply could not afford to keep nonproductive or dangerous people. In difficult economic situations, humanitarian values take second place. Even for modern society, the value system tends to lose its holding power when survival is threatened.

But with increased knowledge and improvements in technology, modern people have become more productive than their predecessors. With economic advancements, society could begin to afford to keep those who were nonproductive, dangerous, or ill, and try to help them. Humanitarian values and social goals have thus become a part of public policy. In an affluent society, moral values can support "human rights," welfare payments, protection of children, and minimum standards for offenders. It is simply a matter of economics and public policy choices.

accomplishing. Unfortunately, there is such a diversity of viewpoints over what should be done with law violators that it is impossible to identify any one mission or goal of corrections. At various times, sentencing practices have reflected demands for retribution, deterrence, incapacitation, rehabilitation, and reintegration.

Retribution

The belief that criminals deserve to be punished as repayment for their misdeeds is one of the oldest reactions to wrongdoing. The "law of retaliation"(*lex talionis*) traces its origins to the Code of Hammurabi as well as the Law of Moses and the Old and New Testaments.

In seeking retaliation, ancient and medieval punishments were violent and bloody—completely out of proportion to the seriousness of offenses. Common penalties were flogging, public boiling, mutilating, using stocks and pillories, blinding, disemboweling (alive), drawing and quartering, cutting out tongues, using the rack (stretching a person by binding ankles and shoulders and pulling in opposite directions), and engaging in similar tortures.[33]

The modern-day concept of retribution is considerably more civilized than its early origins, although some still denounce it "because retribution invokes vengeance and sounds harsh."[34] In fact, it has been noted that retribution differs from revenge in that it is impersonally administered by "disinterested parties" through due process of law, which is designed to "balance the wrong done to the victim" rather than "incite retaliation."[35] As the public has become increasingly fearful of violent crime, frustrated over the inability to control it, and concerned that criminals are not receiving their "just deserts," retribution again has gained in popularity. Proponents of this view maintain that offenders freely elect to engage in criminal activities and therefore should be punished to "pay their debt" to society.

Punishment according to the modern view of retribution is generally in the form of some type of compensation or imprisonment. However, there are those who would argue for less humane conditions of confinement, even advocating a return to corporal punishment, and in fact, the death penalty remains an option in thirty-eight states.[36]

Capital Punishment. The ultimate retribution, of course, is death. As such, it has become a very controversial issue that illustrates the divergence of opinions concerning correctional goals. The death sentence is almost exclusively reserved for those convicted of homicide.[37] If its purpose is vengeance or retribution, capital punishment serves a purpose. On the other hand, if it is designed to prevent such acts of violence, it is aimed at the wrong offenders. Murder is often a crime committed in the heat of passion or emotional strain, and its recidivism rate is low. Those convicted of homicide generally do not repeat their crime on release from prison (and most are imprisoned and ultimately released). Thus, from a pragmatic point of view, retribution is the only goal truly achieved by imposition of the death penalty.

Other Forms of Retribution. Punishment in the form of fines, restitution to the victim, community service, or other methods of "paying back" society are all types of retribution that also recently have received renewed emphasis. In fact, some are convinced that "punishment (insofar as it is justifiable at all) is justifiable only in terms of restitution."[38] In a capitalistic society, it is not surprising to find economics playing a significant role in the sanctioning of criminal behavior. Such sentences have been applauded as both holding offenders responsible for their actions and providing some relief to the victim to compensate at least partially for property loss, hospital bills, pain, and suffering. However, these sentencing practices also have been criticized as discriminating against the poor while allowing the rich simply to "write off" their wrongdoing with a check.

There is no doubt that a $1,000 fine is a severe imposition on a laborer receiving minimum hourly wages but only pocket change to a successful executive. To address this inequity, the Scandinavian system of *day fines* has been suggested, where the judge determines a number of "days" that the offender is to be fined (based on the seriousness of the offense and other related factors), with the amount paid per day based on the person's salary.[39]

While there is no valid evidence that the fear of punishment prevents crime, that is not actually the objective of retribution. Rather, the focus of retribution is on the satisfaction achieved by society in general and the victim in particular when criminals are required to "pay for their crimes"—whether in the form of economic compensation, loss of freedom, or even death.

Deterrence

Unlike retribution, which reacts to past events, deterrence aims to prevent (in other words, to deter) future criminal behavior. Thus, retribution can be considered *reactive*, while deterrence is assumed to be *proactive*.

Despite the proactive emphasis of deterrence, it is not entirely unrelated to retribution. Both believe in holding offenders accountable for their behavior. Both see a relationship between increasing penalties and decreasing crime. In fact, it could be said that through retribution, deterrence can be achieved,[40] or put another way, "deterrence theory is used widely as a cloak for vengeance."[41] Some would feel morally uncomfortable demanding revenge. Seeking to deter criminal behavior entails a more socially acceptable goal, even if the outcome is essentially the same for the offender. The proactive nature of deterrence focuses on two approaches, specific and general: [42]

- *Specific deterrence* is directed toward the individual offender. The rationale is that by making the punishment sufficiently unpleasant, the offender will be discouraged from committing violations in the future. Just as a child is disciplined for inappropriate behavior to prevent its repetition, the idea is that criminals will avoid recidivism if punished properly.

- *General deterrence* is designed to use the offender to "set an example" for those who otherwise might consider engaging in similar criminal acts. The assumption is that crime will be reduced by "terrorizing by-standing citizens so much that they will be afraid to violate the law.[43] It requires punishment that is severe enough to have an impact, assurance that the sanction will be carried out, and enough examples to "remind people constantly of what lies ahead if they break the law." [44] Thus, both certainty and severity of punishment are essential ingredients in general deterrence.

Moral Issues. This approach has been praised as necessary to "send a message" that crime will not be tolerated and that those involved in such activities will be dealt with firmly. On the other hand, general deterrence has been criticized because making an example of an offender "to discourage others from criminal acts is to make him suffer not for what he has done alone but because of other people's tendencies." [45] The issue posed by this line of reasoning is whether justice should be individualized to address specific deterrence, or generalized to serve as a warning to others.

Equity. In addition to this moral issue, generalized penalties also raise the question of equity, particularly when the punishment is out of proportion to the seriousness of the offense or the actual harm caused to society. Again, the death penalty is a good example.[46] The Federal Narcotic Act of 1956 was passed in the midst of what was then thought to be the height of the drug scare. It incorporated the death penalty for a second conviction of sale of drugs to a minor. "As could have been predicted—because the penalty was inordinate—no single individual was ever sentenced to death under this law. Nor did the sale of drugs abate." [47] But despite the historical ineffectiveness of this provision, there are demands today for the death penalty to deter major drug dealers.

Applicability. On the other hand, individualized penalties present the dilemma of applicability, since what may be a deterrent to one may not be to another. People are motivated by different things: status, power, money, personal gratification, and so on. Likewise, they differ in terms of what is a deterrent to fulfilling their motivations. Some children, for example, can be reduced to tears simply by a parent's angry look, while others in the same family will test the extremes of their parents' tolerance, regardless of the penalties. In other words, what is a deterrent to one person is not necessarily equally productive with others.

We cannot take it for granted that "penalty X will have the same influence, whether applied to transgressor A, B, C, or D."[48] To do so would also require assuming that (1) law violators believe they will be apprehended (which most do not), (2) criminals rationally plan their activities—that "burglars think like district attorneys," and (3) "the crime rate will diminish as the penalty scale increases."[49] However, many crimes are acts of passion, spontaneous responses, or committed under the influence of alcohol or drugs, and many criminals are repeat offenders who already have experienced the presumably "deterrent" effect of punishment. For a look at why deterrence theory has failed when applied to drug-related crime, see the "Close-up On Corrections."

 # Close-up On Corrections

THE THEORY AND REALITY OF DETERRENCE

Standard deterrence theory tells us that people calculate the pain and pleasure of their actions, and that if we make the pain of the disfavored conduct great enough, the relative frequency of that behavior will decline. Few people doubt that this theoretical assumption is the driving force behind current national drug policy, as courts and lawmakers have made it increasingly easy to detect, arrest, convict, and punish those who possess the contraband. Some of this movement may be inspired by retributive or incapacitative goals, but overwhelmingly, the political assumption seems to be that the current problems are the result of inadequate brute force, and that if we punish people severely enough, they will change their ways. . . . One difficulty with using the criminal law as the main response to the drug problem is that it necessarily treats all drug users the same . . . as though they had the ability to conform their conduct to the standards the law requires. . . . Many who buy drugs are recreational users who presumably can and would stop if they perceived the risks of detection to be too great. . . . On the other hand, perhaps no realistic penal sanction can deter those who are addicts. . . .

One of the problems with the criminal law model is its failure to distinguish those who can be deterred from those whose reasoning has been sufficiently compromised by drug use that deterrence is ineffective. The result of this one-size-fits-all approach is that the criminal justice system is overwhelmed, and we end up with a far lower deterrent effect than is optimal. . . .

Source: Andrew D. Leipold, "The War on Drugs and the Puzzle of Deterrence," *Journal of Gender, Race and Justice*, Spring/Summer 2002 pp. 111-129.

Measurement. The extent to which either convicted or potential law violators are deterred by severe punishments is virtually impossible to determine accurately, because only those who are not deterred become clients of the criminal justice system. But that does not necessarily mean that the goal of deterrence is sought exclusively through harsh sentencing practices. More recently, "shock" incarceration and even "shock" parole have been experimented with to determine whether the shock of brief imprisonment (or unexpected release) might assist in deterring future law violations. Regardless of whether deterrence is simply a more refined version of retribution or a distinct correctional goal in and of itself, with increased fear of crime, it has gained popular appeal as a result of its association (valid or not) with crime prevention.

Incapacitation

If retribution is viewed as reactive and deterrence as proactive, incapacitation could be characterized as something in between, or perhaps a combination of both. In its reactive sense, incapacitation in a correctional institution is to some degree a punishment for past behavior, although it is not technically "punishment" that is sought by incapacitation, but simply restraint. In a proactive sense, it is designed to prevent criminal activities—not so much in the future, as with deterrence—but more realistically, during the period when an offender is actually incarcerated. Specific deterrence can be achieved, at least temporarily, through incapacitation.

As a result, incapacitation is probably the most pragmatic sentencing goal. It does not specifically seek to prevent future crime, deter potential criminals, or change behavior. It simply focuses on *constraining offenders* to curtail their opportunities to commit additional crimes. That is not to say that criminal acts do not occur behind bars, although they are not usually committed against those in free society.

Such constraint is traditionally (and many would maintain most effectively) accomplished through *isolation* from society in secure correctional facilities. The definition of incapacitation, however, could be extended to include the *community-based controls* imposed through probation, home confinement, or electronic monitoring, but it is incarceration that most closely reflects the fundamental intent of incapacitation—rendering an offender incapable of preying further on the public.

Selective Incapacitation. Theoretically, those who are most likely to be repeat offenders would represent the logical target for isolation to obtain the maximum benefit from incapacitation. Research has demonstrated that among both juvenile delinquents and adult criminals, a relatively small number of "chronic offenders" are responsible for a large portion of offenses.[50] The idea is that if these chronic recidivists could be *selectively incapacitated*, the overall crime rate would be reduced.

Selective incapacitation is reflected in the recent movement toward habitual offender ("three-strikes") laws, which mandate specified sentences for those convicted of a certain number of prior offenses. In contrast, *collective incapacitation* refers to imposing the same sentence for all persons convicted of a designated offense.

While research points to the theoretical validity of selective incapacitation, it also raises several operational and ethical difficulties. Foremost is how to accurately determine which individuals should be confined extensively because of their potential threat to the community. Although detailed "prediction tables" have been formulated,[51] anticipating future behavior is never an exact science, creating the potential for selectively incapacitating some who would not actually pose any further threat to the community (or vice versa, overlooking those who would). In fact, it has been estimated that "for every offender correctly labeled dangerous, at least one offender will be erroneously labeled dangerous."[52]

Then, there is the issue of the moral justice involved in sentencing on the basis of possible future actions. In a democratic system of due process, where defendants are innocent until proven guilty and punishment is presumably related to the offense *committed*, this presents a serious dilemma. Ethically, morally, and legally, can we extend incarceration to a longer term on the basis of what someone might do if released? Even if the answer is affirmative, on a more practical level, selective incapacitation of habitual offenders can be expected to further increase an already overburdened prison population. Thus, while the concept may have popular and political appeal, its implementation is not without drawbacks.[53]

Overall, the goals of incapacitation are quite basic and (apart from selectivity) relatively easy to achieve—assuming that the offender is properly identified. But since "many criminals remain undetected, unapprehended, and unrestrained . . . the . . . value of incarceration may be limited or overrated."[54] In addition, this concept presents a rather pessimistic and short-range outlook.

Collective Incapacitation. Strong advocates of incapacitation would have society abdicate to a "lock-'em up" philosophy, resigned to the belief that no other option will work as well. But a significant drawback to such collective incapacitation is its shortsighted perspective. Although crime may be curtailed during the period of confinement, what happens upon release? With the exception of the relatively few inmates who die in jail or prison, almost all others eventually will return to the community. If "incapacitation" is synonymous with "warehousing," and nothing productive was accomplished during the time they served, little can be expected in terms of long-range effectiveness.

Moreover, the impact of incarceration on crime is not completely clear. Overall, there is no simple correlation between incarceration and crime rates. In the words of one authority on the subject, "As imprisonment increased steadily for ten years, trends in crime rates were inconsistent. This certainly suggests that the relationship between these factors is far more complex than political rhetoric would make it appear."[55]

In a summary of major published research projects addressing collective incapacitation, the most striking finding was that, contrary to popular belief, incapacitation does not appear to achieve the large reductions in crime that might have been expected from a "lock-'em-up" strategy. That does not mean, however, that corrections has been unaffected. While the impact of collective incapacitation on crime reduction has been limited, the effects on prison populations have been substantial.[56] The obvious question, then, is why incapacitation is not producing more dramatic results. Some of the potential answers are contained in the next "Close-up On Corrections."

Close-up On Corrections

WHY BUILDING MORE PRISON CELLS WON'T MAKE A SAFER SOCIETY

Why don't prisons do more to lower the crime rate? . . . The short answer to this puzzle is that we ask too much of prisons. . . . For it is one thing to say that a person will not commit a crime while incarcerated and quite another to say that society's overall crime rate will be affected. Put another way, more prison cells . . . won't reduce crime. Here's why:

- A lot of predatory crime is committed by juveniles too young to be eligible for prison, or by young adults unlikely to be sent to prison for most first-felony convictions. . . .

- Prison terms are usually imposed late in an offender's criminal career when criminal activity, on average, is tapering off. . . .

- Because the justice system only deals with an insignificant proportion of [total] crime, its ability to affect crime levels is minimal . . . [Many crimes are] either unreported or unsolved.

- Studies have shown that much individual crime (particularly violent crime) is an impulsive response to an immediate stressful situation, often under the influence of drugs or alcohol. Rational-choice models require an offender to think clearly about the costs and benefits of committing crime, weigh those costs, and determine that the costs outweigh the benefits. Yet, more than half of all violent offenders are under the influence of drugs or alcohol at the time of their crime, a state of mind with little affinity for rational judgment.

- For imprisonment to deter offenders and potential offenders, it must be stigmatic and punishing. Prison is most likely to deter if the inmate's social standing is injured by punishment and if he or she feels in danger of being excluded from a group about which he or she cares. But many of an offender's peers and relatives also have done time. . . . And estimates indicate that about one-quarter of all males living in inner cities will be jailed at some point in their lives, so the stigma attached to having a prison record in these neighborhoods may not be as great as it was when prison terms were relatively uncommon.

- Imprisonment may increase postrelease criminal activity. RAND analysts studied a "matched sample" of California offenders convicted of similar crimes and with similar criminal records. The two groups differed only in their sentence—members of one group went to prison, the others received probation. After tracking the groups for three years, researchers found consistently higher rearrest rates for offenders sentenced to prison . . .

- Most important, for imprisonment to reduce crime, inmates must not be immediately replaced by new recruits. . . . In [some] instances, an arrest and a prison sentence create a vacancy. Typically, however, that vacancy is filled quickly. . . . In general, new recruits constantly refresh the ranks of active criminals. As a result, crime in the community continues unabated. . . .

Prisons, to be sure, are an important and necessary component of the criminal justice system . . . . But drug clinics do more to rehabilitate drug addicts than prison; job training does more to reduce recidivism than jails; and early childhood prevention programs do more than

(continued)

Close-up On Corrections

Rehabilitation

It is the belief that something positive should be accomplished during the period of incarceration that forms the basis of the rehabilitative approach. Rehabilitation advocates maintain that criminal sanctions should be used as an opportunity to make some type of positive change in the offender. As George Bernard Shaw once pointed out, "if you are going to punish a man retributively, you must injure him. If you are to reform him, you must improve him. And men are not improved by injuries.[57]

Since rehabilitation literally means "to *restore* to good condition," some would maintain that the term is more properly "habilitation," as the condition of many offenders is not one to which corrections would wish to restore them. Regardless of semantics, the objective is to help offenders change their behavior so that they can reenter society as contributing citizens, or at least, not dangerous ones.

Just as retribution, deterrence, and incapacitation form the foundation of the justice model described earlier, rehabilitation is the hallmark of the medical model. Like deterrence, it has a somewhat proactive emphasis, but it differs in its more long-range focus on individual behavior. Like incapacitation, it seeks to reduce crime, but through "radically different means"—that is, by changing the "need or desire to commit crimes," not simply preventing the offender from "having an opportunity to do so."[58] Thus, the goals of rehabilitation are the most ambitious, and, therefore, perhaps the most elusive of the various responses to crime.

Implementation Approaches. Rehabilitative efforts can take many forms—from education and vocational training to detoxification and acupuncture, but most traditional approaches have centered on individual and group counseling, psychotherapy, and other clinical treatment procedures. Although these terms may imply very individualized treatment, such is not always the case. The rehabilitative routine of "counseling for everyone" does not take into account an individual's personal motivation to change or willingness to participate in treatment. Therefore, it has been far from uniformly effective.

It is somewhat ironic that the rehabilitative approach has been denounced for its "rubber stamp" procedures, since it was originally designed to address specific needs of the individual. The intent was to assess the offender's problems, develop a personalized treatment plan, and provide an indeterminate (flexible) sentence whereby the length of confinement largely would be determined by the person's progress toward rehabilitation. That was the theory. In reality, those incarcerated for similar offenses ended up serving widely different amounts of time, which raised the issue of sentencing *equity*. Moreover, the correctional officials, treatment personnel, and parole board members charged with determining when sufficient "rehabilitation" had occurred to justify release were not infallible. Since human nature cannot be precisely predicted, some were inevitably released before it was appropriate, while others were held longer than necessary.

Beyond these operational difficulties, to some extent, the rehabilitative concept was almost destined to flounder from the start because of the manner in which it was implemented. Given the long-term nature of clinical treatment approaches, they have been offered primarily in institutional settings. As a result, offenders must experience the negative impact of incarceration to receive the treatment necessary for their rehabilitation. The coercive nature of high-security correctional facilities is hardly the ideal environment for obtaining treatment and achieving rehabilitation—nor are institutions equally well staffed and equipped to provide such services.

Even among more valid rehabilitative programs, results have been far from encouraging. In his comprehensive report of studies assessing attempts at rehabilitation from 1945 through 1967, Robert Martinson concluded that "with few and isolated exceptions, the rehabilitative efforts that have been reported so far have had no appreciable effect on recidivism."[59] The Martinson report has been widely cited as demonstrating the ineffectiveness of treatment. Its empirical evidence that "nothing works"[60] has become a significant justification for movement from the medical model to the justice model, despite recent attempts to revitalize interest in rehabilitative concepts.

Rehabilitative Demise. Issues of sentencing inequities, untimely releases, and ineffective procedures have plagued the rehabilitative approach since its inception. By the 1980s, these concerns were combined with a more conservative political climate, rising crime rates, increasing recidivism, and the indictment of empirical research. Society seemed to have reached the limits of its tolerance for the unfulfilled promise of the rehabilitative ideal.

As a result of this combination of forces, public policies began to be directed toward determinate (fixed) sentences, elimination of parole, and voluntary (versus mandatory) participation in rehabilitative programs. However, not everyone agrees that society is actually as opposed to rehabilitation as legislators and policymakers would like to think.

Evidence has been offered demonstrating "the myth of the punitive public," which indicates that although support for punitive sanctions is widespread, there is also still considerable belief in rehabilitation as a legitimate correctional goal.[61] Moreover, as a former U.S. cabinet secretary argues in the next "Close-up On Corrections," providing substance-abuse treatment for those behind bars is in the nation's best interest fiscally as well as socially.

RECONSIDERING REHABILITATION—A SECOND FRONT IN THE WAR ON CRIME

Individuals who commit serious or violent offenses . . . should go to prison. But most eventually will be released. So, it is just as much in the interest of public safety to rehabilitate those who can be redeemed as it is to lock up incorrigibles in the first place. . . .

Our political leaders should put some commonsense behind their tough talk by opening up this second front in the war on crime. It would mean a heavy investment in treatment and training for the drug and alcohol abusers they have crammed into our prisons.

But it would pay off handsomely. . . . Some 80 percent [of those behind bars] either violated drug or alcohol laws, were high at the time of their offense, stole property to buy drugs, have histories of alcohol abuse and drug addiction, or share some mix of these characteristics. Among these 1.4 million inmates are the parents of 2.4 million children. . . .

If these hundreds of thousands were helped to live sober lives, they could be law-abiding, tax-paying citizens and responsible parents. . . . [F]or an additional $6,500 a year, an inmate could be given intensive treatment, education, and job training. Upon release, each one who worked at the average wage of a high school graduate for a year would provide a return on investment of $68,800 in reduced criminal activity, savings on the costs of arrest, prosecution, incarceration, and health care. . . .

But that's not all. The potential crime reduction is also big league. Expert estimates of crimes committed by the average drug addict range from 89 to 191 a year. At the conservative end, successfully treating and training just 10,000 drug addicts would eliminate 1 million crimes a year. . . .

Politicians camouflage the failure of their costly punishment-only prison policy by snorting tough rhetoric. . . . They act as though treatment does not work and addiction is a moral failing that any individual can easily change.

The first step toward sensible criminal justice policy is to face reality. Prisons are wall to wall with drug and alcohol addicts and abusers. . . . The normal success rate of treatment in the general population is 20 percent. That's a quarter of a million criminals who could be turned into law-abiding citizens and better parents.

The common denominator among inmates is not race; it is drug and alcohol abuse. . . . Each year the government builds more prisons. . . . In effect, governors, presidents, and legislators keep saying, "If all the king's horses and all the king's men can't put Humpty Dumpty back together again, then give us more horses and give us more men." Instead, give us treatment programs. We know they can put hundreds of thousands of people back together again.

Source: Joseph A. Califano, Jr., "Crime and Punishment—and Treatment, Too," *The Washington Post*, February 8, 1998, C7. Used with permission.

There are also others who argue against abandoning rehabilitation, if for no other reason than because doing so would abandon the humanizing influence it has created in the correctional system. Rehabilitation has played an important role in reforming not only the individual offender, but the system as well—perhaps not as effectively as its lofty goals intended, but not as ineffectively as its abolishment would justify. It is true that nothing works all the time with every inmate. Yet, that is not to say that we should reject all hope that anything ever works with anyone.

Reintegration

To some extent, the demise of rehabilitation also may be related to the difficulty of reintegrating ex-offenders back into the community after long-term confinement. It already has been noted that much of what was pursued in the name of rehabilitation has occurred within the isolated institutional environment of secure correctional facilities. In prison, an inmate's every movement is under scrutiny. Strict compliance with rules is enforced. Established routines regulate everything from requesting an aspirin to eating and sleeping. In response to this "total institutional" climate, an inmate subculture develops to socialize the population into such a "foreign" environment. The negative effects of this regulation, routinization, and socialization into prison life can be intensive and long lasting.

It is one thing to achieve behavioral change among those under such close supervision. It is quite another to assure that any improvements continue upon release—when ex-offenders are again faced with making their own decisions, regulating their own lives, and replacing institutional control with self-control. Reestablishing ties with the community is an essential ingredient in this process, and it is the focus of reintegration. If ex-offenders feel estranged from society, the chances are much greater that they will fall into old patterns of behavior and return to corrections as recidivists. Thus, reintegration efforts such as parole are not simply a privilege for the offender, but also a protection for the community.

Reintegration Challenges. Successful reintegration can be difficult for all but the most motivated. Once convicted and incarcerated, offenders lose a number of privileges, such as eligibility for certain types of employment. They also are stigmatized or "labeled" as high risks for personal relationships and business transactions. Former friends and even family members may distance themselves. Potential employers may be reluctant to "take a chance" by hiring someone with a record. Apartment managers may find excuses to avoid renting to a recent releasee. Banks may deny loans, without which it is difficult to find and keep employment when a car is needed for transportation. The overwhelming sense of frustration from experiencing such rejections can make the ex-offender a prime target for returning to crime.

While parole was designed in part to assist with such community reintegration, parole has a dual mandate of providing both support and continued supervision. When parole caseloads are high and public pressure is strong to detect recidivism among those released, it is not surprising to find parole officers' supervisory functions taking precedence over their supportive role. In addition, offenders serving full mandatory sentences without the possibility of parole can leave the institution without either supervision or support.

Community Transition. Like parole, halfway houses have been established to help the offender gradually phase into community life. At a halfway house, staff are available to help with obtaining employment, transportation, permanent housing, and similar personal needs, such as continuing medication, outpatient therapy, or other postincarceration treatment.

It only has been in relatively recent years that government agencies have invested resources in efforts designed to help with readjustment to the community. The reintegration approach historically has emphasized the role of private citizens in assisting ex-offenders. In fact, for many years, it was socially conscious private agencies (such as the Prisoners Aid Society, the John Howard Society, the Salvation Army, the Volunteers of America, and others) that provided this community service. No sooner had government begun to recognize the need for reintegrative support than public policies changed to embrace the justice model, again creating a greater need for private-sector involvement.

Changing Public Policies. During the 1980s, both rehabilitation and reintegration were deemphasized in favor of retribution, deterrence, and incapacitation, as public policies shifted from the medical model to the justice model. The focus thus has become either deterring criminal behavior, or when prevention is unsuccessful, holding violators accountable for their actions. To the extent that "holding accountable" translates into lengthy prison sentences, there remains a need to address reintegration. The question is whether that need again will be officially recognized, or whether ex-offenders will be left to reestablish socially acceptable lifestyles as best they can. Those who can will disappear with the rest of us into the anonymity of law-abiding society. Those who cannot will continue to provide media headlines and correctional clientele.

Summary

Correctional clients are those against whom society has taken official action because their behavior is in violation of the criminal law. What is considered to be a crime will determine who are identified as "criminals." Even in those cases where the offense is reported, a suspect is apprehended, and official action is taken, a lengthy screening process eliminates many of the accused long before they reach the correctional system.

Many of the decisions, practices, and policies of the justice system are based on public opinions and political pressures. But that does not mean that society is in widespread agreement about how to respond to crime. As a result, we retain a broad range of sentencing options. While indeterminate-sentencing practices still exist in most states, current trends have embraced more determinate-sentencing structures, often implemented through sentencing guidelines, mandatory minimums, and truth-in-sentencing provisions. As a result, U.S. sentencing practices have become fragmented, reflecting a wide variety of correctional goals.

Seeking repayment for the wrongdoing of criminal offenders, retribution guided the community's response to criminal behavior for centuries. As society accepted some responsibility for crime, experiments with rehabilitation occurred. Treatment programs were introduced to change one's motivation to commit crime and to reintegrate the ex-offender more effectively into the community. But when the desired results were not forthcoming, the public became increasingly disenchanted with the ability of corrections to achieve lasting change. Thus, the popularity of retribution reemerged. Efforts were directed toward assuring that criminals received their "just deserts." Offenders were incapacitated in correctional facilities—both to deter them specifically and to send a general deterrence message to the community. Apparently not everyone has received the message. In the next chapter we explore why some have not.

Endnotes

1. Jeremy Travis, "New Challenges in Evaluating Our Sentencing Policy: Exploring the Public Safety Nexus," *Corrections Compendium*, Vol. 25, No. 10, October 2000, p. 26.

2. Federal Bureau of Investigation, *Uniform Crime Reports, 2002*, (Table 29), available at http:www.fbi.gov/ucr/cius_02/pdf/4section4.pdf.

3. Perry Johnson, addressing the Midwinter Meeting of the American Correctional Association, Miami, Florida, January 11, 1993.

4. *Sourcebook of Criminal Justice Statistics*, Washington, D.C.: U.S. Department of Justice, 1999, p. 433.

5. Jeanne B. Stinchcomb and Daryl Hippensteel, "Presentence Investigation Reports: A Relevant Justice Model Tool or a Medical Model Relic?" *Criminal Justice Policy Review*, Vol. 12, No. 2, June 2001, pp. 164-177.

6. Michael Tonry, "Reconsidering Indeterminate and Structured Sentencing," *Sentencing and Corrections: Issues for the 21st Century*, Washington, D.C.: National Institute of Justice, U.S. Department of Justice, September 1999, p. 3.

7. *Ibid.*

8. *Ibid.*

9. "Sentencing Guidelines: A Summary," *Corrections Compendium*, Vol. 24, No. 4, April 1999, pp. 6-13.

10. *Ibid.*, p. 6.

11. *Ibid.*

12. Donald Cressey, "Foreword," in Francis T. Cullen and Karen E. Gilbert, *Reaffirming Rehabilitation*, Cincinnati, Ohio: Anderson, 1982.

13. "Emphasis on Enforcement Not the Answer to the Drug Crisis, ABA Report Says," *Narcotics Control Digest*, January 29, 1992, p. 4.

14. Henry Scott Wallace, "Mandatory Minimums and the Betrayal of Sentencing Reform: A Legislative Dr. Jekyll and Mr. Hyde," *Federal Probation*, Vol. 57, No. 3, September 1993, p. 15.

15. Marc Mauer, *Race to Incarcerate*, New York: The New Press, 1999, p. 74.

16. *Ibid.*, p. 151.

17. *Ibid.*, p. 35.

18. Miles D. Harer, "Do Guideline Sentences for Low-risk Traffickers Achieve their Stated Purpose?" *Federal Sentencing Reporter*, Vol. 7, No. 1,1994.

19. Jonathan P. Caulkins *et al.*, *Mandatory Minimum Drug Sentences: Throwing Away the Key or the Taxpayers' Money*, Santa Monica, California: RAND Corporation, 1997.

20. Peter W. Greenwood *et al.*, *Diverting Children from a Life of Crime*, Santa Monica, California: RAND Corporation, 1996.

21. Allen J. Beck and Christopher J. Mumola, "Prisoners in 1998," *Bureau of Justice Statistics Bulletin*, August 1999, p. 11.

22. Wallace, p. 14.

23. Barbara S. Meierhoefer, *The General Effect of Mandatory Minimum Prison Terms*, Washington, D.C.: Federal Judicial Center, 1992, p. 20.

24. Allen J. Beck, "Prisoners and Jail Inmates at Midyear 1999," *Bureau of Justice Statistics Bulletin*, April 2000, p. 1.

25. Maurer, pp. 124-125.

26. Alfred Blumstein and Allen J. Beck, "Factors Contributing to the Growth in U.S. Prison Populations," in Michael Tonry and Joan Petersilia, eds., *Crime and Justice: A Review of Research*, Chicago: University of Chicago Press, 1999.

27. Joey R. Weedon, "Drug War Undergoes Reform," *Corrections Today*, Vol. 64, No. 5, August 2002, p. 24.

28. "DOJ Says Prison Grant Awards Show Impact of Truth-in-sentencing Laws," *Corrections Digest*, Vol. 28, No. 2, January 10, 1997, p. 3.

29. "Officials Say Building Grants Have Costly Downside for States," *Corrections Journal*, October 7, 1998, p. 7.

30. John Perry, ed., *Repairing Communities through Restorative Justice*, Lanham, Maryland: American Correctional Association, 2002.

31. Leena Kurki, "Incorporating Restorative and Community Justice into American Sentencing and Corrections," *Sentencing and Corrections: Issues for the 21st Century*, Washington, D.C.: National Institute of Justice, U.S. Department of Justice, September 1999, p. 1.

32. Michael Tonry, "The Fragmentation of Sentencing and Corrections in America," *Sentencing and Corrections: Issues for the 21st Century*, Washington, D.C.: National Institute of Justice, U.S. Department of Justice, September 1999, p. 1.

33. Harry Elmer Barnes, *The Story of Punishment: A Record of Man's Inhumanity to Man*, New York: The Stratford Company, 1930, p. 63. Republished by Patterson Smith, Montclair, New Jersey, 1972. *See also* G. Abbott, *Tortures of the Tower of London*, London: David & Charles, 1986.

34. Louis P Carney, *Corrections: Treatment and Philosophy*, Englewood Cliffs, New Jersey: Prentice Hall, 1980, p. 6.

35. Gwynn Nettler, *Responding to Crime*, Cincinnati, Ohio: Anderson Publishing, 1982, p. 11.

36. Tracy Snell, "Capital Punishment 1998," *Bureau of Justice Statistics Bulletin*, Washington, D.C.: U.S. Department of Justice, 1999, p. 1.

37. *Ibid.*

38. Charles F. Abel and Frank H. Marsh, *Punishment and Restitution*, Westport, Connecticut: Greenwood Press, 1984, p. 57.

39. *How to Use Structured Fines (Day Fines) as an Intermediate Sanction*, Washington, D.C.: Bureau of Justice Assistance, U.S. Department of Justice, 1996.

40. *See* H. L. A. Hart, *Punishment and Responsibility: Essays in the Philosophy of Law*, Oxford: Clarendon Press, 1968.

41. Karl Menninger, *The Crime of Punishment*, New York: Viking Press, 1968, p. 206.

42. For a comprehensive review of deterrence literature and an assessment of its effectiveness, *see* Raymond Paternoster, "The Deterrent Effect of the Perceived Certainty and Severity of Punishment: A Review of the Evidence and Issues," *Justice Quarterly*, Vol. 4, No. 20, June 1987, pp. 173-217.

43. Donald R. Cressey "Foreword," in Francis T. Cullen and Karen E. Gilbert, *Reaffirming Rehabilitation*, Cincinnati, Ohio: Anderson Publishing Company, 1982, p. xii.

44. Todd R. Clear and George F. Cole, *American Corrections*, Belmont, California: Wadsworth Publishing Company, 1994, p. 74.

45. Menninger, *Crime of Punishment*, p. 206.

46. The following example is paraphrased from Carney, *Corrections*, p. 7.

47. *Ibid.*

48. *Ibid.*, p. 8.

49. Franklin E. Zimring and Gordon J. Hawkins, *Deterrence*, Chicago: University of Chicago Press, 1973, pp. 19-20.

50. Marvin Wolfgang, Robert Figlio, and Thorsten Sellin, *Delinquency in a Birth Cohort*, Chicago: University of Chicago Press, 1972. Peter Greenwood, "Controlling the Crime Rate through Imprisonment," in James Q. Wilson, ed., *Crime and Public Policy*, San Francisco: Institute for Contemporary Studies Press, 1983. Sholomo Shinnar and Reuel Shinnar, "The Effects of the Criminal Justice System on the Control of Crime: A Quantitative Approach," *Law and Society Review*, Vol. 9, 1975, pp. 581-611.

51. Greenwood, "Controlling the Crime Rate," p. 258.

52. Lee S. Pershan, "Selective Imprisonment Should Not Be Used," in Bonnie Szumski, ed., *America's Prisons: Opposing Viewpoints*, Fourth Edition, St. Paul, Minnesota: Greenhaven Press, 1985, p. 100.

53. For a summary of the objections to selective incapacitation, *see* Jacqueline Cohen, "Incapacitating Criminals: Recent Research Findings," *National Institute of Justice Research in Brief*, Washington, D.C.: U.S. Department of Justice, 1983, p. 4.

54. Dean Champion, *Corrections in the United States*, Englewood Cliffs, New Jersey: Prentice Hall, 1990, p. 17.

55. Mark Mauer, *Americans Behind Bars: U.S. and International Use of Incarceration*, 1995, Washington, D.C.: The Sentencing Project, 1997, p. 11.

56. Kevin E. Meehan, "California's Three-Strike Law: The First Six Years," *Corrections Management Quarterly*, Vol. 4, No. 4, Fall 2000, pp. 22-33.

57. Cited in Louis P. Carney, *Probation and Parole: Legal and Social Dimensions*, New York: McGraw-Hill, 1977, p. 75.

58. Lawrence F. Travis, Martin D. Schwartz, and Todd R. Clear, *Corrections: An Issues Approach*, Second Edition, Cincinnati, Ohio: Anderson Publishing Company, 1983, p. 9.

59. Robert Martinson, "What Works? Questions and Answers about Prison Reform," *The Public Interest*, Vol. 35, Spring 1975, p. 25. It should, however, be noted that Martinson's report did not specifically conclude that "nothing works," but rather, that the methodologies used to evaluate rehabilitative efforts were so inadequate that no effect could be validly measured—which points to the need for implementing more rigorous program-evaluation techniques.

60. Francis T. Gilbert and Karen E. Cullen, *Reaffirming Rehabilitation*, Matthew Bender and Co., 1982. *See also* Paul Gendreau, "The Principles of Effective Intervention with Offenders," in Alan T. Harland, ed., *Choosing Correctional Options that Work*, Thousand Oaks, California: Sage, 1996.

61. Francis T. Cullen, John B. Cullen, and John F. Wozniak, "Is Rehabilitation Dead? The Myth of the Punitive Public," *Journal of Criminal Justice*, Vol. 16, No. 4, 1988, p. 303.

CHAPTER 3

THE DEVELOPMENT OF CORRECTIONS

> 66 In the years to come, it is hoped that . . . citizens will direct a new generation of correctional workers to create more positive chapters in corrections' history. For the harm done through their wrongdoings, offenders are responsible. But for using inappropriate methods for treating offenders, when better methods are known, we are all guilty.[1] 99
>
> —American Correctional Association

Chapter Overview

I f it is true that society is judged by how it treats its prisoners, the methods employed in the past are harsh indictments indeed. For those of us living in this century, it may be difficult to envision the savage treatment of offenders in the past. Life without prisons and jails, or even courts and trials, may be incomprehensible to us—yet these have been relatively recent "inventions." While there have not always been correctional institutions and justice as we know it today, there always has been criminal behavior, and our predecessors were rather ingenious at devising brutal methods of responding to it. It was not without reason that America's forefathers established a constitutional guarantee against "cruel and unusual punishment."

As everything from clothing to child rearing has changed with the times, so has our concept of "cruel and unusual," and along with it, our correctional practices. The tortures, floggings, and public humiliations that characterized "corrections" of the past conflict with today's concept of the worth of life and human dignity. Although there are still countries in which severe physical punishment is employed in response to criminal behavior, the humanitarian values upon which democracy in the United States is based preclude such practices.

Undoubtedly, there are times when, in extreme frustration with our inability to deal with crime, demands arise for a return to the "good old days" when offenders were more likely than not assumed to be guilty, and harsh punishment could be meted out by the victim. (In fact, it is in part for this reason that you occasionally will find graphic descriptions of those times in this chapter—to enable you to view them in the light of rationality rather than with the emotion of nostalgia). Tradeoffs come with every social advancement. Just as we sacrifice some amount of crime for the right to be free of overly restrictive government intrusions, we have traded the barbarity of vengeance for the civilization of due process and respect for human rights.

 # Learning Goals

Do you know:

1. What role the victim played in achieving justice during primitive times?
2. What is meant by the concept of *lex talionis*?
3. How religion influenced early forms of punishment?

Primitive Law

Every society has had methods of social control—ranging from public disapproval to death—that hold individuals to expected standards of behavior. As primitive people formed tribes, group living created certain customs that everyone was expected to observe. "Justice" was a very personal matter. It was also a brutal process. If someone stole game from a neighbor's traps, he could expect to pay for the crime in a pot of boiling oil or a cage of wild beasts.[2]

Ancient cultures developed the idea of justice based on vengeance, retribution, and compensation. When a crime was committed, punishment was carried out by the victim personally, along with help provided by the victim's family. On a practical basis, personal retribution by the victim was still the dominant method of control. In fact, the law of retaliation (*lex talionis*) against the offender was reflected in the Code of Hammurabi, as well as in the Old Testament:

> *Leviticus 24:20* (570 B.C.): "Breach for breach, eye for eye, tooth for tooth, as he has caused a blemish in a man, so shall it be done to him again."

However, the New Testament spoke in opposition to retribution:

> *Matthew 5:38, 39* (A.D. 65): "Ye have heard that it hath been said, 'An eye for an eye, and a tooth for a tooth,' But I say unto you, That ye resist not evil: but whosoever shall smite thee on thy right cheek, turn to him the other also."

Despite this constraint in the New Testament, retribution remained the primary form of social control. The influence of Christian teachings on everyday practice was not to occur for many years. In fact, in a somewhat ironic development, punishments became even more severe with the rise of the major religions. It was believed that sin and crime were offenses against God, and thus became infractions of divine law and God's will, as well as damaging to society.

The many references to "prison" in the Old and New Testaments and other religious books were there long before the modern concept of prison evolved. At that time, they referred to confinement in rooms and facilities not originally designed for punishment—such as old cellars, dens for animals, and other makeshift resources. They were used in a manner not unlike sending an errant child to his or her room for detention. The concept of jails and prisons in the modern sense was still centuries away.

Learning Goals

Do you know:

1. How some offenders were protected in medieval times by the benefit of clergy and the right of sanctuary?
2. How jails were first used, in contrast to their functions today?
3. What impact the breakdown of the feudal system had on the development of debtors' prisons and workhouses?
4. Why banishment and exile were used extensively following the Industrial Revolution?

Medieval Practices

By the medieval period, the influence of the Roman Catholic Church was unmistakable. *Benefit of clergy* provided a reprieve to members of the clergy because of their ability to read and write. Later, it was expanded to include those who could prove their literacy by reading a "test" verse in Psalms 51 (appropriately, the passage begins with the words "Have mercy on me"). However, as those who were illiterate began to memorize this psalm, the practice gradually ended.[3] The *right of sanctuary* was also recognized, through which certain locations (often churches or holy places) were designated as places where an offender might go to escape punishment.

Medieval Punishments

For those who could not escape, medieval punishments were very brutal. Knives, axes, whips, collars, and cuffs were commonly used to inflict pain, along with confinement in cold, dark, damp, vermin-infested dungeons. "Man's primitive fear of being confined in the darkness" was used "as both torture and punishment."[4]

The death penalty was invoked frequently—not in the quick, almost sterile manner in which it is carried out today, but through methods designed to extract as much pain and suffering as possible. Several ingenious devices were designed for this purpose. Among the most grotesque was the "iron maiden"— a boxlike device with the front half hinged like a door so that a person could

In 1790, the Walnut Street Jail became the birthplace of the first penal facility directed toward the correction of convicted felons. Courtesy of Pennsylvania Prison Society.

be placed inside. When the door was shut, protruding spikes, both back and front, entered the body of the victim. Equally barbaric was the "rack"—a device for dragging apart the joints by the feet and hands.

Executions by burning, beheading, and hanging also were employed liberally. These were public events, attended by crowds of gleeful onlookers, as evidenced in the English poem in the next "Close-up On Corrections." Perhaps most reprehensible was the "widespread practice of taking children to see hangings and gibbeted corpses and whipping them soundly on the site."[5] For more than two hundred years, England used capital punishment extensively. During the reign of Queen Elizabeth alone, for example, there were some 72,000 executions.

Those fortunate enough to escape the gallows or the tortures inflicted in castles and dungeons might find themselves confined to the galleys of convict ships that sailed the seas aimlessly with a cargo of felons. These vessels may have been offshoots of the "hulks" or nonseaworthy vessels that had been anchored in the Thames River in London and elsewhere as places of confinement. Like the slave galleys of ancient Rome and Greece, floggings were common and conditions were extremely harsh: "chained to their crowded benches, often for six months at a time and perhaps for longer . . . [t]he rowers were exposed to all weathers and were fed on hard fare, and frequently much stinted in water-supply."[6] In addition, many of these vessels also contained their own torture devices.

Confinement Practices

Originally, incarceration was used only until a confession was obtained or the death penalty was imposed. It was the Roman Catholic Church that first made use of long-term confinement of offenders by locking them into the gatehouse of the abbey during the Middle Ages as a humane gesture to replace execution. In the twelfth century, some private prisons were constructed by wealthy landowners. This enabled those with sufficient power and influence to build their own prisons and incarcerate anyone who interfered with their political ambitions or personal inclinations.[7]

Close-up On Corrections

> Poor John Goose, poor John Goose
> For him not the speed of the hangman's noose
> But the crackle and spit of the ghastly fire
> As inch by inch the flames grow higher.
> Burn him merrily, cry the crowd,
> So he hath no need of a burial shroud.

Source: Shelagh Abbott in G. Abbott, *Tortures of the Tower of London*, London: David & Charles, 1986, p. 60.

Following the signing of the *Magna Carta* by King John in 1215, the crown no longer could imprison or execute subjects unless they first were tried by a jury of fellow citizens. The Magna Carta also reduced much of the king's power and returned it to the local community. A growing philosophy of government by the consent of the governed was evolving. It included provisions for courts, free elections, greater local government control, and theoretically treating all persons alike before the law, whether rich or poor. During this period, the origins of civil and constitutional rights as we know them were emerging. However, these were very rudimentary beginnings, and in reality, "justice" was still largely determined by social class.

Early English Jails

With the development of trials, a place was needed to confine offenders until the king's court could be convened in the county where the crime occurred. That place became the *gaol* (or as it is now spelled, "jail"). In contrast to its use today, offenders did not serve time as punishment in jail. Rather, the jail was employed to confine those awaiting either *trial* or the imposition of *punishment* (functions that are still performed by modern jails). However, during this period of time, the punishment being awaited was more often than not death. It was not uncommon for untried prisoners to wait years to appear before the court.[8]

The crown provided no funds for jail operations. As a result, sheriffs contracted with "keepers" to assure that inmates did not escape. Although the keeper was paid no salary, such contracts were actually quite lucrative. They generated income from *fees* charged to inmates, since prisoners were required "to pay for every service and good provided by the keeper."[9] For example, fees were charged to be booked, to eat, to sleep on a mattress, to obtain a bed, and to be released (even with a judicial order). Because the physical structures were so insecure and prone to easy escape, prisoners were often weighted down by "manacles, shackles, and iron collars, which they also paid the keeper a fee for the privilege of wearing."[10] To pay for their keep, inmates could beg or accept charitable donations, and profit was also made by selling inmate labor. Essentially, offenders were required to "pay for the privilege of being in jail"[11] through a system that basically amounted to extortion. For a vivid account of physical conditions and the fee system in a famous London gaol, see the next "Close-up On Corrections."

Wealthy offenders could pay for the privilege of living in plush quarters. But others "faced virtually intolerable living conditions. Everyone was literally dumped together. Children and adults, men and women, felons and debtors, healthy and sick (including lepers)—all were forced to live communally."[12] Given the extreme crowding, the filthy, rat-infested environment, and the lack of proper nutrition, it was not surprising that the strong preyed on the weak. Rape was common. Illnesses abounded. Many died of starvation or disease. The hopelessness of people confined in such conditions is well-illustrated in the words scrawled on a cell wall by one desperate inmate:

> *To the builders of this nitemare though you may never get to read these words. I pity you; for the crueity [sic] of your minds have designed this hell; if men's buildings are a reflection of what they are, this one portraits the ugliness of all humanity. IF ONLY YOU HAD SOME COMPASSION.*[13]

Breakdown of the Feudal System

As long as people were tied to the land and obliged to landowners through serfdom and tithings, they were relatively easy to control. But with the breakdown of the feudal system and the decline of craft guilds came mass unemployment and poverty. People moved about from county to city, dissolving their ties to neighbors, family, and the land that had held them in bounds for centuries. The hungry and jobless migrated from rural areas to the cities, bringing with them a rise in crime with which society was ill-equipped to cope.

To deal with social outcasts, *debtors' prisons* were established in addition to jails and workhouses.[14] In fact, it has been noted that "the earliest candidates for incarceration in institutions for purposes other than awaiting some bodily punishment were largely the poor and the insane."[15] With the scarcity of laborers following the Black Death, workhouses were used as sources of cheap, forced labor. The city of London established a workhouse at St. Brigit's Well—called Bridewell—in 1557. The use of workhouses became widespread throughout Europe to house the insane and to "reform" minor offenders (such as beggars and pickpockets) by hard work and discipline. Debtors' prisons housed the indigent, who were incarcerated until family, friends, or charitable sources paid their monetary obligations—or until death.

Banishment and Exile

Serious offenders were transported to banishment or exile. *Banishment* was considered an appropriate response to misbehavior, a means of ridding civilized society of nuisances through a sentence to the wilds of the unknown, as reflected in the following decree:

Close-up On Corrections

LONDON'S FAMOUS NEWGATE GAOL

The outside had a nice appearance, but the inside was another matter. The dark and gloomy cells were poorly ventilated, the water supply inadequate, and the stench appalling. These conditions gave rise to outbreaks of gaol fever, which was a form of typhus. The gaol fumes help[ed] spread the disease to many prisoners. . . .

There seems to have been very little, if any, segregation of the Newgaters, with the exception of those cast into the lower dungeons. . . . According to an inmate placed there in 1724, it was "a terrible stinking dark and dismal place situated underground into which no daylight can come. It was paved with stone; the prisoners had no beds and lay on the pavement whereby they endured great misery and hardship."

Those prisoners who could afford to do so had their food and clothing sent to them from the outside. The alternative was to purchase such items from the keeper and his turnkeys, which resulted in tidy profits. . . . The gaol workers also made sums of money from the sale of spirits, candles, food, and even water. Gaolers also charged for the privilege of being released from irons and for allowing prisoners to approach the warming fire.

Source: J. M. Moynahan and Troy R. Bunke, "London's Famous Newgate Gaol (1188-1902)," *American Jails*, 5 (2). May/June 1991, pp. 76-77. Used with permission.

I sentence you . . . but to what I know not—perhaps to storm and shipwreck, perhaps to infectious disorders, perhaps to famine, perhaps to be massacred by savages, perhaps to be devoured by wild beasts. Anyway, take your chance, perish or prosper, suffer or enjoy; I rid myself of the sight of you; . . . I shall give myself no more trouble over you.[16]

Banishment was also a reflection of the economic conditions of the time. Replacement of the feudal system with a developing capitalistic economy occurred with the Industrial Revolution in the mid-eighteenth century. The mechanization provided by the Industrial Revolution made slavery no longer profitable, either on land or in the galleys at sea. Consequently, criminals had to be exported. Russia sent hers to Siberia. Spain and Portugal sent theirs to Africa. France sent hers to South America. England sent her criminals to Australia and America. As one historian has noted, "wilderness was the first penal colony."[17]

In 1717, the British Parliament formally designated America as England's penal colony (although prisoners had been shipped there as early as 1650). By the time of the American Revolution, an estimated 100,000 criminals had been transported in chains to America. Because the exiled prisoners provided a free source of labor in the developing colonies, there was a considerable economic advantage to this practice. At the beginning of the American Revolution in 1776, however, America was closed to British prisoners because the government did not want to risk shipping more able-bodied Englishmen who would take up arms against the mother country. Subsequently, some offenders were confined in "hulks" (old ships anchored in rivers and harbors),[18] while others were sent to Australia until 1879, when that practice was terminated. Prisons eventually substituted for banishment.

✸ Learning Goals

Do you know:

1. What types of punishment were first employed in the American colonies?
2. When and where the first U.S. prison was established?

Early American Corrections

Corrections in America had a harsh beginning. Although the Spanish explored Florida and established the city of St. Augustine in 1564, most of the early development of the United States centered on the northeastern seaboard, where the English came in search of freedom from religious persecution. The Puritans who settled there, however, were equally intolerant of religious views that conflicted with their own.

Colonial Punishments

The colonists brought with them extremely severe criminal codes from England, which, combined with the Puritans' strict concepts of sin, created a rigid system of social control. The famous witchcraft trials in 1692 were prompted by this religious fervor. Even the celebration of Christmas was considered sacrilegious and was outlawed in 1659, and the Connecticut Code of 1650 "stipulated the death penalty for children who disobeyed their parents."[19]

Infractions were dealt with severely. Reflecting the colonists' British heritage, corporal and capital punishment were used frequently and carried out publicly. Branding and various forms of mutilation were employed, both as punishment and to identify the lawbreaker. "The removal of a hand or finger, the slitting of the nostrils, the severing of an ear, or branding usually made it impossible for the marked individual to find honest employment."[20] Minor offenders such as gossips might find themselves subjected to public humiliation through the ducking stool (where they were submerged in water until near drowning).

Stocks and pillories located in the town square secured the offender's head and hands within wooden frames. These devices were not just passive measures. In addition to provoking verbal ridicule, they enabled passers-by to pelt the constrained offender with stones and various other missiles. "The victim might also be whipped or branded while in the stocks or pillory," and when released, "compelled either to tear his ears loose from the nails or have them cut away

During colonial times, minor offenders could find themselves in a revolving pillory, subjected to public humiliation in the town square. Courtesy of Federal Bureau of Prisons, *Handbook of Correctional Institutional Design and Construction.*

carelessly by the officer in charge."[21] For more serious crimes, capital punishment was imposed—by hanging, burning at the stake, or breaking on the rack.[22]

Colonial Correctional Institutions

Along with England's laws and punishments, early settlers brought with them the English system of jails, which became the first correctional institutions in this country. Like British gaols, early American jails housed defendants waiting trial or convicted offenders waiting the imposition of their sentence. The concept of "serving time" in jail was still unknown. Also, like their British counterparts, Americans used the *fee system* for operating jails, along with its resulting abuses and corruption. The first U.S. jails, established in Virginia during the early seventeenth century, charged "two pounds of tobacco" as the fee for admission or release.[23]

Despite the democratic ideals on which this country was founded, the British practice of enabling the rich to avoid jail or live in comfortable quarters was adopted. In contrast to the privileges afforded the wealthy, the poor were confined in gruesome conditions of hunger, filth, and disease spread by communal living. Food was minimal, sanitary conditions deplorable, and discipline nonexistent. Similar to their jailed English counterparts, "it was not uncommon for individuals with no resources to die of starvation."[24]

The first institution intended for long-term punishment rather than pretrial detention was *Newgate* prison, established in Simsbury, Connecticut, just prior to the American Revolution (1773). Actually, Newgate was an abandoned copper mine, with administrative buildings constructed over the mine's shaft. Three excavated caverns with one pool of fresh water constituted the prison. Offenders were confined underground, in the dripping water, foul air, and "horrid gloom" of what has been described as essentially a "dungeon."[25] Men and women, adults and children, sick and well, criminals, and political prisoners

(Tory sympathizers) were all placed together. Escapes were frequent, since "existence in the dungeon was so unbearable that getting out was the one incentive that kept its inmates alive." [26]

 Learning Goals

Do you know:

1. What contributions John Howard made to correctional developments?
2. Why the U.S. Constitution is important to American corrections?
3. What amendments to the U.S. Constitution pertain to corrections?

From Vengeance to Justice

By the mid-eighteenth century, conditions were ripe for major changes in both Europe and the United States. Punishments had become excessively violent and bloody, totally out of proportion to the seriousness of the offense. At the same time, Europe was experiencing the impact of the *Enlightenment* (also known as the "Age of Reason"). Traditional assumptions were challenged, greater emphasis was placed on individual equality, and the barbarity of punishment practices was called into question.

John Howard's Prison Reforms

Among the pioneers insisting on changes in penal practices of the time was the sheriff of Bedfordshire, *John Howard*, a former prisoner himself. The next "Close-up On Corrections" features an account of Howard's personal experiences, which inspired his demands for change.

 # Close-up On Corrections

JOHN HOWARD (1726-1790)

John Howard's interest in prisons began when he was on his way to Portugal in 1754. His ship was captured by a French privateer, and those on board were treated with great severity. While confined, he gained sufficient evidence to show that hundreds of English prisoners had perished because of poor treatment. He was permitted to return to England on parole to negotiate an exchange, and in 1773, he became the high sheriff of Bedfordshire. In that capacity he visited the jail which he was in charge of and found people detained for months until they paid fees for their own release. His first act was to apply for a salary for the jailer to reduce the reliance on fees. From that time on, he devoted himself to penal reform.

Source: D. L. Howard, *John Howard: Prison Reformer*, London: Christopher Johnson, 1958.

Struck by the deplorable conditions that he found when he became responsible for the local gaol, Howard embarked on visits to prisons throughout both England and Europe, documenting what he found and pressing for reform. His blistering essay on *The State of the Prisons in England and Wales* (1777) for the first time called public attention to the plight of incarcerated offenders. Among the improvements that he advocated were the following: [27]

- Segregation of prisoners by age, sex, and severity of their offense

- Cells for prisoners, to reduce moral and physical contamination

- Salaried staff to prevent the extortion of prisoners

- Appointment of chaplains and medical officers to address the spiritual and physical needs of inmates

- Prohibitions against the sale of liquor to prisoners

- Provision of adequate clothing and food to ensure continued good health

Rejecting hard labor, Howard coined the term "penitentiary" to indicate that such institutions should be designed according to the Quaker philosophy of penance and contrition by reflecting on one's sins. The impact of his legacy lives on even today through prison reform groups that commemorate his name—the John Howard Societies.

The U.S. Constitution

Rejecting Europe's class-based aristocracy and monarchy rule, American colonists embraced equality and a democratic system of government. Moreover, the Constitution of the United States was developed during the period of Enlightenment, reflecting many of its humanitarian principles. The colonists followed this line of thinking, introducing a new concept in government—that rights which belonged to them were "inherent and inalienable."

The Constitution is of prime importance to corrections, because it provides the framework for the American system of administering justice. Citizens (including criminal offenders) may lose some of their civil rights but never their constitutional guarantees. While the Constitution itself establishes our democratic system of government, it is the first ten amendments to the Constitution that are of particular importance. These are called the *Bill of Rights. See* the next "Close-up On Corrections" for a look at how those amendments pertain to corrections. This emphasis on the worth of human life, along with the liberty to enjoy it, was in stark contrast to the arbitrary and inhumane practices of the past.

 Learning Goals

Do you know:

1. What group established the Walnut Street Jail and what significance it is to corrections?
2. The differences between the Pennsylvania and the Auburn systems?
3. Why the Auburn system was adopted in the United States?

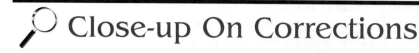

Close-up On Corrections

CONSTITUTIONAL RIGHTS RELATED TO CORRECTIONS

First Amendment

The First Amendment establishes our right to freedom of religion, freedom of speech, and freedom of the press, along with the right to peaceably assemble and "petition government for a redress of grievances." Prisoners have used their First Amendment privileges to challenge the conditions of their confinement.

Fifth Amendment

Among other provisions, the Fifth Amendment requires "due process of law" before anyone can be deprived of "life, liberty, or property." This has implications for such correctional procedures as the revocation of probation or parole.

Sixth Amendment

The Sixth Amendment protects citizens against arbitrary practices of government, and therefore can be invoked in conjunction with disciplinary actions in correctional facilities.

Eighth Amendment

It is this provision that is often cited by inmates challenging the constitutionality of their confinement, since it prohibits the infliction of "cruel and unusual punishment" as well as prohibits "excessive bail and fines."

Fourteenth Amendment

Further applying constitutional guarantees to the states, the Fourteenth Amendment assures all citizens that no state shall "deprive any person of life, liberty, or property without due process of law; nor deny to any person . . . the equal protection of the laws." Among other things, this generally means that corrections cannot provide (or deny) privileges to one group in a manner that is not equivalent to how others are treated.

The Penitentiary Emerges

Even before such protections were established in the Constitution, Pennsylvania had a reform-minded governor, *William Penn*. He replaced existing regulations governing conduct in that colony with the Quaker criminal code. Quite humane in comparison to the extremely severe laws in effect at the time, it called for:

- Abolishing capital punishment for crimes other than homicide
- Substituting imprisonment at hard labor for bloody punishments
- Providing free food and lodging to inmates
- Replacing the pillory and stocks with houses of detention[28]

Penn's humanitarian principles were repealed at the time of his death in 1718, but they later were revived by one of the original signers of the Declaration of Independence, *Dr. Benjamin Rush*, who headed the Philadelphia Society for Alleviating the Miseries of the Public Prisons (which also counted Benjamin Franklin among its members). Under Rush's leadership, the society protested both capital punishment and excessive displays of harsh public reprisals, maintaining that they only served to harden criminals.

The Walnut Street Jail

If the widespread use of corporal and capital punishments was to be abandoned, it was necessary to develop an alternative sanction. It was for this purpose that the Philadelphia Society established the first penitentiary in 1790 at the *Walnut Street Jail.* "Unlike the workhouses, prisons, and jails already in existence, the Walnut Street Jail was used exclusively for the correction of convicted felons."[29] In stark contrast to Newgate, it was the first institution designed for reform—that is, to make the offender penitent (hence the term "penitentiary").

Following many of the concepts advocated by John Howard, men and women were housed in separate facilities. Liquor was prohibited. Inmates were classified by the seriousness of their offense. During the day, they worked on handicrafts in their cells under strict rules of silence. A small exercise yard was attached to each cell. Cells were constructed to provide solitary confinement to eliminate moral contamination from other prisoners. This also served to encourage inmates to meditate at night on the evils of their ways. The Quakers' religious motivation created a more humane prison aimed at treatment by solitary confinement, hard work, religious instruction, and Bible reading. "Nothing was to detract the penitent prisoner from the path toward reform."[30] Despite its relative progressiveness, however, imposed silence and lack of personal contact over extended periods of time took a toll on the inmates' mental health—in terms of both suicides and mental illness.

The Walnut Street Jail served as the model for what became known as the *Pennsylvania system.* It was adopted at Eastern State Penitentiary in Philadelphia, the Western State Penitentiary in Pittsburgh, and in prisons throughout a number of other northeastern states. While we will see that the Pennsylvania system did not survive in this country, it did make a permanent impact on the public's response to criminal behavior and the nature of correctional practices.

The Auburn System

It is somewhat ironic that the major competition to the Pennsylvania system came from Auburn, New York, since the facility constructed there in 1815 was originally based on many of the principles of the Walnut Street Jail. In fact, both systems included solitary confinement in separate cells and enforced silence at all times to prevent inmates from communicating. But while prisoners at

Auburn were locked in their cells at night, during the day they participated together in congregate work. Although the mental distraction of work may appear to create a more humane system, Auburn was far from a humane environment. As described in the next "Close-up On Corrections," inside accounts reveal rigid routines and harsh discipline to control inmate behavior. Adding further to their humiliation, although inmates were not permitted to receive visitors, "citizens who paid admission could come into the prison and look them over," as if they were in a zoo. [31]

Unlike Auburn, the Pennsylvania system incorporated work within one's cell only as a limited diversion from its major emphasis on seeking penance through required Bible reading and reflection on one's sins. Complete solitary confinement was considered essential at all times to maintain discipline, prevent contamination, and more effectively manipulate the inmate's will. In contrast, the Auburn system could confine inmates in smaller units—since they did not need cell space in which to work, and discipline could be assured with on-the-spot lashings for rule violations. But more important, Auburn "could generate productive labor by groups of men working at the same task and by setting up factory areas where machines could be employed." [32] Thus, it became a more profitable system to operate.

For a number of years, intense debate raged in both the United States and in Europe over the relative merits of each system. While Europeans eventually opted for the more humane and treatment-oriented philosophy of the Pennsylvania system, most American states adopted the economical Auburn plan. The Pennsylvania system was geared toward small crafts that rapidly were becoming outdated, whereas Auburn's methods were adaptable to the emerging factory-oriented methods of industrial production. In fact, vestiges of the Auburn system still can be seen in large penitentiaries, and the degrading uniforms with "prison stripes" introduced there more than 170 years ago have made a comeback in some places during recent years.

 # Close-up On Corrections

DISCIPLINE IN THE AUBURN SYSTEM

The prisoners are obliged to obey instantly all orders issued by the foremen, to work quickly and efficiently without pause, in silence, and with downcast eyes. . . . They may not speak to one another except when ordered to do so by their supervisors. . . . They are expressly forbidden to converse with visitors. . . . The least breach of these rules is punished immediately and sternly. Any misdeed shall be penalized instantly and without mercy by flogging with a whip or a cane on the shoulders or the naked back. Every supervisor has the right to mete out punishment, and there is no fixed limit to the number of stripes that may be given. . . .

Source: Torsten Eriksson, 1976. *The Reformers: An Historical Survey of Pioneer Experiments in the Treatment of Criminals*. New York: Elsevier, pp. 56-57.

 # Learning Goals

Do you know:

1. How Alexander Maconochie, Walter Crofton, and Zebulon Brockway influenced correctional developments?
2. What caused the downfall of the industrial era of corrections?
3. The three general types of prison labor still in use?

U.S. Prison Developments

Along with Auburn's philosophy of congregate work, U.S. prisons adopted its stern discipline and degrading practices. Emphasizing strict rules and obedient compliance, infractions were dealt with swiftly and harshly. Staff were relatively free to respond to misbehavior and "disrespect" as they saw fit. This promoted efficiency in terms of administrative operations, but it did little in terms of constructive change for the offenders. Prisons were judged by their "production record and number of escapes, not by the number of inmates rehabilitated," and during much of the nineteenth century, "silence characterized not only prisoners, but the public" as well.[33]

Regional Developments

Most of the significant prisons in populated areas during this period were large, industrial, gothic-style "fortresses," designed to hold as many as 4,000 to 6,000 prisoners in conditions of tight security. In less settled places, territorial jails eventually developed into prisons, and even a few floating hulks emerged in California during the gold rush.[34]

Southern states developed in a different pattern. The agricultural economy there was based on a semifeudal system in which the plantation owners maintained hired help and slaves on large tracts of land. As a result, there was little need for large, central prisons. It was the occupation armies from the North who established the first real prisons in most southern states following the Civil War.

In the postwar South, there were not enough tax funds to support adequate schools, so it is not surprising that correctional institutions received low priority. Arrangements were made in most southern states to *lease* prisoners to the highest bidder. The bidders were generally large landowners, railroad companies, or contractors. Unfortunately, such enterprises were more concerned with making profits than with providing humane conditions for their laborers. The abuses, exploitation, and atrocities that resulted from this system have created a sordid chapter, not just in the history of corrections, but in the overall saga of people's inhumanity to each other.[35] "In retrospect, the most that can be said for this period of American prison history is that . . . it was better than a return to the barbarities of capital and corporal punishment." [36]

The Reform Era

With attention no longer diverted by war, the sorry plight of American prisons finally recaptured public notice by 1870. Reform-minded prison administrators, members of Congress, and prominent citizens gathered in Cincinnati that year to form the National Prison Association, conducting the first meeting of what has now become the American Correctional Association (ACA). The long tradition of the American Correctional Association as a national advocate for correctional improvements was firmly established by the foresighted principles adopted at the 1870 meeting, described in the next "Close-up On Corrections."

 # Close-up On Corrections

PRINCIPLES OF THE 1870 NATIONAL PRISON ASSOCIATION

1. Reformation, not the vindictive infliction of suffering, should be the purpose of penal treatment.

2. Prisoners should be classified on the basis of a mark system patterned after the Irish system.

3. Rewards should be provided for good conduct.

4. Prisoners should be made to realize that their futures rest in their own hands.

5. Indeterminate sentences should be substituted for fixed sentences, and disparities in sentences removed.

6. Religion and education are the most important agencies of reformation.

7. Discipline should be administered so that it gains the cooperation of the inmate and maintains his self-respect.

8. The goal of the prison should be to make industrious free citizens, not orderly and obedient prisoners.

9. Industrial training should be fully provided.

10. Prisons should be small; separate institutions should be provided for different types of offenders.

11. The social training of prisoners should be facilitated; silence rules should be abolished.

12. Society at large must realize that it is responsible for the conditions that breed crime.

Source: Enoch C. Wines, ed., 1871, *Transactions of the National Congress on Penitentiary and Reformatory Discipline*, Albany, New York: Argus. Reprinted by the American Correctional Association, 1970.

Among the leaders influencing deliberations in Cincinnati, and later, developments throughout the country, were the following:

- *Rutherford B. Hayes*, former president of the United States, was elected as the first president of the National Prison Association in Cincinnati, serving until his death in 1893. A progressive social reformer, Hayes pressed for jail reform, separation of offenders by age, indeterminate sentences, and improved academic and vocational education for inmates.[37]

- *Captain Alexander Maconochie* was an Englishman in charge of the British penal colony on Norfolk Island in the South Pacific. When Maconochie arrived at his post in 1840, conditions were so bad that "men reprieved from the death penalty wept, and those who were to die thanked God."[38] While he did not totally abandon the concept of punishment for one's crimes, he maintained that an attempt also should be made to reform offenders by providing incentives to encourage good behavior and some measure of hope for early release. The practice of determinate sentencing offered no chance for release until the full term was served. Maconochie therefore implemented the first form of *indeterminate sentencing*—a "mark system," whereby freedom could be earned through hard work and proper behavior. An elaborate process of earning "marks" through labor and good conduct was developed, with discipline gradually diminished as inmates progressed through the system. The idea was to reward inmates with greater privileges obtained by "marks," thereby providing incentives to reform and better preparation for release. Unfortunately, Maconochie's practices were not well received among the British business enterprises dependent on inmate labor, and he was eventually removed from office. His visionary concepts, however, lived on.[39]

- *Sir Walter Crofton* was chairman of the board of directors of the Irish Convicts Prisons. Influenced by Maconochie's efforts, Crofton also believed that the amount of time served should be related to the prisoner's reformation. Based on that theory, in 1854 he established the Irish *ticket-of-leave* system, essentially, the first form of *parole*. Offenders could earn their release by progression through a series of stages from solitary labor to congregate work. As offenders moved through various later stages, both discipline and the length of their sentences were reduced. During the final stage, they worked outside without supervision, moving freely between the prison and the community. Those who proceeded successfully through all stages were awarded a final "ticket of leave." This was a conditional release that could be revoked any time before the original sentence expired if the offender violated established standards—in much the same manner as parole can be revoked today.

- *Zebulon Brockway* was superintendent of the Elmira Reformatory in New York, which opened in 1876 for young offenders sixteen to thirty years of age. In the United States, it was Brockway who first experimented with these new approaches. With approval of the legislature to permit indeterminate sentencing, release was earned through a modified version of the mark system, combined with the Irish ticket-of-leave. Although

Brockway has been acclaimed for introducing such reforms as education and vocational training at Elmira, he did so with an iron fist. History portrays him as a cruel administrator whose harsh and degrading physical punishments ultimately resulted in serious charges, culminating in an investigation which concluded that "the brutality practiced at the reformatory has no parallel in any modern penal institution in our country."[40] For a disturbing description of conditions at Elmira, *see* the next "Close-up On Corrections."

Nevertheless, with its introduction of education into corrections, it is not surprising that the reformatory movement was gaining strength at a time that society was turning to public education as a solution to many social problems. But the promise of original intentions was diminished by a combination of two drawbacks: (1) the introduction of probation (which diverted the most promising

 # Close-up On Corrections

ELMIRA—REFORM OR REPRESSION?

The nation's model correctional institution was overcrowded, understaffed, and grossly mismanaged. Key treatment programs did not fulfill their stated goals and objectives. Violence, escapes, smuggling, theft, homosexuality, revolts, arson, and other forms of inmate resistance were serious problems. Inmates suffered extraordinarily harsh punishments—including severe whippings and months of solitary confinement in dark, cold dungeons—and deliberate psychological torture. In the words of one inmate [who was removed from his cell with prodding from a hot poker to be punished for failure to complete his work]:

> "A hook was fastened into my shackles, and I was hoisted off the floor. I got a half dozen blows with the paddle right across the kidneys. The pain was so agonizing that I fainted. They revived me, and when I begged for mercy, Brockway struck me on the head with a strap, knocking me insensible. . . . I stayed in the dungeon that night and the next day, shackled, and received only bread and water. The following day I was again hoisted up and beaten, returned to the dungeon, and after one day's rest, beaten again. . . . I remained for twenty-one days on bread and water."

Elmira was, quite simply, a brutal prison. . . . [where] beatings caused discolored faces, bloody noses, and swollen eyes. . . . medical care was inadequate, and inmates had been whipped, punched, and chained in solitary confinement on bread and water. Balancing the conflicting aims of repression and reform proved to be a difficult, if not impossible, task.

Source: Alexander W. Pisciotta, *Benevolent Repression: Social Control and the American Reformatory-Prison Movement*. New York: New York University Press, 1994, pp. 33, 36-37, 57-59, citing the 1884 *Report and Proceedings of the New York State Board of Charities*. Used with permission.

offenders from reformatories); and (2) the lack of qualified staff (who were better prepared to promote discipline than provide education). That is not to say that the visions of these reformers were fruitless, however, for they did stimulate faith in the potential for positive change.

The Industrial Era

Inmate labor has been central to the development of prisons since the first workhouses were opened in Europe during the sixteenth century. Even in the penitence-minded Walnut Street Jail, private contractors furnished raw material that prisoners turned into finished products in their cells for an agreed price. More profitable industrial production has been a feature of corrections since the Auburn Penitentiary and, as we have seen, played a major role in the Auburn versus Pennsylvania debate. Self-supporting prisons have always been popular with taxpayers. As early as 1828, prisons at Auburn and Sing Sing were paying for themselves.

Not until the twentieth century, however, did inmate industries flourish on a large scale. Although the leasing of inmates outside the prison continued, at this time a new system of *contract labor* emerged. Prison factories were constructed within the walls of the institution, and administrators contracted with firms either for wages or for the sale of finished products. In rural areas, offenders worked at manual labor on prison-owned farms. Many of these operations were justified under the guise of achieving reform through disciplined work. But the underlying motive was monetary profit—or more explicitly, achieving the greatest return for the least investment.

Inmates were often virtual slaves of the state, working long hours under harsh conditions with minimal subsistence. A stinging indictment of such practices was issued as early as 1875 in the U.S. attorney general's vivid description of prevalent abuses:

Employment of prisoners to avoid idleness, teach trades, and reduce costs has long been a mainstay of prisons. Here inmates worked in the tailor shop at Folsom State Prison in California. Courtesy of the California Department of Corrections.

> [T]he prisoners work for cruel taskmasters, . . . are improperly fed and clothed, overworked, sometimes severely beaten for slight offenses, and are made a source of large profit to those who avail themselves of this kind of forced labor.[41]

Other accounts further attested to the barbarity of conditions, noting that "a sentence to such imprisonment was, in effect, a life sentence," as most men could not survive the brutal conditions for more than 10 years.[42]

Chain Gangs

Perhaps the most notoriously abusive practices were the infamous chain gangs of this era—intentionally used to repress and humiliate prisoners.[43] Chained together, offenders swung sledgehammers in monotonous unison under the watchful eye of shotgun-toting supervisors who administered lashes to those who could not keep up with the line. Nor did they hesitate to shoot anyone attempting to escape. In one grisly expression of the pent-up anger induced by such treatment, inmates in a labor camp who were breaking up rocks took the sledgehammers and actually used them to break their own legs during an uprising.[44] As one historian put it, the exploitation of inmate labor during this shameful period "embittered the hearts of prisoners to the extent that they came out more vindictive and more ready to injure society than they were when first placed within prison walls."[45]

The chain gangs continued working on road projects and prison construction in some states for many years. However, the late 1920s marked the beginning of the end for large-scale prison industries. This time it was not the progressive views of humanitarian reformers that altered prison practices, but rather, the political realities of the labor market. As organized labor emerged in the industrial northeast, paid workers complained about competing with free inmate labor, which dramatically reduced the price at which their goods could be sold. In response to these concerns, Congress passed the Hawes-Cooper Act of 1929, which subjected prison products to the laws of the state to which they were shipped. This was the first of a number of restrictions on inmate products.

Production Restrictions

With the severe unemployment of the Great Depression in the 1930s, there was even more pressure to prohibit the interference of inmate labor with free markets. Additional legislation was passed to limit prison industries by requiring a "prison-made" label and, ultimately, prohibiting the shipment of prison goods across state lines. By 1940, every state had passed similar restrictions on prison-made products as the power and influence of organized labor increased. Many of these restrictions remain in force today.

Such developments have curtailed the profit motive and dramatically altered the shape of prison industry. But they have not abolished it completely. There are generally three types of prison labor currently in use by various correctional departments throughout the country.

1. *State account system.* Goods are produced in prison and sold on a restricted market within the state.

2. *State use system.* Goods produced are restricted to items that can be used by other state agencies (such as schools and mental health institutions).

3. *Public works system.* Inmates provide labor for construction and maintenance of roads, parks, conservation projects, and other public facilities.

Industrial Renewal

Certainly, the widespread abuse and exploitation of inmate labor prevalent during the Industrial Era called for change. But unfortunately, change came in the form of political restrictions rather than practical reforms. For years, corrections struggled to cope with the complete reversal from forced labor to forced leisure. Although inmate idleness is a problem that still faces correctional administrators, there have been renewed efforts to provide offenders with meaningful labor.

By the mid-1970s, a resurgence of support for prison industries emerged. This reemphasis gained an advocate in 1983 when former Chief Justice Warren Burger called for prisons to be "factories with fences" [46] to provide relief from the boredom of prison life, equip inmates with marketable skills, and create a prison environment more reflective of the real world.[47] Since then, leaders in the field have been pressing to sell the merits of correctional industries to the public in a more proactive fashion.[48] As described in the next "Close-up On Corrections," joint-venture projects between prisons and the private sector have formed a number of successful partnerships that have contributed millions of dollars in taxes, room and board, family support, and victim compensation.[49]

Close-up On Corrections

DEVELOPMENTS IN PRISON INDUSTRIES

In 1979, Congress lifted the ban on interstate transportation and sale of prison-made goods—but only under certain conditions. Participants must meet the requirements of the Private Sector/Prison Industry Enhancement Certification Program (commonly known as PIE), which specifies that:

- Inmate workers are paid the prevailing wage in the local area
- Local unions are consulted before the program starts
- Inmate employment does not displace free-society workers or occur in occupations for which there is a labor surplus in the community

Since then, a number of correctional agencies have been certified under PIE to operate private-sector prison industries; for example:

- If you make a reservation with one of the major airlines, you may be talking to an inmate operator at the California Department of Corrections.
- If you wear a baseball cap featuring the emblem of your favorite team, it may have been produced by inmates working at the Connecticut Department of Corrections.
- If you attended a high school or college commencement ceremony wearing a graduation gown—or if you buy leisure clothes from a major department store—they may have been made in the South Carolina Department of Corrections.

As shown in the following figure, PIE programs not only enhance job skills and reduce prison idleness, but also make significant economic contributions to victims, families, and government.

Source: George Sexton, 1995. "Work in American Prisons: Joint Ventures with the Private Sector," *National Institute of Justice: Program Focus*. Washington, D.C.: U.S. Department of Justice, p. 12.

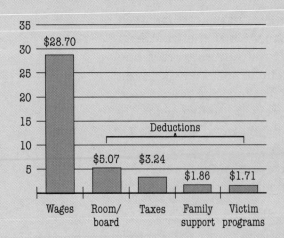

Earnings and contributions of joint-venture workers 1979-1992, in millions of dollars.

Source: George Sexton, "Work in American Prisons: Joint Ventures with the Private Sector," *National Institute of Justice Program Focus*, Washington, DC: U.S. Department of Justice, 1995, p. 12.

Learning Goals

Do you know:

1. What factors stimulated the rehabilitative era of corrections?
2. What basic constitutional rights the Supreme Court recognized on the part of inmates during the 1960s?
3. What social forces during the 1980s generated the move from indeterminate to determinate sentencing and what major correctional problem resulted?
4. How "gain time" has compromised the original goals of the justice model?

Corrections Today

By the late 1930s, the seeds were planted for a dramatic shift that is still influential in modern correctional practices. As punitive punishments became less and less acceptable, a new emphasis on *treatment* and *rehabilitation* emerged. Concerns were raised about the negative effects of imprisonment. Sentencing options other than incarceration became more attractive alternatives. Society began to display a greater awareness of and interest in what was happening behind prison walls. Institutions became more open to public scrutiny. In general, there was excitement and optimism about the possibility of salvaging offenders through treatment—of accomplishing what the term "corrections" is meant to imply.

But improvements did not occur quickly or uniformly. In retrospect, it is apparent that corrections overall was never well equipped to achieve rehabilitative ideals. Nor was the extensive idleness imposed by drastic reductions in prison industries offset by therapeutic, educational, or training programs. Through it all, administrators were forced to accommodate greater numbers of inmates in often-antiquated facilities. At the same time, the courts were beginning to recognize the rights of inmates to challenge conditions and procedures that violated constitutional protections. All of these events—positive and negative—have had an impact on nature of corrections today.

The Rehabilitative Era

With the stock market crash and resulting Great Depression of the 1930s came economic disaster. The security previously enjoyed by society was destroyed. Savings were wiped out virtually overnight. Unemployment skyrocketed to all-time record highs. Hunger reduced distinctions between social classes. Many who had been economically comfortable—even wealthy—were living in poverty. The most desperate committed suicide. Others turned to crime for survival. All of this was due to events they had no ability to control. The long-held explanations of crime as "sins" or personal weaknesses of the offender no longer seemed as valid. Society began to realize that perhaps it was through no fault of their own that some people engage in crime, but rather, that it may be a reaction to forces beyond their control.

At the same time, the psychological and social sciences were making major advances. Freud's theories of *psychoanalytic treatment* offered potential for "curing" criminal behavior. The field of social work gave legitimate recognition to attending to the needs of the underprivileged. With these developments, more attention was focused on corrections, and a new role was created for offenders as psychiatric and social work clients.

Along with changing perspectives on crime and new hope for dealing with it came a new philosophy of corrections—the *medical model*. Emphasis moved from retribution through incapacitation to improvement through rehabilitation. Chain gangs, lockstep marching, and striped uniforms gave way to psychological diagnosis, individual counseling, and group therapy. Determining inmates' needs began to take priority over punishing their deeds. By the 1950s, indeterminate sentences and the widespread use of parole held out the possibility of early release for progress in treatment programs.

That does not mean that all abuses had vanished. Although shifts in ideology pointed the field in a new direction, progress was relative to the dismal conditions of the past. Eventually, it would take outside attention by inmate riots and court intervention to improve the substandard physical conditions and dehumanizing supervisory techniques to which prisoners were still subjected.

Impact of the 1960s

The medical model reached its height in the midst of the turbulent 1960s—a period marked by liberal social attitudes, extensive federal funding, wars on poverty and crime, and massive civil rights demonstrations. The nation was swept up in vocal and sometimes violent protests against the status quo. No longer were traditional practices accepted routinely. Pressure mounted for change. The authority of social institutions was challenged on a widespread, nationwide basis, and corrections was no exception.

In keeping with the euphoria of the 1960s and its advocacy on behalf of the powerless in society, the Supreme Court intervened in the previously sacrosanct world of correctional administrators. Prior to that time, the courts generally had maintained a hands-off approach toward corrections.

That perspective changed dramatically as inmates gained a powerful advocate in the Supreme Court. By the mid-1960s, the Court had recognized the constitutional right of those incarcerated to *maintain access to the judicial process*, and specifically, to *challenge the conditions* under which they are confined.[50] Even more important, the Court later prohibited correctional administrators from *denying or obstructing* that fundamental right.[51] It became the duty of correctional officials to assure that the constitutional protections of inmates under their charge were not violated—opening a floodgate of litigation that held correctional personnel accountable for their actions.

It was also at this point that the public was becoming increasingly concerned about crime and the ability of the criminal justice system to deal with it. Thus, it is not surprising that in 1965, President Lyndon Johnson convened the *President's Commission on Law Enforcement and Administration of Justice*, a prestigious group of national experts, to address the nation's crime problem and make recommendations for improving the police, courts, and corrections. The Commission's Task Force on Corrections was assisted by hundreds of academicians and practitioners, and its *Task Force Report on Corrections* represented the first comprehensive survey of correctional practices in this country.

The task force firmly believed that "above all else" the effectiveness of corrections relies on "a sufficient number of qualified staff."[52] Many of its recommendations therefore called for major improvements in the selection, training, supervision, and accountability of correctional personnel. Moreover, the task force established *correctional standards* for operating institutions and programs. Concern for the proper treatment and well-being of inmates is illustrated in the standards for custodial supervision and discipline, which called for elimination of bread-and-water diets, corporal punishment, and useless "make-work" for purposes of humiliation.[53]

While the President's Task Force was conducting its study, the federal government was also becoming active in providing funds to support new correctional philosophies and innovative approaches. For example, the federal Prisoner Rehabilitation Act of 1965 offered grants to stimulate model projects. Many of these focused on alternatives to institutionalization—thus, for the first time, giving official recognition and status to *community-based corrections*.

Even though national studies, presidentially appointed commissions, and federally funded projects could not change conditions overnight, their impact was certainly felt. By the 1970s, the public had become much more aware of and concerned about the state of corrections. Minimum-security community-based approaches were used far more commonly. Within institutions, inmates were classified and separated by age, offense, and special needs. Specialized treatment facilities emerged. The Commission on Accreditation for Corrections was established to set and monitor standards for everything from cell size to health care. "Guards" were becoming "correctional officers," with job descriptions that focused as much on relating to offenders as on restricting their behavior. (*See* the next "Close-up On Corrections.") In places that were slow to adapt, reforms were stimulated by the courts. But despite improvements, crime was still increasing, much of it committed by repeat offenders who presumably had been rehabilitated.

The Past as Prologue

Belief that "the past is prologue to the future" is perhaps nowhere better illustrated than in the retreat from rehabilitation toward a renewed emphasis on punishment in the 1980s. As the liberal attitudes of the 1960s gave way to the conservative politics of the 1980s, the public became increasingly disenchanted with the unfulfilled promises of the medical model. As concerns were voiced that rehabilitation was not working, Robert Martinson's influential research report [54] appeared to confirm the worst suspicions. As the crime rate continued steadily upward, society became increasingly frustrated with the system's ineffectiveness, as well as impatient with the offender's ability to change.

In retrospect, the extent to which public policies or correctional practices were to blame may have been overstated, in light of the fact that the post-World War II "baby boom" had reached its primary crime-risk age (late teens to young adulthood). It is possible that demographic patterns alone might have produced rising crime, regardless of sentencing procedures or correctional approaches. But the timing was ripe for reassessing America's response to crime. Pressures to "get tough" and assure that offenders receive their "just

Close-up On Corrections

deserts" mounted, resulting in changes in both the length and nature of sentencing. In a number of states, indeterminate sentences and the hope they held out for early release were replaced by determinate (flat, fixed) sentences, often accompanied by the abolishment of discretionary parole.

But the shift from rehabilitation to retribution did not necessarily produce the intended effects. Without the advance planning needed to accommodate longer and more punitive sentences, the justice model was no more equipped to achieve its goals than its predecessor. Just as the funds were never forthcoming to implement the medical model effectively, the facilities needed to incarcerate greater numbers of inmates for longer periods of time were not appropriated. Correctional institutions were unprepared for the massive influx of offenders into already strained facilities. Nor were the courts willing to tolerate vastly overcrowded institutions.

When facilities began drastically exceeding their designed capacity, the courts intervened, requiring that corrections keep the number of inmates being confined within mandated *population caps*. At the same time, correctional officials were becoming concerned about their ability to control inmates in the absence of the incentive that parole provided for good behavior. The answer to both crowding and control came in the form of *gain time*, whereby a specified number of days is automatically deducted from an offender's sentence for every month served without disciplinary infractions. This modification was essential to reduce prison populations to somewhat more manageable levels. However, gain time defeats the original purpose of the justice model to deter crime, incapacitate offenders, and assure that one's "debt to society" is paid by serving a full term without the possibility of early release.

Increasingly dissatisfied with gain time—yet still unwilling to raise taxes in support of massive prison construction—by the mid-1990s, public policymakers had taken yet another turn. Fueled by mounting fear of crime, intolerance of criminals, and exasperation with the system's response to both, corrections policy was propelled into a renewed focus on punishment.[55]

Perhaps because crowding often diminished the length of time behind bars, there was a growing determination to intensify the distastefulness of imprisonment. Responses to the mounting punitive outcry gained steamroller momentum as, one after another, states jumped on the no-frills bandwagon and embraced humiliating practices. For example:

- Mississippi legislators voted in 1994 to return to striped uniforms with the word "convict" emblazoned on the back.[56]

- Alabama, Arizona, and Florida reinstated various forms of chain gangs in 1995,[57] followed by jails and prisons in a number of other locales.

- By 1997, once-basic staples of prison life ranging from weight lifting to TV programming were banned in many facilities throughout the country.[58]

Some of these changes are more symbolic than substantive. There is likewise some disagreement over whether legislators are *responding* to public opinion or *reshaping* it with "get tough" rhetoric designed to project a no-nonsense image at election time.[59]

Regardless of the reasons behind it, reaction from the field of corrections to such legislative micromanagement has been uniformly negative. As is depicted

 # Close-up On Corrections

A nationwide survey of 641 wardens and prison superintendents found that they think taking away such "so-called frills" as bodybuilding equipment, cable TV, education, and recreation programs is misguided—for two reasons:

1. The programs use constructive activities to fill what otherwise would be idle time.

2. They serve important management functions—the "carrots" that can be offered to promote good behavior or withdrawn to control misbehavior.

As the study's author pointed out,

These people understand the day-to-day realities of running huge correctional facilities. They approach the prison from a functional, nonideological perspective. The problem from one respondent's perspective is that "When people think of corrections, they think of people who deserve to be punished, not rehabilitated or provided with other sorts of so-called benefits . . . [but] denying benefits is not a plausible solution."

Source: Compiled from "National Corrections Executive Survey Adds Fuel to 'Frills' Fire," *Corrections Alert*, Vol. 3, No. 1, April 8, 1996, pp. 1-2, citing study author Timothy J. Flanagan and Bernard B. Kerik.

in the prior "Close-up On Corrections," a recent national survey found correctional executives overwhelmingly unsupportive of no-frills mandates. While perhaps politically popular, such measures have been criticized by correctional officials as a "nasty" return to long-abandoned practices [60] that are based on "misconceptions" and "false impressions."[61]

The fact that correctional administrators themselves are largely opposed to what they have condemned as "harsh and mean-spirited" measures does not appear to have made much of an impact.[62] Nor has strong collective opposition emerged to counteract the prevailing tide of legislative oversight that has become characteristic of contemporary correctional policymaking. By and large, leaders in the field have not been influential in shaping the public-policy agendas that guide correctional management.

If, indeed, the past is prologue to the future, it is possible that the philosophy of corrections will again be reassessed in the face of disenchantment with the justice model and its no-frills offspring. In the meantime, at least one critic has observed that "the corrections system is turning back the hands of time when the rest of the world is moving forward."[63]

As an enterprise that deals with the disenfranchised of society, corrections is never likely to attain high priority on fiscal policy agendas. Nevertheless, everything in life is relative. When viewed in comparison to the conditions faced by past reformers, no doubt corrections has made great strides. But the challenge for the future has shifted in recent years—from continuing progressive reforms to curtailing regressive reactions.

Summary

While the victim's role in the criminal justice system has become more active today, it is far removed from the primitive practice in which the victim sought harsh retribution directly against the offender. With the rise of religion, crime was viewed as a sin that violated divine law and God's will, as well as socially unacceptable behavior. As a result, punishments in medieval times were brutal, inflicting extreme pain, suffering, and often death. The more "fortunate" were confined to convict ships or banished.

As the concepts of trials and courts developed, gaols were used to confine suspects until the king's court could convene or punishment could be carried out. Despite the fact that their occupants were still technically innocent, these early jails maintained virtually intolerable living conditions. Men and women, young and old, healthy and sick were forced to live together and pay fees for even the most minor necessities—a system later copied in American jails.

Adhering to strict Puritan religious beliefs, the first American colonists likewise employed extremely severe punishments for criminal offenses. Mutilating, branding, and using stocks, and pillories were all common practices. Just prior to the American Revolution, the first U.S. prison, Newgate, was established in an abandoned copper mine, where conditions were as abysmal as those of the English gaols.

With the Age of Enlightenment and the pioneering work of John Howard, public attention was called to the plight of law violators. Emphasis was placed on punishment in proportion to the offense. The fundamental rights of the individual were formally recognized in the U.S. Constitution. The first U.S.

penitentiary was established by the Quakers at the Walnut Street Jail. But the penitence-oriented philosophy of the Pennsylvania system was challenged by the greater economic benefit of congregate work in the Auburn system. Adopting the stern discipline, imposed silence, and hard work practiced at Auburn, corrections in the United States entered a period marked by abuses and exploitations that were not to be challenged until the beginning of the Reform Era in 1870.

Reformers promoted innovations ranging from indeterminate sentencing to parole and inmate education. Despite their forward thinking, throughout much of the early twentieth century, corrections focused predominately on the generation of profits through inmate leasing, contract labor, prison farms, and factories. With the rise of unions and the Great Depression, society no longer could afford competition from free inmate labor. The Industrial Era thus ended with legislative action restricting the sale of inmate products. Although interest in inmate industries is reviving, the focus today is more on providing meaningful work and career training than on strictly economic gains.

Following the introduction of psychoanalytic and social work techniques, corrections moved into the Rehabilitative Era. The emphasis on offender treatment reached its peak during the 1960s, with national studies, federal funding, and judicial recognition of inmates' rights. Eventually, liberal politics gave way to the conservative agenda of the 1980s. Society became increasingly disillusioned with rising crime, recidivism, and the ineffectiveness of rehabilitation. The medical model was replaced by the justice model, with its determinate sentencing structures.

But correctional facilities were no more equipped to implement the justice model than its predecessor. As institutions filled well beyond capacity, court-ordered population caps forced early release through gain time, thereby defeating the purpose of assuring that offenders receive their "just deserts." These often-contradictory historical fluctuations make it difficult to forecast just where corrections will be tomorrow, as society again reevaluates its priorities. In the meantime, the challenge is to adapt to more punitive sanctions without abandoning more positive solutions.

Endnotes

1.   *American Correctional Association, The American Prison: From the Beginning . . . A Pictorial History*, Laurel, Maryland: American Correctional Association, 1983, p. 261.

2.   James D. Stinchcomb, *Introduction to Criminal Justice: Instructor's Guide*, six audio-visual presentations, Washington, D.C.: Robert J. Brady Company, 1972, p. 6.

3.   Louis P. Carney, *Probation and Parole: Legal and Social Dimensions*, New York: McGraw-Hill, 1977, p. 76.

4.   G. Abbott, *Tortures of the Tower of London*, London: David & Charles, 1986, p. 9.

5.   Keith Baker and Robert J. Rubel, *Violence and Crime in the Schools*, Lexington, Massachusetts: D.C. Heath, 1980, p. 5.

6.   George Ives, *History of Penal Methods*, Montclair, New Jersey: Patterson Smith, 1970, pp. 104-105.

7.   Leslie Fairweather, "The Evolution of the Prison," in Guiseppe de Gennaro and Sergio Lenci, eds., *Prison Architecture*, London: United Nations Social Defence Research Institute, Architectural Press, 1975, pp. 13-14.

8.   Linda L. Zupan, *Jails: Reform and the New Generation Philosophy*, Cincinnati, Ohio: Anderson Publishing Company, 1991, p. 12. (Much of the material on conditions in early jails is paraphrased from this source, pp. 10-14).

9.   *Ibid.*, p. 10.

10. *Ibid.*, p. 11.

11. Henry Burns, *Corrections: Organization and Administration*, St. Paul, Minnesota: West Publishing Company, 1975, p. 148.

12. Zupan, *Jails*, pp. 11 and 13.

13. William G. Nagel, *The New Red Barn: A Critical Look at the Modern Prison*, New York: Walker and Company, 1973, p. 188.

14. For a description of the emergence of correctional institutions as tools of social control, *see* John Irwin, *The Jail: Managing the Underclass in American Society*, Berkeley, California: University of California Press,1985, p. 4.

15. Richard Hawkins and Geoffrey P. Alpert, *American Prison Systems: Punishment and Justice*, Englewood Cliffs, New Jersey: Prentice Hall, 1989, p. 13.

16. Leonard P Liggio, "The Transportation of Criminals: A Brief Political-Economic History," in Randy E. Barnett and John Hagel III, eds., *Assessing the Criminal*, Cambridge: Ballinger, 1977, p. 282, citing the works of Jeremy Bentham.

17. Ives, *Penal Methods*, p. 97.

18. Jay M. Moynahan and V. M. Deitrich, "Prisoners on Ships," *American Jails*, Vol. 13, No. 3, July/August 1999, p. 38.

19. Alexis M. Durham III, "Social Control and Imprisonment during the American Revolution: Newgate of Connecticut," *Justice Quarterly*, Vol. 7, No. 2, June 1990, pp. 315-316.

20. Todd R. Clear and George F. Cole, *American Corrections*, Belmont, California: Wadsworth Publishing Company, 1994, p. 37.

21. Burns, *Corrections*, p. 82.

22. American Correctional Association, *American Prison*, p. 28.

23. Burns, *Corrections*, p. 149.

24. *Ibid.*, p. 153.

25. Durham, *Social Control*, pp. 308-309.

26. Ibid., p. 309, quoting W. Storrs Lee, "Stone Walls Do Not a Prison Make," *American Heritage*, Vol. 18, No. 2, 1967, p. 90.

27. Zupan, Jails, p. 14, quoting D. L. Howard, *The English Prisons: Their Past and Their Future*, London: Methuen & Company, 1960.

28. American Correctional Association, *American Prison*, p. 24.

29   *Ibid.*, p. 29.

30. Clear and Cole, *American Corrections*, p. 76.

31. Clemens Bartollas, "The Prison: Disorder Personified," in John W. Murphy and Jack E. Dison, eds., *Are Prisons Any Better? Twenty Years of Correctional Reform*, Newbury Park, California: Sage Publications, 1990, p. 14.

32. Hawkins and Alpert, *American Prison Systems*, p. 45.

33. American Correctional Association, *American Prison*, p. 55.

34. Moynahan and Deitrich, pp. 37-42.

35. For a documentary on this era, *see* J. C. Powell, *The American Siberia*, 1891 [reprinted, Montclair, New Jersey: Patterson Smith, 1970]. *Also see* David Oshinsky, *Worse than Slavery: Parchman Farm and the Ordeal of Jim Crow Justice*, New York: Free Press Paperbacks, 1996.

36. American Correctional Association, *American Prison*, p. 63.

37. *Ibid.*, p. 75.

38. John V. Barry, "Captain Alexander Maconochie," *Victorian Historical Magazine*, Vol. 27, June 1975, p. 5.

39. For a complete account of Maconochie's efforts, *see* Norval Morris, *Maconochie's Gentlemen: The Story of Norfolk Island and the Roots of Modern Prison Reform*, New York: Oxford University Press, 2003.

40. Alexander W. Pisciotta, *Benevolent Repression: Social Control and the American Reformatory-Prison Movement*, New York: New York University Press, 1994, p. 42, citing the 1884 *Report and Proceedings of the New York State Board of Charities*.

41. Department of Justice, Annual Report of the Attorney General (1875), cited in Paul W. Keve, *Prisons and the American Conscience: A History of U.S. Federal Corrections*, Carbondale, Illinois: Southern Illinois University Press, 1991, p. 18.

42. Keve, *Prisons*, p. 21.

43. Robert Johnson, "American Prisons and the African-American Experience: A History of Social Control and Racial Oppression," *Corrections Compendium*, Vol. 25, No. 9, September 2000, p. 28.

44. John Greene, "Historical Overview: Chain Gangs in the United States, 1800s-1995," Unpublished manuscript: American Correctional Association, 1995, p. 4.

45. American Correctional Association, *American Prison*, p. 95, quoting Louis N. Robinson, *Penology in the United States, 1921*. For a detailed history of prison labor, *see* Richard C. Brister, "Changing of the Guard: A Case for Privatization of Texas Prisons," *Prison Journal*, September 1996, pp. 310-330.

46. "Burger Again Calls for More Prison Industries," *Corrections Digest*, Vol. 14, No. 13, June 15,1983, p. 1.

47. In 1985, retired Chief Justice Burger's National Task Force on Prison Industries published a report through the National Center for Innovation in Corrections, Washington, D.C., outlining fifty recommendations for modernizing, expanding, and strengthening prison industries.

48. *See*, for example, "Is Private Sector Involvement in Prison Industries a Recipe for Success?" *Corrections Alert*, July 29, 1996, pp. 1-3, and Morgan O. Reynolds, *Factories Behind Bars*, Dallas, Texas: National Center for Policy Analysis, 1996.

49. *See Work in American Prisons: Joint Ventures with the Private Sector*, Washington, D.C.: U.S. Department of Justice, 1995.

50. *Coleman v. Peyton*, 302 2nd 904 (4th Cir. 1966).

51. *Johnson v. Avery*, 89 S.Ct. 747 (1969).

52. President's Commission on Law Enforcement and Administration of Justice, *Task Force Report: Corrections*, Washington, D.C.: U.S. Government Printing Office, 1967, p. 93.

53. *Ibid.*, p. 210.

54. Robert Martinson, "What Works: Questions and Answers about Prison Reform," *The Public Interest*, 35, Spring 1975, pp. 22-54.

55. For a more detailed description of changing public perspectives on corrections-related issues, *see* Timothy J. Flanagan, "Community Corrections in the Public Mind," *Federal Probation*, Vol. 60, No. 3, September 1996, pp. 3-9.

56. Adam Nossiter, "Life in Prison Turning into a Real Hard Cell," *Pittsburgh Post-Gazette*, September 18, 1994, p. A-8.

57. Greene, "Historical Overview," p. 5.

58. For a list of the thirteen states that partially or fully banned weight lifting as of 1997 (and a discussion of its merits as well as drawbacks), *see* Susan L. Clayton, "Weight Lifting in Corrections: Luxury or Necessity?" *Corrections Today*, Vol. 20, No. 5, November 1997, pp. 1, 3.

59. Peter Finn, "No-Frills Prisons and Jails: A Movement in Flux," *Federal Probation*, Vol. 60, No. 3, September 1996, p. 36.

60. Stephen J. Ingley, "It's the Wave of the Past: Getting Tough (Nasty) on Criminals," *American Jails*, Vol. 9, No. 4, September/October 1995, p. 7.

61. Bobbie L. Huskey, "Think Twice Before Abolishing Inmate Privileges," *Corrections Today*, Vol. 57, No. 3, June 1995, p. 6.

62. "ACA Develops Legislative Priorities for 1995-96," *On the Line*, Vol. 18, No. 4, September 1995, p. 1.

63. "Back on the Chain Gang," *Corrections Digest*, Vol. 26, No. 10, March 10, 1995, p. 5, quoting Rob Hoelter, director of the National Center on Institutions and Alternatives.

PART II:

CORRECTIONAL SERVICES, PRACTICES, AND INSTITUTIONS

66 While recognizing that offenders are responsible for their own actions, we must also recognize our responsibility for providing the best possible correctional services.[1] 99

—Correctional Service of Canada

One of the difficulties in the field of corrections is that the general public is not aware of what goes on behind prison walls, inside jails, or within the caseloads of probation and parole. Police officers—working directly with the public and easily identifiable by uniforms and marked cars—apprehend and arrest offenders, beginning the process of "putting them away." What happens after that is frequently left to the dark recesses of correctional institutions and caseloads. The correctional process is long, sometimes tedious, and often not very rewarding in terms of public acclaim.

Moreover, society's clamor for punishment appears to give little support to community-based sentencing alternatives that do not involve institutional confinement. Outside the correctional system, few may recognize the merits of such options as diversion, probation, or electronically monitored home confinement, nor do most people appreciate just how restrictive community supervision

Photo, Above: Many small jails are disappearing, giving way to regional jail systems and even mega jails holding a thousand or more inmates. Here is the Cook County Jail's maximum-security detention unit in Illinois. Courtesy of contractor Morse Diesel International and architect Knight/Roula Associates.

actually can be. This may be related to a fundamental lack of understanding, but, in any event, the focus today is on secure confinement.

That does not mean, however, that the public is clear about what correctional institutions should be accomplishing. Although everyone is concerned when prisons and jails fail to "rehabilitate" offenders, society has recognized the futility of achieving long-term behavioral changes. Consequently, it has left correctional institutions with a basic incapacitation mandate. Such a social compromise creates a more realistic mission for corrections but a less optimistic outlook for its clients.

Throughout the next three chapters, these issues are explored as we look at both community-based and institutional corrections—from the types of offenders involved to the types of services provided to them. Beginning with community-based alternatives in Chapter 4, we see how the least visible component of corrections works. The advantages and disadvantages of diverting offenders from the justice system are discussed, along with how electronically monitored home confinement can serve as an intermediate option for those who otherwise would be sent to jail or prison. Even in the midst of the justice model's emphasis on punishment, institutional crowding has necessitated continual use, and even expansion, of such alternatives.

As the oldest and most frequently used sentencing alternative, probation is the next focus of our attention. We will look at who is eligible for probation, what restrictions probationers are subjected to, what services they are provided, and how they are supervised. Of course, not everyone functions effectively under community supervision, so we also must consider under what circumstances this privilege can be revoked. The unsuccessful termination of probation brings us to Chapter 5 and the next level on the sentencing scale: short-term confinement in jail.

Just as the public often is not aware of what actually occurs within community corrections, there is equal uncertainty about the function of jails. Yet, there are far more jails than prisons in the United States and, as a unit of local government, jails are closer to the communities they serve. Because there are so many of them, we will see wide variations among these local correctional institutions—from small, rural facilities to the megajails of major metropolitan areas; from the antiquated, unsanitary facilities built in the past century to the modern direct supervision jails constructed more recently.

Looking at the population of jails, we will find similar disparities. Jail inmates range from those who are convicted to those still awaiting trial; from those serving short sentences for minor offenses to those awaiting transfer to prison for major violations; from alcoholics and drug addicts to juveniles, vagrants, and the mentally ill. In the midst of such diversity, we will see how jails cope administratively with everything from classification to crowding.

This portrait of the jail is followed by a description of those institutions reserved for offenders with longer-term sentences—state and federal prisons. Since they are less numerous than jails, there is more standardization among prisons. But as we see in Chapter 6, they, too, can vary widely—ranging from minimum-security farms, ranches, or work-release centers to the maximum-security custodial institutions that we traditionally tend to associate with the term "prison."

After exploring their various security classifications, we encounter the problems created by the continually escalating prison population in recent years. A review of overcrowding leads us to examine just who is in prison and why they are there. From this perspective, we begin to see that prisons, like jails, may not always be housing those who most need to be kept in secure confinement. Again, this raises the question of what society expects its correctional institutions to accomplish. Finally, we look inside the prison compound to see how the institution is organized, how the warden influences its operations, and to what extent the inmates rather than staff are actually in control.

In summary, whether the topic is community-based or institutional corrections, the bottom line is that a society concerned with crime and recidivism basically has two choices. We can attempt to prepare inmates for a law-abiding lifestyle during confinement, or we can avoid the debilitating effects of institutional life by retaining offenders under control in the community. Both approaches are explored in the following chapters, beginning with community-based treatment alternatives, moving to short-term confinement in jail, and concluding with incarceration in prison. Both options have advocates as well as opponents, benefits as well as drawbacks. But without an understanding of community-based as well as institutional corrections, it is impossible to make informed public policy choices.

Endnote

1. *Mission of the Correctional Service of Canada*, Ottawa, Ontario: Correctional Service of Canada, 1991, p. 7.

CHAPTER 4

COMMUNITY-BASED ALTERNATIVES

> **"** From the very beginning, the direction of the correctional process must be back toward the community. It is in the community that crime will be committed or a useful life lived.[1] **"**
>
> —Ramsey Clark

Chapter Overview

Over the past two decades, community-based alternatives have come to imply excessive leniency—"coddling criminals," "wrist slapping," "being soft on crime"—quite the opposite of the public's demands for "just deserts." In fact, programs that used to be called "alternatives to incarceration" are now labeled "*intermediate sanctions or punishments*," presumably because society does not interpret "alternatives to incarceration" as sufficiently punitive.[2] It has even been proposed that probation be recast as a "surveillance and supervision" program to satisfy the public's need for punishment.[3]

But renewed emphasis on the harsher sentencing practices of the justice model has provided a false sense of security. On the one hand, it was anticipated that potential offenders would think twice before engaging in crime if they knew the severity with which they would be punished. Moreover, even if would-be offenders were not deterred by the threat of punishment (and most were not), there was satisfaction in knowing that incapacitation would prevent further involvement in crime during their period of confinement. This was quite true, but also quite shortsighted. On release, offenders are returning to the very place they came from—free society. How secure are we in the belief that,

The Gwinnett County Comprehensive Correctional Complex in Georgia is one of the few facilities in the country specifically designed to accommodate a community-based corrections program. Photo courtesy of Jim Roof Creative, Inc.

having been exposed to the debilitating effects of prison life and now stigmatized as ex-offenders, they will make the dramatic changes necessary to become law-abiding citizens? If the answer is "not very," then community-based approaches assume greater significance in achieving the goals of the justice system. That does not mean that community corrections is a panacea for solving the crime problem. But even if a community-based approach does not do anything to improve offenders, at least it is not doing anything to worsen them. It is highly unlikely that the same could be said of incarceration.

Certainly, there are some offenders whose crimes are so violent and whose behavior is so uncontrollable that prison or jail is the only feasible option. Nevertheless, there are many others who are harmed more than helped by incarceration. Even in the midst of the "get-tough-on-crime" era, community-based alternatives to secure confinement were never abandoned. In part, this was a result of the inability of new prison construction to keep pace with demand. Overcrowding has forced a reconsideration of priorities, calling attention to the need to reserve costly prison beds for truly violent, hard-core, chronic offenders. Apparently, "out of crisis sometimes comes opportunity."[4] But beyond the practical limitations of space in secure confinement, there remains a fundamental ray of hope in the ability to sanction behavior properly without severing bonds with the community.

Everyone benefits if selected, low-risk offenders can pay their debt to society through alternatives such as diversion, home confinement, community-based treatment, victim restitution, community service, or probation. The offender avoids the social isolation and the stigmatizing impact of imprisonment. Society avoids the economic impact of unproductive confinement in high-cost facilities. However, without awareness of its benefits, community corrections easily can be dismissed as a disagreeable economic compromise rather than a directed effort to control behavior cost-effectively.

To what extent community-based alternatives will be "sold" to the public and maintained in the face of pressure for stiffer sentences will largely determine the shape of future public policy. In that regard, such programs cannot afford to be viewed as "freedom without responsibility" or "sanctions without accountability." Rather, they must be seen as involving real penalties that are as stringent as incarceration would have been.[5] While community corrections has suffered from image problems, there is some evidence that society may not be as unsupportive as we might think. A national survey, for example, found that four-out-of-five people favor community corrections' programs over prison for nondangerous offenders, leading to the conclusion that "Americans are beginning to reformulate their thinking that prison is the only way to punish convicted offenders. It is becoming increasingly clear that America cannot build its way out of the prison crowding crisis. Intermediate sanctions are a viable option to imprisonment and are more cost effective and beneficial to society in the long run."[6] Even if for economic rather than egalitarian reasons, community-based approaches will continue to represent a significant function in the correctional system.

 ## Learning Goals

Do you know:

1. How pretrial intervention differs from other forms of community-based corrections?
2. Why clients of diversion cannot technically be considered "offenders"?
3. How the process of alternative-dispute resolution operates?
4. The advantages and disadvantages of diversion?
5. What net-widening is, and how it relates to diversion?

Pretrial Intervention

Whereas most of the programs discussed in this chapter involve options for keeping offenders out of correctional institutions after adjudication,[7] pretrial intervention is significantly different. It diverts the entire case out of the criminal justice system before adjudication. When first-time, nondangerous offenders are viewed as good risks, they may be eligible for a program of voluntary supervision in the community without being convicted, especially if no constructive purpose would be served by conviction and sentencing.

As the term *pretrial* implies, the system has intervened to remove the case from the criminal justice process *before adjudication*. In essence, the alleged offender is being offered a second chance to avoid prosecution in exchange for voluntary participation in some treatment, counseling, training, or educational program in the community. This type of diversion has been practiced extensively for many years in juvenile court, and various forms of diversion also have been used in the adult system. However, its application to adult offenders did not begin in earnest until the 1960s.[8] By 1973, the National Advisory Commission on Criminal Justice Standards and Goals had recognized diversion

Day treatment centers can serve as alternatives to confinement, or as a transition between prison and the community. Here is the Owensboro, Kentucky, Day Treatment Center. Courtesy of the Owensboro, Kentucky, Day Treatment Center.

as an appropriate alternative when "there is a substantial likelihood that conviction could be obtained and the benefits to society from channeling an offender into an available noncriminal diversion program outweigh any harm done to society by abandoning criminal prosecution."[9] Today, the growing drug court movement is creating treatment-oriented diversion opportunities for many offenders.[10]

We tend to think of corrections as the last phase of the criminal justice system. It, therefore, may appear contradictory to include diversion within the correctional caseload. But recall Chapter 1, where we saw that corrections (specifically, the local jail) is also responsible for pretrial detention—confining those awaiting trial who are not released pending adjudication. Similarly, alleged offenders who have been diverted out of the system before trial could be considered correctional clients. Although they have been accused of criminal behavior, it has been determined that their needs can best be met without official processing, through programs offered in the community.

The Diversion Process

Pretrial intervention is commonly referred to as *diversion*, since the suspect is diverted from official processing, thereby minimizing penetration into the justice system. As Figure 4.1 illustrates, it occurs in the absence of any finding of guilt or innocence—in other words, without subjecting the defendant to trial. Clients of diversion, therefore, cannot technically be considered "offenders," since they have not actually been convicted.

Pretrial intervention represents the system's first opportunity to make a positive change in the defendant's lifestyle, at a point before more serious criminal behavior patterns become firmly established. Through community-based

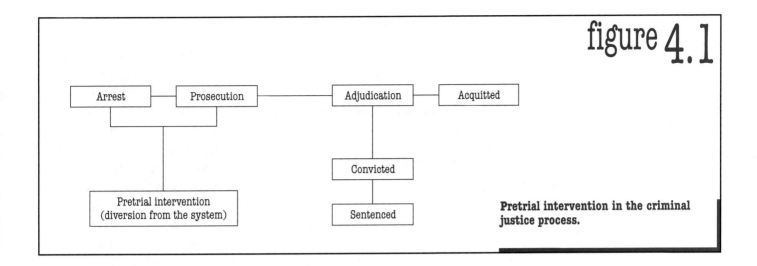

figure 4.1

Pretrial intervention in the criminal justice process.

alternatives, the intent is to help resolve whatever problems led the client to come to the attention of criminal justice authorities.

Diversion can occur at any phase of processing prior to adjudication. In fact, whenever officials decide not to invoke the criminal justice process, they are "diverting the individual from the criminal justice system."[11] Much of the willingness to employ diversion is based on the availability of accessible options. In the absence of options, the process simply becomes diversion *from* the system, rather than *to* a more appropriate alternative.

Particularly if the victim is more concerned with being compensated for losses than seeking a criminal conviction, the prosecutor may arrange an agreement whereby the alleged offender repays the victim in exchange for dropping the charges. In recent years, such approaches have become standardized practice, known in many jurisdictions as *alternative dispute resolution* or *victim-offender reconciliation*. Resolutions can range from victim compensation to community service or simply offering an apology, to "personalize and humanize the criminal justice system."[12] Dispute resolution programs in the United States are similar in some respects to the arbitration of labor-management conflicts. Negotiation between the victim and the alleged offender is mediated by an impartial third party, and an effort is made to reach a satisfactory resolution for all involved.

With the escalation of drug-abuse cases currently flooding the criminal justice system, popular diversionary programs in many jurisdictions have emerged in the form of *treatment alternatives for safer communities* (TASC)[13] or *drug courts*. Such programs are based on the assumption that drug users benefit more from being treated for their addiction than from being adjudicated and incarcerated. They diagnose drug problems, make treatment referrals, and monitor the client's progress. Similar options also exist in many communities for alcohol detoxification, family crisis intervention, and other common problems that are more effectively addressed outside of the justice system. Of course, a defendant's failure to comply successfully with program requirements can result in reactivating the case by proceeding with adjudication.

Advantages and Disadvantages of Diversion

To both the defendant and the system, pretrial diversion offers substantial benefits. Untried offenders who truly are committed to making positive changes in their lives may appreciate this "second chance," as well as the opportunity it presents to obtain help with their problems. At the same time, greater advantage is taken of resources available in the community, thereby supplementing the limited capabilities of the justice system. However, that does not mean that all diversionary options are necessarily treatment-oriented. Victim compensation, for example, while a form of repaying one's debt to society, does not necessarily address the underlying causes of whatever crime was involved, nor does it mean that diversion is without drawbacks, or advantages.

Stigma. Even pretrial interventions that do not address the root causes of behavior at least do no further harm to the defendant. By providing an option to official processing, the stigma of being labeled "criminal" is avoided. Having a criminal record has long been acknowledged as a serious obstacle to employment, social relationships, and even family stability. To defendants facing the prospect of conviction and possible jail or prison time, it is certainly advantageous to elect to participate in a diversionary program. Otherwise, they risk being labeled throughout life as "convicts" or "ex-offenders," along with all the limitations and restrictions that entails.

Leniency. On the other hand, the fact that diversion reduces the consequences of criminal behavior raises the criticism that it is too lenient, doing little to hold offenders accountable for their actions, or to deter future crime. But some diversionary programs are actually harsher than the consequences that probably would follow conviction. For example, in Massachusetts, few defendants elected diversion for first-time drug possession charges: "The anticipated result of prosecution on such charges is a conditional dismissal, largely unsupervised, or a lenient sentence. Diversion, on the other hand, imposes a lengthy treatment period, requires an admission of drug dependency or addiction, and forces the defendant to accept a selected treatment program."[14]

As this example illustrates, we often overlook the fact that community corrections has "significant sanction value" that is "compatible with the demand for retribution."[15] To be taken more seriously as a form of punishment, however, community-based alternatives must demonstrate that they are "tough with the enforcement of court orders—most of all, in quick, decisive and uncompromising reaction to noncompliance."[16] When community corrections takes its mission seriously—firmly supervising its clients and holding them accountable for compliance with established conditions—concern that it is too lenient is diminished considerably.

Normality. Although the effectiveness of diversion remains debatable, the effects of prison are all too well known. In the restrictive, closed environment of prisons and jails, primary emphasis is placed on security. Treatment is a secondary concern (to the extent that it is addressed at all). Operating in the open environment of the community, diversion has been commended for offering an alternative to the counterproductiveness of incarceration, substituting "a normal environment for an abnormal one, and at a substantially reduced cost."[17]

Costs. Compared to the expense of going to trial, the skyrocketing costs of prison construction, and the sophisticated technology needed to maintain institutional security, diversion is significantly less expensive. Cost effectiveness

Community corrections is a growing concept that provides services at a lesser cost than those in prisons and jails. Here is the Decatur, Illinois, Community Correctional Center. Courtesy of the Decatur Community Correctional Center.

is particularly attractive when funds are limited. While economic considerations alone should not determine how extensively pretrial intervention is used, the fact remains that imprisonment is notoriously destructive. If more beneficial results can be achieved in the community, lower costs represent an added incentive to experiment with such options.

Efficiency. Beyond lower costs, diversion presents an opportunity to enhance the efficiency of the criminal justice system. Given the fact that the courts already are overburdened with serious violent crimes, the system probably would crash under its own weight if all previously diverted, less serious offenses were suddenly added to its official workload. Abolishing diversion is neither realistic nor feasible in terms of current staffing or funding.

Flexibility. It is not likely that we would support a justice process that operated routinely by the book, without consideration of either the circumstances of the individual or the management capability of the system. It has been argued that "many offenders' crimes are caused by special problems—vagrancy, alcoholism, emotional distress—that cannot be managed effectively through the criminal justice system." [18] Without the opportunity for diversion and the expanded community resources which it embraces, such cases probably would be dealt with through rather limited, generally punitive, and often inappropriate responses.

Discretion. On the other hand, too much unregulated discretion can result in forcing treatment on those who have committed no crime or for whom there is "insufficient evidence to obtain a conviction." [19] Avoiding a conviction is not the objective of diversion. Rather, it is a tool to facilitate "effective treatment of the social, psychological, or interpersonal problems underlying the deviant act." [20] Pressuring defendants into pretrial diversion programs not only raises ethical questions, but also creates a situation wherein defendants may involuntarily abdicate many of their due process rights—most significantly, the right to trial and protection against self-incrimination. "Even though an overwhelming majority of programs do not require an admission of guilt, there is presumption of guilt inherent in the system." [21]

Net-Widening. Finally, the extent to which diversionary options are available is itself a source of concern. If, for example, the defendant would have been subjected to less interference or less supervision in the absence of diversionary options, are these programs truly serving the purpose for which they were intended? In this regard, it has been noted that "innovations designed to reduce the overall intrusiveness of the system, no matter how well-intentioned, often backfire and instead add to its capacity for social control."[22]

When police, prosecutors, and judges are aware that offenders can obtain help for their problems rather than simply serve time, there is some danger that the system will extend its reach into borderline behavior that otherwise would have been overlooked. For example, when they are aware that the court's options are limited, police officers might ignore a situation involving possession of a small amount of drugs by a young person—concerned that it would be unproductive to see this person incarcerated for such an offense. But when drug treatment is well known as an available diversionary program, the police may be more likely to make an arrest to obtain help for the offender. This illustrates the concept of *net-widening*—when a new program broadens official intervention rather than improves the shortcomings of the existing system.

If diversion results in bringing more clients into the system and/or dealing with them more harshly, it becomes a form of net-widening. On the other hand, it could be argued that the system's initial reluctance to interfere with obviously law-violating behavior before the availability of diversionary options was equally inappropriate and could not be justified simply because effective response alternatives were lacking. In any case, pretrial interventions continue to be useful alternatives that are often benevolent to the offender and beneficial to the victim.

✸ Learning Goals

Do you know:

1. How electronically monitored home confinement works and at what points in the criminal justice process it can be used?
2. With what types of clients electronic monitoring is used most often?
3. The advantages and disadvantages of electronically monitored home confinement in comparison to incarceration?

Home Confinement and Electronic Monitoring

Home confinement through *electronic monitoring* is an innovation that has considerable potential for reducing prison populations, but at the same time, for widening the net as well. With technological advances in recent years, it has become possible to combine diversion with confinement in one's residence, verified by electronic monitors. In fact, as illustrated in Figure 4.2, home confinement under electronic monitoring can be employed at virtually any point in the criminal justice process following arrest—from pretrial to postsentencing, and even postincarceration.

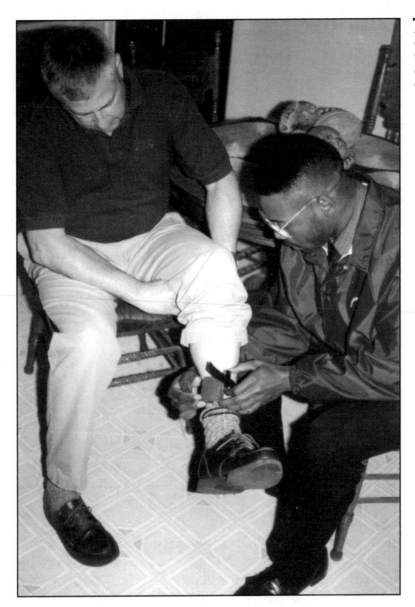

During the period of confinement, participants are placed on a form of curfew and restricted from leaving their place of residence. Exceptions are made during work hours if the client is employed, or for such legitimate reasons as performing community service, grocery shopping, or attending authorized activities (for example, participating in training or treatment programs, attending church services, or going to medical appointments). Otherwise, the client is expected to remain at home, with one's location verified by either computerized devices or, more recently, cellular or satellite tracking systems.

Electronically Monitored Clients

Because of its diverse uses and flexibility, it is not surprising to find that electronically monitored home confinement is being employed with more and more offenders. Since eligibility criteria vary among states, the thousands of offenders being monitored represent a wide range of criminal behavior. Most either have been convicted or accused of *major traffic offenses* (usually DUI—

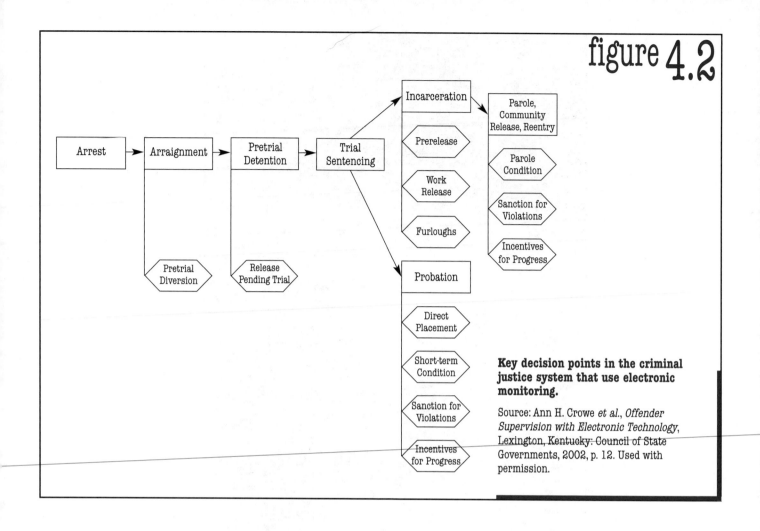

figure 4.2

Key decision points in the criminal justice system that use electronic monitoring.

Source: Ann H. Crowe *et al.*, *Offender Supervision with Electronic Technology*, Lexington, Kentucky: Council of State Governments, 2002, p. 12. Used with permission.

driving under the influence), *property crimes*, or *drug offenses* (possession or distribution).[23] But less than 3 percent of clients in the correctional conglomerate are under such surveillance.[24] While its benefits and drawbacks have been debated, electronic monitoring has become a key ingredient in response to prison crowding and overloaded probation/parole caseloads.[25]

Advantages

Much of the recent popularity of this approach has resulted from the combination of increasingly punitive public attitudes toward crime and decreasingly available space in correctional institutions. With society not in a mood to "coddle criminals," alternatives to prison crowding must be tough, not compromising public safety. Home confinement meets these criteria. Unlike institutional confinement, it also provides greater opportunity for treatment. (In reality, however, that opportunity is rarely fulfilled, since treatment is not often a component of such programs.) When enforced by electronic monitoring, home confinement satisfies the public's demand for retribution and protection without abandoning the system's desire for more productive offender processing. It therefore has produced a reasonable alternative that can simultaneously "satisfy punishment, public safety, and treatment objectives" by:

- Providing a cost-effective community supervision tool

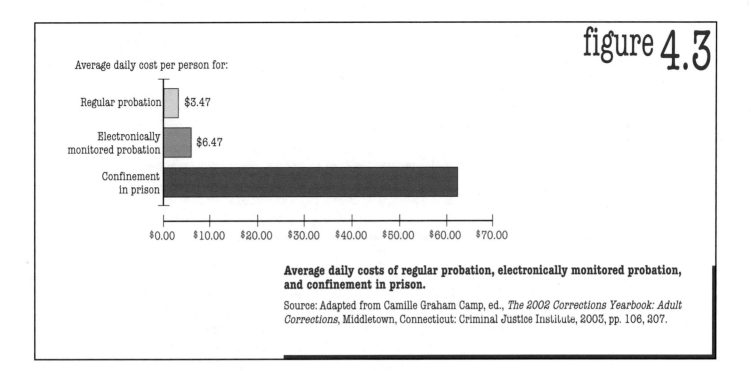

Average daily costs of regular probation, electronically monitored probation, and confinement in prison.

Source: Adapted from Camille Graham Camp, ed., *The 2002 Corrections Yearbook: Adult Corrections*, Middletown, Connecticut: Criminal Justice Institute, 2003, pp. 106, 207.

- Administering sanctions which are appropriate to the seriousness of the offense

- Providing surveillance and risk control strategies [26]

Particularly in times of fiscal shortages, electronically monitored home confinement is especially attractive. As shown in Figure 4.3, the average daily cost for such clients is well below the price of maintaining them in prison, and many programs charge the participants fees to offset expenses.

Beyond monetary considerations, social benefits represent other advantages. The offender can remain employed, continue any treatment initiated in the community, avert family breakup, and avoid the negative effects of prison. In addition, home confinement is well-suited to dealing with special needs offenders who might be particularly vulnerable in prison or jail settings (for example, those who are mentally retarded, pregnant, youthful, or terminally ill). Moreover, it is a speedier and more flexible response to handling vast numbers of clients than would ever be possible through new facility construction.

Disadvantages

Despite its appealing features, home confinement through electronic monitoring is not without drawbacks. To the extent that it becomes a "cheap panacea" for prison, a number of disturbing questions are raised,[27] among them the net-widening potential mentioned earlier. In that regard, it has been observed that "non-violent and low-risk offenders are prime candidates for house arrest; [yet] these offenders are least likely to have been sentenced to prison in the first place."[28] Net-widening provokes concern about the appropriate use of such sanctions. If they are not reserved for the truly prison-bound, cost effectiveness is dramatically reduced. Moreover, the "widened net" in this case can extend

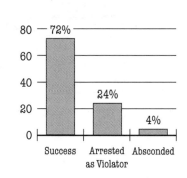

figure **4.4**

Reasons for termination from an electronic monitoring program.

Source: Edward J. Latessa and Harry E. Allen, *Corrections in the Community*, Cincinnati, Ohio: Anderson Publishing, 1997, p. 330. Used with permission.

beyond the individual offender to his or her family as well, particularly when electronically generated calls come in at any time of the day or night.

In that regard, the intrusiveness of electronic monitoring into private residences has also been criticized. One's home, in essence, becomes a prison, generating Orwellian, "big brother" concerns. In response, some maintain that home confinement certainly provides greater privacy than prison or jail, and that in any event, participation is voluntary. But others ask "what's next?" In fact, for over a decade, some community corrections programs have been using telemonitoring, where "visual contacts with offenders are produced via telephone from the offender's home," with a breath-alcohol monitor attached to the video to ensure abstinence from alcohol use.[29] Moreover, such technology has "robo-cop" implications for drastically changing the people-oriented practice of community corrections into a computer-driven emphasis on surveillance.[30]

Not everyone who disagrees with electronic monitoring is opposed to the severity of its intrusiveness. Quite the contrary, there are those who do not believe that it is sufficiently harsh. At the same time, offenders who are not eligible because of the fees involved and the necessity to have a telephone at home have raised the issue of potential discrimination.[31] Nor is electronic monitoring a fail-proof means of preventing criminal activity on the part of those being monitored (although, as shown in Figure 4.4, absconding is relatively infrequent).

These are but a few among the many issues that must be addressed in the future, keeping in mind that "it is all too tempting to employ the equipment simply because the means are available to do so."[32] In the meantime, just as home confinement was originally created as an alternative to incarceration, prison remains an alternative to home confinement.

Learning Goals

Do you know:

1. The definition of probation?
2. How frequently probation is used in contrast to other sentencing options?
3. Why probation often is combined with a suspended sentence?

Among their duties, probation officers are expected to meet with clients, provide supportive assistance, and monitor their compliance with the conditions of probation. Courtesy of Kenneth R. McCreedy.

Probation Services

As a community-based approach, probation has the advantage of dealing with problems in the social environment where they originated. It also avoids the breakdown of social ties that occurs as a result of being institutionalized in a closed environment. When the objective is to assist offenders to adjust to society, it is more effective to work *with* social relationships than to sever them. In short, it is easier and more efficient to maintain the offender's integration as a part of society than to attempt to reintegrate the offender on release from secure confinement. It is also less expensive, since it costs considerably more to maintain a person in an institution than it does to supervise someone in the community.

The courts have recognized these advantages in their sentencing practices, making probation the most widely used correctional disposition in the United States. Of all adults under correctional care or custody, more than half (59 percent) are on probation, representing almost 4 million clients[33] (*see* Figure 4.5).

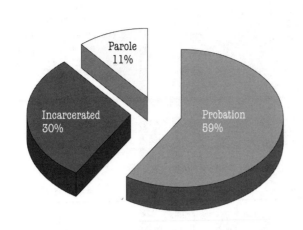

figure 4.5

Parole
11%

Incarcerated
30%

Probation
59%

Percentage of adult offenders on probation.

Source: "One in Every 32 Adults Now on Probation,
Parole or Incarcerated," *Press Release*, Washington, DC:
U.S. Department of Justice, August 20, 2003, p. 1.

In contrast to diversion, which is intervention *before* trial, *probation* is an actual sentence for a *convicted* offender. As we have seen in the preceding section, probation also can be combined with home confinement and electronic monitoring. In addition, it is often combined with a *suspended sentence*, whereby the judge sentences a defendant to prison or jail time and then suspends the sentence in favor of probation. In this way, offenders are presumed to be more motivated to comply with the conditions of probation by knowing what awaits them should they fail to comply. If the conditions imposed by the court during the probationary period are violated, the suspension can be lifted, resulting in confinement. Thus, probation is *a conditional sentence served under supervision in the community.*

Among the conditions that may be imposed on probationers are such restrictions as keeping reasonable hours, remaining employed, and supporting one's family, along with rules that apply to a particular case, such as abstaining from alcohol and drugs, or participating in mandated treatment. Community service work or other forms of restitution likewise can be required. Generally, there is a wider variation among probation rules than among parole regulations, since the conditions of probation generally are set by individual judges rather than by a single state agency as in the case of parole.

Although probation commonly is considered a part of the correctional system because it is a postconviction sanction, technically it is a judicial function, in which convicted offenders are formally placed under supervision of the court. In practice, however, probation officers are usually employed by the state department of corrections, although in a number of jurisdictions, they remain attached to the court system.[34]

Learning Goals

Do you know:

1. How probation as we know it today originated?
2. Who is considered the "father of probation"?

History of Probation

Probation as we now know it in the United States originated in 1841 when a Boston cobbler, *John Augustus*, began visiting the courts. As a temperance crusader, he was interested in the potential of rehabilitating alcoholics. Convinced that he could help such offenders, Augustus would provide their bail or pay their fines, asking the judge to place them under his supervision. He would assist them with remaining sober, finding work, and staying out of trouble. As more and more petty criminals were released to his supervision, his house literally was filled with people whose bail he had paid, almost none of whom violated his trust.[35]

As the "Close-up On Corrections" describes, Augustus was responsible for reporting back to the court on their progress, which the judge usually took into account in deciding a disposition. Reformed offenders were spared incarceration in a correctional facility. Because of his pioneering efforts, John Augustus is considered the "father of probation." As a result of his efforts, the first probation statute was passed in Massachusetts in 1878. By 1954, all states had some form of probation. Moreover, despite recent trends in public attitudes favoring incarceration, probation caseloads have continued to grow dramatically, as shown in Figure 4.6.

 # Close-up On Corrections

THE WORK OF JOHN AUGUSTUS

In the month of August, 1841, I was in court one morning, when . . . an officer entered, followed by a ragged and wretched looking man, who took his seat upon the bench allotted to prisoners. I imagined from the man's appearance that his offense was that of yielding to his appetite for intoxicating drinks, and in a few moments, I found that my suspicions were correct, for the clerk read the complaint, in which the man was charged with being a common drunkard. . . . I conversed with him for a few moments, and found that he was not yet past all hope for reformation. . . . He told me that if he could be saved from the House of Correction, he never again would taste intoxicating liquors, [and] there was such an earnestness in that tone, and a look of firm resolve, that I determined to aid him. I bailed him, by permission of the court. He was ordered to appear for sentence in three weeks from that time. He signed the pledge and became a sober man; at the expiration of this period of probation, I accompanied him into the court room. . . . The judge expressed himself much pleased with the account we gave of the man, and instead of the usual penalty—imprisonment in the House of Corrections—he fined him one cent and costs amounting in all to $3.76, which was immediately paid. The man continued industrious and sober, and without doubt has been by his treatment, saved from a drunkard's grave.

Source: John Augustus, *A Report of the Labors of John Augustus, for the Last Ten Years, in Aid of the Unfortunate*, Boston: Wright and Hasty, 1852, reprinted as *John Augustus, First Probation Officer*, New York: Probation Association, 1939, pp. 4-5.

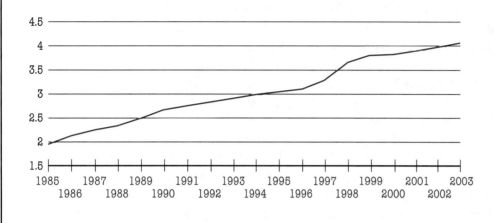

figure 4.6

Growth in adult probation, 1985-2003.

Source: Compiled from Bureau of Justice Statistics, *Correctional Populations in the United States, 1995*, Washington, DC: U.S. Department of Justice, 1997, p. 5 and Lauren E. Glaze and Seri Palla, "Probation and Parole in the U.S., 2003," *Bureau of Justice Statistics Bulletin*, Washington, DC: U.S. Department of Justice, 2004, p.1.

 Learning Goals

Do you know:

1. How probation is organized administratively?
2. What level of education is required for employment in probation today?
3. The difference between general and specific conditions of probation?
4. Why some jurisdictions require probationers to pay supervision fees?

Probation Today

Probation is a function of various governmental jurisdictions. Therefore, staff size, organizational structure, and availability of services vary widely throughout the country. In terms of organizational structure, most jurisdictions administer probation through the state department of corrections. But in others, probation is the responsibility of independent boards, separate departments, the courts, county government, or various combinations thereof. Many states have centralized probation at the state level to make service more uniform and assure that it is available in those counties that cannot afford a probation staff. In these states, the pattern is often to have parole agents also assume the functions of probation. But large counties and metropolitan areas generally maintain their own probation staffs, as does the federal government.

As a result of these differences, there is little uniformity with regard to the quality and quantity of probation throughout the country. In contrast to these administrative factors, staff educational requirements are somewhat more standardized among jurisdictions. Following the lead of federal probation in 1930, most jurisdictions now require a bachelor's degree for entry-level probation or parole officers.[36] But if there is one qualification that probation officers have in common virtually everywhere, it is the personal ability and ingenuity to maximize use of community resources. In addition to their counseling and casework functions, officers are aware of employers who can offer jobs, as well as providers of many other services needed by their clients, from temporary shelter to drug treatment. It is through such personnel and community networking that probation manages to supervise almost 4 million clients, while often unsupported and understaffed.

Conditions of Probation

Among the reasons that the public has not been overly enthusiastic about probation is the common misconception that it involves unrestricted freedom. Probation is often equated with "wrist-slapping, stern lecturing, or a judicial shrug."[37] In reality, however, probationers lose a considerable measure of privacy and liberty. Moreover, they are required to meet a number of conditions, such as:

- Remaining within the geographic jurisdiction of the court
- Reporting to a probation officer on a prescribed schedule
- Refraining from association with certain types of people (for example, known criminals) or places (for example, bars)
- Not possessing a firearm or committing a new offense
- Cooperating with the probation staff

The judge also can mandate such further requirements as maintaining a curfew, fulfilling financial obligations, and remaining employed or seeking employment. These *general* conditions of probation are directed toward controlling the offender's behavior. In addition, *specific* conditions tailored to the client's particular situation or needs may be added that are more individualized or treatment oriented.

For example, family support and/or victim compensation can be required, along with participation in various training, educational, drug treatment, alcohol detoxification, or counseling programs. Offenders are also increasingly being required to pay fees that offset at least some of the cost of their supervision.[38] Additionally, probationers can be subjected to periodic or random drug and alcohol tests to assure that they have not lapsed back into previous patterns of behavior. As detailed in the next "Close-up On Corrections," however, when extreme conditions are mandated, they may be overturned on appeal.

 Learning Goals

Do you know:
1. What types of offenders are eligible for probation?
2. What category of offenses represents the bulk of probation clients?
3. What information is contained in a presentence investigation (PSI)?
4. How a PSI is used?

Close-up On Corrections

Probation Eligibility

The fact that probation does not appear to work equally well with all clients raises the issue of who should be eligible for it, as well as for whom it would be most beneficial. Because probation is a less harsh sentence than incarceration, it might be assumed erroneously that it is reserved for those convicted of misdemeanors rather than felonies. Such is not the case. In fact, not only is probation an available option for sentencing felony offenders, there are actually slightly more felons than misdemeanants on probation. Of the total number of adults on probation in 2002, for example, 50 percent were felons, compared with 49 percent who were misdemeanants. (The status of the remaining 1 percent involved some other type of offense).[39] This is likely because pretrial intervention, fines, and community service are used more often in misdemeanor cases.

In deciding whether to impose probation or incarceration, judges take a number of factors into consideration in addition to the offense. Anticipating future behavior is never an exact science. Even sophisticated "prediction tables" cannot always anticipate the risk an offender poses to society. With the exception of cases in which sentencing guidelines strictly preclude a judge from issuing probation for certain crimes, determination of whether an offender receives probation or incarceration is largely a value judgment and based on the use of discretion.

Presentence Investigations

To assist in their decision making, judges traditionally have relied on a *presentence investigation (PSI) report*. While plea bargaining, mandatory minimum terms, and sentencing guidelines have reduced the role of PSIs in sentencing decisions, they are still important, particularly for assuring that prior criminality is considered.[40]

The presentence investigation is a report generally prepared by a probation officer, although some jurisdictions contract this task to the private sector.

With determinate sentencing and overworked probation staffs in recent years, PSIs have become more of a mechanistic check of prior offenses. But the initial intent was to conduct an in-depth probe not only of criminal history, but also of the defendant's family, educational, medical, and social background, with a view toward working out an effective treatment program. Regardless of whether its contents are more broadly or narrowly focused, the report then is presented to the judge to guide disposition of the case.

In addition to aiding the court in determining the appropriate sentence, a PSI also later can help the correctional officer with probation supervision. Even if the defendant is eventually sentenced to prison, the PSI can assist correctional institutions in planning classification and treatment programs, and ultimately, it can furnish the parole board with information pertinent to the offender's possible release.

 # Learning Goals

Do you know:

1. How the job functions of probation officers can create role conflict?
2. The difference between "brokerage" and "casework" models of probation services?
3. With what types of clients and under what circumstances probation is most successful?

The Role of Probation Officers

As outlined in Figure 4.7, the probation officer's job involves elements of investigation, counseling, service coordination, and rule enforcement. In addition to developing the presentence investigation, probation officers are responsible for the supervision of clients on their caseload. Unfortunately, as a result of the extensive amount of time required to research and prepare thorough PSIs, the time available for client supervision is often less than is necessary to do this complex portion of the job effectively.

Probation supervision includes not only casework and counseling, employment assistance, and personal planning, but also enforcement of the rules and regulations that constitute the conditions of probation. Thus, the role of probation officers involves both *support* and *surveillance*—a combination of social worker and law enforcer. However, it is difficult for one person to fulfill such demands equally effectively. For example, an officer who becomes overly empathetic toward the offender's problems and devotes considerable effort to help resolve them might well be tempted to "look the other way" in the face of minor rule violations. On the other hand, strict rule-enforcing officers may be less inclined to offer much assistance, perhaps even waiting for a chance to "catch" the offender "messing up." Balancing these two contradictory expectations is a challenging task that can lead to *role conflict* for probation officers.

For this reason, a *team concept* is used in some jurisdictions, with services as well as surveillance provided by teams of officers, each specializing in a particular aspect of the probation function.[41] The next "Close-up On Corrections"

figure 4.7

Job Tasks Involved in Probation Work

Investigation
- Presentence investigation reports
- Case documentation
- Violation reports

Counseling
- Initial interview
- Individual supervision
- Family counseling
- Personal counseling
- Financial planning

Service coordination
- Job training
- Educational opportunities
- Employment assistance
- Transportation
- Shelter and subsistence
- Treatment programs

Enforcement
- Probation violation
- Probation-revocation recommendation
- Individual enforcement

Job tasks involved in probation work.

shows how the team concept works. Additionally, some agencies separate responsibility for client supervision from presentence investigation. This enables some officers to prepare PSI reports exclusively, whereas others deal only with the supervision of probationers. Regardless of how the task is organized administratively, the probation staff must find the proper balance between control and treatment that best meets the needs of the offender. This balance may shift over time—initially emphasizing greater control, then gradually reducing the level of supervision. Ultimately, the most important objective is to help clients control their own behavior.

Brokerage and Casework Models

Employment counseling and assistance in finding jobs are major aspects of the probation officer's work. Locating a job is a significant challenge, especially for clients who do not have good work habits or prior employment records. Thus, it is essential for probation staff to be knowledgeable about and take maximum advantage of all resources available in the community. Various treatment programs, family counseling services, employment projects, educational assistance, guidance clinics, mental health facilities, and social work agencies are all of potential help.

This reflects what has been called the *brokerage or resource management approach*—where the "supervising officer is not concerned primarily with understanding or changing the behavior of the offender, but rather, with assessing the concrete needs of the individual" and arranging for the receipt of "services which directly address those needs."[42]

In contrast, a clinical, casework approach focuses more on diagnosis and treatment, toward the goal of changing the offender's law-violating behavior. Based on the original philosophy and humanitarian efforts of John Augustus, the casework method shaped the delivery of probation services for many years. Informal counseling skills are still used by the probation officer in day-to-day work. But in terms of more formal or long-term counseling, most officers are too burdened by heavy caseloads and paperwork to do much more than immediate crisis intervention. One study found that less than 15 percent of probation officers' time is spent on counseling or casework, with even less (6 percent)

Close-up On Corrections

on developing supportive community contacts.[43] Moreover, some would maintain that the authoritative setting of probation is inappropriate to the practice of casework techniques, which again raises the issue discussed earlier of separating probationary functions through teamwork. (For a summary of the differences between the casework and the brokerage/resource management models of probation, *see* Figure 4.8).

Assessing Effectiveness of Probation

The effectiveness of probation can be evaluated from two perspectives—the quality of services provided by staff and the success rates of their clientele. Measuring the diverse services rendered by a probation department is a challenging task. The quality of PSIs, casework, treatment, and community coordination are difficult to assess. In the absence of objective criteria, observing the success or failure of clients over a period of time has been one method used to evaluate the officer's work, assuming that difficult cases are relatively uniformly distributed among the staff.

However, personnel cannot be held responsible for the nature of clients assigned to their caseload. In that regard, it has been found that those with

figure 4.8

	Brokerage	Casework
Goal	(Re)integration	Rehabilitation
Focus	Practical services	Treatment assistance
Approach	Addressing specific, immediate survival needs of the client	Diagnosing/treating problems causing the client's behavioral difficulties
Method	Linking needs of clients with available resources in the community (for example, training, education, employment, health care)	Clinical, therapeutic services (for example, counseling, group work, psychological or social work techniques)
Officer's role	Coordinating community resources	Establishing a one-on-one relationship with the client
Skills needed	Administrative, organizational, managerial	Counseling, treatment, casework
Relationship to clients	Advocate	Counselor

Comparison of brokerage (resource management) and casework models of probation.

several prior felony convictions are "less successful on probation than other offenders." [44] Of felons assigned to probation, 43 percent were rearrested for another felony violation within three years of sentencing in one national study. [45]

Similarly, research indicates that the rate of recidivism varies with a number of client-related factors, as described in the next "Close-up On Corrections."

 # Close-up On Corrections

DOES PROBATION WORK?

In reality there are two stories about probationer recidivism rates. Recidivism rates are low for adults on probation for *misdemeanors*—data suggest that three-quarters successfully complete their supervision. However, recidivism rates are high for *felony* probationers, particularly in jurisdictions . . . where supervision is minimal.

Recidivism rates vary greatly from place to place, depending on the seriousness of the underlying population characteristics, length of follow-up, and surveillance provided. A summary of seventeen follow-up studies of adult felony probationers found that felony rearrest rates ranged from 12 to 65 percent.

Source: Joan Petersilia, "Probation in the United States: Practices and Challenges," *National Institute of Justice Journal*, September 1997, p. 4.

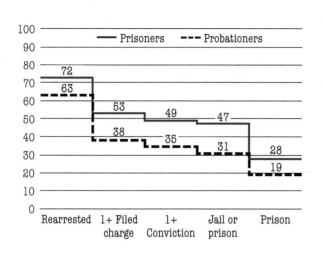

figure 4.9

Recidivism among a matched sample of prisoners and probationers.

Source: Joan Petersilia and Susan Turner, *Prison versus Probation in California: Implications for Crime and Offender Recidivism*, Santa Monica, California: Rand Corporation, 1986, p. 17. Used with permission.

While the effectiveness of probation undoubtedly has been curtailed by inadequate resources, obtaining sufficient funding ultimately depends on whether probation can prove its value, in a "Catch 22" situation that depends on measuring its results.[46] Nevertheless, long-term research has found that compared to those incarcerated, the risk of reoffending is reduced for those in community-based alternative programs,[47] (as illustrated in Figure 4.9) and the addition of a treatment component produces a further reduction in recidivism.[48]

 # Learning Goals

Do you know:

1. How a probationer can be released from supervision?
2. The due-process rights of probationers facing revocation?
3. On what grounds certain conditions of probation have been overruled by the courts?

Rule Enforcement and Revocation

In addition to their counseling and supportive functions, probation officers are authority figures responsible for ensuring that the offender complies with the conditions established when the judge awarded probation. Probation is a privilege, not a right. Violation of the conditions required to maintain that privilege can result in its revocation. It is the probation officer's function to determine that whatever restrictions and mandates the court required, in fact, are being upheld.

There are two ways in which a probationer can be released from supervision: *discharge* or *revocation*. Discharge generally means that the client has successfully completed the probationary period. However, some jurisdictions have developed the practice of discharging persons "not amenable to probation" rather than sending them to prison, which is somewhat similar to the difference between a "dishonorable" and an "undesirable" discharge from the military services. In case of a subsequent conviction, those discharged as "not amenable" are not again placed on probation in that jurisdiction. In contrast, revocation means that the privilege of probation has been withdrawn and that another disposition must be made of the case, such as incarceration.

Generally, there are two reasons for recommending probation revocation: commission of a new crime, or a *technical violation* of the rules. In some jurisdictions, revocation is relatively automatic with the commission of a serious offense, although there may be exceptions. Technical violations involve breaking one or more of the conditions of probation. Whatever the general and specific conditions are for a particular person, violation of them can result in a recommendation of revocation by the probation officer. In practice, the enthusiasm with which officers enforce these regulations varies considerably. While it is a rare officer who will overlook many technical violations before taking action, that is not to say that misconduct will result in removal from the community—in fact, one study found that although 49 percent of probationers violate their conditions, only 20 percent are incarcerated as a result.[49]

Legal Issues

Probation is not automatically terminated on an officer's recommendation. Both probationers and parolees facing revocation have been extended a number of due-process rights by the courts—among them, a formal hearing. At this revocation hearing, the judge and the probationer hear the probation officer's recommendation for revocation (based on detailed information in the violation report), and the judge makes a decision. In 1967, the U.S. Supreme Court determined in the *Mempa v. Rhay* case [50] that the probationer is entitled to representation by an attorney before being resentenced after a probation revocation. With this ruling, the court began to emphasize the revocation process as a "critical phase" in the justice system, which falls within the due-process protections of the Fourteenth Amendment. The criticality of the hearing, of course, refers to the fact that it can involve the loss of liberty, since having probation revoked may result in a jail or prison sentence.

Due-process protections were extended further in the 1973 *Gagnon v. Scarpelli* [51] case, which initiated a two-stage hearing process. In addition to the actual revocation hearing, this case established a *preliminary hearing* to determine whether there is probable cause to revoke probation (similar to the function of a preliminary hearing, when the defendant is originally accused of a crime). At both the preliminary hearing and the subsequent revocation hearing, this case also provided the probationer with certain minimum due-process rights, including:

- Prior notice of the hearing
- Written notice of the alleged violation
- The right to:
  — be present at the hearing
  — present evidence and witnesses
  — be judged before a neutral and detached official

But despite these protections, just as disparities occur in sentencing, they also appear in probation revocation. Petty, unrealistic, or irrelevant conditions invite violations, which do not necessarily reflect poor adjustment. It is in such instances that appellate courts have intervened, particularly when the conditions established do not specifically address the needs of the client. For example:

> Consider the California case involving a female convicted of robbery who was ordered as a condition of probation not to become pregnant until she was married. After she violated this condition, she was sent to prison. But the revocation of probation was overturned by the appellate court, which then prohibited trial court judges from imposing conditions for probation that have *no relationship to the offender's original crime*, that relate to conduct that is *not in itself criminal*, or that forbid conduct *not reasonably related to future criminal* conduct by the offender [52] [emphasis added].

On the other hand, some rather unusual conditions have been upheld when they related directly to the client's offense. Examples include requiring a rapist to undergo a vasectomy, forbidding a bookie to have a telephone in his home [53] and even mandating weight loss (as described in the next "Close-up On Corrections"). In essence, the courts tend to overrule conditions that are irrelevant to the case and uphold those that have a direct bearing on the original conviction.

General conditions of probation also have been subject to challenge, especially when they are vague or ambiguous. How, for instance, does one objectively determine whether the client is "cooperating" with the probation officer? What about the client who lives on a state border and "travels out of state" to seek employment in the nearest city, which happens to be across the state line? When such questions are raised, they can provide the basis for legal challenges regarding fairness and practicality, as well as denial of due process, since the conditions are not necessarily related to the offender's circumstances.[54] In response, the courts have tended to dismiss the enforcement of conditions that "are unreasonable," "endanger the offender's welfare," or prohibit the client from "engaging in an innocuous activity."[55] Such cases appear to point in the direction of reserving revocation for meaningful, constructive purposes, rather than for arbitrary reasons or petty harassment.

✵ Learning Goals

Do you know:

1. How classification helps probation officers manage large caseloads?
2. The difference between "traditional" and "intensive supervision" probation?
3. The purpose and limitations of "shock" probation?

Close-up On Corrections

THE CASE OF THE PORTLY PROBATIONER

The 505-pound man's initial brush with the law came following the closure of his weight-loss business—ironically called "Inches Be Gone." Although slapped with probation after an ensuing forgery conviction, he cited his weight as the reason he was unable to pay restitution. . . . The judge subsequently ordered him to shed pounds as a condition of probation. When he twice violated the condition, . . . the offender was sentenced to ninety-three days in jail, despite his attorney's contention that the court's order to lose weight was cruel and unusual.

Source: "Portly Prisoner Poses Peculiar Problem," *Corrections Alert*, Vol. 2, No. 20, January 29,1996, p.1.

Probation Caseloads

Although they supervise the majority of all convicted offenders, probation agencies receive less than 10 percent of state and local correctional expenditures. Moreover, in relation to other components of the justice system, their budgets are actually declining.[56] As a result, one of the primary difficulties in the field of probation is large caseloads. In fact, 92 percent of probation directors responding to a national study indicated that they needed more officers to handle increased caseloads.[57]

In California alone, probation caseloads had grown so much by the 1990s—to more than 500 per officer—that over half of the probationers in Los Angeles were tracked solely by computer, with no face-to-face contact.[58] In fact, the situation has grown even worse in recent years—to the point that by 1998, some probation officers were reporting caseloads of 3,000 offenders, and more than half of the state's probationers were "likely to serve their entire term without ever meeting or even speaking with a probation officer."[59]

Classification

One of the ways that strained probation staffs are attempting to cope with ever-increasing caseloads in the absence of accompanying fiscal increases is through classifying cases according to the level of supervision needed. Clients vary in terms of the number and types of contacts that they should have because of such factors as the nature of their offense, their prior record, the variety and intensity of their problems, and the potential risk they pose. Classification recognizes these distinctions, providing differing levels of services according to the requirements of the client. For example, some states vary the intensity of probation from maximum to medium, minimum, and even mail-in supervision. Others screen cases on intake to divert low-risk clients into nonreporting status.

Although there is no direct evidence that lower caseloads reduce recidivism, the amount of time in supervision does appear to have a positive effect, along with how that time was spent (in other words, on surveillance that would increase technical violations, or counseling that would improve adjustment).[60] Workload reduction alone is not sufficient to achieve maximum effectiveness unless there is a commitment to specific treatment programs. But it is apparent that officers laboring under excessively high caseloads simply cannot provide the necessary time and attention to their clients.

Intensive Supervision Probation

Many of the first efforts designed to classify and manage probation caseloads actually contained early versions of what has become known as intensive supervision probation (ISP). Florida, for instance, passed legislation in 1983 to slow down prison admissions through "community control"—a "punishment-oriented program of intensive supervision" that combines home confinement with strong surveillance.[61]

ISP programs have become recognized over the years as a "response to pressures created by a demand for incarceration which exceeds prison capacity."[62] As illustrated in Figure 4.10, ISP has changed over the years from a focus on treatment and service delivery to an emphasis on control and surveillance to reduce prison crowding. When public policy toward crime became increasingly punitive without an accompanying expansion of prison space, the need emerged for an intermediate sanction—something stronger than traditional probation but not as harsh as incarceration. For selected offenders, the solution came in the form of more intensively supervised probation, which is designed to:

- Provide a cost-effective community option for offenders who would otherwise be incarcerated

- Promote public safety by providing surveillance and risk-control strategies

- Increase the availability of treatment resources to meet offender needs

- Promote a crime-free lifestyle by requiring ISP offenders to be employed, perform community service, make restitution, and remain substance free[63]

To meet these objectives, ISP programs differ from more traditional probation in a number of respects. As its name implies, ISP requires a more intense level of supervision, which is achieved through such measures as:

- Manageable caseloads

- Frequent face-to-face contacts

- Home confinement and electronic monitoring

- Regular visits to the client's home and workplace

- Verification of treatment participation

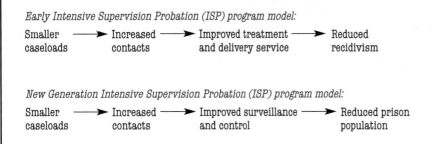

figure 4.10

Early Intensive Supervision Probation (ISP) program model:

Smaller caseloads → Increased contacts → Improved treatment and delivery service → Reduced recidivism

New Generation Intensive Supervision Probation (ISP) program model:

Smaller caseloads → Increased contacts → Improved surveillance and control → Reduced prison population

Changing nature of intensive supervision probation (ISP) programs.

Source: Edward J. Latessa and Harry E. Allen, *Corrections in the Community.* Material has been adapted from *Corrections in the Community* for use in this text. Copyright 1997 Matthew Bender and Company, Inc., a member of the Lexis Nexis group. Used with permission.

- Drug and alcohol screening
- Clear revocation guidelines that are administered consistently and firmly

In addition, those on ISP also may be required to make restitution payments, perform some type of community service, and pay supervision fees.

Early studies of ISP programs operating in Georgia, New York, Texas, and New Jersey were quite positive, indicating lower recidivism rates for serious crimes, high rates of successful completion, and greater cost effectiveness.[64] However, at least one major national study found that effectiveness was related to whether the program set out to reduce costs and prison crowding or to provide a stricter form of traditional probation.[65]

ISP programs also have been noted for often limiting participation to low-risk, property offenders[66]—thus potentially inflating their success rate. In fact, research indicates that "offender selection is one of the most problematic areas of ISP."[67] When ISP becomes a form of net-widening, many of its objectives are defeated. Moreover, when recidivism does occur, it is not necessarily a reflection of the fact that the public is not being protected. Given the stringent conditions of ISP, there is more opportunity for technical violations to occur. In that respect, it has been argued that removing offenders from the streets because of technical violations precludes further criminal behavior, thereby enhancing public safety.[68]

On the other hand, ISP's heavy emphasis on surveillance functions might be producing an underestimate of its potential. If the proper clients were selected and focus on treatment were expanded, it is possible that ISP could be more effective. This issue was addressed in a study examining ISP programs for serious offenders with prior records at three locations in California. The results revealed that at all sites, offenders who participated in treatment programs had lower recidivism rates than those who did not.[69] Others agree that although ISP should be continued, its emphasis should shift from "punitive measures to a more integrated approach," since the current conditions of ISP provide short-range crime control, "while rehabilitation has been associated with long-term behavioral change."[70]

Shock Probation

Another intermediate alternative is *shock probation*, which combines a brief exposure to incarceration with subsequent release on probation. The idea is that the "shock" of a short stay behind bars will make such an indelible impression that offenders will be deterred from future crime. With shock probation, the negative effects of lengthy imprisonment can be avoided, while still giving the offender a "taste" of institutional life, and still maintaining postrelease control through probation supervision.[71] The advantages of probation are therefore combined with the use of confinement.

Although Ohio experimented with shock probation as early as 1965, it has not enjoyed widespread popularity. Reluctance to embrace this approach may be based on concern that "any institutional stay interferes with therapeutic efforts," and even limited prison exposure can produce negative attitudes and promote resentment.[72] In fact, this type of detrimental effect has been suggested in some of the research on shock probation, resulting in the conclusion that "the negative effects of exposure to prison begin to occur very quickly—much sooner than shock probation programs are designed to release offenders."[73]

Moreover, shock probation is not always implemented as originally intended. If the true value of "shock" is to be maximized, it is logical to presume that these programs would be reserved for first-time offenders, or at least those who have not previously served time. In short, studies of the effectiveness of shock probation "suggest great caution in exposing persons to confinement who can be safely supervised in the community."[74] As we will see in upcoming chapters on jails, prisons, and their effect on the inmate population, that is sound advice.

Summary

Community-based alternatives to incarceration were developed to deal more effectively with the offender's problems where they originated, to avoid breaking social ties, and to prevent exposure to the negative effects of secure confinement. As prison crowding provided additional incentives to retain offenders under community supervision, much of what previously had been called "community-based alternatives" became known as intermediate sanctions, reflecting more punitive attitudes and concerns that such programs assure the safety and protection of society.

Pretrial intervention represents the least-intrusive community-based intervention, since it diverts the case out of the criminal-justice system prior to adjudication. In addition to providing a "second chance," diversion avoids the stigma of a criminal record. It also takes advantage of community resources and enhances the efficiency, flexibility, and cost effectiveness of the justice system. However, it has been criticized, on the one hand, as being too lenient, and, on the other hand, as having the potential for net-widening.

One form of community-based supervision that has become popular in both pre- and postadjudication phases of the justice system is home confinement, which often is combined with electronic monitoring to assure compliance with curfew restrictions. Use of this alternative is increasing dramatically as a cost-effective alternative to prison crowding. But it also has raised questions with regard to net-widening, and the intrusiveness of electronic monitoring has been especially vulnerable to the criticism that government is now invading the privacy of home. At the same time, there are those who do not believe that home confinement is a sufficiently serious penalty.

While home confinement and electronic monitoring have been very recent developments, probation originated more than 160 years ago with the work of John Augustus. Since probationers are *convicted* offenders, they represent felons or misdemeanants, in contrast to the unconvicted status of those diverted through pretrial intervention.

In determining whether to sentence someone to probation or incarceration, judges often rely on a presentence investigation report, which contains information on the offense and the offender's background, along with a recommended disposition. In addition to preparing such reports, the probation officer is responsible for supervising clients, which involves both support and surveillance functions. Officers vary in terms of their supervisory styles, with some focusing on casework/counseling, while others act more as "brokers," linking the needs of clients with resources in the community.

Probationers can be released from supervision either through discharge (successful completion) or by revoking probation and making another disposition of the case. Those facing revocation have certain due-process rights, including a two-stage hearing. Revocations involving technical violations have tended to be upheld by the courts if the conditions established were related directly to the offender's circumstances.

As probation officers struggle with high caseloads, efforts have begun to classify cases according to the level of supervision needed. Likewise, intensive supervision probation (ISP) has emerged as a more punishment-oriented alternative to traditional probation. Often combined with home confinement and electronic monitoring, ISP provides more frequent face-to-face contacts, regular contacts, and consistently enforced rules. Shock probation combines a brief exposure to incarceration with subsequent release on probation.

These alternatives are among the varieties of programs that serve as intermediate sanctions. They are becoming increasingly attractive as society continues to explore options for dealing with prison overflow, keeping costs in line with what taxpayers will support, and providing help to those who can remain in the community without endangering public safety. For those who cannot, there always will be prisons and jails—as explored in the next chapters on institutional corrections.

Endnotes

1. Ramsey Clark, *Crime in America*, New York: Simon and Schuster, 1970, p. 220.

2. Ken Kerle, "Jails and Intermediate Punishment," *American Jails*, Vol. 5, No. 1, March/April 1991, p. 4.

3. Orville B. Pung, "Let's Abolish 'Probation and Treatment,'" *Overcrowded Times*, Vol. 4, No. 2, April 1993, p. 3.

4. Thomas J. Quinn, "Delaware—A Structural Response to Correctional Overcrowding," *American Jails*, Vol. 5, No.1, March/April1991, p. 14.

5. Perry Johnson, addressing the Midwinter Meeting of the American Correctional Association, Miami, Florida, January 11, 1993.

6. "Community Corrections Survey: Public Indicates Strong Support," *Corrections Today*, Vol. 53, No. 7, December 1991, p.134, citing Neil Tilow, president of the International Association of Residential and Community Alternatives.

7. Note that this chapter is focused exclusively on nonresidential community-based alternatives. Community residential centers are included in the discussion of minimum-security facilities in Chapter 6.

8. President's Commission on Law Enforcement and Administration of Justice, *Task Force Report: The Courts*, Washington, D.C.: U.S. Government Printing Office, 1967, pp. 97-107.

9. National Advisory Commission on Criminal Justice Standards and Goals, *Courts*, Washington, D.C.: U.S. Government Printing Office, 1973, p. 32.

10. *See* Richard S. Gebelein, *The Rebirth of Rehabilitation: Promise and Perils of Drug Courts*, Washington, D.C.: National Institute of Justice, 2000.

11. Belinda Rodgers McCarthy and Bernard J. McCarthy, Jr., *Community-Based Corrections*, Second Edition, Pacific Grove, California: Brooks/Cole Publishing Company, 1991, p. 21.

12. Gordon Perry and John Walker, "Intermediate Sanctions in Canada," *American Jails*, Vol. 5, No. 1, March/April 1991, p. 124.

13. Karen V. Chappel and Mary Shilton, "Innovative Initiatives of Treatment Accountability for Safer Community (TASC) Programs," *Corrections Today*, Vol. 66, No. 6, October 2004, pp. 92-95.

14. Raymond T. Nimmer, *Diversion: The Search for Alternative Forms of Prosecution*, Chicago: American Bar Foundation, 1974, p. 99.

15. David E. Duffee, "Community Corrections: Its Presumed Characteristics and an Argument for a New Approach," in David E. Duffee and Edmund F. McGarrell, eds., *Community Corrections: A Community Field Approach*, Cincinnati, Ohio: Anderson Publishing Company, 1990, p. 4.

16. Benjamin F. Baer, "Good PR Programs Enhance Public Acceptance," in *Intermediate Punishment: Community-Based Sanctions*, Laurel, Maryland: American Correctional Association, 1990, p. 16, quoting Barry J. Nidorf.

17. Louis P. Carney, *Corrections and the Community*, Englewood Cliffs, New Jersey: Prentice Hall, 1977, p. 58.

18. Todd R. Clear and George F. Cole, *American Corrections*, Belmont, California: Wadsworth Publishing Company, 1994, p. 159.

19. McCarthy and McCarthy, *Community-Based Corrections*, p. 48.

20. Nimmer, *Diversion*, p. 47.

21. Stephen E. Doeren and Mary J. Hageman, *Community Corrections*, Cincinnati, Ohio: Anderson Publishing Company, 1982, p. 37.

22. Clear and Cole, *American Corrections*, p. 159.

23. Marc Renzema and David Skelton, "Use of Electronic Monitoring in the United States," *National Institute of Justice Reports*, November/ December 1990, p. 11.

24. Ann H. Crowe *et al.*, *Offender Supervision with Electronic Technology*, Lexington, Kentucky: Council of State Governments, 2002, p. 3.

25. *See* David W. Rasmussen and Bruce L. Benson, *Intermediate Sanctions: A Policy Analysis Based on Program Evaluations*, Washington, D.C.: Collins Center for Public Policy, 1994.

26. Bureau of Justice Assistance, *Electronic Monitoring in Intensive Probation and Parole Programs*, Washington, D.C.: U.S. Department of Justice, 1989, p. 3.

27. *See*, for example, Ronald Corbett and Gary T. Marx, "No Soul in the New Machine: Technofallacies in the Electronic Monitoring Movement," *Justice Quarterly*, Vol. 8, No. 3, September 1991, pp. 399-414.

28. Joan Petersilia, "House Arrest," *National Institute of Justice; Crime File Study Guide*, Washington, D.C.: U.S. Department of Justice, 1988, p. 1.

29. Gail Townsend, "Kansas Community Corrections Programs," *American Jails*, Vol. 5, No. 1, March/April 1991, p. 30. *See also* Joan Farrall and Dick Whitfield, "Voice Verification and Offender Monitoring," *Journal of Offender Monitoring*, Vol. 12, No. 3, Summer 1999, pp. 14-15.

30. Ronald Corbett, "Electronic Monitoring," and Gary Graham, "High-Tech Monitoring: Are We Losing the Human Element?" in *Intermediate Punishment: Community Based Sanctions*, pp. 21-25, 35-39. *See also* Edward J. Cosgrove, "ROBO-PO: The Life and Times of a Federal Probation Officer," *Federal Probation*, Vol. 58, 1994, pp. 29-30.

31. For a review of related legal issues, *see* David T. Skelton, "Appellate Litigation Involving the Electronic Monitoring of Offenders: A Ten Year Retrospective," *Journal of Offender Monitoring*, Vol. 12, No. 2, Spring 1999, pp. 13-20 (Part 1), Vol. 12, No. 3, Summer 1999, pp. 18-22 (Part 2).

32. Ray Wahl, "Is Electronic Home Monitoring a Viable Option?" in *Intermediate Punishment: Community-Based Sanctions*, p. 27.

33. "One in every 32 Adults is now on Probation, Parole or Incarcerated," *Press Release*, Washington, D.C.: U.S. Department of Justice, August 20, 2003, p. 1

34. For a more detailed description of the providers of probation services, *see Vital Statistics in Corrections*, Lanham, Maryland: American Correctional Association, 2000, pp 128-129.

35. *See* Louis Gesualdi, "The Work of John Augustus: Peacemaking Criminology," *ACJS Today*, September/October 1999, pp. 1-4.

36. Although states vary from 33 percent to 100 percent in terms of the percentage of their jurisdictions minimally requiring a bachelor's degree for probation or parole officers, the vast majority of locations in most states maintain this requirement for entry. *Vital Statistics in Corrections*, p. 161.

37. Orville B. Pung, "Let's Abolish 'Probation and Treatment,'" *Overcrowded Times*, Vol. 4, No. 2, April 1993, p. 3.

38. For example, in one year Texas spent more than $106 million to supervise probationers, but collected more than $57 million in fees. *See* Peter Finn and Dale Parent, "Making the Offender Foot the Bill: A Texas Program," *National Institute of Justice: Program Focus*, Washington, D.C.: U.S. Department of Justice, 1992, pp. 2.

39. Lauren E. Glaze, "Probation and Parole in the U.S., 2002," *Bureau of Justice Statistics Bulletin*, Washington, D.C.: U.S. Department of Justice, August 2003, p. 1.

40. Jeanne B. Stinchcomb and Daryl Hippensteel, "Presentence Investigation Reports: A Relevant Justice Model Tool or Medical Model Relic?," *Criminal Justice Policy Review*, Vol. 12, No. 2, 2001, 164-177.

41. *See* Walter L. Barkdull, "Probation: Call It Control—and Mean It," in Lawrence F. Travis, Martin D. Schwartz, and Todd R. Clear, eds., *Corrections: An Issues Approach*, Second Edition, Cincinnati, Ohio: Anderson Publishing Company, 1983, pp. 154-155.

42. Edward J. Latessa, "Community Supervision: Research, Trends, and Innovations," in Travis et al., p. 163. *See also* Paul F. Cromwell et al., *Probation and Parole in the Criminal Justice System*, St. Paul, Minnesota: West Publishing Company, 1985, pp. 109-110.

43. Jean Jester, "Technologies of Probation and Parole," in David Duffee and Edmund F. McGarrell, eds., *Community Corrections*, Cincinnati, Ohio: Anderson Publishing, 1990, pp. 143-144.

44. McCarthy and McCarthy, *Community-Based Corrections*, p. 120.

45. Patrick A. Langan and Mark A. Cuniff, "Recidivism of Felons on Probation, 1986-1989," *Bureau of Justice Statistics Special Report*, Washington, D.C.: U.S. Department of Justice, 1992, p. 1.

46. Barry J. Nidorf, "Surviving in a 'Lock Them Up' Era," *Federal Probation*, Vol. 60, No. 1, March 1996, p. 10.

47. "Alternatives to Incarceration Mean Less Recidivism," *Corrections Digest*, Vol. 27, No. 18, 1996, pp. 1-3.

48. Paul Gendreau, Francis T. Cullen, and Donald A. Andrews, "The Effects of Community Sanctions and Incarceration on Recidivism," *Forum on Correctional Research*, Vol. 12, No. 2, May 2000, p. 12.

49. P. A. Langan, "Between Prison and Probation: Intermediate Sanctions," *Science*, May 6, 1994, pp. 791-794.

50. *Mempa v. Rhay*, 389 U.S. 128 (1967).

51. *Gagnon v. Scarpelli*, 411 U.S. 778 (1973).

52. Holten and Lamar, *The Criminal Courts*, p. 304, citing Hazel B. Kerper and Jansen Kerper, *Legal Rights of the Convicted*, St. Paul, Minnesota: West Publishing Company, 1974, p. 250.

53. *Ibid.*, p. 257.

54. "Serve or Surveil?" in Travis et al., *Corrections: An Issues Approach*, p. 119.

55. David A. Jones, *The Law of Criminal Procedure: An Analysis and Critique*, Boston: Little, Brown, 1981, p. 540.

56. William M. DiMascio, *Seeking Justice: Crime and Punishment in America*, New York: Edna McConnell Clark Foundation, 1997, p. 6.

57. "NIJ Survey of Probation and Parole Agency Directors," *National Institute of Justice Update*, Washington, D.C.: U.S. Department of Justice, 1995, p. 1.

58. Dan Richard Beto, Ronald P. Corbett, Jr., and John J. DiIulio, Jr., "Getting Serious about Probation and the Crime Problem," *Corrections Management Quarterly*, Vol. 4, No. 2, Spring 2000, p. 3.

59. Eric Schlosser, "The Prison-Industrial Complex," *The Atlantic Monthly*, December, 1998, p. 68.

60. M. G. Neithercutt and D. M. Gottfredson, *Case Load Size Variation and Differences in Probation/Parole Performance*, Pittsburgh, Pennsylvania: National Center for Juvenile Justice, 1974. *See also* American Probation and Parole Association, *Results-Driven*

Management: Implementing Performance-based Measures in Community Corrections, Lexington, Kentucky: American Probation and Parole Association, 1995.

61. Donald Cochrane, "Corrections' Catch 22," *Corrections Today*, Vol. 51, No. 6, October 1989, p. 16.

62. Bureau of Justice Assistance, *Intensive Supervision Probation and Parole (ISP): Program Brief*, Washington, D.C.: U.S. Department of Justice, 1988, p. 7.

63. *Ibid.*, p. 9.

64. *Ibid.*, pp. 17-20. *See also* Frank S. Pearson, "Evaluation of New Jersey's Intensive Supervision Program," *Crime and Delinquency*, Vol. 34, No. 4, 1988, pp. 437-448.

65. Joan Petersilia and Susan Turner, "Evaluating Intensive Supervision Probation/ Parole: Results of a Nationwide Experiment," *National Institute of Justice Research in Brief*, Washington, D.C.: U.S. Department of Justice, 1993.

66. *See*, for example, Todd R. Clear and Patricia L. Hardyman, "The New Intensive Supervision Movement," *Crime and Delinquency*, Vol. 36, No. 1, 1990, p. 49, who maintain that "there are almost certainly numerous persons on regular probation who represent a considerably higher public safety problem than the ISP client."

67. Betsy Fulton and Susan Stone, "Evaluating the Effectiveness of Intensive Supervision," *Corrections Today*, Vol. 54, No. 8, December 1992, p. 82.

68. *Ibid.*, citing Barry Nidorf.

69. Joan Petersilia and Susan Turner, "Objectively Evaluating ISPs," *Corrections Today*, Vol. 53, No. 3, June 1991, p. 28.

70. Fulton and Stone, "Evaluating Intensive Supervision," p. 85. *See also* American Probation and Parole Association, *Restructuring Intensive Supervision Programs: Applying "What Works,"* Lexington, Kentucky: American Probation and Parole Association, 1994.

71. Diane Vaughan, "Shock Probation and Shock Parole: The Impact of Changing Correctional Ideology," in David M. Petersen and Charles W. Thomas, eds., *Corrections: Problems and Prospects*, Second Edition, Englewood Cliffs, New Jersey: Prentice Hall, 1980, p. 216.

72. *Ibid.*, p. 217.

73. Wayne Logan, "Description of Shock Probation and Parole," in Dale G. Parent, *Shock Incarceration: An Overview of Existing Programs*, Washington, D.C.: U.S. Department of Justice, 1989, p. 53.

74. *Ibid.*

CHAPTER 5

JAILS: PRETRIAL DETENTION AND SHORT-TERM CONFINEMENT

❝ The 'jail problem' is a complex collection of problems, including jurisdictional authority and responsibility, Constitutional rights, sociological and medical opinion, basic public safety, and perhaps most difficult, the allotment of increasingly scarce resources for the benefit of an exceedingly unpopular constituency. [1] **❞**

—Advisory Commission on Intergovernmental Relations

Chapter Overview

J ails are the oldest component of the criminal justice system. Yet, they also have been the most neglected. Tracing their origins back to the abysmal conditions and corrupt fee system of English gaols, American jails have endured a legacy of insufficient funding, inappropriate facilities, idle inmates, inadequate staffing, and a public largely indifferent to it all.

Modern, reform-minded jail administrators have faced the extraordinary challenge of overcoming these historical obstacles and bringing today's jails into the twenty-first century. It has not been an easy task, for despite how long they have been with us and how many people they incarcerate, jails are not highly visible.

Just as corrections is the least-known function of the criminal justice system, jails represent the "silent majority" of the correctional system—"silent" because of their low profile and "majority" because they actually process more clients than any other correctional institutions. Although the average stay in jail is much shorter than in prison, jails admit twenty times more inmates than prisons.[2] Moreover, all jail inmates do not necessarily go on to prison, but practically all prison inmates have experienced time in jail.

Beyond their lack of visibility, jails must struggle with a role that has never been well defined. If society is uncertain about whether corrections should be a symbol of deterrence, a place of incapacitation, or a method of rehabilitation, the role of the jail is even more unclear. With a mixture of sentenced/unsentenced, convicted/unconvicted, and felon/misdemeanant populations, jails must balance multiple missions. Their functions range from the first stop for the police after making an arrest to the last resort for a community when no other resources exist to deal with the problem. As a result, anyone from homeless hitchhikers to homicide offenders can be found in jail.

But where challenges seem endless, the potential for change is equally limitless. With obstacles also come opportunities. Creative administrators have begun to seize these opportunities to make a positive impact on the status of the nation's jails. Particularly in major metropolitan areas, the dirty, dark, decrepit jails lingering from the past century have begun to be replaced by clean, well-lighted, modern facilities that no more resemble the traditional image of jails than today's computers resemble yesterday's typewriters. Under the "new generation" approach, jails are structured to produce a normal environment. They are secured by doors rather than bars. They are staffed by officers trained in direct supervision techniques. But most of all, they confirm that there is, indeed, hope on the horizon for turning jails from virtual dungeons into viable detention centers.

Admittedly, there is still a long way to go toward securing the public attention, funding, and support that jails require to fulfill their potential. The day may come when society realizes that more effectively dealing with those in jail may well reduce the demand for so many prisons. But until that time, there is reassurance in knowing that no matter what the future holds for jails, it inevitably will be an improvement on the past.

Learning Goals

Do you know:

1. How many jails there are in the United States and why the number has been decreasing?
2. The definition of a jail?
3. What size of facility makes up the majority of the nation's jails?
4. In what size of jail the majority of inmates are confined?
5. What problems are experienced by very small jails?
6. What regional jail consolidation is and what impact it has had?

Number and Types of Jails

No one knows exactly how many jails operate in the United States. As surprising as this may seem, it relates to society's uncertainty about the function of jails. Because we do not agree on what jails should be doing, it is difficult to determine what types of facilities are performing whatever that role is. Definitions of what a jail is vary throughout the country, ranging from massive detention centers operating in large urban counties to small "lockups," "holdovers," or "drunk tanks" in police stations. In this chapter, the term jail will be limited to locally administered confinement facilities that hold persons awaiting trial (for more than forty-eight hours) or those serving a sentence (usually a year or less).[3]

Using that definition, there were 3,365 jails in the United States during 1999,[4] which actually represents a *decrease* from the 3,493 jails that were operating in 1978.[5] This does not mean that fewer people are going to jail, nor does it mean that there is less need for jails. Rather, it reflects two trends: (1) the number of small jails that are being consolidated into large detention centers, and (2) the number of extremely old jails that are being phased out of service.

Jail Size

A major obstacle in the path of modernization is the large number of relatively small jails. As Figure 5.1 illustrates, facilities housing fewer than fifty inmates actually make up the majority (71 percent) of the nation's jails. That might create the assumption that most of the people in jail are confined in small facilities, but they are not. Despite their dramatically fewer numbers, large jails account for far more inmates: 290,574 are in jails of a thousand or more, compared with 102,683 in jails of less than 150 inmates.[6] In other

Facilities confining a thousand inmates or more represent the types of jails that are increasing in number throughout the United States. When it opened in 1990, the Orient Road Jail in Tampa, Florida, was the largest direct supervision jail in the United States. It has a rated capacity of 1,711. Courtesy of the Hillsborough County (Florida) Sheriff's Department Aerial Unit.

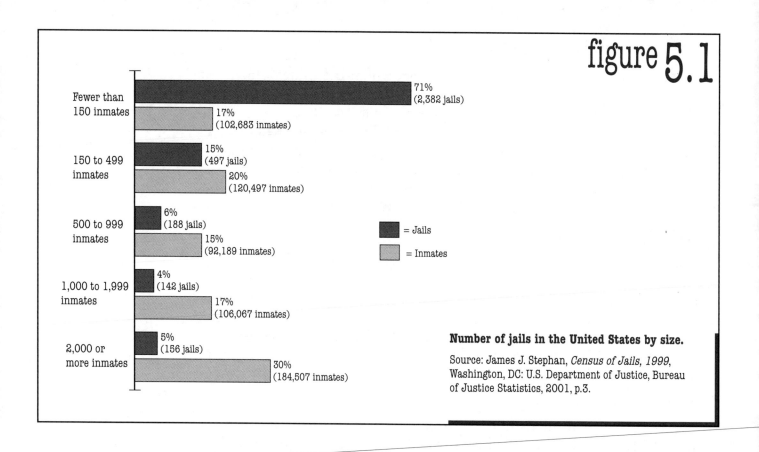

figure 5.1

- Fewer than 150 inmates: 71% (2,382 jails) / 17% (102,683 inmates)
- 150 to 499 inmates: 15% (497 jails) / 20% (120,497 inmates)
- 500 to 999 inmates: 6% (188 jails) / 15% (92,189 inmates)
- 1,000 to 1,999 inmates: 4% (142 jails) / 17% (106,067 inmates)
- 2,000 or more inmates: 5% (156 jails) / 30% (184,507 inmates)

■ = Jails
▨ = Inmates

Number of jails in the United States by size.

Source: James J. Stephan, *Census of Jails, 1999,* Washington, DC: U.S. Department of Justice, Bureau of Justice Statistics, 2001, p.3.

words, 9 percent of the nation's jails—the largest facilities—house 47 percent of the total number of inmates.

In very small, rural jails, even segregating only the most obvious groups (male/female; young/old; felons/misdemeanants) can create crowded conditions, despite the fact that the total population may be within the facility's overall capacity. Moreover, it is virtually impossible to provide the training, range of treatment services, and varieties of personnel that are available in larger, urban jails.[7] The most pressing issues facing small jails include staff shortages, lack of round-the-clock coverage, maintenance difficulties, and inability to provide adequate physical separation of special inmates (for example, juveniles, females, mentally ill, and so forth). The lack of ability to properly classify and separate inmates also can accelerate other operational problems such as attacks, assaults, and the introduction of weapons and other unauthorized items.

Consolidating Small Jails

For many of these reasons, there has been considerable movement in recent years toward the *consolidation* of small jails into larger regional detention centers. Just as the centralization of purchasing reduces the cost of items to each department involved, regional-jail consolidation enhances cost effectiveness, along with providing expanded and improved services.

Some states are even taking the lead by encouraging local jails to regionalize. In Virginia, for example, the state has reimbursed up to half of the new construction or renovation costs when three or more jurisdictions consolidate. As a result, twelve regional jails in Virginia represent a total of twenty-four counties and eleven cities that otherwise would have to maintain their own small jails. The savings in construction and operating costs alone have been cited as "economically staggering."[8]

Such cooperative efforts also enable a jail to offer programs that jurisdictions functioning independently could not afford to staff or operate. In addition, regionalization assures that minimally acceptable standards can be met. Wide variations in staffing patterns, training programs, operational procedures, and inmate services can be reduced significantly.

Thus, it is not surprising to find that the type of facilities that have been declining the most in recent years are jails housing fewer than fifty inmates. At the other extreme, megajails confining a thousand or more inmates are rapidly increasing. In short, while we still have far more very small jails, they are dropping in number. By the same token, while we still have few very large jails, they are increasing in number.

 # Learning Goals

Do you know:

1. What functions are performed by jails?
2. What percentage of the jail population is pretrial (versus convicted)?
3. For what types of offenses most people are in jail?
4. To what extent alcohol and drug abuse affect the jail population?

Functions of the Jail

As noted in Chapter 3, early English gaols originated as places to confine those awaiting either trial or imposition of the death penalty. (In contrast to today, at that time, the defendant could expect to wait much longer for the former than the latter.) Those on death row are now housed in state prisons. But local jails have retained their pretrial function to this day. In terms of their conviction status, the bulk of the jail population breaks down into two general categories:

- *Accused* defendants awaiting trial

- *Convicted* offenders serving short-term sentences (usually one year or less)

Pretrial Detention and Convicted Offenders

Since incarceration is considered a form of punishment, it would be logical to expect that jails would house more *convicted* offenders serving sentences than *accused* suspects waiting for trial. That is not the case. Jail populations over the past several decades generally have been equally divided, with approximately half awaiting trial and half serving sentences.

Obviously, jails have little control over the sentences of those convicted. But efforts have been made to reduce pretrial populations through alternatives such as release on recognizance, pretrial intervention, and electronic monitoring. However, as pretrial release rates declined throughout the late 1990s, the unconvicted population has been steadily advancing. In fact, it is the increasing number of pretrial detainees that accounts for the majority of the jail population growth in recent years.[9] By 2002, the proportion of convicted inmates had dropped to 40 percent,[10] which means that the majority of the jail population (60 percent) is technically innocent in the eyes of the law.

Other Jail Inmates

Beyond confining pretrial detainees and those serving short sentences, as illustrated in Figure 5.2, jails also are responsible for:

- Booking those arrested
- Holding convicted offenders awaiting sentencing
- Holding sentenced offenders awaiting transfer to other correctional facilities
- Readmitting probation, parole, and bail/bond violators or absconders

Of these functions, holding inmates waiting to be transferred to prison is the most controversial. Lately, it has become a source of conflict between some local and state jurisdictions. As prisons fill above capacity, an overflow of sentenced inmates can quickly back up in already crowded jails. For example, by the end of 2002, local jails were holding 71,256 state and federal prisoners.[11] When the state refuses to accept such inmates in a timely manner, it can

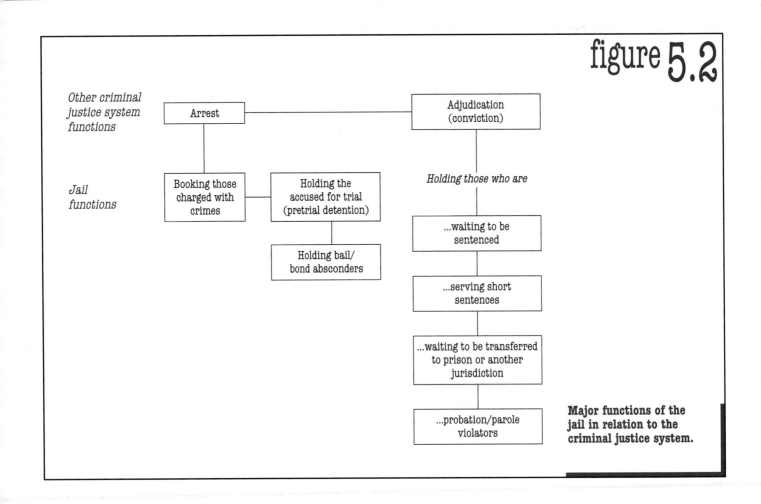

figure 5.2

Major functions of the jail in relation to the criminal justice system.

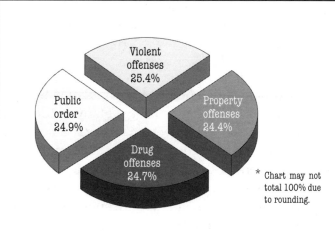

figure 5.3

Violent
offenses
25.4%

Public
order
24.9%

Property
offenses
24.4%

Drug
offenses
24.7%

* Chart may not
total 100% due
to rounding.

Most serious offenses of jail inmates. *

Source: Doris J. James, "Profile of Jail Inmates, 2002,"
Bureau of Justice Statistics Special Report,
Washington, DC: U.S. Department of Justice, 2004, p. 1.

create conflict between the local jail and state prison officials. As noted in a lawsuit filed by several sheriffs against a state department of corrections, "holding felons for long periods in local jails is not only illegal, but dangerous, expensive, and unfair."[12]

The jail also serves other purposes for which it was not intended. For example, jails can hold juveniles (pending their trial in adult court or transfer to other correctional facilities); probation and parole violators (pending their revocation hearings); the mentally ill (pending their transfer to mental health facilities when such resources are available); and indigent transients—who, unfortunately, are usually not pending transfer anywhere but back on the streets, since the jail is often the only facility available twenty-four hours a day to shelter them.

Offenses of Jail Inmates

From this wide assortment, it is apparent that the jail serves many purposes and confines a diverse population. Although the public may be under the impression that local jails are incarcerating primarily hardened, violent offenders, the data in Figure 5.3 challenge that assumption.

While the types of offenses for which people are confined in jail vary with local policies, a national picture of the jail population presents some interesting findings. In terms of their most serious offense, only *one fourth* (25.4 percent) of the population is confined for such violent offenses as murder, kidnaping, rape, robbery, or assault.[13] Of these, most are in *pretrial* status, since those suspected of such violent crimes are less likely to qualify for bail or release on recognizance, and once convicted, they are more likely to receive an extensive prison sentence.

Thus, as Figure 5.3 illustrates, three out of four inmates are *not* in jail for the types of violent personal crimes most feared by society—but rather, for property crimes, drug-related offenses, or public order offenses, (such as traffic violations, obstruction of justice, weapons charges, or—most commonly—driving while intoxicated). This is not meant to imply that jail crowding should be reduced by legalizing drugs or that drunk driving is not a significant threat to public safety, but it does point out that the public's perception of the "typical" jail inmate may not conform with who is actually in jail.

Alcohol and Drug Abusers

As is apparent from this inmate profile, much of the jail's population is experiencing some type of difficulty with either alcohol or drugs. Many of the jail's residents are homeless, drifters, vagrants, or "skid row" inhabitants. Since public intoxication remains an offense in most jurisdictions, a sizable number of these people find themselves incarcerated for drunkenness, vagrancy, or disorderly conduct. A chronic drinker who has been arrested dozens of times cumulatively can spend a decade in jail on short-term sentences. Despite some efforts to replace "drunk tanks" with detoxification centers and to decriminalize public inebriation, the "common drunk" remains a headache for local jails.[14]

Moreover, recent crackdowns on Driving While Intoxicated (DWI) offenders and "zero tolerance" drug policies have contributed substantially to the jail population. But that does not mean that jails are well equipped to help alcohol and drug abusers. Considering that it costs more than $15,000 annually to house an inmate in jail,[15] incarceration is an expensive option, and most jails are not able to provide necessary treatment for substance abusers. It has been reported, for example, that only 4 percent of jailed DWI offenders are in treatment programs, compared with 46 percent of those on probation. Even when such self-help efforts as Alcoholics Anonymous (AA) are included, the numbers increase to only 17 percent of those in jail, in contrast to 62 percent of those on probation.[16]

Likewise, jails continue to warehouse drug offenders, despite research indicating that drug treatment is more effective than punitive sentences.[17] Substance abuse continues to generate inmates with problems that jails were not designed to handle. But as long as society continues to focus more on building jails than developing treatment programs, the cycle of drug- and alcohol-related crime can be expected to continue.

Jail Turnover

Regardless of their offense, in most jurisdictions, the jail usually is not authorized to hold inmates serving longer than one year. Thus, as a general rule, those with a sentence of a year or less will serve it in jail, while those with longer terms will serve their time in prison. As with most general statements, however, there are exceptions. Some counties enable inmates to serve a number of years in jail. But since there are about as many *admissions* to as *releases from* jails on an annual basis, it is apparent that there is a high turnover among the jail population—in other words, few stay there very long. Stated another way, it takes the U.S. prison population two years to turn over once, whereas the jail population turns over twenty to twenty-five times each year.[18] This has significant implications for jail management, programming, and inmate supervision.[19]

 Learning Goals

Do you know:

1. What the differences are between first-, second-, and third (new) generation jails?

2. How architecture and management style shape behavior in direct-supervision facilities?

3. Why direct-supervision jails do not result in higher operating costs?

4. The difference between direct-supervision facilities and traditional jails in terms of violence, escapes, vandalism, and property damage?

5. Why direct-supervision/new-generation jails cannot be run with "old generation" management?

Direct Supervision (New Generation) Jails

If you bought a computer several years ago, you probably have found that it is obsolete. Newer, faster, more sophisticated models are constantly replacing each previous "generation" of computers. As society progresses and new advancements are made, one might expect that similar changes would be reflected in our jails. But even facilities constructed as recently as twenty-five to thirty years ago "are not radically different, in most respects, from the nation's first penitentiary—the Walnut Street Jail of 1790."[20] They may be cleaner. They may be better lighted. They may include more high-tech security, but their basic features have remained essentially the same.

Philosophy

In response to the need for a "new generation" of correctional facilities, several jails were constructed during the mid-1970s that no more resemble traditional jails than manual typewriters resemble today's computers. The rationale behind this movement is based on several fundamental principles:

- At least half of those in jail have *not yet been convicted*. It is therefore questionable whether pretrial inmates should be punished by subjecting them to worse conditions than what they would experience if convicted and sentenced to prison.

- The *physical design* of a correctional facility shapes inmate and staff behavior. When people are degraded to the point of putting them in cages otherwise reserved for animals, it should not be surprising if their reactions more closely resemble animal than human behavior. When staff are overstressed by the noise, confusion, and depressing environment of the jail, it should not be surprising if they become frustrated, quit, or act unprofessionally.

- The *control of behavior* within a correctional facility should be a function of staff rather than inmates. When jail personnel cannot adequately observe what all inmates are doing at all times, gaps are created.

This is a linear jail with cells arranged in a line. Courtesy of the American Correctional Association, Lanham, Maryland.

Inmates will be quick to fill the vacuum, with the strong preying on the weak.

- The fundamental purpose of jails is to *maintain custody* of those who have been deprived of their liberty. In other words, the role of the jail is not to inflict greater punishment than the loss of freedom. Exposure to substandard living conditions, sexual attacks, demeaning treatment,

Direct-supervision jails are based on the concept that inmates will behave more normally when they are confined in a more normal environment. Here is the day-room of the Bernalillo County Detention Center. Courtesy of Mark Goldman and Associates, project architect and engineers, Joint Venture of CBL/DCSW (Custer-Basarich, Ltd. and Design Collaborative of the Southwest) with the Durrant Group.

and inmate dominance are not what the courts have authorized as part of an inmate's "sentence."

In recognition of these problems, the courts have intervened to improve jail conditions. As successful cases challenged the constitutionality of the jail environment on grounds of cruel and unusual punishment, many localities were forced to upgrade their jails. Rather than waiting to react to court decisions, the new-generation philosophy assumes a *proactive* approach—creating facilities that not only meet basic standards of human decency, but come as close to replicating a "normal" environment as can be achieved in confinement.

Architecture and Inmate Supervision

The two major features that set direct supervision facilities apart from traditional jails—and to which much of their success in behavioral control can be attributed—are *architecture* and *management style*. These features work hand-in-hand to shape behavior and are reflected in the three generations through which jails have progressed.[21]

1. *First-generation* jails are those we most typically would think of if asked to describe a jail. Inmates are confined in multiple-housing cells that are lined in rows along a corridor. The end of each row comes together toward a central control area, similar to the spokes on a wheel (*see* Figure 5.4). Officers patrol the corridors (or "catwalks") on an intermittent, infrequent basis. They cannot observe everyone in all cells at any one time. Their interaction with inmates is generally through bars as they pass by. As a result, activities often occur in the cells without staff knowledge or control. Because of the linear layout of the cells and the lack of constant supervision, the inmate-management style of first-generation jails is known as *linear remote* (or *intermittent*) *surveillance*.

2. In *second-generation* jails, inmate housing surrounds a secure control booth (*see* Figure 5.5). Officers can see directly into the housing units. Thus, rather than physically patrolling corridors, staff can observe inmates directly from their glass-enclosed booth. Although this design increases visual surveillance, isolation in the booth reduces verbal interaction. Communication with

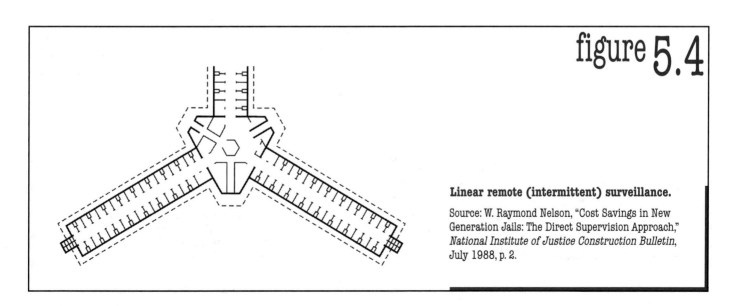

figure 5.4

Linear remote (intermittent) surveillance.

Source: W. Raymond Nelson, "Cost Savings in New Generation Jails: The Direct Supervision Approach," *National Institute of Justice Construction Bulletin*, July 1988, p. 2.

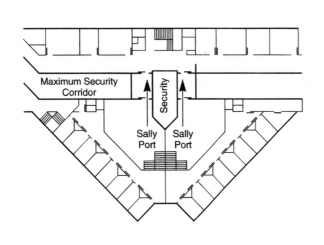

figure 5.5

Indirect (remote) surveillance.

Source: W. Raymond Nelson, "Cost Savings in New Generation Jails: The Direct Supervision Approach," *National Institute of Justice Construction Bulletin*, July 1988, p. 2.

inmates is accomplished through an intercom. Because of the lack of personal contact, the inmate-management style of second-generation jails is known as indirect (or remote) surveillance.

3. The *third (or new) generation* of jails combines the principles of continual surveillance with personal interaction. Individual housing units are located around an open area, where an officer is stationed permanently (*see* Figure 5.6). No barrier separates personnel from residents. Inmates freely move throughout the unit, under the continual supervision of the officer in charge. For this reason the new-generation jails are known as *direct-supervision* facilities. As one advocate of direct supervision jailing notes:

> It's a throwback to the old days, when cops used to walk a certain beat every day, [and] the people of the neighborhood would develop a relationship with him. . . . Gradually, the neighborhood would accept him and feel comfortable enough to share their daily life and concerns with him. This kept the officer informed and intimately

figure 5.6

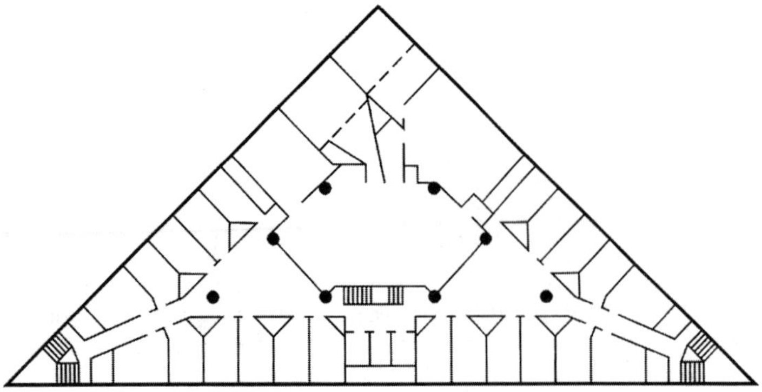

Direct supervision.

Source: W. Raymond Nelson, "Cost Savings in New Generation Jails: The Direct Supervision Approach," *National Institute of Justice Construction Bulletin*, July 1988, p. 3.

aware of neighborhood dynamics. . . . Having an officer in the pod [unit], among the inmates at all times, resembles in many respects walking a neighborhood beat.[22]

To reduce unnecessary movement and related staffing costs, all services are provided directly in the unit—meals, telephones, showers, laundry, counseling, visits, and the like.[23] Although the relative freedom may give the impression that security is lacking, new-generation jails concentrate security on the outside perimeter. Internal security devices are designed to be as unobtrusive as possible. For a summary of architectural and management differences between traditional and direct-supervision jails, see the next "Close-up On Corrections."

 # Close-up On Corrections

COMPARISONS BETWEEN TRADITIONAL AND DIRECT SUPERVISION JAILS

Architecture	Traditional Supervision	Direct Supervision
CELLS	Arranged in linar style along access corridors	Surround a common dayroom
FURNISHINGS	Security grade (indestructible)	Institutional grade
EXERCISE AREA	Centralized, with limited access and need for additional staff	Outdoor area extending from day room for each housing pod

Management/ Supervision		
INTERACTION	Discouraged by barriers	Encouraged, with no physical barriers
SUPERVISION	Intermittent	Continuous observation
DISCIPLINE/INMATE MANAGEMENT	Primarily a function of administrators	Primarily a function of pod officer supervisors
VANDALISM	Rampant	Rare

Source: Compiled from W. Raymond Nelson and Russell M. Davis, *American Jails*, July/August 1995, p. 12.

Physical Features

Visitors to a direct-supervision facility are almost immediately struck by how unlike a "jail" it looks. The atmosphere is calm. You practically can feel the lack of tension. In fact, it is so quiet that some visitors have thought the inmates were "tranquilized." [24] The floors are carpeted. Windows provide natural light. There are no communal cells with bars. Instead, there are individual rooms with doors. The atmosphere is similar to what you might find in a college dorm.

The initial reaction to direct-supervision facilities is how totally contrary they are to our traditional concept of what a jail has been (and to some, what jails should still be today). But in addition to the fact that a sizable portion of jail inmates are accused citizens rather than convicted criminals, there are specific operational reasons for each of the amenities provided. For example:

- *Carpeting, (or vinyl tile), acoustical tile, and open spaces* reduce noise and the tension it creates by absorbing sounds.

- *Solid walls and doors* (instead of gates and bars) eliminate the constant irritation of metal clanging against metal.

- *Natural lighting and soft colors* create a soothing behavioral effect and reduce the impression of an institutional environment.[25]

Through such measures, new-generation jails attempt to provide more natural surroundings, based on the belief that the environment in which we live is self-reinforcing. In other words, the conditions to which people are exposed have a significant effect on their behavior—with normal conditions producing more normal behavior.

Nevertheless, it has been their physical features that have provoked the greatest criticisms of direct-supervision jails. As public attitudes toward offenders have hardened over recent years, critics maintain that such facilities are too "plush"—that they are "coddling" criminals. In response, some jurisdictions have modified the physical structure by removing carpeting, replacing porcelain fixtures with stainless steel, increasing the ratio of inmates to officers, and even replacing unique wall colors with industrial beige and white paint. But in direct-supervision facilities, "positive expectations are generated in part by an environment that is noninstitutional in appearance," and when such jails have compromised physical-design principles, they also have experienced less successful results. [26]

Costs and Effectiveness

The appearance of direct-supervision jails may give the impression that they are more expensive to construct and operate than traditional jails. But evidence indicates that exactly the opposite is the case. Such facilities are both easier to manage and more economical.[27] Cost savings are achieved in a number of ways, including: [28]

- The use of *standard, commercial-grade fixtures* rather than high-security, vandal-proof materials

- The efficiency resulting from the *need for fewer staff*, since personnel are in constant contact with the inmates and are not required to transport them as often because most services are offered directly in the housing unit

- The *reduced use of sick leave* by personnel

- The *lower maintenance costs* resulting from the absence of vandalism and graffiti

For just one unit housing forty-eight inmates, it has been estimated that direct-supervision jails save more than $200,000 in construction costs alone.[29] Moreover, annual operating costs are significantly reduced as well. For example, one jurisdiction debating whether to construct a second- or third-generation jail compiled figures estimating that by the time a new-generation jail is in operation for twenty years, the county will have saved more than $97 million.[30]

Although cost savings are certainly a high priority for any responsible government official, they usually come only at the expense of reducing the quality of service. But again, new-generation jails represent an exception to this rule of thumb. As noted previously, direct-supervision facilities provide a more natural environment, with the anticipation that inmate behavior, in turn, will be modified. Evidence of this self-reinforcing effect is extensive:

- *Violent incidents* overall are reduced by 30 to 90 percent.[31]

- *Homosexual rape* virtually disappears.[32]

- *Aggravated assaults* are substantially reduced.[33]

- Inmates experience fewer symptoms of *stress*.[34]

- The numbers of *suicides, attempted suicides*, and *escapes* are considerably lower.[35]

- The introduction of *contraband* (unauthorized items) is practically nonexistent.[36]

- Significantly *fewer formal rule violations* occur,[37] and disciplinary problems are substantially reduced.[38]

- *Vandalism* and *destruction of property* are almost completely eliminated. For example, in one facility, the number of TV sets needing repair dropped from two per week to two in two years.[39]

- Additionally, direct-supervision administrators report *improved staff morale* and *lower stress* as benefits,[40] along with reductions in violence, assaults, and other aggressive behavior.[41]

These positive results do not mean that direct-supervision jails are intentionally designed for the purpose of treatment or rehabilitation. Rather, they simply are designed to improve security and prevent inmates from deteriorating further as a result of their jail exposure. But they can promote positive outcomes by providing a setting in which any treatment programs that are offered have a better chance to work.[42] By creating a more normal environment, it is expected that those confined will behave more normally, and research thus far has confirmed this expectation.

Training and Management

The residents, of course, are quite receptive to direct-supervision jails. Beyond their basic comforts, they are much safer facilities in which to be confined. No longer do inmates constantly have to fear for their safety or make weapons for their own defense. Officers, however, sometimes experience difficulties with the transition to a new-generation jail. Those who have become accustomed to being physically separated from the inmates quite naturally feel safer being on the "other side of the bars." As a result, they initially may resist being placed directly into a housing unit which "seemingly places officers at the mercy of inmates."[43]

Personnel are not permitted to carry weapons inside of any correctional facility, because of the potential that weapons would encourage attacks on staff and fall into the wrong hands. When officers are separated from inmates by secure metal bars, this is not viewed as a major disadvantage. But it is an entirely different situation when removing the bars requires staff to interact face-to-face with inmates continuously, relying only on verbal skills to control their behavior.

Thus, training is critical to the effective implementation of direct-supervision jails.[44] Such training focuses on the underlying principles of new-generation jailing, the significance of staff to its success, and the interpersonal skills needed to deal with inmates in such an environment. With direct supervision, officers are taught to respond *proactively* to minor issues before they become major problems, rather than dealing *reactively* with the consequences.

By being in constant contact with inmates, officers "get to know them well. They learn to recognize and respond to trouble before it escalates into violence; . . . negotiation and communication become more important than brute strength."[45] In fact, after staff have experienced the relative tranquility, reduced tension, and improved inmate behavior of such jails, they usually are reluctant to work in any other type of facility.

Just as officers must be prepared for their new role in direct-supervision jails, supervisors also must become familiar with a new management style. In traditional jails, lower-level staff tend to have routine assignments, management is centralized, and upper-level administrators make all important decisions. In contrast, new-generation jailing only will be effective when management adopts a more decentralized approach.

As the personnel in charge of the units, officers require much more autonomy to carry out their job. Thus, they must be granted more authority to participate in jail management, make their own decisions, and provide leadership within their unit. In other words, "you can't run a new-generation jail with old-generation management."[46] The physical design is only half of the formula for the success of direct-supervision jails—as in any correctional facility, it is staffing and training that are really the key ingredients. In fact, it is when these critical features are compromised that direct-supervision jails have failed to fulfill their expectations, despite the most advanced architectural design.[47]

Do you know:

1. At what level of government most jails function, and where the exceptions are?

2. How the "elected sheriff" model of jail management differs from the "appointed administrator" model?

Jail Administration and Operations

While the number of direct-supervision facilities increases each year, the vast majority of jails still reflect varieties of first- and second-generation architecture. The major reason that there is so little consistency in terms of everything from size to facility design is that jails are primarily financed, operated, and controlled by *local governments*.

Although there are federal jails for inmates serving short sentences or awaiting trial on federal charges, they represent only eleven of the nation's jails.[48] The majority of jails function at the *local level* of government. Because most jails are local facilities housing a relatively short-term, transient population, they have not received much attention or priority. As a result, they have been referred to as the "stepchild of the criminal justice system." [49]

Counties and municipalities are relatively free to set their own policies and procedures with regard to jail operations. Again, however, there are exceptions. In most states, jails are a function of local government. But in six states—Alaska, Connecticut, Delaware, Hawaii, Rhode Island, and Vermont—jails are a responsibility of the *state level* of government.[50] In addition, even when the jail is locally controlled, states may intervene in jail operations. Some, for example, require that jails adhere to state-mandated standards; others provide fiscal incentives to improve jail conditions.

Two Models of Jail Administration

Despite these exceptions, most of the nation's jails are administered at the *county level* of government. As a result of its English origins, the typical jail today is run by the *county sheriff*, who (like the early shire-reeve) generally is responsible for both *enforcing the law* and *administering the jail*. Again, however, there are the inevitable exceptions. In some counties, the sheriff's functions do not include law enforcement, but rather, are limited to jail administration, court security, and the serving of legal documents.

As an elected official, the sheriff is ultimately accountable to the citizens. This can be advantageous to the jail if the public is concerned about maintaining safe and sanitary conditions in its correctional facilities. But more often, voters place a higher priority on reducing crime than improving jails, and the sheriff who does not respond to public pressures is not likely to be reelected. There are certainly many professional sheriffs who take their responsibilities for jail administration as seriously as their law enforcement duties. But there

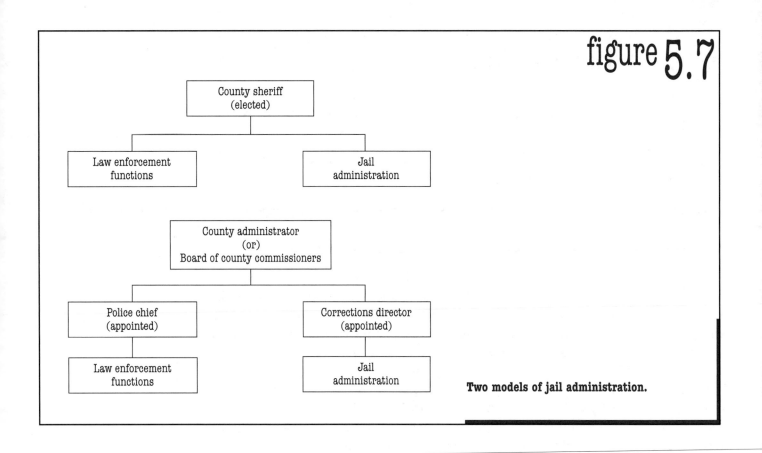

figure **5.7**

County sheriff
(elected)

Law enforcement
functions

Jail
administration

County administrator
(or)
Board of county commissioners

Police chief
(appointed)

Corrections director
(appointed)

Law enforcement
functions

Jail
administration

Two models of jail administration.

are also others who neglect the needs of the jail in favor of higher-visibility enforcement activities that are more likely to generate votes.

To balance law enforcement and correctional responsibilities more equitably, some counties have either created separate budgets for law enforcement and correctional functions or actually have abolished the office of sheriff, establishing in its place a local department of corrections that is independent from the county's police department. Under this arrangement, both the police chief and the corrections director are *appointed* by the county administrator rather than elected by the public. In this type of management system, the jail has a separate administrator advocating for its needs and may not be as subject to political pressures. (For an illustration of these two models of jail management, *see* Figure 5.7.)

The Administrator's Role: Setting the Tone for Staff

Regardless of whether the person in charge of the jail is appointed or elected, it is that individual who sets the tone for how the facility will operate. As public servants, jail administrators serve the general public—especially that part of the public under their custody in jail. It is the administrator who makes it clear—by actions as well as inactions—just what will and will not be acceptable.

When the facility's leadership is indifferent to what is going on, staff members get the message that their work is unimportant, and inmates will be quick to take advantage of the situation. For example, institutions with poor morale are more vulnerable to escape attempts than those with good morale. Such an organizational culture can make even the most modern, well-designed jail an unpleasant place to be—for both inmates *and* staff. On the other hand, there are modern jail administrators who are using a combination of staff accountability and computer-based management information systems to improve the operation of their facilities (as described in the next "Close-up On Corrections").

Jail managers who display visionary leadership take an active interest in daily operations and assure that rules and regulations are enforced firmly, fairly, and consistently so that they can create a positive climate, even in a less-than-desirable physical facility. As we have seen with new-generation jailing, although humane physical conditions are essential, operational staff are actually the key ingredient to managing any correctional facility effectively.

Close-up On Corrections

COMPSTAT BREAKS INTO JAIL

Law-enforcement administrators are becoming increasingly familiar with the term "Compstat," the New York City Police Department's innovative method of statistics-based management. . . . Still, despite the recognition and success that NYPD has achieved, little thought has been given to Compstat's adaptability outside the context of "police management"—until now.

The New York City Department of Correction has achieved a series of astounding results by applying Compstat. The number of inmate slashings has substantially declined. Overtime spending is down. Use of sick leave has dropped. These achievements have been brought about, in large part, by adapting the Compstat model to what is called a TEAMS approach. TEAMS is the Department of Correction's Total Efficiency Accountability Management System. The theory behind TEAMS is that performance in every area of the department affects how it performs its mission—the care, custody, and control of the inmate population.

Wardens are held accountable for implementing improvements in their jails, reporting on facility operations, explaining unusual incidents, and charting operational strategies. During monthly TEAMS sessions, wardens provide a detailed description of their jail's operations. Inmate violence, searches, contraband seizures, overtime, sick leave, and facility conditions are just some of the operational issues discussed during these sessions. Executive staff use the information presented by each of the facilities to assess jail operations and conditions, to identify "best practices," to ensure accountability, and to provide direction regarding individual jail or systemwide issues.

TEAMS has created a culture of accountability. Statistical data are analyzed as a means of acquiring continuous feedback and making prompt and effective operational decisions. Today, the Department of Correction monitors more than 100 performance indicators to assess and continuously improve agency operations.

Source: Paraphrased from Paul O'Connell and Frank Straub, "For Jail Management, Compstat's a Keeper," *Law Enforcement News*, September 30, 1999, p. 8.

Staff Roles: Setting the Tone for Inmates

Just as the jail administrator creates the organizational culture for staff, it is operational personnel who, in turn, establish the climate for inmates. They are the people who are in day-to-day, continuous interaction with the jail's population. Inmates are completely dependent on them—for everything from the time they eat, to what they can keep in their cells, to whether they can get an aspirin for a headache. Staff control virtually every aspect of an inmate's life during confinement, in accordance with the rules and regulations of the facility.

Effective administrators today recognize that "a jail's most important resource is staff."[51] As a result, personnel have progressed from being viewed as "turnkeys" or "guards" to inmate managers and leaders,[52] who are recognized for their critical role in facility operations. (For more insights into this issue, see the next "Close-up On Corrections.") Because of their tremendous diversity, jails vary considerably with regard to how extensively they have improved employee salaries, training, screening, and management practices over the years. But the bottom line is simply that physical facilities notwithstanding, any jail will be only as good as the people staffing it.

Learning Goals

Do you know:

1. How intake affects one's adjustment to jail?
2. In contrast to prison, why jails are particularly vulnerable to suicides?
3. How public policy changes resulted in more of the mentally ill being confined in jails?

Close-up On Corrections

GUARDS OR CORRECTIONAL OFFICERS?

Are we guards or correctional officers? . . . A "guard" is one who watches over, protects and prevents escape, etc., but more than that, a "guard" is a technician trained to do a rather specific task, maintain security/custody. On the other hand, an "officer," by definition, is one who . . . serves other people in a holistic way, concerned about the total person . . . and the surrounding environment. They learn how to care for the physical health of a person, how to promote mental/emotional well-being, and how to lift the spirit by promoting self-esteem. They learn how to provide a safe and secure environment. Above all, they are respecters of persons, individuals, and their rights.

Source: Larry W. Bergman, "Corrections as a Holistic Profession?" *The Keepers' Voice*, Vol. 15, No. 1, Winter 1994, p. 43.

Intake Procedures

To the extent that first impressions are lasting, it is during initial intake that the jail has the greatest potential for making a positive or negative impression. The attitudes of staff, the way inmates are handled, and the level of professionalism displayed during the receiving process do much to establish the frame of mind for the inmate's adjustment to jail. An offender who is rough handled physically, demeaned verbally, or simply treated discourteously during intake is likely to form lasting impressions of distrust and disrespect that will influence subsequent interactions with the jail's personnel. On the other hand, when new arrivals are treated with dignity, courtesy, and respect, the effect often can be reinforcing in terms of how they, in turn, interact with staff.

Inmates are usually received by way of an outside enclosure called a sallyport, through which the police or sheriff's car transporting the offender passes. To accommodate those coming directly from court, many jails have an enclosed walkway connected to the courtrooms. This reduces the security risks involved during outside transportation. But one's first contact with the jail will be through the sallyport on arrest. Once the police vehicle is inside and the gate secured, the suspect is removed to the receiving area of the jail. The arrest form must be checked carefully during the intake and booking process, since legal problems can arise when a person is deprived of liberty without adequate and completely legal documentation. Assuming that immediate medical attention is not needed, most jails then conduct a *pat-down* or *frisk search* (often followed later by a full strip search).

All valuables confiscated are carefully recorded, placed in an envelope, and signed for on a property receipt. Since cash and expensive jewelry are not permitted in most jails, these items are placed in a property storage room, to be collected on release. Needless to say, the proper handling of money and valuables is very important.

Basic information is then taken—such as name, address, physical description, occupation, specific charges, name and phone number of anyone to be notified in case of emergency, attorney's name and address, and name/address of those who may be expected to visit the inmate. In addition, some jails record a particularly personal item of information that only the person being admitted would be likely to know, such as mother's maiden name. The purpose of this procedure is to ensure that on release, the correct inmate is being discharged, since several inmates may share exactly the same name and even bear a physical resemblance, especially in very large jails.

Photographing and *fingerprinting* follow next, with a complete set of prints sent to the FBI to check on outstanding warrants and file with the National Crime Information Center. The FBI, in turn, sends back a "rap sheet," which is a criminal record history based on the times the person has been fingerprinted. This gives jail personnel a more complete picture of whom they are dealing with to determine whether the person poses any identifiable security or safety risks.

Operational Considerations

Because no one can be held "incommunicado" in jail, inmates also must be given opportunities to make arrangements for bail (or release on recognizance) and to contact their attorney. Visits must be carefully controlled, with a record

Jail inmates often pay for basic services and goods. Here, a Davidson County Sheriff's Office employee issues items to an inmate that are covered by the agency's processing fee. Courtesy of the Davidson County Sheriff's Office.

made of who visits and when. No person can be denied access to counsel at any time. Incoming packages have to be inspected to prevent the introduction of drugs, alcohol, weapons, or other contraband items. Medicines must be carefully controlled—issued by qualified medical staff and taken in their presence.

These are but a few of the legal and security-oriented operational considerations that must be handled effectively by jail personnel. Since most jail operational practices also pertain to prisons, a more detailed discussion of these procedures is contained in Chapter 7. But it is noteworthy that in many respects, jails incur greater security risks than prisons. Not only is there a constant flow of inmates into and out of the jail, but the sizable pretrial population must be transported to all of their preliminary court appearances, as well as to and from the courtroom during each day of their trials. Such continuous movement presents a significant security challenge, requiring jail personnel to be alert at all times to the potential for escape.

Treatment and Industrial Programs

In the past, most inmates lingered unproductively in jails, making security matters even more difficult as residents sought "creative" outlets for their boredom. In part, this is a reflection of the jail's early history as a holding facility, which did not include reform or rehabilitation among its goals. Moreover, both treatment and constructive employment are particularly difficult in jails because of the high turnover of the population as a result of their short-term confinement. But "without appropriate programs that focus on changing the criminal behavior of inmates, the jail becomes a 'revolving door,' releasing individuals into the community simply to readmit them in a few months, weeks, days, or even hours, when they are arrested for another crime." [53] Progressive administrators today therefore are attempting to provide activities that promote job skills, occupy time, and in some cases, even reduce the cost of jail management.

Most jails now at least have reading materials available in a library, recreational opportunities, arts and crafts, and organized religious programs. Many also have added various forms of educational classes, correspondence courses, group counseling sessions, and even self-paced computer-assisted instruction. Even television is being programmed with topics ranging from drug- and alcohol-dependency to educational improvement, employment readiness, parenting skills, and anger management, to turn idle TV watching into useful skills training.[54]

In addition, productive labor is expanding under a federally sponsored industries initiative, through which inmates can earn privileges, learn job skills, and earn wages that go toward repayment of custodial costs and compensation to crime victims.[55] Beyond reducing idleness, such programs are designed to improve work habits, develop new skills, and generate revenues or reduce costs. Activities in which inmates are engaged range from landscaping to assembling electronics components. Thus, inmate labor is beginning to expand beyond the routine facility maintenance functions to which jail inmates largely had been limited in the past.

Medical Services

In recent years, court cases resulting from deaths related to lack of proper medical attention, as well as increasing pressure for adequate medical standards, have focused more attention on health care in jails.[56] Although they are voluntary, the standards established by the Joint Commission on Correctional Health Care and the American Correctional Association have had a substantial influence on improving institutional medical services.

The importance of an initial medical exam is perhaps best illustrated by the fact that some suspects who have been arrested for apparent drunkenness later were found to have had a fractured skull, diabetes, or other illnesses or

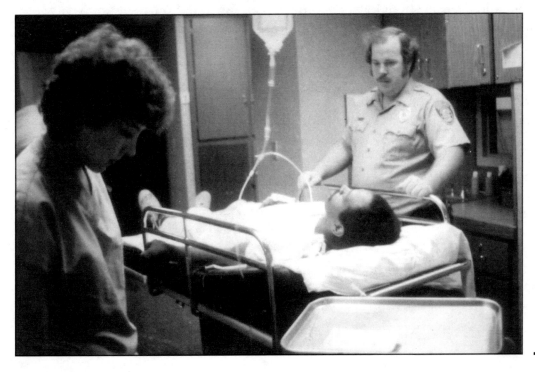

Providing for routine health care, as well as emergency medical services, is an essential feature of modern jails. Courtesy of the Miami-Dade County Department of Corrections and Rehabilitation, Miami, Florida.

injuries which caused physical behavior that easily could be misinterpreted as intoxication, particularly with alcohol on the breath.

Moreover, infectious diseases (such as hepatitis, tuberculosis, and AIDS) are common among those most frequently brought into jail, and treatment is often unavailable to them in the community. Recognizing this, a special task force has been established by the Centers for Disease Control and Prevention to focus on the public health risks related to these diseases among those behind bars. While society has those with such communicable illnesses in custody, it has an opportunity to diagnose and treat them—not only for the benefit of the individual patient, but for the ultimate benefit of the entire community by reducing the spread of infection.

Suicide Vulnerability

Another critical element of the intake process is identifying those who may be displaying signs and symptoms that indicate they are intent on taking their own life. This is a particularly significant problem, since suicide accounts for

 # Close-up On Corrections

TRAGEDY BEHIND BARS

In a northwestern state a young man encountered a snowstorm as he drove from his office to a distant town. For reasons perhaps caused by his psychiatric problems, together with the stress of driving in a snowstorm, the man developed a sense of helplessness and confusion. He parked outside of a hospital and made a phone call to his father asking for help because he was confused and did not know what to do. His father told him that he would send his brother to be with him and that he should wait at the hospital for him. So he sat and waited. The desk receptionist observed the young man sitting in the snow without a coat during the blizzard and decided to call the police.

The police officer who responded to the call accused him of being on drugs and therefore took him away to the small local jail. At the prisoner's request, the officer called the boy's father who informed him of the boy's psychiatric history. Unconcerned with this information, the officer told the boy's father that he was going to hold the young man on suspicion of drug possession. The young man was placed in a cell without being booked or charged with any crime. At that time, a traffic accident was reported and because he was the only one on duty, the officer left the man alone in the cell for the rest of the evening. The prisoner was frightened and begged the officer not to lock him up. The officer did not return that evening. When shifts changed, the replacement officers discovered the prisoner was dead; he had hanged himself by his shoelaces.

Source: Used with permission of the Charles Press, Publishers, Inc., from *Suicide Behind Bars: Prediction and Prevention* by David Lester and Bruce Danto. © 1993 by the Charles Press, Publishers, Inc.

more than one-third of inmate deaths in local jails.[57] In contrast, it is the cause of only 5 to 9 percent of the deaths in state and federal prisons.[58] Nor do statistics on jail suicides reflect the many additional but unsuccessful attempts that were prevented by alert staff.

Those in jail are especially vulnerable to the potential for suicide. Many jail inmates are suffering from various forms of mental illness, which can be aggravated by exposure to jail, as the tragic case in the accompanying "Close-up On Corrections" reveals. But even among otherwise mentally healthy inmates, the jail includes high percentages of the types of people most prone to suicide—such as young, unemployed, unmarried males.

Moreover, admission to jail can be a traumatic experience for a young person who has never been incarcerated before. By the time offenders go through the full legal process and are sentenced to prison, they have more or less accepted and adjusted to the reality that they are facing a period of confinement. But the uncertainty of how long they will be kept in jail—combined with the sense of loss and hopelessness resulting from one's first exposure to jail—can promote suicidal thoughts, as reflected in the fact that more than half of all suicides occur within the first twenty-four hours of incarceration.[59]

Added to this is the fact that a sizable percentage of inmates arrive in jail intoxicated or under the influence of drugs.[60] When the effects of the alcohol or drugs wear off, depression can set in, along with realization of the seriousness of their situation. In fact, one study found that more than half of jail suicide victims were intoxicated at the time of incarceration,[61] and another reported that all of the victims studied had used excessive amounts of alcohol and drugs prior to their admission to jail.[62]

Suicide Prevention

Thus, it is essential that intake staff and custodial officers be familiar with warning signs and suicidal "profiles."[63] The role of intake is especially important, since most suicide attempts in holding areas occur within the first three hours of incarceration.[64] Moreover, research on jail suicides reveals that the vast majority (89 to 97 percent) did not undergo any form of intake screening as part of their booking process.[65]

Even after inmates have completed intake and been assigned to a cell, officers must be able to "tune in" to subtle signals and remain alert to any sudden behavioral changes. In this regard, direct supervision presents obvious advantages over remote, intermittent surveillance, as illustrated by the inside accounts of suicide attempts in the next "Close-up On Corrections." It is therefore not surprising to find fewer suicides in direct-supervision jails.[66]

When the possibility of suicide is suspected, personnel must take immediate action. Unfortunately, the ability of many jails to deal with mentally disturbed suicidal inmates may be limited to isolating them from the general population. But this approach can be counterproductive, since isolation "tends to create fear and suspicion . . . further undermining their mental state" and increasing the potential for suicide.[67]

Precautions taken to respond adequately to suicide risks will depend on the situation. Based on the seriousness of the symptoms, responses can range from simply talking with the inmate, to removing any items that could be used for self-destruction, to arranging for more frequent (or even constant) monitoring,

Close-up On Corrections

to reassignment in special management units or "suicide-proof" cells.[68] The most serious cases, of course, also should be referred for psychiatric evaluation. But no matter how trivial they may seem, no suicidal threats can be taken lightly in the vulnerable atmosphere of the jail.

The Mentally Ill in Jails

Beyond identifying those prone to suicide, intake screening long has been noted as "one of the most significant mental health services that a jail can offer."[69] That is because, for a number of reasons, the mentally ill are overrepresented in the jail population.[70] Every year, more than 11 million days are spent in jail by the seriously mentally ill.[71] Moreover, "men in urban jails are three times more likely to be afflicted by such illnesses as schizophrenia, severe depression, and mania than the population at large."[72]

Nearly 70 percent of those in jail report a history involving mental health services, compared to less than half of those in prison.[73] According to the National Coalition for the Mentally Ill in Criminal Justice, there are about 33 percent more mentally ill people in jails than in mental hospitals.[74] The situation has come to the point that "the three largest de facto psychiatric facilities in the United States are now the Los Angeles County Jail, Rikers Island

Jail in New York City, and Cook County Jail in Chicago." [75] In fact, one judge estimates that:

> Psychiatric inmates languish in jail eight times longer than other inmates. They wait for court-ordered evaluations. They wait for medication to make them competent to stand trial. They wait for beds in treatment facilities. [76]

Jails today are additionally faced with growing numbers of "dually diagnosed" offenders—those suffering from a combination of mental health and substance abuse problems. [77] It has been estimated that more than half of those with a mental health diagnosis also have a co-occurring substance-abuse disorder. [78]

Even if the resources are not available to properly treat them (as is often the case), it is important that such inmates be identified to better assure their safety during confinement. But determining who is mentally ill among jail inmates does not answer the question of why they represent such a sizable portion of the jail population.

Deinstitutionalization of Mental Health Services

For many years, psychiatric patients were warehoused in large, substandard mental health institutions. In response, there was a major move throughout the country during the 1960s to close these "insane asylums" and replace them with community-based mental health facilities. This process of deinstitutionalization, in fact, did result in the closing of many of the worst mental hospitals, but the local outpatient treatment services envisioned to replace them were not as readily forthcoming:

> In 1955, there were over half a million severely mentally ill patients in public psychiatric hospitals. In 1994, there were 71,619. Based on population growth, estimates are that there would have been over 885,000 patients in state hospitals in 1994. [79] Where have they gone?

As communities closed their mental health institutions without providing other alternatives, many former patients were found wandering the streets, vulnerable to arrest. Of the 600,000 people who are homeless in America, it is estimated that at least a third are mentally ill. [80] In addition, closer restrictions designed to ensure that only the truly ill are confined to mental hospitals have made involuntary commitment procedures more difficult. [81] As a result of these circumstances, "people whose bizarre behavior might have landed them in a hospital bed a few years ago, are now being arrested and are ending up in jail." [82]

Criminalization of the Mentally Ill

While most of those with mental disorders are no longer being warehoused in substandard mental-health institutions, many are still being warehoused in jails—"the only place left to 'put' them and the only institution that cannot say 'no'." [83] This has resulted in what has become known as "criminalization" of the mentally ill.[84] It raises a fundamental public policy question in terms of whether jails are the appropriate government agency for responding to mental illness.[85] Such revolving-door policies are also costly. Taxpayer dollars are paying for police officers to repeatedly arrest, transport, and process mentally disturbed defendants for the jail costs associated with treatment and crisis intervention, for the salaries of judges and court staff, prosecutors and defense attorneys, and for many more hidden costs.[86]

A recent study found that stabilizing the homeless and mentally ill resulted in $16,000 annual savings per person in terms of social, mental health, and jail expenses.[87] Moreover, there can be serious repercussions when the mentally ill are released back into the community without follow-up. For example, upon discharge from the New York city jail system, a class action lawsuit contends that 93 percent of inmates who have received treatment for mental illness are released without any further planning—simply "dropped off at a subway station between 2:00 a.m. and 6:00 a.m. with two subway tokens and $1.50 in cash."[88]

That does not mean that correctional facilities are simply ignoring this unwanted responsibility. To the contrary, some are making substantial efforts to provide behavioral health care.[89] In Milwaukee, an outpatient community-support program combines therapeutic services and money management with day reporting and close monitoring.[90] In several states, jail officials collaborate with mental health professionals to divert potential jail inmates from confinement to community-based treatment.[91] In a number of jurisdictions from California to Alabama, mental health treatment courts have been established on the basis of successful drug court models.[92] But in many other places, mentally disturbed clients land in jail, prompting the American Jail Association to adopt the resolution highlighted in the next "Close-up On Corrections."

 Learning Goals

Do you know:

1. How inmates are managed through classification?
2. What the difference is between the "design" and "rated" capacity of jails?
3. What can be done to reduce jail crowding?

Classification

Just as certain inmates may need special attention because they are suicidal or mentally disturbed, other groups also need to be housed separately to promote the safety of all inmates and the security of the institution. This is what is meant by classification—the "systematic grouping of inmates into categories based on shared characteristics and/or behavioral patterns."[93] Classification helps to promote inmate safety and the smooth operation of the facility.

Correctional facilities did not always group inmates separately. As we saw in the early origins of the jail, men and women, young and old, and even sick

Close-up On Corrections

THE MENTALLY ILL IN JAIL

WHEREAS, the growing number of inmates with mental illness and the lack of appropriate resources in jails to screen, treat, and properly house these individuals, strain daily jail operations and weaken staff morale. Additionally, the problem compromises the safety of staff and inmates alike, exacerbates crowding, and increases the costs of operating our nation's jails.

WHEREAS, the American Jail Association feels strongly that the jail setting is not the proper therapeutic milieu for effective, long-term treatment of mental illness. . . .

THEREFORE, BE IT RESOLVED that the American Jail Association urges its members to improve the response to people with mental illness who come into contact with the criminal justice system by developing and promoting programs, policies, and legislation that accomplish the following goals:

- Improve collaboration among stakeholders in the criminal justice and mental health systems;

- Integrate mental health and substance abuse services to more effectively address the needs of individuals who have co-occurring mental health and substance abuse disorders;

- Focus efforts toward providing the mental health system with resources and training regarding the criminal justice system;

- Recognize that the solution to this complex problem depends on an effective and accessible community mental health system;

- Support efforts to establish mental health courts that would effectively divert nonviolent offenders from the criminal justice system into appropriate treatment and/or supporting services. . . .

[NOTE: The resolution also calls for Congress, federal agencies, and local government officials to increase funding programs, collect information, facilitate partnerships, and improve research on this topic].

Source: "Newly Adopted Resolutions [of the American Jail Association]," *American Jails*, July/August 2003, p. 7. Used with permission.

and healthy inmates were all housed together. In the history of correctional institutions, "separation by sex came first, then separation by age, followed by separation by problems."[94] In today's jails, classification serves to segregate:

- *Pretrial* defendants from *convicted* inmates
- *Sentenced* from *unsentenced* inmates
- *Males* from *females*

- *Adults* from *juveniles* [95]

- *Violent* from *nonviolent* inmates

- *General* population from *special-need* inmates (for example, drug/alcohol abusers, emotionally disturbed, sexual predators, elderly, physically disabled)

Jail personnel determine an inmate's housing assignment on the basis of classification procedures. The information used to classify inmates comes from a number of sources, including observations and interviews, along with review of available court reports, the inmate's personal history, and medical or psychological screening records. Ideally, staff look at such things as the offense committed (or charged), and the offender's legal status, background, attitude, work record, and education.

The objective classification techniques that are typically employed in both prisons and jails today are discussed in greater detail in Chapter 8. Using such procedures, a basis is established for making decisions in terms of everything from housing assignment to degree of supervision needed and eligibility for various work, and educational or treatment programs. But jails do not have access to as much information about these short-term clients as their prison counterparts. Nor do they have as many varied institutional security levels and programming options. Thus, there is a tendency to somewhat overclassify inmates in jail.

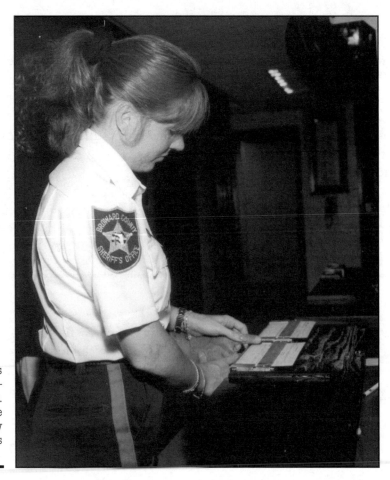

An exact set of fingerprints is essential for establishing personal identification on intake. Fingerprinting is one of the aspects of classification. Courtesy of the Broward County Sheriff's Office, Ft. Lauderdale, Florida.

Regardless of what specific programs or services an inmate might receive, most jail operations are no longer provided exclusively at taxpayer expense. Nearly every state has passed legislation authorizing assessment of inmate fees for jail services and operations, generating annual revenues in the millions of dollars.[96] In many jurisdictions today, in fact, there is no such thing as a "free lunch,"[97] and fees for medical services have reduced demand by as much as 60 percent.[98] Nevertheless, there are concerns that such fees also can discourage inmates from seeking necessary treatment and that they are not as cost effective as might appear, since the administrative burden of collecting fees is not always matched by the revenues generated.[99]

Crowding

Even the best intentioned and most sophisticated programs cannot achieve their objectives in institutions that are seriously crowded. When space is limited, just having enough room for screening, booking, and classifying inmates becomes a luxury. Moreover, when space is severely restricted, inmates must be "fit in" wherever a spare bed can be found (or added). Under such conditions, the integrity of the classification system is compromised. Although the seriousness of this situation is apparent, the next "Close-up On Corrections"

 # Close-up On Corrections

UNANTICIPATED DEMANDS AND JAIL CROWDING

It was a beautiful Saturday morning—the birds were singing, the sky was blue, and a blessed event was just about to be bestowed on a friend of mine. Most new fathers would probably worry at this point, but not him—he [had] thoroughly planned ahead. . . .

Two months after marrying his lovely wife, they decided to have their first child . . . they bought an affordable new two-bedroom house. Next, they spent a fortune on the furnishings for the baby's room, but it was worth it. A real oak crib, a real oak two-drawer dresser, a wind-up swing set to rock the little tyke to sleep. You should see the cute little baby bath—it's one of a kind. The wallpaper, the new paint, the new carpet, the new clothes, and, let us not forget, the oak rocker for mom to rock and feed the child. . . .

They performed some pretty steady planning. Unfortunately, like all well-planned events, Murphy's Law paid my friends a visit . . . they had triplets. That's right, not one, not two, but three adorable babies. . . . Mother and babies are doing fine. Dad is on the brink of despair. Why, you ask? For the same reason that most administrators of overcrowded . . . facilities are on the brink of despair. Too many people requiring services which were designed for the . . . number of people that a well-thought-out and planned budget allowed for.

Source: James Myers and Michael Kramer, "The Effect of Overcrowding on Direct Supervision: The Experiences of Washoe County," *Direct Supervision Jails: Proceedings of the Fifth Annual Symposium*, Hagerstown, Maryland: American Jail Association, 1990, p. 47. Used with permission.

offers a humorous comparison between jail crowding and a family-planning scenario that everyone can appreciate.

A correctional facility is generally considered to be crowded when it exceeds either:

- *Design capacity*: the number of inmates that it was originally constructed to confine; or

- *Rated capacity*: the number of inmates that an acknowledged expert (such as a state prison inspector) estimates the jail can hold safely, which is generally a less conservative figure.

As inmates became more active in challenging crowded conditions, the courts became increasingly active in correcting the situation. Many of the nation's jails are subject to court-mandated population caps, and others are under court order or consent decree for a number of conditions related to crowding—such as fire hazards or lack of sufficient medical services, staffing patterns, visiting practices, library services, or inmate classification.

The fact that the judicial branch of government has determined that the situation is so serious as to warrant court action itself is illustrative of the severity of the problem. New construction, expansion of existing facilities, community supervision, and early release are among the many options that have been used to reduce crowding. However, many of these innovations are short-term, stop-gap measures, and new facilities often fill to capacity quickly. The issue cannot be addressed effectively without systemwide attention to everything from public policies and sentencing practices to consideration of the community-based alternatives described in Chapter 4. In fact, jails in recent years have begun placing some of their clients under various forms of community supervision, as reflected in Figure 5.8.

But jail administrators cannot be the only personnel who take responsibility for the crowding crisis. To the contrary, the jail itself can implement very few changes to alleviate crowding, since it does not enact penal codes, prescribe sentences, or determine release dates. In fact, jails actually have little or

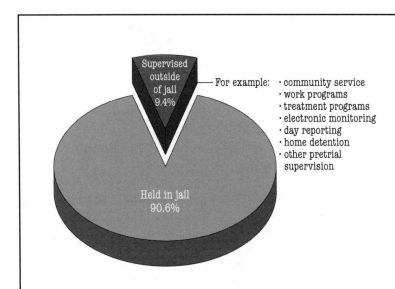

figure **5.8**

Supervised outside of jail 9.4%

For example: · community service
· work programs
· treatment programs
· electronic monitoring
· day reporting
· home detention
· other pretrial supervision

Held in jail 90.6%

Confinement status of jail inmates.

Source: Paige M. Harrison and Jennifer C. Karberg, "Prison and Jail Inmates at Midyear 2003," *Bureau of Justice Statistics Bulletin*, Washington, DC: U.S. Department of Justice, 2004, p. 7.

Close-up On Corrections

SYSTEMWIDE STRATEGIES TO ALLEVIATE CROWDING

Law Enforcement

Decisions surrounding local arrest practices are critical determinants of jail population size. In that regard, police can increase the use of citations for minor offenders and divert those with special problems to community treatment programs.

Jail Administrators

While having little direct control over admissions and length of confinement, jail administrators nevertheless can help to reduce crowding by:

- Assuring ready access to pretrial release screening and bail review

- Keeping judges continually informed of the status of the jail population

- Establishing time frames for case disposition

- Supporting such options as electronic monitoring or day reporting

- Improving contact with state legislators—requesting changes that would offer alternatives to jail sentences, allow deferred sentencing, and increase jail funding

Prosecutors

Early case screening by prosecutors can reduce unnecessary length of confinement by eliminating or downgrading weak cases as soon as possible. Greater use of risk assessment, diversion, and delegated release authority also would contribute to reducing the jail population.

Pretrial Services

Providing background information on defendants, release-on-recognizance recommendations, case flow information, and other pretrial assistance can be important components of solutions to crowding.

Judiciary

Judges make more decisions affecting jail populations than anyone else. As such, they can:

- Make greater use of alternatives to jail, including pretrial release and diversion programs

- Speed up court proceedings

- Make magistrates available twenty-four hours per day, seven days per week for release decisions

- Expedite all court proceedings, whenever possible

- Provide intake staff who can screen out people inappropriate for jail (including the mentally ill) and place them in alternative programs

(continued)

Close-up On Corrections

no control over the two primary determinants of the jail population—the number of bookings and the average length of stay.[100] Moreover, there is little the jail can do when judges become less willing to grant bail, more offenders violate probation or parole conditions, and state prisons slow down transfer of sentenced inmates as a result of their own crowded conditions.

But there are many other decision makers in the local justice system who exercise discretion in small ways that can add up to sizable reductions in the jail population without releasing serious offenders. Several examples are highlighted in the prior "Close-up On Corrections."

While these illustrations are indicative of the significant steps being taken, managing crowding requires a comprehensive understanding of the dynamics that create changes in jail occupancy levels.[101] Jail crowding is a complex challenge that cannot be adequately addressed by one or two isolated changes. Rather, it requires comprehensive strategies based on information gathered from sources ranging from surveys of criminal justice officials to analysis of arrest data bases, court files, and aggregate trends.[102]

The long-term plight of crowded jails will be resolved only when jails are reserved for those who actually need to be confined behind bars—who are not there simply because the system is slow in processing them, or because there is no other resource in the community to deal with their problems. Moreover, as long as society continues to respond to the symptoms rather than the causes of behavior for which people are confined, the public will continue to be disenchanted with the performance of its jails. As long as jails remain the primary vehicle for responding to such social problems as mental illness, alcoholism, and drug abuse,[103] their role will continue to be unclear; their performance will continue to be unsatisfactory; and their space will continue to be filled beyond capacity. Direct-supervision/new-generation jails can change living conditions for those confined, but only a new generation of public policies can challenge long-held practices concerning who should be confined.

Summary

As the oldest component of the justice system, jails have historical legacies, which remain evident today in antiquated facilities that have long outlived their usefulness. While more small jails are being consolidated into regional detention centers, there are still far more jails housing fifty inmates or less than megajails confining a thousand or more. However, the largest facilities still hold the greatest percentage of the overall inmate population.

Of those in jail, less than half are convicted offenders, while the remainder are accused defendants awaiting trial. Jails also book arrestees, hold those awaiting sentencing or transfer, and readmit probation, parole, or bail/bond violators. Many inmates confined in jail have not been involved in violent crimes, but rather, are being held for drug-related, public order, or property offenses. In fact, alcohol and drug abusers represent a sizable portion of the jail's clients, despite the lack of adequate resources to address their problems while incarcerated.

Since jails generally do not have authority to confine offenders with sentences of more than one year, there is a high turnover among the inmate population. To improve management and operational practices, a number of jurisdictions have embraced a new generation of jailing, which attempts to create as "normal" an environment as can be achieved in confinement. Architecture, physical amenities, and management style all work together to shape behavior in such jails. In contrast to the intermittent or remote style of surveillance in traditional facilities, these jails rely on direct supervision. Officers interact directly with inmates, unobstructed by bars or glass enclosures. While such facilities have been criticized as too "plush," their basic intent is not to promote comfort but to provide a safe and secure environment where staff—rather than inmates—are in control. Consequently, they tend to experience lower rates of violent incidents, suicides, escapes, and vandalism. Despite their effectiveness and pleasant appearance, direct-supervision facilities are actually less costly to build, operate, and maintain.

Because jails are administered primarily at the local level of government, they represent considerable diversity with regard to everything from size to facility design and management style. Most jails are under the supervision of an elected sheriff, and it is this administrator who sets the tone for how the jail will operate—just as staff, in turn, establish the climate for inmates. Because proper staffing is so important to the jail's functions, increasing attention is being given to improving the compensation, training, and selection of personnel.

Inmates are admitted to jail through the process of intake, which includes such tasks as booking, taking information, searching, photographing, and fingerprinting. Once admitted, many jails now provide recreational, educational, and counseling services, and some have initiated jail industries to enable inmates to engage in productive work.

The availability of medical services is a necessity in jails, not only to provide appropriate treatment to the inmate, but also to curtail the spread of infectious diseases. Because suicide is the primary cause of death in jail, personnel must be especially alert to its signs and symptoms, taking immediate precautions whenever the potential for suicide is suspected. Like those vulnerable to suicide, the mentally ill are overrepresented among the jail population, largely as a result of the deinstitutionalization of mental health facilities. Because of the lack of resources to deal with them in the community, the mentally ill are often confined in jails, which are poorly suited to address their problems.

To better ensure safety and security of all inmates, the jail population is classified according to their conviction/sentencing status, sex, age, offense, and needs. But it is difficult to provide proper classification in crowded facilities, where limited space does not always enable the appropriate separation of inmates. Jails are considered crowded when the number of persons they are holding exceeds either the facility's design or rated capacity. A number of severely crowded jails are operating under court order or consent decree to reduce their population. New construction, renovations, community supervision, and early release all have been employed to address the crowding problem. The situation is not much better in prisons, as we will see in the following chapters.

Endnotes

1.   *Jails: Intergovernmental Dimensions of a Local Problem*, Washington, D.C.: Advisory Commission on Intergovernmental Relations, 1984, pp. 5-6.

2.   For example, in the entire year of 1999, prisons admitted 617,387 inmates in comparison to the 219,408 new admissions to jails during *one week* of that same year. Paige M. Harrison and Jennifer C. Karberg, "Prison and Jail Inmates at Midyear 2002," *Bureau of Justice Statistics Bulletin*, Washington, D.C.: U.S. Department of Justice, April 2003, p. 6; and James J. Stephan, *Census of Jails, 1999*, Washington, D.C.: U.S. Department of Justice, August 2001, p. 5.

3.   Paraphrased from Harrison and Karberg, "Prison and Jail Inmates," p. 7.

4.   Stephan, *Census of Jails*, 1999, p. iii.

5.   *Sourcebook of Criminal Justice Statistics*, 1990, Washington, D.C.: U.S. Department of Justice, 1991, p. 582.

6.   Stephan, *Census of Jails*, 1999, p. 3.

7.   *See* Mark Kellar and Shelley Parker, "Operating a Small Jail in Texas: An Administrative Challenge," *American Jails*, September/October 2003, p. 19-23.

8.   Morton J. Leibowitz, "Regionalization in Virginia Jails," *American Jails*, Vol. 5, No. 5, November/December 1991, pp. 42-43.

9.   Allen J. Beck, "Jail Population Growth: National Trends and Predictors of Future Growth," *American Jails*, May/June 2002, p. 12.

10. Harrison and Karberg, "Prison and Jail Inmates," p. 9.

11. Paige M. Harrison and Allen J. Beck, "Prisoners in 2002," *Bureau of Justice Statistics Bulletin*, Washington, D.C.: U.S. Department of Justice, July 2003, p. 6.

12. "Three VA Sheriffs Sue Department of Corrections," *On the Line*, Vol. 18, No. 2, March, 1995, p. 2. *See also* David M. Bogard, "State-Ready Inmates in Local Jails: Are You in Jeopardy?" *American Jails*, January/February 1995, pp.75-78.

13. Doris J. James, "Profile of Jail Inmates, 2002," *Bureau of Justice Statistics: Special Report*, Washington, D.C.: U.S. Department of Justice, July 2004.

14. Kenneth E. Kerle, "Introduction," in Joel A. Thompson and G. Larry Mays, eds., *American Jails: Public Policy Issues*, Chicago: Nelson-Hall, 1991, p. xiv.

15. Craig A. Perkins, James J. Stephan, and Allen J. Beck, "Jails and Jail Inmates, 1993-94," *Bureau of Justice Statistics Bulletin*, 1995, p. 10.

16. Laura M. Marushak, "DWI Offenders under Correctional Supervision," *Bureau of Justice Statistics: Special Report*, Washington, D.C.: U.S. Department of Justice, June 1999, p. 1.

17. Jonathan P. Caulkins *et al.*, *Mandatory Minimum Drug Sentences*, Santa Monica, California: RAND Corporation, 1997.

18. Joey R. Weedon, "The Role of Jails is Growing in the Community," *Corrections Today*, April 2003, p. 18.

19. *A Second Look at Alleviating Jail Crowding*, Washington, D.C.: Bureau of Justice Assistance, October 2000, p. 26.

20. Stephen H. Gettinger, *New Generation Jails: An Innovative Approach to an Age-Old Problem*, Washington, D.C.: U.S. Department of Justice, 1984, p. 2.

21. Much of the following architectural descriptions are summarized from Lois Spears and Donald Taylor, "Coping with Our Jam-Packed Jails," *Corrections Today*, Vol. 52, June 1990, p. 20; and W. Raymond Nelson, "Cost Savings in New Generation Jails: The Direct Supervision Approach," *National Institute of Justice Construction Bulletin*, July 1988, p. 2.

22. Brent Swager, "County Jail without Doors," *Corrections Technology and Management*, Vol. 3, No. 2, March/April 1999, pp. 46-47, quoting Sgt. Don Kracke.

23. For an alternative to this approach, which encourages inmates to take responsibility for themselves by moving through the facility to obtain services rather than having the services delivered to them, *see* Sandra Thacker, "A New Principle, a New Generation," *American Jails*, March/April 2000, pp. 43-52.

24. Richard Werner, F. W. Frazier, and Jay Farbstein, "Direct Supervision of Correctional Institutions," in *Podular, Direct Supervision Jails*, Boulder, Colorado: National Institute of Corrections Jail Center, 1991, p. 3.

25. For more information on the relationship between color schemes and inmate behavior, *see* I.S.K. Reeves V, "Soothing Shades: Color and Its Effect on Inmate Behavior," *Corrections Today*, Vol. 54, No. 2, April 1992, pp. 128-130.

26. Christine Tartaro, "Examining Implementation Issues with New Generation Jails," *Criminal Justice Policy Review*, Vol. 13, No. 3, September 2002, pp. 231, 234.

27. David M. Parrish, "The Evolution of Direct Supervision in the Design and Operation of Jails," *Corrections Today*, Vol. 65, No. 6, October 2000, p. 127.

28. Summarized from Nelson, "Cost Savings in New Generation Jails," pp. 4-6.

29. *Ibid.*, p. 6.

30. "Dade County Stockade Expansion: Comparative Analysis of Design Schemes," in *Podular, Direct Supervision Jails*, p. 71.

31. Richard Werner, William Frazier, and Jay Farbstein, "Building Better Jails," *Psychology Today*, Vol. 21, No. 6, June 1987, p. 42.

32. *Ibid.*

33. P. G. Jackson, *Detention in Transition: Sonoma County's New Generation Jail*, Washington, D.C.: National Institute of Corrections, 1992.

34. Linda L. Zupan, *Jails: Reform and the New Generation Philosophy*, Cincinnati, Ohio: Anderson Publishing Company, 1991, p. 160.

35. Jeffery D. Senese, "Evaluating Jail Reform: A Comparative Analysis of Podular/Direct and Linear Jail Inmate Infractions," *Journal of Criminal Justice*, Vol. 25, No. 1, 1997, pp. 61-73.

36. Herbert R. Sigurdson, *Pima County Detention Center: A Study of Podular Direct Supervision*, Washington, D.C.: National Institute of Corrections, 1987; Herbert R. Sigurdson, *Larimer County Detention Center: A Study of Podular Direct Supervision*, Washington, D.C.: National Institute of Corrections, 1987.

37. Jeffery D. Senese, "Evaluating Jail Reform: A Comparative Analysis of Podular/Direct and Linear Jail Inmate Infractions," *Journal of Criminal Justice*, Vol. 25, No. 1, 1997, pp. 61-73.

38. James L. Williams, Daniel G. Rodeheaver, and Denise W. Huggins, "A Comparative Evaluation of a New Generation Jail," *American Journal of Criminal Justice*, Vol. 23, No. 2, Spring 1999, pp. 223-246.

39. Werner *et al.*, "Building Better Jails," p. 42. For a more detailed comparison of traditional and direct-supervision jails in terms of rule violations resulting in incident reports, *see* Jeffrey D. Senese *et al.*, "Evaluating Jail Reform: Inmate Infractions and Disciplinary Response in a Traditional and a Podular/Direct Supervision Jail," *American Jails*, September/October 1992, pp. 14-23.

40. Byron Johnson, "Exploring Direct Supervision: A Research Note," *American Jails*, March/April 1994, pp. 63-64.

41. Gerald J. Bayens, Jimmy J. Williams, and John O. Smykla, "Jail Type and Inmate Behavior: A Longitudinal Analysis," *Federal Probation*, Vol. 61, September 1997, pp. 54-62.

42. Werner *et al.*, "Direct Supervision," p. 6.

43. Werner *et al.*, "Building Better Jails," p. 42

44. Dillard H. Hughes, "The New Generation Jail: Ten Years After," *American Jails*, May/June 2003, p. 44.

45. *Ibid.*

46. Gettinger, *New Generation Jails*, p. 20. *See also* Jerry W. Fuqua, "New Generation Jails—Old Generation Management," *American Jails*, March/April 1991, pp. 80-83.

47. W. Raymond Nelson and Russell M. Davis, "Podular Direct Supervision: The First Twenty Years," *American Jails*, July/August 1995, pp. 16-22; Christine Tartaro, "Survey: Direct Supervision Jails," *American Jails*, May/June 2003, pp. 77-79.

48. James J. Stephan, "Census of Jails, 1999," Washington, D.C.: U.S. Department of Justice, *Bureau of Justice Statistics*, 2004, p. 7.

49. Belinda R. McCarthy, "The Use of Jail Confinement in the Disposition of Felony Arrests," *Journal of Criminal Justice*, Vol. 17, No. 4, 1989, p. 241.

50. N.E. Schafer, "State Operated Jails: How and Why," *American Jails*, September/October 1994, pp. 35-44.

51. Robbye Braxton-Mintz and Mike Pinson, "Personnel: Your Most Important Resource," *Corrections Today*, Vol. 62, No. 6, October 2000, p. 96. *See also* Gary E. Christensen, Steven T. Lifrak, and Anthony Callisto, "Twenty-first Century Outcomes: Organizational Assessment and Officer Hiring," *American Jails*, November/December 2003, pp. 25-31.

52. Braxton-Mintz and Pinson, "Personnel," p. 96.

53. Calvin A. Lightfoot, Linda L. Zupan, and Mary K. Stohr, "Jails and the Community: Modeling the Future in Local Detention Facilities," *American Jails*, September/October 1991, p. 50. *See also* Dennis Gilbertson, "Jail Industry Programs and Offender Reentry," *American Jails*, May/June 2003, pp. 9-13.

54. "Reno Announces Grant for New TV Programming in State and Local Jails," *Corrections Digest*, Vol. 26, No. 24, June 16, 1995, p. 9.

55. Rod Miller, George E. Sexton, and Victor J. Jacobsen, "Making Jails Productive," *National Institute of Justice: Research in Brief*, Washington, D.C.: U.S. Department of Justice, 1991, p. 1. *See also* Barbara Auerbach, "Private Sector Jail Industries," *American Jails*, May/June 2003, pp. 15-18.

56. *See*, for example, Ken Kerle, "Jail Health Care" and John Clark, "Correctional Health Care Issues in the Nineties: Forecast and Recommendations," *American Jails*, September/October 1991, pp. 5, 22-23.

57. Stephan, *Census of Jails, 1999*, p. 13.

58. James J. Stephan and Jennifer C. Karberg, *Census of State and Federal Correctional Facilities, 2000*, Washington, D.C.: U.S. Department of Justice, 2003, p. 8.

59. Laura Tahir, "Supervision of Special Needs Inmates by Custody Staff," *Corrections Today*, Vol. 65, No. 6, October 2003, p. 110.

60. Caroline Wolf Harlow, "Drugs and Jail Inmates, 1996," *Bureau of Justice Statistics Special Report*, Washington, D.C.: U.S. Department of Justice, 1998, p. 1.

61. Ronald Jemelka, "The Mentally Ill in Local Jails: Issues in Admission and Booking," in Henry J. Steadman, ed., *Jail Diversion for the Mentally Ill*, Washington, D.C.: National Institute of Corrections, n.d..

62. P. Marcus and Philip Alcabes, "Characteristics of Suicides by Inmates in an Urban Jail," *Hospital and Community Psychiatry*, Vol. 44, No. 3, 1993, pp: 256-261.

63. Thomas A. Rosazza, "Suicide Litigation: Common Problems Seen in Training, Assessment, Housing, Observation, and Referral," *American Jails*, September/October 1999, pp. 27-30.

64. Jemelka, "The Mentally Ill in Local Jails," p. 42.

65. *Ibid.*, p. 43.

66. However, the direct supervision model is unlikely to be successful in reducing suicide vulnerability unless all aspects of it are properly implemented. *See* Christine Tartaro, "Suicide and New Generation Jails: A National Study," *American Jails*, September/October 2003, pp. 37-42.

67. *Jails: Intergovernmental Dimensions of a Local Problem*, p. 179. *See also* Tartaro, "Suicide and New Generation Jails," p. 38.

68. For more information on the training, screening, supervision, and intervention needed to prevent suicides, *see* Lindsay M. Hayes, *Prison Suicide: An Overview and Guide to Prevention*, Longmont, Colorado: National Institute of Corrections, 1995, as well as *Jail Suicide/Mental Health Update*, published quarterly by the National Institute of Corrections (website: http://www.ncianet.org/ncia/suicide.html).

69. H. J. Steadman, D. W. McCarty, and J. P. Morrisey, *The Mentally Ill in Jail: Planning for Essential Services*, New York: Guilford Press, 1989, p. 34.

70. Zupan, *Jails*, p. 31. *See also* Michael P. Maloney, Michael P. Ward, and Charles M. Jackson, "Study Reveals that More Mentally Ill Offenders are Entering Jail," *American Jails*, April 2003, pp. 100-103.

71. Jayne Russell, "International Conference to Target Treatment and Diversion of Mentally Ill Offenders," *American Jails*, May/June 1993, p. 49.

72. Donna Crawford, "Alternatives to Incarceration for Mentally Ill Offenders," *Community Corrections Report*, Vol. 3, No. 1, November/December 1995, p. 1.

73. Stephanie W. Hartwell and Karin Orr, "Release Planning and the Distinctions for Mentally Ill Offenders Returning to the Community from Jails or Prison," *American Jails*, November/December 2000, p. 11.

74. William M. DiMascio, *Seeking Justice: Crime and Punishment in America*, New York: Edna McConnell Clark Foundation, 1997, p. 22.

75. Thomas N. Faust, "Shift the Responsibility of Untreated Mental Illness Out of the Criminal Justice System," *Corrections Today*, Vol. 65, No. 2, April 2003, p. 6.

76. "Mentally Ill Relegated to Jail Cells," *The Herald*, May 23, 2004, p. 20A, quoting Judge Steve Leifman.

77. Holly Atkins, Brandon K. Applegate, and Gillian F. Hobbs, "Mentally Ill and Substance Abusing Inmates," *American Jails*, March/April 1998, p. 70.

78. Laura Gater, "The Problem of Mental Health in Prison Populations," *Corrections Forum*, March/April 2004, p. 30.

79. E. Fuller Torrey, *Out of the Shadows: Confronting America's Mental Illness Crisis*, John Wiley and Sons, 1997, pp. 8-9.

80. Evelyn L. Stratton, Scott Blough, and Kristina Hawk, "Solutions for the Mentally Ill in the Criminal Justice System," *American Jails*, January/February 2004, p. 15.

81. *Mentally Ill Offenders in the Criminal Justice System: An Analysis and Prescription*, Washington, D.C.: The Sentencing Project, 2002, p. 5.

82. Rob Wilson, "Who Will Care for the 'Mad and Bad'?" *Corrections Magazine*, February, 1980, p. 14. *See also* Daniel Patrick Moynihan, "Defining Deviancy Down," *American Educator*, Winter 1993/1994, p. 13.

83. *Jails: Intergovernmental Dimensions of a Local Problem*, p. 180.

84. *Mentally Ill Offenders in the Criminal Justice System*, p. 7.

85. *See Criminalizing the Seriously Mentally Ill: The Abuse of Jails as Mental Hospitals*, Washington, D.C.: Joint Report of the National Alliance for the Mentally Ill and the Public Citizen's Health Research Group, 1992.

86. Stratton, Blough, and Hawk, "Solutions for the Mentally Ill in the Criminal Justice System," p. 15.

87. *Ibid.*, p. 17, citing research by the Corporation for Supportive Housing. Additionally, the Mentally Ill Offender and Crime Reduction Act of 2003 (Senate Bill 1194) provides federal seed money for collaboration, planning, and implementation of such alternatives.

88. *Mentally Ill Offenders in the Criminal Justice System*, p. 9.

89. *See* Susan W. McCampbell, "Finding Friends in the Right Places—Coalitions to Address the Mentally Ill in Jails," *American Jails*, July/August 1999, pp. 52-55.

90. "Managing Mentally Ill Offenders in the Community," *National Institute of Justice: Program Focus*, Washington, D.C.: U.S. Department of Justice, 1994. *See also* Valerie Hildebeitel, "Addressing the Needs of the Mentally Ill Inmate," *American Jails*, November/December 1992, pp. 60-61.

91. Edward W. Szostak and Marisa L. Beeble, "Mental Health Jail Diversion," *American Jails*, July/August 2003, pp. 35-41.

92. Deborah Linden, "The Mentally Ill Offender: A Comprehensive Community Approach," *American Jails*, January/February 2000, p. 58. Ronald E. Truss, "Birmingham Municipal Court Mental Health Approach," *American Jails*, November/December 2003, pp. 32-34.

93. The following list, as well as much of the remaining information on classification, is summarized from School of Justice and Safety Administration, "Classification," Miami, Florida: Miami-Dade Community College: unpublished lesson plan, n.d., p. 1. *See also* James Austin, *Objective Jail Classification Systems: A Guide for Jail Administrators*, Longmont, Colorado: National Institute of Corrections, 1998.

94. Vernon Fox, *Correctional Institutions*, Englewood Cliffs, New Jersey: Prentice Hall, 1983, p. 61.

95. *See* Chapter 12 on Juvenile Corrections for a discussion of the prohibitions restricting placement of juveniles in adult jails.

96. "Fees Paid by Jail Inmates," *Special Issues in Corrections*, Longmont, Colorado: National Institute of Corrections, 1997, p. 2. *See also* Karla Crocker, "Inmate Fee for Services," *Corrections Today*, July 2004, pp. 82-85.

97. "Charging Inmates for Food Gaining Popularity," *Corrections Digest*, January 26, 1996, p. 6.

98. Pat Nolan, "Inmate User Fees: Fiscal Fix or Mirage?" *Corrections Today*, August, 2003, p. 23.

99. *Ibid.* For views on the opposite side of this debate, which supports the use of inmate fees, *see* Michelle M. Sanborn, "The Pay-to-Stay Debate: Inmates Must Take Financial Responsibility," *Corrections Today*, August 2003, p. 22.

100. *Jail Population Reduction Strategies*, Washington, D.C.: National Institute of Corrections, April 1995, p. 2. *See also* Mark A. Cunniff, *Jail Crowding: Understanding Jail Population Dynamics*, Washington, D.C.: National Institute of Corrections, 2001.

101. Robert C. Cushman, "Jail Crowding: Understanding Jail Population Dynamics—A Practical Guide," *American Jails*, November/December 2003, pp. 62-67, and Mark A. Cunniff, "Jail Crowding: Understanding Jail Population Dynamics—How Can We Forecast Future Needs?" *American Jails*, May/June 2003, pp. 55-58.

102. Robert C. Cushman, "Jail Crowding" Understanding Jail Population Dynamics—Understanding the Sources of Jail Crowding," *American Jails*, January/February 2004, p. 45.

103. One study of local policymakers, for example, found that "the most favored goal was to use jails to meet the needs of people with mental health, drug, or alcohol problems." *See* Brandon K. Applegate *et al.*, "The Multifunction Jail: Policy Makers' Views of the Goals of Local Incarceration," *Criminal Justice Policy Review*, Vol. 14, No. 2, June 2003, p. 164.

CHAPTER 6

PRISONS AND OTHER CORRECTIONAL FACILITIES

> 66 "We ask an awful lot of our prisons. We ask them to correct the incorrigible, rehabilitate the wretched, deter the determined, restrain the dangerous, and punish the wicked. We ask them to take over where other institutions of society have failed.....We ask them to pursue so many different and often incompatible goals that they seem virtually doomed to fail."[1] 99
>
> —Charles H. Logan

Chapter Overview

If jails are the last resort for a community that has no other alternatives to deal with its social problems, prisons presumably represent the last resort for a criminal justice system which has exhausted all other alternatives. Although a first-time offender may be sent to prison for a serious offense, the majority of prison inmates have had previous experience with the criminal justice process. Some had been afforded a "second chance" through probation; others had served prior time. But whatever their previous experience, it was obviously unsuccessful in changing long-term behavior—leaving the prison to attempt to accomplish what other sanctions failed to achieve. In most cases, however, it is equally unable to do so. About the only thing that prisons are able to achieve with consistent success is suppressing further involvement in street crime during the period of incarceration. Whether the offender becomes better or worse as a result of prison experience is no longer the issue. Society apparently has settled for this compromise.

Even as community-based alternatives to incarceration have expanded, prison populations have steadily increased. As the most visible image of corrections, it is prisons that first come to mind when the public considers responses to crime. Like anything else that is not easily comprehended, isolation behind thick walls, barbed-wire fencing, and high-powered rifles protruding from guard towers creates an aura of mystique. The public is at the same time both fearful of and fascinated by its prisons.

Prisons provide the direct, external control demanded when such indirect social controls as norms, values, and even laws have proved ineffective. Because of their significance and their impact on the historical development of corrections, prisons tend to disproportionately influence the philosophy of the entire correctional system.

 # Learning Goals

Do you know:
1. What levels of government are responsible for the operation of prisons?
2. How many prisons there are in the United States?
3. How much it costs to build and operate a prison?
4. Which level of government carries the burden for the bulk of correctional expenditures?

Number and Types of Institutions

Prisons range from large, high-security complexes to small, rural road camps. Like jails, some date to the turn of the century, whereas others are much more modern. But because they do not trace their history as far back as jails, prisons overall have been constructed more recently. Conditions in the worst jails are therefore likely to be inferior to the worst prisons. But on the other hand, conditions in the best jails may surpass those in the best prisons, since the new-generation philosophy has yet to significantly influence prison construction.

Frequently, federal facilities have several levels of security on one campus, which saves taxpayer dollars. In the Federal Correctional Complex at Beaumont, Texas, the low security's three housing buildings have dormitory-style cubicles that encourage interaction between staff and inmates. Courtesy NBBJ.

Federal, State, and Military Facilities

Beyond their more recent development, prisons are also far less numerous than jails, thereby enabling greater uniformity. Since jails are a function of the local level of government, every county and municipality potentially has the authority to operate a jail. Prisons, however, are a responsibility of the state and federal levels of government, which represent only 51 jurisdictions. Thus, in contrast to the 3,365 jails spread throughout the country, there are less than half as many (1,404) state and federal prisons in the United States, along with another 264 that are privately operated,[2] (as will be discussed in more detail in Chapter 15).

In addition, the U.S. Army, Navy, Air Force, and Marine Corps maintain correctional facilities for some 2,377 imprisoned military personnel.[3] Some of these prisoners have been turned over to the military for trial, sentencing, and imprisonment after committing crimes in civilian jurisdictions. Others have been convicted of violations of the Uniform Code of Military Conduct (for example, desertion, disrespect for a superior officer, or being AWOL [absent without official leave]). In this respect, military corrections differs somewhat from its civilian counterparts, since the primary objective is restoration of the offender to active duty.

Costs of Imprisonment

How expensive any particular correctional institution is to build and operate will depend on a number of factors—where it is located, the number of inmates it confines, the number of personnel needed to adequately staff it, how secure it is designed to be, the extensiveness of programs offered, and so on. In general, the larger and more secure a prison is, the more expensive it will be. Construction costs range from:

- More than $92,000 *per bed* for maximum-security state prisons, to
- More than $39,000 *per bed* for minimum-security facilities[4]

But that is just for initial construction. Annual operating costs average almost $22,650 per inmate.[5] As a result, more than three out of four dollars spent on corrections go to prisons (*see* Figure 6.1). To offset these escalating costs, more and more facilities are charging inmates fees for room and board, and for special services, such as medical treatment.[6] It is, however, security that is far more expensive than treatment. For example, in the late 1990s, California spent approximately $21,000 per inmate each year; of that:

- $11,000 (52 percent) was spent on security
- $3,125 (14 percent) was spent on health care
- $900 (4.5 percent) was spent on education and training[7]

Because the majority of prisons operate at the state level of government, it is not surprising to find that (as shown in Figure 6.2) it is the states that are bearing the primary brunt of this fiscal burden. Moreover, the burden is ever-increasing. State correctional spending has been climbing in recent years at more than double the rate of increase for state educational expenditures.[8]

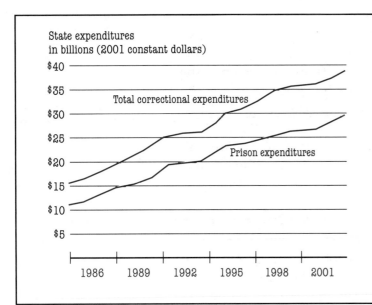

figure 6.1

State prison expenditures. Prison operations consumed about 77 percent of state correctional costs in 2001. The remaining 23 percent was spent on juvenile justice, probation and parole, community-based corrections, and central office administration.

Source: James J. Stephan, *State Prison Expenditures, 2001,* Washington, DC: U.S. Department of Justice, 2004, p. 1.

Undoubtedly, imprisonment is an expensive option. For what it costs to keep a prisoner in maximum custody for a year, a student could attend one of the best universities in the country; two dozen offenders could be supervised on probation or parole in the community; or hot meals could be provided to thousands of needy people. It is for such reasons that this country's extensive use of incarceration frequently comes under fire.

But others argue that the costs of prison must be balanced against the costs of crime. At least one study indicates that an average crime costs society $2,300 in losses to victims, court costs, and police expenditures. Given a yearly median crime rate of twelve offenses per criminal, this research estimates that it actually costs less to keep someone in prison (twelve times $2,300 = $27,600, versus $14,000 for incarceration at the time of the study).[9] Regardless of whether such sizable fiscal savings are achieved by incarceration, the costs of imprisonment must be weighed against the alternatives.

Offender Fees

Despite the economic arguments pro and con, the fact remains that current public policies emphasize the use of imprisonment. As correctional costs

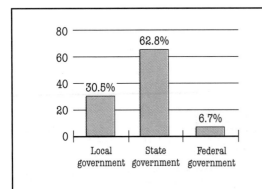

figure 6.2

Responsibility for correctional expenditures.

Source: Compiled from Bureau of Justice Statistics, *Sourcebook of Criminal Justice Statistics, 2002,* Washington, DC: U.S. Department of Justice, 2003, p. 5.

have skyrocketed in recent years, some jurisdictions have turned to the private sector to operate prisons more cost effectively (a topic discussed further in Chapter 15). In addition, "the notion that offenders should contribute to their own supervision costs has gained widespread political support" in recent years.[10] To offset expenses, states have authorized inmate fees for items ranging from special health services to room and board for those on work release. In fact, one analyst goes so far as to propose an annual $100 "user fee" tax on *all* men (not just inmates) to offset the costs of their disproportionate involvement in crime, with proceeds used to expand tutoring, counseling, and prison education programs.[11]

To some, charging offenders for their confinement brings back memories of the inequities involved in the fee system that was common during the early history of corrections. Thus, it is not surprising to find that there is significant debate surrounding these practices, which have been subjected to court challenges[12] and criticized as being "impractical, unprofessional, or inherently unfair."[13] But when government revenues are increasingly limited while demands continue to escalate, there is also considerable support for requiring users to pay for the services they receive—even if the "users" are inmates and the "services" are food, clothing, and shelter in a prison cell.

Time Served and Jurisdiction

Regardless of whether they are paying "rent" for being there, prison inmates face longer periods of confinement than their jail counterparts. Prisons generally confine those sentenced to minimum terms that are *longer than one year*. The maximum, of course, can extend to life imprisonment, and states that provide for capital punishment also hold inmates awaiting execution on death row.

In terms of *where* they are confined, there may be a misperception that those serving longer sentences or convicted of more serious offenses are incarcerated in federal prisons. In fact, whether one's time is served in a *federal* or a *state* facility depends not on the length of sentence or the seriousness of the

Calculation of time served is a critical function which must be done accurately. Photo by Michael Dersin. Courtesy of the American Correctional Association.

offense, but rather, on whether it was a federal or a state law that was violated. Murder, for example—considered the most serious violent offense—is typically a violation of a state statute, resulting in state imprisonment. On the other hand, federal prisons hold offenders guilty of such federal offenses as interstate commerce violations, tax fraud, or international drug trafficking, as well as crimes involving federal property (for example, post offices or banks covered by the Federal Deposit Insurance Corporation).

✸ Learning Goals

Do you know:

1. The difference between various security levels in correctional institutions?
2. At what level of security most inmates are assigned?
3. How an inmate's custody classification is determined?

Security Classifications

Beyond their jurisdictional differences, prisons also operate at varying levels of *custody classification*. For security purposes, correctional institutions are classified into maximum, high/close, medium, and minimum—depending on the level of control they exert.

The security level of a particular institution is based on such factors as how heavily the outside perimeter is controlled, the presence or absence of "guard" towers, the extent of external patrols, the number of detection devices, the security of housing areas, and the level of staffing.[14] An entire facility may be classified at one level (for example, maximum), or various levels of security may be established for different units within an institution. Thus, within the same compound might be found sections designated as maximum, close, medium, or even minimum security.

Maximum/Close Security

A *maximum-security* facility is characterized by a walled (or heavily fenced) outside perimeter, armed towers, searchlights, alarms, electronic detection devices, and similar high-security measures. Often located in remote rural areas, these institutions have been characterized as "fortresses" that are placed "out in the country as if they were for lepers or for people with contagious diseases."[15]

External security is physically obvious, and *internal* security is tight as well. Movement within the institution is closely restricted. Visits are limited and carefully controlled. Inmate counts are conducted frequently (as often as every two hours). Because surveillance is so continuous, privacy is essentially eliminated.

Larger, more populated states usually have one or more maximum-security prisons. In states with fewer institutions, a portion of a medium-security compound might be designated for maximum-internal security. In still other locations, an additional category of *close security* has been added, which is not quite as restrictive as maximum but more closely supervised than medium.

The supermax Wallens Ridge State Prison, Big Stone Gap, Virginia, sits atop a mountain. As other supermax facilities, it is physically remote and relies on a complex system of cameras, electronics, and controlled movement.

At the other extreme, a number of states have now added *supermax* prisons, where impersonal controls keep staff at a distance, virtually all privileges have been stripped away, and "segregation is the end in itself."[16] Inmates "banished" to these facilities are confined to their cells for twenty-three hours a day under extremely tight security. Denounced as the "Marionization" of U.S. prisons—after the notorious federal penitentiary in Illinois where the practice apparently originated[17]—such facilities have been criticized for imposing "extreme social isolation," "limited environmental stimulation," and "extraordinary control over every movement."[18] For a glimpse inside a supermax prison, *see* the next "Close-up On Corrections."

York Correctional Institution for Women (Niantic, Connecticut), in contrast to supermax prisons, uses centralized programs and services that require frequent inmate movement.

Close-up On Corrections

Medium Security

A *medium-custody* institution usually has a wire fence, along with a strong perimeter that can include towers or booths. Increasingly, however, armed towers are being replaced by lethal fencing—a development that has led to the controversy described in the upcoming "Close-up On Corrections." From the exterior, some medium-security physical plants may not be noticeably different from maximum-security prisons. But they contain fewer restrictions inside the fences—fewer counts, more privileges, greater freedom of movement, and more interaction with other inmates. However, all of these "liberties" are relative to the virtual isolation of those in maximum confinement. There will still be such controls as alarms, closed-circuit television, and locked gates, with the flow of traffic restricted to certain specified areas.

These types of institutions house a wide variety of offenders—virtually anyone who is not dangerous enough to require maximum/close security, but not a sufficiently low risk to be entrusted to a minimum level of security. Because their inmates are potentially viewed as more "salvageable," medium-security prisons tend to offer more training, treatment, and work programs.

Close-up On Corrections

Minimum Security

In contrast, a *minimum-custody* facility has extremely little external control or regimentation. It frequently possesses only a single fence or no exterior obstruction at all. There are no towers or outside patrols. Inside, there are no cells, bars, or other obvious security measures. Housing is generally arranged in dormitory fashion. The physical structure itself may look like a farm, ranch, or college campus.

In fact, minimum-security facilities are rarely referred to as "prisons." More likely, they are called halfway houses, work release centers, or prerelease centers. Especially in urban areas, where minimum-security facilities are located directly in the community, they have recently come to be known by the generic term *community residential centers*, which can "be used as a pretrial detention option, as a condition of probation, as part of a sentence of confinement, as a transitional setting for offenders about to be released into the community from jail or prison, and as an intermediate sanction for violations of community supervision requirements."[19]

In this type of setting, "custody is a function of classification rather than of prison hardware."[20] In other words, only those sufficiently trustworthy are assigned to minimum custody, so there is little need for elaborate physical security systems. Administrators concerned with reducing the public's fears about being neighbors to a community-based facility are sensitive to the need for both careful screening and proper supervision. In that regard, residential programming has been described as "strict, intensive, and accountability-oriented."[21] Verifying the close supervision, one offender who was fulfilling the last months of his sentence at a community residential center stated on national television that serving time there was harder than in prison.[22] In minimum security, the stern imposition of external control is replaced by the firm expectation of self-control.

Inmates in such institutions may hold jobs or attend classes in the community by day, returning to the facility after work or school. Most commonly, the programs offered are a combination of work release and drug treatment.[23] Although those returning from outside assignments are likely to be searched, much of the facility's security depends on the "honor system," which most tend to respect to avoid losing the greater freedoms and privileges of minimum security.

Inmates confined in minimum security tend to be nonviolent offenders serving short sentences, preparing for release, or those who have earned a lower custody classification through good behavior in higher-security facilities. Phasing inmates into the community through minimum security near the end of their sentence enables them to resume life in free society while still under some supervision and lessens the trauma of their readjustment.

Security Distribution

Maximum-security prisons undoubtedly have the greatest notoriety among the public. Institutions such as San Quentin, Alcatraz (now closed), and Attica have been the subject of numerous books, songs, television programs, and movies. But despite this publicity, as shown in Figure 6.3, nearly two out of every three inmates are confined in medium or minimum custody.[24]

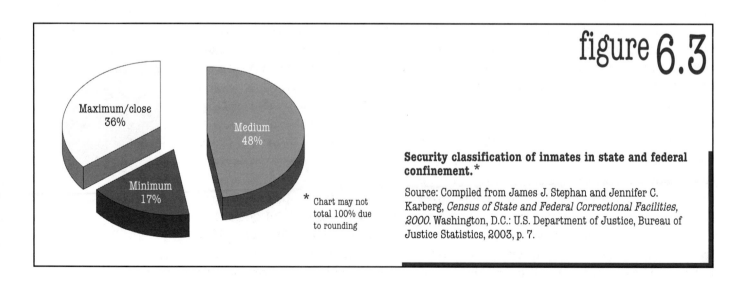

figure 6.3

Maximum/close 36%

Medium 48%

Minimum 17%

* Chart may not total 100% due to rounding

Security classification of inmates in state and federal confinement.*

Source: Compiled from James J. Stephan and Jennifer C. Karberg, *Census of State and Federal Correctional Facilities, 2000.* Washington, D.C.: U.S. Department of Justice, Bureau of Justice Statistics, 2003, p. 7.

Classification Procedures

Custodial classification relates to the level of *externally imposed* control needed by those whose behavior indicates that they have not developed sufficiently strong *internal* controls. As we saw earlier, classification refers to the separation of inmates into groups according to characteristics they share in common. Those sentenced to serve their time in prison represent a wide range of seriousness in terms of both their current offense and prior criminal history. Prison inmates therefore are classified primarily according to the degree of security they require.

During initial intake, an evaluation assessment is conducted, often at a central reception or diagnostic center, where new inmates are transferred on arrival. The reception process itself ranges considerably in terms of sophistication. Some systems simply may conduct a medical exam and review the official documents accompanying the inmate's transfer (court papers, arrest forms, the presentence investigation report, and so forth). Others may include an in-depth interview with the offender, along with a psychological evaluation, intelligence and aptitude testing, and vocational interest measures.

After this information is gathered, the classification unit makes determinations with regard to custodial classification, housing assignment, and what (if any) types of educational, treatment, or work programs the inmate will be offered. Throughout this process, efforts are made to predict both security risk and treatment potential. Greatest emphasis, however, is on determining the level of risk or dangerousness of the offender, both to protect other inmates and to promote order and safety of the total institution. For example, in deciding a person's custody classification, the U.S. Bureau of Prisons ranks offenders on such factors as "severity of current offense, expected length of incarceration, type of prior commitments, history of escape attempts, and history of violence," along with additional internal management considerations, such as racial balance and degree of crowding in various facilities.[25]

But as we have seen in terms of how classification operates in jails, the process does not always work effectively, particularly when a system is faced with such severe crowding that inmates must be placed where there is room rather than where they can function most effectively. In that regard, evidence indicates that a substantial majority of new inmates are classified as minimum custody upon intake, although limited space in such facilities may not necessarily enable them to be confined there.[26]

Reclassification

Initial classification does not preclude a change in status at a later time. The process is not foolproof, and it may turn out that someone either was over-classified or inappropriately classified at too low a level of security. Additionally, as inmates prove themselves worthy of greater trust over the years, their custodial classification could be reduced. It is in the institution's interest to classify offenders at the lowest security level that is safely feasible. The less security, the less expensive the supervision, and simultaneously, the closer the correctional process is to reintegrating the offender into society. Thus, during the period of their incarceration, prisoners may be reclassified and assigned to new housing, jobs, or programs any number of times.

Do you know:

1. How rapidly the prison population has been growing in recent years?
2. What health and safety risks accompany prison crowding?
3. What nation has the highest incarceration rate?

The Prison Population

Just as there are concerns that people such as vagrants, alcoholics, and the mentally ill are being detained in jails inappropriately, the question has been raised as to whether prisons are being reserved for those who truly need or deserve to be behind bars. For example, the perception that only high-risk, dangerous offenders are going to prison is challenged by one study which found that only 18 percent of new admissions could be ranked "serious" on the basis of the offense for which they were committed.[27] But others point out that some inmates are entering prison with a long criminal history (even though the offense they are being admitted for may be nonviolent).[28] Such issues have come under considerable debate as it has become apparent that the United States is entering a fourth decade of continually increasing prison populations,

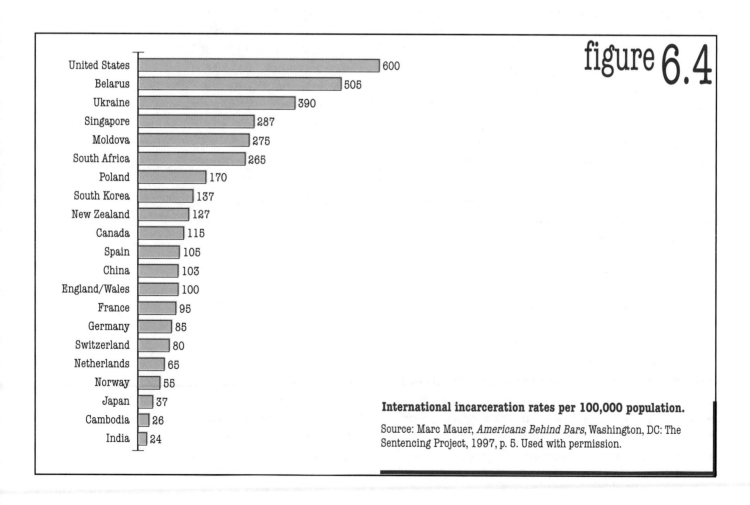

figure 6.4

International incarceration rates per 100,000 population.

Source: Marc Mauer, *Americans Behind Bars*, Washington, DC: The Sentencing Project, 1997, p. 5. Used with permission.

figure 6.5

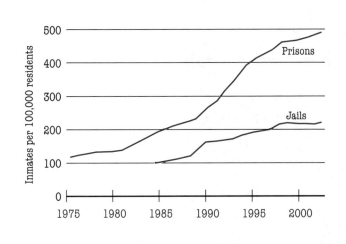

Incarceration rates in the United States over the past twenty-five years.

Source: Allen J. Beck, "The Impact of Drug Crimes on State and Federal Prison Population Growth," presented at the American Correctional Association 2004 Winter Conference, January 11, 2004.

with no end in sight. As Figure 6.4 shows, the United States also maintains the world's leading incarceration rate.

Number of Inmates

The number of inmates in state and federal prisons has been increasing steadily since the 1970s. By 2002, the total number of state and federal prisoners had reached a record high of 1,367,856 [29]—representing a doubling of the incarceration rate since 1985 (*see* Figure 6.5). While the pace of prison growth has slowed somewhat in recent years, many facilities are still overcrowded. By the end of 2002, state prisons were operating between 1 percent and 16 percent above capacity, while federal prisons were operating at 33 percent above capacity. One in five correctional facilities was under court order or consent decree to reduce crowding or address conditions of confinement.[30]

Prison Crowding

Numbers and charts, of course, do not begin to portray the misery of living conditions to which inmates are subjected in overflowing prisons. The consequence of housing too many people in too little space means that inmates are double-bunked in small cells designed for one or forced to sleep on mattresses in unheated prison gyms, day rooms, hallways, or basements. Others sleep in makeshift trailers, tents, or converted ferries. Space that had once been devoted to work, study, and recreational programs is being turned into dormitories. [31]

Under such conditions, it is not surprising to find that inmates have fewer opportunities for everything from visits to training or treatment programs. Even more important, there are serious health and safety risks associated with packing more inmates into less space. Studies have linked crowding with higher rates of violence, aggression, and stress-induced mental disorders.[32] Additionally, crowded institutions promote such communicable medical problems as colds, flu, infectious diseases, tuberculosis, and sexually transmitted diseases.

Double-bunking is one measure that both jails and prisons use to address the crowding issue. Here is the Bernallilo County Detention Center. Courtesy of Mark Goldman and Associates (Custer-Basarich, Ltd. and Design Collaborative of the Southwest) and the Durrant Group.

Additionally, prison staff are not able to exert as much control over the population of excessively crowded facilities:

> As the numbers of prisoners increase, the space normally used for recreation or education is diverted to dormitory use. Incidents of violence between prisoners increase, and control of the institution gradually slips to the most aggressive groups. . . . The exhaustion of services and the limitation on recreational activities further lead to tension, boredom, and conflict. . . . Eventually, there is a degradation of morale among the staff, greater staff turnover, and a vicious cycle of diminished control.[33]

Moreover, the greater potential for violence in crowded facilities is not limited to incidents between inmates. During the early-to-mid 1990s, the inmate population increased 158 percent, but assaults on officers occurred at twice that rate. In 1990, "there was one assault for every 321 inmates," but by 1995, "there was one assault for every 171 inmates."[34]

Responses to Crowding

Reactions to the crowding crisis have included both the expansion of existing facilities and the construction of new institutions. In recognition of the futility and expense of this approach, a range of additional options has been advocated—from a *front-end reduction* in the number of people *going into* prisons to a *back-end increase* in the number *coming out*.

The intent of front-end solutions is to keep more people from being incarcerated, through the use of community-based alternatives (diversion, electronic monitoring, probation, and so forth). Back-end approaches are designed to release more of those already confined, through such options as time off for good behavior, parole, weekend confinement, and other forms of early or temporary release.

Some would argue that neither front- nor back-end solutions have been pursued very vigorously. In any event, these approaches have yet to significantly reduce the escalating size of the prison population.

 # Learning Goals

Do you know:

1. The characteristics of a typical prison inmate?
2. What percentage of those in prison are recidivists?
3. For what types of offenses prisoners are serving time?

Characteristics of Inmates

With so many people incarcerated, it is reasonable to ask just who exactly is in all these prison cells—or, if trends continue in the same direction, the more pertinent question may become who is not. As the data in Figure 6.6 indicate, the typical profile of a state prison inmate is a relatively young, black male. The average inmate is unmarried (either single, separated, divorced, or widowed), undereducated, and employed at a low-paying job before incarceration (to calculate your chances of going to prison, during your lifetime, *see* the next "Close-up On Corrections").

figure 6.6

Sex	Male	94%
Race/Ethnicity	White (non-Hispanic)	33%
	Black	47%
	Hispanic	17%
Age	Under 25	19%
	Under 35	57%
Marital Status	Unmarried (or separated)	83%
Education	Less than high school	43%
Prearrest employment	Employed full-time	56%
Income prior to arrest	Less than $12,000	54%

Characteristics of state and federal prison inmates.

Source: Bureau of Justice Statistics, *Correctional Populations in the United States, 1997*, Washington, DC: U.S. Department of Justice, 2000, p. 48.

Close-up On Corrections

Offenses of Inmates

Prisoners generally are familiar with the criminal justice system—the vast majority (75 percent) have previously served time on probation or behind bars.[35] In terms of the type of violation for which they are presently incarcerated, slightly less than half of those in state prison (49 percent) are serving time for violent offenses—predominantly murder (13 percent) and robbery (13 percent) [36] (*see* Figure 6.7).

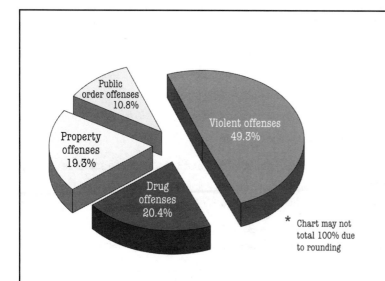

figure 6.7

* Chart may not total 100% due to rounding

Current offenses of state prison inmates. *

Source: Compiled from Paige M. Harrison and Allen J. Beck, "Prisoners in 2002," *Bureau of Justice Statistics Bulletin*, Washington, DC: U.S. Department of Justice, 2003, p. 10.

figure 6.8

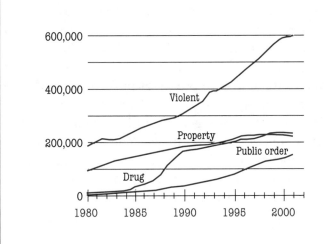

Trends in most serious offenses of state prisoners.

Source: Available at www.ojp.usdoj.gov/bjs/glance/corrtyp.htm.

There always will be some differences between looking at incoming inmates and those already serving time. But as the effects of mandatory minimum sentencing guidelines began to take effect, the prison profile has been changing, as reflected in Figure 6.8. Evidence also indicates that there is a trend toward greater use of imprisonment overall.[37] The question then becomes what return society expects for the costly investment it is making in institutional confinement.

 Learning Goals

Do you know:

1. What goals society has had for prisons over the years and how they have changed today?
2. To what extent the public supports punishment versus rehabilitation for inmates?

The Purpose of Prisons

What does society expect its prisons to accomplish? There is no consensus on the answer to that question. As a result, we cannot evaluate how effective our prisons are, because we are not entirely sure what they should be doing—as the saying goes, "If you don't know where you're going, how will you know when you get there?"

As described in earlier chapters, correctional institutions were first developed to provide a more humane alternative to corporal or capital punishment. In line with their Quaker-initiated origins, they were viewed as a place where inmates could read the Bible, reflect on past wrong-doings, and ultimately, repent for their sins. As one historian said, "the founders of the American prison were idealists who believed that prisons and other total institutions could be used to change human beings for the better."[38]

With the advent of the Industrial Era, achieving penitence gave way to attaining profits. Then, as the promise of the medical model renewed hope for rehabilitation, the purpose of prisons shifted again. The degrading pictures of chain gangs, forced labor, and physical punishment diminished in favor of the uplifting potential of counseling, therapy, and treatment. There are probably few who would advocate a return to the barbaric practices of the past, but society's frustrations with the apparent inability to accomplish long-term behavioral changes in prison, coupled with the fears generated by increasing crime rates, again called for a new prison agenda. In summary, "each generation has criticized the prisons and penal philosophies of its predecessor and has offered new rationales and management theories. . . . Time and again in American history, men and women have looked to penal institutions for solutions to individual and social problems. Time and again, they have been disappointed."[39]

Social Compromise

By the early 1980s, the justice model's concern for retribution, deterrence, and certainty of punishment had found a receptive public audience. From the unfulfilled promises of the medical model came an unconditional plan for change. If it was too much to hope that prisons could improve people, at least they could incapacitate them. If rehabilitation was an impossible expectation, at least retribution would ensure that "justice was served." If criminals were not mindful of penalties, at least they would be reminded through punishment. And if this did not deter them, at least they would pay their debt.

When society came to the conclusion that the situation was out of control, it settled for these compromises. Essentially, we elected to "pull drowning people out of the river without going upstream to find out why they are drowning in the first place."[40] The problem is that they are "drowning" for many complicated reasons that we cannot comprehend, cannot respond to effectively, or simply do not wish to address. Thus, we continue to pull offenders out of the social mainstream and put them into secure institutions. There they find a fertile environment to nourish isolation, frustration, and antisocial behavior—as we see in the upcoming "Close-up On Corrections."

Public Opinion

However, there is some doubt that the public in general is truly as punitive as advocates of the justice model would like to believe. For example, in 1995, people throughout the country were asked whether they thought the crime rate could be lowered by spending money on social and economic problems or on prisons, police, and judges. Given the presumed popularity of the justice model, it would be reasonable to assume that the response would have been overwhelmingly in favor of the latter. Not so. Overall, only 27 percent supported criminal justice spending in comparison to the 68 percent favoring social and economic options.[41]

Likewise, once offenders are in prison, public support for rehabilitation (48 percent) far outdistances that for punishment (15 percent).[42] But that does not mean that the public believes prisons are doing a good job—82 percent rated the ability of prisons to rehabilitate inmates only "fair" or "poor."[43] In that regard, some maintain that the dominance of blacks in today's prisons has

Close-up On Corrections

PRISON LIFE AND HUMAN WORTH

There is a slang phrase, which probably originated far from prison but which applies better to prison life than do any other two words in the English language, "put down." It eloquently describes the emotional effect of being squelched, and . . . it tells sadly, bitterly just what prison is. To the person who never has served time, it is hard to realize just how much of a daily humiliating "put-down" prison life can be even in a well-run institution.

It is not necessary to look for a venal warden, or even a merely inept one. It is not necessary to look for sadistic guards, political chicanery from the governor's office, inadequate food, or stingy budgets from an uncaring legislature . . . . When we look for such factors, we are missing the real guts of the problem, which is that in the best of prisons with the nicest of custodians and the most generous of kitchens, the necessary minutiae of management tend to dcny and even insult the basic needs of individuals . . . . Sooner or later, the prisoner must lose his spirit, or he must rebel.

Source: Paul W. Keve, *Prison Life and Human Worth*, Minneapolis, Minnesota: University of Minnesota Press, 1974, pp. 15, 41-42.

resulted in these institutions virtually being "written off as useless by the larger white society . . . serving no useful purpose for those confined."[44] Moreover, support for treatment-oriented imprisonment does not necessarily equate with a willingness to pay for it.

 # Learning Goals

Do you know:
1. How politics influence the administration of prisons?
2. The differences between the operations, program services, and support services units within a correctional institution?
3. What career opportunities exist within correctional facilities?

Prison Organization

The fact that society's true sentiments may not always be accurately represented in the public policy does not necessarily mean that public opinions are not reflected in the way prisons are operated. Quite the contrary, the attitude of the public influences the political leadership, which, in turn, is responsible for appointing correctional leadership. For example, every state's director (or commissioner) of corrections is appointed by the governor. Thus, the type of administration that prevails at any institution is ultimately a reflection of public preferences, as expressed through the political process. Prison directors themselves also develop a reputation for having a certain operational "style" and are attracted to locations where public sentiments are consistent with their approach.

Political Influence

This system of political influence can be a positive benefit when it works to the advantage of its stakeholders. However, it also can be a negative factor when "politics" unduly interfere with correctional practices. For example, following a highly visible escape or institutional disturbance, the correctional administrator or warden may be fired, serving as a political scapegoat for public disenchantment with the system. Moreover, when a new governor is elected, it is almost certain that new cabinet appointments will be made, including the director of corrections.

This is a legacy dating back to the time when states were small, the correctional "system" consisted of one prison, and the warden was the sole correctional administrator, appointed by and responsible to the governor, under a system of political patronage. Thus, much of the early history of prisons reflected mediocre performance by those who were appointed more for their political connections than their prison-related capabilities. "There were some [who] . . . administered with intelligent dedication, but part of the reason for their outstanding leadership was the wasteland of mediocrity around them." [45]

Today, some correctional departments are still politically motivated, which can result in appointing a director with little knowledge of or experience in corrections. But even when more qualified candidates are appointed, it is essential for them to know the political system and be able to work adeptly within it. When a career correctional expert is placed in a turbulent political environment and does not understand the political maneuvering required to survive, the outcome can be disastrous.

It is for such reasons that those in charge of state correctional systems experience an average longevity of just over three years,[46] often regardless of their talent. This brief tenure is "hardly long enough for the inexperienced appointee to learn the job and assess the adequacy and competence of staff available, let alone weigh the need for change." [47]

As a result, it is not uncommon to find directors who have experienced a virtual career of "musical chairs," having been in charge of corrections in any number of states. Even where there is more stability in the upper ranks, it may be attained at the cost of continually adjusting to the changing political climate. Needless to say, such instability is neither personally desirable nor organizationally productive.

Institutional Organization

Relatively frequent leadership turnover is one of the few organizational features that many correctional facilities have in common. The specific manner in which prisons are organized and operated varies according to their size, purpose, and degree of security. Correctional institutions range from large, sprawling prison complexes to road camps or halfway houses that hold as few as ten or twenty people. The manner in which they are organized varies likewise.

In medium-to-large facilities, the administrative structure of the organization is typically divided into three general components:

- Operations (also called custody or security)

- Program services (also called treatment or inmate programs)

- Support services (also called administrative or staff services)

In larger institutions that provide their own in-house medical staff (rather than contracting with an outside provider), there also may be a separate unit for health services. A general overview of the organization for a typical prison housing about 2,000 residents is shown in Figure 6.9.

Operations. The operational division includes all of the custodial staff and activities directly related to providing both internal and external security, and inmate supervision. Staff authority is assigned on the basis of rank—starting with officers (or "line" staff), and moving up the supervisory hierarchy to sergeants, lieutenants, and captains. Ultimately, all sworn personnel report to a deputy or assistant warden for operations. However, it is expected that they will do so through the "chain of command," starting with their immediate supervisor and working upward if the issue cannot be resolved.

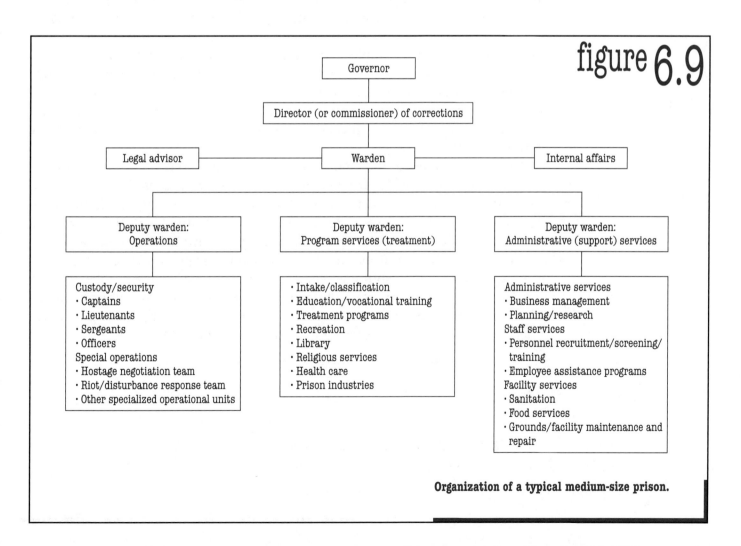

figure 6.9

Organization of a typical medium-size prison.

The number of operational staff will vary with the size of the facility, as will the officer/inmate ratio. Throughout the country, there is an average of one correctional officer for every 4.8 inmates in state confinement.[48]

Program Services. Within the program-services division are all of the units providing inmate programs and treatment: for example, vocational training, education, prison industries, the library, recreation, casework, counseling, and the like. Other responsibilities related to inmate welfare also are likely to fall within this division, such as the maintenance of records, the chaplain's office, health care, and the classification unit. In contrast to the operational division, personnel in program services tend to be nonsworn civilians (although sworn staff on specialized assignments may be included).

Because of differences in backgrounds, job classifications, and the nature of their work, there is considerable potential for mistrust between operational and program personnel. The goals of custody and treatment differ substantially, and each needs to understand the other to maintain effective and productive relationships. If the overall interests of the total institution are to be served, they must avoid conflict and pursue mutual cooperation.

Administrative (Support) Services. Administrative (or support) services encompass the many activities within a prison that assist treatment and custody functions. In some prisons, this unit may be further divided into two separate sections: one addressing *facility maintenance* and one focusing on *staff support*. Within facility maintenance are such services as physical plant maintenance (electricity, water, heat, sanitation, and so forth), clothing issue and laundry, food preparation, fire protection, locksmithing, and other functions related to the physical complex. Business management, accounting, purchasing, planning, research, and new construction may be considered support services, or these functions may be provided through a separate administrative unit. Support services related to staff include the recruiting, screening, and training of personnel (described in Chapter 13), as well as various employee assistance programs.

Career Opportunities. Regardless of how the prison is organized administratively, the overall compound of a large institution functions as a community within itself. Because of their self-contained nature, correctional institutions offer a wide variety of career opportunities. To operate effectively, they need everyone from teachers, health care professionals, psychologists, social workers, and correctional officers to the less visible people working behind the scenes, such as clerical staff, dieticians, electricians, and maintenance personnel. As a result, wide varieties of career opportunities are available, even for those who do not desire security-related work. In fact, corrections has been among the top growth industries for a number of years.[49]

 Learning Goals

Do you know:

1. What the responsibilities of a prison warden are?
2. How the warden's style influences prison operations?
3. To what extent inmates exert control in prisons?

Prison Administration

Just as the organization of a prison differs according to the size and complexity of the institution, so do the demands on the leader. Each correctional institution within a state is headed by an appointed administrator, whose title is typically warden or superintendent and who generally is responsible for:

- *Coordination* of the various administrative divisions, to assure that all are working toward organizational goals

- Establishment of the institution's *policies and procedures*, which guide the work of staff on a day-to-day basis

- Authority for *personnel decision making* (for example, hiring, promoting, making demotions and terminating staff)

- Preparation and oversight of the facility's *budget*

- Development of *external relationships* with civic groups, professional associations, and the like—ranging from "image-building" public relations to substantive discussions of problems and needs

It is the warden or superintendent who is in charge of both internal operations and external interactions—who ultimately is responsible for the institution. Thus, it is also the warden who establishes the priorities and sets the tone for the entire facility and its organizational culture.[50]

Leadership Styles

While the visionary leadership capabilities of wardens vary, their fundamental principles are expected to be in line with the director who appointed them. Whatever their leadership style, it is reflected throughout the prison. For example, there are some administrators who seek to exert complete control, to be "on top" of any situation. This type of warden clearly establishes who is in charge. But demands for tight control also can result in rigidly regimented prisons with strict rules and stern discipline, where the organizational culture is characterized by tensions and apprehensions.

Other correctional administrators are more treatment-focused. Those whose careers began with work in inmate programs and remained committed to rehabilitative ideals throughout their career represent a treatment orientation. The type of treatment emphasized may range widely—from programs directed toward education and vocational training to sophisticated therapy based on group living, guided group interaction, and other clinical approaches.

This is not meant to imply that correctional leaders are exclusively "treatment" or "punishment" oriented. Some have made efforts to combine elements of both. Others emphasize neither—but rather, simply focus on custody, or what might be termed "warehousing." Still other administrators may try to simplify procedures so that prison life is as nearly "normal" as possible. There are also those whose primary objective is to run the facility as quietly as possible—that is, to "keep the lid on."

Operational Impact

Regardless of what particular leadership style is established by upper-level management, there is little doubt that it will affect policies and procedures throughout the entire system—which, in turn, will have an impact on both operational practices and inmate behavior. As a result, the organizational culture of even the same institution can vary dramatically over the years, depending on who is in charge, as described in the next "Close-up On Corrections."

Inmate Control

Institutions with some level of disorder may not necessarily be inferior to those with a calmer appearance. Just as society "tolerates" some amount of crime to ensure the preservation of individual freedoms, prisons must seek a compromise between widespread chaos and overly rigid control. But just who is in control of prisons?

Some correctional administrators have noted that most institutions actually are run by inmates—if not officially, at least unofficially. It is, of course, the inmates who outnumber officers and civilian staff. But the extent to which inmates rather than staff are in charge of a prison depends in part on the capacity in which inmates are used within the institution.

In previous years, it was common for many of the clerical and technical jobs in prisons to be assigned to inmates, particularly when budgets were too limited to hire enough staff. In fact, well into the twentieth century, some states went so far as to rely on "inmate guards" to maintain order among the prison population. For an inside account of how brutal these unofficial "staff" could be in dealing with fellow inmates, see the following "Close-up On Corrections."

Even in prisons where inmates were prohibited from using physical force against other inmates, they might be used for such sensitive assignments as delivering and picking up supplies or equipment, bookkeeping, or accounting. Needless to say, these practices were open to considerable abuse. Freedom to travel outside the compound made the introduction of contraband quite tempting. Moreover, even "trusties" in clerical jobs often used their positions to personal advantage—as a basis for gaining authority over other inmates by extending favors to them.

As the corruption resulting from such practices captured administrative attention, strong arguments were made to provide sufficient fiscal support to enable prisons to function without extensive dependence on inmate skills. As a result, inmates now tend to work in much less sensitive areas and generally have been absolved of any custodial supervision over other prisoners. But even today, many institutions rely extensively on residents for carpentry, plumbing, general maintenance, and other nonsecurity-related tasks.

Eliminating inappropriate job assignments, however, has not eliminated inmate influence. Particularly in those institutions that assign new correctional officers to work without sufficient training, security personnel may well find themselves relying on "friendly" inmates to teach them their job. The American Correctional Association (ACA) now has standards that call for the provision of a minimum of forty hours of training prior to job assignment (followed by an additional 120 hours).[51] But in addition to the fact that this is

 # Close-up On Corrections

STATEVILLE: FIFTY YEARS OF FRUSTRATIONS

Partisan Politics, 1925-1936

From its opening in 1925, the Stateville Penitentiary in Illinois began a dismal legacy. This was the era of the "spoils system"—when influential politicians gathered in smoke-filled back rooms to reward those who had supported their election with government appointments. Corrections was no exception. The warden and many staff members at Stateville owed their positions to political patronage. With neither prior correctional experience nor any particular commitment to the field, they were motivated by little more than pleasing their political sponsors. "Job security was nonexistent. Wages were barely above subsistence. Rules were made on the spot. Discipline was arbitrary and capricious." For inmates with political connections, favoritism and corruption flourished, while those in solitary were "handcuffed to the bars for eight hours a day," living on "one glass of water and one slice of bread."

Charismatic Dominance, 1936-1961

Realizing the seriousness of the situation by 1936, a reform governor appointed a no-nonsense administrator who came to be known as "Mr. Prison"—Joseph E. Ragen. Sure enough, Ragen drastically changed things. But not everyone would agree with the manner in which he did so. In a complete turnaround from the chaotic conditions he found, Ragen implemented an authoritarian system that he personally dominated. "His daily inspection of the prison, accompanied only by his two dogs, symbolized his highly personalistic rule. He alone managed all contacts with the outside, thereby reinforcing his personal power. From his staff, he demanded absolute loyalty. . . ."

For the inmates as well as the staff, discipline was rigid. Punishments were severe. Criticism was not tolerated. Inmate leaders were coopted to support the system by good jobs. Ragen's totalitarian rule and charismatic leadership left no doubt about who was in charge or how Stateville should be run—a system of dominance that survived for a quarter-century.

Drift, 1961-1970

For most of the next decade, the institution would drift between control and chaos. Although Ragen's successor was a hand-picked assistant warden who had risen through the ranks under "Mr. Prison's" leadership, he had neither the charismatic style nor the formal authority of his predecessor. Education, recreation, and rehabilitative programs were implemented. But at the same time, the euphoria of the mass demonstrations of the 1960s was being felt inside the walls. Black Muslims organized to challenge the authority of the system— a move that was met with massive administrative resistance and repression. As the courts intervened, the Illinois legislature was also changing sentencing and parole policies. Old-time "con's" who had been inmate leaders were suddenly released, creating a power vacuum. The inmates were no longer in control. But neither was the traditional system of authority. The timing was ripe for a crisis.

(continued)

Close-up On Corrections

(CONTINUED)

Crisis, 1970-1975

Stateville had come a long way from the abuses of the spoils system and the autocracy of "Mr. Prison." The next two wardens were "well-educated professionals" who believed in rehabilitation and the "human relations model of management." In place of the authoritarian regime, they attempted to establish a system based on the consent of subordinates. But many who had been groomed under Ragen saw these changes as too "permissive." Among the staff, treatment personnel lined up against custodial personnel. Among the inmates, gangs lined up against other gangs. And everyone lined up against the administration. "Inmates simply refused to follow orders, refused to work, and refused to follow the rules." Strikes and riots erupted. Hostages were taken. Gang fights broke out. As confrontations escalated, crackdowns ensued. "Having no other strategy to maintain control, the reform regimes periodically reverted to measures even more repressive than those of previous decades." Conditions "deteriorated to a level of violence and destruction beyond anything previously seen in Illinois."

Restoration, 1975-

The next administrator had no where to go but up, and he met the challenge with determination and enthusiasm. Beginning with sweeping upper-level management changes, he completely reorganized the facility. Improvements were made in everything from the disciplinary process to institutional security and inmate services. The human-relations model of management was replaced with a "highly-rational, problem-oriented" strategy. Administration resembled "corporate" more than correctional management in its emphasis on professionalism, detachment, and cost-consciousness.

Epilogue

The study on which this synopsis is based did not continue long enough to assess the results of these alterations, and in the ensuing years, leadership has changed hands again. It will be up to a future generation of researchers to document the administrative styles of subsequent wardens. But those of the past have certainly left their mark on Stateville in the political patronage of the spoils system; the paragon of toughness; the "puppet" of Ragen; the human relations of the participatory managers; the objective professionalism of the rational businessman. Each has had his own style. Each has shaped the prison culture, the people within it, and the public's perception of both.

Source: With the exception of the epilog, this material is paraphrased along with direct citations (in quotes) from James B. Jacobs, *Stateville*, Chicago: University of Chicago Press, 1977.

Close-up On Corrections

clearly a minimum requirement, as we will see in later chapters, compliance with ACA standards is voluntary. Until training standards are mandated, there are potentially places where the bizarre situations reflected in the next "Close-up On Corrections" can occur.

 # Learning Goals

Do you know:

1. How informal social control works among the inmate population?
2. How participatory management has been used in prison settings?
3. How inmate self-governance relates to Maslow's hierarchy of needs?

Informal Social Control

In every facility, there is informal control among the inmates that enables the institution to run smoothly. Some have a personal stake in a trouble-free prison—whether they are in positions of responsibility or simply want to "do their own time" as quietly as possible. Because of this personal investment, they will take steps to preserve the system and will help to keep other inmates in control. Naturally, administrators must be alert to ensure that the "peace-keepers" themselves do not become disorderly by physically taking authority into their own hands (as we saw earlier in the case of the building tenders).

But even if it is not formally endorsed by the administration, this type of *informal social control* is imposed by the inmate body on itself and can help to run the prison without disturbance. In return for healthy self-government, the administration may extend certain privileges to the inmate population, ranging from work release to conjugal visits. Participants in such programs will guard these benefits carefully and informally pressure others to conform when their behavior threatens the system. Everyone knows, for example, that if those on work release take advantage of this liberty by attempting to escape, the privilege will be revoked for everyone. Similarly, engaging in disruptive behavior

Close-up On Corrections

INMATES TRAINING OFFICERS

Most who entered the prison service prior to when a training academy was established, reported that they were simply issued "a badge, a club and a hat," shown the yard, and told to go to work. . . .

[W]ith reluctance on the part of the experienced officers to instruct the rookie correction officers, new men were in many cases forced to turn for advice to the inmates over whom they had authority. . . . When a rookie officer was sent to an area of the institution with which he was unfamiliar, there always seemed to be an inmate there who knew what was supposed to happen. . . . [T]he new officer had virtually nowhere else to turn to discover what was going on in the prison but to the inmates. . . . "The guy that broke me in[to] the mess hall was a murderer. You couldn't work for a nicer guy. . . . Inmates trained officers. Really! He told me to stand back, and he showed me how and where to frisk. He hit the table top to sound it out. Rap the bars to see if they were solid. . . .

Such an experience must have made the new officer wonder about the primacy of the security aspect of his job. . . . This . . . might lead an officer to place more trust in the inmate than in the administration or in his fellow officers, both of whom failed to provide him with much guidance.

Source: Lucien X. Lombardo, *Guards Imprisoned: Correctional Officers at Work*, Second Edition, Cincinnati, Ohio: Anderson Publishing Company, 1989, pp. 35, 39-40. Used with permission.

results in additional supervision, restriction, and scrutiny that inmates do not want forced upon them.

Participatory Management

There have been efforts to formalize such inmate self-control through various degrees of official recognition—from simple "suggestion boxes" to full-fledged "inmate councils" with decision-making power. The idea behind increased involvement of inmates in institutional procedures is based on the principles of *participatory management.*

According to participatory management, people are more likely to be *committed* to decisions or policies which they were involved in making. If, for example, the warden determines that high-fat foods will be eliminated, the change probably will meet with considerable resistance. If, on the other hand, inmates themselves become sufficiently concerned about the unhealthy effects of such foods that they propose a ban on them, the change will encounter greater support. The idea is that people inherently resist being *told* what to do (often regardless of whether they actually favor doing it). But when the idea is *theirs*, they have "ownership" of it and are therefore more likely to support it.

Because of the need for security-related restrictions, prisons are obviously not the ideal environment for inmate participation in facility management. Quite the contrary, correctional institutions are usually well noted for exercising "total control" over everything from the movement of inmates to the timing of meals.

But prison administrators also have recognized that such impotence can produce disastrous consequences when resulting frustrations explode into violence. Moreover, officers dealing with inmates on a day-to-day basis experience their frustrations firsthand as they attempt to resolve a series of seemingly endless complaints before situations escalate into serious disruptions. In addition, the courts have become more active with regard to intervening on behalf of inmates when prison conditions fall below constitutionally acceptable levels of safety, sanitation, or security. From this perspective, the advantage underlying some form of inmate participation is that it enables the administration to respond *proactively* to concerns before they get out of hand.

Inmate Self-Governance

Recognizing the benefits of involving inmates in prison management is not a new concept. But failure to install sufficient protections and controls resulted in abolishing many early efforts, as a few powerful inmate leaders began using the process to further their own self-interests.

In any inmate self-governance experiment, adequate administrative controls are essential. Caution must be exercised in determining to what extent the governing body will be able to exercise authority, assuring that established limits are not exceeded. Self-governance is a form of participatory management—a method of involving inmates in decisions and negotiating problems and grievances with them. As such, it is a form of *sharing* power and decision making with inmates, not *abdicating* authority to them.

Inmate governing councils have existed in varying forms in a number of institutions. One of the most widely used has been that in which elected inmates discuss policies and complaints with management staff. In this form of inmate involvement, elected representatives do not have the power or authority to change policies or implement new procedures. Rather, they simply bring to administrative attention issues that are of concern to the resident population. For example, they might forward inmate grievances, make suggestions, identify problem areas, help to work out unnecessary conflicts, and interpret administrative decisions to the general population.

The results can be quite favorable to all involved when proactive adjustments are made in response to the inmates' concerns. In doing so, not only can potential disruptions be curtailed, but inmates also begin to see that the administration cares about their welfare, potentially resulting in improved relationships with staff.

Self-Governance Critique

Of course, not all forms of inmate self-governance are equally effective, as illustrated in the next "Close-up On Corrections." The question then becomes why it is that so many experiments with inmate involvement in institutional management have not succeeded. One might assume that those institutions where inmates have a greater "say" in rules and regulations affecting them would tend to be less disruptive. To the contrary, at least one researcher has concluded that there is "little evidence . . . to support the belief that prisons where inmates enjoy more self-government are better than prisons where they enjoy less."[52] The reasons for this apparent contradiction are as varied as the types of inmate self-governance that have been implemented, but they may relate to such issues as timing, authority, relationships, and inmate maturity.

- *Timing.* It is not uncommon for inmate governance to be implemented as a result of the threat of a riot or a strike. In such a situation, the population apparently has reached such a high level of frustration with existing administrative procedures or institutional conditions that they believe these are the only tactics that will get the attention of those in charge. In other words, they are reacting (or at least threatening reaction) to the lack of an administrative climate that proactively seeks to address grievances before they build up to the point of violence. If inmates are to be involved in facility management, the time to do so is *before complaints* escalate to such a dangerous point. Otherwise, the perception is created that the administration is abandoning its responsibilities by "giving in" to demands, thereby opening the door for exploiting such signs of "weakness."

- *Authority.* Particularly if the expansion of inmate participation is seen as a concession by management, inmates may tend to get somewhat carried away with their newfound source of power and authority. Those who have been docilely subservient for many years may well find it difficult to cope with any amount of power without abusing it. Obviously, it must be emphasized in both written policy and unwritten practice that inmate involvement is *advisory* only (unlike the "Bikers" example in the following "Close-up On Corrections"). It must be clear that inmates are not *running* the facility, but rather, simply making suggestions for how it *could be run* better. Reducing inmate roles to an advisory capacity still involves some

Close-up On Corrections

INMATE SELF-GOVERNANCE

[H]ere was the recipe for an ostensibly new and better form of prison government . . . invest responsibility in inmate leaders . . . and everything from inmate-staff relations to recidivism rates will improve. In essence, this was the recipe for participative prison management. To many . . . it seemed like a recipe for disaster. As one veteran of two experiments with participative prison management recalled:

> Boil it down, and the thing was to be nice to the inmates, to let them have a real hand in running the show. Some so-called experts discovered that these men had never had enough responsibility for themselves and that was why they had killed people, beat up teachers, raped, and so forth. So that was the main thing now . . . let them organize themselves. We used to say "do your own time." Now we said "do time in your own way"—you organize the place, you run it. Just don't try to escape or get too crazy on us.

[O]ne of the most forthright experiments in inmate self-government was made . . . in response to inmate strikes and threats to riot. The formal prison administration abdicated in favor of inmate leaders. Among those who came to rule the prison were the "Bikers," a prison gang which, when not terrorizing other inmates or the staff, extended [to] its members the privilege of racing their motorcycles on the prison yard. The experiment ended when the internal situation became so thoroughly chaotic that public pressure mounted to regain control of the institution.

Source: John J. Dilulio, Jr., *Governing Prisons*, New York: Free Press, 1987, pp. 36-38.

risks, however, since those representing the population have the power to bring forth or withhold issues for administrative consideration.

- *Relationships*. Even the most clear-cut guidelines restricting the authority of the inmate governing body will produce ineffective results if the system is nothing more than a public relations "gimmick." If the primary concern is improving the image of the administration instead of making fundamental changes in response to legitimate concerns, the effort will be self-defeating. When communication consists of one-way, inmate-to-staff "gripe sessions," trust and confidence in the process quickly disappear. Not only are two-way dialog and feedback needed, but staff also must take inmate concerns seriously and make good-faith efforts to act on those that reasonably can be changed without jeopardizing institutional safety or security.

- *Inmate maturity.* Needless to say, those inmates selected to represent the prison population in any form of participatory government will play a crucial role in whether the process works. When inmate representatives are given too much authority, the process can break down as a result of their lack of experience with power, resulting in their inability to use it responsibly. Many of those in prison are simply not accustomed to making their own decisions or taking personal responsibility for their actions. In fact, it could be argued that some actually subconsciously may be seeking the secure environment of an institution to avoid facing the demands of adult life in free society.[53]

In this regard, Maslow's *hierarchy of needs* is a useful tool for assessing the motivation of inmates to participate in and benefit from self-governance. As illustrated in Figure 6.10, Maslow maintains that our behavior is determined by our personal motives or needs, which can be arranged in a hierarchy:

- *Physiological* (or physical) needs—food, clothing, shelter—dominate initially. These are our most powerful motivators until they are at least somewhat satisfied.

- Once our needs for physical well-being are gratified, *safety* dominates—the need to be secure, free of risk, danger, or concern for our physical needs.

- When both physiological and safety needs are relatively well met, we are motivated by the need for *social* affiliation—to belong to various groups and to be accepted by them.

- But once we belong to a group, we often want to be more than a member, perhaps a leader, trusted advisor, or at least someone held in respect—reflecting our need for *esteem.*

- Finally, it is no longer sufficient to be recognized by others, which leads to our desire for *self-actualization*—that is, to become everything within our capability, to be "all that we can be."

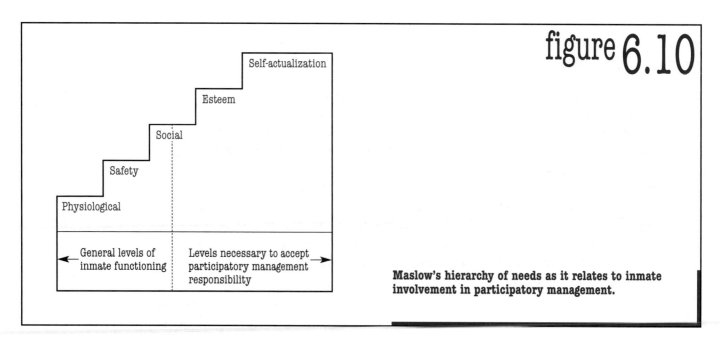

figure 6.10

Maslow's hierarchy of needs as it relates to inmate involvement in participatory management.

Very few people reach the top of Maslow's hierarchy (self-actualization), and prison is certainly not the ideal environment for achieving one's full potential. Nor are the majority of inmates likely to be functioning on the level of self-esteem, since many tend to characterize themselves as "losers," "dropouts," or "failures." In essence, "the hierarchy of needs attainment stops at the safety and security level in the correctional setting." [54] It is therefore likely that the bulk of the inmate population is functioning at the physiological, safety, or at most, social levels of Maslow's hierarchy.

However, participatory management will be effective only insofar as the participants are sufficiently emotionally mature—that is, motivated at the upper levels of Maslow's hierarchy [55] Only when the participants are mature enough to accept the responsibilities of being involved in making their own decisions will true participatory management work effectively. Otherwise, it is similar to parents involving their children in making daily decisions about what to eat, when to go to bed, or anything else concerning their welfare. They are simply not mature enough to make such decisions in a responsible manner.

This, of course, does not negate the need to be responsive to inmate complaints. But it is perhaps for this reason more than any other that the ideals of actual participation in management have met with so much failure when implemented in the reality of the prison environment. Nor, as the next chapter reveals, is the nature of the environment itself conducive to the rationality of behavior that we associate with life in free society. Prisoners may or may not be substantially "different" from the rest of society. But they are imprisoned, and that, if nothing else, distinguishes them from everyone else.

Summary

As a responsibility of the state and federal levels of government, prisons are less numerous than local jails. But while prisons are typically more standardized than jails, they still reflect considerable diversity—from high-security custodial institutions to minimum-security community residential centers. In addition, the military operates correctional facilities confining enlisted personnel and officers.

Compared to other alternatives, prisons are the most expensive component of the correctional system. Most of their costs are paid by the state level of government, although many jurisdictions have begun to collect fees from inmates to offset expenses. Generally, prisons confine those serving sentences of longer than one year. The type of institution in which an inmate will serve time is determined by the person's security classification. Those requiring the greatest amount of control are assigned to maximum security, which imposes a high level of both external and internal restrictions. At the other extreme, the most trustworthy offenders are assigned to minimum security, which provides far greater freedoms and privileges.

The offender's custody level is determined through the classification process, which identifies the person's level of risk or dangerousness. During classification, the inmate is received into the system, processed, and assigned to housing. Prisoners may be reclassified at any time during their confinement.

In recent years, the number of inmates sentenced to state and federal correctional institutions has been increasing at a steady pace, causing many facilities to become crowded. The effects of crowding not only reduce the availability and quality of inmate programs and services, but they also pose serious health and safety risks. Responses to the crowding issue have ranged from expansion and new construction to "front-end" alternatives designed to keep people out of prison, and "back-end" approaches to release more of those already confined.

The typical profile of a state prison inmate is a relatively young, black male, who is unmarried, undereducated, and was employed at a low-paying job before confinement. The majority are recidivists, and many have been incarcerated previously. While society has not clearly expressed what it expects its prisons to accomplish with these offenders, changing from the medical model to the justice model has reduced the emphasis on rehabilitation.

Organizationally, state departments of corrections are headed by a director (or commissioner) appointed by the governor. As a result, there is potential for political influence, and directors often are replaced with the election of a new governor. The state director appoints the warden (or superintendent) of each facility, who is responsible for internal coordination, institutional policies and procedures, personnel decision making, and external relationships. It is the warden's job to assure that the organizational units within the prison (operations, program services, and support services) are working together toward mutually compatible goals. The leadership style of the warden has an impact on the prison itself and the people within it.

While the management of prisons is formally in the hands of the warden, the inmate population has considerable informal control. To prevent inmates from exercising too much unofficial authority, efforts have been made to restrict them to less-sensitive work assignments and to remove them from direct supervision over other inmates. However, prisoners still exert significant informal social control, which in some institutions has been formalized through participatory management. Where participatory management has expanded into inmate self-governance, some difficulties have occurred—particularly when officials abdicate authority to the inmates rather than share power with them. Many offenders may not be sufficiently mature to accept the responsibilities of self-governance in a responsible manner. Moreover, the security-conscious nature of the prison environment is not always conducive to the types of rational behavior associated with life in free society, as we will see more clearly in the upcoming chapter.

Endnotes

1.   Charles H. Logan, "Criminal Justice Performance Measures for Prisons," in Timothy J. Flanagan, James W. Marquart, and Kenneth G. Adams, *Incarcerating Criminals: Prisons and Jails in Social and Organizational Context*, New York: Oxford University Press, 1998, pp. 262-263.

2.   James J. Stephan and Jennifer C. Karberg, *Census of State and Federal Correctional Facilities, 2000*, Washington, D.C.: U.S. Department of Justice, Bureau of Justice Statistics, 2003, p. iv.

3.   Paige M. Harrison and Allen J. Beck, "Prisoners in 2002," *Bureau of Justice Statistics Bulletin*, Washington, D.C.: U.S. Department of Justice, 2003, p. 8.

4.   Camille Graham Camp, ed., *The 2002 Corrections Yearbook: Adult Corrections*, Middletown, Connecticut: Criminal Justice Institute, 2003, p. 86.

5.   James J. Stephan, *State Prison Expenditures, 2001*, Washington, D.C.: U.S. Department of Justice, Bureau of Justice Statistics, 2004, p. iv.

6.   "Special Focus: Charging Prisoners for Medical Treatment," *Corrections Alert*, Vol. 1, No. 18, December 26, 1994, p. 1-2.

7.   Karen Fein, "Women Prisoners," in Roslyn Muraskin, ed., *Key Correctional Issues*, Upper Saddle River, New Jersey: Prentice Hall, 2004, p. 265.

8.   Stephan, *State Prison Expenditures*, p. 1.

9.   "Study Shows Prison Cheaper Than Having Criminals on the Street," *Community Crime Prevention Digest*, January 1991, p. 4, citing John J. DiIulio's study of prison inmates, conducted for the Wisconsin Policy Research Institute.

10. Dale Parent, *Recovering Correctional Costs through Offender Fees*, Washington, D.C.: U.S. Department of Justice, 1990, p. 1.

11. June Stephenson, *Men are not Cost-effective: Male Crime in America*, New York: Harper Perennial, 1995.

12. Susan W. McCampbell, "The Paying Prisoner . . . Room with a View, At a Price," *American Jails*, March/April 1997, p. 39. Note: The litigation described herein refers to fees charged in a jail setting.

13. Parent, *Recovering Correctional Costs*, p. 1.

14. Paraphrased from *Federal Bureau of Prisons: Facilities*, Washington, D.C.: U.S. Department of Justice, nd., p. 3.

15. Prison Research Education Action Project, "Prisons Cannot Protect Society;" in Bonnie Szumski, ed., *America's Prisons: Opposing Viewpoints*, Fourth Edition, St. Paul, Minnesota: Greenhaven Press, 1985, p. 46.

16. Dick Franklin, "Supermax Prisons: More of the Same in the 21st Century? Where Do We Go from Here?" *Training Manual: NIC Executive Training for New Wardens*, Longmont, Colorado: National Institute of Corrections, February 2000, pp. 2-4.

17. M. Olivero and J. Roberts, "The United States Federal Penitentiary at Marion, IL: Alcatraz Revisited," *New England Journal of Criminal and Civil Confinement*, Vol. 16, 1990, pp. 21-51.

18. Human Rights Watch, *Cold Storage: Super-maximum Security Confinement in Indiana*. New York: Human Rights Watch, 1997, p. 14.

19. Bernard J. McCarthy, "Community Residential Centers: An Intermediate Sanction for the 1990s," in Peter J. Benekos and Alida V Merlo, eds., *Corrections: Dilemmas and Directions*, Cincinnati, Ohio: Anderson Publishing Company; 1992, p. 190.

20. National Advisory Commission on Criminal Justice Standards and Goals, *Corrections*, Washington, D.C.: U.S. Government Printing Office, 1973, p. 345.

21. Bobbie L. Huskey "The Expanding Use of CRCs," *Corrections Today*, Vol. 54, No. 8, December 1992, p. 73.

22. *Ibid.*, p. 72.

23. *Ibid.*

24. James J. Stephan and Jennifer C. Karberg, *Census of State and Federal Correctional Facilities, 2000*. Washington, D.C.: U.S. Department of Justice, Bureau of Justice

Statistics, 2003, p. 7. Actual inmate statistics are: maximum/close = 442,970; medium = 594,916; minimum = 206,688.

25.   *Federal Bureau of Prisons: Facilities*, p. 3.

26.   Jack Alexander and James Austin, *Handbook for Evaluating Objective Prison Classification Systems*, San Francisco: National Council on Crime and Delinquency, 1991.

27.   John Irwin and James Austin, "Who Goes to Prison?," in *It's About Time: America's Imprisonment Binge*, Belmont, California: Wadsworth Publishing, 2001, p 27.

28.   Comments made by Larry Greenfeld, Chief, Correctional Statistics Program, Bureau of Justice Statistics, at the December 4, 1991, National Teleconference, "Who Goes to Prison?"

29.   "One in Every 32 Adults Now on Probation, Parole, or Incarcerated," *Press Release*, Washington, D.C.: U.S. Department of Justice, August 20, 2003, p. 1.

30.   Stephan and Karberg, *Census of State and Federal Correctional Facilities*, p. 9.

31.   William DiMascio, *Seeking Justice: Crime and Punishment in America*, New York: Edna McConnell Clark Foundation, 1997, p. 4.

32.   Eric Schlosser, "The Prison-Industrial Complex," *The Atlantic Monthly*, December 1998, p. 68.

33.   Alfred Blumstein, "Prison Crowding," *National Institute of Justice: Crime File Study Guide*, Washington, D.C.: U.S. Department of Justice, n.d., p. 1.

34.   "Assaults against Corrections Officers Rise," *Corrections Digest*, August 16, 1996. p. 5.

35.   Bureau of Justice Statistics, *Correctional Populations in the U.S., 1997*, Washington, D.C.: U.S. Department of Justice, 2000, Table 4.10.

36.   Paige M. Harrison and Allen J. Beck, "Prisoners in 2002," *Bureau of Justice Statistics Bulletin*, Washington, D.C.: U.S. Department of Justice, 2003, p. 10.

37.   Marc Mauer, *Race to Incarcerate*, New York: The New Press, 1999.

38.   James B. Jacobs, "Inside Prisons," *National Institute of Justice: Crime File Study Guide*, Washington, D.C.: U.S. Department of Justice, n.d., p. 1, quoting historian David Rothman.

39.   *Ibid.*

40.   Paraphrased from Dennis Rosenbaum's analogy comparing reactive to proactive policing in Andrew H. Malcolm, "New Strategies to Fight Crime Go Far beyond Stiffer Terms and More Cells," in John J. Sullivan and Joseph L. Victor, eds., *Annual Editions: Criminal Justice 91/92*, Guilford, Connecticut: Dushkin Publishing Group, 1991, p. 27.

41.   The remaining 5 percent had no opinion. Bureau of Justice Statistics, *Sourcebook of Criminal Justice Statistics, 2001*, Washington, D.C.: U.S. Department of Justice, 2002, p. 128.

42.   Bureau of Justice Statistics, *Sourcebook of Criminal Justice Statistics, 1998*, Washington, D.C.: U.S. Department of Justice, 1999, p. 129.

43.   Bureau of Justice Statistics, *Sourcebook, 2001*, Washington, D.C.: U.S. Department of Justice, 2002, p. 112.

44. Robert Johnson, "American Prisons and the African-American Experience: A History of Social Control and Racial Oppression," *Corrections Compendium*, Vol. 25, No. 9, September 2000, p. 29.

45. Paul W. Keve, *Prison Life and Human Worth*, Minneapolis, Minnesota: University of Minnesota Press, 1974, pp. 63-64.

46. Camille Graham Camp, ed., *The 2002 Corrections Yearbook: Adult Corrections*, Middletown, Connecticut: Criminal Justice Institute, 2003, p 150.

47. Joseph Rowan, "Politics and Corrections in America: A Good System Goes Bad in Wisconsin," in *The Americas*, Vol. 5, No. 3, June/July 1992, p. 7.

48. American Correctional Association, *Vital Statistics in Corrections*, Lanham, Maryland: American Correctional Association, 2000, p. 144.

49. James D. Stinchcomb, *Opportunities in Law Enforcement and Criminal Justice Careers*, New York: McGraw Hill, 2003, p. 118.

50. *See* Clemens Bartollas, *Becoming a Model Warden: Striving for Excellence*, Lanham, Maryland: American Correctional Association, 2004.

51. *Standards for Adult Correctional Institutions*, 4th ed., Lanham, Maryland: American Correctional Association, 2002.

52. John J. DiIulio Jr., *Governing Prisons*, New York: Free Press, 1987, p. 38.

53. *See* Karl Menninger, *The Crime of Punishment*, New York: Viking Press, 1968, p. 176.

54. David B. Kalinich and Terry Pitcher, *Surviving in Corrections*, Springfield, Illinois: Charles C Thomas, 1984, p. 12.

55. *See* Paul Hersey, Kenneth H. Blanchard, and Dewey E. Johnson, *Management of Organizational Behavior: Leading Human Resources*, Upper Saddle River, New Jersey: Prentice Hall, 2001.

PART III:

CORRECTIONAL INSTITUTIONS: CUSTODY, TREATMENT, CONFINEMENT, AND RELEASE

> ❝ The possibility should at least be examined that the reason for the high levels of violence in American prisons may have as much to do with the way in which prisons have been managed and staffed on the cheap, and the fairness and dignity with which prisoners are treated, as it has with the qualities that criminals bring with them into prison.[1] ❞
>
> —Roy King

To a society fearful of crime, it is undoubtedly reassuring to know that convicted offenders are confined behind bars. In the short term at least, the public can take some comfort in knowing that an offender cannot continue to victimize society while serving time in a correctional facility, but a short-term sense of safety does little to address long-term solutions. Very few offenders die in prison, which is another way of saying that almost all inmates

Photo, Above: Prisons use a variety of perimeter-security devices. Here microwave systems are used to detect movement between perimeter fences. Courtesy of Alan Latta.

eventually are released to society—replacing our sense of comfort today with a renewed concern for our safety tomorrow.

In the upcoming chapters, we explore this issue by looking at just what does happen when an offender is incarcerated. The logical starting point is an inside view of prisons and their custodial procedures. If nothing else, correctional institutions are expected to retain inmates in custody. In Chapter 7, we will see how this is accomplished—from the formal controls achieved through physical restrictions, rules, and regulations, to the informal controls encouraged through supervisory relationships between staff and inmates.

However, the overall objective of protecting society is better served in the long run by treatment. Thus, in Chapter 8, we turn our attention to the various clinical, educational, and training approaches that have been provided within correctional institutions. Some of these efforts focus on improved behavioral adjustment. Others emphasize developing self-respect and social responsibility. Still others target the need for marketable job skills. Regardless of their specific approach, all have in common the goal of better preparing the offender for a law-abiding lifestyle on release.

But, as we will see in Chapter 9, the ability to accomplish this far-reaching goal is constrained by the very environment within which such programs are offered. Correctional institutions are notorious for the negative impact they have on those confined. Even the most humane, progressive institutions are, in the final analysis, just that—institutions. They are not rehabilitation centers. They are not job training facilities. They are not personal treatment programs. They are, first and foremost, institutions—where residents are closed off from normal relationships, unable to make even the most minor personal decisions, and pressured by others to fit into the inmate society and conform to its "informal code" of conduct. For many, prison reinforces rather than reduces antisocial tendencies. As a result, it is perhaps not surprising that so many offenders return to a life of crime, but rather, more surprising why some do not.

It is to this issue of life after confinement that Chapter 10 is devoted—considering such issues as how well institutional regimentation prepares one for success after release; how likely former inmates are to recidivate; and how the shift from the medical model to the justice model has influenced the nature of parole in terms of release criteria, time served, and postrelease supervisory practices.

Exploring this transition from confinement, it becomes apparent that a society reassured by incapacitation is unlikely to welcome the reintegration of those same offenders back into the community. But that is exactly where more than 99 percent are eventually returning. And it is when they are released that the public must confront the issue of how prudent it is to dismiss long-term solutions for a short-term sense of security.

Endnote

1.   Roy King, *The Rise and Rise of Supermax: A Solution in Search of a Problem* (in progress), cited in "Contemporary Issues in Prison Management," *Training Manual: NIC Executive Training for New Wardens*, Longmont, Colorado: National Institute of Corrections, 2000.

CHAPTER 7

INSTITUTIONAL PROCEDURES: CUSTODY

> **❝** The clanging of the metal doors to the main entrance . . . is unlike any sound you have ever heard. It is loud, heavy and harsh. An exclamation point hammering home the fact that you are now inside a prison.[1] **❞**
>
> —Grace L. Wojda, et al.

Chapter Overview

Providing *safety, security,* and *preventing escapes* are the major functions of custodial institutions. This requires such practices as counting, controlling movement, conducting searches, staffing tower observation points, regulating contact with the outside, and managing inmate behavior. Some inherent restrictions are built into the physical plant itself. Others result from custodial procedures implemented by staff. All emphasize maintaining compliance with rules and regulations. When such compliance is not achieved, the results can be disastrous—ranging from escapes or violent assaults to riots or other disturbances. But custodial features represent only one aspect of maintaining institutional control. Often overlooked are the more informal, noncoercive controls emerging from the relationship established between correctional officers and the inmate population.

For many years, the fact that those dealing directly with the inmates have significant potential for achieving a positive impact on their behavior was largely overlooked. But it has now become clear that operational staff are perhaps even more influential than treatment staff because of their continuous interaction with those incarcerated. Like the teachers a child encounters at school, treatment personnel play a major role. But teachers cannot completely replace the impact of the family, with whom the child interacts more intimately on a daily basis. In a correctional institution, it is the operational staff who are to some extent the inmate's surrogate "family"—whose firm-but-fair supervisory style can go far toward creating a more receptive environment for treatment.

This recognition of a broader role for line staff began the transition from punitive, rule-enforcement "guards" to the modern concept of "correctional officers" whose responsibilities extend beyond custody toward establishing a genuine relationship based on mutual respect. That does not mean overlooking security measures, but rather, developing the type of respectful relationship that is more likely to produce enough voluntary compliance to reduce the need to rely exclusively on coercive techniques. With even the most efficient custodial procedures, it is difficult to control those who do not voluntarily consent to be controlled. Thus, in the long term, developing effective working relationships not only promotes treatment but serves security objectives as well. It is this combination of conventional control and informal influence that best enables an institution to achieve its custodial mandate.

Learning Goals

Do you know:

1. The primary function of custody?
2. The operational objectives of custody?
3. What impact custodial security has on treatment effectiveness?

Functions of Custody

The primary function of custody is to provide *external control* for those who do not have sufficient internal controls to function effectively in free society. Ideally, custody should provide only that amount of external control which is immediately necessary. It is for this reason that correctional institutions function at various levels of security—from minimum to maximum. Even for those who are initially assigned to a high-security classification, the level of control can be reduced gradually for those who increasingly demonstrate the ability to function on their own as they better internalize self-control.

While correctional facilities represent the ultimate form of control, less restrictive social controls also are maintained by many other institutions in society, such as the family, schools, churches, and civic organizations. It is through these institutions that we learn morals, values, and socially acceptable behavior. But when the socializing influences of these other institutions fail, correctional control takes over.

Purposes of Custody

Custodial procedures are designed to control individual behavior for the overall well-being of the institution. More specifically, the immediate *operational objectives of custody* are to:

- Prevent *escape*
- Maintain *order and safety*
- Promote *efficient functioning* of the facility

In the long term, the types of behavioral restraints involved in maintaining custody also are designed to shape the offender's behavior upon reentry into society. Undoubtedly, other programs offered during confinement—counseling, vocational training, work release, and the like—contribute significantly to this long-term goal. But it is custody that enables such programs to function.

Custody/Treatment Relationships

Referring back to the previous discussion of Maslow's hierarchy of needs, it is apparent that at least some minimal level of physiological well-being, safety, and security must be established before higher-level motivations can be fulfilled. In more practical terms, it is difficult, if not impossible, to develop meaningful programs when work schedules are "frequently interrupted by violence" or classrooms become "battlegrounds." [2] If an inmate is constantly concerned about self-protection and institutional disruption, the appropriate environment for working, learning, or changing behavior is simply lacking. As one officer put it: "Security doesn't mean keep them from going over the wall. It means you try to make the guy feel secure, that he's not going to get killed or hurt. . . . So he doesn't have to worry about something happening. . . . If they want to go out, they'll find a way. It's not that kind of security." [3]

There is, in fact, a "correlation between good security and good inmate programming," and blending the two creates a system that is "responsive to the needs of both inmates and staff." [4] Most staff "realize that effective programs cannot exist in a disorderly, dangerous institution. . . . [and] that offering a variety of institutional programs actually helps them manage the institution more effectively." [5] In short, custody and treatment go hand in hand.

Even under the best of conditions, correctional institutions are far from the ideal environment for the implementation of meaningful treatment programs. But in those facilities where basic control is absent, treatment faces a formidable obstacle. On the other hand, the most secure institution might keep the inmates closely confined to their cells. But that would make it next to impossible to provide effective inmate programming. Nor does such restriction prepare inmates for the interaction with others who they inevitably encounter when released. Consequently, the institution is faced with finding the appropriate balance between program operations and security needs.

Security Techniques

Correctional facilities seek to achieve this balance in different ways. In part, emphasis will depend on the security classification of the institution. Certainly, more freedoms and opportunities for program participation are available in minimum-security facilities. However, that does not mean that services must be sacrificed to achieve custodial security. To the contrary, *custody* is a necessary condition for *treatment*.[6]

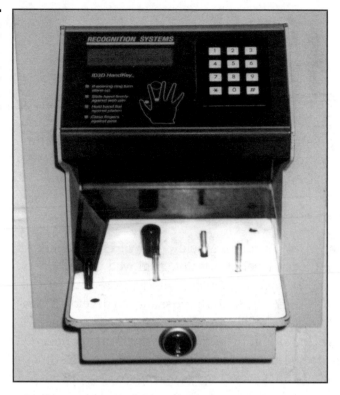

Even with the most sophisticated electronic devices, such as biometric recognition, security is primarily dependent on the men and women who make the system work. Courtesy of Tamms, Illinois, Correctional Center, a supermax facility.

Custody is achieved in part through the architectural features and security hardware of the *physical plant* itself. But even the most architecturally sound institution designed for the highest level of security also requires such *control procedures* as separation, restricted movement, counts, searches, and the regulation of everything from visiting and correspondence to tools and property. Throughout the remainder of this chapter, we will see how physical features, combined with control techniques, function together to maintain custodial security.

Learning Goals

Do you know:

1. How security is incorporated into the physical design of a correctional institution?
2. What external-security features prevent unauthorized entrance or exit?
3. How such high-tech procedures as biometric recognition can improve security?
4. What "double door" security and "vulnerability analysis" are?

Architectural Design

The physical design of a correctional facility largely reflects its philosophy. As an example, look at the forbidding prison "fortresses" surrounded by thick, impenetrable concrete walls that were built before the turn of the century. The

cold, uninviting atmosphere of such a sternly institutional structure immediately communicates a morbid impression of the prison as a symbol of punishment.

Although prison architecture has progressed beyond such harsh origins, the need to incorporate *security* remains a primary consideration. The challenge now has become integrating the "dual mission" of treatment and security into facility design.[7] In addition, the American Correctional Association has established certain minimum standards that institutions seeking ACA accreditation are required to meet. Although the internal and external security measures built into prisons today may be somewhat more subtle, upon entering a prison, there is little doubt about where you are. For an inside account of the impact of prison security on a newly arriving visitor, see the next "Close-up On Corrections."

External Security

Simply by looking at the external physical plant, it is often possible to determine the security classification of a correctional institution. The higher the security classification, the more specific "reminders" there will be of the institution's custodial function.

As noted earlier, maximum-security institutions traditionally have had a perimeter composed of high walls. Building miles and miles of walls around a prison compound, however, has become extremely expensive. More recently, walls have tended to be replaced by the type of fencing common in medium-custody facilities, topped with rows of razor wire for added security. Beyond

Close-up On Corrections

Welcome to Lebanon

More than the miles of razor-sharp concertina wire that surround the institution, more than the guard towers that loom over the compound, it is the clanging of the three-inch thick steel doors that defines what life is like inside the prison.

In some respects, your first view of Lebanon is disappointing. There's no shoving and pushing going on. Nobody is manacled. The inmates don't march in lock step; the officers don't even carry guns. In fact, it all seems pretty tame.

But a senior correctional officer quickly puts things into focus. "This is not a boys' camp," he says, "You never forget what they're here for." Adds another officer, "You can't totally relax in here. If you do, you're a fool." . . .

Tuesday is laundry day. . . . In the space of 35 minutes, all 2,000 inmates walk the length of the prison, deposit their old sheets and pillowcases in large hampers, pickup clean linen, and head back to their cells. It is the single biggest mass movement among the inmates that takes place at Lebanon, and it presents . . . security problems.

During the exchange, inmates are required—as always—to walk along the right-hand wall. . . . The sheets are . . . folded and placed over the left shoulder, allowing the officer to watch the inmates' hands and ensure that no weapons or contraband are being transported.

The most obvious security problem, however, is the simple fact that 2,000 inmates are in one place at one time. That's a lot of men to watch.

Source: Grace L. Wojda, Raymond, G. Wojda, Norman Erik Smith, and Richard K. Jones, *Behind Bars*, Laurel, Maryland: American Correctional Association, 1990, pp. 1-3, 11.

keeping prisoners inside, a wall or fence also serves to reduce the passage of contraband into the institution.

At various points throughout the perimeter, guard towers are located, sometimes surrounded by bulletproof glass and equipped with search lights. From these towers, armed officers with binoculars constantly survey the area for signs of disturbances, escapes, or anything else that is out of the ordinary. In fact, it has been said that "if there is any doubt as to the nature of the institution . . . the inmate may merely glance at the walls. The tower guard symbolizes the stern hand of the community that has placed him in exile."[8]

In addition, ground posts may be situated between towers on the outside perimeter. These are staffed during times when there is low visibility from the towers, such as during fogs or storms. In some very high-security facilities, ground sensors—designed to sound an alarm or alert personnel when activated—also may be installed in areas inside the perimeter fences that are off-limits.

Internal Security

The entrance to a correctional facility (called the sallyport) is secured by a series of locked gates, with passage in and out controlled by the officer on duty. Search procedures for those entering the compound will vary according to the security classification of the prison. However, even prisons with the same security level may vary the intensity of searches according to the particular administrative policy of the institution. Procedures range from a superficial "frisk" to the use of a metal detector or even the inspectroscope equipment used to screen carry-on baggage for airline security. The difficulty with the metal detector is, of course, that a belt buckle, a money clip, or a pocket full of change can set it off. But the greater limitation in terms of its use in corrections is that while it can detect metal weapons, it does not identify such nonmetallic contraband items as drugs.

Once inside, the physical plant is constructed to limit and monitor movement throughout the compound. In addition to the ground posts and guard towers, this can be accomplished through closed-circuit TV monitors, centralized locking devices, control booths, alarms, magnetic data strips, and computer-controlled door access.[9] However, it will not be long before existing methods of electronic security are surpassed by *biometric recognition*—use of various parts of the body (for example, retina, voice, fingerprints, and so forth) to confirm personal identification.[10] For an inside look at some of the sophisticated technology that increasingly will be used to maintain security, *see* the next "Close-up On Corrections."

Not all facilities have such high-tech equipment, but virtually every maximum or medium security institution will have a system of *double door security* monitored from control booths, whereby no two consecutive doors or gates can be opened at the same time. Movement therefore occurs sequentially, from one security post to the next, with the rear gate always closing behind you before the upcoming gate is opened. In this way, if a disturbance occurs during movement, it can be separated from the rest of the population, or one entire area of the compound can be closed off to keep an uprising from spreading further.

Vulnerability Analysis

All of these security features—from external hardware to internal rules and regulations—function together to promote the custodial security of the institution. They help to assure that those who are not authorized to do so neither come in nor get out. But at an even more sophisticated level, *vulnerability analysis* now has enabled techniques employed to protect the homeland security of military and domestic assets to be adapted to the correctional environment. Using both performance and policy-compliance measures, this unique technique defines threats and identifies potential vulnerabilities, actually putting a quantifiable number on the level of risks in the physical-protection system:

> The key to an effective vulnerability analysis program is to evaluate staff compliance with policy and the performance of security systems (both physical and human). . . . Sound correctional policies and procedures are the foundation for institutional security, but an ongoing assessment of staff and system performance is necessary to ensure the safety of staff, inmates, and the public.[11]

TECHNOLOGICAL ADVANCES IN THE NEW CENTURY

In the area of inmate identification, a variety of applications will be available. Retina imaging and scanning will be faster and more reliable. . . . Barcoded wristbands, access cards with magnetic data stripes, and enhanced use of video cameras will . . . enable staff to control, track, and record movements within the institution. Electronic bracelets . . . make it possible to determine the wearer's exact position. . . .

Ingenious new technologies also will aid in detecting contraband and illicit activity. Vastly improved X-ray capabilities will detect weapons, explosives, and other contraband. . . . Highly sensitive air-sampling equipment placed in prison ventilation systems will be able to detect the presence of drugs or explosives. Thermal-imaging, night-vision eyewear will hold out the possibility of running more secure institutions with a minimum of light. Staff will be able to see, but inmates in unauthorized areas will not. . . .

Electronic keys, meanwhile, promise to make it more difficult than ever for inmates to successfully tamper with locking devices. Electromagnetic locks will make such tampering virtually impossible. . . .

Variable-threat lasers will be able to detect and track an escaping inmate and escalate the response until the inmate stops. First, a warning to stop would be issued to an inmate detected by the laser system to be approaching a restricted area; then, a laser burst would be directed at the inmate's eyes to cause momentary blindness; that would be followed by a laser blast that would physically stun the inmate, and if the inmate kept advancing, a fatal laser blast would be issued. . . .

Video conferencing will reduce the number of times inmates will have to be escorted out of an institution. . . . Telemedicine technology will drastically reduce the need for transporting inmates to community medical facilities. . . . Virtual reality technology will be used to train correctional officers . . . enabling them to respond to escapes, medical emergencies, and disturbances from the relative comfort of the classroom . . . helping staff stay one step ahead of inmates.

Source: John W. Roberts, "Yesterday and Tomorrow—Prison Technology in 1900 and 2000," *Corrections Today*, Vol. 57, No. 4, July 1995, pp. 118-120.

 Learning Goals

Do you know:

1. The purpose of segregating inmates?
2. The difference between protective custody, administrative segregation, and disciplinary segregation?

Control Procedures

Even the best and most modern physical plant represents only part of what is needed for secure custodial control. The structure and hardware work hand in hand with the people and procedures used to ensure institutional security. Electronic gadgetry cannot replace the need for operational procedures that provide further controls within the physical structure. As correctional administrators have cautioned, it is not the hardware that catches escapees or breaks up fights—"behind every good security system stand the people who make it work."[12] In the end, security is primarily dependent on personnel.

Facilities differ considerably with regard to the degree of operational restrictions imposed and how rigorously they are enforced. Obviously, those with high-security classifications will have the most severe restrictions and will be less tolerant of infractions. But again, even within prisons of similar custodial classification, there will be variations in terms of how extensively inmates are segregated, how strictly movement is controlled, how frequently counts and searches are conducted, how much effort is devoted to property and tool control, or how often visits are permitted. Moreover, the specific rules and regulations governing inmate behavior will vary in terms of content, enforcement, and resulting penalties. But regardless of the implementation differences, there are certain general techniques that are relatively universal.

Principles of Segregation

Just as the prison itself is physically separated from the outside world, *segregation* within the institution isolates inmates from each other. It is based on the premise that *minimizing interaction* between inmates also minimizes their opportunity for disruptive behavior—everything from planning escapes and dealing in contraband to engaging in fights and assaults.

In the most secure prisons, each inmate is confined in a separate cell. Unlike the individual living units of new-generation jails, however, the cells do not open into a dayroom to which inmates have free access. Rather, movement in and out of the cell is strictly regulated—often confined to brief periods of recreation or visiting—and always under the close supervision of a correctional officer. While such an approach serves security interests of the institution, there are trade-offs in terms of the psychological effects of isolation, as well as the limits it imposes on the development of social skills or participation in institutional programs.

With the pressures of crowding in recent years, more and more inmates are being doubled-up in cells originally intended for single occupancy. As a result, many facilities have two or more inmates in a cell, while others use the dormitory concept. Group living has definite social and psychological advantages over single-cell isolation. But here, too, there are trade-offs, since it is far more difficult to control group behavior, particularly when observation is limited to an officer occasionally passing by the cellblock on routine "patrol."

Types of Segregation

Of course, not everyone is equally capable of living amicably in a dormitory, and the weak are easy prey for the strong in such an environment. Thus, segregation also can be used to respond to problems created by group living. For instance, an inmate who fears for his safety in a dormitory can request isolation for personal protection. Some inmates are administratively assigned to protective custody, as in high-profile cases or those involving former judges, police, or correctional officers whose safety in the general population would be in jeopardy. Once someone is assigned or moved to *protective custody*, it is, however, very difficult to assimilate into (or return to) the general population, since that person now has a reputation for being unable to stand up for himself.

Administrative segregation refers to any number of reasons for which an inmate may be separated other than disciplinary infractions. Examples might include those experiencing deteriorating mental health, undergoing "mood swings," or requiring gradual reentry following hospitalization. In essence, any circumstances that call for greater attention and supervision than would be available in the general population could result in administrative segregation. In such cases, the inmate has not necessarily done anything that would be a violation of institutional rules.

In contrast, *disciplinary segregation* is used for punitive purposes in response to rule infractions. Disciplinary segregation may include various levels of supervision (ranging from "close" to "maximum"). But it is most often associated with solitary confinement. Under solitary conditions, inmates spend all but a few recreational hours in their cells. Additional privileges such as commissary and visiting also may be restricted. Inmates are confined to such conditions for a specified length of time following a disciplinary hearing (unlike administrative segregation, which is more subject to staff discretion). The function of disciplinary segregation is to isolate and control those whose behavior presents a problem for others or for the overall security of the facility.

Without violating constitutional protections, there are a relatively limited number of benefits and privileges that can be withdrawn through disciplinary action. When these have been exhausted, there may be no other alternative but to separate the offender physically, protecting others from assaults, homosexual attacks, or strong-arm tactics. Thus, segregation can be used to confine those who are threatening to others, dangerous to themselves, or in need of protective custody from other inmates.

✹ Learning Goals

Do you know:

1. In what ways movement is controlled within a correctional institution?
2. How and why periodic counts are conducted?
3. In contrast to media portrayals, how most prison escapes occur?

Controlled Movement

Another way in which inmates are physically restricted is through closely *controlled movement* within the institution. This is an important feature of custody, since every time inmates are moved—particularly in groups—there is a potential *security risk* (as noted in the laundry situation described in an earlier "Close-up"). In addition, it is essential to know where all inmates are at all times, which becomes increasingly difficult with frequent movements.

The amount of movement allowed within a facility will largely depend on the institution's security classification. In minimum-security facilities, there are few restraints—inmates are permitted to move relatively freely from their living quarters to work assignments, recreation areas, and dining halls. But maximum-security prisons reduce the potential for escapes by (among other things) closely supervising and very strictly limiting the amount of movement.

Individual Movement. In the past, a system of passes typically has been used to control movement. For example, a prisoner needing to go from a work assignment to a counselor would get a pass from a correctional officer, which would include the time of departure and designated location. The pass then would be signed by the correctional officer at the identified destination. Upon the inmate's return, the officer would note the time and fill in the pass.

This manual method of recording movement has many shortcomings. It is "time-consuming, subject to error," and potentially dangerous, since each time officers log one person's transfer, they are "temporarily unable to keep a close watch on other inmates."[13] More recently, a modern high-tech approach that automatically records all transfers has become available as an alternative to the pass system. Each inmate wears a bracelet which contains a bar code that is scanned at various locations throughout the facility whenever the inmate is moved. Like the bar code system used at supermarket checkout counters, an electronic scanning device produces a printout that records precisely when and where the inmate was moved throughout the day. In fact, the same system can be used to obtain books from the library or to charge items purchased at the commissary to an inmate's account.[14]

External Transportation. To limit the need for transportation outside prisons, most large institutions provide as many services as possible within the compound. For example, through the use of "telemedicine," medical professionals

Often inmates need to be transported from jail to prison, to court, or to medical or other appointments in the community. Specially designed buses are used for this purpose. Courtesy of the Miami-Dade County Department of Corrections and Rehabilitation, Miami, Florida.

have been able to confer with inmate patients without ever setting foot in the facility or transporting the inmate. (*See* the next "Close-up On Corrections.") Judges likewise can conduct various types of proceedings through two-way video monitoring. In fact, some correctional facilities even have installed video visitation systems,[15] and others treat mentally ill inmates through "telepsychiatry." [16] However, there will always be a need for some *external movement* to transport inmates to other correctional facilities, hospitals, trials, funerals, and so on.

Although staff do not carry weapons while supervising inmates within the facility, those transporting inmates to the outside almost always are armed. The inmates themselves are restrained by handcuffs, which are sometimes attached to waist chains. Leg irons also may be used to control a prisoner's stride and eliminate a foot race.

All outside trips must be well planned. If, for instance, an inmate is being transported to a hospital or funeral parlor, the local police should be contacted in advance to verify the relative's illness or death. The precise route should be determined carefully and scheduled, with law enforcement officials notified if additional police protection is needed. In particularly dangerous situations, a "chase" vehicle may follow the transporting vehicle to provide backup assistance in case an escape is attempted.

But aside from the ever-present threat of a setup or escape attempt, perhaps the greatest danger of outside movement is staff complacency when such assignments are viewed as boring routines.[19] Given the risks, costs, and labor involved, it is not surprising to find more and more correctional agencies contracting with private companies for transportation services.

Close-up On Corrections

TELEMEDICINE IN ACTION

In 1995, a Colorado Department of Corrections inmate was transported from a state correctional facility to a Denver hospital for a follow-up appointment related to an earlier knee injury. During the trip to the hospital, he managed to release himself from his restraints. . . . When the vehicle arrived and the deputies opened the door, the inmate bolted, knee injury notwithstanding. He sprinted through the hospital parking lot and escaped into a residential neighborhood, and has not been seen since. His timing in this escape was fortuitous, since in early 1997, his correctional facility implemented a telemedicine program which would have eliminated the need to transport him off-site.

Telemedicine involves linking primary care and specialty doctors with inmates via video or other electronic media for selected medical consultations, which eliminates the need to transport some inmates to an outside medical facility. Telemedicine can be used to increase access to health care, (particularly in remote areas), improve access to specialists, and provide faster diagnosis and treatment.

The overall impact of this technology falls into three categories:

- *Cost*: If the savings in transportation outweigh the cost of the telemedicine equipment and its operation, the facility realizes an economic benefit. One projection of these costs and benefits for eight different types of facilities found annual net savings potentially as high as $45,000.[17] Another study reported the cost of a conventional consultation with a specialist at approximately $108, compared with $71 using telemedicine—a $37 difference which adds up to $44,400 in annual savings for a facility with 100 monthly consultations.[18]

- *Quality of care*: The issue of cost savings also involves more subjective measures of service quality. For example, some facilities use telemedicine to replace some of their existing medical staff, thus attempting to maintain the current level of service at a lower per-inmate cost. Others augment existing staff by using it to provide access to more specialized expertise, thus attempting to increase the level of service at a similar cost.

- *Security*: An inherent advantage of telemedicine is that it allows the facility to keep the inmate in custody, thereby reducing escape vulnerability.

Telemedicine even has been used to improve the management of inmates needing mental health services. It also entails a number of intangible benefits—for example, one facility in Virginia which now provides cardiology-related care through telemedicine has noticed a reduced number of chest pain complaints because inmates know they no longer will be taken off-site for diagnosis.

Sources: Compiled from Kevin Raines, Joni Toenjes, and Allan Liebgott, "Telemedicine . . . It's not Just for Rural Jails," *American Jails*, May/June 1998, pp. 9-21; Mark F. Fitzgibbons and Tracy Gunter-Justice, "Telemedicine and Mental Health in Jails: A New Tool for an Old Problem," *Corrections Today*, Vol. 62, No. 6, October 2000, pp. 104-107; and Barbara Drazga, "Telemedicine and Corrections," *Correctional News*, July/August 2000, p. 43. *See also* "Telemedicine Can Reduce Correctional Health Care Costs: An Evaluation of a Prison Telemedicine Network," available online at http://www.ncjrs.org/telemedicine/toc.html.

Conducting Counts

The purpose of restrictions on inmate movement is naturally to keep track of precisely where everyone is at all times. The location of inmates is also confirmed periodically through *headcounts*. In the past, counts were only able to be conducted physically by correctional officers. But here, too, technology now exists in terms of a sensor device worn like a wristwatch that not only has an automated headcount feature but also can be used by the inmate to signal for help in a dangerous situation.[20]

Counts are one of the most important functions of custody. Because the count is so significant, other activities stop when it is conducted. Inmates may be required to stand in order to be properly identified. But regardless of the specific procedures employed, officers must be extremely careful to identify each inmate personally. Assuming, for instance, that a bulky form under blankets on a bed is actually the cell's occupant gives an escaping inmate valuable time until the next count is conducted. On the other hand, inefficient counting which erroneously indicates that an inmate is missing can cause serious disruption of normal institutional operations while a needless recount or search is mounted. Any count that does not match the number on the official roster (whether over or under) results in everyone being "locked down" in the living units while a rapid recheck is made and another full count is conducted. If the discrepancy still exists, emergency search procedures are activated.

Escapes

Having exactly the right number of inmates in custody at any given time is critical to every correctional institution. Any fewer than there should be results in activating an escape alarm, notifying appropriate law enforcement agencies, and closing down normal operations while an extensive search is mounted. For a firsthand account of the adrenalin-pumping response to a missing inmate, *see* the next "Close-up On Corrections."

The overdramatized television and movie accounts of prison breakouts would lead us to believe that escapes are accompanied by elaborate plotting, high suspense, and violent outcomes. But in real life, escape attempts take many forms. In one case, a telephone call from a "probation officer" requested the release of a prisoner, but a return call to the officer indicated that no such request had been made. The prisoner himself was discovered telephoning from the institution's pay phone.

Many escape attempts are simply "walk-aways," often in conjunction with visiting, outside work assignments, or a low level of institutional security. While there are few escapes from inside the walls of high-security facilities, those are the ones that make the headlines. But as shown in Figure 7.1, almost all escapes are from minimum-security facilities or in conjunction with furloughs, work release, or home confinement.

Most are eventually apprehended.[21] Although escapees do not generally avoid capture for very long, there are always the isolated exceptions. For example, one man who escaped in 1957 from an Alabama prison (where he was sentenced to a fourteen-year term for stealing pigs) was discovered living in Detroit some forty-five years later—although Alabama officials were no longer

Close-up On Corrections

interested in reincarcerating him.[22] Today, chances of eluding the authorities are not as great. With the numerous "electronic bulletin boards" available in recent years through such nationally broadcast television programs as *America's Most Wanted*, the high visibility given to dangerous escapees assists in their recapture.

Learning Goals

Do you know:

1. What types of searches are conducted in a correctional institution?
2. The definition of contraband?
3. Under what conditions cells can be searched?
4. The differences between frisk, strip, and body-cavity searches?

Contraband, Searches, and Equipment Control

The type of search resulting from an escape extends throughout the institution as well as to the outside community. But other more restricted searches are conducted within the facility on a daily basis. These can include both *cell searches* and *personal (body) searches*.

Searches of cells or dormitories (generally referred to as "shakedowns") are conducted routinely, with frequency depending on the facility's security level. The purpose of conducting cell searches is to detect contraband. It therefore stands to reason that the searches should not be so routinely scheduled that inmates are well aware of when they will occur.

Contraband

Contraband consists of any item (or quantity of items) that is *not authorized within the institution* or an authorized item that is *altered from its original state*. For example, a certain amount of food may be permitted in one's cell, but hoarding large amounts would be prohibited. A normally authorized item that has been altered could be something as simple as a pen or a plastic eating

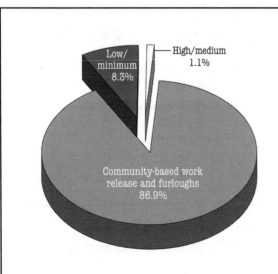

figure 7.1

Low/minimum 8.3%

High/medium 1.1%

Community-based work release and furloughs 86.9%

Percentage of total escapes by security level.

NOTE: The remaining 3.7 percent occurred in other types of facilities or circumstances.

Source: Camille Graham Camp, ed., *The 2002 Corrections Yearbook: Adult Corrections*, Middletown, Connecticut: Criminal Justice Institute, 2003, p. 49. Used with permission.

utensil that is melted down and sharpened into a "shank" (weapon). Some unauthorized items are traditionally forbidden in all correctional institutions, such as liquor, drugs, knives, guns, or other potential weapons. But with modern technology has come new additions to contraband lists, such as the rapidly growing problem of smuggling cell phones.[23]

Facilities vary widely, however, in terms of what is and is not considered contraband. Some go so far as to prohibit such seemingly innocent things as family photos. Some permit inmates to keep a specified amount of money (although it would be a violation to be in possession of a quantity greater than the authorized amount). Others do not permit any money at all to discourage theft and gambling. When inmates wish to make purchases from the commissary (inmate store), the transaction is made by computerized account system through which no actual cash changes hands.

The purpose of removing contraband from the facility is to reduce the potential for escapes, fights, threats, and assaults that it creates, thereby promoting the safety and security of both inmates and staff. Moreover, dealing in contraband allows some inmates to have power over others by being the distributors of illicit resources that are in wide demand.[24] But contraband never can be eliminated completely. There are simply too many sources through which it can pass into the institution—from a kiss or embrace during visiting, to interaction with the vendor on a food delivery truck, to contact with a staff member in need of extra money.

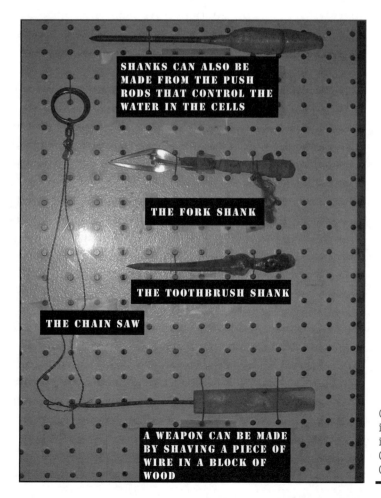

Contraband is a major security issue. Here are some contraband items taken from one prison. Courtesy of the American Correctional Association.

Cell Searches (Shakedowns)

In free society, it would generally not be legal for a police officer to search your home without a court-issued warrant based on probable cause. The right to be free from illicit searches is protected under the Fourth Amendment. But it is entirely different in a correctional facility. While inmates do not lose their Constitutional protections, they do not enjoy as much privacy because of the overriding need to maintain institutional security. Within a correctional institution, general searches can be authorized at any time without specific cause. Thus, searches may be conducted:

- *Routinely*, at certain predetermined (but unannounced) times

- *Randomly*, at undetermined, unannounced times or

- Deliberately, based on *reasonable suspicion*, such as information received from a reliable informant

Correctional officers do not need a warrant or probable cause to justify a search. But they cannot recklessly destroy property in the process of the search. Nor can searches be used to single out any particular person for harassment by, for example, continuously focusing on one person's cell to the exclusion of all others for no particular reason.

Inmates can be ingenious at finding unsuspected hiding places, particularly in the many cracks and crevices of older institutions. Conducting a thorough cell search therefore can become quite physically disruptive. Tearing apart what is for all practical purposes an inmate's "home" will create ill will if the contents are left carelessly scattered around. Moreover, it is particularly irritating if one's personal possessions were disturbed only to confiscate some insignificant item on the contraband list.

One method that has been used on occasion to uncover contraband without disrupting individual cells is to deceive inmates into discarding their own contraband. For example, sometimes an institutionwide shakedown is announced by officials, who actually begin the search but abandon it shortly thereafter. Once the search procedures start and the word spreads, inmates often will take actions to avoid being caught with contraband. They may flush homemade liquor, drugs, or illegally obtained food down the toilets, while throwing "shanks" or other items out of their cells. Needless to say, however, a pattern of fake shakedowns can create distrust and animosity (not to mention plumbing problems).

Personal Searches

Since contraband somehow must be transported to one's cell, personal *body searches* are also routine features of prison life, particularly when an inmate enters or leaves the facility. The intrusiveness of personal searches ranges from a simple frisk (or "pat down"), to an unclothed strip search, to a body-cavity search. A *frisk search* is an external inspection of a fully clothed person. It is the least intrusive, since the officer only feels exterior surfaces to determine if any items are being concealed within one's clothing, hair, shoes, and so on.

Much more intrusive is the *strip search*, in which the naked body and its cavities are visually inspected from all angles. Because strip searches can be very personally degrading, it is important to conduct them in a manner that retains as much dignity as possible.

As inmates became increasingly creative in their efforts to conceal contraband, the need for *internal body-cavity searches* emerged. In fact, body-cavity searches have yielded items ranging from drugs to ammunition, weapons, and tools. This is the most intrusive type of search. It therefore demands justification based on reasonable suspicion. Special permission from a higher authority (such as the prison warden) generally is required, and such searches can only be performed by appropriate medically trained staff. However, a recent technological innovation may one day put an end to exploratory body cavity searches. Called "the body-orifice scanning system," it enables the inmate to simply sit in a chair specially designed to detect metal contraband that is concealed internally.[25]

Learning Goals

Do you know:

1. What procedures are used to control tools and keys in correctional institutions?
2. How inmates are supervised during daily prison operations?

Tool Control

It is apparent by now that the major purpose of searches is to detect contraband. But even within the same institution, certain items generally may be regarded as contraband yet permitted under some circumstances. For example, scissors or tire irons normally would be prohibited. But it would be difficult to offer a sewing or auto repair course without such tools.

The proper control of tools is essential because of their potential use as weapons. The foundation of a tool control program is a rigid check system, with receipts kept for the tools available in shops, and a classification system used to store different types of tools. For example, tools that can cut steel (such as welding torches) must be stored in a secure area overnight. Knives used in the kitchen for food preparation can be attached to tables by wire cables.

Not all tools, however, can be immobilized. In accounting for industrial or vocational training tools, a *shadow board* is helpful. This is a sort of bulletin board on which tools are physically stored. The outline of each tool is painted on the board so that the supervisor can readily determine what pieces are missing. When tools are checked out, each inmate using any particular piece of equipment surrenders a chit with his assigned number on it and signs a receipt for the tool. If the tool is not returned, the "chit" indicates who last checked it out.

Key Control

Because keys provide the most direct access to escape, key control is of primary importance in correctional institutions. Keys inadvertently left unattended for even a few brief moments have been pressed into a bar of soap for models. Inmates have even been known to observe keys and manufacture replicas from visual recall. When a key is lost, there is no recourse but to change the locks and issue new keys to the affected areas—a time-consuming and expensive process. Of course, as electromagnetic locking devices become more prevalent, such tampering should become obsolete.

Inmate Supervision

It may seem somewhat illogical to discuss careful tool and key control when, at the same time, items such as knives and industrial scissors are available to trusties working in the prison kitchen or sewing shop. Even if these implements are controlled carefully to assure that they do not leave the area, they could be used in a stabbing attempt while in the hands of inmate workers. Naturally, careful classification screening is essential when determining such work assignments.

In addition to cautious selection, those on various work details must be closely supervised. Particularly when assignments involve work outside the prison compound, unauthorized contacts and the acquisition of contraband must be prevented. Otherwise, those on external work details can be used as a "trafficking service" in contraband items or an underground "messenger service" between other inmates and the outside. Even within the prison, certain work details can provide opportunities for graft, corruption, and contraband trading if officers do not maintain close oversight of inmate activities.

Nor is the correctional officer's responsibility limited to those engaged in work assignments. Throughout the day, the inside of the institution is supervised by operational personnel assigned to each school, factory, or shop, as well as such other areas of the prison as the infirmary, counseling offices, and recreation yard. During these assignments, officers are responsible for constantly observing all activities to detect signs of danger. It is largely through training and experience that operational staff develop the insights and intuition that alert them to the warning signs of imminent danger, as described in the next "Close-up On Corrections."

But in the final analysis, it is not so much the explicit control of staff as the implicit cooperation of inmates that enables the system to operate effectively. In that regard, the prison is completely dependent on the willingness of inmates "to leave their daytime activities and return at night to their cells for lockup. It is equally dependent on their willingness to keep their activities reasonably and delicately balanced between licit and illicit behavior."[26]

 Close-up On Corrections

Never Stop Observing

[A]n officer supervising a recreation period in the gymnasium notices that two basketball games are going on, one at each end of the court. On one end, the game consists of eight black inmates. On the other end, the players are six white inmates. An inexperienced person might observe the make-up of the two teams, watching carefully that neither game gets out of hand. Another, more experienced officer observes that same scene, however, couples that observation with his knowledge of other circumstances, and makes conclusions. He knows that for the past three months, the fourteen players have been playing together, both black and white, in the same basketball game. The officer is sensitive to any racial problems in [the] prison and is uneasy about his current observation. He also recalled reading the log from the last shift, which noted an unusual amount of racial segregation at the chow line the same day. He records his observation and notifies his shift commander. He then continues to carefully observe the inmates and their moods and interactions with each other, being extremely sensitive to any racial provocation on anyone's part.

Source: David B. Kalinich and Terry Pitcher, *Surviving in Corrections*, Springfield, Illinois: Charles C. Thomas, 1984, pp. 51-52.

Learning Goals

Do you know:

1. Why inmate contact with the outside must be restricted but not eliminated?
2. How correctional institutions limit outside contacts by phone and mail?
3. What restrictions are imposed on visits to inmates?

Contacts with the Outside

Beyond controls that restrict freedom within the compound, everyone confined to a correctional institution is subject to some degree of isolation from the rest of society. It is largely through visits, phone calls, and letters that inmates maintain ties with the community.

On the one hand, it is important to retain such communication with the outside because of its constructive influence in terms of inmate behavior and morale. External contacts help to reduce the negative impact of socializing only with other criminals day after day. They promote a more civilizing atmosphere, serve as a reminder of what life is like on the outside, and assist with eventual readjustment to society.

On the other hand, such interactions present security risks. They can facilitate both escapes and the introduction of contraband. The key is to find the proper balance between overly restricting outside contacts and overly jeopardizing institutional security. As a result, limits have been placed on phone calls, written correspondence, and visiting.

Telephone

Although all correctional institutions permit inmates to use the telephone, the number of calls authorized generally is limited according to one's security classification. Minimum-security facilities might have a centrally located telephone for all to use with few restrictions. In contrast, medium and maximum custody are more likely to involve individual arrangements for telephone access, such as using modular outlets to enable a phone to be moved into cells during designated times.

Since many of the calls inmates make are long-distance, it is essential for the institution to avoid being held accountable for individual phone bills. Some facilities employ a process of placing phone charges on the inmate's commissary account. In others, phones are designed to accommodate only collect calls. But those in prison often demonstrate a great deal of creative ingenuity in circumventing even the most sophisticated systems.

Mail

Since prisoners do not have the immediate convenience of e-mailing or picking up the phone, written correspondence is of great importance to them. Anyone who has ever been away from home in an unfamiliar environment for an extended period of time can appreciate how much letters from family help to ease loneliness, tension, and anxiety.

In the past, all incoming mail and packages were very closely scrutinized—to the point of censorship. Arbitrary censorship has now been replaced by practices that can be justified on the basis of institutional security, such as inspection for contraband. As prison populations expanded, it became increasingly difficult and labor-intensive to read and censor all correspondence. In some institutions, the inspection of mail may be limited to a spot-check for contraband. Of course, letters from attorneys, judges, or other government officials cannot be either censored or read. However, inmates may be required to open such correspondence in the presence of a correctional officer if transmission of contraband is suspected.

Visiting Policies

During the initial intake process, approved visiting and correspondence lists are made up for each inmate. Visiting lists generally will be more limited than those approved for written correspondence. Immediate family members are almost always approved, and one's attorney can visit at any time. Other relatives and friends may need further justification, particularly in maximum-security institutions.

In addition to who can visit, prisons regulate how often they can come. Again, the number of visits allowed may depend on custody classification. Moreover, a

Inmates who retain links with their families have an easier transition back to the community. Here an inmate reads with his daughter during visitation at the Monroe Correctional Complex in Washington. Courtesy of Volunteers of America.

severely crowded facility may need to further restrict the frequency of visits simply because of operational inability to manage the necessary movements.

Beyond the obstacles presented by institutional regulations, it may be difficult for an inmate's family to visit when the prison is located in a rural area far from home and not accessible to public transportation. It is indeed a dedicated family member who will go to the expense, take the time, and suffer the humiliation often involved in visiting someone in prison. That is hardly conducive to maintaining family unity.

Part of the reluctance to visit those in prison relates to the abnormal atmosphere surrounding the conditions under which outside contact takes place. Privacy is virtually nonexistent. Visits are supervised and carefully monitored by uniformed correctional officers to reduce the introduction of contraband. Inmates generally are searched before and after each visit, and visitors themselves may be subject to frisk searches as well.

In very high-security situations, visitors and residents are placed in two different rooms. They are separated by a window of plate glass, with a telephone device used for communication. Visits in a lower-security environment may be conducted around long tables, with inmates sitting on one side and visitors on the other, sometimes monitored by video surveillance cameras. The least restrictive are contact visits, which permit physical contact between inmates and visitors (within specified rules). Of course, with greater visiting freedom also comes greater potential for the introduction of contraband.

Not all inmates are granted contact visits. The video visiting booths at the Pinellas County Visitation Center reduce the need for staff involvement and eliminate contraband problems. Courtesy of Datapoint, Inc.

Learning Goals

Do you know:

1. Why some states permit conjugal visits?
2. The advantages and disadvantages of conjugal visiting?
3. What furloughs are designed to accomplish?

Conjugal Visits

Even the most liberal and informal visiting procedures cannot replace the intimacy of heterosexual relationships. Confinement in prison can severely strain a marriage and actually represents grounds for divorce in a number of states. Some believe that sexual deprivations are to be expected as an inherent part of the punishment function of incarceration. Others express concern about the promotion of homosexual activities when the legitimate expression of basic sexual drives is denied.

In response to such concerns, several states have authorized inmates to participate in conjugal visits. Unsupervised visits from members of the opposite sex have been common in a number of South American and Scandinavian countries. But the more conservative nature of North American sexual and social attitudes has restrained their development in the United States.

Although it was not openly admitted, conjugal visiting has actually been available in American prisons from time to time on an informal basis. South Carolina initiated such visits in the late nineteenth century, and Mississippi started the practice informally at the state penitentiary in Parchman early in the twentieth century. Over the years, several other states did likewise, but currently, only five states have retained conjugal visiting.[27]

Studies have found that conjugal visiting has a significant positive effect on family stability, as well as a significant negative effect on involvement in prison violence.[28] Other advantages of conjugal visits include fewer pressures to engage in homosexuality, improved morale, and a strengthening of family bonds. The potential loss of conjugal visiting privileges is also a strong restraint on behavior. But these visits are not without drawbacks. For one thing, if visits are limited to married inmates, everyone will not qualify, and the provocation of seeing others participate may promote homosexuality among those who are ineligible. Additionally, some wives may not participate for a variety of reasons, particularly if the process is viewed as degrading. Even if it is handled in a sensitive manner, the pain of subsequent separation may override any immediate benefits.[29] Participants also are faced with issues surrounding pregnancies and sexually transmitted disease.

For the correctional institution, both administrative and operational issues are involved. Administratively, there are concerns surrounding the verification of marriages and the question of whether to accept common-law relationships. Operationally, potential problems include the difficulty of controlling contraband and enforcing appropriate behavior, along with resentment on the part of those who do not have access to conjugal visits.[30] Thus, the question becomes whether the benefits outweigh the risks. For more insights into the answer, *see* the point/counterpoint debate in the next "Close-up On Corrections."

Furloughs

Many correctional administrators who are opposed to conjugal visits favor the use of *furloughs* instead. Essentially, furloughs involve a brief period of *temporary release*—often over a weekend—with the understanding that the prisoner will return to the institution at a specified time. Because a large portion of those incarcerated are single or divorced, more inmates will qualify for furloughs. Moreover, the emphasis with furloughs is on broader social reintegration rather than the exclusive sexual focus of conjugal visits. Another benefit is that rather than seeing their parent in a prison setting, children can interact with mom or dad at home during furloughs.

Offering inmates temporary freedom does, however, entail obvious dangers. Although efforts are made to select those awarded furloughs carefully, there is always the possibility that the desire to live on the outside again will be too great to resist. Absconding is generally not as great a problem as might be expected, since there is considerable pressure from other inmates to abide by the rules so that the privilege is not revoked for everyone. In fact, only about 1 percent of furloughs result in either escape or commission of a new crime.[31]

But there is always the potential of awarding a furlough to someone who does not have sufficient self-control to avoid becoming involved in crime. This concern was propelled into a major national issue that affected the 1988 presidential election when an inmate who was granted a weekend pass in Massachusetts (Willie Horton) engaged in a series of violent crimes that ultimately reflected upon the campaign of former Governor Michael Dukakis.[32]

As a result of the public outcry following the Horton case, a number of correctional administrators implemented much more restrictive measures governing furlough eligibility. The tightening of furloughs following this public backlash created a situation of "zero tolerance"—similar to reducing the driving

Close-up On Corrections

Conjugal Visits . . . A Matter of Logic

Besides preparing inmates for re-entry, private family visits can also maintain and strengthen family bonds. At the same time, such visits are a behavior management program that rewards positive behavior among inmates. . . .

For many now drug-free inmates, this may be the first time they are accepting their parental responsibilities. Thus, although parents and children living for a few days in a motel-type setting on the prison grounds or furloughed to a nearby motel may be a very artificial setting, such visits could begin to address some of the problems that every family must solve to function properly.

[A review of] all previous studies on visitation concluded that an inmate who receives visits is six times less likely to recidivate. . . . Besides the family, private family visits can be beneficial to prison administration and staff by providing inmates incentive to follow prison rules. Such a program is by far one of the best ways to reward positive inmate behavior.

Source: Charles Sullivan, "Private Family Visits are A Matter of Logic," *Corrections Today*, Vol. 65, No. 3, June 2003, p. 18.

Costs Outweigh Benefits

Instead of promoting healthy family bonding, the unsupervised nature of conjugal visits may actually lead to an increased risk to the physical safety of family members in some cases. . . . Supervised visitation that enables interaction in a more secure environment may better serve families involved in such dysfunctional relationships. . . .

[Moreover], conjugal visitation increases the risk of spreading sexually transmitted diseases by an already identified high-risk population. . . . States that have initiated such visitation programs are forced to address the tough moral and ethical dilemma of permitting conjugal visitation for offenders known to be infected. . . .

Conjugal visitation also presents an ethical dilemma by increasing the chance of pregnancy when the incarcerated partner often lacks the ability to provide financial and emotional support to the partner and resulting child. Children born as the result of conjugal visitation are denied important emotional bonding with the incarcerated parent. . . .

The high-risk nature of conjugal visitation also makes it an expensive program when providing for necessary security precautions. [Additionally, there is] a disinclination of the public to accept programs that provide extra privileges to convicted felons at a cost to the taxpayer . . . a public demand for limiting all extraneous inmate privileges.

Source: Reginald A. Wilkinson, "The Cost of Conjugal Visitation Outweighs the Benefits," *Corrections Today*, Vol. 65, No. 3, June 2003, p. 19.

speed limit to ten miles per hour to prevent traffic crashes. While their use began to increase in a number of states by the 1990s,[33] even the designation of "furlough" has changed to "transitional control," presumably in an effort to portray an unpopular practice in a more positive light.

Nevertheless, research indicates that participation in furloughs "appears to have a pronounced and consistent positive impact on lowered recidivism."[34] Like conjugal visits, they are not without risks. A reasonable compromise must be found between an excessively liberal furlough policy that completely disregards public safety and overly restrictive practices that deny the benefits of social interaction to virtually everyone except a handful of the most model prisoners.

 Learning Goals

Do you know:

1. What types of rules and regulations govern inmate conduct?
2. What disciplinary procedures are employed when an inmate violates the rules?
3. What rights inmates have when facing severe disciplinary action?
4. What sanctions can be imposed for rule violations?

Institutional Rules and Discipline

All of the procedures discussed thus far—from segregating prisoners within the institution to restricting their contacts with the outside—are designed to control inmate behavior. Not all prisons are so rigidly controlled. All do, however, have provisions for shaping individual behavior for the benefit of the overall population. As we saw with movement, counts, and outside contacts, these provisions will be more relaxed in minimum-security facilities. But inmates in higher-custody classifications presumably lack the self-control necessary to constrain their own behavior. Therefore, they must be constrained by external restrictions.

The purpose of institutional rules and regulations is to provide the *guidelines regulating conduct* through which an effort is made to achieve *orderly group life*. While institutional regulations compel compliance within the prison, resulting frustrations can be counterproductive to reintegration. If one's prison experience was embittering and degrading, bottled-up hostilities may be unleashed as soon as institutional controls are removed. Recognition of these drawbacks, however, does not negate the need for correctional facilities to control behavior through rules and regulations during confinement.

Rules and Regulations

One of the first things that a newly arriving inmate receives upon initial reception is the rulebook outlining the "do's" and "don'ts" that are expected during confinement. Rules are designed to promote one's adjustment to the institutional routine and thereby maintain order. The nature of inmate rules will vary depending on the size and security classification of the facility. But virtually all institutions will have at least some general rules governing such things as:

- *Inmate-officer relationships* (addressing employees respectfully; immediately obeying orders issued by officers)

- *Relationships with other inmates* (no fighting, assaults, homosexual behavior, or conspiring with other inmates)

- *Prohibited activities* (no profanity, gambling, trafficking, bartering, trading, attempting escape, running, and so forth)

- *Prohibited items* (no unauthorized items that are designated as contraband)

- *Personal hygiene/grooming* (requirements regarding personal attire and cleanliness)

- *Outside contacts* (mail, phone, and visiting restrictions)

- *Overall institutional regulations* (prohibited areas of the compound; personal property limitations; disciplinary and grievance procedures; the schedule of daily routines governing eating, sleeping, and so forth)

In addition to these general rules, some institutions extend regulations to very precise details. But the longer and more complex the list of rules, the more difficult they are to enforce. Additionally, the more rules are viewed as petty harassments, the more likely they are to be violated. On the one hand, too much rigidity can promote resistance. On the other hand, too little regulation can produce confusion and lack of control.

Rule Enforcement

Whatever the institution's specific rules are, it is up to the operational staff to assure that they are being observed, and if not, to deal with infractions. How firmly regulations are enforced will vary considerably, depending on the institution, the situation, and the particular officer involved. Ultimately, it is through both formal disciplinary measures (in other words, rule enforcement) and informal communication that a process for managing inmate behavior develops.

Correctional officers have the day-to-day authority to enforce rules. That does not mean that they have the power to inflict formal punishment for disciplinary infractions. Operational staff have some limited authority to handle minor misconduct. Major violations, however, are "written up" on official *disciplinary action reports* and submitted through the organizational chain of command.

Typically, major violations in prisons involve gambling, sexual activities, fighting, and assaults. Anything involving physical harm or a major security violation is most likely to be officially referred for formal disciplinary action. But as the employee guidelines of one prison state, "Minor matters of discipline, where no danger to life, security or property exists, shall be handled quietly and routinely." [35]

Disciplinary Procedures

When a major infraction is reported, upper-level command staff must determine if further action is warranted. If so, the inmate is afforded a hearing before either a *hearing examiner* or a *disciplinary (or hearing) committee*. While some institutional committees are drawn from the ranks of custodial, treatment, and/or classification staff, the current trend is to invoke the services of an outside hearing examiner. This has developed in response to concerns that using staff in disciplinary proceedings is inherently biased against the inmate, tending to favor institutional concerns. The outside hearing examiner is viewed as more impartial. Additionally, committees also can take up excessive staff time. Since the hearing examiner is only one person, the process is more cost effective. It also enables the examiner to concentrate on the cases at hand, rather than viewing the hearing as an inconvenience added to one's regularly scheduled job.

In the past, inmates had no universally recognized due process rights during disciplinary hearings. In fact, correctional administrators were free to impose penalties without a hearing. Needless to say, this widespread discretion was open to potential abuse, particularly in prisons with little public oversight or administrative restraints. To assure more objective and impartial proceedings, the Supreme Court ruled that inmates are entitled to certain due process protections when facing severe disciplinary action (for example, that which would further restrict their freedom or extend their confinement). Thus, with the *Wolff v. McDonnell* [36] case (1974), inmates facing such penalties now are entitled to:

- Advance written notice of the charges

- The right to a fair and impartial hearing

- The right to present evidence and call witnesses on their behalf (when permission to do so "will not be unduly hazardous to institutional safety or correctional goals")

- Use of counsel or counsel substitute for illiterate accused persons or those who otherwise cannot understand the proceedings

- Written statement of the decision reached and the reasons for it

However, more recently in the 1995 case of *Sandin v. Conner*, the Supreme Court modified its position, no longer requiring the procedural protections outlined in *Wolff v. McDonnell* in disciplinary cases where sanctions are limited to segregation (and therefore do not affect the inmate's "liberty interest" in being free from restraint). [37]

Inmates are not legally entitled to appeal the outcome of disciplinary hearings. Nevertheless, many institutions provide for an appeal to the prison warden, and some allow appeals beyond the institution to the state director of corrections. Nor does internal disciplinary action preclude subsequent criminal prosecution. If warranted by the offense, that would not constitute double jeopardy. [38]

Disciplinary Penalties

Aside from solitary confinement or disciplinary segregation, the most severe penalty inmates can receive is loss of credits reducing the length of their sentence (for example, good time or gain time). No inmate wants to jeopardize a release date. Time credits therefore represent both a major incentive to maintain good behavior and the ultimate penalty for misconduct.

Moreover, many of the harsh punishments used in the past (such as bread-and-water diets and corporal punishment) have been ruled unconstitutional. Restricting visits, commissary privileges, recreation, and the like also must be done within legal limits. As a result, the loss of time credit is the one primary behavioral control mechanism that correctional personnel still have to induce compliance with institutional rules and regulations.

 # Learning Goals

Do you know:

1. How officers exercise formal and informal controls to regulate inmate behavior?
2. What results occur when officers either over- or underenforce institutional rules?

Inmate Management

Some inmates recognize that the rules exist largely for their own protection and therefore tend to support their enforcement. Older, long-timers who simply want to "do their time" as quietly as possible are likely to hold such cooperative attitudes. Those who are younger, recent arrivals, and more militant, however, are more likely to view institutional regulations as a form of repression and a personal challenge. When voluntary compliance is not forthcoming, it is the correctional officer's job to initiate the disciplinary process. In fact, it has been noted that "whatever else they may be," correctional officers are "primarily agents of social control." [39]

Although officers must be observant to detect violations, the responsibility of managing inmates is certainly not restricted to simple visual surveillance. If that were the case, closed-circuit television largely could replace the need for human supervision. This point was vividly made in one minimum-security institution when a perimeter fence was installed: "Staff were taken from interacting with inmates and committed to operating and monitoring a fence. Perhaps it was not surprising that the fence did not reduce the number of escapes." [40]

It is the officer's ability to *communicate verbally* that is of greatest importance—a skill that is not confined to issuing orders, but rather, one which, when used properly, establishes an *effective working relationship* with the inmate population.

Major violations are logged into daily records, documented on disciplinary action reports, and forwarded through the agency's chain of command. Photo by Joseph Fuller, II.

Rules and Relationships

Just as the rules themselves must be properly balanced between too much rigidity and too little regulation, officers also find that they must steer a middle course between severity and laxity in enforcing them. Institutional regulations represent the "tools of discipline." It takes experience, sensitivity, and training to learn how to use them properly, just as it takes practice and instruction to use any other kind of tool.

The extent to which regulations are enforced varies from institution to institution. As we saw earlier, some differences reflect the administrative style of the warden. But even within the same institution, enforcement styles can vary from one shift to another and from one officer to another. It is the administrator's job to assure that there is general enforcement consistency, which cannot be achieved simply by telling operational staff that they are expected to "fully enforce all rules at all times." Like police officers enforcing society's laws on the street, correctional officers find that it is neither possible nor practical to do so. Faced with a wide variety of regulations, many of which are ambiguous, they have a great deal of discretion in deciding what rules will be enforced, against whom, and under what circumstances.

Formal and Informal Controls

It is not only by enforcing the rule book that inmates are managed. As in free society, institutional behavior is controlled through both *rules* and *relationships*. Parents, for example, establish certain boundaries (rules) governing their children's actions. At one extreme, an excessively stern parent immediately might resort to punishment whenever a child crosses the established boundaries. At the other extreme, an overly lenient parent might avoid any type of punishment, trying instead to reason, bribe, or coax the child into compliance. In-between these extremes are those who attempt to find a reasonable compromise—developing a nurturing relationship that communicates concerned support, guiding the child toward self-restraint but resorting to some form of discipline when these informal controls do not work.

Correctional officers likewise employ a great deal of discretion in the management of inmate behavior. Faced with choices between relying on rules or developing relationships, the actions they take can be directed toward:

- *Formal controls*: initiating the disciplinary process by officially "writing up" the offender through a disciplinary action report

- *Informal controls*: using informal verbal communication to either prevent or deal with a situation, to foster voluntary compliance without the need to resort to official action

Within a correctional institution, neither excessive reliance on formal disciplinary action (overenforcement) nor too much informality (underenforcement) is an effective approach. Rather, the key is to find the proper balance between these two extremes.

Overenforcement

Some officers enforce rules strictly "by the book," writing up every inmate for even the most minor infractions. Such practices are obviously resented. That can create a dangerous process of retribution, as illustrated in the following scenario:

> At approximately 5:15 P.M., the officer on duty in C cellhouse was standing just inside the office door when an iron weight of about five pounds was dropped from an upper range. It landed on the metal screen covering the office. It is believed this was a measure of retaliation against the officer, who was performing his job in a manner seen as "overzealous" by inmates.[41]

Nor do inmates have to resort to physical attacks to avenge an officer's heavy-handed rule enforcement. Simply being uncooperative can cast a negative light on the officer's supervisory abilities. Such tactics vividly point out the difference between rule enforcement within correctional institutions and law enforcement in free society. Outside a court of law, police officers may never again encounter those against whom they take action. But it is entirely different in the enclosed environment of corrections, where officers must continue to interact on a daily basis with those against whom they enforce the rules. As a result, one's safety and even job security may be jeopardized by a "hard-line" approach.

In addition, correctional officers are closely scrutinized by their colleagues. Hard-liners do not earn much respect from their peers or supervisors. They are generally viewed by other staff members as being too weak to manage inmate behavior without using the rule book as a crutch. Moreover, because of the resentment and retaliation that their actions may create among the inmates, those who rely excessively on the formal disciplinary process can place their co-workers in danger as well. For a look at the ineffectiveness of overreliance on formal sanctions in one institution, see the next "Close-up On Corrections."

Underenforcement

On the other hand, there are those who rarely take any formal action at all. Such officers simply may be intimidated by fear. Or they may be overly sympathetic to the plight of those incarcerated. Or they may be trying to avoid ill will. For whatever reasons, they attempt to remain in the good graces of the population simply by "looking the other way" when rules are violated.

 # Close-up On Corrections

POWER IN A PRISON

A formal disciplinary procedure existed at all Massachusetts state prisons which consisted in essence of the following. When an inmate broke a rule, the officer in charge could "write-up" the incident in a Disciplinary Report ("D Report" or "ticket"). The case would then be heard by the prison Disciplinary Board ("D-Board"). If the inmate was found guilty, the Disciplinary Board was empowered to impose sanctions.

Two problems undermined this system. First, frequent recourse by an officer to writing D-Reports was not deemed an acceptable means of maintaining control. Although a few officers "didn't let a sneeze go by without writing a ticket," such behavior typically led to derision from fellow officers, threats of reprisal from inmates, and routine reversal of tickets by the D-Board. ([One] officer who resorted too often to writing tickets was reportedly pulled from the yard by his supervisors and placed for months in the towers). "They lose respect when a person writes a lot of tickets," for he indicates thereby that he cannot otherwise maintain control. . . .

Second, the sanctions the D-Board could impose were few in number. . . . an inmate could lose "good time" (thereby making his stay in prison longer); he could be locked in his own cell for a few days or weeks ("isolation time" or "ice time"); he could be removed from the minimum end to the more restrictive maximum end or from either [the] minimum or maximum end to Block 10. . . . Each step involved more of the same: more restraint, more isolation, more deprivation. [In addition], Block 10 . . . was often not viewed as punishment at all. Despite confinement to one's cell twenty-three hours a day or more in squalid conditions . . . many inmates preferred to be in Block 10. It was often safer than the maximum or minimum blocks. . . . By committing an obvious offense (preferably assault on an officer), and being "sentenced" to Block 10, an inmate could effect his withdrawal from the prison population without losing his standing among fellow inmates.

Source: Reprinted by permission from the publisher from Kelsey Kauffman, *Prison Officers and their World*, Cambridge, Massachusetts: Harvard University Press, 1988, pp. 62-63, copyright © by the President and the Fellows of Harvard College.

Even those who may not be concerned about how they are viewed by the inmates can fall into a laid-back supervisory style if they come to the conclusion that their disciplinary actions will not be supported by upper-level management. Consider, for example, how you would react after experiencing the following situation:

> On one occasion, I witnessed an officer break up a fight between two inmates. He waded in among some twenty-five spectators and separated the two combatants. He informed each that they were to be reported for fighting and ordered them to return to their cells. At this point, he was accosted by the spectators, who argued that there was no apparent reason for reporting them, as it had merely been a friendly argument. Nonetheless, the officer stood his ground, reported the inmates, and returned them to their cells. Later that day, he learned that the captain had returned them to normal status, and that no Disciplinary Board was recommended, as there had been no animosity involved.[42]

When officers are confronted continually with situations in which they feel that their efforts were not backed up by the chain of command, it can become very frustrating. In some cases, lack of further action may be justified on the basis of mitigating circumstances that the officer was unaware of, but officers who believe that the administration "doesn't care anyway" are likely to be considerably less enthusiastic about taking action in the future.

Some prisoners use the greater freedoms they are afforded under a *laissez faire* approach to manipulate staff and see how much they can "get away with." Others find themselves victimized as strong inmate leaders emerge from the vacuum created when rules are not enforced. Officers likewise come to resent the additional burden placed on them when some are not carrying out their full responsibilities. Needless to say, neither inmates nor staff members respect those who actively avoid rule enforcement on a continuous basis.

 # Learning Goals

Do you know:

1. Why the relationship between officers and inmates has been called a "corrupt alliance"?
2. What characterizes a consistent inmate-management style?
3. How officers can use interpersonal communication skills to manage inmate behavior proactively?

Corrupt Alliance

To a certain extent, almost all officers will overlook some things. In fact, one study found that "experienced and effective officers" never went completely "by the book," for several reasons: "First, the many complex human situations that must be dealt with could not be adequately covered by any set of rules, so that flexibility in rule enforcement was necessary. Moreover . . . bending correctional rules is necessary to secure compliance from inmates so that control can be maintained. . . . In this way, negotiation secures compliance in a situation where coercive enforcement . . . would produce resentment and hostility."[43]

In other words, a willingness to tolerate violations of "minor" rules and regulations enables the officer to obtain compliance with "major" custodial requirements.[44] The resulting system of informal compromises has been cited as usurping official authority by developing a "corrupt alliance" between the inmates and custodial staff. In this respect, "corrupt" is not used in the sinister sense of exploitation for illicit gain, but rather, in the more benign sense of seeking a workable accommodation.

In normal settings, it is in the subordinate's best interests to comply with the orders issued by those in charge. Whether the order is issued by a parent or an office manager, there is a certain "sense of duty" that motivates compliance. But correctional institutions are not normal settings, and inmates are primarily confined to their custody because they have not demonstrated such internal moral controls in the past. In prison, "the custodians find themselves confronting men who must be forced, bribed, or cajoled into compliance."[45]

Needless to say, submission through physical force is no longer permissible. Nor, as we have seen earlier, are there many incentives left with which to "bribe" inmates into compliance: "Mail and visiting, recreational privileges, the supply of personal possessions–all are given to the inmate at the time of his arrival . . . . The prisoner, then, finds himself unable to win any significant gains by means of compliance, for there are no gains left to be won."[46]

Beyond this lack of incentives, the close working relationships established between officers and inmates throughout the course of weeks, months, and years of confinement can serve to inhibit stern reactions to misbehavior. Moreover, we have seen that those writing too many disciplinary reports often are frowned on by their supervisors. As a result, a situation can be created in which the officer, "under pressure to achieve a smoothly running tour of duty not with the stick but with the carrot . . . finds that one of the most meaningful rewards he can offer is to ignore certain offenses or make sure that he never places himself in a position where he will discover them. . . . In effect . . . buy[ing] compliance or obedience in certain areas at the cost of tolerating disobedience elsewhere."[47]

Balanced Enforcement

The disobedience tolerated obviously represents relatively minor rule infractions, the excessive enforcement of which could be viewed as unnecessary harassment. In addition, officers who find themselves chronically overworked in overcrowded prisons with an overwhelming number of rules must develop some system of prioritizing simply to survive. Whether the result is considered a "corrupt alliance" achieved by implicit bargaining or a "calculated arrangement" accomplished by impartially balancing priorities is largely a matter of perspective.

Ultimately, the enforcement of discipline must be reasonable, steering a middle course between severity and laxity, and neither ignoring nor overenforcing the rules. Since regulations are not absolutes, it is essential to employ a common-sense approach to discipline in which "regulations are subject to interpretation."[48]

Consistency

There are some who would maintain that a consistent inmate-management style means treating everyone exactly alike. But such an approach is no more effective with inmates than it would be if parents responded to all of their children in precisely the same manner, or if employers used the same tactics in supervising all their employees.

Like everyone else, the needs and behavioral motives of inmates differ widely. Some will respond promptly to a mild verbal warning. Others will openly defy even a direct order. The key is to remain fair and objective without showing favoritism.[49] In other words, the most effective officer is one "who is flexible, who adapts to various situations, who can change from authority figure to counselor, depending on the type of interaction required, who has the good judgment to realize which rules and regulations need to be rigidly enforced and which ones can be bent."[50] Moreover, when inmates are treated firmly, fairly, and consistently, they well may reciprocate when the tables are turned and an officer needs help—as actually happened in the true story featured in the upcoming "Close-up On Corrections."

In addition to variations among inmates, the particular circumstances involved also may call for considerably different responses. An emergency situation obviously requires immediate take-charge action, whereas a minor infraction

---

 # Close-up On Corrections

THE IMPORTANCE OF LISTENING

Officer Richard Sawyer was working in the minimum security unit . . . when he began to feel sick. He leaned against a wall, turned to an inmate and said, "I'm not feeling well. . . ." Seconds later, Sawyer began to slide down the wall to the floor. The inmate helped lower him to the floor and called for assistance from other inmates. Before passing out, Sawyer asked the inmate to phone for help.

Several inmates helped place Sawyer in a more comfortable position and began checking his vital signs. Although they had access to his keys, they knew it would take too long to find the right one to open the unit and run for help. They also were unsure how to use the unit's security phone system. Finally, one inmate took the officer's radio and called for assistance. . . . Help arrived a short time later and Sawyer was taken to a nearby emergency room, where he regained consciousness. . . .

One reason for the assistance he received may have been Sawyer's good relationship with the inmates: "I had an excellent relationship with them—not in terms of friendship, but in terms of being able to talk. . . . I always had good communication back and forth with most inmates in the facility, and that might have helped a lot."

Source: "Inmate Comes to Officer's Aid," *On the Line*, Vol. 16, No. 4, September 1993, p. 2.

---

could be handled on a more informal basis. Developing a *consistent manage-ment style* means responding to a similar circumstance or type of behavior in a similar manner whenever it occurs, as opposed to treating all inmates and situations alike.

Informal Controls

To be effective, correctional officers must realize the ultimate objective of discipline—that is, developing control from within—rather than focusing on the external imposition of rules and regimentation. Thus, the question becomes how order can be promoted without either ignoring or excessively writing-up inmate violations. The answer involves how officers use both informal disciplinary action and verbal communication.

Simply because an infraction is not officially recorded on a disciplinary action form does not necessarily mean that it was ignored. In addition to a verbal warning, officers may be able to reduce television privileges, remove an inmate from a work detail, or initiate similar informal responses to misconduct. Although the range of privileges that can be restricted is somewhat limited and temporary in nature, there are means short of official action that can be used to achieve compliance.

But it is obviously far more effective to prevent violations *proactively* than to deal *reactively* with misbehavior after it occurs. In other words, it is best to encourage *voluntary compliance* to reduce the need to resort to official action. This is quite a challenge when dealing with those whose lack of internal restraints often has much to do with why they are incarcerated. It calls for developing appropriate interpersonal working relationships that are neither too close nor too distant.

Social Distance

Naturally, there must be some social distance between officers and inmates. There is a fine line between properly displaying some degree of empathy and improperly becoming overly sympathetic. Those who become sympathetic and emotionally involved with prisoners are inevitably vulnerable to deception and manipulation. Inmates are quick to identify staff weaknesses and prey on them. It is for such reasons that officers have been encouraged to avoid such things as using nicknames to address inmates, making "deals," discussing their personal life, giving legal advice about inmates' legal or family matters, and the like.[51]

At the other extreme, there are those who are coldly detached from the inmates—performing their duties in a routine, bureaucratic manner, and making it clear that they are unapproachable, regardless of the inmate's personal needs. Like the physician who must maintain a caring but clinical relationship with patients, correctional officers must balance personal concern with professional caution. Those who are successful in doing so develop a style of *detached commitment*, whereby their professional commitment to the well-being of the inmate is tempered with a degree of personal detachment that promotes objective judgments and rational decision making.

Interpersonal Communications

Since so much of an officer's time is spent interacting with inmates, the development of effective *interpersonal communication skills* is an essential ingredient of the job. The manner in which officers build and maintain relationships with inmates will have much to do with their success or failure in managing behavior. It also will largely determine whether they can proactively control inmates or whether they must rely on reactive measures.

In corrections, staff are sometimes so inundated with "requests, complaints, and stories from inmates on a daily basis that listening skills become tainted and weakened as time goes by."[52] Like the narrator on a guided tour, it is difficult to maintain the same enthusiasm with the last group in the evening as the first group in the morning. Day after day, correctional officers hear the same troubles, gripes, and pleas—often from the same inmates, and many times concerning things that the staff can do nothing about. But simply

 # Close-up On Corrections

THE IMPORTANCE OF LISTENING

I listen. You find out you gain more respect if you listen. Give them your attention. It's appreciated. I spent half my career listening to personal problems. . . . [G]uys come up to you with personal problems like sickness, a death in the family, and want to see a counselor. It might take three to five days before he does. You have to deal with this then and there. . . .

One guy was shaking and upset. He said he was in a big jam. . . . He gave me a check he'd gotten in the mail; (correspondence had overlooked it). I took the check, gave the guy a receipt and put it in his account. It's not a big thing, just little things to take the edge off. Sometimes if you're helpful, you can correct things and save trouble. When they can't handle it, they just swing out.

I had a guy working for me, a good worker. . . . Everybody was down on him. They said he'd be a bum. I said let's see what he does. I asked what his problem was and he said that he got a bad letter. His little girl had had an operation. He didn't know how serious it was, but he was worried. I tried to make arrangements for him to make a phone call. . . . He got his phone call and perked up.

I went by a guy's cell and he was crying. He says for me to go, but if he tips, he might hurt six or seven people. I opened his cell, walked in and started talking and got him calmed down. . . . Other inmates asked me what was happening when I went by I told them "Nothing's going on." You don't spread the word on a thing like that. If the inmate knows this, it takes the edge off and he feels better.

Source: Lucien X. Lombardo, *Guards Imprisoned: Correctional Officers at Work*, Second Edition, Cincinnati, Ohio: Anderson Publishing Company, 1989, pp. 54, 62, 63, 81, 82. Used with permission.

being there to listen is often just the "safety valve" that is needed to prevent an inmate's frustration from exploding into violence. For some examples of this in the words of officers themselves, *see* the previous "Close-up On Corrections."

As a result, the ability to listen may be an officer's most effective asset. As noted earlier, verbal communication is not limited to a one-way issuing of orders and commands. Rather, it involves engaging in a two-way dialog that establishes an effective working relationship. Proactively listening can be a far more powerful management tool than reactively responding. Quite simply, a good inmate manager is a good inmate listener.

 # Learning Goals

Do you know:

1. How unit management improves correctional practices?
2. What benefits unit management involves?

Unit Management

In fact, proactive management of inmate behavior is one of the hallmarks of an initiative that is transforming administrative and operational practices in a number of prisons throughout the country—in other words, the concept of unit management. Similar in many respects to the principles of direct supervision jailing, unit management (originally called "functional unit management") was likewise initiated by the federal government during the mid-1970s. Although designed originally to decentralize classification and treatment services, unit management is not a treatment program, nor is it a custodial strategy. Rather, it is a system whereby custody and treatment work hand-in-hand within a setting that promotes their close cooperation in achieving two primary goals:

- To establish a safe, humane environment for both staff and inmates that minimizes the detrimental effects of confinement

- To deliver a variety of counseling, social, educational, and vocational training programs designed to aid offenders in making a successful return to the community [53]

The units themselves consist of a small, self-contained living and staff office area. They can be either comprehensive units that house a variety of general population inmates, or specialized units serving those with particular needs, such as alcohol or drug abusers. Thus, unit management offers a flexible approach to the classification and management of different groups of offenders.[54] Whether they present special risks or special needs, inmates can be placed accordingly, and their situation can be addressed appropriately.

More of the operational details about unit management are described in the next "Close-up On Corrections." In that regard, unit staff generally approve visitors and correspondence lists, process requests for job assignments, and review requests for program changes. During team meetings among unit staff,

Close-up On Corrections

UNIT MANAGEMENT—OBJECTIVES AND OPERATIONS

The concept of unit management is designed to:

- Divide large groups of inmates into smaller, well-defined clusters

- Increase contact and the quality of relationships between staff and inmates

- Better observe inmate activities, detecting problems before they become critical

- Improve inmate accountability and control

- Provide different programs, strategies, and interventions for each inmate, depending on individual needs, abilities, and ambitions

- Place special emphasis on institutional adjustment, work skill acquisition, interpersonal communications, positive self-esteem, self-motivation, problem-solving techniques, realistic goal-setting, education, and training.

But unit management only will be effective to the extent that it adheres to the basic requirements for its success, which include:

- *Leadership*: Since it involves decentralizing power and decision-making more broadly throughout the organization, top-level administrators must be supportive and committed to the concept.

- *Unit plan and mission*: Each unit requires a written plan specifically defining its purpose, which provides documentation of the goals against which progress is measured.

- *Population size*: Each unit's population size is based on its mission—a general unit can accommodate 150-250 inmates; a special unit, 75-125 inmates.

- *Staffing*: In each living unit, staffing consists of a unit manager, one or two case managers, counselors, and a secretary, along with mental health staff and twenty-four-hour correctional officer coverage.

- *Assignment stability*: Inmates and unit staff are permanently assigned to the unit (barring changes in the inmate's status). Correctional officers are stationed for a minimum of nine months.

- *Training*: Personnel receive formal training on their roles and responsibilities.

- *Cooperation*: Because unit management cannot work in a vacuum, interdisciplinary cooperation is essential.

- *Monitoring and evaluation*: A systematic approach to the evaluation of unit management is necessary to determine if its goals are being achieved.

Sources: Compiled from James D. Henderson, W. Hardy Rauch, and Richard L. Phillips, 1987. *Guidelines for the Development of a Security Program*, Lanham, Maryland: American Correctional Association, 1987), pp. 14-15; and Robert B. Levinson, *Unit Management in Prisons and Jails*, Lanham, Maryland: American Correctional Association, 1999, p. 9.

program decisions are arrived at jointly, with staff listening to the inmate and explaining their decisions. On a day-to-day basis, staff interact closely with the inmate, taking a proactive approach that enhances communication, enables closer observation, and promotes order and control. While that is more costly, the extra expenses are made up in savings as a result of less over-time, fewer repairs to damage from vandalism, fewer disturbances, and even less litigation.[55]

Because the centralized power typical of correctional operations is redis-tributed under this concept, the unit manager serves as a "subwarden," and each unit is in a sense a "mini-institution," operating semi-autonomously within the confines of a larger institution. All decisions and problems concern-ing the inmates are handled in the unit. The idea is to decentralize authority by dividing the prison into smaller, more manageable components:

> The arrangement is analogous to neighborhoods in a city. Each neighborhood can be intimate, but is part of and has access to the amenities of the city. . . . Autonomy lets units develop their own cul-tures and identities. But the unit still functions as part of the whole prison. [56]

One of the major advantages of unit management is that it "works as well in high-security institutions as it does in low- or medium-security facilities." [57] Moreover, studies have found that in such facilities, there are fewer inmate-on-inmate assaults, fewer escapes while on furlough, and considerably less cus-tody-treatment rivalry among staff.[58] But its success is perhaps best illustrated by the fact that unit management is operational in at least thirty-three states,[59] and thus far, no correctional system that has adopted this approach has later abandoned it.[60]

Summary

Because many of those in prison have not displayed sufficient self-control to function effectively in society, an elaborate system of external controls is imposed to maintain security. The operational objectives of custody are to pre-vent escape, maintain order and safety, and promote efficient functioning of the institution. Moreover, custody is a necessary condition for effectively imple-menting treatment programs.

Custodial security is achieved through the architectural design and techno-logical hardware of the physical plant, as well as the control procedures enacted by prison staff. Externally, high-security features include perimeter walls, fences, and razor wire, along with guard towers, ground posts, locks, alarms, and double-door security. Internally, control procedures include inmate segre-gation, controlled movement, periodic counts, cell searches, personal searches, and control of tools, keys, and equipment. Since these provisions are less rigid in minimum-security facilities, they are the most vulnerable to escapes. Most inmates who abscond are, however, eventually apprehended.

To detect and remove contraband items from the institution, cell searches are conducted either routinely, randomly, or for reasonable suspicion. Personal searches are also conducted, which range in intrusiveness from a simple frisk, to a full strip search, to a body-cavity examination.

To further reduce the risk of escape or the introduction of contraband, correctional institutions control inmate contact with the outside. Use of the telephone is restricted, mail is checked, and the number of visits is limited. Some states permit conjugal visits to reduce homosexual activities, improve morale, and strengthen family bonds. But not all inmates qualify for conjugal visits, which can create resentment. Some institutions therefore favor the use of furloughs, through which inmates can better maintain social integration and interaction. However, furloughs present the obvious risk of absconding or committing new crimes during the period of freedom.

To achieve orderly group life, a number of rules and regulations govern individual conduct within correctional institutions. Officers are responsible for enforcing the rules, and they possess considerable discretion in this regard. Although minor infractions may not be fully enforced, major violations are documented through official disciplinary action reports. If it is determined that further action is necessary, the inmate is afforded a hearing before a disciplinary committee, which has the authority to impose sanctions when a penalty is warranted.

Obtaining compliance without taking official action can create an accommodation between officers and prisoners, whereby officers accept some degree of minor misconduct as a tradeoff for the observance of major rules. This is the result of an effort to avoid either over- or underenforcing the rules. Overly strict enforcement is viewed by the inmates as unnecessary harassment, whereas nonenforcement diminishes respect for both the officer and the rules. Ultimately, the purpose of discipline is developing internal self-control.

Yet, formal regulations represent only one aspect of maintaining institutional control. Often overlooked are the more informal, noncoercive controls emerging from the relationship established between correctional officers and the inmate population. Encouraging voluntary compliance involves the need to develop an appropriate interpersonal working relationship with the inmates. But officers must be careful to maintain a certain social distance, balancing personal concern with professional caution. Much of an inmate's frustration, anxiety, and tension can be reduced simply by having someone who is willing to listen without passing judgment. Establishing a two-way dialog rather than a one-way dictation of commands not only lessens potential hostility, but also creates a more proactive management atmosphere. In that regard, unit management demonstrates considerable potential for both controlling and changing inmates while they are subject to correctional custody. It is the subject of changing behavior that will be explored more extensvely in the next chapter.

Endnotes

1.   Grace L. Wojda, Raymond G. Wojda, Norman Erik Smith, and Richard K. Jones, *Behind Bars*, Lanham, Maryland: American Correctional Association, 1991, p. 3.

2.   John J. DiIulio, *Governing Prisons: A Comparative Study of Correctional Management*, New York: Free Press, 1987, p. 92.

3.   Lucien X. Lombardo, *Guards Imprisoned: Correctional Officers at Work*, Second Edition, Cincinnati, Ohio: Anderson Publishing Company, 1989, p. 64.

4.   Anthony Travisono, "Editorial," *On the Line*, Vol. 13, No. 2, March 1990, p. 1.

5.   *Correctional Officer I Correspondence Course: Security Issues*, Lanham, Maryland: American Correctional Association, 1997, p. 12.

6.   Paraphrased from DiIulio, *Governing Prisons*, p. 41.

7.   Scarlett V. Carp and Joyce A. Davis, "Planning and Designing a Facility for a Special Needs Population," *Corrections Today*, Vol. 53, No. 2, April 1991, p. 102. For a description of how the structure of prisons has changed over time, *see* Courtney A. Waid and Carl B. Clements, "Correctional Facility Design: Past, Present, and Future," *Corrections Compendium*, Vol. 26, No. 11, November 2001, pp. 1-5; 25-29. *See also* Leonard Witke, ed., *Planning and Design Guide for Secure Adult and Juvenile Facilities*, Lanham, Maryland: American Correctional Association, 2000.

8.   James B. Jacobs and Harold G. Retsky, "Prison Guard," *Urban Life*, Vol. 4, No. 1, April 1975, p. 19.

9.   John W. Roberts, "Yesterday and Tomorrow—Prison Technology in 1900 and 2000," *Corrections Today*, Vol. 57, No. 4, July 1995, pp. 114-120.

10. Janice Joseph and Rupendra Simlot, "Technocorrections: Biometric Scanning and Corrections," in Roslyn Muraskin, ed., *Key Correctional Issues*, Upper Saddle River, New Jersey: Prentice Hall, 2004, pp. 128-148.

11. John S. Shaffer, "Vulnerability Analysis in the Correctional Environment," *Corrections Today*, Vol. 65, No. 7, December 2003, p. 120.

12. Susan B. Cohen "Never Forget . . . Behind Every Good Security System Stand the People Who Make it Work," *Corrections Today*, Vol. 53, No. 4, July 1991, pp. 86-88.

13. Warren Rohn and Trish Ostroski, "Advances in Technology Make It Easier to Monitor Inmates," *Corrections Today*, Vol. 53, No. 4, July 1991, p. 144.

14. *Ibid.*

15. "Two New Jails Hold World's Largest Video Visitation System," *Correctional News*, May/June 2004, p. 35.

16. Laura Gater, "The Problem of Mental Health in Prison Populations," *Corrections Forum*, March/April 2004, p. 31.

17. Kevin Raines, Joni Toenjes, and Allan Liebgott, "Telemedicine . . . It's not Just for Rural Jails," *American Jails*, May/June 1998, p. 21.

18. Douglas McDonald, Andrea Hassol, and Kenneth Carlson, "Can Telemedicine Reduce Spending and Improve Prisoner Health Care? An Evaluation of a Prison Telemedicine Network," *National Institute of Justice Journal*, April 1999, p. 23.

19. "Don't Let Prisoner Transport Become a Vacation," *Corrections Alert*, Vol. 3, No. 5, June 3,1996, pp. 1-2.

20. Philip J. Boyle and James G. Ricketts, "Using Technology to Achieve Higher Efficiency in Correctional Facilities," *Corrections Today*, Vol. 54, No. 5, July 1992, pp.78-80.

21. Camille Graham Camp, ed., *The 2002 Corrections Yearbook: Adult Corrections*, Middletown, Connecticut: Criminal Justice Institute, 2003, pp. 48-49.

22. Cecil Angel and Dan Shine, "Fugitive of '57 Can Stay A Free Man," *The Herald*, April 1, 2001, p. 26A.

23. "Cell Phones Proliferate as Inmate Contraband," *Correctional News*, July/August 2004, p. 25.

24. Stan Stojkovic, "Social Bases of Power and Control Mechanisms among Prisoners in a Prison Organization," *Justice Quarterly*, Vol. 1, No. 4, 1984, p. 526.

25. Jay Lowe, "Technology Enhances Public Safety in Texas," *Corrections Today*, Vol. 66, No. 4, July 2004, p. 69.

26. Paul W. Keve, *Prison Life and Human Worth*, Minneapolis, Minnesota: University of Minnesota Press, 1974, p. 67.

27. Christopher Hensley, Sandra Rutland, and Phyllis Gray-Ray, "The Effects of Conjugal Visits on Mississippi Inmates," *Corrections Compendium*, Vol. 25, No. 4, April 2000, p. 1. The five states are California, Mississippi, New Mexico, New York, and Washington.

28. *Ibid.*, p. 20.

29. A. Crosthwaite, "Punishment for Whom, the Prisoner or His Wife?" *International Journal of Offender Therapy and Comparative Criminology*, Vol. 19, No. 3, 1975, pp. 275-284.

30. "Family Visitation," *Corrections Compendium*, Vol. 4, No. 7, January 1980, pp. 2-5.

31. Camp, *The 2002 Corrections Yearbook*, p. 148.

32. In fact, as late as 1992 (by which time Willie Horton was confined in a Maryland prison), he was still being widely referred to in conjunction with presidential campaigning, having been cited on 420 occasions in newspapers and magazines throughout the country—prompting a *Wall Street Journal* editorial which called for "a furlough" of the Willie Horton issue. *See* Paul A. Gigot, "Willie Horton: The Mother of All Diversions," *The Wall Street Journal*, April 17, 1992, p. A-10.

33. "Number of Prison Furloughs Increases," *On the Line*, Vol. 15, No. 2, March 1992, p. 5.

34. Daniel P. LeClair and Susan Guarino-Ghezzi, "Does Incapacitation Guarantee Public Safety? Lessons from the Massachusetts Furlough and Prerelease Programs," *Justice Quarterly*, Vol. 8, No. 1, March 1991, p. 9.

35. Lombardo, *Guards Imprisoned*, p. 100.

36. *Wolff v. McDonnell*, 418 U.S. 539 (1974).

37. *Sandin v. Conner*, 2293 U.S. S. Ct. (1995).

38. "Double Jeopardy for Prison Rioting," *Corrections Alert*, Vol. 2, No. 8, July 24, 1995, p.7, citing *U.S. v. Brown*, 9th Circuit.

39. John R. Hepburn, "Prison Guards as Agents of Social Control," in Lynne Goodstein and Doris Layton MacKenzie, eds., *The American Prison: Issues in Research and Policy*, New York: Plenum Press, 1989, pp. 214-215.

40. Adria Lynn Libolt, "Technology Cannot Be a Replacement for Creative Planning and Programming," *Corrections Today*, Vol. 53, No. 4, July 1991, p. 21.

41. Anthony L. Guenther and Mary Quinn Guenther, "Screws vs. Thugs," in Ben M. Crouch, ed., *The Keepers: Prison Guards and Contemporary Corrections*, Springfield, Illinois: Charles C Thomas, 1980, p. 171.

42. Leo Carroll, *Hacks, Blacks, and Cons: Race Relations in a Maximum Security Prison*, Lexington, Massachusetts: Lexington Books/D.C. Heath, 1974, p. 55.

43. Frances E. Cheek and Marie Di Stefano Miller, "A New Look at Officers' Role Ambiguity," *Correctional Officers: Power, Pressure and Responsibility*, Lanham, Maryland: American Correctional Association, 1983, p. 12.

44. Gresham M. Sykes, *Society of Captives: A Study of a Maximum Security Prison*, Princeton, New Jersey: Princeton University Press, 1958, p. 58. The following discussion

of the "corrupt alliance" between inmates and officers is based on Chapter 3, "The Defects of Total Power" of this reference.

45. *Ibid.*, p. 47.

46. *Ibid.*, p. 51.

47. *Ibid.*, pp. 56-57.

48. G.L. Webb and David G. Morris, "Prison Guard Conceptions," in Crouch, *The Keepers*, p. 151.

49. David B. Kalinich and Terry Pitcher, *Surviving in Corrections*, Springfield, Illinois: Charles C Thomas, 1984, p. 39.

50. Robert Blair and Peter C. Kratcoski "Professionalism among Correctional Officers: A Longitudinal Analysis of Individual and Structural Determinants," in Peter J. Benekos and Alida V. Merlo, eds., *Corrections: Dilemmas and Directions*. Cincinnati Ohio: Anderson Publishing Company, 1992, p. 117.

51. Kalinich and Pitcher, *Surviving in Corrections*, pp. 45-53.

52. *Ibid.*, 55.

53. Robert B. Levinson, *Unit Management in Prisons and Jails*, Lanham, Maryland: American Correctional Association, 1999, p. 10.

54. Robert Johnson, *Hard Time: Understanding and Reforming the Prison*, Belmont, California: Wadsworth Publishing, 1996, p. 262.

55. James Houston, *Correctional Management*, Chicago: Nelson-Hall, 1999, pp. 326-327.

56. Hans Toch, "Functional Unit Management: An Unsung Achievement," *Federal Prisons Journal*, Vol. 2, No. 4, Winter 1992, pp. 15-16.

57. James H. Webster, "Designing Facilities for Effective Unit Management," *Corrections Today*, Vol. 53, No. 2, April 1991, p. 38.

58. Houston, *Correctional Management*, p. 329.

59. "Survey Summary: Special Housing," *Corrections Compendium*, Vol. 26, No. 7, July 2001, p. 6.

60. Robert B. Levinson, "The Future of Unit Management," *Corrections Today*, Vol. 53, No. 1, April 1991, p. 46.

CHAPTER 8

INSTITUTIONAL PROCEDURES: TREATMENT

66 We must accept the reality that to confine offenders behind walls without trying to change them is an expensive folly with short-term benefits—winning battles while losing the war.[1] **99**

—Former U.S. Supreme Court Chief Justice Warren Burger

Chapter Overview

Treatment in correctional institutions involves all of the programs and services that bring socializing influences to bear on the inmate. Viewed comprehensively, treatment refers to all of the processes that ordinarily promote the normal socialization of people in the free community—such as schools, religion, and recreation—as well as the psychological, psychiatric, and social work services that are traditionally associated with the term "treatment." To the extent that they contribute to the inmate's socialization, a wide variety of factors can be broadly viewed as treatment—from the work habits learned in prison industries, to the high school equivalency diplomas earned in general equivalency degree (GED) classes, to the discipline instilled by compliance with regulations.

Despite society's shift from the specific rehabilitative emphasis of the medical model to the more punitive focus of the justice model, corrections has not abandoned the broad scope of treatment. In part, this may be a reflection of practical considerations. A prison in which training, education, work, or religious activities are lacking is one in which boredom and idleness prevail, compounding the already difficult task of maintaining custody and control.

Institutional programs not only enable better supervision than custodial staff alone can provide, but they also help neutralize feelings of frustration.

In addition, despite the presumably voluntary nature of treatment under the justice model, it is inevitably corrections which is criticized when ex-offenders become recidivists. Even if the public views the mission of corrections as restricted to incapacitation, it does not seem to be willing to absolve prisons of at least some blame when they fail to make positive changes among those confined. The *legal* responsibility of the prison may be limited to the court's demand for humane custody and security. But the public's *protective* demand ultimately is to return the offender to society as a law-abiding citizen. In that regard, "education, mental health, substance abuse, and other rehabilitative programs . . . are not a bleeding heart coddling of inmates, but rather, are directly related to public safety and are cost beneficial." [2]

Moreover, correctional administrators themselves continue to express a belief in rehabilitation. As one warden expressed it, "although society's concern in recent years has been to get tough on crime, most corrections professionals never really gave up on program interventions." [3] Basic literacy, GED, and vocational training programs are among the "amenities" least favored for reduction or elimination by prison wardens. [4] While "maintaining custody and institutional order are dominant concerns," there is also clear "support for rehabilitation as a secondary but fundamental goal." Not only do wardens feel that rehabilitation programs have an important place in their institutions, they also express a desire to expand inmate treatment opportunities. [5] As we will see in this chapter, that is a legitimate concern, since treatment in the traditional clinical or casework sense is sadly lacking in most correctional facilities.

Treatment is not confined to a single program or service. But neither is it merely a process for helping the inmate adapt to the institutional environment with a minimum of irritation and anxiety. Rather, it is related to what every officer, counselor, work supervisor, chaplain, or other institutional employee does that has a positive impact on the inmate's long-term social adjustment. Even in those facilities lacking sophisticated clinical or therapeutic programs, much can be done on a routine day-to-day basis to promote the overall treatment effort by introducing socializing influences into lives that often have been characterized by personal disorganization and social dysfunction. In other words, the correctional process must be directed toward "*changing behavior*, rather than just *containing behavior*." [6]

 ## Learning Goals

Do you know:

1. For what purposes inmates are classified?
2. How the emphasis of classification has changed over time?
3. On what basis classification decisions are made?
4. How classification decisions affect the offender?

Inmate Classification

Through the classification process, inmate risks and needs are identified. As such, classification decisions become the basis for assigning inmates to varying programs and institutions to meet their requirements. We may not think of classification as a part of life in free society, but there are also many ways in which it functions outside of prisons. For example, every time that you go to the "express" line in the supermarket, the "cash-only" checkout in a convenience store, or the "self-service" pump at a gas station, classification is being used to expedite your transactions.

Within corrections, classification refers to the *grouping of inmates according to characteristics that they share in common*. It is therefore a helpful tool in managing large numbers of cases more efficiently than they could be handled on an individual basis. By identifying general patterns and grouping services to match them, the unique requirements of large numbers of people can be met more efficiently. Thus, classification promotes homogeneous grouping of offenders for the purpose of maximizing resources, minimizing risk, and/or promoting change. Treatment goals can range from learning auto mechanics through vocational training, to becoming functionally literate through computer-assisted instruction, to achieving social adjustment through group therapy. As noted in the next "Close-Up on Corrections," classification serves a number of objectives that are related to both institutional concerns and inmate considerations.

Historical Developments

The rudimentary origins of classification were established when the Quakers separated men and women in the Walnut Street Jail of 1790. Children began to be segregated from adults around 1825 with New York's establishment of private Houses of Refuge, followed by public juvenile training schools in Massachusetts (1847) and the Elmira Reformatory (1876). Following emphasis

Classification of prisoners by sex, age, health, and crime is a relatively new phenomenon. Early prisons held men and women, along with children as well as violent criminals and nonviolent debtors. Courtesy of the Federal Bureau of Prisons, *Handbook of Correctional Institution Design and Construction*, 1949.

Close-up On Corrections

on gender and age, inmates were later separated on the basis of severity of offense. These early beginnings represented the *segregation period* of classification[7]—when offenders were isolated from one another primarily for safety and security, to promote the orderly functioning of correctional institutions.

Separation for treatment purposes began to appear in France with the development of the first intelligence (IQ) test, which was brought to New Jersey's Vineland Training School in 1911. This stimulated the period in which classification was used for *diagnosis and planning*, which shifted the focus from institutional security considerations to identification of offender needs.

With the introduction of the medical model and psychoanalytic techniques in the 1930s, many state correctional systems adopted classification, since diagnosis of individual needs was considered essential for proper treatment intervention. This ushered in the *classification-for-treatment* era. Many of the treatment developments discussed in this chapter—from counseling to group therapy—were initiated in the 1950s and 1960s, during the height of the medical model.

By the 1980s, however, the rehabilitative goals of the medical model gave way to the emphasis on confinement and voluntary treatment of the justice model. This resulted in the use of classification for *security and custody*, as opposed to rehabilitative purposes: [8]

The treatment concept—changing the criminal into a law-abiding citizen by therapeutic intervention—generally has grown out of

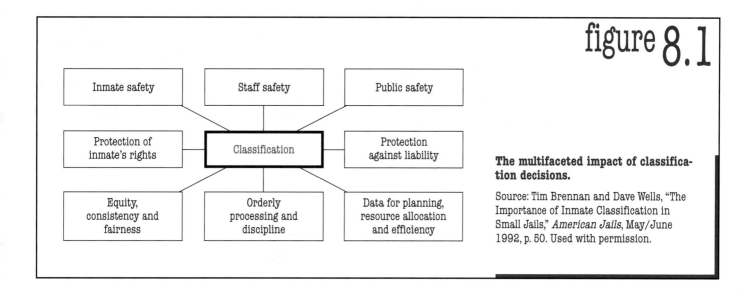

figure 8.1

The multifaceted impact of classification decisions.

Source: Tim Brennan and Dave Wells, "The Importance of Inmate Classification in Small Jails," *American Jails*, May/June 1992, p. 50. Used with permission.

favor and has been replaced by the notion of safety. We are concerned more with running safe, secure, industrious, and relatively lawful institutions than with treating the million or more prisoners in them.[9]

Identifying treatment needs is not necessarily excluded from current classification decision making. But neither is it any longer the exclusive objective, as is apparent in the multifaceted impact of classification illustrated in Figure 8.1.

Reception and Diagnosis

The initial step in classifying inmates is the diagnostic process that occurs during reception and intake. Incoming inmates are interviewed, tested, examined, and evaluated. Additionally, the contents of their presentence investigation report and background information are reviewed. Before the adoption of classification on a statewide basis, judges could sentence offenders to a particular prison within the state. Thus, classification was essentially a function of the court. Today, state-controlled classification places everyone sentenced by the courts under the central authority of the state department of corrections.

Classification Decisions

On the basis of diagnostic information, decisions are made concerning an inmate's housing, level of security, program assignments, and special needs (such as anger management training, alcohol/drug treatment, psychiatric referral, and so forth). This is how classification is designed to operate, but the process is far from being either foolproof or completely objective. The sheer volume of cases can create routinized decisions that are based more on efficient processing than effective prognosis. It is in part for such reasons that more clearly defined, objective criteria are now being used in many correctional classification systems.

However they are made, classification decisions can have a long-term impact on the offender. Everything from job placement to educational programming and parole eligibility is tied to classification outcomes. In essence, classifying people "channels destinies and determines fate,"[10] and at times becomes a self-fulfilling prophecy.

✹ Learning Goals

Do you know:

1. How classification relates to both the medical model and the justice model?
2. Why classification decisions can result in "overclassifying"?
3. What the benefits and drawbacks are of using objective models for classification decision making?

Relationship to the Medical Model

The reception-and-diagnostic process was compatible with the medical model's focus on the unique pathologies of individual offenders. Since this perspective was based on a belief that criminal acts were essentially a "cry for help," early and accurate diagnosis was essential, "followed by prompt and effective therapeutic intervention," as outlined in the treatment plan during classification.[11]

Whether or not the inmate desired treatment was not the point. The offender's own motivation to seek help—or lack thereof—was largely ignored. Rather, the treatment plan was based on the classification committee's view of inmate *needs*, as opposed to what the person *wanted* or had the motivation to *do*. Realizing that "going along with the system" would provide the only avenue to freedom naturally created a strong incentive for doing what was prescribed, even if that might mean simply going through the motions to demonstrate eligibility for release. Although there is some evidence that court-ordered treatment can be even more effective than voluntary treatment,[12] the shift from the medical model to the justice model, in part, was intended to deemphasize mandated treatment in favor of voluntary participation.

Institutional Implications

As correctional facilities have become increasingly crowded, however, it is not always feasible to place inmates in the institutions and programs that are best suited for them. It has, for instance, been noted that "[a] state with 75 percent maximum security spaces will tend to classify 75 percent of its intake population as maximum security."[13] Studies have indicated that subjective classification systems tend to violate "one of the cardinal rules of classification by 'overclassifying'"—that is, "unnecessarily placing many inmates in higher levels of security than required, given the risks they pose."[14] While the process may not always work as intended, the aim of a properly implemented classification system is to match the security and treatment needs of the inmate with the resources available within the correctional system.

Objective Models

Throughout the history of classification progress, professional treatment personnel were needed to make the initial diagnosis and develop the related custody and treatment plans. This was not only costly, but also vulnerable to subjective opinions. As early as 1967, the President's Task Force on Corrections expressed a desire for a more objective and easily administered classification tool, "capable of administration in general day-to-day correctional intake procedures, that would group offenders according to their management and treatment needs."[15]

To streamline the process and make it more objective, there has been a move in recent years toward more empirically valid classification measures. As described in the objective classification guidelines developed by the National Institute of Justice, improved classification of inmates is an essential component of the response to prison crowding:

> With proper classification . . . only those inmates requiring high levels of security are placed in costly, tight custody facilities, while those evidencing less threat can be assigned to lower security institutions. Appropriate classification also can assist in determining which inmates can be considered for early release or for retention in the community with appropriate supervision. Most importantly, effective classification helps assure the safety of the public, agency staff, and prisoner population.[16]

By removing personal opinions and subjective judgments, objective models are designed to be more equitable to all inmates, as well as more valid and reliable predictors. (For more details on how they operate, *see* the next "Close-up On Corrections"). Methods that are used to classify for treatment purposes are directed toward understanding causes of criminal behavior and identifying specific targets for change. In contrast, objective systems use standardized decision-making criteria that are focused more on classification for institutional management or inmate adjustment to confinement.

Relationship to the Justice Model

It is not surprising that *objective classification models* have gained support under the justice model, when sentencing guidelines and selective incapacitation prediction formulas also have become popular. All of these numerical formulas, models, and prediction devices may owe much of their prominence to concerns for achieving consistency and rational decision making, along with our fascination with the capabilities of computers. If decisions are numerically derived, there is a tendency to view them as more valid and trustworthy, despite the fact that the variables being analyzed are still a product of human choice. In that regard, it has been noted that "the objectivity of a classification system is a matter of degree, for the creation of these systems involves subjective judgments, and all of the systems currently in existence incorporate at least some subjective staff judgment."[17]

Certainly, the variables taken into consideration in objective prediction models are considerably more moderate in scope than the widespread tests

Close-up On Corrections

and measures on which previous classification decisions were based. As outlined in the above "Close-up On Corrections," criteria are limited to relatively few clearly defined and legally based variables that are designed to predict one's institutional adjustment and future behavior. Notable by their absence are indicators related to clinical assessments of offender needs. Objective prediction models therefore are directed more toward determining the necessary level of institutional security than individual treatment prescriptions. Thus, their acceptance in the field represents another reflection of the movement from the rehabilitative focus of the medical model to the custodial orientation of the justice model.

Assessment of Objective Classification

To the extent that objective classification can reduce needless overclassification without increasing misconduct or escapes, it can represent a significant accomplishment—especially in light of the potential relationship between misclassification and rule infractions, adjustment difficulties, and treatment progress (*see* Figure 8.2). In that regard, objective classification has been credited

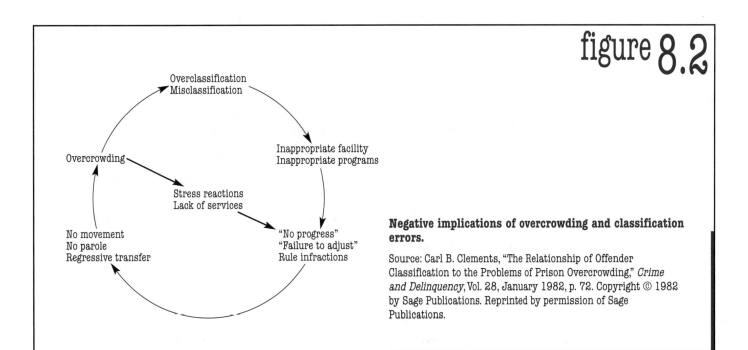

figure 8.2

Negative implications of overcrowding and classification errors.

Source: Carl B. Clements, "The Relationship of Offender Classification to the Problems of Prison Overcrowding," *Crime and Delinquency*, Vol. 28, January 1982, p. 72. Copyright © 1982 by Sage Publications. Reprinted by permission of Sage Publications.

with helping to reduce violence, escape attempts, inmate manipulation of housing assignments, and staffing costs.[18]

But there is also some resistance to objective classification techniques, since they change the role of classification personnel from diagnosticians and therapists to something closer to that of an accountant or a bookkeeper. Such an impersonal approach can dehumanize classification, to the point where it simply becomes a bureaucratic process devoid of personal discretion.

Nor do classification experts themselves agree on the "best" way to classify inmates. Thus, it is recommended that whatever system is employed be reviewed regularly.[19] Some caution against relying on one instrument in a "one-size-fits-all" approach, arguing for discretionary input within the framework of an objective instrument.[20] Others continue to question whether removing the human element from classification decision making is truly more *equitable* or whether *efficiency* is merely disguised as equity. In other words, do the rigors of empirical analysis produce more equitable results than the richness of clinical assessments?

Regardless of the answer, once classified, the inmate is faced with adjusting to the decisions made during the intake process. Offenders may find themselves assigned to a minimum-, maximum-, or medium-security institution; to a facility with a wide range of programs and services or to a place where an hour a day of solitary recreation is the single diversion; to a prison with a variety of employment opportunities or a location where work is confined to routine maintenance duties. Given these variations, the remainder of this chapter focuses on the change-oriented activities, services, and programs typically provided in correctional facilities.

Do you know:

1. What role religion plays in a correctional facility?
2. To what extent correctional chaplains are accepted by inmates and staff?
3. How faith-based programming is related to correctional treatment?

Faith-Based Programming

Ever since the powerful religious impact of the Quakers on the first penitentiary at the Walnut Street Jail, religion has played a significant role in prison life. More than 200 years later, virtually every state offers faith-based instructional programs and worship services.[21] Such activities still attract more inmate participation than any other programs.[22] Perhaps that is because religion performs essential functions in prison life—ranging from dealing with guilt to finding a new way of life, and coping with loss, especially that of freedom.[23]

Historically, chaplains represented the first example of what could be considered treatment staff in correctional institutions. During the early development of prison systems, they were the unofficial therapists, dedicated to "saving souls," before there were teachers, social workers, or counselors.[24] Even in facilities with limited or nonexistent treatment programs, inmates virtually always have access to a chaplain. As seen in the next "Close-up On Corrections," it is the chaplain who is there to break bad news, soothe sorrows, and make life somewhat more tolerable for those incarcerated—who holds out promise for a future better than the past.

For those behind bars, religious studies can be an important source of hope, optimism, and potential change. Courtesy of the Roanoke County (Virginia) Sheriff's Office.

Close-up On Corrections

Inmate Acceptance

Unquestionably, chaplains play an indispensable role in correctional institutions. But while chaplains always have been involved in prisons, their acceptance has never been complete or unreserved. Some inmates consider religion as representing the authority of an "establishment" of which they are not a part. On the other hand, inmates who are experiencing guilt and remorse can seek out religious programs for support and forgiveness. With little but time on their hands, even some of the most seemingly hard-core inmates—in the original Quaker tradition—do indulge in reading the Bible and attending faith-based programs. There are those who undoubtedly find a measure of personal solace in religion. Others find it a useful aid to help them adjust to their situation, or simply a "crutch" to lean on in hard times. Still others actually may use religious conversion as a manipulative tool to convince officials of their reform and eligibility for release. But regardless of their motives, it is not uncommon for prisoners to "find God" during their incarceration.

Staff Acceptance

By the same token, chaplains have not been universally well accepted by prison staff. Some operational personnel may look upon the chaplain as a threat to security, since the job calls for being on somewhat "friendly" terms with the inmates. A chaplain who is naive with regard to the manipulative capabilities of inmates can become an "easy touch." For example, in one small rural prison, the chaplain was told by the inmates that they did not have pens to write to their loved ones. The prisoner communicating this sad news indicated that his wife would gladly donate pens if the chaplain would pick them up. Inside each of the pens was a small quantity of marijuana. As illustrated by this "con game," chaplains must minister to the religious needs of the population while being alert to the security concerns of the institution. Doing so requires maintaining a delicate balance between being useful and being used.

Current Challenges

Finding dedicated people to fill a position that is often underpaid, unappreciated, and overworked can be a challenge. In addition, as prison populations reflect greater cultural and ethnic diversity, faith-based personnel representing the traditional Catholic/Jewish/Protestant denominations may not be as relevant to the broader-based religious orientations of current inmates. Although it is no longer assumed that a chaplain's training must reflect the specific religious denomination of the inmate being counseled, it is equally inappropriate to overlook the need for greater diversity among religious staff. In that regard, some correctional institutions maintain a religious advisory board, composed of faith-based representatives from throughout the community, which serves as a potential source of volunteers.[25] Other institutions have implemented such creative approaches to meeting religious needs as broadcasting faith-based programs through the facility's television sets.[26]

Treatment Impact

The chaplain's contribution to treatment can be substantial. Just having someone to talk to, share grief with, or listen to problems can exert a powerful influence. Imprisonment can be a lonely, soul-searching experience. It is often faith-based personnel who make existence there more bearable. Moreover, finding structure in religion provides many offenders with the internal stability needed to make a successful adjustment not only to prison, but also to society upon release.[27] In that regard, research indicates that "religion seems to give hope, meaning, optimism, and security" to people, that it is "positively related to personal and emotional well-being," "has beneficial health effects,"[28] and most significantly, also appears to have a positive influence on recidivism.[29]

As the most consistent representative of treatment over the years, the chaplain probably has contributed more than any other position to the correctional process. In fact, faith-based cognitive programs are now emerging that blend biblical perspectives with cognitive-therapeutic techniques. In this "healing environment," faith-based counselors encourage self-awareness and teach new ways of thinking through cognitive restructuring:

> For example, Thinking Error No. 2 is Victimstance, which is defined as the tendency to see oneself as a victim of circumstances such as social conditions, family history, past negative experiences, and so

forth. It involves blaming others for one's actions instead of accepting responsibility for bad choices. For insight into this behavior, students are directed to look at the story of Adam and Eve's disobedience . . . [and] are led to see that failure to admit crime and accept responsibility is a barrier to rehabilitation.[30]

Thus, the oldest and most modern approaches to treatment have established a unique working partnership. But as religious principles have merged more and more intimately with secular programs, questions have been raised about the constitutionality of using public funds for faith-based initiatives. For some insights into how this issue might be addressed, *see* the next "Close-up On Corrections."

 # Close-up On Corrections

PRINCIPLES GOVERNING FAITH-BASED INITIATIVES IN GOVERNMENT-FUNDED SETTINGS

- The primary criterion for whether any provider is eligible to participate in the delivery of government-funded social service must be its effectiveness in meeting the needs of beneficiaries.

- If any individual objects to the religious character of the faith-based organization that is providing services, the individual should have the option of participation in alternative programs without negative consequences. . . .

- The same standards of financial accountability should be applied to religious as to non-religious providers of services regarding the use of government funds.

- Nondiscrimination with respect to religion must be maintained in all relations between government and organizations providing services. . . . well-established Constitutional principles should govern the relationship (*see Bowen v. Kendrick*, 487 U.S. 589, 1988).

- Existing legal and civil rights protections for all beneficiaries and providers of government-financed social services must be preserved; but faith-based groups must be allowed to maintain employment standards that support their quality and character.

Source: Pat Nolan, "Prison Fellowship and Faith-based Initiatives," *On the Line*, Vol. 25, No. 5, November 2002, p. 2.

Do you know:

1. The extent of functional illiteracy among those incarcerated?
2. The benefits of providing academic and vocational instruction in correctional institutions?
3. Why computer-assisted instruction is particularly well suited to teaching inmates?

Education, Training, and Other Services

Following religion, the introduction of education was the second major change in the history of correctional institutions, and the need for inmate education has not diminished over the years. As recently as 2003, more than half (52 percent) of state prison inmates under twenty-five years of age did not have a high school degree or general equivalency degree (GED)—a rate double that of the general population in free society.[31] Even more startling, nearly 60 percent of inmates are completely or functionally illiterate (*see* Figure 8.3), meaning that they cannot fill out a job application, read a newspaper, or balance a checkbook. Lack of education may or may not have promoted their involvement in crime. Nevertheless, it is clear that their postrelease employment opportunities will be severely limited in a culture where high school education is a minimum requirement for most jobs. In today's society, functional literacy is essential for basic survival.

The difficulties resulting from inadequate education are not restricted to employment limitations. Those who have insufficient schooling probably also have missed the socialization and cultural conditioning that are equally important. Education is not just learning knowledge or skills, but also the development of work habits, feelings of accomplishment, and the self-discipline it takes to succeed.

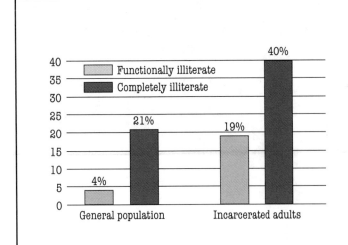

figure 8.3

Literacy levels for U.S. adults.

Source: *Research Brief: Education as Crime Prevention*, New York: Center on Crime, Communities, and Culture, 1997, p. 7, citing U.S. Department of Education, *1992 National Adult Literacy Survey*, Washington, DC: National Center for Education Statistics, 1992. Used with permission.

Institutional Programs

Promoting literacy and marketable job skills saves money in the long term by better equipping inmates with the resources they need to survive in free society. Making inmates productive is the first step to keeping them out of prison, and making them literate is the first step toward making them productive.[32] In that regard, an examination of ninety-seven published articles revealed "solid support for a positive relationship between correctional education and lower recidivism." [33] Likewise, the National Institute for Literacy reported that correctional education programs reduced the probability of reincarceration by 29 percent, with a similar 33 percent reduction for those who participated in vocational training. [34]

The primary purpose of *academic education* and *vocational training* programs in correctional facilities is to provide offenders with the tools of literacy, a trade, or specific job skills. But important secondary advantages include enhancing the inmate's work habits, pride, dignity, and self-esteem. Merely being able to read a story to a child during visiting can be an uplifting experience for a formerly illiterate inmate.[35] For those who have experienced a lifetime of being "losers," these indirect benefits often prove to be even more significant than more immediate objectives. For a personal account of how this happened in one case, *see* the inmate's story in the following "Close-up On Corrections."

Educational Challenges

When educational programs are conducted within prison walls, unique challenges are presented. For one thing, maintaining order in the classroom is essential. It is not conducive to learning if inmates view classes as a break from normal discipline. Some institutions reserve separate cellblocks for those involved in various educational activities. Housing all inmates participating in a particular program together enables them to study together and mutually reinforce learning. In addition, it promotes security by minimizing the need for movement to and from classes. But wherever they are housed, it is essential to

Close-up On Corrections

PLEA FROM A PRISONER

The youngster appeared in front of my tiny "house" on an afternoon when I was short on patience and long on aggravation. All of his possessions were in side a pillowcase slung over his shoulder.

"I'm your new cellie," he informed me. "Jackson's my name and crack's my game."

"Perfect . . ." I mumbled to myself, looking at a kid half my age. . . . Just what I needed, a 20-year-old street punk sharing my 5' x 9' cubicle. . . .

Fortunately, we worked different jobs, and different shifts, allowing occasional cell privacy. . . . Jackson stayed on his bunk, pacified by television. There was no animosity on my part, just no interest in lame conversation.

One thing I did notice. He would perk up when the guard came around our cell at mail call. But there was never anything for Jackson. A couple of times he had commented sarcastically about all the letters I wrote, and the stack of magazines and books cluttering my shelf space.

A day came when Jackson did get a letter. Lying on my lower bunk, I could hear him above, rattling the pages while I flipped through a new magazine. He swung his bare feet off the upper bunk and hopped to the floor. . . .

With unusual meekness he asked, "Say man, you got a minute?"

"What for?"

"Would you read my momma's letter to me?"

I was just able to hold back the question, You can't read? But surprise surely registered on my face. It always comes as an astonishing revelation to encounter an adult American who is functionally illiterate.

"Sure," I told him. The letter was two simple pages from a mother worried about her boy confined in a harsh world of bricks and bars. He was silent after I read the final few words: "We love you son. Be careful and come home soon, Momma."

"Would you help me write back to her?" he asked. Gone was the cocky criminal, replaced by a sad, vulnerable youngster barely out of his teens. I hesitated, then made a decision.

"Yeah, I'll write the letter, but it's going to cost you."

"How much?" he asked suspiciously. Everything costs something in the penitentiary.

"An hour of your time, *every* night at lock up. You're gonna learn to read and write."

He looked hard at me. "What's the catch?"

"You've got nothing but time," I reminded him. "Might as well get something out of being here."

"You won't tell nobody?" he asked sheepishly.

"Isn't anybody's business."

"Deal!" he said, sticking out his hand to seal the bargain. . . .

Jackson obviously hadn't absorbed much in the six years he attended school. The basic alphabet was a cloudy concept. His written vocabulary was barely double digit. But within a few weeks, two things were readily apparent: I had a lot to learn about patience, and Jackson was a very bright young man.

(continued)

Close-up On Corrections

avoid labeling students in such classes as "stupid" or "illiterate." As was clearly demonstrated in the last Close-up, illiteracy is a personal embarrassment that many inmates will attempt to conceal.

Computer-Assisted Instruction and Distance Learning

Schools in correctional institutions are also unlike those in free society in another respect—they are not able to run on a regular, September-to-June calendar. Inmates arrive continuously throughout the year. Moreover, unlike the public schools, smaller facilities may not have the luxury of dividing classes by grade levels. Addressing the educational needs of inmates who function at varying grade levels was especially difficult before the introduction of *computer assisted instruction* (CAI). With the programmed instruction available through CAI, however, many deficiencies in the academic offerings of correctional institutions can be eliminated.

As a self-paced instructional tool, CAI enables each student to progress at his or her own rate. It also enables the institution to address widely varying educational levels without the need for separate classrooms for each grade. CAI presents material in short and easy steps, keeps the learner actively involved, and provides immediate feedback of results. Moreover, it is considerably more prestigious to work on a computer than to be in a regular classroom setting. Another major benefit is reduced staffing, which is a significant factor, given the shortage of prison teachers. With CAI, fewer instructors can serve more students.

Every correctional institution obviously cannot afford the investment in equipment and software that would be necessary to enable all inmates with educational deficiencies to participate in computer-assisted instruction. But *distance learning* presents another high-tech solution that is more cost effective than on-site instructors. In those facilities where inmates have access to TV, interactive instructional programming is available free of charge through the Corrections Learning Network. Broadcast by satellite throughout the country, the network's adult education programs help juvenile offenders continue their educational progress, provide literacy skills for adults, and assist offenders with developing the skills needed to obtain employment and make a successful transition into the community.[36]

Postsecondary Education

In addition to basic remedial education, college course work is also available now through distance learning, and from local institutions of higher education. But providing postsecondary education to inmates has generated protests among taxpayers who resent providing inmates with the advantage of college study while they have to pay the costs of educating their children. This argument overlooks the expense of continuing to support recidivating offenders who might be prompted by a college education to make a change in their lifestyle.

As shown in Figure 8.4, the higher the inmates' level of education, the less likely they are to recidivate. Moreover, a summary of studies on this topic concludes that a significant body of research "demonstrates a positive correlation between higher education and post-release success." [37] Nevertheless, public backlash can be a strong deterrent to offering educational programs that go beyond what is available in secondary schools.

This was perhaps best illustrated by the 1994 congressional action barring inmates from receiving Pell grants for postsecondary education. As a result, by

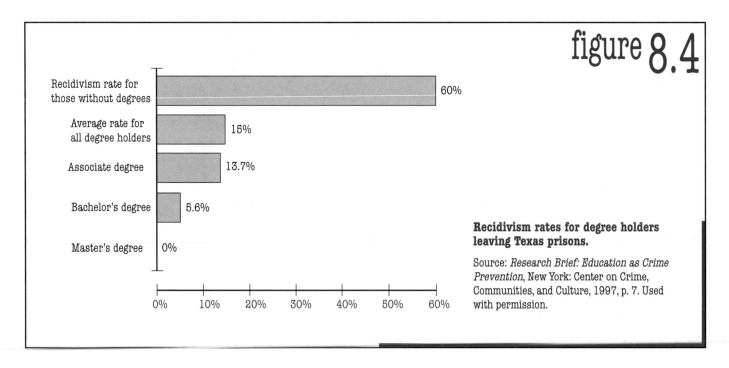

figure 8.4

Recidivism rates for degree holders leaving Texas prisons.

Source: *Research Brief: Education as Crime Prevention*, New York: Center on Crime, Communities, and Culture, 1997, p. 7. Used with permission.

Close-up On Corrections

1995, a national survey of prison wardens found 68 percent reporting that college education programs had been reduced or eliminated in their facilities during the previous year.[38] By the year 2000, more than two out of three state and federal prisons were not offering postsecondary coursework.[39] Even where college courses are still available, inmates now generally pay for their own classes. As described further in the previous "Close-up On Corrections," the Congressional prohibition has undoubtedly had an impact.

 # Learning Goals

Do you know:

1. The major deficiency of vocational training programs in corrections today?

2. How the private sector has become involved in prison industries and what issues this raises?

3. Why the provision of recreational activities is important in correctional facilities?

Vocational Training

Work has been a central feature of prisons throughout the history of corrections—from the handicrafts assembled in the Walnut Street Jail, to the large prison industries of the nineteenth century, to the contract labor systems used throughout the South. While such labor may have instilled discipline, the demeaning work and dehumanizing manner in which inmates were often supervised on the job did more to degrade self-esteem than to develop skills. Moreover, the primary purpose was not to promote an inmate's potential, but rather, to produce an institutional profit. As a result, "during the first half of the twentieth century, the unregulated use of prison labor led to exploitation of prisoners and unfair competition with free-world labor." [40]

Currently, more than half of prisons and many jails have some type of industrial or vocational training program.[41] Since its origin in the Elmira Reformatory (1876), vocational training has expanded to include everything from auto mechanics to welding, printing, construction trades, woodworking, horticulture, data processing, bookkeeping, and cosmetology. In contrast to the days of pressing license plates, there is greater concern today that many offenders will end up back in the correctional system unless we develop some way of integrating them into "meaningful occupations with a future."[42]

But that does not mean that there is consistent agreement about what vocational training programs should accomplish. Depending on one's perspective, such activities can be seen as a method of providing meaningful work, teaching skills and work habits, preparing for a trade on the outside, earning wages, or overcoming idleness (*see* Figure 8.5). Nor are these varied goals necessarily contradictory. As demonstrated by the true stories in the upcoming "Close-up On Corrections," inmate labor can provide practice in a trade, service to the community, and a source of personal satisfaction to the inmate.

Private-Sector Involvement

Despite this enthusiasm, however, many prisons and jails are unable to accommodate everyone desiring to participate in vocational training. Less than

---

figure 8.5

Offender-based	Institution-oriented	Societal
Good work habits	Reduces idleness	Repayment to society
Real work experience	Structures daily activities	Dependent support
Vocational training	Reduces the net cost of corrections	Victim restitution
Life management		
Gate money		

Differing perspectives on the goals of prison labor.

Source: Randall Guynes and Robert C. Greiser, "Contemporary Prison Industry Goals," *A Study of Prison Industry: History, Components, Goals,* College Park, Maryland: American Correctional Association, 1986, p. 21.

Close-up On Corrections

a third of those in prison have ever received such training.[43] Even though more than two out of three prison inmates have work assignments, most involve janitorial duties or food preparation (26 percent), with only 4 percent involved in any type of production.[44]

A promising response to the lack of readily available vocational training is the expanding *private-sector involvement* in prison industries. In addition to removing certain restrictions on the sale of prison-made products, federal legislation in 1979 authorized the establishment of Prison Industry Enhancement pilot projects (discussed in Chapter 3). These projects now operate in thirty-five states and are generating millions of dollars in government revenues, inmate family support, and victim-compensation payments.[45]

Such partnerships between public prisons and private enterprises are not, however, problem-free. The challenges of recruiting private industries into prisons and determining salaries and benefits for inmate employees remain major issues. Attracting industries into prisons undoubtedly would be promoted by the payment of lower salaries. But others argue that only union or prevailing wages will protect the free market from the unfair competition of prison-made products. Furthermore, such accepted practices of the private sector as collective bargaining can conflict with prison policies. In other words, "the goals of private enterprise and of running an efficient and safe prison are by no means complementary."[46]

Recreation

Unlike vocational training or other forms of treatment, virtually all inmates are entitled by court rulings to some form of recreation. Even in maximum security, inmates are afforded recreation, although it may be restricted to an hour of solitary workout under the close supervision of correctional staff. In lower-security facilities, recreational pursuits can range from individual or group athletics to arts and crafts, music, drama, table games, hobbies, television, and movies. However, some of these activities have generated considerable controversy and public criticism in recent years.[47] For a look at both sides of the debate surrounding inmate "amenities," *see* the next "Close-up On Corrections."

While the future of recreational TV may be in jeopardy, some institutions have turned television into a productive tool through programming that

Recreation can be a beneficial activity for coping with confinement. Courtesy of the Broward County Sheriff's Office, Ft. Lauderdale, Florida.

Basketball is a popular recreational outlet in many correctional facilities. Courtesy of Kenneth R. McCreedy.

features instruction on everything from basic education to life skills and conflict resolution.[48]

Additionally, meaningful recreation may be one of the most beneficial activities in correctional facilities. Beyond occupying leisure time, recreation can help inmates cope with confinement and relieve the stress and anxiety of incarceration. Moreover, people do not get into trouble while busily occupied and working off excess energy. Trouble almost always starts during the boredom caused by too much leisure time.

 ## Learning Goals

Do you know:

1. To what extent correctional treatment was available under the medical model?
2. Whether inmates have a constitutional right to treatment?
3. The most commonly available form of treatment in correctional facilities?

Counseling, Casework, and Clinical Services

Everyone would not necessarily agree that religious services, educational programs, vocational training, or recreation meet a strict definition of "treatment." But there is little doubt that counseling, casework, and clinical services represent traditional long-term approaches to offender rehabilitation. Given its rehabilitative emphasis, one might assume that such treatment services were

Close-up On Corrections

TIGHTEN THE REINS?

YES

The way prisoners see it, anything [the] Alabama Prison Commissioner can do to make their lives miserable, he will. But [he] says he's turning the state's penal institutions into a real deterrent against crime. . . .

Rules instituted by the commissioner include cutting television hours and chopping female inmates' hair to collar length. Video cassette recorders have been removed and cable service cut. Smoking is no longer allowed in prisons. A new phone system limiting the numbers prisoners can call and the time they can talk is being installed. A recording will be played several times during the conversation to remind people they are talking to a prisoner.

"It's all cosmetic attempts to look tough. What it creates for inmates is an opportunity to get angry, frustrated and abusive," said criminal attorney Bryan Stevenson. . . .

But the most striking example of the anti-crime mood sweeping the nation is in Mississippi. There, in addition to denying inmates weight-lifting equipment, individual television sets, and air conditioners, the state legislature . . . decreed that inmates must wear striped uniforms with the word CONVICT emblazoned across the back.

"Politicians want people to believe that these sorts of actions are going to stem the tide of crime," said Tim Fahy, president of the National Correctional Recreation Association. "The thinking is, if we make prison bad enough, no one will want to go to prison."

Source: "Commissioner Tightens Reins in Alabama Prisons," *Corrections Digest*, July 7, 1995, p. 5, and "Hard Time Gets Harder," *On the Line*, January 1995, p. 1.

NO

Correctional officers are well aware such inmate diversions as TV, weight rooms, basketball, ping-pong, and horseshoes are not politically popular. But they say they are necessary to reduce inmate stress and prevent them from taking it out on their keepers or each other.

"The public wants their pound of flesh," said Sgt. William Laney. "That's fine, but don't do it at the expense of safety for the correctional officers."

Televisions in the state's prisons were purchased, in effect, by the inmates. Profits from the small items and snacks sold in the canteens were used to purchase the sets. But a mandate passed by the Legislature . . . forbids such purchases of new televisions in the future.

"I think they're making a big mistake," said Sgt. Dennis Crawford. . . . "At least with the television you got something you can use to leverage them," he said. "You say, 'Now you all get loud, that TV's going off.' They will police themselves and quiet down. That's their only tie to the outside world. Take that away, it's like a caged animal."

At the heart of the debate over inmate privileges is the age-old issue of punishment versus rehabilitation. What some consider frills, such as televisions and exercise equipment, others see as components of the rehabilitation process and as critical prison management tools. Banning inmate privileges runs counter to the spirit of the American Correctional Association's

(continued)

Close-up On Corrections

widely available in prisons under the medical model. That, however, was not the case.

Rhetoric versus Reality

Even at the height of the medical model, in-depth psychological counseling, social casework, and psychiatric therapy have never been prominent features of correctional institutions. A survey of state and federal prisons conducted in the mid-1950s, for example, found that the vast majority of staff held jobs related to the security needed to keep prisoners *in*, with less than 8 percent classified as people who were "there to get them ready to go out and stay out" (and even many of these were clerical positions).[49] At that time, there were only twenty-three full-time psychiatrists in U.S. correctional institutions—a number that would provide an average of eighty-two seconds of psychiatric help each month per inmate (assuming equal distribution throughout the country). The psychological staff numbered sixty-seven—able to provide about four minutes monthly for individual attention. The 257 caseworkers averaged less than sixteen minutes per inmate each month.

By the mid-1960s, the percentage of treatment personnel had increased. But it was still estimated that more than 20,000 additional specialists were needed to address the "drastic scarcity" of treatment staff.[50] During a time that represented the peak years of the medical model, these figures do not say much for practical as opposed to ideological commitment to rehabilitation. In fact, most correctional administrators responding to a national survey in 1975 maintained that treatment programs had never really been tried, because they had not been adequately funded.[51]

Others have observed that "it is not uncommon for an institution that houses a thousand or more inmates to define itself as being committed to rehabilitation when there is no full-time staff member who holds an advanced degree in any of the helping professions, or, when there are full-time and more or less adequately qualified staff members, to find that the ratio of inmates to qualified treatment staff is a hundred or more to one." [52] As a vocal critic put it:

> One might conclude [that] we went through a great renaissance in corrections in the 1960s—characterized by massive infusions of funds into rehabilitative programs, psychoanalysis, psychotherapy, intensive treatment programs, and so forth This, of course, is a great myth. The language of rehabilitation was popular—the reality was virtually nil.[53]

Additionally, during this period of time, treatment represented an "invasion" of what previously had been a custody-dominated system. Those in the custodial ranks tended to view treatment personnel with varying degrees of skepticism, mistrust, or at best, grudging tolerance. Mere acceptance was still a long way off, let alone the establishment of a mutual custody-treatment partnership.[54] For all of these and many other reasons, it would appear that the medical model focused more on rhetoric than rehabilitation.

Treatment Availability Today

Undoubtedly, staffing over recent years has increased well beyond twenty-three psychiatrists, sixty-seven psychologists, and 257 caseworkers—but then, so has the number of people behind bars. At the same time that the inmate population has been escalating, the availability of mental health services in the community has been declining. Over the past decade, "forty state mental hospitals have closed, while more than 400 new prisons have been opened." [55] This shifts more and more of the mental health burden to the correctional conglomerate. Yet as Figure 8.6 illustrates, custodial/security employees still far outnumber educational or professional/technical personnel. Even where treatment staff are available, many of them work in classification, where they are *processing* prisoners rather than *counseling* them.

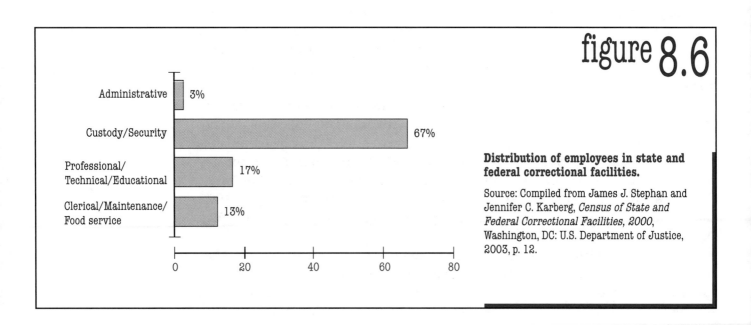

figure 8.6

Distribution of employees in state and federal correctional facilities.

Source: Compiled from James J. Stephan and Jennifer C. Karberg, *Census of State and Federal Correctional Facilities, 2000*, Washington, DC: U.S. Department of Justice, 2003, p. 12.

However, treatment has not been recognized as a constitutional right. The Supreme Court has held that correctional administrators cannot maintain an attitude of "deliberate indifference" to the serious mental, physical, or emotional illness of offenders, but treatment may be limited to those with an identified medical necessity, and to procedures that can be provided within reasonable time and costs. [56] In fact, the courts rejected a sex offender's argument that the failure of prison officials to provide a therapeutic program tailored to his needs constituted cruel and unusual punishment.[57] In short, legal opinion to date has not supported an inherent constitutional right to treatment for adult prisoners.

Changing "Treatment" Orientation

Additionally, the overall objective of "treatment" has changed in recent years. With emphasis shifting toward the public-safety orientation of the justice model, it has been observed that the major rationale for prison programming is no longer treatment, but security. Thus, a program's impact on future criminality has become secondary to "more immediate concerns of keeping inmates busy and out of trouble." As a result, prison programs today are more likely to be viewed "as a means of riot prevention than crime prevention."[58]

Inmate Motivation

On the other hand, it also must be acknowledged that many inmates do not actively seek treatment with a great deal of enthusiasm. They may procrastinate even in the face of very clear expectations about the types of programs they must participate in to earn various privileges (such as parole, work release opportunities, a lower security classification, and so forth). Then, when it becomes apparent that entering a specified program is the only avenue to achieve these objectives, space may not be available. Under such circumstances, packed "therapy sessions" are more likely to provide attendance certification than an avenue for meaningful change.

Generic Counseling

Counseling represents the one type of treatment that has been most commonly available in correctional facilities, and remains so today (*see* Figure 8.7). In fact, generally speaking, counseling could be considered an approach used by almost everyone in the correctional setting. As a result, the word *counseling* can be a very misleading term when used within institutions.

In the outside world, counselors are considered to be those with appropriate academic credentials and a license to practice, who address a client's problems through such professionally recognized practices as individual or group therapy. In corrections, however, this title can take on a much broader meaning and might not actually refer to someone with formal educational preparation in counseling. Rather, "the term can be used much more generically in corrections—for example, having been used at times to refer to nonprofessional staff and to untrained volunteers."[59] (For a closer look at how counselors' credentials can affect long-term outcomes, *see* the following "Close-up On Corrections".)

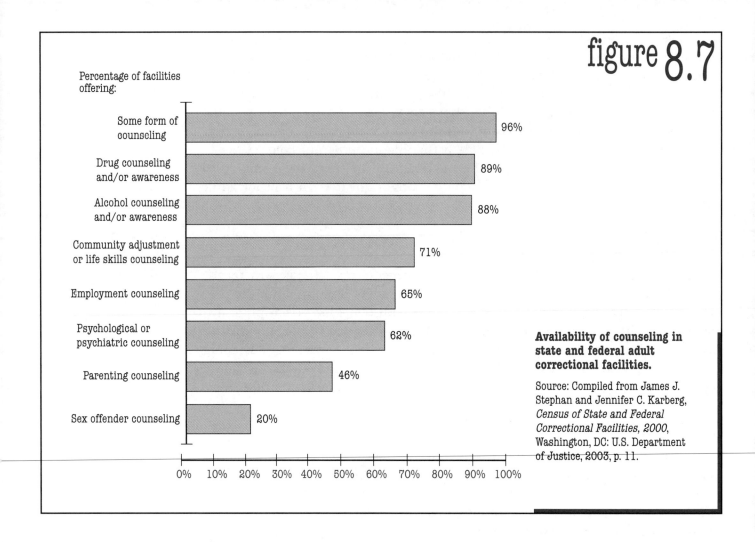

figure 8.7

Percentage of facilities
offering:

Some form of counseling 96%

Drug counseling and/or awareness 89%

Alcohol counseling and/or awareness 88%

Community adjustment or life skills counseling 71%

Employment counseling 65%

Psychological or psychiatric counseling 62%

Parenting counseling 46%

Sex offender counseling 20%

0% 10% 20% 30% 40% 50% 60% 70% 80% 90% 100%

Availability of counseling in state and federal adult correctional facilities.

Source: Compiled from James J. Stephan and Jennifer C. Karberg, *Census of State and Federal Correctional Facilities, 2000,* Washington, DC: U.S. Department of Justice, 2003, p. 11.

The title "correctional counselor" within a facility might be attributed to anyone from professionally licensed clinical practitioners to unlicensed civilian personnel who handle inmate requests for commissary items, passes, medical attention, and so on. This does not mean that there are not uncertified personnel who can and do perform generic counseling functions. Correctional officers, for example, probably conduct more "cellblock counseling" than any other staff members, since they are readily accessible to the inmates and are with them for more extended periods of time than the official treatment personnel.

Clinical Counseling

Unlike those who engage in informal "counseling" without professional training, some correctional staff are certified counselors with academic credentials in psychology. In contrast to psychiatrists, who search for deep-rooted causes of behavior, psychologists deal with how behavior is expressed. The goal is to help the offender better manage conflict, rather than to completely resolve it.

Basic to psychological therapy are the methods used to preserve one's ego or sense of worth—that is, *defense mechanisms,* such as *rationalization.* All of us have rationalized our behavior at some time, seeking to justify what we do. Whether this defense mechanism is socially harmful or not depends on what is being rationalized—the shoplifter's theft of merchandise because "that store

Close-up On Corrections

is ripping off customers anyway," or the student's inability to remember historical dates because "they don't really matter."

Offenders are often noted for the defense called *projection*—transferring the blame for one's own shortcomings to others. Such projections essentially are excuses to avoid accepting responsibility. A common pattern among correctional clients, for example, is the projection of blame on society or "the system." Using this line of thinking, offenders can convince themselves that they are not in trouble because of their own fault, but rather, because of cops who were "out to get" them, judges who were "corrupt," a victim who "asked for it," or a lawyer who was "incompetent." The reality or unreality of these attitudes does not matter—the fact remains that they exist.

Counseling Challenges

In treating criminal behavior, clinical psychologists attempt to divert the offender from socially unacceptable activities. This is done by channeling aggression, frustrations, and other stress and tensions in more socially acceptable directions. However, problem-solving through counseling in the correctional setting is often directed more toward facilitating the inmate's adjustment to the institution than to their long-term adjustment to life in free society.[60] This does not necessarily mean that counselors take an overly narrow view of their role. But the limited availability of treatment personnel in correctional institutions can impose a system of prioritizing. And obviously, the difficulties associated with incarceration are the immediate concerns of the inmates.

Beyond large caseloads, counselors face a number of additional challenges unique to the institutional setting. Correctional counselors must be able to cope with everything from lack of administrative support and a heavy volume of paperwork to the difficulty of maintaining confidentiality, the potential for being "conned" by manipulative clients, and the necessity to work with those who have been "coerced" into counseling. Given these considerations, the effective correctional counselor is one who is both patient and persistent; skilled and streetwise; optimistic and realistic.

✴ Learning Goals

Do you know:

1. Why group rather than individual methods tend to prevail in correctional treatment?
2. The advantages of peer counseling and self-help groups?

Group Methods

Because individual counseling is conducted in one-on-one sessions between the client and therapist, it does not enable as many inmates to receive services as group methods, where a number of clients can be handled simultaneously. The key difference between group and individual counseling is the presence of other clients during the intervention process.[61] In addition to being more economical and meeting the needs of a greater number of inmates, group techniques provide an opportunity for obtaining feedback and reinforcement from one's peers.

In its pure sense, *group therapy* is a treatment process in which a trained therapist (often a psychiatrist or clinical psychologist) works with small groups, guiding interaction, exploring problems, and developing social skills through the establishment of supportive relationships within the group. Group therapy, group counseling, guided-group interaction, sensitivity training, and psychodrama are among the group-oriented techniques that were introduced into correctional institutions in the decades between the late 1940s and the mid-1960s. While some of these techniques (such as psychodrama and sensitivity training) by now have fallen out of favor, group methods in general have become a widely used alternative in correctional settings, within both institutions and community-based services such as probation, parole, and halfway houses. As described in the upcoming "Close-up On Corrections," guided-group interaction is making a comeback today in the treatment of young gang members.

Self-Help Groups

Beyond merely participating in groups initiated by the correctional administration, inmates for many years have been involved in *self-help groups* of their own creation. The basic premise of these affiliations is that people with similar needs can be a source of mutual support. Both within and outside

# Close-up On Corrections

GUIDED GROUP INTERACTION

Philosophy: Assumes that delinquency depends on identification with a peer group (for example, gang) rather than on individual pathologies (for example, personality shortcomings).

Goal: To form affiliations with new peer groups that have strong positive values and behavioral expectations.

Technique: Uses peer groups to change individuals—based on the belief that if individuals bond with the group, they will alter their behavior to win support and acceptance.

Phase I: (Averages seven months): In this intensive phase, participants spend most of their time in structured activities (for example, school, work, recreational activities). During one-to-two hour daily group sessions, "here-and-now" problems are discussed and dealt with by the group (rather than staff). Group leaders gradually share more power and decision making with the members.

Phase II: (Lasts up to one year): Graduates are regularly visited at home and come to the program center each week for a group meeting that reinforces the behavioral norms learned in Phase I. They also help establish new groups, give participants a visible goal to strive for, and serve as role models.

Source: Adapted from Albert G. Smith, "Juvenile Program Created in 1950s May Stem 1990s Youth Violence," *Corrections Today*, August 1994, p. 180.

correctional institutions, prisoners and ex-offenders have become involved in such groups as Alcoholics Anonymous, Narcotics Anonymous, and Gamblers Anonymous. In addition to treatment-oriented groups, they also have participated in such social organizations as the Jaycees and various religious associations.

There are a number of advantages to the peer involvement of such self-help groups. For one thing, many of those involved have recognized that they have a problem with which they need help. Whether the motivation to change is the result of external intervention or internal self-awareness, these groups involve positive peer pressure through association with other people undergoing similar problems. The person comes to realize that he or she is not alone in experiencing such difficulties, and that others can help in developing the inner strength necessary to overcome the problem. Moreover, they provide a vehicle through which the offender can learn responsibility, decision-making, problem-solving, and other life skills. In fact, in one state where budget cuts have eliminated most drug treatment programs, the only types of treatment available to prisoners in need of such services now will be AA and NA.[62]

An additional benefit of these groups is the fact that they operate both inside prisons and within the outside community, and therefore can serve as a "bridge" back into the mainstream of life for newly released ex-offenders.

✳ Learning Goals

Do you know:

1. How behavior modification has been used as well as misused?
2. How reality therapy differs from traditional therapeutic techniques?
3. Why social casework is more frequently used in community-based corrections than in institutional settings?
4. What therapeutic communities are?

Behavior Modification

Because prisons are closely controlled environments, they represent a setting that is adaptable to *behavior modification*. This treatment technique is based on the assumptions that criminal behavior is learned, and that it can be altered through a system of rewards and punishments in an institutional setting. However, it also has been criticized for reducing human dignity through manipulative stimulus-followed-by-response types of interaction.

Most often used in juvenile facilities, behavior modification often has taken the form of a "token economy." In this system, tokens that can be used to purchase institutional privileges are awarded for good behavior and taken away for misconduct. One of the difficulties, of course, has been identifying effective reinforcers of approved behavior, since what may be motivating to one person may have little relevance to another. The process is also vulnerable to manipulation by inmates who quickly "learn the system" and superficially comply without altering their fundamental behavior. Additionally, there is concern that even valid changes which do occur may be temporary features of the rigidly controlled environment of prisons, rather than long-term behavioral improvements, which carry over to the freedom of life on the outside.

Most disturbing, however, is the fact that some of the correctional procedures dubiously referred to as "behavior modification" have gone well beyond what was originally meant by the term—turning into "fiendish forms of punishment." [63] Examples include the use of electroshock, aversive therapy, mind-altering drugs, and psychosurgery. In response to the abuse of these techniques, litigation was generated that has helped to eliminate many of these forms of "behavior modification" from prison systems.[64]

Drug Therapy and Other Behavioral Controls

Tranquilizing drugs, however, have continued to be used because of their sedative effect in controlling violent, angry, or unruly offenders. As recently as 2000, officials admitted that nearly 10 percent of the state prison population receives psychotropic medications, and in five states, that figure is nearly double (20 percent) [65]—despite criticisms that such tranquilizing drugs represent "an inconspicuous form of repression" that "disguises control as therapy."[66] In fact, it was only in 1990 that the Supreme Court determined that "a prison could not forcibly medicate a mentally ill person as punishment nor . . . forcibly medicate a mentally healthy inmate to achieve security objectives."[67]

The administration of drugs as a substitute for treatment has been one of the unfortunate byproducts of an inadequate number of therapeutic personnel. But even when used more for the control of personality disorders than for managerial convenience, such medications do not specifically attempt to change criminal behavior.

Reality Therapy

If there is one area of correctional treatment that has been almost as controversial as behavior modification, it is *reality therapy*. Originally, reality therapy was developed by a psychiatrist who became disenchanted with traditional therapeutic techniques and created a system diametrically opposed to orthodox psychoanalytic approaches.[68] It takes the position that excuses for deviant behavior should be faced realistically, and that the most appropriate therapeutic approach is getting involved with the client, rejecting irresponsible behavior, and encouraging acceptance of responsibility for one's own actions.

Some of the key words in reality therapy are "responsibility," "involvement," "here and now," and "facing the consequences." Focus is on discussing the client's current situation as one of his or her "own choosing," while still making the person feel loved and worthwhile. The idea is that aggressively dealing with reality in a therapeutic frame of reference can communicate love (sometimes called "tough love") and generate self-respect through firm but caring steps.

More recently, several new forms of reality-based behavior therapy have emerged that appear to hold considerable potential—including anger management and cognitive-restructuring programs. Such efforts emphasize changing inappropriate behavioral responses and antisocial thought patterns that have played a significant part in igniting the offender's conflicts with society.

On the one hand, this technique may be helpful in encouraging young offenders to take responsibility for their problems and regaining control over their lives. But on the other hand, its weakness may lie in oversimplification of human behavior and the potential for worsening some types of mental illness by expectations that are too demanding.

Cognitive Restructuring

One of the most recent therapeutic trends has been in the area of cognitive restructuring—attempting to change first the way people think, and ultimately, the way they act. The basis of this theory is that criminals do not think like law-abiding prosocial people. Rather, their thinking "rationalizes and justifies" their behavior by making excuses, blaming others, and playing the role of victim.[69]

Therapists have identified a number of these common errors or distortions in cognitive processing that can have serious implications for subsequent behavior.[70] Programs that use this approach are based on the premise that changing thinking patterns changes self-image, and ultimately, behavior. Through cognitive restructuring, offenders learn how to identify and change their thought patterns. They learn that "by controlling their thinking and changing their perceptions of events around them, they gain the ability to make appropriate choices."[71] Prosocial reasoning, self-control, and problem-solving strategies are emphasized in an open, empathetic atmosphere.[72]

One such program, for example, works with violent juvenile offenders to help them develop insights into and strategies for dealing with such characteristic problems as expressing anger, lying, and projecting blame. They learn how to take responsibility for their actions and to defer immediate gratification. Self-reflections are used to explore the inmate's thought processes, and participants eventually begin to see how "certain events trigger cycles or patterns of thinking." The object is then to "design and practice interventions to derail the cycle and avoid the thought patterns that led to violent behavior."[73] Since cognitive restructuring is relatively new, it has not been subjected to extensive long-term evaluations, although at least one three-year study has shown positive results.[74] Moreover, the reaction of participants appears to be favorable. As one summarized the process, "I guess I don't have to do the same old stuff if I don't think the same old way."[75]

Psychiatric and Psychoanalytic Treatment

Psychiatric involvement in corrections is generally limited to initial diagnosis, treatment prediction, and subsequent consultation with the psychologists, social workers, and other counselors who make up the bulk of institutional treatment staff. As shown in Figure 8.8, the extremely small number of psychiatrists working in the correctional field suggests that long-term *psychoanalytic techniques* designed to uncover deep-rooted causes of behavior have not frequently been employed in prison settings. Within the criminal justice system, most psychiatrists function outside of corrections in the pretrial and courtroom phases of the process—to determine whether defendants are of sufficient mental competence to be held legally responsible for their actions.

When an extremely disturbed inmate is in need of mental health services, referral is usually made to a psychiatric hospital for treatment. In fact, some correctional departments, in conjunction with the state mental health agency, maintain a separate forensic facility exclusively for the criminally insane. (For a more detailed account of how the mentally ill are handled in corrections, *see* Chapter 11.)

Social Casework

Historically, the partnership between social work and corrections began early in the twentieth century, when private charities and reform groups were becoming increasingly involved with offenders. As the field progressed toward development of the concept of self-determination, social work became the art of "helping people help themselves."

Because of this emphasis on empowerment of the individual client, however, social work has not been as amenable to the authoritarian setting of institutional corrections. As a result, social casework is used more frequently in community corrections (particularly probation and parole), minimum-security institutions,

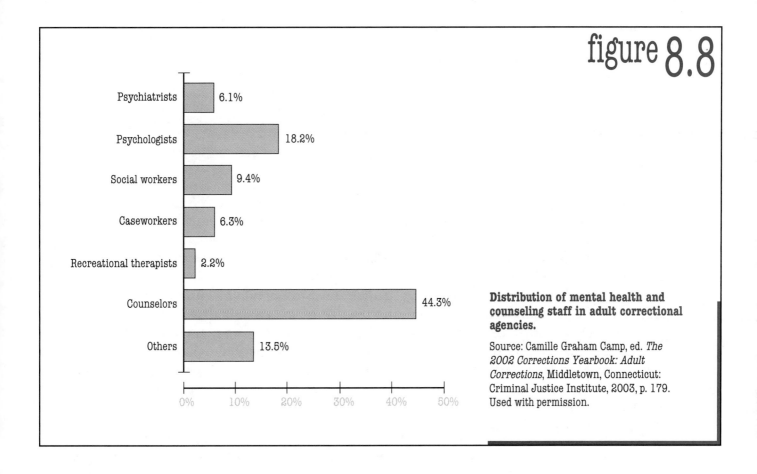

figure 8.8

Psychiatrists 6.1%

Psychologists 18.2%

Social workers 9.4%

Caseworkers 6.3%

Recreational therapists 2.2%

Counselors 44.3%

Others 13.5%

Distribution of mental health and counseling staff in adult correctional agencies.

Source: Camille Graham Camp, ed. *The 2002 Corrections Yearbook: Adult Corrections*, Middletown, Connecticut: Criminal Justice Institute, 2003, p. 179. Used with permission.

juvenile facilities, and diagnostic processing, as opposed to the direct delivery of services in high-security prisons.

Social work techniques typically include social casework and group work, along with practices ranging from community organization and individual problem solving to Freudian diagnostic and therapeutic approaches. But generally, the emphasis is more on dealing with one's immediate situation than on in-depth psychotherapy. Caseworkers help clients maintain constructive relationships, solve problems, and function independently.[76]

Nontraditional and Interdisciplinary Techniques

The psychoanalysis practiced by psychiatrists, the casework methods used by social workers, the group and individual therapy performed by psychologists, and the informal counseling conducted by many others all represent traditional approaches to working with people. Those who have become disenchanted with these orthodox procedures have advocated such nontraditional concepts as transactional analysis, primal therapy, systematic desensitization, nondirective therapy—and more recently—even acupuncture, pet therapy, and transcendental meditation, along with many others. Generally, these new techniques have been directed toward a certain group representing a proportionally small segment of the total correctional caseload. For an exception to this narrow approach, *see* the nontraditional strategy described in the next "Close-up On Corrections," where productivity, decision making, and accountability are emphasized throughout the institution in preparation for the realities of life on the outside.

Close-up On Corrections

Preparing for Life on the Outside—Missouri's Parallel Universe

Recognizing the disconnection between life inside and outside of prison, the Missouri Department of Corrections has overhauled its approach to prison management. The new strategy, "parallel universe," is based on the notion that life inside should resemble life outside, and that inmates can acquire values, habits, and skills that will help them become productive, law-abiding citizens.

In conventional prison management, institutional control eliminates any opportunity for prisoners to make decisions and be held accountable. The primary staff activity is surveillance, and the prison environment prevents normal social interaction. Avoiding punishment becomes the primary occupation. In exercising strong control, traditional prison management does not develop two important skills that offenders need—making decisions and accepting their consequences. But in Missouri, the structure of prison life has been re-engineered to include four interactive components:

(1) *Productivity*: Every inmate is engaged in productive activities that parallel those of free society. During "work hours," they go to school, jobs, and treatment programs. During "nonwork hours," they participate in community service, recreation, and reparative activities, such as victim-offender mediation, victim-impact classes, and specific projects designed to repair the harm suffered by victims. Treatment is the first step. Relapse prevention is the second.

(2) *Prevention*: Everyone must adopt relapse-prevention strategies and abstain from unauthorized activities, including drug/alcohol use and sexual misconduct. Because they are aware of their need for treatment as well as the risk of reoffending, they are better able to make related decisions.

(3) *Decision making*: Most offenders can earn opportunities to make choices, and they are held accountable for them.

(4) *Motivation*: Offenders are recognized for good conduct and can improve their status by obeying rules and regulations.

From an institutional management standpoint, this approach also has obvious advantages, since most inmates do not commit crimes while productively engaged in work or school activities. But the real evidence of its effectiveness occurs when they are released.

On admission, felons in the Missouri prison system could be considered failures on a number of counts. The vast majority were high school dropouts. Many were unable to obtain or hold a job. Most had abused drugs and/or alcohol. But since Missouri prisons adopted components of the parallel universe, many failures have been transformed into successes. Now, more than 98 percent of the inmate population is engaged in some combination of full-time

(continued)

Close-up On Corrections

(CONTINUED)

education, work, and/or treatment. Lawsuits initiated by prisoners have dropped substantially. But perhaps most impressive, between 1994 and 1999, recidivism was reduced by one-third (from 33 percent to 20 percent). This clearly translates into a correctional system that is more effectively preparing those on the inside for life on the outside.

Source: Compiled from Dora Schiro, "Correcting Corrections: Missouri's Parallel Universe," *Sentencing and Corrections: Issues for the 21st Century*, Washington, D.C.: U.S. Department of Justice: May 2000.

None of the traditional or nontraditional approaches works with everyone, but each seems to work with someone. Some offenders are reformed through psychiatric help; others because they learned a job skill; others because they found religion; and still others simply because someone took an interest in them. It is apparent that no single type of treatment is demonstrably superior to any other one. No single program or process represents the ideal solution for every client. Each has its unique strengths and weaknesses. Each works better with some offenders or at some point in their lives than others.

Although treatment personnel might like to draw from a broad array of techniques, the extensive training needed to become a professional in any one area creates a narrowly focused perspective. As a result, most identify with one or two approaches, neglecting the larger body of knowledge outside of their professional discipline. Similarly, budgetary constraints combined with political ideologies often result in correctional institutions adopting a narrowly limited range of techniques to offer everyone within their custody. Given this "one-size-fits-all" approach, it is not surprising that researchers often have reported disappointing results of correctional treatment. However, a review of some 700 studies indicates that when offenders participate in programs that are appropriate to their specific needs, reductions in recidivism range from 25 to 30 percent.[78]

Therapeutic Communities

Some institutional settings have embraced a much wider variety of treatment alternatives that are not based on a single method. An example of such a multifaceted approach is the prison that functions as an overall *therapeutic community*. As the next "Close-up On Corrections" describes, these "communities" are based on the concept that multiple interdisciplinary techniques focusing on prosocial values, combined with a treatment-oriented custodial staff, and a supportive peer culture can produce an institutional environment directed

Close-up On Corrections

INSIDE A THERAPEUTIC COMMUNITY

In comparison to prisons, therapeutic communities are nonbureaucratic. There is a minimum of clearly defined rules, and decision making is decentralized to facilitate the goal of individualized treatment. The staff are either trained professionals or lay personnel who receive extensive and continuous training in treatment skills . . . In their relations with clients, the staff is expected to minimize status distinctions, to encourage open and spontaneous communication, and to develop close, personal relations in an effort to gain client cooperation and identification with the staff and the goals of the institution. . . . Misconduct by clients is interpreted as symptomatic of an underlying problem, and any punishment is consistent with therapeutic recommendations. Punishment is thus minimized and highly individualized.

The client is expected to develop a life as similar as possible to life in the free community through involvement in the work, educational, religious, and recreational programs provided. . . . Relations within residential units are expected to resemble family relations. Group therapy sessions are conducted within the residential unit, perhaps on a daily basis. Further, each cottage is largely a self-governing unit, and administrative and maintenance problems are resolved by means of group decisions.

What distinguishes TCs [therapeutic communities] is the "community" or group as the primary facilitator of growth and change. . . . Clients live isolated from the rest of the prison population and receive treatment to change negative patterns of behavior, thinking, and feeling. . . .

Participation generally lasts for an extended period. The time and the isolation are primary resources; the isolation, in particular, shields clients from competing demands of street, work, friends, and family. TCs have other features in common: use of ex-offenders and ex-addicts as staff, use of confrontation and support groups, a set of rules and sanctions to govern behavior, and promotion of prosocial attitudes. . . . Transformations in conduct, attitudes, values, and emotions are monitored and mutually reinforced. It may be this multiple focus that explains why TCs are more likely to be successful in the long run.

Source: Adapted from Douglas S. Lipton, "Prison-Based Therapeutic Communities: Their Success with Drug-Abusing Offenders," *National Institute of Justice Journal*, February 1996, p. 13.

toward behavioral change.[79] In this manner, everyone works together toward providing a cohesive, supportive network. As one treatment administrator put it, "Acupuncture would not work without counseling, counseling would not work without job development, and job development would not work without education."[80]

In fact, some therapeutic communities extend into postrelease aftercare, which has been reported to have positive results with drug-involved offenders.[81] While there has been some exception taken to the "premature" belief in

Close-up On Corrections

PRINCIPLES OF EFFECTIVE INTERVENTION

1. *Services should be intensive and behavioral in nature*—occupying 40 percent to 70 percent of the offenders' time over three-to-nine months in a program based on the principles of operant conditioning, which uses positive reinforcers that are contingent on behavior.

2. *Behavioral programs should target the criminogenic needs of high-risk offenders*—matching treatment with the offender's risk level.

3. *Characteristics of offenders, therapists, and programs should be matched*—thereby avoiding the temptation to treat all offenders as if they had identical personality traits, attitudes, and beliefs.

4. *Program contingencies and behavioral strategies should be enforced in a firm but fair manner*—with positive reinforcement exceeding punishment by a ratio of at least four to one.

5. *Therapists should relate to offenders in interpersonally sensitive and constructive ways and should be trained and supervised appropriately*—thereby better assuring that treatment personnel actually adhere to the principles and employ the techniques of the therapy they purport to provide.

6. *Program structure and activities should be designed to disrupt the delinquent/criminal network by placing offenders in situations where prosocial activities predominate*—as another behavioral modeling reinforcer.

7. *Relapse-prevention strategies should be provided in the community to the extent possible*—with significant others, such as family and friends, trained to provide reinforcement for prosocial behavior.

8. *A high level of advocacy and brokerage should be attempted*—wherever possible, referring offenders to community-based services that can address their problems.

Source: Compiled from Paul Gendreau, "The Principles of Effective Intervention with Offenders," in Alan T. Harland, ed., *Choosing Correctional Options that Work: Defining the Demand and Evaluating the Supply*, Thousand Oaks, California: Sage, 1996, pp. 120-125.

---

the substantial impact of therapeutic communities,[82] studies have reported recidivism among therapeutic community graduates at 26-29 percent, compared to 63-74 percent for prison-based treatment groups.[83]

The Future of Prison Programming

Every approach does not work equally effectively with every offender. The question then becomes just what *does* seem to work best? The two "Close-up

Close-up On Corrections

ELEMENTS OF A SUCCESSFUL TREATMENT PROGRAM

1. *It provides specific guidelines for the use of positive reinforcement.* Behavioral programs have been found to be more successful than nondirective or "talking" programs. This element implies that there should be clear and consistent procedures for awarding positive reinforcements.

2. *It draws from a variety of sources.* This may be the most effective mode of service delivery, in that some elements may work for different types of offenders.

3. *It is heavily scripted.* The value of this element is that it reduces the chance of counselor bias or diminishing program content through counselor apathy or lack of training. A heavily scripted program implies that one should be able to go to several different locations and observe the same program.

4. *It is based on evaluated results.* Obviously, it is a waste of time or money if the program has not been evaluated or results indicate no change is induced in program participants.

5. *It requires structured activity of the learner.* This principle is consistent with other learning theory that supports the notion that we learn by doing, not by listening or watching.

6. *It requires transfer of training to everyday life.* Programs that have little applicability to the offender's life will be forgotten as soon as the offender is released.

7. *It includes a method of teacher monitoring.* This is to reduce the possibility that the program is made less effective or is changed by the individual counselor.

8. *It contains an outcome evaluation.*

9. *It contains a technique and rationale for client selection.* This is consistent with studies that indicate that certain types of programs work better for certain types of offenders.

10. *It is repetitive and integrated.*

11. *It requires active participation from the teacher.*

12. *It is constructed for a specific purpose and for a specific client.*

Source: Joycelyn Pollock, "Rehabilitation Revisited," *Prisons: Today and Tomorrow*, Sudbury, Massachusetts: Jones and Bartlett Publishers, 1997, p. 206-207. Reprinted with permission.

On Corrections" features on pages 291-292 provide some answers—identifying the fundamental principles of effective intervention and the elements of a successful treatment program. Especially with so much focus today on the negative aspects of corrections and the failures among its clients, it is important to keep in mind that properly structured programs based on appropriate treatment techniques *do* hold promise and have potential to alter lives.

But with the change from the therapeutic focus of the medical model to the incapacitation emphasis of the justice model, enthusiasm for prison-based rehabilitative efforts has diminished. What the future holds remains to be seen, but it is apparent that the orientation of prison programming has shifted from treatment to security.[84]

It is equally clear that if insufficient resources were available to implement the mandates of the medical model, it is not very realistic to expect more during times of greater fiscal restraint and political conservatism. Prison-based programming simply has not kept pace with the dramatic growth in institutional populations.[85] Yet, research indicates that "effective treatment results in savings to society that outweigh the costs of treatment by a factor of at least four to one." [86] In fact, when managed effectively, alcohol and drug treatment have been cited as saving $7 for every $1 spent.[87]

Limited resources and lessened enthusiasm are not the only current drawbacks to treatment. Prison-based rehabilitative programs are inherently difficult to manage and administer, regardless of the specific modality, qualifications of staff, or sincerity of participants. Correctional institutions "are simply ill-suited for intensive treatment programs." [88] Moreover, transferring treatment progress to the real world from the artificial environment of a correctional institution represents a significant challenge. In that respect, the better option is to expand the availability of treatment programs outside of the correctional conglomerate. As one researcher has pointed out, "instead of advocating treatment in prison, we should be trying treatment *instead of prison.*" [89]

Summary

Some would maintain that correctional treatment is limited to therapeutic intervention by licensed professionals following a clinical diagnosis. In contrast, this chapter has reflected a broader perspective encompassing many of the programs and services provided within correctional facilities that promote socializing influences among the inmate population.

Whatever one's perspective of treatment, within corrections, the process begins with initial classification. Through proper classification, the institution is better able to manage large groups of offenders, meet individual requirements, prioritize needs, and distribute scarce resources. Recently, objective models have been used to streamline classification. But concerns have been expressed that such a highly structured process dehumanizes classification, substituting administrative efficiency for an in-depth assessment of needs. Additionally, prison crowding can prohibit placing inmates in those facilities and programs best suited to their needs. Nevertheless, classification outcomes have a long-term impact on the offender.

Regardless of how an inmate is classified, religious services represent one form of "treatment" to which everyone is entitled. Beginning with the Quakers, religion always has played a key role in corrections. Although chaplains are not always fully accepted by either inmates or staff, they can be very influential. Beyond providing worship services and faith-based studies, one of the most significant roles of the chaplain is simply being a willing listener.

Following religion, education and vocational training were the next major rehabilitative programs to be introduced into correctional institutions. Because so many inmates have not completed high school or are functionally illiterate, correctional clients are especially in need of remedial education. Computer-assisted instruction has been helpful in this respect, since it enables classes to be provided on an ongoing basis and tailors learning to individual capabilities.

Work has been a central feature of prisons throughout the history of corrections. But it has only been in relatively modern times that employment and vocational training have been directed toward developing marketable job skills rather than making financial profits. Although wide varieties of vocational programs are available throughout corrections today, they are still insufficient to meet the demand. Efforts therefore have been underway to encourage the private sector to become involved in establishing prison and jail industries.

While such vocational opportunities are limited, virtually all inmates have access to recreation, which can encompass everything from team sports to arts and crafts, music, drama, table games, hobbies, television, and videos. Recreation programs not only relieve boredom and idleness, but also can help to reduce the stress and anxiety of incarceration.

The more traditional forms of treatment provided in corrections include counseling, casework, and clinical services. Even during the height of the medical model, such programs have not been readily available, and many treatment personnel find themselves more immersed in routine processing than in direct service delivery. Of all forms of treatment, counseling represents that which is most commonly available (although the term counseling has sometimes been interpreted very broadly in the correctional setting). In contrast to one-on-one counseling sessions, group therapy can serve more clients in a less-threatening atmosphere. Inmates themselves also have formed such self-help groups as Alcoholics Anonymous and Narcotics Anonymous.

Another form of treatment, behavior modification, originally was designed to change behavior through the conditioning power of rewards and punishments. However, efforts to modify behavior at times have extended to such aversive techniques as electroshock and mind-altering drugs. Although many of these practices have been terminated as a result of legal intervention, tranquilizing drugs are still used to control violent, angry, or disruptive inmates.

Numerous additional techniques have been attempted at one time or another—ranging from reality therapy to cognitive restructuring. However, long-term psychoanalysis has not been frequently employed in corrections. Similarly, social work has not been a part of the treatment program of many correctional institutions, in part because its focus on self-determination and individual empowerment can conflict with an authoritarian setting. Social casework, however, has been used much more extensively in juvenile facilities and community corrections.

Historically, correctional institutions have offered a limited range of treatment techniques, despite the fact that no one alternative will work equally well with all inmates. To provide a multifaceted approach that incorporates a number of disciplines, therapeutic communities direct the total environment toward behavioral change. A broader array of treatment alternatives certainly presents greater potential for meeting the needs of any particular person. But with society's move from the medical model to the more punitive justice model, issues surrounding how best to diagnose, treat, and change behavior are no longer prominent concerns of the correctional conglomerate.

Endnotes

1.   Quoted in J. M. Taylor, "Pell Grants for Prisoners," *The Nation*, January 25, 1993, p. 90.

2.   Richard G. Kiekbusch, "Leadership Roles: How Are We Doing?" *American Jails*, November/December 1992, p. 6.

3.   Margaret C. Hambrick, "Intervention Programs: Setting Change in Motion," *Corrections Today*, Vol. 53, No. 5, August 1991, p. 6.

4.   W. Wesley Johnson, Katherine Bennett, and Timothy J. Flanagan, "Getting Tough on Prisoners: Results from the National Corrections Executive Survey, 1995," *Crime and Delinquency*, Vol. 43, No. 1, January 1997, p. 31.

5.   Francis T. Cullen, Edward J. Latessa, Velmer S. Burton, and Lucien X. Lombardo, "The Correctional Orientation of Prison Wardens: Is the Rehabilitative Ideal Supported?" *Criminology*, Vol. 31, No. 1, 1993, pp. 84-85.

6.   W. Ray Nelson, "The First International Symposium on the Future of Law Enforcement," *Direct Supervision Network*, Vol. 1, April/June 1991, p. 4.

7.   The titles of classification periods used throughout this section generally reflect those identified by Leonard J. Hippchen, "Trends in Classification Philosophy and Practice," in Leonard J. Hippchen, Edith E. Flynn, Chester D. Owens, and Alfred C. Schnur, eds., *Handbook on Correctional Classification: Programming for Treatment and Reintegration*, Cincinnati, Ohio: Anderson Publishing Company, 1978.

8.   Michael W. Forcier, "The Development of the Modern Classification System," in Bruce I. Wolford and Pam Lawrenz, eds., *Classification: Innovative Correctional Programs*, Richmond, Kentucky: Department of Correctional Services, 1988, p. 1.

9.   Simon Dinitz, "The Transformation of Corrections: 50 Years of Silent Revolutions," *Training Manual: Executive Training for New Wardens*, Longmont, Colorado: National Institute of Corrections, February 2000, p. 15.

10. Hans Toch, "The Care and Feeding of Typologies and Labels," *Federal Probation*, Vol. 34, No. 3, September 1970, pp. 15-19.

11. Donal E. J. MacNamara, "The Medical Model in Corrections: *Requiesat in Pace*," *Criminology*, Vol. 14, No. 4, February 1977, pp. 439-440.

12. In one alcohol/drug treatment program, for example, it was found that court-ordered referrals had better success rates than did voluntary entrants. Marie Ragghianti and Toni Glenn, *Reducing Recidivism: Treating the Addicted Inmate*, Center City, Minnesota: Hazelden, 1991, p. 12.

13. Hans Toch, "Inmate Classification as a Transaction," *Criminal Justice and Behavior*, Vol. 8, No. 1, March 1981, p. 4.

14. Forcier, "Modern Classification System," p. 2, citing James Austin, "Assessing the New Generation of Prison Classification Models," *Crime and Delinquency*, Vol. 29, No. 4, October 1983, pp. 561-576.

15. President's Commission on Law Enforcement and Administration of Justice, *Task Force Report: Corrections*, Washington, D.C.: U.S. Government Printing Office, 1967, p. 20.

16. Robert A. Buchanan and Karen L. Whitlow, *Guidelines for Developing, Implementing, and Revising an Objective Prison Classification System*, Washington, D.C.: National Institute of Justice, 1987, p.1. *See also Jail Classification System Development: A Review of the Literature*, Longmont, Colorado: National Institute of Corrections, 1992, p. 12-13.

17. Jack Alexander and James Austin, *Handbook for Evaluating Objective Prison Classification Systems*, Washington, D.C.: National Institute of Corrections, 1992, p. 1.

18. James Austin, "Objective Offender Classification is Key to Proper Housing Decisions," *Corrections Today*, Vol. 56, No. 4, July 1994, pp. 94-96.

19. Mary Dallao, "Keeping Classification Current: Old Systems Must Adjust to Changing Times," *Corrections Today*, Vol. 59, No. 4, July 1997, p. 88.

20. Carl B. Clements, "Offender Classification: Two Decades of Progress," *Criminal Justice and Behavior*, Vol. 23, No. 1, March 1996, p. 139.

21. "Survey Summary: Faith-based Programming," *Corrections Compendium*, Vol. 28, No. 8, August 2003, p. 8.

22. Allen Beck *et al.*, *Survey of State Prison Inmates, 1991*, Washington, D.C.: U.S. Department of Justice, 1993, p. 27.

23. Todd Clear, *et al.*, *Prisoners, Prisons, and Religion: Final Report*, Camden, New Jersey: School of Criminal Justice, Rutgers University, 1992

24. Judith Coleman, "Chaplains: God's Partners in Prison," *Corrections Today*, Vol. 67, No. 7, December 2003, p. 122.

25. For additional suggestions, *see* Robert Toll, "How a Multifaith Chaplaincy Program Operates in a County Detention Facility," *American Jails*, January/ February 2004, pp. 19-24.

26. Phil Danna, "Lights, Camera, Religion," *American Jails*, July/August 1992, pp. 60-62.

27. Melvina T. Sumter and Todd R. Clear, "Religion in the Correctional Setting," in Roslyn Muraskin, ed., *Key Correctional Issues*, Upper Saddle River, New Jersey: Prentice Hall, 2004, p. 113.

28. Byron R. Johnson and David B. Larson, "Linking Religion to the Mental and Physical Health of Inmates: A Literature Review and Research Note," *American Jails*, September/October 1997, pp. 29-30.

29. Pat Nolan, "Prison Fellowship and Faith-based Initiatives, *On the Line*, Vol. 25, No. 5, November 2002, p. 1.

30. Stephen T. Hall, "Faith-based Cognitive Programs in Corrections," *Corrections Today*, Vol. 65, No. 7, December 2003, p. 113. *See also* Rebecca L. Propst, *Psychotherapy in a Religious Framework: Spirituality in the Emotional Healing Process*, New York: Human Science Press, 1988.

31. Caroline Wolf Harlow, "Education and Correctional Populations," *Bureau of Justice Statistics Special Report*, Washington, D.C.: U.S. Department of Justice, 2003, p. 1.

32. "High-Tech Tutors: Wisconsin Uses Literacy Program Statewide," *Corrections Today*, Vol. 52, No. 7, December 1990, p. 142.

33. Dennis J. Stevens, "Educational Programming for Offenders," *Forum on Correctional Research*, Vol. 12, No. 2, May 2000, p. 30.

34. Michelle Tolbert, *State Correctional Education Programs: State Policy Update*, Washington, D.C.: National Institute for Literacy, 2002.

35. For a description of a reading programs that is designed to strengthen bonds between incarcerated parents and their children, *see* Sara Urrutia, "Words Travel: A Model Family-strengthening and Literacy Program," *Corrections Today*, Vol. 66, No. 2, April 2004, pp. 80-83.

36. "STEP: Star Network Expands Distance-learning Services," *Correctional Education Bulletin*, Vol. 3, No. 2, November 1999, pp. 1, 6.

37. Sylvia G. McCollum, "Prison College Programs," *The Prison Journal*, Vol. 73, No. 1, March 1994, p. 51. *See also* Stevens, "Educational Programming," p. 30, where "solid support for a positive relationship between correctional education and reduced recidivism" was noted in the vast majority (85 percent) of ninety-seven studies published between 1969 and 1993.

38. Johnson, Bennett, and Flanagan, "Getting Tough on Prisoners," p. 33.

39. James J. Stephan and Jennifer C. Karberg, *Census of State and Federal Correctional Facilities, 2000*, Washington, D.C.: U.S. Department of Justice, Bureau of Justice Statistics, 2003, p. 11.

40. Barbara J. Auerbach, George E. Sexton, Franklin C. Farrow, and Robert H. Lawson, *Work in American Prisons: The Private Sector Gets Involved*, Washington, D.C.: U.S. Department of Justice, 1988, p. 9.

41. James J. Stephan and Jennifer C. Karberg, *Census*, p. 11.

42. Simon Dinitz, "The Transformation of Corrections: 50 Years of Silent Revolutions," *Training Manual: Executive Training for New Wardens*, Longmont, Colorado: National Institute of Corrections, February 2000, p. 15.

43. Allen Beck *et al.*, *Survey of State Prison Inmates, 1991*, Washington, D.C.: U.S. Department of Justice, Bureau of Justice Statistics, 1993, p. 27.

44. *Ibid.*

45. Barbara Auerbach, "Private Sector Jail Industries," *American Jails*, May/June 2003, pp. 15-18.

46. Timothy Flanagan, "Prison Labor and Industry," in Lynne Goodstein and Doris Layton MacKenzie, eds. *The American Prison: Issues in Research and Policy*, New York: Plenum Press, 1989, p. 153.

47. Peter Finn, "No-Frills Prisons and Jails: A Movement in Flux," *Federal Probation*, September 1996, pp. 35-43.

48. "TV or Not TV? Programming for Inmates to Get Educational Spin," *Law Enforcement News*, October 15,1996, p. 1.

49. Alfred C. Schnur, "The New Penology: Fact or Fiction?" *Journal of Criminal Law, Criminology and Police Science*, Vol. 49, November/December 1958, pp. 331-334.

50. President's Commission on Law Enforcement and Administration of Justice, *Task Force Report*, p. 97.

51. Michael S. Serrill, "Is Rehabilitation Dead?" *Corrections Magazine*, Vol. 1, No. 5, May/June 1975, pp. 3-7, 10-12, 21, 32.

52. Charles W. Thomas and David M. Petersen, *Prison Organization and Inmate Subcultures*, Indianapolis, Indiana: Bobbs-Merrill,1977, p. 36.

53. Jerome Miller, "Sentencing: What Lies between Sentiment and Ignorance?" *Justice Quarterly*, No. 3, 1986, p. 231.

54. For a look at how one system has more recently established such a custody-treatment partnership, *see* Sherry Macpherson, "Collaboration between Clinicians and Custody Staff Benefits the Entire Prison," *Corrections Today*, Vol. 66, No. 2, April 2004, pp. 116-119.

55. *Mentally Ill Offenders in the Criminal Justice System: An Analysis and Prescription*, Washington, D.C.: The Sentencing Project, 2002, p. 3.

56. *Estelle v. Gamble*, 97 S. Ct. 285 (1976). In this case, an inmate sued on the grounds that he was denied parole because of a psychological evaluation indicating that he would not complete the parole period successfully; yet the institution had not offered psychiatric services to deal with his problems.

57. Daniel Pollak, "Legal Briefs: *Bailey v. Gardebring*, U.S. Court of Appeals, 8th Circuit, *Corrections Today*, Vol. 54, No. 2, April 1991, pp. 26-28.

58. Kenneth Adams, Timothy J. Flanagan, and James W. Marquart, "The Future of the Penitentiary," in Timothy J. Flanagan, James W. Marquart, and Kenneth G. Adams, eds., *Incarcerating Criminals: Prisons and Jails in Social and Organizational Context*, New York: Oxford University Press, 1998, p. 326.

59. *The National Manpower Survey of the Criminal Justice System*, Vol. 3, Corrections, Washington, D.C.: U.S. Department of Justice, 1978, p. 77.

60. Michael Braswell, "The Purpose of Correctional Counseling" in David Lester, Michael Braswell, and Patricia Van Voorhis, eds., *Correctional Counseling*, Second Edition, Cincinnati, Ohio: Anderson Publishing Company, 1992, p. 25.

61. David Lester and Patricia Van Voorhis, "Group and Milieu Therapy," in Lester *et al.*, *Correctional Counseling*, p. 175. *See also* Ed Jacobs and Nina Spadaro, *Leading Groups in Corrections: Skills and Techniques*, Lanham, Maryland, American Correctional Association, 2003.

62. "Budget Cuts Affect Drug Treatment," *Correctional News*, Vol. 8, No. 3, May/June 2002, p. 1. The state referred to is Florida.

63. Wayne Sage, "Crime and Clockwork Lemon," *Human Behavior*, Vol. 3, No. 9, September 1974, pp. 16-25. See also "Behavior Modification Program Report Released by GAO," *Corrections Digest*, Vol. 6, No. 17, August 30,1975, pp. 1-2.

64. *See* "Symposium—The Control of Behavior: Legal, Scientific, and Moral Dilemmas, Part I," *Criminal Law Bulletin*, Vol. 2, No. 5, September/October 1975, pp. 598-636. Court cases have supported the right of an individual to freedom or privacy of the mind [*Stanley v. Georgia*, 394 U.S. 559 (1968)] and raised serious questions regarding "tinkering" with mental processes through the use of drugs [*Mackey v. Procunier*, 477 F. 2d 877 (1973)].

65. Allen J. Beck and Laura M. Maruschak, "Mental Health Treatment in State Prisons, 2000," *Bureau of Justice Statistics: Special Report*, Washington, D.C.: U.S. Department of Justice, 2001, p. 1 and 4.

66. Richard Speiglman, "Prison Drugs, Psychiatry, and the State," in David F. Greenberg, ed., *Corrections and Punishment*, Beverly Hills, California: Sage Publications, 1977, pp. 155-163.

67. *Washington v. Harper* case (110 S. Ct. 1028); *see* Fred Cohen, "A Closer Look at Mentally Disordered Inmates and Forcible Medication," *Correctional Law Reporter*, Vol. 2, No. 2, May 1990, p. 20. More recently, the Louisiana Supreme Court held in 1992 that "an incompetent inmate cannot be forced to take drugs that might make him sane enough to be executed." *See* "National News Briefs," *Corrections Today*, Vol. 54, No. 8, December 1992, p. 16.

68. *See* William Glasser, *Reality Therapy*, New York: Harper and Row, 1965.

69. Boyd D. Sharp, *Changing Criminal Thinking: A Treatment Program*, Lanham, Maryland: American Correctional Association, 2000, p. 2.

70. Richard A. Wells, *Planned Short-Term Treatment*, New York: The Free Press, 1994, pp. 214-215. *See also* Jessica B. Konopa, *et al.*, "Recovery from the Inside Out: A Cognitive Approach to Rehabilitation," *Corrections Today*, Vol. 64, No. 5, August 2002, pp. 56-58.

71. Miriam Haworth, "Program to Improve Inmate Behavior Also Helps Boost Staff Relations," *Corrections Today*, Vol. 55, No. 7, December 1993, p. 120.

72. Paul Gendreau, "The Principles of Effective Intervention With Offenders," in Alan T. Harland, ed., *Choosing Correctional Options that Work, Defining the Demand and Evaluating the Supply*, Thousand Oaks, California: Sage, 1996, p. 121.

73. Pamela K. Withrow, "Cognitive Restructuring: An Approach to Dealing with Violent Inmates," *Corrections Today*, Vol. 56, No. 5, August 1994, pp. 112-115.

74. Sharp, *Changing Criminal Thinking*, pp. 125-27.

75. Jeanette Germain, "Addictions Recovery Cognitive Restructuring, and a Team Effort," *Corrections Today*, Vol. 58, No. 1, February 1996, p. 70.

76. Howard Abadinsky, *Probation and Parole*, Seventh Edition, Englewood Cliffs, New Jersey: Prentice Hall, 2000, p. 286-287.

77. *See*, for example, Shannon J. Osborne and Renee Bair, "Healing Inmates' Hearts and Spirits with Man's Best Friend," *Corrections Today*, Vol. 65, No. 2, April 2003, pp. 122-123, 146; Todd Harkrader, Tod W. Burke, and Stephen S. Owen, "Pound Puppies: The Rehabilitative Uses of Dogs in Correctional Facilities," *Corrections Today*, Vol. 66, No. 2, April 2004, pp. 74-79, and Charles N. Alexander *et al.*, eds., *Transcendental Meditation in Criminal Rehabilitation and Crime Prevention*, Binghamton, New York: Haworth Press, 2003.

78. *Principles of Effective Correctional Programming*, Toronto: Correctional Service of Canada, 2003.

79. *See* Faye S. Taxman and Jeffrey A. Bouffard, "Assessing Therapeutic Integrity in Modified Therapeutic Communities for Drug-involved Offenders," *The Prison Journal*, Vol. 82, No. 2, June 2002: 189-212.

80. Peter Finn and Andrea Newlyn, "Miami's Drug Court: A Different Approach," *National Institute of Justice: Program Focus*, Washington, D.C.: U.S. Department of Justice, 1993, p. 14.

81. James A. Inciardi *et al.*, "Therapeutic Communities and Work Release: Effective Modalities for Drug-involved Offenders," *NIJ Research Review*, Vol. 1, No. 3, September 2000, p. 2.

82. James Austin, "The Limits of Prison Drug Treatment," *Corrections Management Quarterly*, Vol. 2, No. 4, 1998, p. 73.

83. Brian Shapiro, "The Therapeutic Community Movement in Corrections," *Corrections Today*, Vol. 63, No. 1, February 2001, pp. 26, 32, citing research conducted by Douglas Lipton. *See also* the similar findings of M. L. Hiller *et al.*, "Prison-based Substance Treatment, Residential Aftercare, and Recidivism," *Addiction*, Vol. 94, No. 6, 1999, pp. 833-842.

84. Flanagan, Marquart, and Adams, *Incarcerating Criminals*, p. 326.

85. Daniel P. Mears, Sarah Lawrence, Amy L. Solomon, and Michelle Waul, "Prison-based Programming: What It Can Do and Why It is Needed," *Corrections Today*, Vol. 64, No. 2, April 2002, pp. 66-67.

86. *Substance Abuse Treatment for Women Offenders: Guide to Promising Practices*, Rockville, Maryland: U.S. Department of Health and Human Services, 2002, p. 12.

87. *For Our Health and Safety: Joining Forces to Beat Addiction*,   Sacramento, California: Little Hoover Commission on California State Government Organization and Economy, 2003.

88. Austin, "The Limits of Prison Drug Treatment," p. 73.

89. *Ibid.*

CHAPTER 9

THE EFFECTS OF INSTITUTIONAL LIFE

" A prison confines, punishes, and hopefully deters. It is neither designed nor inclined to foster, cure, or rehabilitate.[1] **"**

—Victor Hassine (Inmate AM4737)

Chapter Overview

The effects of being incarcerated are difficult for those in free society to fully appreciate. They range from the simple irritation of being required to eat the same monotonous food at precisely the same time day after day to the serious impact of being restricted from normal social relationships. They include the dehumanizing influence of everything from being subjected to strip searches to losing material possessions, personal privacy, and individual autonomy. They are the product of an environment in which inmates are secluded from the outside, subservient to the staff, subdued by the rules, subjected to the control of other inmates, socialized into the prison subculture, and silenced by the lack of public concern.

Under such conditions, hopelessness, frustration, and alienation find fertile breeding grounds. Some express their feelings in passive resignation, others in physical rebellion. Assaults, homicides, and suicides occur in virtually every correctional institution. Although considerably less frequent, riots represent the ultimate expression of built-up hostilities. The public is inevitably shocked when violence flares into a widespread riot. But it is perhaps more surprising that such major disturbances are relatively unusual events.

Those in free society might argue that by stripping the offender of human dignity, imprisonment will make the type of lasting, negative impression that will serve as a strong deterrent to recidivism. Quite the contrary, instead of leaving with a determination to avoid another prison term, many become accustomed to prison life and resigned to the inevitability of returning to it. Some become so acclimated to the prison routine and so apprehensive of their ability to "make it" on the outside, that, ironically, they are reluctant to leave.

Given the fact that even the best of the treatment techniques described in the previous chapter take place within such a dehumanizing environment, it is little wonder that they have been less than totally successful. Undoubtedly, there are those who have overcome the effects of prison to become law-abiding citizens. But they may well have done so despite—rather than because of—their experiences in confinement. In many respects, imprisonment represents more an obstacle to overcome than an opportunity to reform. It simply may be illogical to expect corrections to change behavior, given the incongruity of trying to teach offenders to adjust to society by removing them from it.

Learning Goals

Do you know:

1. What "prisonization" is?
2. How the importation model and the deprivation model differ in terms of their explanation of inmate socialization?
3. What behaviors characterize an "institutionalized" personality?
4. How social rejection contributes to the prisonization process?

The Process of Prisonization

Through the process of prisonization, inmates become socialized into prison life.[2] It involves adapting to the culture, values, norms, and behavioral expectations of the prison environment and virtually begins immediately on entry. In fact, incarceration has been found to promote prisonization among both new and experienced inmates.[3] The entering inmate is stripped, showered, deloused, given a uniform, assigned a number, and issued the rule book. Personal property is searched, inspected, and inventoried. Items that are not allowable are stored or shipped elsewhere. Hair is cut to standardized regulations. Stripped of these sources of individual identity, the depersonalization of imprisonment begins. As one inmate describes it, "One of the cruelest aspects of a penitentiary is the way it leaves one isolated and lonely despite the overcrowded surroundings."[4]

Reactions to the prisonization process range from physical or mental rebellion to abnormal hunger and the incapacity to sleep.[5] But free will and self-direction can be repressed only so far, even in the most regimented institution. In opposition to the authoritative controls of the administration, inmates create their own status hierarchy, code of conduct, and subcultural value system—governing everything from verbal communications to sexual activities. It

is not long before new inmates learn how personal autonomy finds expression within confinement. They quickly determine who wields power, controls privileges, and imposes punishments. Nor is it long before those imprisoned realize that they are subject not only to the formal rules and regulations established by the official administration, but also to the informal code imposed by their fellow prisoners. And among the inmate population, violation of the informal code is a far more serious infraction than violation of the official regulations.

Importation or Deprivation?

But just how does prison socialization take place? Is it simply a result of confining together large groups of offenders who share similar values, attitudes, and behaviors? If so, the attributes of prisonization are *imported* (in other words, brought into the institution) by the particular types of people who commit crime. Thus, we would not expect to find the same behaviors if prisons confined those of a different socioeconomic class or value background.

Certainly, one's moral values are bound to be affected by close, continuous association with others who do not adhere to socially acceptable norms. But is there also something about the nature of correctional institutions that creates an unnatural response among those who otherwise would not react the same way in a different environment? If so, the behavior of those confined may reflect a normal response to being abnormally *deprived* of everything from physical amenities to social status and personal self-esteem.[6] Figure 9.1 illustrates the differences between the importation and deprivation models of prisonization.

Regardless of which theory is ascribed to, it is apparent that prisons produce a unique culture that reflects either "response to the deprivations of

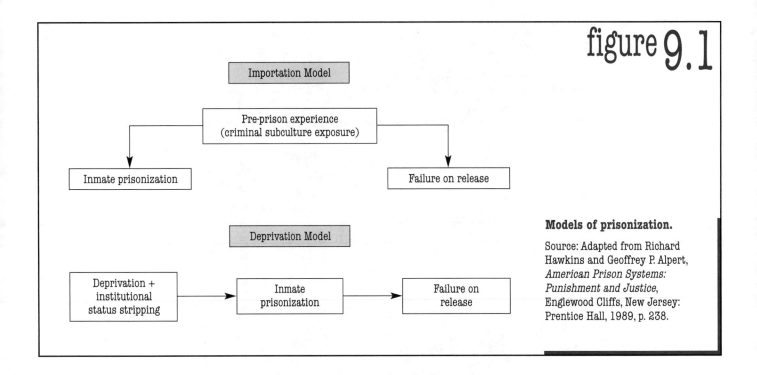

figure 9.1

Models of prisonization.

Source: Adapted from Richard Hawkins and Geoffrey P. Alpert, *American Prison Systems: Punishment and Justice,* Englewood Cliffs, New Jersey: Prentice Hall, 1989, p. 238.

prison existence or . . . re-creation of [one's] external environment within the walls." [7] Actually, it may be a little of each, with the two models complementing rather than contradicting each other.[8]

The Stanford Prison Experiment

A landmark experiment conducted with two dozen male college students acting in roles as inmates and officers may shed some light on this issue.[9] Those selected were mature, emotionally stable, intelligent students from middle-class backgrounds. None had any criminal record. In fact, they appeared to represent the "cream of the crop" of their generation. By the flip of a coin, half were assigned to play the role of "prisoners." The other half were designated as "guards," instructed to make up their own rules for maintaining law, order, and respect in the mock prison setting established by the researchers. How do you think you would react if placed in the role of an inmate or correctional officer? According to this experiment, your response might be quite different from what you would expect! *See* the next "Close-up On Corrections" for the chilling details of what actually happened.

The outcome of that experiment tends to support the deprivation model in a number of respects. The student inmates displayed many of the same prisonization characteristics as their real-life counterparts, despite the fact that their backgrounds were not at all representative of the typical prisoner. Additionally, the officer "guards" quickly assumed roles that reflected a repressive environment. As a result, the researchers concluded that we underestimate the power and pervasiveness of situational controls over behavior.[10]

At the same time, it should be noted that this brief experiment involved not "hardened criminals" but defenseless students, who were placed in an environment that was very different from that to which they were accustomed. In contrast, inmates entering correctional institutions today are more likely to have

Close-up On Corrections

THE PATHOLOGY OF IMPRISONMENT

The "prisoners" were unexpectedly picked up at their homes by a city policeman in a squad car, searched, handcuffed, fingerprinted, booked . . . and taken blindfolded to our "jail." There they were stripped, deloused, put into a uniform, given a number, and put into a cell with two other prisoners, where they expected to live for the next two weeks. The pay was $15 a day, and their motivation was to make money. . . .

At the end of only six days, we had to close down our mock prison because what we saw was frightening. It was no longer apparent to most of the subjects (or to us) where reality ended and their roles began. The majority had indeed become prisoners or guards, no longer able to clearly differentiate between role-playing and self. There were dramatic changes in virtually every aspect of their behavior, thinking, and feeling. In less than a week, the experience of imprisonment undid (temporarily) a lifetime of learning; human values were suspended, self-concepts were challenged, and the ugliest, most base, pathological side of human nature surfaced. We were horrified because we saw some boys (guards) treat others as if they were despicable animals, taking pleasure in cruelty, while other boys (prisoners) became servile, dehumanized robots who thought only of escape, of their own individual survival, and of their mounting hatred for the guards.

We had to release three prisoners in the first four days because they had such acute situational traumatic reactions as hysterical crying, confusion in thinking, and severe depression. Others begged to be "paroled," and all but three were willing to forfeit all the money they had earned if they could be paroled. By then (the fifth day), they had been so programmed to think of themselves as prisoners that when their request for parole was denied, they returned docilely to their cells. . . . By the last days, the earlier solidarity among the prisoners (systematically broken by the guards) dissolved into "each man for himself." Finally, when one of their fellows was put in solitary confinement (a small closet) for refusing to eat, the prisoners were given a choice . . . give up their blankets and the incorrigible prisoner would be let out, or keep their blankets and he would be kept in all night. They voted to keep their blankets and to abandon their brother.

About a third of the "guards" became tyrannical in their arbitrary use of power, in enjoying their control over other people. They were corrupted by the power of their roles and became quite inventive in their techniques of breaking the spirit of the prisoners and making them feel they were worthless. Some of the guards merely did their jobs as tough but fair correctional officers. . . . However, no good guard ever interfered with a command by any of the bad guards; they never intervened on the side of the prisoners, they never told the others to ease off because it was only an experiment, and they never even came to me as prison superintendent or experimenter in charge to complain. . . .

The consultant for our prison . . . [was] an ex-convict with sixteen years of imprisonment. . . . [He] would get so depressed and furious each time he visited our prison, because of its psychological similarities to his experiences, that he would have to leave. A Catholic priest who was a former prison chaplain . . . talked to our prisoners after four days and said they were just like the other first-timers he had seen.

Source: Phillip G. Zimbardo, "Pathology of Imprisonment," *Society*, Vol. 9, No. 2, 1972. Copyright 1972 by Transaction Publishers. Reprinted by permission of the publisher.

progressed through a number of intermediate sanctions or shorter terms in jail prior to experiencing prison. It, therefore, would be expected that their "criminal identity" would be better developed.

Nor did those playing the role of "guards" have the benefit of the academy training and more rigorous selection that would be characteristic of a real setting. In that respect, the experiment's most significant message actually may be the danger inherent when unskilled, untrained, and unsupervised personnel control the destiny of the powerless. As a result of such factors, the effects on the students were rather drastic and spontaneous, whereas becoming "prisonized" in reality is a more long-term, gradual process. In fact, this message was reinforced more recently with the 2004 scandal at Abu Ghraib prison during the Iraq war.

The Impact of Incarceration

As the mock prison experiment illustrated, the pervasive effects of incarceration can occur in even a very brief period of time. Consider, then, how detrimental the effects of long-term imprisonment can be, especially for those in maximum custody, where everyone is subjected to strict regulation for the safety and security of the institution, where inmates are taught to line up and move in unison, where aggression is met with aggression, where orders dictate every movement, where lights never go out, where life is highly structured around a well-regulated routine, where there are few individual decisions to be made—other than whether to go along or resist.

In such a setting, close emotional relationships are nonexistent. Little things—from the food menu to TV programming—take on an exaggerated importance. The minimal standard of living drains the very meaning from life. Goals and aspirations become readjusted downward or are given up completely. Long-timers learn to live from day to day. In the words of one ex-offender, it is the strict rules, combined with the lack of opportunity to make decisions that produces inmates who are "emotionally crippled."[11]

The Institutionalized Personality

The result is a dehumanizing environment that forms an institutionalized personality. Such a personality is similar to moving like a robot according to a routinized pattern: losing all initiative, living on a day-to-day basis, blocking off the past, and avoiding the future. To the extent that the institutionalized inmate looks forward to anything, it is only to such simple diversions from the dullness of routine as a weekly movie. As one inmate describes this depersonalization, "The longer a person remains in prison, the less likely it is that he will be able to share sincere feelings with anyone."[12]

It may be difficult for those on the outside to appreciate how issues as seemingly minor as getting a smaller portion of food or disagreeing over what TV program to watch can explode into violent attacks. But such apparent overreactions to trivial details are not nearly as irrational when viewed from within the confines of a totally controlled environment.

This transformation to an institutionalized personality represents the inmate's accommodation to long-term control through processes that have been variously described as "desocialization,"[13] "prisonization,"[14] "imposed socialization,"[15] "total institutionalization"[16] or adapting to the "pains of imprisonment."[17] It is largely generated by the abnormal features of the prison environment, particularly those tangible as well as intangible things that the prisoner is deprived of—including everything from personal property to goods and services, civil rights, heterosexual relationships, personal status, autonomy, and security. Contrary to what those in free society may believe, it is not the extent to which inmates are deprived of material possessions that imposes the greatest punishment. Rather, it is the deprivation of being "locked away from one's family and friends, being totally out of control of one's life," that "dwarfs the significance of television, stereos, and designer jeans."[18]

Personal Adaptations

Many institutionalized offenders simply attempt to "get along" in a regimented society by "playing the nods" with supervisors and "doing their own time" with peers. They conform to the norms and values considered socially acceptable by other inmates—for example, disdain for the system and those in authority, use of vulgar language, name calling, distrust of fellow prisoners as well as staff, and acceptance of the status quo.

The resulting stereotypical pattern of behavior allows inmates to "get into the routine" with a minimum of irritation and anxiety. In some respects, it is similar to breaking the spirit of a wild horse to shape its response to the commands of the rider. Like horse and rider—who develop a working accommodation with each other—the subsequent relationship is characterized by routines of dominance, surrender, and behavior on cue. Among inmates, this conformity creates a facade of courtesy toward authority figures and promotes flat, noncommittal responses to others, which are devoid of any emotional investment. In essence, "the most common effect of the prison experience is a

Isolated from free society, many inmates are aware of their social rejection, experiencing feelings of helplessness, frustration, and loss of hope. Photo by Michael Dersin.

slow, water-drip disfigurement of the human spirit. The greatest tragedy is that those who adjust to it best are damaged most."[19]

✳ Learning Goals

Do you know:

1. What types of inmates are most susceptible to the debilitating effects of prisonization?
2. What factors contribute to an inmate's adjustment to confinement?
3. What personality factors influence one's behavior in prison?

Adaptations to Confinement

To some extent, everyone is affected by this "wearing-down" process of imprisonment. Those who are younger, more emotionally vulnerable, and confined for longer periods of time will be particularly susceptible. But even among the physically strong and emotionally healthy, few escape the long-lasting influence of incarceration. Of course, not everyone reacts exactly the same way to the dehumanizing effects of imprisonment nor do all correctional institutions exert the same impact. In local jails, for example, the shorter terms of confinement—combined with the high turnover of their population—do not provide the intense, long-term interactions that promote prisonization.

One of the adaptations to prison concerns is eating prison food at a set time. Employment as a cook provides transferable job skills. Photo by Michael Dersin.

The treatment or custodial orientation of a facility also can be influential. Generally, research has suggested that the counterproductive influences of the inmate subculture are diminished in settings focused more on treatment than custodial control. For example, the prisonization process seems to be reduced among inmates who are "actively involved in prison-based therapeutic communities."[20] When people are locked into cages and treated like animals, it should not be surprising that their behavior is less than civilized. In other words, behavior often conforms to expectations.

Individual Adjustments

Because of the unique nature of this interaction, it is not surprising to find a wide range of *adaptative behaviors*. Some simply try to maximize their personal benefits and minimize discomforts. Some try to remain aloof, not risking involvement with others and attempting to keep a social distance from the rest of the population. Others rebel, become aggressive, or exploit fellow inmates—exercising whatever control they can exert over those who are even more powerless. Still others rebel passively, sullenly biding their time until release.

First-timers may be particularly vulnerable to intimidation by other inmates, as well as more cautious and apprehensive in their dealings with staff. Youthful offenders tend to react to institutional conditioning even more intensely than their older counterparts—potentially developing antisocial grudges, feelings of inequality, and a diminished self-concept that can shape their outlook for years to come. Among adults, some portray a "tough guy" image. Others attempt to enhance self-esteem by boasting about their criminal past. Still others become crafty, deviant, or secretive.

Inmate Attitudes and Values

There is little doubt that the coercive nature of imprisonment does much to shape inmate responses to it. Nevertheless, there are also certain attitudes and values prevalent among the population that influence behavior. To some degree, these represent traits that may have brought offenders into contact with the law on the outside, although they also can be further nurtured by the institutional environment.

For example, many inmates have experienced a lifetime of difficulty with appropriately responding to authority—particularly if they were products of dysfunctional families or abusive homes, where violence was an acceptable means of exerting power. To such offenders, the constant supervision, adherence to the demands of those in power, and subservient role of inmates in prison further reinforce their distrust and disrespect for authority. Their reference to correctional officers as "screws" reflects what they perceive the staff as doing to them. Officers are authority figures who are out to "get" them.

Defense Mechanisms

Nor is it only the correctional staff who "have it in" for them. The very fact that they are in prison often is blamed on someone else—or simply "the system" or society in general. In a social structure where one sees oneself as "born to lose," it is easy to assume the self-concept of a scapegoat. Unwilling or unable to accept personal accountability for their actions, it is convenient for offenders to neutralize blame by rationalizing their actions (for example, "I needed the money." "People who never get caught steal a lot more than I did"). Through various forms of rationalizing their guilt and/or projecting blame on others, they can psychologically:

- *Avoid responsibility*: "It wasn't my fault." "I just went along with the gang."

- *Deny injury*: "They can afford it." "Nobody got hurt."

- *Blame the victims*: "They had it coming." "They should have done what I said."

- *Minimize guilt*: "Yes, I sold drugs, but not to kids." [21]

In part, such attitudes are further reinforced by the inmate's concept of the social system as composed of those who got caught and those who got away. Those incarcerated were just unfortunate enough to get caught. In a world filled with perceptions of exploitation and injustice, those society has labeled as "offenders" often view themselves as "victims." Whether it was a teenager "asking" for sex, a poverty-ridden family, or an abusive childhood, their self-image as the unwitting victims—the "innocent pawns" of society—enables them to avoid accountability.[22] This line of thinking may seem quite convoluted to law-abiding citizens in free society. But in the words of one inmate, "the more hostile the environment, the more they saw themselves as victims, and the less responsible they felt for their own actions." [23]

Tolerance for Anxiety

An inmate's *tolerance for anxiety* is another factor to be taken into consideration in predicting institutional behavior. Many are worried about their spouse, family, or loved ones. A disturbing letter from home (or lack of correspondence) can create a state of severe anxiety. Yet, those incarcerated can do nothing about anything on the outside—they are utterly powerless.

During the first few months of incarceration, inmates routinely experience high levels of anxiety. This anxiety tends to level off as the offender adjusts to institutional routines and then rise again nearing release, as the inmate confronts the uncertainties of what will be faced in free society.[24] This helps to explain why some inmates escape only a week or so before they are scheduled for parole. It also sheds some light on the bizarre post-release behavior of the inmate after thirty-two years behind bars that is described in the upcoming "Close-up On Corrections."

 Learning Goals

Do you know:
1. How the inmate subculture operates within prisons?
2. What functions are served by the inmate code?
3. How new inmates are initiated into the informal code of conduct?
4. What action Congress has taken to reduce prison rape?

Close-up On Corrections

RELEASE ANXIETIES

Around age fifteen, Bill was imprisoned for rape. He served his time and was released, and he went on to join the Army during World War II. When he was released from active duty, Bill found himself without a family, a skill, or the basics for living outside of a prison or the wartime military. He purposely committed another crime and reentered prison in 1948. There he was provided basic care and saved the $3,000 he earned by washing staff cars. Life was secure.

In 1980, Warden Judy Anderson reviewed Bill's inmate record and found he had been granted parole ten years earlier with the conditions that he secure a job and a place to live in the community prior to release. Unable to do either from his prison cell and having slipped through the social services cracks, Bill had spent ten years in prison under paroled status.

Anderson contacted the Alston Wilkes Society, who arranged to have Bill released to a halfway house and to start an entry-level job as a dishwasher. Bill walked free for the first time in thirty-two years. This was a new beginning for Bill. He did not have another incident of law breaking, and he did not bounce from job to job. In fact, he was so excited to have a job that he was never out sick and had to be forced to take annual leave.

However, Bill did have some new problems. He did not know how to live outside prison. For example, he had never slept alone. In the institution, with others around, he slept soundly. Now, alone in his room, he was terrified and woke up often.

One night Bill heard staff making routine rounds, but he didn't know who it was or what they were doing. He barricaded his door as the sounds came his way. Staff could not get in. Finally, they broke in, worried that something had happened to Bill. They found him huddled in a corner, like a frightened child.

Receiving his first paycheck was another intimidating experience for Bill. As he came home down the street, staff saw him zig-zagging across the road with a stick in his hand. He was not drunk or sick. He was afraid. He had never had that much money in his pocket and he was sure someone would try to take it from him.

Bill was not prepared for independent living. At age sixty-one, with no family support, he found it difficult to face living outside the halfway house. Although the average length of stay for most residents is four to six months, the Alston Wilkes Society offered Bill a permanent home in exchange for a small rent fee and help around the facility.

Though Bill is free to leave at any time and has thought of doing so, he always decides to stay. After thirteen years, the Society has become Bill's family.

Postscript: Bill stayed at the halfway house until 1997, when he was able to be placed in the retirement facility where he still lives today. He has never re-offended.

Source: S. Anne Walker, "South Carolina Volunteer Agency Plays Vital Role in Corrections," *Corrections Today*, August 1993, p. 99.

Those who share certain values, attitudes, beliefs, ethnicity, or other similar traits often group together into subcultures within free society. The same occurs within prison walls. And just as different patterns of behavior, standards of conduct, and even language characterize subcultures on the outside, they also do within prison.

Inmates organize into a separate *subculture* in reaction to the deprivations and isolation of institutional living, as well as in their interaction with institutional authority. It serves as an expression of autonomy in a setting that attempts to suppress individuality. It provides a self-defensive solidarity in an environment where a "we versus they" social boundary prevails. As prisoners become increasingly integrated into the inmate society over long periods of confinement, antisocial behavior is continuously reinforced.

Prison Language (Argot)

This society is manifested in a unique language, as reflected in the terms used to identify various inmate roles (for example, "straight," "tough," "wolf"), as illustrated in the "Close-up On Corrections" on page 314. It should, however, be noted that inmate slang is neither universal nor static, but rather, it is continually evolving at each institution. These examples, therefore, represent prison *argot* in one area of the country at one particular point in time. Like the secret codes of childhood games, learning the inmate argot not only enables prisoners to communicate with each other in a language unfamiliar to outsiders, but also establishes an identity which only they can share. Moreover, within the terms used in the language of the inmate subculture are elements of:

- Mockery of the system (for example, "the man;" "goon squad")
- Superficial resignation to authority (for example, "play for the gate;" "play the nods")
- The inmate social hierarchy (for example, "right guys" versus "straights")
- Adherence to the inmate code ("don't snitch;" "get backs")

But to the extent that language is simply a means of communicating and reinforcing values, it is the inmate *code of conduct* that most significantly identifies the prison subculture. In opposition to the institutional rules and regulations, it sets informal standards for controlling behavior in a manner designed to counteract official authority.

The Inmate Code

The informal social control maintained by inmates through adherence to the inmate code serves the vested interests of powerful and long-term prisoners. Those who have been around the institution long enough to know the routines and the authority structure can achieve power by gaining the trust of administrative officials and the acquiescence of other inmates. It is through the inmate code that such compliance is maintained.

The code defines what actions are proper or improper from the inmate's perspective. By establishing these prescriptions for "do's" and "don'ts," it clearly distinguishes between the values of the official administration and those of the unofficial social system. As shown in the following "Close-up On Corrections," the code forbids "any type of supportive or nonexploitative liaison with prison officials. It seeks to confer status and prestige on those inmates who stand most clearly in opposition to the administration."[25]

In free society, breaking the laws of the community results in punishment, and an inferior social status for the offender. In much the same manner, violation of the inmate code produces alienation from fellow prisoners, reduced status on the social hierarchy of the institution, and punitive sanctions. In fact, it can result in severe physical retaliation, as we will see later in the vicious treatment of "snitches" when inmates broke into the protective custody unit during the Santa Fe, New Mexico, riot.

Violence in Prison

Newly arriving inmates (referred to in a predatory manner as "fish") are rapidly initiated into the code of conduct through exaggerated accounts of what lies ahead, threats, and intimidation by other inmates, situations where they are required to "prove themselves," and both real and fabricated stories of what happens to those who are noncompliant. Moreover, visual observations quickly reinforce the power of inmate control:

> The first day I got to Soledad, I was walking from the fish tank to the mess hall and this guy comes running down the hall past me,

 # Close-up On Corrections

THE INMATE CODE

1. DON'T INTERFERE WITH THE INTERESTS OF OTHER INMATES: Never rat on a con. Don't be nosy. Don't have a loose lip. Don't put a guy on the spot.

2. DON'T QUARREL WITH FELLOW INMATES: Play it cool. Don't lose your head. Do your own time.

3. DON'T EXPLOIT OTHER INMATES: Don't break your word. Don't steal from cons. Don't sell favors. Don't welsh on bets.

4. MAINTAIN YOURSELF: Don't weaken. Don't whine. Don't cop out. Be tough. Be a man.

5. DON'T TRUST THE GUARDS OR THE THINGS THEY STAND FOR: Don't be a sucker. Guards are hacks or screws. The officials are wrong and the prisoners are right.

Source: Adapted from Gresham M. Sykes and Sheldon I. Messinger, "The Inmate Social System," in Richard A. Cloward, Donald R. Cressey, George H. Grosser, Richard McCleery, Lloyd E. Ohlin, Gresham M. Sykes, and Sheldon I. Messinger, eds., *Theoretical Studies in the Social Organization of the Prison*, New York: Social Science Research Council, 1960, pp. 6-8.

Close-up On Corrections

INMATE SLANG AND ARGOT TERMS

TERM	MEANING
Fish	New inmates.
Get-backs	Revenge in prison. "Those guys got some get-backs coming for what they done to Johnny last week."
The man	Any person in authority.
Play for the gate	To adjust your conduct so that you can compile a record as a model prisoner and be paroled sooner.
Pull your own time	To mind your own business. "You're gonna have to learn to start pulling your own time for a change."
Script	Prison "money."
Shank	A knife or other sharp-edged weapon.
Snitch	A prison informer.
Waste	To kill someone. "They're going to get themselves wasted."
Watch your back	To protect oneself from attack.
What goes around comes around	A commonly used expression meaning: "You eventually have to pay for what you do to others in here."

Source: Inez Cardozo-Freeman, *The Joint: Language and Culture in a Maximum Security Prison*, Springfield, Illinois: Charles C. Thomas, 1984, pp. 480-541.

TERM	MEANING
Bug out	To act crazy.
Boss	When spelled backwards, the letters stand for "sorry S-O-B." Used by inmates to call staff an "SOB" without actually doing so.
Chill out	To take on a low profile, stay out of sight or calm down.
Hack	A correctional officer.
Hole	The administrative detention unit or the disciplinary segregation unit.
To roll over	To become an informant.

Source: Eugene Ray, *Dictionary of Prison Slang*, Federal Bureau of Prisons, Computer Printout, November 30, 1986.

yelling, with a knife sticking out of his back. Man, I was petrified. I thought, what the f- kind of place is this? [26]

Along with being oriented to the inmate code, the new offender is "sized-up." He is evaluated by others according to such features as age, race, offense, fighting ability, and social connections. The prisoner who does not establish his "turf," demonstrate his masculinity, or prove able to defend himself during this initial assessment process is likely to be relegated to a low position on the inmate hierarchy—subject to manipulation, intimidation, and domination throughout his prison term.[27] In fact, research indicates that "the vast majority of inmates experience feelings of vulnerability to victimization and attack, creating a mental state in which they are constantly on guard against danger that one cannot hope to locate, to anticipate, or to guard against." [28] Nor does it take a great deal of insight to realize that those subjected to such vulnerability and brutality in prison "are likely to pass on their trauma once released." [29]

Prison Rape Elimination Act

One of the most brutal and prevalent forms of violence behind bars—inmate rape—ultimately reached national attention. In 2003, Congress passed the Prison Rape Elimination Act, which established three programs in the Department of Justice that are devoted to:

(1) Collecting prison rape statistics throughout the United States, with special focus on those prison systems where the incidence of rape greatly exceeds the national average

(2) Disseminating information and procedures for combating prison rape—including prevention, investigation, and punishment

(3) Providing grant funding to state and local programs that enhance the prevention and punishment of prison rape

Additionally, this legislation created a National Prison Rape Reduction Commission to examine all related physical, medical, mental, and social issues, as well as to propose national standards for investigating and eliminating prison rape. Once these standards are established, they become applicable to the Federal Bureau of Prisons, and states which adopt them by statute receive increased federal funding. Moreover, new prison accreditation processes are required to examine rape-prevention practices as a critical component of their accreditation reviews, unless they want to risk becoming ineligible for the receipt of any federal funds.

 # Learning Goals

Do you know:

1. Why inmates join prison gangs?

2. What activities are engaged in by inmate gangs?

3. What prison administrators are doing in response to security-threat groups?

Inmate Gangs

In the hostile setting of prisons, it is not surprising to find a prevalence of gang-related violence. In fact, the "sizing-up" of new "fish" is in some respects similar to the initiation rights performed before accepting new members into a gang—where torturous rituals seek to determine the proposed member's loyalty and manhood.

With the emergence of gangs, the prison subculture is no longer as simple as "us" (inmates) against "them" (staff). Inmate solidarity has not disappeared. But beyond overall resistance to institutional authority, specific allegiance to inmate associations has developed, largely along racial, ethnic, or religious lines—as evidenced by such gangs as the White Mafia, Aryan Brotherhood, Afro-American Society, Black Guerrilla Family, Black Muslims, Mexican Mafia, La Nuestra Familia, and Latin Kings. Just as with gangs in free society, such divisiveness further intensifies power struggles within correctional institutions, generating "an almost relentless cycle of violence and vengeance."[30]

The organization of inmates within power-wielding subgroups has long been a feature of prison life. Some fifty years ago, the Washington State Penitentiary at Walla Walla became infamous for being the birthplace of the first documented prison gang, the Gypsy Jokers Motorcycle Club.[31] But it was not until the 1970s that correctional administrators recognized the widespread development of gangs in American prisons.[32]

Purpose of Gang Membership

Like their counterparts on the outside, prison gangs often are united by a common language and shared values. Given the fact that gangs in free society tend to attract those seeking acceptance, recognition, and a sense of belonging, it is apparent that fertile recruiting grounds exist among those in confinement. The racial or ethnic pride promoted by a gang can serve as a substitute for lack of personal identity. Status in a gang can upgrade low self-esteem. Viewing those in power as "oppressors" can provide a cause for uniting militant inmates. The protection and excitement offered by a gang can fill voids in an unsafe and boring existence. In essence, gangs meet unfulfilled needs. But whatever the reasons for their existence, they also seriously jeopardize the order and safety of correctional institutions.

Nature of Prison Gangs (Security-Threat Groups)

Gangs tend to share such traits as loyalty, unity, and identity. But unlike nonviolent groups that may do likewise, gangs engage in criminal behavior. In fact, they reward the antisocial activities of their members.[33] It is for this reason that they are more recently becoming known by the term "disruptive groups" or "security-threat groups." For a look at the activities of some of the gangs operating inside prison, *see* the next "Close-up On Corrections."

Gangs are becoming an increasing problem in prisons and jails throughout the United States. For example, one national survey found that more than 147,000 inmates were members of some 755 security-threat groups operating in U.S. prisons.[34] Moreover, a recent study of jail-based gangs concluded that there is a much higher prevalence of gang membership than was uncovered in earlier research.[35]

Close-up On Corrections

PRISON GANGS

Mexican Mafia

The Mexican Mafia is considered the most powerful gang in the California correctional system. It . . . is totally crime-oriented. As its name suggests, the gang is very homogeneous, with membership composed almost entirely of first or second generation Mexican-Americans. . . . Membership is for life. Voluntary dropouts are prohibited.

Formed in 1958 . . . in a relatively short time, the gang was in control of most illicit activities valued by other inmates, including gambling, narcotics, homosexual relations, and debt collection. Attempts . . . to weaken the gang through transfer resulted in the spreading of membership throughout the correctional system. By the mid-1960s, the gang regulated heroin traffic and controlled much of the inmates' activities. . . .

Black Guerrilla Family

The Black Guerrilla Family is a black terrorist gang that follows a Marxist-Maoist-Leninist revolutionary philosophy. Its primary goal is to control the destiny of black inmates, particularly through educating them about racism and helping them maintain pride and dignity while incarcerated. The gang also advocates forceful overthrow of the U.S. government. They accept any black inmates, except homosexuals, who are willing to meet their standards.

The Black Guerrilla Family is highly organized. It has a formalized rank structure consisting of a central executive committee, field generals, captains of arms, captains of squads, lieutenants, and soldiers. . . . [It] follows a precise code of ethics, with punishments for violations. . . . Once accepted, a member must take a death oath affirming a lifelong commitment to the gang. . . .

The gang considers law enforcement and correctional authorities to be its number one enemy . . . [and] is responsible for the most serious assaults on and murders of California correctional staff.

Source: Management Strategies in Disturbances and with Gangs/Disruptive Groups, Washington, D.C.: U.S. Government Printing Office, 1992, pp. 3-4.

Large states such as California, Illinois, New York, and Texas are especially susceptible because of the size of their prison populations and the influence of gangs in these highly populated states. For example, it has been estimated that in one year alone, between 80 and 90 percent of the inmates in the Illinois correctional system had some affiliation with street gangs.[36] Among the street gangs that are infiltrating correctional institutions today are the Bloods, Crips, Vice Lords, Hells Angels, Skinheads, and Latin Kings. In fact, there is more and more overlap between groups defined as "prison gangs" and those identified as "street gangs," [37] which is also complicating parole supervision of gang members.[38]

While many gangs originally may have been formed for self-protection, finding strength in unity has bolstered their power, and if uncontrolled, they will "influence every conceivable aspect of prison life."[39] As shown in Figure 9.2, prison gangs develop sequentially through several stages, which can result in deadly consequences.

Institutional Responses

In Texas alone, the two most violent years in the history of the correctional department resulted in fifty-two inmate homicides and more than 7,000 inmate and staff assaults—with 92 percent of the homicides and 80 percent of the assaults attributed to gang-related activities.[40] In response, Texas has implemented strategies ranging from hiring more staff to providing additional training, aggressively prosecuting in-house violence, and placing confirmed

figure 9.2

Inmate (Stage 1)	• Feeling fearful of new setting • Sensing danger • Feeling isolated • Feeling lonely
Clique (Stage 2)	• Sense of belonging • No rules for acceptance • No commitment to group • No rules of conduct • Members can come and go • No formal or informal leadership exercised • No involvement in criminal activity
Protection Group (Stage 3)	• Self-identity • Existence of simple general rules • Existence recognized by inmates and staff • No involvement in criminal activity • Does not initiate violence unless provoked • Informal leadership based on charisma • No formal code of conduct
Predator Group (Stage 4)	• Discussion of formalizing rules of conduct • Beginning to realize strength • Exclusion of "undesirable" or "unwilling" members • Involvement in inmate/staff intimidation • Involvement in retaliation and assaults • Initial entry as a group into illegal activity • Emergence of strong leadership, although informal • Existence and activity limited to inside penal setting
Prison Gang (Stage 5)	• Formal rules and constitution • Well-defined goals and philosophy • Hierarchy of formal leadership with clearly defined authority and responsibility • Membership for life • Members wear gang tattoos • Wholesale involvement in criminal activity both inside and outside the penal setting • Ongoing criminal enterprise

Prison gang development.

Source: Robert S. Fong, Ronald E. Vogel, and Salvadore Buentello, "Prison Gang Dynamics: A Research Update," in J. Mitchell Miller and Jeffrey P. Rush, eds., *Gangs: A Criminal Justice Approach*, Cincinnati, Ohio: Anderson Publishing, 1996, p. 107. Used with permission.

prison gang members in administrative segregation. Other states are providing cognitive restructuring training to redirect gang members toward more prosocial lifestyles. Even experiments with behavioral contracting (for example, promising "no further gang activity" in exchange for institutional privileges) have been tried,[41] along with the strategies outlined in the next "Close-up On Corrections." Although these tactics have undoubtedly helped to ease the problem, they have not eliminated it, and officials still continue to view gangs as a "serious and continuous threat." [42]

Well-organized gangs can exert considerable control over such illicit prison enterprises as gambling, sex, and drug transactions. They can intimidate other inmates through coercion, threats, and physical violence. But aside from their strong-arm tactics and corrupt activities, one of the greatest threats of gangs to institutional security is their ability to unite the inmate population into *polarized groups* prepared for *collective violence.*

 # Close-up On Corrections

CORRECTIONAL RESPONSES TO SECURITY-THREAT GROUPS

Methods for designating that an inmate is a security threat group (STG) member usually include two or more of the following, although some agencies use self-admission alone:

- Self-admission by inmate
- Identifiable security-threat group tattoo
- Possession of security-threat group paraphernalia
- Information from an internal investigation, confidential informant, or law enforcement sources
- Restrictions placed on security-threat group members:
- Frequent cell shakedowns; strip searches
- Increased custody level
- Work and/or program limitations
- No contact visits
- Monitoring of mail, phone, inmate accounts
- Administrative segregation
- Within-state transfers

Source: William Toiler and Basil Tsagaris, "Managing Institutional Gangs: A Practical Approach Combining Security and Human Services," *Corrections Today*, Vol. 58, No. 6, October 1996, p. 111.

 Learning Goals

Do you know:

1. When and where the first prison riot occurred?
2. What predisposing conditions can make an institution vulnerable to a riot?

Prison Uprisings

Correctional institutions may be physically isolated from the outside world. However, they are not immune from the influence of the social, political, racial, and ethnic tensions that also have an impact on society in general.

The explosion of urban street riots in Los Angeles following the acquittal of police officers involved in the beating of Rodney King revealed the mounting hostility that had been lurking beneath a surface of superficial tranquility. If frustrations can erupt into such outrage in free society, the "chemistry for violence" is that much greater in prison. The words of a former director of corrections, although written some three decades ago, echo a warning no less relevant today:

> All around us, the ghetto streets have periodically burst with violent indignation at the demeaning inequities suffered by the have-nots. If we listen closely to what the ghetto rioters are saying, we find that they are not just angered by their lack of jobs and income, but angered more by those societal conditions and attitudes which frustrate their efforts to improve their lot and enhance their dignity. When such people come into our prisons, they find there a microcosm of the ghetto's frustrations, denied opportunities, and purposeless living. To bring this explosive potential to a critical point needs only the right leadership and the right incident for a spark.[43]

Expressions of personal frustration can take many forms. Some seethe inwardly—resisting authority in subtle ways and mouthing silent words of defiance. Others are much less constrained—belligerently challenging "direct orders" and asserting their individuality at all costs. Still others act-out aggressively by physical attack—destroying property; assaulting staff or other inmates. In fact, prison violence to some extent has come to be viewed as almost a routine expectation, for reasons ranging from overcrowding and understaffing to changes in good time and parole policies.[44]

But these forms of violence are largely individual, self-defeating expressions of frustration or discontent. As long as inmates are predominantly loners who usually cooperate with institutional procedures, controls can be concentrated on the relatively few mavericks. It is when prisoners unite into close-knit groups under leaders promoting intentional, collective violence that the stability of the "fragile truce" between the keepers and the kept is clearly endangered.[45]

The aftermath of a riot in Ohio shows the extensive property damage that can result from inmate insurrections. Photo courtesy of the Ohio Department of Correction and Rehabilitation.

Riots and Disturbances

Among the public, corrections is narrowly judged by its ability to maintain custody and control. Losing either is a correctional administrator's worst nightmare. Unless the prisoner is particularly notorious, there is generally little public attention paid to an individual escapee, and quickly regaining custody of the absconder can restore public confidence. Riots, however, are a far more notable threat. Unlike the solitary escapee, riots represent the correctional authority's loss of control over "a significant number of prisoners, in a significant area of the prison, for a significant amount of time."[46]

The intensive media scrutiny occurring when such a widespread disturbance breaks out can devastate the image of corrections. That would be a relatively minor price to pay, however, if instantaneous notoriety generated long-lasting public support for change. If so, it would be possible that positive byproducts could result from destructive events. But the impact is likely to be a fleeting concern expressed by demands for tighter security, rather than a fundamental commitment directed toward substantial improvements.

Perhaps because of this inability to learn from the past, riots and disturbances are as old as prisons themselves. In fact, the first recorded U.S. prison riot predates the American Revolution. It occurred in 1774 at the Newgate Prison built over an abandoned mine shaft at Simsbury, Connecticut.[47] Since then, correctional institutions throughout the country have been plagued by hundreds of riots and numerous less serious disturbances.

Causal Factors

Inmates have never won a prison riot, either in the short-term sense of maintaining their freedom or in the long-term sense of drawing lasting attention to their plight. Knowing the ultimate outcome, why do they engage in such futile actions? There is no single answer or simple explanation. Although some riots may be well-planned protests, most appear to be more spontaneous events. One study found that riots are more likely in older, larger, and maximum-security institutions, as well as those where there is less recreation, fewer meaningful work opportunities, and less contact between the warden and inmates.[48] But it has also been noted that:

> [I]t isn't necessary to have a callous or inept warden to have a riot. It isn't necessary to have sadistic guards, bad food, or any of the other classic grievances that supposedly provoke a riot. Those will be only surface complaints. The real problem is that even in a prison with good food and humane custodians, life is still a put-down, day after day. Boredom, pettiness, and repetitive meaningless activities are inherent in prison existence, and it should be no surprise that at some point the inmate population has had all it can stand.[49]

In other words, prison riots are to a considerable extent natural consequences of unnatural circumstances. An active volcano is bound to erupt. Likewise, prisons are virtually destined to burst into violence periodically. Just as geological factors alert us to the potential for volcanic eruption, there are signals that can warn perceptive staff of an impending disturbance. For example, in the two days preceding the 1987 riot at the U.S. Penitentiary in Atlanta, there was evidence that a riot might be impending. Inmates had remained dressed overnight, and the outgoing mail volume was several times heavier than normal, much of it containing photographs.[50] Later, it was learned that inmates were mailing the photos home to prevent their loss or destruction in the riot. *See* the next "Close-up On Corrections" for other changes in institutional atmosphere that can serve as early-warning indicators of inmate unrest.

 Learning Goals

Do you know:

1. What predisposing conditions and precipitating events spark prison riots?
2. Through what stages riots develop?

Predisposing Conditions

Although there is no single overall explanation that accounts for all prison riots, various features of prisons either can *reduce* or *reinforce* the potential for violent explosion. In other words, there are certain *predisposing conditions* that can serve to make an institution vulnerable to organized violence. For example, the American Correctional Association has identified the following as underlying contributors to institutional disturbances:[51]

- *Environmental stressors*: regimentation, personal deprivations, freedom limitations, boredom, idleness, brutality, racial conflicts, and gangs

- *Substandard facilities*: overcrowded living quarters, depersonalized surroundings, poor or monotonous food, and inadequate plumbing, heating, lighting, or ventilation

- *Inappropriate staffing*: insufficient numbers of staff to provide basic services, as well as inadequate management, security, and supervision

- *Public apathy*: indifference, punitive attitudes, singular focus on incapacitation, and lack of concern for treatment—prompting feelings of alienation as inmates see themselves increasingly ostracized from society

- *Inadequate funding*: the basis of many of the staffing, physical plant, and program deficiencies that set the stage for potential problems

 # Close-up On Corrections

EARLY WARNING SIGNALS: CONDITIONS CONDUCIVE TO UNREST

- Dining hall indicators
  - Alteration of noise levels
  - Removal of food staples
  - Refusals/requests not to attend meals

- Housing unit indicators
  - Increase in contraband
  - Alteration of noise levels
  - Increase in misbehavior reports /incidents
  - Increase in cell change requests
  - Increase in assaults on staff

- Recreation yard indicators
  - Large gatherings of ethnic, racial, or other groups
  - Polarization of known inmate rivals
  - Increase in verbal defiance of staff members
  - Decrease in yard attendance

- Other indicators
  - Increase in buying of staples from commissary
  - Alteration of visiting activity
  - Increase in smuggling of contraband by visitors
  - Increase in manufacture/possession of weapons
  - Increase in sick call attendance
  - Increase in protective custody admissions

Source: Condensed from *Early Warning System: Introduction and Implementation Manual for Employees*, Albany, New York: Department of Correctional Services, n.d., pp. 5-9.

Pleas for Dignity

While all of these and many other conditions serve to predispose correctional institutions to riots, perhaps the most pervasive underlying factor is the simple *lack of personal dignity.* As was expressed in the riots at both Attica and Santa Fe, "prisoners came to believe the only way to prove their humanity was by dying; . . . [t]hey saw nothing short of death that would regain their individuality and give them an identity." [52] Stated in their own words, "If we cannot live like people, we will at least try to die like men" (Attica); "If I'm going to die, I'm going to die like a man" (Santa Fe).

Undoubtedly, such alienation exists in many prisons, along with the additional institutional conditions and social forces described above. The question thus may be not why there are so many prison riots, but rather, why there are so few. As one correctional official put it, "dignity and respect should not be currency in human relationships to be doled out as a reward or withheld as punishment." [53]

Precipitating Event

Inmates may endure any number of predisposing conditions for quite extensive periods of time without erupting into organized violence. At some point, however, a completely unanticipated event may precipitate mass action in violent response. Creating a strong perimeter with extreme pressure inside is the basic technique for building a bomb. It is also the recipe for creating a riot. Then, all that is needed is to ignite the fuse.

Any number of *precipitating events* can serve as the spark that ignites a riot. An altercation between an inmate and an officer, a momentary breech of security, a fight between two inmates, or any variety of other random incidents can trigger a riot. Even publicized accounts of events outside the prison can serve as precipitating events, as in the case of federal immigration actions that set off the Atlanta and Oakdale riots of 1987. In fact, it is probably due to the alert attention of correctional officials that widespread violence throughout the country did not spread into correctional institutions following the verdict in the 1992 trial related to the Rodney King case.

When a number of predisposing conditions come into contact with both a precipitating event and a breakdown in security, the stage is set for a riot. Such was the case in Attica—where in 1971, the most lethal riot in correctional history resulted in the deaths of thirty-two inmates and ten staff members.[54] *See* the upcoming "Close-up On Corrections" for an account of the conditions, events, and bloodshed surrounding a disturbance which some thirty years later remains a vivid reminder that society will not permit reforms to be forced by riots.

Stages of a Riot

Although riot activities are not easily categorized into uniform patterns, as illustrated in the Attica scenario, they generally tend to proceed in five stages:

1. *Initial explosion*: the spontaneous (or in some cases, planned) uprising during which inmates gain control of part of the institution.

Close-up On Corrections

ATTICA

The Setting

Serenely located among the orchards and dairy lands of upstate New York, the maximum-security Attica Correctional Facility was not a traditional trouble spot among the state's institutions. Yet, the critical events that transpired there between September 9 and 13, 1971, thrust Attica into the national spotlight—symbolizing it as representative of correctional problems everywhere.

Surrounded by a gray concrete wall, with gun towers spaced along the top, this concrete fortress housed some of New York State's most notorious inmates. Many of Attica's 2,243 inmates were repeat offenders convicted of violent crimes, and by 1971, the population was increasingly composed of young, black, or Puerto Rican offenders from urban areas.

Administrative Shortcomings

In contrast to the inmates, Attica's 380 correctional officers were predominately white, recruited from the rural countryside surrounding the facility. With little or no training (three weeks at most, depending on when the person was hired), the officers considered their function to be primarily custodial. In light of the shortage of psychological staff, however, counseling was often their responsibility by default.

Not only were they largely untrained, but by virtue of a 1970 union contract, it was the youngest and most inexperienced officers who were in most frequent, direct interaction with the inmates. The contract enabled staff to bid for their assignments, and the older, more senior officers were quick to opt for the choice posts—those which involved the least contact with inmates. Administrative policies enabled the day-to-day changing of duty posts, thereby further deterring any development of inmate/officer rapport. No more than one-third of the officers were on duty at any one time, resulting in considerable apprehensiveness about being understaffed.

Caught in a statewide budget squeeze, employees' salaries were low, and little was spent on inmate programs or rehabilitative efforts. As State Corrections Commissioner Russell G. Oswald expressed it: "On the one hand, the state budget for . . . government had never been more stringent, and the taxpayers had never been so tax-conscious. On the other hand, the inmates in the maximum security institutions had rarely seemed more dangerous." [55]

Overall, Attica was no better or worse than other maximum-security facilities that were operating with meager numbers of inadequately prepared staff, receiving increasingly militant inmates, and forced by all of these constraints to place greater emphasis on security. The fact that these unfortunate circumstances resulted in the most lethal prison uprising in American penal history indeed may be the only thing that set Attica apart. History made Attica, justifiably or not, symbolic of the plight of corrections nationwide.

(continued)

(CONTINUED)

Precipitating Events

To this day, there are conflicting versions of whether the Attica riot was a well-planned attack by an organized group of militants or a spontaneous burst of violence resulting more from angry frustrations than revolutionary plans. The truth may never be known. But regardless of its confusing origins, the outcome was undeniably tragic.

The initial explosion on September 9 occurred in response to an event the previous day from which angry feelings lingered. In that incident, a misunderstanding resulted in an inmate striking a correctional lieutenant—an unheard-of violation of regulations. Two offenders involved were assigned to special disciplinary housing quarters. Rumors that officers retaliated with physical abuse against the disciplined inmates kept the situation tense. Then, as one of the officers involved in the incident attempted to return a group of inmates to their cells after breakfast, he was attacked. The uprising was under way.

At this point, the physical design of the building should have enabled the cellblock where the disturbance originated to be sealed off. But several conditions permitted the violence to spread, including a defective gate, an outdated communications system, insufficient staff, and extensive confusion in the absence of a riot-control plan. With these advantages, homemade weapons emerged, and the initial violence spread. Inmates from other areas joined in, got swept along, or fled in search of security. In less than two hours, extensive property had been destroyed, several officers had been critically injured, and more than 1,200 inmates were in command of four cellblocks and more than forty hostages.

The Organization Phase

Now, a crucial decision was necessary—whether to send state police troopers in to face the rioters directly. Recognizing their limited strength and lacking enough of the type of tear gas most effective under riot conditions, it was obvious that weapons would have to be fired in a direct attack. Since there would be no way to protect the hostages, offensive moves were postponed.

Intent upon avoiding unnecessary bloodshed, the director of corrections agreed to negotiate with the inmates himself. This violated long-standing policy against negotiations when hostages are being held. It was perceived by many as "giving in," bolstering the inmates' confidence. When an immediate decision to retake the institution was not made, tensions among both the state police and the correctional employees heightened further, creating an atmosphere of edgy anticipation and nervous strain.

Negotiations

The state police were not yet fully mobilized for an attack. Still hoping that a nonviolent settlement could be reached, the corrections director agreed to additional unprecedented steps—personally meeting with the rioters on territory held by them and conceding to admit

(continued)

(CONTINUED)

the news media. In retrospect, many criticized the decision to open the riot up to the glare of publicity. The media offered inmates a new source of power and reinforced their sense of importance, making it "almost impossible to persuade them to give up the limelight and return to anonymity."[56] But time was needed to assemble a sufficient supply of tear gas, and concern for the safety of the hostages if an attack were launched kept hope alive.

By this time, the list of inmate demands was growing. Added to it were a court injunction protecting them from subsequent administrative reprisals and the names of outside observers with whom they wanted to meet. Still anxious to negotiate a settlement, the state concurred. By the end of the day, there was optimism that a peaceful resolution could be reached.

But the next morning, in a gesture symbolic of their increasing defiance, a rebel leader tore the court injunction in half, accompanied by hearty cheers. As frustrations were vented before the cameras, a shouting, name-calling melee resulted during the next meeting with the corrections director. A move was made to take him hostage, but leaders kept their earlier guarantee of safe passage.

With this ominous change of atmosphere, any remaining confidence in the ability to obtain voluntary release of the hostages shifted to the efforts of the observers' committee. The observers were well-known liberal and radical leaders who had been chosen by the inmates themselves. But the committee's effectiveness was severely limited by its unmanageable size and confusion over its role. Eventually, the committee negotiated a compromise consisting of twenty-eight points regarding physical facility improvements, staff upgrading, and greater freedom from administrative controls. But the committee's tireless efforts ended in the early hours of September 12 with the inmates' refusal to accept any plan that did not include unconditional amnesty, transportation to a "nonimperialist" country for those desiring it, and removal of the existing Attica superintendent.

By this point, tremendous pressure was building to retake the facility. State police, correctional officers, and the national guard had been assembled for two days and were becoming seriously demoralized, impatient, and anxious to get a direct offensive under way. So, following the inmates' rejection of one final message asking for release of the hostages in exchange for the twenty-eight points, reluctantly preparations were initiated for the retaking of Attica.

Termination

At almost precisely the hour that the rebellion had begun four days previously, the state launched its counterattack. Less than ten minutes later, thirty-nine people were dead, and eighty others were wounded—with all deaths the result of firepower, not at the hands of inmates as initially reported.[57] While twenty-eight of the remaining thirty-eight hostages were saved, a variety of flaws contributed to the carnage:

- Although a general order was issued to use the minimum amount of force necessary, another order to avoid hand-to-hand combat (to prevent the loss of weapons) forced reliance on firepower.

(continued)

(CONTINUED)

- Final decision making relative to the firing of weapons was left to the discretion of individual troopers. The long wait experienced by the officers resulted in stress and tension, potentially intensifying their perception of a threatening situation.

- Inadequate advance planning, lack of proper controls, and uncoordinated leadership contributed to confusion and misinterpretation. For example, the wide variety of weapons and ammunition used did not always enable precise firing (for example, shotguns loaded with "00" buckshot). Moreover, inappropriate plans for evacuation and treatment of the wounded resulted in the availability of only two doctors and eight other medical personnel to provide assistance until the national guard's mobile unit could reach the scene.

- Confusion over who was actually in charge and lack of communication further contributed to the uncoordinated nature of the attack. Even when precise orders were issued, gas masks (not equipped with communication devices) restricted ability to hear verbal orders. Since no plan was developed for visual commands, it was impossible to transmit orders to begin or halt firing.

Postscript

If nothing else, Attica thrust corrections into the national spotlight for nearly five days. Americans were forced to become aware of things about its correctional system which until then, had remained secluded from public scrutiny. In terms of the specific grievances of Attica's rebelling inmates, conditions undoubtedly improved over what existed in 1971. But officials were careful to associate any changes with an existing commitment to prison reform rather than a response to pressures generated by the uprising. In Attica, as elsewhere throughout the country, officers are better trained; physical facilities have been upgraded; and more inmate programs are available. But progress is relative to previous conditions. As one Attica commentator noted, "No matter how badly we fare, the legacy we pass on cannot be worse than the one we inherited."[58]

2. *Organization*: the emergence of inmate leadership, as staff mobilize to prepare to respond.

3. *Confrontation*: the stage when inmates are confronted, either through negotiation or by force. This phase can range from long, drawn-out discussions to quickly issuing a warning, followed by an ultimatum and a show of force. Tactics employed may depend on whether hostages have been taken.

4. *Termination*: the point at which custodial control is regained, either through firepower, nonlethal force, or negotiated agreement.

5. *Explanation*: the subsequent investigation, designed to identify the cause of the disturbance and assure the public that necessary remedies are undertaken.

 # Learning Goals

Do you know:

1. How most riots are terminated?
2. What techniques were used in the negotiated settlement of the Oakdale riot?
3. What proactive steps can be taken to prevent riots?

Riot Control: Planning and Negotiating

To prevent widespread loss of life, injuries, and property, the best point at which to intervene in a riot is before the inmates can become organized under strong leadership. Unfortunately, that is also the time when correctional staff may be equally disorganized. As a result, institutions have devoted more attention in recent years to developing riot control plans designed to locate and isolate the disturbance, evacuate unsafe areas, and quickly resolve the situation.

Rioting inmates know who has the advantage of weapons and firepower. In such a situation, "negotiation" takes on a different connotation from labor mediation, where the power of both sides is more equally balanced. In prison disturbances, negotiation is more a form of "keeping them talking" until group cohesion begins to break down, then offering an honorable and face-saving way out for the inmate leadership.

Officers practice techniques for regaining control of the facility in the event of a riot or major disturbance. Photo by Diane Geiman.

Lengthy negotiations with rioters have always been politically unpopular, particularly in light of the disastrous results at Attica following four days of extended discussions. In addition, if disorders are not dealt with immediately and decisively, the initiative is lost. It is for such reasons that most riots have been resolved by either use of force, show of force, or force combined with other factors.[60] More recently, however, a study of eight prison riots between 1986 and 1991 revealed that half were settled through some form of negotiation.[61] In one such example (Oakdale, Louisiana), surrendering inmates cleaned up the yard, planted flowers, and formed a gauntlet through which the hostages were released—receiving flowers and open signs of affection as they passed through.[62]

Riot Prevention

Once a major disturbance has occurred, there is generally considerable reluctance to "give in" to any demands that were not part of an official negotiation agreement. Especially if lives were lost, the public is not likely to support responses which appear to send a message that endorses violence as a means of achieving change. In fact, during the explanation phase, a "scapegoat" often is identified (such as the warden or director of corrections) whose physical dismissal also may serve as a symbolic dismissal of the entire incident.

Obviously, the days following a riot are not the ideal time to address conditions underlying the disturbance. What is needed are not *reactive responses* after the damage has been done, but rather, *proactive procedures* designed to prevent riots from occurring in the first place.

Admittedly, there may be little that correctional administrators can do to alleviate public apathy, social inadequacies, and stressors inherent in the environment of prisons. Moreover, there is not much that can be done without public willingness to support substantial additional funding to improve everything from physical facilities to staff training. But there are some less costly steps that can be taken to reduce the tension, anxiety, and frustration which make an institution particularly vulnerable to rioting. One of the primary examples is simply having in place a formal grievance procedure to respond to inmate complaints before minor irritations become major issues. Of course, if inmates do not have confidence that the grievance procedure will result in action, it may only serve as a further source of frustration. Although there undoubtedly will be complaints that are not within the authority or fiscal ability of the administration to resolve, efforts can be made to explain the reasons for inaction.

Riots: Language of the Unheard

In this regard, *effective communication* with the inmate population represents another area that can be addressed without additional resources. In fact, from one perspective, a riot can be viewed as a method of communicating—"a dramatic one that is seldom used unless other forms of communications have been tried and failed."[63] Perhaps Martin Luther King stated it best when he described riots as "the language of the unheard."[64]

In an atmosphere of open, two-way interaction, inmates do not have the need to resort to violence to get administrative attention. While even the best communication process is not likely to create an atmosphere of true mutual trust within a prison, listening and responding to inmate problems demonstrates administrative concern, allows for the airing of legitimate complaints, and enables staff to detect signs of impending unrest. In other words, "the most effective approaches to prevention are founded on good management, visibility and accessibility of top administrative staff, and constant alertness to symptoms of possible problems."[65]

This does not, however, mean that communication should focus on nurturing sources of intelligence information through informants (or "snitches," as they are disreputably referred to by prisoners). The use of inmate "tipsters" creates a

 ## Close-up On Corrections

"GET BACKS" FOR "SNITCHES" IN SANTA FE

The first killings took place in Cell Block 3, soon after the block was under inmate control. In one case, inmates armed with steel pipes gathered in front of the victim's cell. One of the assailants said, "We've got to kill this son-of-a-bitch, man. . . . We've got to kill him. . . . He snitched on [inmate's name]." They beat and then knifed him to death. . . .

Another unpopular resident of Cell Block 3, seeing what was coming, jammed the door of his cell so successfully that it couldn't be opened for two days after the prison was recaptured. But it did him no good. He was shot in the face through the window of his cell with one of the grenade launchers taken from the control center.

These murders created a model for retribution against "snitches" and enemies. Thereafter, it was as if inmates vied with each other to produce imaginative modes of murder and mutilation. . . . Begging for his life, [one] victim was kicked and then bludgeoned to death with a pipe. . . . Another victim had his eyes gouged out, a screwdriver driven through his head. . . .

Inmates killed no hostages. . . . [T]he guards may actually have been less hated by the inmates than the "snitches" were. . . . The demonstrative means used to kill "snitches" suggest a virtually ritualistic "purging" of traitorous elements. . . . Guards, on the other hand, however disliked, do what they are expected to do in imprisoning inmates, and do not bear the stigma of treason.

Source: From *States of Siege: U.S. Prison Riots, 1971-1986* by Bert Useem and Peter Kimball, copyright © 1991 by Oxford University Press, Inc. Used by permission of Oxford University Press, Inc.

Postscript: Although no correctional officers were killed, it should be noted that they did suffer "stabbings, beatings, and brutal degradation during their captivity."

Source: Adolph B. Saenz and T. Zane Reeves, "Riot Aftermath: New Mexico's Experience Teaches Valuable Lessons," *Corrections Today*, Vol. 51, No. 4, July 1989, p. 66.

paranoid atmosphere, encourages corruption, and is demeaning to employees and inmates alike.[66] Moreover, the "snitch system" can put the lives of informants in grave danger. The worst example of the sadistic cruelty with which inmates have reacted to informants was demonstrated in the 1980 Santa Fe, New Mexico, disturbance—when rioters broke into the section of the institution holding those in protective custody. The viciously brutal treatment of informants by the rioters is described in the prior "Close-up On Corrections."

Beyond accounting for thirty-three inmate deaths, rioters in Santa Fe violently expressed their vengeance through widespread property damage, creating the most costly disturbance in U.S. prison history. Totaling some $36 million, the "cost of the event reached almost exactly one million dollars an hour; the riot lasted thirty-six hours."[67]

Aftermath

Undoubtedly, $36 million could have been used much more effectively for remedies directed toward preventing the disturbance than for repairs to the resulting damages. However, it is inevitably easier to generate public concern and fiscal support *after* an institution explodes into all-out violence—when the ambiguity of unheeded warnings is replaced by the clarity of undeniable consequences. As a prison manager noted, "Every time there's a riot, half of us cries and half is happy because we know it means more attention and probably more money for everything—salaries, programs, you name it,"[68] a benefit of which the prisoners themselves may well be equally well-aware. In the words of one inmate, "What incentive is there to keep prisons safe and humane? Violence and hatred in prison mean more money, more guards, more overtime, and more prisons."[69]

In the face of the immediate fiscal cost of institutional disruptions, it is easy to become distracted from the greater long-term social costs incurred by the more subtle day-to-day threat of brutality and degradation. Some would contend that exposure to such conditions is "just deserts"—that it is fitting for those who were victimizers in the free community to become victims themselves in the prison community. Aside from basic human dignity, what that argument conveniently overlooks is the fact that their membership in the prison community is temporary. Thus, "permitting them to serve their punishment in an atmosphere at least as free from terror and violence as the outside world is a test of our collective self-respect, and ultimately, a matter of our collective self-interest."[70]

Summary

Inmates are socialized into the institutional setting through the process of prisonization, by which they adapt to the culture, values, norms, and behavioral expectations of the environment. Some maintain that this process is a feature of similar values, attitudes, and behaviors that offenders bring into the prison setting (importation), while others attribute it to natural adjustments made to an unnatural environment (deprivation).

Whatever the cause, the result is often adaptation through development of an "institutionalized personality"—characterized by such noncommital features as routinized behavior, automatic responses, loss of initiative, submission to power, and avoidance of any emotional investment. To those exhibiting such a personality pattern, seemingly minor diversions or incidents can take on exaggerated importance.

But everyone does not accommodate to imprisonment in exactly the same manner. Individual characteristics, environmental conditions, and interaction between the two all shape one's adjustment. Defense mechanisms ranging from outright rebellion to rejecting authority, projecting blame on others, and rationalizing behavior also assist the inmate in psychologically coping with confinement.

In response to the dehumanizing nature of institutional conditions, the inmate subculture serves to protect personal identity and autonomy. Through this subculture, inmates reinforce values, attitudes, and standards of conduct that are in direct contrast to those of the administration. The subculture is distinguished by a unique language (argot), as well as an inmate code of conduct that establishes informal regulations in opposition to the formal rules of the institution.

Beyond their organization into a separate subculture, inmates also unite through gangs. Prison gangs polarize the population along racial, ethnic, and religious lines. In addition to their involvement in corrupt activities, gangs present a serious concern for order and safety as a result of their collective violence. Intentional violence by well-organized, close-knit groups is considerably more difficult to control than individual expressions of frustration.

When correctional officials lose control of a number of prisoners in a sizable area of the compound for a significant amount of time, an institutional riot has occurred. Many underlying conditions can promote the potential for a riot—from the regimentation, deprivations, and lack of personal dignity of the environment itself to crowding, substandard physical facilities, inadequate staffing, public apathy, and perceptions of inequities. Such predisposing conditions may be tolerated for long periods of time. Then, a completely unanticipated event suddenly can provide the "spark" that precipitates a riot.

Once the institution explodes into a violent uprising, riots generally progress in stages—moving from organization under inmate leaders, to confrontation with authorities, to termination (through firepower, nonlethal force, or negotiated agreement), and subsequent explanation. In addition to improved riot-control planning, correctional officials can take proactive steps to address predisposing conditions. Examples include implementing formal grievance procedures and providing open, two-way communications between inmates and staff.

Beyond the loss of life and injuries resulting from riots, extensive property damage can require massive fiscal investments to restore the institution to a fully operating condition. Undoubtedly, such funding could have been spent more productively to remedy conditions provoking the disturbance, rather than to repair the subsequent damage. Doing so is in the best interest of all of us, since (as the next chapter describes), almost all inmates are eventually released.

Endnotes

1. Victor Hassine, *Life without Parole: Living in Prison Today*, Los Angeles: Roxbury Publishing, 1999, p. 40.

2.   One of the classic works on this concept is Donald Clemmer, *The Prison Community*, New York: Hold, Rinehart and Winston, 1958.

3.   Glenn D. Walters, "Changes in Criminal Thinking and Identity in Novice and Experienced Inmates," *Criminal Justice and Behavior*, Vol. 30, No. 4, August 2003: 399-421.

4.   Hassine, *Life without Parole*, p. 47.

5.   In fact, these same reactions were reported among students confined to a room in their home for just forty-eight hours as an assignment for a college course. *See* Jeanne B. Stinchcomb, "Prisons of the Mind: Lessons Learned from Home Confinement," *Journal of Criminal Justice Education*, Vol. 13, No. 2, 2002, pp.463-478.

6.   *See* Nicolett Parisi, "The Prisoner's Pressures and Responses," in Nicolett Parisi, ed., *Coping with Imprisonment*, Beverly Hills, California: Sage Publications, 1982, pp. 9-11, who maintains that both *internal and external* stimuli contribute to pressures and strategies of coping in prison.

7.   Jim Thomas, Harry Mike, Jerome Blakemore, and Annmarie Alyward, "Exacting Control Through Disciplinary Hearings: 'Making Do' with Prison Rules," *Justice Quarterly*, Vol. 8, No. 1, March, 1991, p. 41.

8.   Charles W. Thomas and David M. Petersen, *Prison Organization and Inmate Subcultures*, Indianapolis, Indiana: Bobbs-Merrill,1977, p. 55.

9.   Philip G. Zimbardo, "Pathology of Imprisonment," in Lawrence F. Travis, Martin D. Schwartz, and Todd R. Clear, eds., *Corrections: An Issues Approach*, Second Edition, Cincinnati, Ohio: Anderson Publishing Company, 1983, pp. 99-104. (The remainder of the discussion of what has become known as the "Zimbardo experiment" is summarized from this source.)

10. *Ibid.*, p. 101.

11. Meg Laughlin, "Ex-convicts Learn How to Embrace Freedom," *The Herald*, February 15, 2004, p. 3B, quoting Bernie DeCastro.

12. Hassine, *Life without Parole*, p. 35.

13. Peter O. Peretti, "Desocialization-Resocialization: Process within the Prison Walls," *Canadian Journal of Corrections*, Vol. 12, No. 1, January 1970, pp. 59-66.

14. Clemmer, *The Prison Community*.

15. John J. Vollmann, "Imposed Socialization: A Functional Control in a Total Institution," *Sociological Research Symposium VIII*, Richmond, Virginia: Virginia Commonwealth University, 1978.

16. Erving Goffman, *Asylums: Essays on the Social Situation of Mental Patients and Other Inmates*, Garden City, New York: Anchor Books, 1961, who describes a "total institution" as a "place of residence and work where large numbers of like-situated individuals, cut off from the wider society for an appreciable period of time, together lead an enclosed, formally-administered round of life," p. xiii.

17. Gresham M. Sykes, *The Society of Captives: A Study of a Maximum Security Prison*, Princeton, New Jersey: Princeton University Press, 1958.

18. John Irwin and Rick Mockler, "Prison Comforts Make Little Difference," in Bonnie Szumski, *America's Prisons, Opposing Viewpoints*, St. Paul, Minnesota: Greenhaven Press, 1985, p. 86.

19. Charles Campbell, *Serving Time Together: Men and Women in Prison*, Fort Worth, Texas: Texas Christian University Press, 1980, p. 229.

20. Walters, "Changes in Criminal Thinking," p. 401.

21. Boyd D. Sharp, *Changing Criminal Thinking: A Treatment Program*, Lanham, Maryland: American Correctional Association, 2000, pp. 2, 48.

22. *Ibid.*, p. 53.

23. Hassine, *Life without Parole*, p. 39.

24. D. B. Kennedy, "A Theory of Suicide While in Police Custody," *Journal of Police Science and Administration*, Vol. 12, 1984, pp. 191-200. Similarly, a U-shaped pattern of compliance in correctional facilities has been observed—with those closest to either the beginning or the end of their sentence more likely to support staff and reject the inmate code. *See* Stanton Wheeler, "Socialization in Correctional Communities," *American Sociological Review*, Vol. 26, 1961, pp. 697-712.

25. Lloyd Ohlin, *Sociology and the Field of Corrections*, New York: Social Science Research Council, 1956, p. 28. *See also* Sharp, *Changing Criminal Thinking*, pp. 39-41.

26. John Irwin, "The Prison Experience: The Convict World" in George G. Killinger and Paul F. Cromwell, Jr., eds. *Penology: The Evolution of Corrections in America*, St. Paul, Minnesota: West Publishing Company, 1973, p. 202, quoting an interview with a Soledad inmate, and p. 207.

27. Because they represent the vast majority of prisoners, as well as the subject of much of the prison-related research, this discussion focuses on male inmates. For more information on the unique aspects of socialization in female prisons, *see* Chapter 11. *See also* Joann Morton, *Working with Women Offenders in Correctional Institutions*, Lanham, Maryland: American Correctional Association, 2004.

28. Craig Hemmens and James W. Marquart, "Race, Age, and Inmate Perceptions of Violence in Prisons," *Corrections Compendium*, Vol. 24, No. 2, February 1999, p. 4.

29. Steve Lerner, "Prisons Are Violent and Dehumanizing," in Szumski, *America's Prisons*, p. 70.

30. Peter Scharf, "Empty Bars: Violence and the Crisis of Meaning in the Prison," in Michael Braswell, Steven Dillingham, and Reid Montgomery, Jr., eds., *Prison Violence in America*, Cincinnati, Ohio: Anderson Publishing Company, 1998, p. 139.

31. William Riley "Taking a Two-Pronged Approach to Managing Washington's Gangs," *Corrections Today*, Vol. 54, No. 5, July 1992, p. 68.

32. Harold W. Clarke, "Gang Problems: From the Streets to Our Prisons," *Corrections Today*, Vol. 54, No. 5, July 1992, p. 8.

33. *Management Strategies in Disturbances and with Gangs/Disruptive Groups*, Washington, D.C.: U.S. Government Printing Office, 1992, p 2.

34. "Gangs in Correctional Facilities: A National Assessment (Preliminary Results)," unpublished handout, Lanham, Maryland: American Correctional Association, 1993, p. 4.

35. Ed Tromanhauser *et al.*, "Gangs and Guns: A Task Force Report," *American Jails*, May/June 1995, p. 63.

36. Michael P. Lane, "Inmate Gangs," *Corrections Today*, Vol. 51, No. 4, July 1989, p. 99.

37. Craig H. Trout, "Taking a New Look at an Old Problem," *Corrections Today*, Vol. 54, No. 5, July 1992, p. 64.

38. Irving Spergel *et al.*, *Gang Suppression and Intervention*, Washington, D.C.: Office of Juvenile Justice and Delinquency Prevention, 1994, p. 15.

39. Lane, "Inmate Gangs," p. 99.

40. Salvador Buentello, "Combating Gangs in Texas," *Corrections Today*, Vol. 54, No. 5, July 1992, p. 58.

41. William Toller and Basil Tsagaris, "Managing Institutional Gangs: A Practical Approach Combining Security and Human Services," *Corrections Today*, Vol. 58, No. 6, October 1996, p. 111.

42. Buentello, "Combatting Gangs in Texas," p. 60. *See also* Jeanne B. Stinchcomb, "Promising (and Not-so-Promising) Gang Prevention and Intervention Strategies: A Comprehensive Literature Review," *Journal of Gang Research*, Vol. 10, No. 1, 2002, pp. 27-46.

43. Paul Keve, *Prison Life and Human Worth*, Minneapolis, Minnesota: University of Minnesota Press, 1974, p. 6.

44. "Violence on the Rise at Federal Prisons," *Corrections Digest*, Vol. 26, No. 4, January 27,1995, p. 5.

45. Keve, *Prison Life*, p. 67.

46. Bert Useem and Peter Kimball, *States of Siege: U.S. Prison Riots, 1971-1986*, New York: Oxford University Press, 1991, p. 4.

47. Steven D. Dillingham and Reid H. Montgomery, Jr., "Prison Riots: A Corrections' Nightmare since 1774," in Braswell *et al.*, *Prison Violence in America*, p. 19.

48. Dillingham and Montgomery, "Prison Riots," pp. 23-24.

49. Keve, *Prison Life*, p.15.

50. Bert Useem *et al.* "Resolution of Prison Riots," *National Institute of Justice: Research in Brief*, Washington, D.C.: U.S. Department of Justice, 1995, p. 7.

51. Summarized from American Correctional Association, *Causes, Preventive Measures, and Methods of Controlling Riots and Disturbances in Correctional Institutions*, Lanham, Maryland: American Correctional Association, 1998, pp. 8-11. *See also* Richard C. McCorkle, Terance D. Miethe, and Kriss A. Drass, "The Roots of Prison Violence: A Test of the Deprivation, Management, and 'Not-So-Total' Institution Models," *Crime and Delinquency*, Vol. 41, No. 3, July 1995, pp. 317-331.

52. Sue Mahan, "An 'Orgy of Brutality' at Attica and the 'Killing Ground' at Santa Fe: A Comparison of Prison Riots," in Parisi, *Coping with Imprisonment*, p. 76.

53. Dick Franklin, "Contemporary Issues in Prison Management," *Training Manual, NIC Executive Training for New Wardens*, Longmont, Colorado: National Institute of Corrections, February 2000, p. 8.

54. James A. Hudson, *Attica*, New York: Kimtex Corporation, 1971, p. 3.

55. Russell G. Oswald, *Attica—My Story*, New York: Doubleday, 1972, pp. 7-11.

56. New York State Special Commission on Attica, *Attica*, New York: Bantam Books, 1972, p. 212.

57. *Ibid.*, 332.

58. D. M. Rothman, "Attica System: You Can't Reform the Bastille," *Nation*, March 19, 1973, p. 366.

59. Summarized from Vernon Fox, *Correctional Institutions*, Englewood Cliffs, New Jersey: Prentice Hall, 1983, p. 120.

60. Ellis MacDougall and Reid H. Montgomery, Jr., "American Prison Riots, 1971-1983," unpublished paper, Columbia, South Carolina: College of Criminal Justice, University of South Carolina, p. 26.

61. Bert Useem *et al.*, "Resolution of Prison Riots," *National Institute of Justice: Research in Brief*, October, 1995, p. 13.

62. Clinton Van Zandt and G. Dwayne Fuselier, "Nine Days of Crisis Negotiations: The Oakdale Siege," *Corrections Today*, Vol. 51, No. 4, July 1989, p. 24. *See also* Thomas J. Fagan, *Negotiating Correctional Incidents: A Practical Guide*, Lanham, Maryland: American Correctional Association, 2003.

63. American Correctional Association, *Causes, Preventive Measures and Methods of Controlling Riots and Disturbances in Correctional Institutions*, p. 23.

64. Quoted by Scott Minerbrook, "A Different Reality for Us," *Newsweek*, May 11, 1992, p. 36.

65. *Management Strategies in Disturbances*, p. 47.

66. *See* Perry Johnson, "The Snitch System: How Informants Affect Prison Security," *Corrections Today*, Vol. 51, No. 4, July, 1989, pp. 26-28, and Van Vandivier, "Do You Want to Know a Secret? Guidelines for Using Confidential Information," *Corrections Today*, Vol. 51, No. 4, July 1989, pp. 30-32.

67. Mahan, "Orgy of Brutality," p. 68.

68. John J. Dilulio, Jr., *Governing Prisons: A Comparative Study of Correctional Management*, New York: Free Press, 1987, p. 33, quoting an anonymous prison manager.

69. Hassine, *Life without Parole*, p. 78.

70. Lerner, "Prisons Are Violent and Dehumanizing," p. 72.

CHAPTER 10

TRANSITION FROM CONFINEMENT TO THE COMMUNITY

66 America is the land of the second chance, and when the gates of the prison open, the path ahead should lead to a better life.[1] 99

—George W. Bush

Chapter Overview

Given the effects of prison life described in Chapter 9, it is apparent that incarceration is far from the optimal means of preparing offenders for a law-abiding lifestyle in the community. No matter how punitive the public may be, the fact is that at some point, nearly all inmates are eventually eligible for release. The inevitable may be postponed temporarily, but in most cases, it cannot be totally prevented.

As we saw in previous chapters, those in confinement are isolated from the rest of society, both physically and psychologically. They are constrained by strict rules. They are constantly supervised. Their movements are closely regulated. They "survive" the experience by adaptation. Some become subservient automatons. Others become rebellious activists. Most subscribe to an inmate behavioral code that is counter to the norms and values of official authority.

At the other extreme, those of us in free society are physically integrated with that society. Our actions are unhampered by direct scrutiny. We are free to come and go as we wish. We are able to live our lives much as we please, guided only by self-discipline and the implicit deterrence of social controls. In exchange for these freedoms, however, society requires certain expectations.

Thus, former inmates rejoining free society must be able to replace external controls with internal constraints. They must substitute compliance with social laws for adherence to inmate codes. In other words, they have to adapt to community integration from controlled isolation.

An inmate cannot be subjected to the rigidities of a tightly controlled institutional environment one day and walk confidently into the freedom of society the next without mishap. Yet, that is exactly what is expected in the absence of parole: "One day these predatory inmates are locked in their cells for twenty-three hours at a time and fed all their meals through a slot in the door, and the next day they're out of prison, riding a bus home."[2]

Making the transition between these two extremes is obviously not an overnight process that can occur effectively without assistance. Much like the deep-sea diver who cannot rise too quickly to the surface without proper decompression, the parole process is designed to de-escalate external controls gradually to ease reintegration into the community.

Changing Nature of Parole

Parole involves both regulatory and rehabilitative functions. Much like the dual responsibilities of probation discussed in Chapter 4, parole officers face the need to balance their supportive and surveillance duties. But beyond the dual nature of its mission, parole also has encountered vocal opposition, especially as public sentiments have shifted.

Under the medical model, it was assumed that there was an optimum time for releasing an offender from incarceration. With indeterminate sentencing, establishing when an inmate should be released was largely the subjective decision of the paroling authority.

In the absence of clear, objective guidelines, eligibility for parole became the source of complaints about apparent inequities. In some cases, parole policies even have been cited as causing prison riots. Attica was a prime example—where the official investigation concluded that "the operation of the parole system was a primary source of tension and bitterness within the walls."[3] In Attica and elsewhere, those who were satisfied with decisions of the parole board were out in the community, while those turned down for parole remained in prison venting their frustrations. Nor was the credibility of the decision-making process enhanced by high rates of recidivism or the public outrage that followed when a parolee engaged in a particularly notorious crime.

Release under the Justice Model

Movement to the justice model's determinate sentencing was designed to eliminate the uncertainty of prison terms based on the release-through-parole feature of indeterminate sentencing. As a result, sixteen states have abolished parole,[4] and mandatory release is now increasing, while discretionary parole releases are decreasing.

This does not mean that parole no longer exists. However, paroling authorities are now more likely to be responsible for *supervising offenders* in the community following mandated discharge rather than for *making decisions* about when to release. Despite more restrictive functions and a less supportive public, parole remains a key component of the correctional conglomerate.

As long as the environment of correctional institutions differs so extremely from free society, assistance is needed to help released offenders from becoming repeat offenders.

✸ Learning Goals

Do you know:

1. The origin and definition of "parole"?
2. What legislative authorization is necessary to implement parole?
3. Why some states have returned to determinate sentencing?

Historical Background

The word *parole* originated with the French term *parole d'honneur*, which means "word of honor."[5] But because inmates are not generally considered to be highly honorable, parole always has been controversial.

As noted earlier, Captain Alexander Maconochie experimented with a *mark system* that enabled inmates to earn freedom through credits awarded for hard work and proper behavior. For this and similar progressive but provocative efforts, Maconochie was removed as superintendent of the Norfolk Island (Australia) penal colony. Returned to England, he was subsequently dismissed from prison service for employing methods that were too lenient. Maconochie's visions lived on, however, in the Irish *ticket-of-leave* concept pioneered in 1854 by Sir Walter Crofton. Under this system, inmates earned release by gradually progressing through a series of stages involving reduced discipline, which eventually could earn them a ticket of leave—or what we now know as parole.

Parole Developments in the United States

Massachusetts was the first state to officially establish parole service when an agent was appointed in 1846 to assist released prisoners. By legislative action some twenty years later, Michigan became the first state to introduce *indeterminate sentencing*. This was necessary to enable correctional officials to provide early release on parole, under the philosophy that "the prisoner's destiny should be placed . . . in his own hands."[6]

Combined with use of the indeterminate sentence, the possibilities of parole were discussed on a national basis in 1870 during the meeting of the National Prison Association. At that meeting, Zebulon Brockway argued that preemptory (fixed) sentences should be replaced with indeterminate sentences. With such a change, prisoners could be released early after exhibiting some evidence that they had been reformed rather than being released after a mere lapse of time.[7] He further suggested providing some type of supervision for three years after release from prison. Brockway later became superintendent of the Elmira Reformatory, where parole was an integral feature from its opening in 1876.

By 1910, thirty-two states and the federal government had established parole systems.[8] By the 1950s, all states had implemented indeterminate sentencing, and all jurisdictions throughout the country had adopted some form

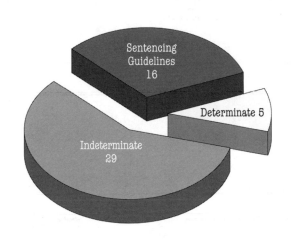

figure 10.1

Sentencing Guidelines 16

Determinate 5

Indeterminate 29

Sentencing practices in the fifty states.

Source: Compiled from Bureau of Justice Assistance, *National Assessment of Structured Sentencing*, Washington, DC: U.S. Department of Justice, 1996, p. 23.

of parole. But a quarter-century later, the tide began to turn. Public disillusionment with the medical model's indeterminate sentencing was fueled by reports citing the futility of rehabilitation, along with alarming recidivism rates. As a result, in 1976, Maine became the first state to fully embrace determinate sentencing and abolish parole. Since then, a number of states and the federal government have adopted some form of structured sentencing practices (as reflected in Figure 10.1), which have had considerable implications for parole.[9]

Parole Defined

While some form of parole remains the primary method through which inmates are released from prison, the nature of parole has changed considerably from its early origins. Generally, parole is considered to be *supervised conditional release* from a correctional institution prior to sentence expiration, under requirements that permit reincarceration if violated. In other words, parole is simply a continuation of one's sentence in the community. The inmate is released under supervision and expected to abide by certain provisions, violation of which could result in revocation of parole. The conditions imposed are quite similar to those required of probationers—such as remaining drug/alcohol-free, reporting periodically to a parole officer, avoiding criminal associations, obeying the law, and the like.

 Learning Goals

Do you know:

1. Which branch of government has authority over parole?
2. How the functions of parole have changed in recent years?
3. What conflicting objectives are involved in parole?

Parole Authority

Unlike probation, which is primarily a judicial function of the courts, parole is an *executive function* of correctional authorities. In fact, under indeterminate sentencing practices—when parole boards had virtually unlimited discretion to determine release dates—correctional officials in many respects had a greater impact than judges in terms of establishing the length of sentences.

Typically, the functions of parole involve:

- *Selection for parole*: reviewing cases to identify which inmates should be released from prison before the expiration of their sentence.

- *Preparole preparation*: classroom sessions, counseling, and other assistance designed to prepare new parolees for the decisions and self-discipline needed to resume life in free society.

- *Parole supervision*: assistance, treatment, and oversight provided in the ex-offender's home environment to ease transition from the institution and to control behavior in the community.

- *Parole termination*: either through routine dismissal of the case (successful completion) or revocation for violation of parole conditions.

Today, correctional authority is more limited to parole supervision and termination, with release determination often a function of legislative guidelines. But there is some debate over whether this actually represents a departure from past practices, rather than new terms for old practices.

Objectives of Parole

Ultimately, the major objective of parole has been and continues to be *reducing recidivism*. In the past, parole attempted to achieve this objective by a combination of selecting the most appropriate candidates for release and providing them with support and supervision as they made their transition into the community. With responsibility for selection diminishing, the focus of parole today is directed more toward postrelease procedures. But parole is still expected to *help the offender* successfully reintegrate into the community, while at the same time *safeguard the public* by continuing to control the parolee under community supervision.

As with probation, parole officers struggle to find a balance between providing support and supervising activities so that public safety is not compromised. In fact, it is ironic that the effectiveness of parole is largely judged on the basis of whether its clients return to prison—since it is incumbent on parole authorities to do exactly that when a client is not functioning effectively in society. Moreover, as we will see, parole can neither be fully credited with its successes nor blamed for its failures.

Do you know:

1. Who is eligible for parole?
2. Why parole is preferable to unsupervised release?
3. On what basis appointments to parole boards have been subject to criticism?

Eligibility for Parole

Once an inmate has served whatever minimum sentence was established, he or she is generally eligible to be considered for release. Unless the sentence specifically includes a stipulation that it is issued with no possibility of parole, even those with "life" sentences are eligible for early release in a number of states. That does not, however, mean that inmates can initiate an application for parole. While they voluntarily may turn down an opportunity to be paroled, they have no direct control over when it will be offered.

Also, eligibility for parole does not mean that parole will be granted automatically. Discretionary parole legally is considered a *privilege* rather than a *right*. No constitutional right to be released on parole has been recognized by the courts.

Those turned down at their first opportunity for consideration are often routinely scheduled for a rehearing after a designated period of time. While some offenders are paroled at the first opportunity, particularly notorious criminals may proceed through numerous rehearings unsuccessfully. For example, parole hearings are still conducted periodically for Charles Manson, under California's provision for rehearing the cases of those serving life terms every three years.

Many of the jobs available to inmates do not prepare them for gainful employment in urban areas on release. Courtesy of the Florida Department of Corrections, Tallahassee, Florida.

Obviously, inmates repeatedly denied parole are likely to be the most serious, potentially dangerous offenders. But in states that do not provide for life without parole, only death in prison can completely assure the prevention of one's eventual release. In that respect, it is an irony that long-termers who ultimately exit prison on the expiration of their sentence—without community supervision—are often those who need the scrutiny of parole the most. *See* the next "Close-up On Corrections" for the tragic account of one such case. While some may denounce the availability of parole as "too lenient," it is the desire to prevent such unfortunate events that motivates many to support postrelease supervision.

 # Close-up On Corrections

The Truth About Polly Klaas

Richard Allen Davis was a dangerous, violent felon. He was sentenced to life in prison in 1976 for kidnaping and other violent crimes. His criminal record was littered with instance after instance of predatory behavior. The paroling authority in the State of California knew this. His disregard for human life and safety, even while in prison, was a profound reminder of the need to keep this individual isolated from the community as long as possible. While in prison, the parole board reviewed his case six times, and six times the parole board rejected any possibility of release.

But the forces of change were at work in California. Politicians pledged to be "tough on crime." The obvious answer—"Abolish parole." And they got their wish. The requirement of earning the approval of the parole board before even a dangerous offender could be released was abolished. New standard sentences mandated automatic release after service of a set portion of the sentence. Offenders already incarcerated came under the provisions of the new law.

Release dates were churned out by the prison system's computers for thousands of prisoners then in custody. When the computers had done their job, there was no turning back. Richard Allen Davis had already served the amount of prison time that the new law and its mandatory release provisions demanded. . . . On the night of June 27, 1993, Richard Allen Davis walked out of prison, a free man. Less than four months later, in the safe darkness of a girlhood slumber party, Richard Allen Davis is alleged to have kidnaped and brutally murdered a little girl. Her name was Polly Klaas.

No one can say with certainty all that would have happened to Richard Allen Davis if parole had not been abolished in California. But there is overwhelming evidence that if the parole board had still been in control of release, Richard Allen Davis would have been in prison the night that Polly Klaas was murdered. [Information from California Board of Prison Terms.]

Source: Abolishing Parole: Why the Emperor Has No Clothes, Lexington, Kentucky: American Probation and Parole Association, 1995, p. 2. Used with permission.

Parole Boards

Parole selections in most states have been administered by a commission or board appointed by the governor, which may be subject to confirmation by the legislature. Given the relatively small size of most parole boards, it has been noted that "[in] no other part of the system is so much power concentrated in so few hands."[10]

Much of the concern surrounding parole has centered on how that power has been used. Appointments often have been a reward for political service to the successful gubernatorial candidate. It is therefore not surprising that parole commissioners in the past have been suspected or accused of corruption—awarding parole on the basis of political and/or financial motivations.

To reduce the potential for political involvement, recommendations of the President's Crime Commission in 1967 called for appointments based solely on merit, with qualifications including "broad academic backgrounds, especially in the behavioral sciences."[11] Yet, three decades later, parole boards in most states were still being cited for making appointments according to political patronage, without relevant background or educational requirements.[12] One study found that in twenty-nine states, "there were no professional qualifications, defined by statute, for parole board membership."[13] Even among the remaining twenty-one jurisdictions, statutes establishing qualifications may be written in "very general terms," thus giving the governor rather "wide latitude and generous discretion."[14]

 # Learning Goals

Do you know:

1. How the procedures used to grant parole have changed over time?
2. What (if any) due-process protections are involved in parole decision making?
3. On what basis parole boards make selection decisions?
4. On what grounds parole decisions have been criticized?

Selection Procedures

Generally, the prison or institutional treatment staff prepare a preparole progress report for the board's review.[15] This report usually includes such information as:

- A summary of the inmate's *case history* (including prior record, presentence investigation report, classification results, and the like)

- The *institutional programs* in which the offender has participated

- Evidence of *adjustment* during confinement (particularly any disciplinary action taken)

- A *proposed plan* for postrelease transition (such as employment and residence)

- Other documents relevant to *behavioral predictions* (such as a psychological profile)

- A *recommendation* by the institutional staff for or against parole, along with supporting reasons

Due-Process Considerations

Due-process procedures surrounding parole hearings have undergone changes over the years. Surprisingly, however, these modifications have not been a result of court intervention. Quite the contrary, courts have been reluctant to interfere in what they traditionally have viewed as the administrative decision-making function of parole boards.

The courts have not recognized that inmates have a constitutional right to parole nor have they established due-process requirements in the parole selection process. For example, in one particular case (*Menechino v. Oswald*),[16] an inmate challenged his parole denial on the basis that he should have been entitled to counsel, the right to cross-examine and produce witnesses, notice concerning the information being reviewed, and specific grounds for the denial. The court ruled that these due-process rights did not apply to parole hearings, under the rationale that:

1. Denying parole did not alter the status of the inmate (in other words, the inmate did not possess something that was being lost), and

2. The parole board's interests in rehabilitation and readjustment were not contrary to those of the inmate (in other words, the board was not in an adversarial position with regard to the inmate)

Nevertheless, although not legally required, most parole hearings today do allow the inmate to be represented by an attorney and to introduce witnesses. Generally, the proceedings are recorded in written transcripts, with the inmate advised in writing of the final decision (although again, this is not constitutionally required).[17] Recommendations of the American Correctional Association further call for consistently applied written criteria on which to base decisions, along with informing those denied of both their future hearing date and recommendations for improving their prospects at that time.[18]

Selection Criteria

The popular perception of parole boards may be that they make every effort to select inmates who have good potential for early release, but that is not exactly how the system operates. This does not mean that parole boards do not take their mission seriously or that they are overly lenient. Given the candidates they are faced with assessing, however, their function is often limited to screening out the *worst*, rather than selecting the *best*.

Despite having access to volumes of records, reports, data, interview transcripts, and other information concerning the offender, determining parole eligibility ultimately has been a product of the individual judgments of parole board members. Factors deemed important by any single member might include anything from cleanliness to church attendance.

Some members refuse to parole anyone who steadfastly maintains innocence despite having been convicted. Others base decisions on rehabilitative considerations—reviewing the inmate's outlook, self-improvement, change in work habits, and similar indicators of capacity to adapt to society. Some place heavy emphasis on victim-impact statements and anticipated public reaction if the offender is paroled. Still others reluctantly will support releasing a high-risk offender nearing sentence expiration, using the rationale that it is preferable to be released under supervision than unconditionally. In the absence of solid, tangible evidence, parole boards have acted largely on faith in the inmate's intentions and capacity to "make good."

In short, all of these varied decision-making criteria reflect the individual preferences, values, beliefs, and biases of parole board members. Given this extensive discretion, combined with concerns about the political independence and professional qualifications of those entrusted with it, it is not surprising that the parole selection process has been subject to complaints and controversy.

Decision-Making Criticisms

Needless to say, inmates denied parole often have been dissatisfied with what they consider arbitrary and inequitable features of the process. Particularly when inmates are not personally involved in parole decision making, it is difficult to appreciate how an anonymous group of people can fairly determine an unknown inmate's destiny. Even those who have an opportunity to present their case through a personal interview are sent out of the room while discussions of the case take place (being recalled only to hear the ultimate decision and a summary of the reasons for it). This common practice protects the confidentiality of individual member's actions. But it does not enable the candidate to hear objective discussions of the case, evaluations of strengths and weaknesses, or guidance in terms of how to modify behavior to improve subsequent chances for successful consideration. Without such insights, it is unlikely that those denied parole understand the basis for the decision or attach any sense of justice to it.

Parole boards also are subject to manipulation by clever inmates. For example, some prisoners initially fake illiteracy, reasoning that when they later appear to be doing extremely well educationally, they will have tricked the parole board into "believing they had worked hard to make a positive change in their lives."[19]

Nor are criticisms of parole limited to the inmate population. Friction between prison wardens and parole boards can be generated because of differences in viewpoints. Like the candidates themselves, prison officials may wonder why some were paroled while others were not. On the other hand, parole boards may view some of the recommendations of institutional staff as favoring the "warden's pet" or advocating the release of certain inmate leaders to manage the facility better. In essence, no matter what the board's decision, it is unsatisfactory to *someone*.

Learning Goals

Do you know:

1. The differences between conditional and unconditional release?
2. How a commutation differs from a pardon?
3. How good time and gain time are related to release?

Impact of the Justice Model

Beyond inmate discontent and staff disagreement, however, it is ordinary citizens who often express the most vocal dissatisfaction with parole. For it is not the long-term successes but the legendary failures that capture public attention. As a result of a few notorious cases, public opinion has had a substantial impact on stimulating change toward the determinate sentencing of the justice model.

In retrospect, it is perhaps surprising (but not illogical) to discover that it was actually inmates who originally advocated determinate sentences—to avoid being coerced into rehabilitation and to better assure that those convicted of similar offenses received similar prison terms. As one inmate phrased the frustration of his fellow prisoners, "Don't give us steak and eggs; . . . free us from the tyranny of the indeterminate sentence!"[20] But the complaints of inmates about involuntary treatment or sentencing inequities might well have fallen on deaf ears had the public been satisfied with the existing system.

To many observers, however, by the late 1970s and early 1980s, the system simply did not appear to be working:

- The unspecified length of indeterminate sentences created strong suspicion that potential law violators were not being *deterred* by the certainty of punishment.

- High rates of recidivism provided evidence that criminals were apparently not being *rehabilitated.*

- The likelihood of early release on parole generated concern that offenders were not paying their "*just deserts*" to society.

Parole itself was termed a tragic failure and a cruel hypocrisy. It was viewed as deceiving both the inmate looking for help and the public looking for protection,[21] providing neither security to the law-abiding nor fair treatment to law violators.[22] The premise that parole safeguards society by keeping criminals in prison until they are ready for release was dismissed as nonsense.[23] Although the criminal justice system never can be free of failures, parole was charged with providing more than its share of them. As a result, an increasingly conservative society—lacking trust in rehabilitation and fearful of rising crime rates—called for *fixed, determinate sentences* with a more *objective method* of establishing release dates (preferably upon completion of full sentences). Yet, as the next "Close-up On Corrections" reveals, abolishing parole does not necessarily improve public safety.

Close-up On Corrections

WHICH OF THESE ALTERNATIVES MAKES YOU FEEL SAFER?

Scenario 1: Parole as Part of Responsible Sentencing

A prisoner, convicted of assault upon his wife, received a sentence of seven years that included eligibility for parole after service of three years in prison. . . . The board deemed a minimum of five years in prison as appropriate. Concerned that the wife might still be endangered if the prisoner were to be released, the board ordered polygraph testing of the offender and interviewed fellow inmates about threats made in their presence. . . . In addition, the board invited the wife to a confidential interview so that they could hear directly from her about her concerns. Convinced that the wife was still at considerable risk, the board continued the prisoner in custody, and indicated that they would not consider release until he had completed an anger management program, identified a residence in a completely different part of the state from his wife, and agreed that he would accept a "no contact" condition if parole were to be granted at a later date. Because the wife indicated that his episodes of violence usually occurred while the offender was drinking alcohol, the board also required alcohol screening and treatment as a condition of parole. In all, the offender served six years in prison, was released under strict conditions designed to protect the wife, and completed his sentence in the community without incident.

Scenario 2: The Impact of Abolishing Parole

This same prisoner has been convicted of assault in the same state. However, the state has recently abolished parole to be "tougher" on crime. As the result of a plea, the offender has . . . pled guilty to simple assault, an offense that allows the judge to impose a sentence of four years. With good time credits, he will serve twenty-four months in prison before he is released. He has boasted many times to his cell mates that he will make his wife "pay" when he gets home, but no one ever learns of these threats. Indeed, he has even made threatening phone calls and sent letters to his wife, but she does not know where to turn. She never appeared in court for fear of angering her husband, and does not know the name of the judge in the case, who, in any event, has rotated off the criminal bench . . . . Unaware that her husband was to be released, she was home the day he arrived from prison. Her husband is drinking heavily again, and has instigated several arguments that have resulted in further injury to her and her children. [Based on an actual case.]

Source: *Abolishing Parole: Why the Emperor Has No Clothes*, Lexington, Kentucky: American Probation and Parole Association, 1995, p. 15. Used with permission.

Conditional versus Unconditional Release

With the transition from the medical model to the justice model, the method by which inmates are released from confinement has changed, although not necessarily in the manner anticipated. Ever since the first indeterminate sentencing legislation was enacted more than 130 years ago, inmates have been released from correctional institutions either:

- *Conditionally*: with continued freedom dependent on adhering to the requirements established by the paroling authority or

- *Unconditionally*: with no conditions attached, because the offender had served the full sentence, been pardoned, had the sentence commuted, or received some other form of legal modification

Beyond the simple expiration of one's sentence, unconditional release can occur as a result of clemency extended by the executive branch of government (in other words, the governor of a state or the president of the United States, although parole boards in some states have this power as well). *Executive clemency* ordinarily takes one of the following forms:

- *Commutation*. One's sentence is reduced, such as when "time served" is substituted for a longer original sentence. However, a commutation does not necessarily lead to release—as, for example, when life imprisonment is substituted for a death sentence.

- *Pardon*. The offender's conviction is forgiven. While pardons do not erase the offender's criminal record, they do restore the rights of citizenship. Originally designed to undo miscarriages of justice (for example, when a person was wrongfully convicted), pardons often are unconditional. But conditional pardons can be issued, which depend on subsequent performance of the person being pardoned.

Corrections can maintain supervisory authority only over those offenders who are *conditionally released*. Conditional release is similar to the situation of probationers who face the imposition of a suspended sentence for failure to abide by the conditions of probation. Likewise, parolees face the possibility of returning to prison to complete their original term if parole is revoked for failure to comply with the conditions attached. Those receiving unconditional release, however, are no longer under any legal authority of the correctional system.

Parole Trends Today

The movement toward determinate sentencing presumably was designed to achieve certainty in punishment—with *fixed, flat terms* replacing *flexible ranges*. One might therefore assume that more full sentences would be served, more unconditional releases would occur, and parole populations would decline. Nothing could be further from reality.

Despite the intent of the justice model, inmates continue to be released from prison before serving their full potential terms. The average time served by those released from state prisons is still only about half of their original sentence.[25] Unconditional releases, however, are not replacing conditional supervision. Most of those coming out of prison are still being released under some form of conditional supervision in the community (*see* Figure 10.2). Nor is the number of people on parole diminishing—quite the contrary. By 2002, the parole population had reached a record high of more than 750,000.[26] What can account for these discrepancies?

figure 10.2

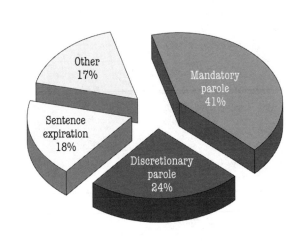

Methods of release from adult correctional agencies.

Source: Timothy A. Hughes, Doris James Wilson, and Allen J. Beck. "Trends in State Parole, 1990-2000," *Bureau of Justice Statistics Special Report*, Washington, DC: U.S. Department of Justice, 2001, p. 4.

As was described in earlier chapters, the major element that public policy changes failed to take into account when shifting to determinate sentencing was prison space. Under the justice model, more offenders have been more likely to be sentenced to at least some time in a correctional institution. Yet, sufficient funding has not been available to accommodate them either through new construction or expansion of existing facilities.

The primary method for dealing with this escalating inmate population has become the awarding of "gain time" or "good time." These terms are widely used interchangeably. But technically, *gain time* refers to time that is *automatically* deducted by law, based on the length of the sentence, the length of time served, and/or the seriousness of the offense. For example, some states credit an increasing number of days per month the longer a person remains incarcerated. Under such a system, an inmate could earn five days each month during the first year of imprisonment, six days per month during the next year, and so on. On the other hand, *good time credit* (or what is also called "incentive" or "meritorious" time) is *earned* for proper institutional conduct. In some jurisdictions, it also can be awarded for participation in certain treatment, training, educational, or work programs.

Learning Goals

Do you know:

1. How mandatory and discretionary parole differ?
2. How objective prediction instruments have changed parole decision making?

Mandatory versus Discretionary Release

If the primary intent of the justice model was to increase the severity of sentencing, its goal will not be realized until institutional crowding is eliminated. If, however, the major intent was to achieve certainty in sentencing, its mission is closer to accomplishment. This does not mean that the full sentence imposed by the court is the one that will be served. But after crediting inmates with time deductions, it is a straightforward mathematical calculation to determine one's earliest possible release date. Assuming that the prisoner does nothing while confined to jeopardize time credits, release is virtually required at that point.

Thus, in states with determinate sentencing, inmates now become eligible for what is known as *mandatory supervised release* (or *mandatory parole*) when they have served their original sentence minus any gain/good time accrued. In that respect, there is more than some truth to the observation that new language simply has been introduced for continuing practices—with "supervised release" replacing "parole," but very little actually changing with regard to the parole officer's supervisory role.[27] Another indicator that meaningful change may not have actually occurred is the earning of good time for program participation—a practice that bears close resemblance to basing parole decisions on treatment progress.

Supervised mandatory release (mandatory parole) is essentially a form of what has been described earlier as conditional release. The ex-offender is subject to conditions which, if violated, could result in reincarceration to serve out the remainder of the sentence (in other words, that portion which was relieved by time credits). It is therefore not the postrelease supervisory function of parole that has changed with the justice model. Nor is that unfortunate, since replacing conditional with unconditional releases could create far greater public safety hazards.

What has been fundamentally altered is how release decisions are made. As the term "*mandatory* supervised release" or "*mandatory* parole" implies, more inmates are now coming out of prison because the statutory authority to confine them has expired. In other words, they have served at least their minimum sentence, minus time credits. It is this mandated element that distinguishes it from the traditional form of discretionary parole. Once gain/good time credit has been deducted from the original sentence, release becomes a *compulsory* result of mathematical calculations, as opposed to a *discretionary* decision of parole boards.

In the mid-1970s, nearly three out of four persons discharged from prison (about 72 percent) were released on the basis of parole board decisions.[28] But

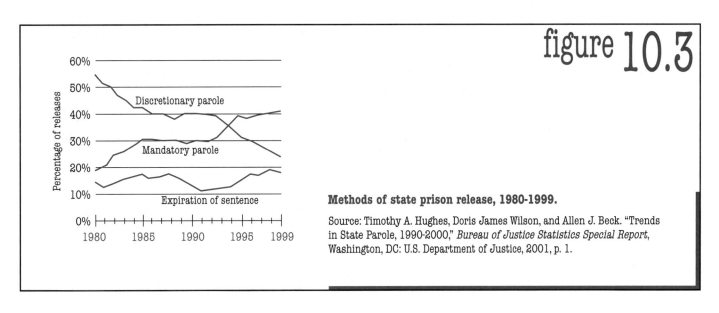

figure 10.3

Methods of state prison release, 1980-1999.

Source: Timothy A. Hughes, Doris James Wilson, and Allen J. Beck. "Trends in State Parole, 1990-2000," *Bureau of Justice Statistics Special Report*, Washington, DC: U.S. Department of Justice, 2001, p. 1.

by 2002, discretionary parole accounted for only 39 percent of prison releases.[29] As illustrated in Figure 10.3, at the same time that discretionary releases have been *decreasing*, mandatory releases have been *increasing*.

Parole Implications

Despite the significance of this change, few of those in free society fully understand it. The scenario in the next "Close-up On Corrections" provides a vivid example of how such misconceptions can fuel public anger.

It is easy to see how the public has become confused. Obviously, the trend over recent years has been toward less discretionary and more mandatory supervised releases. But that does not mean that parole board decision making has been completely abolished. The majority of states still have various forms of indeterminate sentencing. And even in states with determinate sentencing, parole boards must continue to address those inmates sentenced earlier under indeterminate statutes.

While the releasing authority of parole boards has been declining steadily, it has not been destroyed completely. It has, however, been subject to much greater *accountability*—"parole has been called on to be more responsive to the competing concerns of offenders, victims, and the public."[30] Consequently, parole discretion also has been subject to much greater control. Not only are paroling authorities more restricted in terms of which inmates can be selected for release, but today they also function under more structured release decision-making guidelines.

 # Close-up On Corrections

LET'S GET IT STRAIGHT—WHO'S DOING THE RELEASING?

All too frequently, the media fail to understand and clearly distinguish between basic concepts. . . . As a result, the public does not get an accurate story. Few reporters understand the difference between . . . discretionary release and mandatory release, or the function of earned time or gained time and its effect in radically altering a sentence structure.

A recent example provides a valid illustration. A California man who had raped and severed the arms of his victim was widely reported to have been on parole release after serving only a portion of his sentence. The public voiced understandable outrage at the thought that parole board members would consider early release for such an individual. In fact, the inmate was not released as a matter of discretion, but because the law mandated it. Virtually no media reports pointed out that important aspect of the story.

Source: John J. Curran, Jr., "A Priority for Parole: Agencies Must Reach Out," *Correctional Issues: Probation and Parole*, Laurel, Maryland: American Correctional Association, 1990, pp. 34-35.

Structured Decision Making

The trend toward structuring the discretion of parole boards reflects much of the same reasoning as the sentencing guidelines and objective classification procedures discussed previously. In other words, it is designed to replace the *subjectivity* of personal decisions with the *objectivity* of formulas that predict risk on the basis of empirical research.

The search for valid instruments to identify what types of offenders represent the best risks for parole began well before current infatuation with the capabilities of computers. As early as the 1920s, rudimentary forms of *parole prediction tables* began to appear.

As corrections assumed a more legalistic direction guided by constitutional issues during the 1960s and 1970s, increasing emphasis was placed on due-process considerations, definable standards, and defensible procedures. Parole was no exception. By the late 1970s, for example, a number of states moved to *parole contracting,* whereby a target date is determined, which becomes the parole release date if all provisions are met by the inmate. These contracts set specific goals in such areas as education, training, counseling, and institutional behavior.

By the 1980s, most states had adopted various forms of written guidelines governing the granting of parole.[31] Some of these documents are essentially lists of criteria that parole board members are implicitly supposed to take into account in making release decisions. Others are much more explicit statistical tables that assign specific weights to various factors, with one's total score determining the candidate's prognosis for success or failure on parole. All are designed to base the granting of parole on more *objective criteria.*

One of the best known and most widely used of the statistical risk prediction tables is the *Salient Factor Score*, originally pioneered by the U.S. Parole Commission in the 1970s. Under this system, scores of varying weights are assigned to six factors pertaining to the offender's background (shown in Figure 10.4). As that chart indicates, better risks are reflected by high scores (for example, those who are older or who have no prior convictions). Low scores, on the other hand, reflect greater risk of subsequent violations.

While a number of states use the Salient Factor Score in parole decision making, other forms of objective risk assessment are employed as well. Among the most common items that they include are the following:

- Number of parole revocations
- Number of adult or juvenile convictions
- Number of prison terms served
- Number of incarcerations served
- Whether the current crime involves violence [32]

Of course, mitigating or aggravating factors that have a bearing on the case are not reflected in the mechanical calculations of statistical scores. As with sentencing guidelines, structured parole guidelines provide the option of overriding the results. Discretion therefore has not been totally eliminated. But deviations from the guidelines generally are restricted to specific reasons that are documented in writing.

The result—like sentencing guidelines—is designed to enable some flexibility within a standardized framework. Even the most sophisticated statistical techniques cannot fully substitute for human judgment. While objective instruments can provide valuable tools to guide human decision making, they cannot replace it.

A Model for Transition from Prison to the Community

A new, more comprehensive approach developed by the National Institute of Corrections and recently tested in several states is the Transition from Prison to the Community Initiative (TPCI). The prime objective of this model is "to safeguard the public from harm" by released offenders.[33] As such, it uses validated risk-assessment tools to identify offender needs, which are then linked with appropriate interventions. Rather than dealing with release as an

figure 10.4

Item A:	*Prior convictions/adjudications (adult or juvenile)*	_____
	None	=3
	One	=2
	Two or three	=1
	Four or more	=0

Item B:	*Prior commitment(s) of more than thirty days (adult or juvenile)*	_____
	None	=2
	One or two	=1
	Three or more	=0

Item C:	*Age at current offense/prior commitments*	_____
	Age at commencement of the current offense	
	26 years of age or more	=2*
	20-25 years of age	=1*
	19 years of age or less	=0
	*Exception: If five or more prior commitments of more than thirty days (adult or juvenile), place an "x" here _____ and score this item	=0

Item D:	*Recent commitment-free period (three years)*	_____
	No prior commitment of more than thirty days (adult or juvenile) or released to the community from last such commitment at least three years prior to the commencement of the current offense	=1
	Otherwise	=0

Item E:	*Probation/parole/confinement/escape/status violator this time*	_____
	Neither on probation, parole, confinement, or escape status at the time of the current offense; nor committed as a probation, parole, confinement, or escape status violator this time	=1
	Otherwise	=0

Item F:	*Heroin/opiate dependence*	_____
	No history of heroin/opiate dependence	=1
	Otherwise	=0
	Total Score	_____

Salient Factor Score Sheet.

NOTE: For purposes of the Salient Factor Score, an instance of criminal behavior resulting in a judicial determination of guilt or an admission of guilt before a judicial body shall be treated as a conviction, even if a conviction is not formally entered.

isolated procedure, it is viewed as part of a broader transition process that uses evidence-based practices at key decision points, including:

- Initial assessment and classification
- Institutional programming
- Release preparation
- Release decision making
- Community supervision
- Responses to violations
- Discharge from supervision

Because of its comprehensiveness, TPCI is implemented through the collaboration of multi-agency partnerships—including criminal justice and human service agencies, along with community and faith-based organizations. But perhaps the most significant feature of the TPCI model is its commitment to "consider the effect of returning an offender to the community *from the time the offender enters the prison system*," [emphasis added].[34] Such a long-term perspective requires a fundamental shift in everything from agency priorities to operating procedures and management practices. If nothing else, that should bring the varying missions of correctional facilities and post-release community-based supervision into closer alignment.

 # Learning Goals

Do you know:

1. How the supervisory functions of parole and probation officers differ?
2. What transitional services assist offenders preparing to return to society?
3. How today's reentry population differs from previous releasees?

Parole Supervision

In addition to more closely structuring decision making, objective parole guidelines also have been used to determine the level of supervision needed by those released. Again, this is not unlike another practice discussed earlier—the classification of probation caseloads. We already have seen how classifying probationers according to the level of risk they pose enables staff to allocate scarce resources more appropriately and manage heavy workloads more efficiently. In much the same manner, objective-prediction instruments can serve similar functions for parole officers.

In fact, the supervisory responsibilities of parole staff in many respects are quite similar to those of probation officers. Their clients, however, are not necessarily similar. Parolees are generally more difficult to supervise than probationers. Whereas probationers have been considered sufficiently hopeful to avoid being sent to prison, parolees have been incarcerated as poor risks for probation. In addition, they have adapted to institutional life. Many have learned to acquiesce to authority on a superficial basis while maintaining a behavior pattern that basically is unchanged. Others have learned to manipulate their way through prison life. All have been screened out as ineligible for probation and conditioned by their prison experience.

That does not mean that they are unsalvageable. However, the fact that parolees have been removed for some period of time from the community not only increases the difficulty of their supervision but also subjects them to additional personal stresses not encountered by probationers. Despite their indifferent external demeanor, freedom can have an overwhelmingly emotional impact on those institutionalized. Successful planning for parole, therefore, must begin well before an inmate exits the prison gate, although that often is not the case. In fact, underfunding has made parole in many jurisdictions "more of a legal status then a systematic process of reintegrating returning prisoners."[35]

Prerelease Planning

From their perspective, ex-offenders already have been rejected for years by the mainstream of society. When they encounter continued rejection upon reentering a hostile environment, feelings of inadequacy and failure are reinforced. It may not take long for even the most hopeful parolee to find the optimism of "starting over" replaced by the realism of being stigmatized. The ultimate effect is often a self-fulfilling prophecy, as those society expects to fail do exactly that. In the words of one ex-offender: "They walk through the gate in the big brick wall, which confined them for months or years or lifetimes, only to hit the wall of solid self-righteousness that so many people erect . . . perhaps in an attempt to feel that they are somehow morally superior to all of us ordinary folk out here breathing common air."[36]

At the same time, just as the community must be prepared to accept ex-offenders, they, in turn, must be prepared to be realistic about what they will confront and what adjustments they must make when released. Those who have adapted well to years of institutional life face the formidable challenge of reorienting to an entirely different lifestyle in free society. Few can successfully make that adjustment alone.

For an inside view of the fear and apprehensions of someone being released, read the next "Close-up On Corrections," which puts you in the place of a long-term inmate leaving prison (and also illustrates the unrevealing "social veneer" described previously). As that scenario points out, in the final analysis, it is in everyone's best interests to extend the help needed to prevent releasees from becoming readmissions.

Because the reception extended to ex-offenders is often more antagonistic than accepting, it is important for the parolee to locate *supportive peer associations*. Relying on such groups can do much to make the transition from confinement less frightening. It may be difficult to imagine a "hardened ex-con" fearing anything—much less the expectation of imminent freedom. As we saw in the last scenario, however, even with official assistance, parole can be a very lonely experience. In the upcoming "Close-up On Corrections," (page 361) an inmate's plea to Ann Landers is further evidence that the prospect of getting out can create more panic than the possibility of staying in. Note her response, particularly in terms of the critical role of self-help groups.

Close-up On Corrections

HESITANT TO GO HOME

Next Wednesday you will be walking out those front gates as a free man. This last time around cost you ten years. It was your third hitch. You have spent thirty of the last forty years of your life behind bars. Sixty-two years of life's ups and downs have softened your disposition. You have no excuses left; you feel that the time you got was coming to you. In fact, the last hitch was one you purposely set up.

You had been released on a cold gray morning in February. There was no one on the outside waiting for you; your friends were all in prison. You had been divorced for over fifteen years and your former wife had remarried. Your parents were dead, and your two sisters had given up on you long ago. Besides, there were too many decisions to make in the free world. You were not used to all of that freedom; it was frightening. No one cared about you like they did inside the joint.

You got a job as a busboy in a restaurant, but the hustle and bustle was too much, and besides, no one wanted to make friends with an old ex-con. Finally you had all you could take, so you stole all the money from the cash register one night during a lull in the business. You did not spend any of it, but instead went home, had a beer, and waited. In less than two hours, the police arrived at your apartment. Once the restaurant manager realized you and the money were missing, it was not long before you were arrested. You refused an attorney and told the judge that you would keep committing crimes until he sent you back. He reluctantly sentenced you to ten years. You passed up parole each time it came around.

So, here you are again. You have been measured for your new suit of street clothes and your one hundred fifty dollar check for transitional expenses has been processed. The labor department representative has arranged for you to have a stock-clerk job in a small grocery store in a nearby town. Your social worker has also arranged for you to stay in a small apartment near where you will work. You remember your last prerelease counseling session with her and how she offered all the words of encouragement a young, energetic, and well-meaning counselor could muster. You just smiled and nodded your approval. What good would it have done to burst her idealistic bubble? She could never understand how frightening the outside world had come to be for you. All of her friends lived in the free world; none of yours did.

You would like to make it on the outside if you could, but the odds are against you. And besides, it's just too lonely out there. You know you ought to feel happy about leaving prison, but the truth is, you are miserable about it. You would like to be able to make it on the outside, but deep down inside, you feel you are doomed before you start.

Source: Reprinted by permission of Waveland Press, Inc. from Michael Braswell, Tyler Fletcher, and Larry Miller, *Human Relations and Corrections*, Third Edition, Long Grove, Illinois: Waveland Press, Inc., 1990, pp. 83-84. All rights reserved.

Preparing the Offender

Not all institutions offer prerelease guidance before discharge.[37] But some correctional facilities do make an effort to prepare offenders for what to expect and how to cope on release. In fact, much of the success of reintegration depends on how well the inmate is prepared prior to release.[38] This can be accomplished through a variety of prerelease counseling and planning programs, and through *work release* or by phasing-out through *prerelease centers*.

Prerelease centers. In some cases, prisoners are phased-out through gradual reduction of their security classification. In this manner, the last months of one's sentence are served in a minimum-security facility or prerelease center—where there are fewer rules governing behavior, less staff monitoring, and greater trust placed in the inmate. The goal is to enable those about to be released to take more personal responsibility for decision making, and to encourage them to replace external staff control with internal self-control.

Inmates in prerelease centers may spend daytime hours at work assignments or educational programs in the community. Thus, they are able to become better accustomed to the freedoms of outside life. They can "practice" living in society while remaining under supervision during their unoccupied time. Beyond these general functions, additional assistance is provided in terms of plans to obtain housing, employment, transportation, and other essentials for surviving on the outside.

Work release. Not all correctional agencies have a prerelease center or sufficient bedspace in it to meet demands. But arrangements can be made for *work release* without transferring inmates from their assigned institution. Particularly where preparation for parole is viewed as a long-term process, opportunities for work release may be provided well in advance of one's anticipated departure. It enables inmates to be employed on salary in the community during the day, while returning to the facility at night.

Work release is an alternative to total confinement that has a number of advantages—among them, enabling offenders to help support their families and reducing the financial burden on taxpayers. Perhaps most important, it enhances the inmate's job skills, confidence, sense of responsibility, and ties with the community.

Not everyone, however, is equally enthusiastic, nor is work release without risks. Despite its advantages, not all correctional systems have adopted work-release programs. Even where it is available, the number participating is extremely small, representing only 2 percent of the total prison population.[39] Undoubtedly, there have been isolated problems with inmates absconding or returning under the influence of alcohol or drugs. But for the most part, it would appear that the benefits of reintegrating the offender into society through work release outweigh the drawbacks. Except for the extremely few prisoners sentenced to death or confined to life without parole, virtually everyone is subject to potential release at some time. With those who are eligible, it would seem logical that the time to take the risks associated with work release is while they are still subject to continued custody.

Close-up On Corrections

Today's Reentry Population

Offenders being released today are not only often ill-prepared for their return to free society, but they also differ from their earlier predecessors in a number of ways. For one thing, they have been incarcerated for longer periods of time. For another, they have been involved in fewer prison programs; for example:

- In 1991, 31 percent of prisoners scheduled to leave in the next year had participated in a vocational program. By 1997, that rate had dropped to 27 percent.

Inmates who prepare for release while still incarcerated are more likely to succeed on parole. Here a caseworker discusses prerelease planning with an inmate. Photo by Joseph Fuller, II.

- In 1991, 43 percent had participated in an education program. By 1997, that rate had dropped to 35 percent.

- In 1991, 25 percent had participated in a drug treatment program. By 1997, that rate had dropped by more than half, to 10 percent.

- In both years, only 10 to 12 percent of those scheduled for release in the next year had participated in formal prerelease programs designed to help them transition to the community.[40]

To the extent that shorter sentences—combined with education, training, treatment, and prerelease planning—increase the potential for successful completion of parole, these are foreboding statistics. They are a result of "sharp reductions" in programs at all levels of the correctional conglomerate—federal state, and local—that provide offenders with the skills necessary to prepare them for reintegration into society. Yet, at the same time that corrections is required to manage the reentry process for increasing numbers of offenders, the very programs on which successful reentry is built are being scaled back or eliminated as a result of shifting priorities driven by budget cuts.[41]

 ## Learning Goals

Do you know:

1. What general conditions are usually established for parolees?
2. What functions parole officers perform?
3. How reentry courts assist with the transition process for parolees?

Conditions of Parole

For the most part, the conditions of parole are quite similar to the probation stipulations described earlier. As with probation, *general conditions* refer to the standard requirements governing behavior that are imposed uniformly. Designed to reduce the chances of renewed involvement in crime, they may require steady work, restrict travel, limit personal associations, prohibit the use of alcohol, and the like. Within a particular jurisdiction, these general conditions will be imposed on all parolees. Although they are not identical throughout the country, some are commonly imposed in the majority of states, as shown in Figure 10.5.

In addition to such universal requirements, *specific conditions* can be added for a particular client to address any unique treatment needs or behavioral restrictions. For example, a habitual DUI (driving under the influence) offender also may be required to attend Alcoholics Anonymous sessions regularly, to abstain completely from the use of alcohol, to refrain from driving a car, and even to submit to random breath, blood, or urinalysis testing.

General trends in the overall parole process also have been moving toward greater *objectivity*. As a result, parole authorities have begun to reduce the number of conditions, focusing more on those related to crime control than on those related to social activities. Regardless of what the requirements are, however, the client must agree in writing to abide by them.

Functions of Parole Officers

It is the parole board in the state's central office that authorizes general conditions by which clients must abide. But it is the parole officer in the field

---

figure 10.5

Condition	Percentage of Jurisdictions
Obey all federal, state, and local laws	98.0%
Report to the parole officer as directed and answer all reasonable inquiries by the officer	96.1%
Refrain from possessing a firearm or other dangerous weapon unless granted written permission	92.2%
Remain within the jurisdiction of the court and notify the parole officer of any change in residence	90.2%
Permit the parole officer to visit the parolee at home or elsewhere	82.4%
Obey all rules and regulations of the parole supervision agency	78.4%
Maintain gainful employment	78.4%
Abstain from association with persons with criminal records	60.8%
Pay all court-ordered fines, restitution, or other financial penalties	52.9%

General conditions of parole found in most jurisdictions.

Source: Edward E. Rhine, William R. Smith, and Ronald W. Jackson. *Paroling Authorities: Recent History and Current Practice*, Laurel, Maryland: American Correctional Association, 1991, p. 106.

who is responsible for assuring that they are upheld. Previously, field services were an administrative unit of the parole board. But since the 1970s, community supervision has become increasingly independent and is now usually housed separately (primarily within the state department of corrections).[42]

On the part of the officer, field services call for—among many other attributes—being skilled in working with the client and his or her family, developing relationships with law enforcement agencies, and becoming thoroughly familiar with available resources in the area. Like probation supervision, the parole officer's role involves similar conflicts between providing support and imposing sanctions. But encouraging *change* is actually what both are designed to accomplish.[43] To achieve change, parole officers are simultaneously expected to:

- Furnish assistance to help the ex-offender readjust

- Monitor signs indicating how well or poorly that adjustment is occurring

- Take appropriate action to control behavior when necessary

Soon they may be getting some assistance in that regard from a powerful but unlikely source—the courts. In a unique strategy designed to bring the prestige and resources of the judiciary to bear on the challenges of making a successful transition from prison, the upcoming "Close-up On Corrections" describes the parole equivalent of drug courts—that is, reentry courts. While this new initiative is just beginning to make an impact, at least one early assessment indicates that the extensive supervision provided to the client (for example, monthly court appearances, individualized attention, and three to four personal contacts per week) improves chances for success, even among drug and sex offenders, who are not traditionally considered good parole risks.[44]

 Learning Goals

Do you know:

1. What collateral consequences of conviction affect parolees returning to the community?
2. What federal benefits can be denied to drug offenders?
3. How occupational licensing restrictions limit employment for ex-offenders?

Collateral Consequences of Conviction

Among the many *collateral consequences* of being incarcerated[45] is the loss of family ties over the years spent behind bars, often in remote locations far from the offender's home community. As a result, many parolees have neither the supportive family nor the financial resources to help them get settled. Thus, it has been estimated that 20 to 25 percent of ex-offenders are homeless on release. As one person described it, temporarily they are "staying on someone's couch, but it won't last long."[46]

Along with residence, employment is an immediate concern. Research indicates that the quality and quantity of employment are the most consistent

Close-up On Corrections

TRANSITION THROUGH REENTRY COURT

The reentry-court concept involves drawing on the authority of the court to promote positive behavior by offenders returning from prison, much like drug courts manage the behavior of drug offenders. Two of the key components in drug courts are that they represent the exercise of judicial authority toward a beneficial end, and that offenders respond positively to the fact that a judge is taking an interest in their success. Frequent appearances before the court, combined with the offer of assistance and predictable consequences for failure, assist offenders in taking the steps necessary to get their lives back on track.

The reentry court involves applying these principles at another stage in the justice process—as inmates leave prison. But the core elements are similar:

- *Assessment and planning*: Following assessment of inmates' needs, corrections officials—working in conjunction with the reentry court—establish linkages to social services, family counseling, health care, housing, job training, and work opportunities to support successful reintegration.

- *Active oversight*: The reentry court sees clients frequently—probably once a month—beginning right after release and continuing until the end of their parole (or other form of supervised release).

- *Management of supportive services*: A case manager brokers a broad array of supportive resources, including substance-abuse treatment, job training, faith institutions, housing assistance, and community services.

- *Accountability to the community*: There are mechanisms for drawing on diverse community perspectives that are incorporated, such as a citizen advisory board.

- *Graduated and parsimonious sanctions*: A predetermined range of sanctions for violations of release conditions would be swiftly, predictably, and universally applied (although they would not automatically require return to prison).

- *Rewards for success*: Milestones in the reentry process trigger recognition and rewards through positive judicial reinforcement (for example, graduation ceremonies; early release from supervision).

Based on the concept that the judiciary provides a powerful public forum for encouraging positive behavior, the expectation is that focusing on reentry issues in the courts will help reduce the recidivism rate of returning prisoners and will encourage a broad-based coalition to support their successful reintegration.

Source: Compiled from "Re-entry Courts: Managing the Transition from Prison to Community," A Call for Concept Papers, U.S. Department of Justice: Office of Justice Programs, September, 1999, pp. 1-9.

predictors of success on parole.[47] Yet, many jobs are restricted because of the ex-offender's ineligibility. Those who have not participated in institutional education programs will especially find many doors closed to them, since even entry-level jobs today tend to require at least a high school diploma. In one state alone, it has been estimated that about half of the prisoners released on parole are illiterate, and about 85 percent are substance abusers[48]—hardly good qualifications for seeking postrelease employment.

Even those with the required educational credentials, however, will find that they are faced with another of the collateral consequence of conviction in the form of *occupational licensing* restrictions. Often based on "good moral character," such restrictions effectively exclude ex-offenders. As shown in the next "Close-up On Corrections," positions requiring state licenses are difficult to obtain by those with a criminal record and can include a long list of occupations.

Moreover, Congress has provided federal and state courts with the ability to deny federal benefits to those convicted of drug possession or trafficking. Among the benefits that can be denied are grants, contracts, loans, and licenses. Thus, students can lose college loans, pilots can lose their FAA license, business-owners can lose federal contracts, and researchers can lose academic grants.[49]

Additionally, denial of welfare benefits and public housing—combined with restrictions on employment prospects—can present a virtual "brick wall" for returning ex-offenders.[50] Beyond these pragmatic barriers is yet another collateral consequence of a felony conviction that has generated widespread controversy in recent years—the disenfranchisement of millions of potential voters on the basis of their criminal record.

While nearly 4 million Americans (one of every fifty adults) are currently or permanently disenfranchised,[51] several states are beginning to restore voting rights to ex-offenders (*see* the "Close-up On Corrections" on page 368), as well as remove arbitrary restrictions on job opportunities for ex-offenders. Some states also have begun prohibiting the denial of employment or licensing because of a conviction unless it involves "unreasonable risk" or there is a direct relationship between the offense and the specific type of job or license.[52]

The U.S. Department of Labor provides free bonding for parolees and also has compiled a guide for making occupational plans during confinement and identifying employment resources on release.[53] A similar guide specifically directed toward women preparing to leave prison also provides advice for everything from getting a job and locating affordable housing to accessing medical benefits, getting financial help, and handling the stress of change.[54]

In his January, 2004, State of the Union address, the president proposed a four-year $300 million prisoner reentry initiative "to expand job training and placement services, to provide transitional housing, and to help newly released prisoners get mentoring."[55] But the fact remains that while individual states vary, and eventually may relax restrictive regulations in response to federal funding, many positions still require licensing that would disqualify parolees.

Combined with such legislatively imposed restrictions is the basic hesitancy of many employers to "take a chance" by hiring ex-offenders. For example, a recent survey discovered that in five major U.S. cities, 65 percent of all employers said they would not knowingly hire an ex-offender.[56] Finding jobs for parolees is also especially difficult in times of high unemployment, when even

Close-up On Corrections

ONE STATE'S EMPLOYMENT RESTRICTIONS

Until civil rights have been restored, a felon cannot:

- Hold public office
- Serve on a jury
- Vote
- Carry a firearm
- Work in pest control
- Be an investigative agent
- Join the military services
- Get a passport

On conviction of a felony, a person cannot be a:

- Member of the state board of dentistry
- Bartender
- Minister (in most churches)
- Firefighter
- Guardian
- Police or correctional officer
- Funeral director or embalmer
- Sanitarian
- Deception detector
- Armed security guard

On conviction of a felony, licenses may be refused, suspended, or revoked for (partial list):

- Accounting
- Architecture
- Barber
- Cosmetology
- Court reporting
- Insurance
- Land sales
- Landscape architecture
- Massage
- Mortgage broker
- Nursing
- Occupational therapy
- Optometry
- Pharmacy
- Physical therapist
- Teacher
- Veterinary medicine

Source: Office of Executive Clemency, State of Florida, Tallahassee, Florida, 1992.

those without the stigma of being "ex-cons" have a hard time finding meaningful work. Thus, it sometimes appears almost impossible to place parolees in jobs with a livable salary, much less career mobility or advancement.

Easing Reentry through Restorative Justice

For these and many other reasons, some communities are turning to a unique, broad-based approach to reentry that involves not only the correctional system, but collaborative partnerships with the community as well. Through *citizens' circles* involving a widespread array of local representatives, (*see* Figure 10.6), the root causes contributing to the parolee's involvement in crime are addressed, offender accountability is established, and linkages are developed with those in the community who have a direct stake in the outcome, based on the principles of restorative justice:

 # Close-up On Corrections

FELON VOTING

States that have relaxed voting prohibitions since 1996:

- CONNECTICUT: Repealed a voting ban for felons on probation.

- DELAWARE: Repealed a lifetime voting ban for some felons, but requires a five-year waiting period.

- MARYLAND: Repealed a lifetime ban for most repeat offenders, but requires a three-year waiting period.

- NEVADA: Repealed a ban on voting for first-time nonviolent felons.

- NEW MEXICO: Repealed a lifetime ban for felons.

- TEXAS: Eliminated a two-year waiting period before felons can vote.

- VIRGINIA: Made it easier for nonviolent, first-time felons to get their voting rights restored.

- WYOMING: Repealed a ban for first-time nonviolent felons, but requires a five-year waiting period.

States that have placed additional restrictions on voting rights since 1996:

KANSAS: Expanded its prohibition on voting rights to felons on probation.

MASSACHUSETTS: Eliminated the right of felons to vote while in prison.

UTAH: Eliminated the right of felons to vote while in prison.

Source: "States Study Voting Rights for Felons," *The Washington Times*, September 24, 2003, citing The Sentencing Project.

The process itself is based on negotiation and consensus-building between the offender and circle members. The circles embrace local citizens, support systems, community agencies, the corrections depart-ment, and the offender in decision-making and case management related to rehabilitation and reentry. Circle members meet on a regular basis . . . [and] offer a powerful forum for citizens to

 # Close-up On Corrections

NATIONAL PUBLIC CORRECTIONAL POLICY ON RESTORATION OF VOTING RIGHTS FOR FELONY OFFENDERS

INTRODUCTION:

People convicted of crimes are expected to become responsible citizens after being discharged from correctional supervision. However, many individuals are excluded from exercising their civic rights because they are banned from voting in many jurisdictions. The laws that prohibit offenders from voting, even after they have been discharged from correctional supervision, frustrate the offenders in their attempts to fully reenter society successfully, reduce the voting constituency, and disproportionately exclude a large number of people from participating fully in society.

Nearly all states place some form of restriction on felon voting rights. Some states have developed processes to restore voting rights, but many felons are unaware of them, do not present the proper documentation, or the processes are often very cumbersome and have the effect of discouraging voting.

POLICY STATEMENT:

The American Correctional Association affirms that voting is a fundamental right in a democracy and it considers a ban on voting after a felon is discharged from correctional supervision to be contradictory to the goals of a democracy, the rehabilitation of felons and their successful reentry to the community.

Therefore, ACA advocates:

A. Restoring voting rights for felony offenders once they have been discharged from incarceration or parole;

B. Developing protocols for federal, state and local correctional agencies that inform inmates near their release about the means by which their voting rights will be restored and provide education and assistance to felony offenders in completing the restoration process to regain their civil rights; and

C. Developing state election agency procedures that permit eligible felony offenders to vote in elections after completing and filing all necessary paperwork.

This Public Correctional Policy was unanimously ratified by the American Correctional Association Delegate Assembly at the Winter Conference in Phoenix, on January 12, 2005.

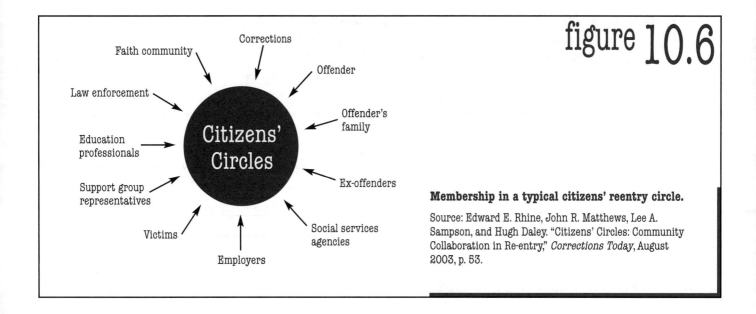

Membership in a typical citizens' reentry circle.

Source: Edward E. Rhine, John R. Matthews, Lee A. Sampson, and Hugh Daley. "Citizens' Circles: Community Collaboration in Re-entry," *Corrections Today*, August 2003, p. 53.

figure 10.6

communicate their expectations for successful reentry. They also help offenders recognize the harm their behavior has caused . . . and develop a viable plan of action to promote responsible citizenship. . . Most importantly, the circle helps offenders understand that acceptance back into the community requires the fulfillment of certain obligations and commitments.[57]

In this way, the community can exert its capacity to provide informal social control, build supportive relationships with ex-offenders, and promote prosocial lifestyles. At the same time, ex-offenders can obtain opportunities to alter their self-image, earn redemption, repair the harm they have caused, and rebuild community trust through civic engagement.[58]

Field Supervision

Once survival needs have been addressed, the officer's attention can turn more toward monitoring the parolee's *reintegration progress*. Much of this component of the job relates to enforcing the conditions established for the client. It is helpful if both the officer and the client can view parole conditions as tools to shape behavior rather than as *limits* being imposed. Of course, that is not often the case. When it is obvious that the parolee is becoming unresponsive and in danger of getting into further trouble, the officer may recommend revocation. If a new offense is committed, such action will be virtually certain.

As with probation, parole officers might be reluctant to take formal action on a first violation, especially when it involves a technical or minor matter. But unlike probation, parole officers are dealing with more serious and/or repeat offenders and, therefore, do not tend to exercise as much discretion. Public criticism has not gone unnoticed when a client's criminal actions capture media headlines. Unfortunately, that is when parole is most likely to make the news. In that regard, parole has taken its share of criticism from many quarters:

> Crime-control advocates have denounced parole supervision as largely nominal and ineffective; due-process advocates have criticized

Monitoring the offender's reentry into the community is an essential duty of parole officers. Courtesy of Kenneth R. McCreedy.

parole revocation as arbitrary and counterproductive; social welfare advocates have decried the lack of meaningful and useful rehabilitation services.[59]

While parole has not responded with equal vigor to all of these concerns, authorities have become increasingly responsive to the need to protect community safety. As a result, more parole agencies are turning to intensive supervision programs, tightening standards, and adopting a *sanction orientation* that stresses "swift and uncompromising response to noncompliance."[60] That does not mean that parole officers have now become police officers, or that they take pleasure in recommending revocation, or that they have abandoned rehabilitative goals. But "[i]f a criminal cannot or will not change within the environment of the community, then the sanction orientation requires that community corrections must, for the sake of community protection, immediately . . . act to change the environment in which the criminal functions."[61]

 Learning Goals

Do you know:

1. What due-process protections are required for parole revocation?
2. Why measures of recidivism are not always valid indicators of parole's success or failure?
3. What types of offenders are more likely to complete parole successfully?

Parole Revocation

Since parole is a form of conditional release, it can be *revoked* for failure to maintain the conditions on which it was awarded. But while the supervising officer can make such a recommendation, only the parole board is authorized to revoke parole. In other words, those with the authority to grant parole are also those with the power to repeal it.

In contrast to parole selection, however, inmates *are* entitled to certain *due-process protections* in parole-revocation proceedings. The rationale for this distinction is, as the Supreme Court has phrased it, that there is a "difference between losing what one has and not getting what one wants."[62] That is, those denied the opportunity to be *released* on parole are not subject to a change in status. They remain in the institution to which they are already confined. On the other hand, those denied the opportunity to *remain* on parole may suffer a substantial change in status.

Due-Process Protections

For many years, parolees had no legal means of challenging the discretion of parole board revocation actions. The concept then was that parole was extended by the "grace" of the executive branch of government and that it could be withdrawn at any time. The granting of parole is still legally considered a privilege. Nevertheless, the Supreme Court determined in the 1972 *Morrisey v. Brewer* case[63] that revocation of parole represents a "grievous loss" which falls within the due process provisions of the Fourteenth Amendment. This does not extend to parolees the full due-process protections of defendants facing adjudication in a criminal court. Parole revocation is not considered either a stage of criminal prosecution nor an adversarial proceeding. But the Supreme Court's ruling did establish that parole revocation must include two stages:

1. A *preliminary hearing*, at which point it is determined if there is probable cause to believe that a violation of parole conditions was committed, and if so,

2. A full *revocation hearing*, at which the parolee must be afforded:
   — Written notice of the alleged violation
   — Disclosure of the evidence related to the violation
   — An opportunity to be heard in person and to present witnesses and documentary evidence
   — An opportunity to confront and cross-examine adverse witnesses (unless good cause can be demonstrated for prohibiting confrontation)
   — Judgment before a neutral and detached hearing body (such as a parole board)
   — A written statement regarding the evidence relied on and the reasons for revoking parole

Note that one of the fundamental due-process protections—the right to counsel—is *not* included among these requirements. This issue was addressed the very next year (1973) in the *Gagnon v. Scarpelli* case. But that ruling did *not* extend due-process protections to the provision of counsel for indigent clients facing possible probation or parole revocation. Rather, it was held that the decision to appoint counsel could be made by the state on a case-by-case basis, using its discretion as to whether the parolee's version of an issue being disputed can only be fairly presented by an attorney. Nor have any court decisions thus far mandated the provision of a revocation-appeal process. It therefore may be surprising to find that, although not constitutionally required, about half of the states (48 percent) do offer an opportunity to appeal.[65] Overall, both legally and administratively, trends point toward affording greater due-process rights when liberty will be restricted.

Revocation Results

The next question is what *consequences* might occur if parole is revoked. Many would immediately answer that the offender would be *returned to prison* to complete the remainder of the original sentence. That is certainly a possible outcome, particularly if another crime has been committed. In fact, the readmission of parolees accounts for a substantial share of prison crowding.[66] In recognition of that fact, one state has substantially reduced the number of technical violations that can send a parole violator back to prison, such as not having a job or missing a meeting with a parole officer.[67] But reincarceration is not the only possibility. To the contrary, in many states, the parole board also may elect to *restore parole* status—either with no change or a modification of conditions.

Ultimately, parole, along with much of the entire correctional conglomerate is judged by measures of its effectiveness. Such measures and judgments often are based on *recidivism rates*.

Recidivism

To recidivate means to "revert" or "repeat." The question is, what is being reverted to or repeated? In that regard, one of the major challenges in determining recidivism rates is how its definition fluctuates. For example, recidivism could be defined as:

- *Rearrest.* Are criminals considered "recidivists" when they are rearrested? If so, does the type of crime make any difference? Would a juvenile car thief be considered a recidivist if taken back into custody for running away from home?

- *Reconviction.* What about those rearrested who are not *reconvicted*? Can they be classified as recidivists if they are innocent in the eyes of the court?

- *Reincarceration.* Even if reconvicted, does it matter whether they are *reincarcerated*? What if their only punishment is a fine?

- *Parole violation.* Are parole violators recidivists? What if they only committed a minor technical violation?

- *Parole revocation.* Are those whose parole is *revoked* recidivists? What if they are not reincarcerated?

For example, a recent national study found that within three years of their release:

- 67.5 percent of the prisoners were rearrested for a new offense (almost exclusively a felony or a serious misdemeanor)

- 46.9 percent were reconvicted for a new crime

- 25.4 percent were resentenced to prison for a new crime

- 51.8 percent were back in prison, serving time for a new prison sentence or for a technical violation of their release, such as failing a drug test, missing an appointment with their parole officer, or being arrested for a new crime [68]

In addition to questions concerning what type of conduct is considered recidivism, there is the further issue of how long a period of time should be taken into consideration. In other words, how long should offenders be monitored to establish valid recidivisim rates? One year? Ten years? For the rest of their lives?

Using different *failure measures* and *follow-up periods* obviously will produce different outcomes. For instance, one study found that when "arrest within one year" is used as the failure criterion, only about 15 percent "recidivated." But by the end of six years, 42 percent had failed. When more stringent criteria than arrest data are used, results appear to be more encouraging. For example, if "commitment to a correctional institution for sixty days or more" is used to measure failure, only about 5 percent "recidivated" within the first year (compared to the 15 percent who failed because of rearrest). By the end of six years, only 19 percent were unsuccessful if the measure is reincarceration for sixty days or more, whereas a total of 42 percent failed if arrest is the criterion (*see* Figure 10.7). These are among the complications that make it not only difficult to measure recidivism, but also virtually impossible to compare studies, which use varying definitions of it.

If successful discharge is any indicator, parole may not be as ineffective as sensationalized media accounts might lead us to believe. The likelihood of successfully completing parole, however, depends on a number of factors. Overall, 42 percent of parole discharges in 1999 successfully completed supervision. But as illustrated in Figure 10.8, *success rates* were higher for discretionary parolees (54 percent) than those who received mandatory parole (33 percent). Parole outcomes also vary by a number of other factors. In that regard, success rates are higher among parole discharges who have the following characteristics:

figure 10.7

Criteria	1 year	2 year	3 year	4 year	5 year	6 year	Total
Arrest	14.8%	9.4%	7.7%	3.6%	3.5%	3.0%	42.0%
Commitment of 60 days or more	4.8%	4.8%	3.6%	2.1%	2.6%	1.1%	19.0%

Measuring Recidivism.

NOTE: Recidivism rate is given as the percentage with unfavorable outcome each year by differing criteria and follow-up periods for adult parolees.

Source: Reprinted from *Journal of Criminal Justice*, Vol. 3, No. 1, Peter Hoffman and Barbara Stone-Meierhoefer, "Reporting Recidivism Rates: The Criterion and Follow-up Issues," p. 60, Copyright 1980, with permission from Elsevier.

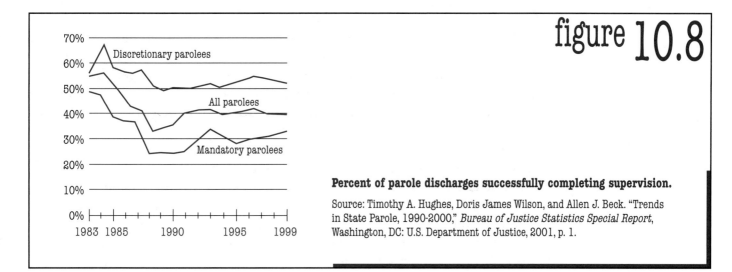

Percent of parole discharges successfully completing supervision.

Source: Timothy A. Hughes, Doris James Wilson, and Allen J. Beck. "Trends in State Parole, 1990-2000," *Bureau of Justice Statistics Special Report*, Washington, DC: U.S. Department of Justice, 2001, p. 1.

- First-prison releases (63 percent success rate) rather than re-releases (21 percent)

- Age fifty-five or older (54 percent) rather than under age twenty-five (36 percent)

- Female (48 percent) rather than male (39 percent).[69]

Research also indicates that the profile of the typical violator is that of a "single male who does not seek or obtain a job following release, has a known history of abusing alcohol and/or drugs, has not taken academic or vocational courses while incarcerated, is a minority, and more often, is a repeat offender."[70]

In summary, the effectiveness of parole depends on many factors—from what variables are being measured to what types of offenders are being assessed over what period of time. For such reasons, standardization of recidivism criteria is necessary if accurate evaluations of parole are to be obtained. But even with nationally standardized guidelines for determining recidivism, parole cannot be held completely accountable for either its successes or failures.

The willingness or unwillingness of correctional institutions to provide inmates with meaningful programs during confinement will have an impact on parole's effectiveness. For example, one study found that offenders who leave prison without any transition had a 21.4 percent recidivism rate after one year but those who participated in a faith-based transitional recovery program had only a 1.4 percent recidivism rate.[71]

Perhaps most influential, however, is the acceptance or rejection of the client by the community. In that regard, "there is always an instinct to shun the disgraced, especially when they appear to be blameworthy. . . . But we must help them all, for their sake and our own."[72] Beyond the offender's desire and capacity to change, the success of parole is therefore dependent on everything from correctional practices to community responsiveness.

Summary

Originating with Maconochie's "mark system" and Crofton's "ticket of leave," parole was initiated in this country at the Elmira Reformatory in 1876. By the

1950s, every state had implemented the indeterminate sentencing necessary to enable offenders to be released on parole. But some twenty-five years later, trends began to change. Several states moved back to determinate sentencing, abolishing or limiting the functions of parole. Nevertheless, whether based on mandatory or discretionary discharge, parole retains its role of supervising those released prior to sentence expiration, under conditions that permit reincarceration if violated. In that respect, parole is still grappling with contradictory expectations—for example, safeguarding the community while serving the client and extending support without overlooking surveillance.

Parole is considered a privilege rather than a right. Unlike probation, parole is a responsibility of the executive branch of government. In most states, it is administered by a board or commission appointed by the governor. Given their extensive power, recommendations have been made to enhance the qualifications of board members, with appointments made solely on the basis of merit.

The decision-making component of parole has experienced both the greatest criticism and the greatest change over recent years. Extensive information is taken into account in deciding whether to grant parole. But personal preferences, values, and backgrounds of individual board members can influence the process. The final selection decision may come down to a basic trust or mistrust with regard to both the inmate's intention and capacity to change. As a result, parole decisions have been vulnerable to criticism. Some contend that discretionary parole does not provide sufficient deterrence or punishment, has been used to coerce inmates into treatment, and creates disparities in the sentences of offenders convicted of similar crimes.

All of these issues have generated pressure to return to determinate sentencing, with release specified by sentence length rather than subject to parole board discretion. But in light of the severe prison crowding that followed changes in sentencing practices, good/gain time provisions have been established. Once these time credits are deducted from one's sentence, release is essentially mandatory. But because the full original sentence was not served, release is still conditional on the offender's good behavior under community supervision. Current trends clearly point toward a significant increase in such mandatory supervised releases. At the same time, discretionary releases are decreasing. Even where parole boards still have discretion over release decisions, objective parole-prediction devices (for example, the Salient Factor Score) often are used to reduce the subjectivity of decision making.

Despite these changes in the selection process, parole retains its postrelease supervisory functions. Much of the parole officer's initial work with a client involves arranging to meet basic survival needs, such as locating housing and employment. The hesitancy of employers to hire ex-offenders, combined with occupational licensing restrictions and education/experience limitations, often make it difficult for parolees to obtain suitable employment. Once these needs have been addressed, the officer's role shifts toward monitoring the reintegration process.

When the parolee is not adjusting successfully to the freedom of the community, it is also the officer's duty to recommend revocation if warranted by evidence that conditions are being violated. The sanction orientation, which such actions reflect, maintains that the welfare of all involved requires swift and sure enforcement of parole rules. In contrast to the parole-selection process, those facing possible revocation are entitled to certain due-process rights.

Although parole is judged largely on the basis of recidivism rates, such figures can be misleading. Differing failure measures over differing follow-up periods have produced vastly differing results. The effectiveness of parole is not only difficult to quantify but is also subject to variations in terms of programs offered during confinement and community attitudes toward ex-offenders. Beyond the inmate's desire and capacity to change, the success of parole is therefore dependent on everything from correctional practices to community responsiveness.

Endnotes

1. Excerpt from President George W. Bush's State of the Union Address, January 20, 2004, cited in Joey R. Weedon, "Presidential Support is A Start But Still Not Enough," *Corrections Today*, April, 2004, p. 24.

2. Eric Schlosser, "The Prison-Industrial Complex," *The Atlantic Monthly*, December 1998, p. 70.

3. "Prison without Walls: Summary Report on New York Parole; Citizens' Inquiry on Parole and Criminal Justice, Inc." in Calvert R. Dodge, ed., *A Nation without Prisons*, Lexington, Massachusetts: D.C. Heath, 1975, p. 83, quoting the New York State Special Commission on Attica.

4. Timothy A. Hughes, Doris James Wilson, and Allen J. Beck, "Trends in State Parole, 1990-2000," *Bureau of Justice Statistics Special Report*, Washington, D.C.: U.S. Department of Justice, 2001, p. 2. Four additional states have abolished discretionary parole for certain violent offenders.

5. Howard Abadinsky, *Probation and Parole: Theory and Practice*, Upper Saddle River, New Jersey: Prentice Hall, 1997, p. 209.

6. Edward Lindsey, "Historical Sketch of the Indeterminate Sentence and Parole System," *Journal of the American Institute of Criminal Law and Criminology*, Vol. 16, 1925, p. 9.

7. John Lewis Gillin, *Criminology and Penology*, New York: Appleton-Century Company, 1915, p. 510.

8. George G. Killinger, "Parole and Other Release Procedures," in Paul W. Tappan, ed., *Contemporary Corrections*, New York: McGraw-Hill, 1951, pp. 361-362.

9. Bureau of Justice Assistance, *National Assessment of Structured Sentencing*, Washington, D.C.: U.S. Department of Justice, 1996, pp. 26-27.

10. Peggy McGarry, *Handbook for New Parole Board Members*, Second Edition, Washington, D.C.: National Institute of Corrections, 1988, p. 18.

11. President's Commission on Law Enforcement and Administration of Justice, *Task Force Report: Corrections*, Washington, D.C.: U.S. Government Printing Office, 1967, p. 67.

12. Howard Abadinsky, *Probation and Parole: Theory and Practice*, 6th ed., Upper Saddle River, New Jersey : Prentice Hall, 1997, p. 233.

13. Edward E. Rhine, William R. Smith, and Ronald W. Jackson, *Paroling Authorities: Recent History and Current Practice*, Laurel, Maryland: American Correctional Association, 1991, p. 37.

14. *Ibid.*

15. Since the mid-1970s, an increasing volume of cases has significantly expanded the workload of parole boards. In response, the U.S. Parole Commission and many of the larger states have adopted the use of hearing examiners, who are not members of the parole board. Under this system, the board acts in executive session on the recommendations of the hearing examiner.

16. *Menechino v. Oswald*, 430 F.2d 402, 407 (2d Cir. 1970).

17. *Greenholtz v. Inmates*, 442, U.S. 1 (1979).

18. *See Standards for Adult Parole Authorities*, 2nd ed., Lanham, Maryland: American Correctional Association, 1980, and *Standards Supplement: 2004*, Lanham, Maryland: American Correctional Association.

19. Victor Hassine, *Life without Parole: Living in Prison Today*, Los Angeles: Roxbury Publishing, 1999, p. 11.

20. Jessica Mitford, "Kind and Usual Punishment in California," in Jerome H. Skolnick and Elliott Currie, eds., *Crisis in American Institutions*, 2nd ed., Boston: Little, Brown, 1973, p. 512.

21. "Citizens' Study Calls for End to Parole," *LEAA Newsletter*, Vol. 4, No. 2, July 1974, p. 23.

22. Herman Schwartz, "Let's Abolish Parole," *Reader's Digest*, August 1973, pp. 185-190.

23. *Ibid.*

24. Without benefit of a pardon, for example, some 4 million ex-offenders in a number of states throughout the United States are disenfranchised. *See* "States Study Voting Rights for Felons," *The Washington Times*, September 24, 2003, quoting Marc Mauer of the Sentencing Project.

25. Paula M. Ditton and Doris James Wilson, "Truth in Sentencing in State Prisons," *Bureau of Justice Statistics Special Report*, Washington, D.C.: U.S. Department of Justice, 1999, p. 1.

26. Lauren E. Glaze, "Probation and Parole in the United States, 2002," *Bureau of Justice Statistics Bulletin*, Washington, D.C.: U.S. Department of Justice, 2003, p. 1.

27. Orville B. Pung, "Introduction," *Correctional Issues: Probation and Parole*, Laurel, Maryland: American Correctional Association, 1990, p. vi.

28. *Correctional Populations in the United States, 1995*, Washington, D.C.: U.S. Department of Justice, 1997, p. 126.

29. Lauren E. Glaze, "Probation and Parole in the United States, 2002," *Bureau of Justice Statistics Bulletin*, Washington, D.C.: U.S. Department of Justice, 2003, p. 6.

30. William K. Smith, Edward E. Rhine, and Ronald W. Jackson, "Parole Practices: Survey Finds U.S. Agencies Undergoing Changes," in *Correctional Issues: Probation and Parole*, Laurel, Maryland: American Correctional Association, 1990, p. 37.

31. "Hitting the Boards," *Corrections Compendium*, Vol. 5, No. 5, November 1980, p. 1. (However, using a more rigorous definition, it has more recently been found that only twenty-three states report using "formal, structured guidelines" in making parole-release decisions.) *See* Rhine *et al.*, *Paroling Authorities*, p. 67.

32. Joan Petersilia and Susan Turner, "Guideline-Based Justice: Prediction and Racial Minorities," in Don Gottfredson and Michael Tonry, eds., *Prediction and Classification: Criminal Justice Decision Making*, Chicago: University of Chicago Press, 1987, p. 158. (Items listed were found in more than 75 percent of instruments identified).

33. Kermitt Humphries, "Transition from Prison to the Community," *Corrections Today*, Vol. 66, No. 5, August 2004, p.16.

34. *Ibid.*, p. 30.

35. Jeremy Travis, "But They All Come Back: Rethinking Prisoner Reentry," *Sentencing and Corrections: Issues for the 21st Century*, Washington, D.C.: U.S. Department of Justice, 2000, p. 1.

36. Kim Wozencraft, "The Scarlet Letter," *Prison Life*, June, 1994, p. 22.

37. For a list of prerelease services and programs offered by correctional agencies throughout the country, *see* "Survey Summary: Parole," *Corrections Compendium*, Vol. 26, No. 6, June 2001, pp. 15-16.

38. Samuel F. Saxton, "Reintegration: Corrections' Hope for the Future," *American Jails*, Vol. 5, No. 3, July/August 1991, p. 45.

39. Calculated from Camille Graham Camp, ed., *The 2002 Corrections Yearbook: Adult Corrections*, Middletown, Connecticut: Criminal Justice Institute, 2003, pp. 1, 146.

40. Jeremy Travis, "Prisoner Reentry: The Iron Law of Imprisonment," in Roslyn Muraskin, ed., *Key Correctional Issues*, Upper Saddle River, New Jersey: Prentice Hall, 2004, p. 65-66.

41. Joey R. Weedon, "The Foundation of Re-entry," *Corrections Today*, Vol. 66, No. 2, April 2004, p. 6.

42. Rhine *et al.*, *Paroling Authorities*, pp. 102-103.

43. Barry J. Nidorf, "Probation and Parole Officers: Police Officers or Social Workers?" in *Correctional Issues: Probation and Parole*, p. 73.

44. Jeffrey Spelman, "An Initial Comparison of Graduates and Terminated Clients in America's Largest Re-Entry Court," *Corrections Today*, Vol. 65, No. 5, August 2003, pp. 74-77, 83.

45. *See* Marc Mauer and Meda Chesney-Lind, eds., *Invisible Punishment: The Collateral Consequences of Mass Imprisonment*, Washington, D.C.: The Sentencing Project, 2002.

46. John J. Larivee, "Returning Inmates: Closing the Public Safety Gap," *Corrections Compendium*, June 2001, pp. 4, 10. *See also* Linda Connelly and John Larivee, "Community-based Treatment for Homeless Parolees," *Corrections Today*, Vol. 66, No. 6, October 2004, pp. 100-103.

47. Marilyn D. McShane and Wesley Krouse, *Community Corrections*, New York: Macmillan, 1993, p. 238.

48. Eric Schlosser, "The Prison-Industrial Complex," *The Atlantic Monthly*, December 1998, p. 69. The state referred to is California.

49. Nancy E. Gist, "Denial of Federal Benefits Program and Clearinghouse," *Bureau of Justice Assistance: Fact Sheet*, November 1997, p. 1.

50. Vanessa St. Gerard, "Study Cites Legislation Too Tough on Ex-Inmates," *Corrections Today*, Vol. 65, No. 5, August 2003, p. 18.

51. *Felony Disenfranchisement Laws in the U.S.*, white paper prepared by The Sentencing Project, Washington, D.C., November 2003, p. 1.

52. Howard Abadinsky, *Probation and Parole*, p. 361-62.

53. *Getting a Job—Another Chance to Make It*, Washington, D.C.: U.S. Department of Labor, 1993.

54. *Reuniting: Money, Family and You: A Guide for Women Leaving Prison*, Denver, Colorado: National Endowment for Financial Education, 2004.

55. President George W. Bush, *State of the Union Address*, January 20, 2004.

56. "When Ex-con's Come Home to the 'Hood, Will Police Be Ready?," *Law Enforcement News*, February 14, 2001, p. 6.

57. Ed Rhine, John R. Matthews, Lee A. Sampson, and Hugh Daley, "Citizens' Circles: Community Collaboration in Re-entry," *Corrections Today*, August 2003, pp. 53-54.

58. Gordon Bazemore and Jeanne Stinchcomb, "Promoting Successful Re-entry through Service and Restorative Justice: Theory and Practice for a Civic Engagement Model of Community Reintegration," *Federal Probation*, Vol. 68, No. 2, September 2004, pp. 14-24.

59. Cheryl L. Ringel, Ernest L. Cowles, and Thomas C. Castellano, "Changing Patterns and Trends in Parole Supervision," in *Critical Issues in Crime and Justice*, Newbury Park, California: Sage Publications, 1997, p. 299.

60. Nidorf, "Probation and Parole Officers," p. 70.

61. *Ibid.*, p. 74.

62. *Greenholtz v. Inmates of the Nebraska Penal and Correctional Complex*, 442 U.S. 1 (1979).

63. *Morrisey v. Brewer*, 408 U.S. 471 (1972).

64. *Gagnon v. Scarpelli*, 411 U.S. 778 (1973). As was discussed earlier, in this case, the Supreme Court extended many of the same due-process procedures to probationers.

65. Smith *et al.*, "Parole Practices Survey," p. 42.

66. Allen J. Beck, "Prisoners in 1999," *Bureau of Justice Statistics Bulletin*, Washington, D.C.: U.S. Department of Justice, 2000, p. 11. Those returning for parole or other conditional release violations represent a 54 percent increase since 1990.

67. Vanessa St. Gerard, "Connecticut Focuses on Breaking Recidivism Cycle," *Corrections Compendium*, Vol. 28, No. 10, October 2003, p. 26.

68. Patrick A. Langan and David J. Levin, "Recidivism of Prisoners Released in 1994," *Bureau of Justice Statistics: Special Report*, Washington, D.C.: U.S. Department of Justice, 2002, p. 1.

69. Timothy A. Hughes, Doris J. Wilson, and Allen J. Beck, "Trends in State Parole, 1990-2000," *Bureau of Justice Statistics: Special Report*, Washington, D.C.: U.S. Department of Justice, 2001, p. 11.

70. Dale J. Ardovini-Brooker, "Correctional Education: The History, the Research, and the Future," in Roslyn Muraskin, ed., *Key Correctional Issues*, Upper Saddle River, New Jersey: Prentice Hall, 2004, p. 216.

71. Meg Laughlin, "Ex-convicts Learn How to Embrace Freedom," *The Herald*, February 15, 2004, p. 3B, citing a 2003 study conducted by the Florida Department of Corrections, Florida State University, and the Corrections Privatization Commission.

72. George Ives, *A History of Penal Methods*, Montclair, New Jersey: Patterson Smith, 1970, pp. 382-383.

PART IV:

SPECIAL POPULATIONS, LEGAL ISSUES, AND THE FUTURE

> **❝** [There is a] nagging voice in all of us that says we should be doing more to effect change. Not necessarily change for every inmate. Not necessarily change that attempts to completely reverse damage done by lifelong neglect. But small change. Incremental change. Change that can be built upon—for this generation and for generations to come.[1] **❞**
>
> —Margaret C. Hambrick

The discussions of correctional services, facilities, and programs in earlier chapters primarily have described current practices and procedures for dealing with conventional adult offenders. However, this does not provide the entire picture of either where corrections is today or where it should be heading in the future.

Among the major correctional populations that have not yet been addressed are groups that present special problems or unique challenges—from

Photo, Above: Health care needs are increasing, but budgets are not. The next generation of correctional staff will be faced with addressing the growing population of offenders with special needs. Photo by Joseph Fuller, II.

female offenders to those who are older, AIDS-afflicted, alcoholic, drug-addicted, physically challenged, or mentally disordered. Some of these groups (such as women) traditionally have been in the minority within correctional caseloads and facilities. Others (such as the addicted or mentally ill) represent sizable proportions of correctional clientele. Regardless of their numbers, the focus of Chapter 11 is on the special difficulties they face within corrections, which in the past have not always been well-addressed.

Among those who clearly fit that category and whose involvement in the justice system persists at alarming rates are juvenile offenders. Many current prisoners and probationers had their first contact with the law as juveniles. Thus, much of the hope for reducing adult correctional populations rests with the juvenile justice system.

But as with adults, as we will see in Chapter 12, even the best intentions are not readily fulfilled. Nor do youthful offenders escape the impact of the justice model. Not only are more juveniles being transferred into the adult criminal justice system, but the juvenile system itself is beginning to look more like its adult counterpart. Regardless of the underlying reasons, the substantial impact of juveniles on the future justifies their significance as a topic of special consideration.

Whether adult or juvenile, special or typical, institutional or community-based, convicted offenders ultimately come under the supervision of correctional staff. As Chapter 13 emphasizes, staff are the key ingredient. Even the most elaborate security systems or sophisticated rehabilitative approaches cannot be implemented effectively without qualified, motivated personnel.

From the director of the department to the entry-level officer in the cell-block or the probation/ parole officer in the community, it is the dedication of its employees that enables corrections to function. It is these faceless names on organizational charts who actually operate the system twenty-four hours a day, seven days a week, often with little compensation and even less recognition. It is therefore fitting that we turn our attention to staff in Chapter 13—how they are recruited, selected, trained, compensated, and supervised. For it is these thousands of men and women who are the vital factor, not just in terms of how corrections performs today, but more important, what potential it has for tomorrow.

Aside from staffing, there is probably nothing more likely to shape tomorrow's correctional practices than liability and litigation—the subjects of Chapter 14. To the extent that the past is prolog to the future, a logical starting point for discussion of what lies ahead is legal issues, since past and present correctional operations often have been substantially altered by judicial intervention. The courts have been somewhat more restrained in recent years, and legislative actions have discouraged frivolous lawsuits. Nevertheless, the future will continue to be affected by legal actions and social change. A prime example is the continuing public debate and legal challenges surrounding the death penalty. Chapter 14, therefore, considers major legal cases that have influenced the correctional system and lingering controversies that await resolution.

Certainly, no consideration of the future would be complete without devoting attention to the fundamental mission of corrections and how it has changed over time. Again, by looking at past trends, public opinion, and legislative actions in Chapter 15, we can begin to glimpse what tomorrow may hold. Will more proactive crime prevention reduce the system's reliance on reactive responses? If not, will we continue to struggle with the dilemma of finding the right balance between punishment and treatment? Will corrections forever be plagued with excessive caseloads and crowded facilities? Will it remain a government function or increasingly become a component of the private sector? Will promising treatment techniques ignite new hope for its potential? And most critically of all, will corrections be able to attract and retain the quality of personnel necessary to meet the challenges of change? If so, there is hope for a future that is brighter than the past. But whatever the outcome, there is no one with a greater stake in assuring its success than each and every one of us.

Endnote

1.   Margaret C. Hambrick, "Intervention Programs: Setting Change in Motion," *Corrections Today*, Vol. 53, No. 5, August 1991, p. 6.

CHAPTER 11

SPECIAL POPULATIONS IN CORRECTIONS

> 66 Because of the nature of the business, we are responsible for people who are not at liberty to make choices and have fewer options than the larger society, and therefore we should be held to a higher standard.[1] 99

—Janie L. Jeffers

Chapter Overview

The ordeals of adjusting to imprisonment and the obstacles to readjusting when released can be particularly difficult for inmates with special needs—from childbearing females to those who are elderly, physically or mentally disabled, alcoholic, drug-addicted, or AIDS-infected. If the negative effects of incarceration described previously can be so profound for healthy males—who, within correctional institutions, represent the majority of inmates—the impact can be even more significant for those who differ in some respect from the rest of the inmate population. Women, for example, do not react to the conditions of confinement in the same manner as men. Their concerns, social relationships, and adaptation to imprisonment are somewhat different. Although still in the vast minority among the institutional population, their numbers are increasing. Consequently, there is a need for both greater consideration of their unique requirements and greater parity of services in comparison to those extended to men.

Other groups that also were incarcerated in vastly smaller numbers in the past include AIDS-infected and elderly inmates. But with longer mandatory sentences, as well as the spread of AIDS in society at large, more and more of these offenders are appearing in correctional facilities, and bringing with them special medical needs.

Still others, such as alcoholics and the mentally ill, always have been represented in sizable numbers among those under correctional supervision. The necessity to provide better care and treatment for them is no less acute today. Now, however, they are joined by growing numbers of drug-addicted offenders. Although corrections has made strides in providing treatment for such clients, demand still exceeds capacity.

To some extent, the lack of correctional services for inmates with special needs reflects similar shortcomings in the community at large. Once removed from society through incarceration, they become an even lower priority on the public agenda—essentially, a minority within a minority.

Some are subject to victimization by other inmates in a subculture where the weak are quickly overcome by the strong. Some simply languish in a system hard-pressed to meet basic necessities of conventional inmates, much less divert scarce resources to special needs. It is an unfortunate irony that in many cases, attention is largely directed toward them reactively in proportion to the growth of their numbers, rather than proactively to prevent their numbers from growing.

✳ Learning Goals

Do you know:

1. For what types of crimes women are more likely to be arrested?
2. What proportion of inmates in prison and jail are female?
3. What offense is largely accounting for increases in female arrest and incarceration rates?

Female Offenders

In comparison to males, females have always been (and continue to be) less frequently convicted of crimes and incarcerated in correctional facilities. Some maintain that this reflects a tendency of the justice system to treat women with more leniency. For example, when a woman is the sole support for her children, the decisions of criminal justice officials may be influenced by realizing the hardship that imprisonment would create for the family. On the other hand, some believe that females—especially those engaged in the types of violent crimes usually committed by men—are dealt with more severely by a system that views such acts as particularly unacceptable for women.

Beyond potentially chauvinistic attitudes, the fact remains that women generally do not pose as clear a danger to society. In comparison to men, they are far more likely to be arrested for property offenses than for violent crimes.[2]

Nor are women as likely to be arrested in the first place. Of all police apprehensions in 2002, the vast majority (77 percent) were male offenders.[3] However, from 1992 to 2002, arrest rates for women have *increased* by 14 percent, whereas those for men have *decreased* by 6 percent.[4] Whether there is

Most women in prison do not have education, training, or work opportunities equivalent to male inmates. Photo by Vince Lupo.

any causal connection between social trends and criminal tendencies, women are beginning to appear more often in police reports, and subsequently, in prison populations.

Female Prison Inmates

Given their more limited involvement in crime, it is not surprising to find that women represent only 6.9 percent (89,044) of all prisoners nationwide,[5] which means that there are fewer female prisons. A total of only ninety-eight federal and state prisons exclusively house women, which represents just 8

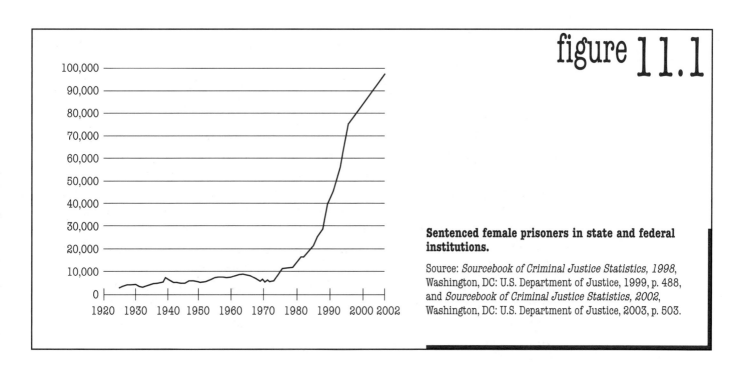

Sentenced female prisoners in state and federal institutions.

Source: *Sourcebook of Criminal Justice Statistics, 1998*, Washington, DC: U.S. Department of Justice, 1999, p. 488, and *Sourcebook of Criminal Justice Statistics, 2002*, Washington, DC: U.S. Department of Justice, 2003, p. 503.

figure **11.2**

		Females	Males
Race/Ethnicity	White (non-Hispanic)	33%	33%
	Black	48%	46%
	Hispanic	15%	18%
Age	Under 35	55%	57%
Marital Status	Unmarried (or separated)	83%	83.5%
Education	Less than high school	44%	39.4%
Employment	Employed full-time	40%	60%
Welfare	Receiving assistance	30%	8%

Comparison of male and female prison inmates.

Source: Laurence A. Greenfeld and Tracy L. Snell. "Women Offenders," *Bureau of Justice Statistics: Special Report*, Washington, DC: U.S. Department of Justice, 1999, p. 7-8, and *Correctional Populations in the U.S., 1997*, Washington, DC: U.S. Department of Justice, Bureau of Justice Statistics, 2000, p. 49.

percent of all prisons.[6] Since arrest data show that about 23 percent of offenders apprehended were female,[7] it initially may appear that the criminal justice system is, indeed, going easier on women. But beyond those under state and federal jurisdiction, local jails confine another 77,369 women, representing 11.6 percent of the jail population.[8]

In addition, the nonviolent property crimes that are more characteristic of female offenders are more likely to make them candidates for probation, community service, restitution, or other nonincarceration alternatives. Although the rate of imprisonment for males is considerably higher, the number of women serving time has increased significantly in recent years (*see* Figure 11.1), and the female-inmate population continues to grow faster.[9] In fact, there is some empirical evidence that more punitive action is taken against women offenders.[10] To get a better idea of what may be accounting for this discrepancy, we need to take a closer look at what types of female offenders are being incarcerated.

In many respects, the characteristics of female inmates resemble those of their male counterparts. Like male prisoners, females tend to represent minorities who are relatively young and unmarried (either single, separated, divorced, or widowed). As Figure 11.2 reflects, they are less likely to have been employed prior to their arrest, and much more likely to have been on welfare. They also are more likely to have suffered physical and sexual abuse as children.[11] (For a profile of the typical female offender, *see* the next "Close-up On Corrections").

These characteristics are also reflective of drug-related offenders—a relationship that is demonstrated in Figure 11.3, which shows that the proportion of women confined for violent and property crimes has been decreasing at the same time that the proportion of female drug and public-order offenders (often DUI's) has been increasing. Arrests among women for drug-related violations increased 50 percent in the past decade—more than for almost any other offense.[12] In that regard, it has been suggested that the "war on drugs has translated into a war on women."[13] Moreover, when drug-convicted women are released, they may be subjected to a lifetime ban on welfare benefits, a penalty that affects more than 135,000 children.[14]

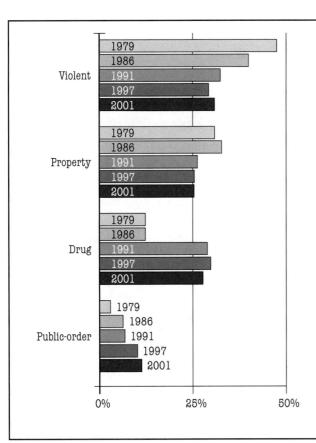

figure 11.3

Trends in most serious offenses of female prison inmates.

Source: Laurence A. Greenfeld and Tracy L. Snell. "Women Offenders," *Bureau of Justice Statistics: Special Report*, Washington, DC: U.S. Department of Justice, 1999, p. 7, and Paige M. Harrison and Allen J. Beck. "Prisoners in 2002," Bureau of Justice Statistics, Washington, DC: U.S. Department of Justice, revised August 27, 2003, p. 10.

Close-up On Corrections

NATIONAL PROFILE OF WOMEN OFFENDERS

- Disproportionately women of color

- In their early-to-mid-thirties

- Most likely to have been convicted of a drug-related offense

- From fragmented families that include other family members who also have been involved with the criminal justice system

- Survivors of physical and/or sexual abuse as children and adults

- Individuals with multiple physical and mental health problems

- Unmarried mothers of minor children

- Individuals with a high school or general equivalency diploma (GED) but limited vocational training and sporadic work histories

Source: Barbara Bloom, Barbara Owen, and Stephanie Covington, *Gender-Responsive Strategies: Research, Practice, and Guiding Principles for Women Offenders*, Washington, D.C.: U.S. Department of Justice, National Institute of Corrections, 2003, p. 8.

Learning Goals

Do you know:

1. How concerns about their children affect female inmates?
2. In contrast to men, how women adapt to the conditions of confinement?
3. The advantages and disadvantages of coed prisons?

Concerns for Children

In fact, if there is one major issue that separates female from male inmates, it is worrying about their children. That is not to imply that men are unconcerned, but despite social progress toward achieving sexual equality, child-rearing largely remains a female responsibility. The majority of women in correctional facilities (64 percent) lived with their minor children prior to being incarcerated, while only 44 percent of male inmates did so.[15] Together, they account for almost 1.5 million children under eighteen years of age.[16] Since we have already seen that almost 80 percent of female prison inmates are unmarried or separated, it is apparent that many of these mothers are single parents. Additionally, half of them were unemployed in the month before their arrest, and 18 percent had been homeless at some point in the past year.[17]

While male inmates traditionally have counted on the mother of their children to look after their children, women cannot necessarily depend on the father to do so. As shown in Figure 11.4, 90 percent of male-inmate fathers report that their children live with the child's mother. In contrast, only 28 percent of inmate mothers have their children living with the child's father. Whereas the male offender's family may remain relatively intact, it appears that a woman's family can be seriously disrupted when she is removed from the home.[18] Added to the "pains of imprisonment" for women, therefore, is the further frustration, conflict, and guilt of being separated from and unable to care for their children.

figure 11.4

	Percent of state inmate parents, 1997	
	Male	Female
Lived with children prior to admission	43.8%	64.3%
Current caregiver*		
Child's other parent	89.6%	28.0%
Child's grandparent	13.3%	52.9%
Other relative	4.9%	25.7%
Foster home/agency	1.8%	9.6%
Friends/other	4.9%	10.4%

*Some prisoners had children in different homes

Current caregiver for children of state prison inmates.

Source: Christopher J. Mumola. "Incarcerated Parents and Their Children," *Bureau of Justice Statistics: Special Report*, Washington, DC: U.S. Department of Justice, 2000, p. 1.

Maintaining Maternal Bonds

Only twelve states permit infants born in prison to remain with their mother—usually just until the mother is released from the hospital. However, special programs established in California, Nebraska, New York, and Washington State enable children to remain with their mothers for up to eighteen months.[19]

While they may not permit live-in arrangements, most states do attempt to nurture mother-child relationships during visiting. (Exceptions are South Carolina and Wyoming, where mother/child visitation is prohibited).[20] Almost all other states have a room or an area set aside to simulate a "home setting," and most provide special activities for visiting children. For example, in addition to arts, crafts, and games, some facilities sponsor storytelling sessions, summer camp, reading programs, birthday celebrations, and holiday events. Several even permit overnight visits on camping trips in conjunction with programs such as Girl Scouts Behind Bars (described in the next "Close-up On Corrections"). In other places, inmates and their children are allowed to cook meals in the kitchen, take naps together, and enjoy outside playgrounds or picnic areas.[21]

Yet, because there are fewer women's prisons, female offenders are likely to be incarcerated at a greater distance from their children than males. In that regard, the average female inmate is more than 160 miles farther from her family than a male inmate.[22] To maintain parental bonds in facilities too remote for regular visitation, Florida is experimenting with a unique program that allows inmate mothers to visit with their children technologically through videoconferencing.[23] But despite these brief reprieves, women often find the

 # Close-up On Corrections

GIRL SCOUTS BEHIND BARS

The girls enter the gym one by one. They scan the room, spot a smile and run for their mothers' arms. The older girls start talking about their friends, schoolwork, their hair. The younger ones are content to be swung in the air, cradled and kissed.

This is a prison. The women are criminals. Their daughters are Girl Scouts. And they're about to have a meeting. They will do arts and crafts, sing songs, and say the Girl Scout pledge. But at the end, after the holding and sharing and giggling, the girls will board a bus for home. The mothers will go back to their cells.

"It hurts," says [one inmate]. . . . "You want to go with them." . . .

"Is there ever going to be a time when I won't feel so guilty?" [asks another inmate]. . . . "I really didn't know that my life affects so many people."

Source: Nicole Carroll, "Girl Scouts Help Inmates, Daughters Bond," *USA Today*, October 19, 1993, p. 8D.

loneliness of prison filled with anxious thoughts about the collateral consequences for their "prison orphans."[24]

This anxiety about how their children are getting along without them is not without cause. Studies show that children of incarcerated parents have lower than average self-esteem, are more likely to end up behind bars themselves, and have a much greater than average chance of getting pregnant and having learning or emotional problems.[25] In recognition of such risks, some states extend outreach efforts, social services, and group support to the children of offenders.[26] Moreover, the American Correctional Association's policy on crime prevention calls for considering the children of offenders as integral partners in treatment programs.[27]

Some may think that the children of drug abusers, alcoholics, and property criminals might be better off growing up without their influence, but this is not what studies show. It is more likely that imprisonment of parents is more harmful to children, even when they come from dysfunctional families. Once the parent is removed from the household, the quality of alternative care arrangements for the children may be worse, which only enhances the trauma of separation.[28]

More than half of female prison inmates never have personal contact with their children,[29] and such separation can provoke considerable stress, along with a threat to the inmate's self-esteem.[30] In a society where women who violate the law are not only social outcasts but almost automatically assumed to be inadequate parents as well, the inmate mother's self-respect is inevitably bound to suffer. It is not the burden of children alone, however, that distinguishes female from male inmates.

Adaptation to Confinement

Women face many of the same debilitating effects of imprisonment as men. But there are some differences in the manner in which they adapt to the prison environment. These distinctions result from both dissimilarities between male and female correctional institutions and inherent differences between the sexes.

Women generally find institutional adjustment more difficult than men do, for a number of reasons. They tend to value privacy more, and consequently, experience greater difficulties adjusting to communal living, the intrusion of rules, and the degrading nature of body searches.[31] At the same time, they do not have as much support from spouses and significant others on the outside. They may fear being abandoned and worry about the inability to cope with the loneliness they might experience on release. Thus, female inmates are more likely to substitute *emotional intimacy* with other inmates for the loss of family and social ties. These bonds are often expressed in *quasi-family patterns*, with certain inmates taking on the roles of mother, father, and children within the institution.

Inmate Relationships

The value of family life—and the woman's role within it—are so firmly established in American culture that female inmates try to avoid the alienating and dispiriting effects of imprisonment by creating family structures. Unlike men, who tend to form gangs, women establish power and authority relationships through the model that they were familiar with on the outside—the family.[32] In other words, they imitate the "real world" that they came from:

> This is an affectionate world of families . . . [where] some women play the parts of men . . . cutting their hair short, wearing slacks, walking and talking in a masculine way. . . . Other women play the traditional role of mother or wife. . . . [T]hey wander into relationships . . . much like friendships we have on the outside—where, for instance, you guide and counsel a friend as though he or she were your own child. The difference in prison is that you most often call that friend your "child" or your "mother" openly. It is a family that allows a sense of belonging and eases the loneliness of feeling isolated. . . . It creates a common bond that eases the pressures of doing hard time.[33]

Thus, homosexuality in female institutions is characterized more by mutual affection and caring relationships than the violent submission to force of homosexual behavior in male prisons. In contrast to male prison subcultures, the resulting subculture among female inmates is more an attempt to establish a "substitute social world" in which they can play roles related to their lives on the outside.[34]

Prison Conduct

Women are, therefore, less likely than men to experience sexual attacks during incarceration, and also appear to be less victimized in general by other inmates.[35] In fact, "many women inmates report feeling safer in prison than they did on the streets."[36] This does not mean that women's institutions are peaceful, tranquil environments that are managed with ease. Quite the contrary, a number of correctional staff tend to prefer being assigned to male institutions—despite the fact that they may fear for their safety more when working in male prisons. "The reasons usually given for this preference are that the male inmates are perceived as more cooperative and respectful than female inmates, who usually are seen as more manipulating and emotional."[37]

There is also debate about why female inmates seem to accrue more disciplinary infractions than their male counterparts. There is some evidence that rules in women's prisons may be more strict and cover more petty details than those in male institutions, and that staff may be less tolerant of violations.[38] In that regard, minor misbehavior can assume more significance in a female institution. Petty violations might not generate as much concern in a male facility, where more serious infractions (such as physical assaults) demand more frequent attention. As a result of their emotional bonds, women also differ in their reaction to staff disciplinary actions:

> Male inmates generally do not care if another inmate is disciplined or "locked up"—it's "every man for himself." Female inmates, however, tend to support the inmate involved in the misconduct or fight [even if they themselves were uninvolved].[39]

Women, likewise, relate to staff in a somewhat different manner than men. In contrast to their male counterparts, women tend to "ask more questions, question authority, . . . and challenge decisions. Staff who are inexperienced with these differences become irritated" and therefore are more likely to write-up female inmates for disciplinary infractions.[40] On the basis of such realities, 70 percent of prison administrators in one study recommended using a different management style for women—one that involves greater capacity to respond to expressions of emotion, along with a willingness to communicate openly in a less authoritarian manner.[41]

Conditions of Confinement

Although conditions of imprisonment for women have come a long way from the abuses reflected in the historical origins described in the next "Close-up On Corrections," they still have a long way to go in many respects. In fact, the issue of staff sexual misconduct has received increasing attention in recent years. Sexual misconduct can take many forms, including inappropriate language, verbal degradation, intrusive searches, sexual assault, unwarranted visual supervision, denying privileges, and the use (or threat) of force.[42] Particularly among women who enter prison with an abusive past, such mistreatment can trigger a retraumatization that can result in depression, anxiety, and other disabilities that diminish the offender's ability to participate in rehabilitative programs during confinement, as well as reintegrate effectively when released.[43]

 # Close-up On Corrections

WHEN WOMEN HAD IT WORSE

Rachel Welch didn't know it at the time, but her unfortunate plight at the Auburn, New York, prison in 1826 did much to advance women's correctional reforms throughout the United States. Welch was a prisoner at the Auburn State Prison. She and many other women like her were herded into a large attic room in the prison, where they were confined . . . for twenty-four hours a day. Food was sent up once from the kitchen daily, and "slops" were removed once a day as well. One of the Auburn correctional officers raped Welch, impregnated her, and, after learning that she was five months pregnant, flogged her so severely that she died soon afterward. . . . A committee investigated her death, and . . . the condition of women at Auburn was publicly revealed.

Source: Dean J. Champion, *Corrections in the United States: A Contemporary Perspective*, Upper Saddle River, New Jersey: Prentice Hall, 1998, pp. 512-13; citing Nicole Hahn Rafter, "Prisons for Women: 1790-1980," in Michael Tonry and Norval Morris, eds., *Crime and Justice: An Annual Review of Research*, Chicago: University of Chicago Press, 1983, p. 135; and Susan M. Hunter, "Issues and Challenges Facing Women's Prisons in the 1980s," *The Prison Journal*, Vol. 64, 1984, pp. 129-135.

In terms of the facilities in which they are confined, there are advantages and disadvantages of being a female inmate. Virtually every state has maximum-, medium-, and minimum-security institutions for men. But because of their fewer numbers, there is *less custodial classification* among women's prisons. Those convicted of a wide variety of offenses representing a considerable range of seriousness therefore may be confined together. In fact, a number of states do not have enough female offenders to justify more than one women's prison. Thus, it is not unusual to find a women's prison housing all levels of custodial security. This also means that they are likely to be *more geographically remote* than male facilities, requiring families to travel considerable distances for visiting.

Because they serve a more limited population, female institutions are likewise substantially smaller in size. The average daily population of male prisons (700) is almost double that of female institutions.[44] That does not necessarily mean that female facilities are less crowded. But they are generally less likely to suffer from the impersonal conditions of male facilities. The physical environment of women's prisons is less oppressive, and there is more emphasis on rehabilitation. At the same time, however, because of their smaller size, female institutions are less likely to be able to economically justify a wide variety of programming.

In that regard, research has cited inadequacies ranging from medical services to education, vocational training, prison industries, and law libraries.[45] As a result, rehabilitative efforts in women's prisons may be limited to such stereotypical activities as sewing, typing, and the like—or at best, other nontraditional programs that do not need sizable enrollments to be cost effective. In contrast, the more diverse, large-scale industrial and vocational training offered in male facilities provides better preparation for obtaining jobs and achieving upward mobility on release. For example, research indicates that:

- Women are generally offered a narrow range of stereotypical job-training programs for conventionally "female" occupations, such as cosmetology and low-level clerical work.

- Male prisons typically provide a greater variety of educational and vocational programs and training for more skilled (and better compensated) occupations.

- Women in prison receive fewer institutional work assignments and lower rates of pay than male inmates, and men have greater access to work-release programs.[46]

- In comparison to the more than 35,000 professional/technical staff employed in male facilities, there are less than 3,000 in female facilities.

- In contrast to nearly 11,000 educational personnel in male facilities, fewer than 900 provide educational services for women.[47]

Under the equal protection clause of the U.S. Constitution, female offenders have filed suit to obtain programs similar to those provided for male inmates. But while one court ruling rejected that claim,[48] another found that state prisons receiving federal funds "are required by Title IX to make reasonable efforts to offer the same educational opportunities to women as men."[49]

In recent years, some improvements undoubtedly have been made to upgrade services provided in female prisons, particularly in such areas as health care, drug treatment, and accommodating children (*see* the upcoming "Close-up On Corrections"). Although needs still tend to outdistance available resources, the American Correctional Association has developed policy guidelines calling for equity in terms of correctional services for male and female offenders.[50] To what extent they will be implemented remains to be seen.

Co-correctional (Coed) Prisons

Although it would be quite costly to establish services in women's prisons that are equivalent to those received by men, one way to better assure parity between male and female offenders would be to incarcerate them together in *co-correctional (coed) prisons.* The first experiments with coed prisons for adults date back to 1973-1974, when the Massachusetts Correctional Institution at Framingham and the Federal Correctional Institution at Fort Worth, Texas, became co-correctional.

 # Close-up On Corrections

THE NEW WOMEN'S PRISONS

Coffee Creek, Oregon, is a special facility for mother/child bonding. Situated outside the secure perimeter in secluded woods, it functions as a day school with a bona fide Head Start program, where inmates work with at-risk youths. Female offenders learn valuable parenting skills while children reap the rewards of motherly attention.

Another fresh transitional-housing application is found at the new Denver Women's Correctional Facility, which includes "reintegration" apartments. These residential-style units, each with its own outdoor patio, are arranged around a central common room and children's play area. As they near release, inmate mothers are placed in these apartments with their children for stays ranging from a day to a week, allowing counselors to monitor their progress.

At the Kentucky Correctional Institute for Women, spatial provisions include places for women to retreat (designed as a result of awareness of the ways in which women deal with conflict, primarily by withdrawal). Medical and psychiatric services take precedence because a large number of women have experienced sexual or physical abuse and arrive at the prison with sexually transmitted diseases, as well as psychological problems and issues of mistrust. The treatment they receive in prison may be the only serious attempt to intervene in generational cycles of criminality.

Source: Compiled from "Inmates/Women/Mothers: The New Women's Prisons," *Correctional News*, March/April 2002, p. 14-15.

To attain greater cost effectiveness (as well as in some cases provide a more natural environment for both male and female inmates), some ninety-three state and federal prisons operate on a coed basis, housing more than 77,000 inmates of both sexes.[51] Obviously, these facilities do not remotely resemble the communal quarters in which women were housed during the early history of corrections. Yet, it is somewhat ironic that after successfully achieving separate institutions, we have come full circle one hundred years later. While such changes undoubtedly reflect shifting social attitudes, they are also to some extent an indicator of the limited potential for achieving full parity between male and female institutions.

Men and women in U.S. coed prisons are prohibited from sharing living quarters or engaging in sexual contact. In some institutions, they may interact socially during meals, recreational periods, or while attending various institutional programs. However, rules governing unacceptable conduct are quite specific and carefully supervised. Although the public may have visions of these facilities as havens of sexual freedom where rampant promiscuity results in many illegitimate births, nothing could be further from reality. Moreover, it may be preferable to deal with the few instances of improper heterosexual contact in coed institutions than the widespread homosexuality characteristic of single-sex prisons.

For both male and female inmates, serving time in coed facilities has both benefits and drawbacks. Men are not pressured to portray the hardened, macho image required to avoid appearing weak in a male institution. They tend to behave better in the presence of women and engage in fewer fights, since proving one's toughness does not become the "badge of honor" that it is in male institutions. For women, such facilities provide a greater range of recreational, educational, training, and work programs than traditionally would be available in female prisons. However, researchers have found that women do not tend to take advantages of these expanded opportunities, and because there are more men than women, programming is still largely targeted toward men.[52] In fact, research evidence concludes that co-correctional facilities overall are not as beneficial for female offenders:

> Serving time with men evidently reinforces traditional sex stereotypes, since women tend to concentrate on relationships and not self-improvement, and recreate dysfunctional relationships similar to those that got them into trouble on the outside.[53]

If, as these studies suggests, traditional co-correctional facilities are not actually beneficial to women (and perhaps even somewhat detrimental), a more effective approach may be implementation of the gender-responsive guidelines developed by the National Institute of Corrections.[54] In any event, whatever strategies are pursued to reduce recidivism among female offenders, the results are destined to have a wide collateral impact—potentially reducing the intergenerational cycle of crime and improving outcomes for their children as well.[55]

✷ Learning Goals

Do you know:

1. Why the rate of AIDS is higher within correctional institutions than among the public at large?
2. What AIDS and viral hepatitis have in common among correctional populations?
3. What responses correctional administrators have implemented to reduce the spread of HIV/AIDS?
4. What the arguments are for and against the distribution of condoms in correctional facilities?
5. What position the courts have taken on the mandatory testing of inmates for HIV/AIDS and the separate housing of those who test positive?

AIDS (Acquired Immune Deficiency Syndrome) and other Infectious Diseases

In recent years, a disease that knows no gender, racial, or class boundaries has created a devastating impact on society. No particular social or demographic groups are inherently at risk of contracting the disease; it is the high-risk *behaviors* in which they engage that place them in danger,[56] nor is anyone immune. Many of those being infected today, such as women and children, are the inadvertent victims of those involved in such high-risk behaviors as sharing drug needles or engaging in unsafe sexual practices.

Infectious Diseases in Corrections

Although AIDS has received the most notoriety, it is likely that even more inmates are infected with various types of viral hepatitis—the results of which can range from minor discomfort (hepatitis A) to acute liver failure (hepatitis C). Of those behind bars, it has been estimated that 22 to 39 percent are infected with the hepatitis A virus with 16 percent to 41 percent showing signs of hepatitis C infection.[57]

AIDS in Corrections

Like hepatitis, without mandatory testing, it is impossible to know exactly how many inmates are infected with HIV, since the virus can linger undetected for years before developing into AIDS. But we do know that the rate of confirmed AIDS cases is three times higher among prison inmates than the general population[58] (*see* Figure 11.5).

Some of this difference may be a result of either reduced rates of increase among the population at large and/or improved reporting and record-keeping among correctional systems. Nevertheless, prisons and jails do confine a population with a *higher concentration* of individuals who have histories of high-risk behavior, particularly IV drug use. In that regard, the National Commission on

figure 11.5

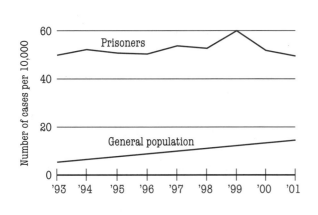

Rate of confirmed AIDS cases among the general population compared to state and federal prisoners.

Source: Laura M. Marushak. "HIV in Prisons, 2001," *Bureau of Justice Statistics: Bulletin*, Washington, DC: U.S. Department of Justice, 2004, p. 5.

AIDS points out that, "By choosing mass imprisonment as the federal and state governments' response to the use of drugs, we have created a de facto policy of incarcerating more and more individuals with HIV infection."[59]

Since there is not yet a vaccine to prevent either AIDS or hepatitis C,[60] the vital concern of correctional administrators is to reduce expansion of these diseases. A number of approaches have been implemented in response to this concern, primarily:

- *Educating* both inmates and staff on how the diseases are spread

- *Issuing condoms* to protect inmates engaged in homosexual activities

- *Testing* (either voluntary or mandatory) to identify those who are infected

- *Separately housing* those in various stages of AIDS

Education and Training

Practically everyone agrees that educational efforts are needed. As one national study found, "most correctional administrators feel strongly that AIDS education and training are not options but absolute requirements," and virtually all prisons and jails reported offering or developing AIDS training or educational materials.[61] Such programs are essential to provide facts concerning how the disease is transmitted—thereby hopefully changing high-risk behaviors. In addition, they can help to eliminate the myths surrounding casual transmission that can lead to overreaction and unwarranted discrimination.

Ideally, programs should be offered for both inmates and staff in a *proactive* manner—well before widespread concern promotes panic. Among inmates, for example, at least one study has found that there is considerable confusion about the manner in which AIDS can be transmitted. Moreover, lower levels of knowledge are also associated with higher perceptions of the risk of contracting AIDS while incarcerated.[62] In other words, the *less inmates* know about objective facts concerning AIDS transmission, the *more fearful* they are of acquiring the virus in prison. Nor is there any reason to believe that similar lack of knowledge on the part of institutional personnel is any less influential.

AIDS training for staff can diminish such unfounded fears while encouraging basic precautionary measures.

Condom Distribution

While support for AIDS education is widespread, there is one particular policy of some facilities that is another matter entirely: the distribution of condoms. On the one hand, this practice has been widely criticized as giving official sanction to unauthorized sexual activities. But on the other hand, there are advocates who maintain that since it is virtually impossible to prevent inmates from engaging in homosexual behavior, it is better to provide them with protection than to risk spreading the disease throughout the institution. As one doctor practicing in corrections has argued: "Facilities that have decided to issue condoms to inmates have not decided to permit sex. Instead, the programs are established as an acknowledgment that sex occurs. In the absence of such programs, I challenge prison administrators to stop sex altogether."[63]

HIV Testing

Like the condom issue, testing inmates for HIV has both supporters and critics. Recent advances in HIV treatment that delay the onset of AIDS underscore the need for early detection and intervention. In light of this medical incentive, more people in the general population are undergoing diagnostic tests. But, of course, they are doing so of their own free will. Within corrections, few would argue against providing tests and follow-up medical services on a *voluntary* basis for those requesting such help—as evidenced by data showing that 75 percent of prisons and 90 percent of jails make testing available on request.[64] But it is the *mandatory* testing of everyone that is in dispute.

This involuntary means of identifying HIV-positive inmates increasingly has come under fire from both sides of the issue. On the one hand, some inmates have demanded mandatory mass testing for everyone's protection. In opposition, others have challenged such practices as an invasion of their right to privacy. Thus far, the courts have neither uniformly upheld nor denied either side.

In one case, for example, an appellate court refused to order correctional officials to administer AIDS tests to all inmates and staff on the basis that "the risk alleged by the inmates was based on unsubstantiated fears and ignorance." [65] From the opposite perspective, a prisoner in another jurisdiction challenged the constitutionality of the state's policy of testing all inmates for the AIDS virus. In this case, the court ruled that the inmate's invasion of privacy was "far outweighed" by the prison's interest in treating those infected and taking steps to prevent further transmission of the disease.[66] In yet another case, the outcome was more ambiguous, with the court finding that the prison administrators had no evidence on which to base an AIDS-testing procedure.[67]

Overall, however, the courts have been relatively consistent in upholding the constitutionality of state laws permitting mandatory testing. But at the same time, they have supported the right of correctional administrators to refuse to implement mandatory testing. Thus, current judicial reasoning appears to be that testing is not constitutionally *required* under the Eighth Amendment (which forbids cruel and unusual punishment); but neither is it *prohibited* under the Fourth Amendment (which protects privacy).[68] As a compromise between the extremes of mandatory and voluntary screening, some states target AIDS testing toward *high-risk* groups (such as IV drug users, homosexual men, and prostitutes).

Some jurisdictions have discontinued mass screening for reasons ranging from funding shortages to the realization that it was "creating more problems than it was intended to solve." [69] In that regard, the American Correctional Health Services Association has gone on record as opposing mandatory testing, based on the concern that it is "costly and serves no useful public health function."[70] With less mass testing, there are undoubtedly inmates in prison who have undetected AIDS. But that does not mean that they necessarily *contracted* the disease in prison. To the contrary—although correctional facilities may be perceived as "fertile breeding grounds" for the spread of HIV, a number of studies suggest that this is not the case. Research to date indicates that actually, very few inmates have become HIV positive as a result of activities that took place within a correctional facility.[71]

Separate Housing

Regardless of whether inmates are screened on arrival or submit to testing voluntarily, once AIDS is detected, the issue becomes what actions are appropriate to take. As the National Commission on AIDS has observed, "there is certainly no point in screening without a clear notion of what is to be done with information uncovered in the screening process." [72] From a humanitarian point of view, it is obviously essential to provide appropriate medical care. Meeting this obligation can create serious financial difficulties as the number of cases escalates, since "it costs a minimum of $76,500 to house and treat a prisoner with end-phase HIV." [73] Moreover, because of the overwhelming emotional impact of AIDS, most would agree that counseling and other supportive services are equally critical. But it is the question of *where to locate* inmates who have tested positive that has become most controversial.

As with mandatory/voluntary testing, correctional administrators are again caught between two contradictory arguments. On the one hand, inmates free of AIDS have raised Eighth Amendment challenges, maintaining that it is "cruel and unusual punishment" to be unprotected from others with this communicable disease. But at least one court has held that prisoners must specifically show how the conditions of confinement they are challenging put them at risk of contracting AIDS.[74] In a similar case, inmates demanded mandatory screening and housing segregation of those who test positive. The judge rejected their arguments, ruling that the state had taken reasonable precautions to minimize the risk that inmates would contract the virus.[75]

At the same time, HIV-positive inmates have questioned whether it is a violation of *their* rights to be housed separately from the general population. In this respect, one court has declared that inmates shall not be segregated solely because they are HIV-positive, although they may be isolated on a case-by-case basis according to security or medical needs.[76] But in another case, the court supported the argument of correctional administrators that "the segregation of infected prisoners was mandated to protect both the AIDS victims and other prisoners from tensions and harm that could result from fears of other inmates."[77] While most judicial rulings have upheld the constitutionality of separate housing, as with testing, "the courts have concluded that the Constitution neither requires nor prohibits segregation."[78]

Legal Implications

As these cases reflect, such disputes have raised a number of legal issues. An immediate legal implication of a separate housing policy is that it readily identifies those with HIV, thereby compromising the confidentiality of AIDS testing. State laws and court rulings vary in terms of how strictly they protect the confidentiality and anonymity of those tested for HIV.[79] States with such protections generally limit notification to the inmate and attending physician. Only a few jurisdictions have official policies of notifying correctional officers.

Staff, however, are not always satisfied with these confidentiality provisions. As one officer has argued, "the nation now has right-to-know laws dealing with dangerous and toxic substances in the workplace; . . . an inmate with AIDS is a dangerous person, and his or her blood is definitely a toxic substance."[80] In response, it has been pointed out that "disclosures may, in fact, lull correctional officers into a false sense of security, leading them to believe that all infected prisoners have been identified."[81]

In addition to revealing the confidentiality of their health status, separately housing those who are HIV-positive can have further repercussions. The National Commission on AIDS notes that not only is there "no legitimate public health basis for segregating prisoners with HIV disease," but also, those who are so isolated:

- Often lose access to religious services, work programs, visitation rights, libraries, educational and recreational programs, and drug/alcohol treatment

- Serve in virtually solitary confinement within small prisons, and in larger institutions, are often grouped together indiscriminately, regardless of their security classification[82]

It therefore is not surprising that such practices have represented a sizable proportion of the lawsuits related to AIDS. Undoubtedly, these cases have generated some of the impetus toward the current trend away from segregation—toward the "mainstreaming" of HIV-positive inmates with the rest of the general population. But beyond the threat of legal action, this change in housing policy has resulted from a combination of additional factors, including increased costs, less fear, more compassionate attitudes, and the rising numbers of inmates with HIV infection or AIDS—which is making segregation both impractical and not feasible."[83]

A compromise between the extremes of complete integration and total segregation has been recommended that would take into account both high-risk behavior and HIV/AIDS infection. This approach would classify the person according to a continuum reflecting institutional behavior and the health status of those who are HIV-positive. Housing and supervision then would be designed to both reduce opportunities for high-risk activities and provide for the medical needs of those who are becoming progressively ill.[84]

In summary, there are no clear-cut guidelines on how corrections should respond to the threat of AIDS. As a result, some administrators have experimented with preventive measures, ranging from providing condoms to promoting education. Identification approaches likewise have varied from requiring mandatory mass testing, to selectively screening high-risk groups, to simply making tests available on a voluntary basis. In reaction to the results, some systems have implemented housing segregation policies. Others have explored compromises, such as increasing segregation on the basis of how far the disease has progressed. Many either have continued or returned to mainstreaming those who are HIV-positive with the rest of the population. The only thing that is sure about AIDS is that until there is a cure, the issues surrounding this disease undoubtedly will continue to create further conflict, confusion, and court cases.

 # Learning Goals

Do you know:

1. What percentage of prison inmates were involved with drugs prior to their offense?

2. For those convicted of drug offenses, what sanction is imposed most often by the justice system?

3. To what extent those in prison or jail are participating in drug-treatment programs?

Other Special Offender Populations

Beyond women and those who are afflicted with HIV/AIDS, any number of inmates with special needs are in the correctional conglomerate. Some (such as those who are alcohol/drug-addicted or mentally disordered) represent a sizable portion of the correctional population. Others merit attention either because they often have been overlooked as a result of their limited numbers (for example, the physically impaired), or their growing numbers are causing increasing concern (for example, the elderly). While these groups certainly do not exhaust all categories of special offenders, they do illustrate the scope of unique problems that correctional administrators face.

Drug Abusers

It is well known that intravenous (IV) drug use with unsanitary needles is a major transmitter of AIDS and hepatitis. Earlier in this chapter, we found that drug involvement is an increasing problem among female offenders. But drug abuse is hardly limited to these two groups. Almost half of those in prison admit to having committed their offense under the influence of drugs or to get money for drugs.[85]

Perhaps because poverty and discrimination can be so degrading to self-esteem, drug abuse traditionally has been associated with low-income and minority groups. The use of drugs knows no social or racial boundaries today, but

Because so many inmates enter the correctional system as a result of problems with alcohol, drugs, or both, substance-abuse treatment is an essential ingredient in reducing recidivism. Courtesy of the Roanoke County (Virginia) Sheriff's Office.

minorities are still disproportionately affected. Growth in the minority population of juvenile detention facilities, for example, has been linked to the "extremely large increase in the number of these youth referred to juvenile court for drug offenses," along with "a substantial change in how juvenile courts respond to [such] cases."[86] As with adults, the juvenile justice system is becoming more inclined to incarcerate those involved in drug offenses. And if they do not find effective treatment for their problem in juvenile facilities, it can be anticipated that they later will appear in the adult correctional system.

Institutional Profiles

In fact, there is already evidence that such trends are occurring among the nation's jails. Because they are more likely than state prisons to house young, first-time, or minor drug offenders, it is not surprising to find significant percentages of drug users among the jail population. Nearly three-fourths (70 percent) of jail inmates either committed a drug-related offense or used drugs regularly.[87] Similarly, 70 percent to 80 percent of federal and state prison inmates reported prior drug use. [88]

Like its juvenile counterpart, it is apparent that the adult criminal justice system has become tougher on drug crimes. The majority of adults convicted of drug offenses are being *sentenced to confinement* (67 percent)—either in jail (29 percent) or prison (38 percent).[89] Moreover, the average sentence for drug offenses (thirty months) is greater than for any felony except violent offenses.[90] Thus, drug violators have contributed significantly to the growth of inmates in both jails and prisons over the past decade, (*see* Figure 11.6), despite the fact that treatment is far less expensive than imprisonment (*see* Figure 11.7).

Treatment Programs

The U.S. Office of National Drug Control Policy reports that up to 85 percent of state prisoners need drug treatment, but only 13 percent will receive it

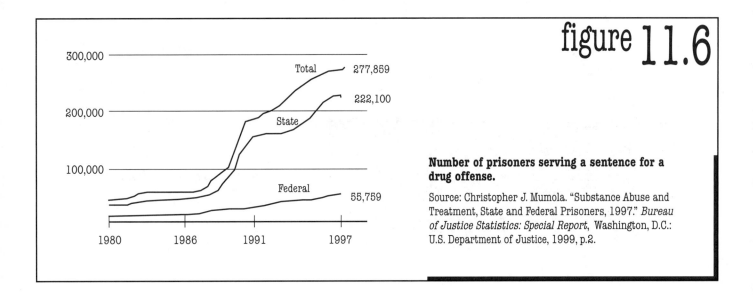

figure 11.6

Number of prisoners serving a sentence for a drug offense.

Source: Christopher J. Mumola. "Substance Abuse and Treatment, State and Federal Prisoners, 1997." *Bureau of Justice Statistics: Special Report*, Washington, D.C.: U.S. Department of Justice, 1999, p.2.

while incarcerated.[91] Likewise, a national survey discovered 84,000 offenders on program waiting lists for drug treatment.[92] As shown in Figure 11.8, even those needing treatment for severe drug abuse have not been likely to obtain it throughout the 1990s. Among those programs that are being offered in correctional institutions, the focus ranges widely—from group counseling, intensive therapy, and self-help groups to the use of acupuncture and the therapeutic community technique featured in the next "Close-up On Corrections."

To address the nationwide shortage of treatment programs, the U.S. Department of Justice had allocated $64 million to support Residential Substance Abuse Treatment (RSAT) Programs in local and state correctional facilities.[93] However, by 2004, funding for RSAT was eliminated from the federal budget.[94] RSAT-funded initiatives had been designed to work closely with community-based substance-abuse programs to continue treatment after

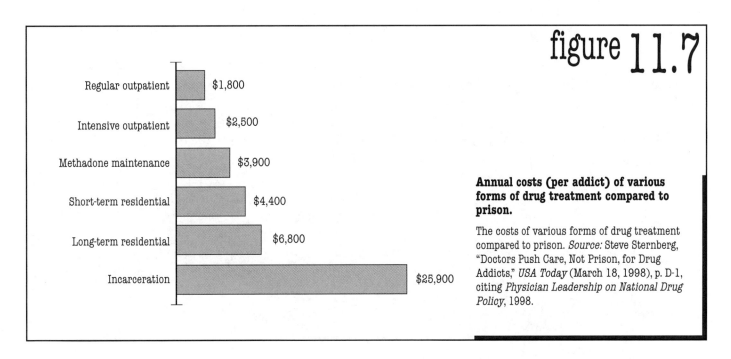

figure 11.7

Annual costs (per addict) of various forms of drug treatment compared to prison.

The costs of various forms of drug treatment compared to prison. *Source:* Steve Sternberg, "Doctors Push Care, Not Prison, for Drug Addicts," *USA Today* (March 18, 1998), p. D-1, citing *Physician Leadership on National Drug Policy*, 1998.

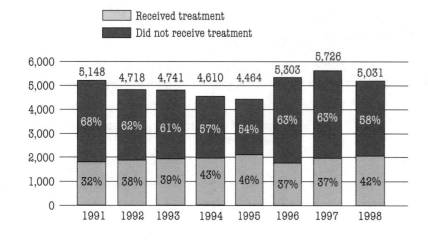

figure 11.8

Received treatment
Did not receive treatment

							5,726	

6,000
5,148   4,718   4,741   4,610   4,464   5,303   5,031
5,000
68%   62%   61%   57%   54%   63%   63%   58%
4,000
3,000
2,000
32%   38%   39%   43%   46%   37%   37%   42%
1,000
0
1991   1992   1993   1994   1995   1996   1997   1998

Estimated number of persons needing treatment for severe drug abuse and the percentage who received treatment.

Source: *National Drug Control Strategy: 2000 Annual Report*, Washington, DC: Office of National Drug Control Policy, 2000, Table 39.

 ## Close-up On Corrections

SUCCESS OF THERAPEUTIC COMMUNITIES WITH DRUG-ABUSING OFFENDERS

In recent years, drug abuse treatment in prison has been influenced by the development of therapeutic communities (TCs). Grounded in the self-help tradition and the fellowship concept of Alcoholics Anonymous, TCs typically house clients in residential settings that offer opportunities for intensive intervention and support that may not be available on an outpatient basis.

What distinguishes TCs is the "community" or group as the primary facilitator of growth and change. As applied to corrections, clients live isolated from the rest of the prison population and receive treatment to change negative patterns of behavior, thinking, and feeling that predispose them to drug use.

Among the other features that TCs have in common are the use of ex-offenders and ex-addicts as staff, use of confrontation and support groups, a set of rules and sanctions to govern behavior, and promotion of prosocial attitudes. The drug user's transformation in conduct attitudes, values, and emotions is monitored and mutually reinforced. It may be this multiple focus that explains why TCs are more likely to be successful in the long run.

In addition to keeping people drug-free and out of prison, these programs are cost effective—the savings in crime-related and drug-use-associated costs pay for the treatment in about two to three years. It is an inescapable conclusion that treatment lowers crime and health costs as well as related social and criminal justice costs.

Source: Compiled from Douglas S. Lipton, "Prison-based Therapeutic Communities: Their Success with Drug-abusing Offenders," *National Institute of Justice Journal*, February 1996, pp. 12-17.

release. Along with the multiple ingredients listed in the next "Close-up On Corrections," such postrelease follow-up is among the most significant factors that have been associated with successful programs, which include:

- *Target population*: Selecting offenders identified as "addicts" rather than entrepreneurial "criminals" involved in the drug trade is a more effective approach.

- *Field-tested curriculum*: Using a treatment curriculum that has been empirically tested is a primary key to success.[95]

- *Program length*: The longer the program, the greater the success rate. For example, optimum time for a therapeutic community approach is apparently nine-to-twelve months. Anything shorter tends to have less effect on recidivism.

- *Age of participants*: Younger offenders are less likely to be successful on release.

- *Follow-up*: Programs that maintain continuing services in the community have better outcomes than those that do not.[96]

 # Close-up On Corrections

WHAT WORKS IN CORRECTIONAL DRUG TREATMENT?

The National Task Force on Correctional Substance Abuse Strategies has identified the following elements of effective approaches to drug treatment in corrections:

- Individualized treatment plans that are multidisciplinary

- Matching offenders with supervision, control, and treatment programs that are appropriate to their assessed needs

- A full range of services, from drug education to intensive residential treatment

- Prerelease treatment programming

- Integrated treatment/ custody staffing

- Use of incentives and sanctions to increase prisoners' motivation

- Self-help groups as an adjunct to treatment and for aftercare

- Targeted programs for special-needs populations

- Education and treatment for relapse prevention

Source: National Task Force on Correctional Substance Abuse Strategies, *Intervening with Substance Abusing Offenders: A Framework for Action*, Washington, D.C.: U.S. Department of Justice, National Institute of Corrections, 1991, p. 27.

In fact, a major weakness of many drug-rehabilitation efforts in corrections is that they operate without the benefit of postrelease treatment and continuing support.[97] Research has found that drug treatment alone, without an accompanying comprehensive range of rehabilitation services "can rarely effect stable, long-term behavioral change."[98] For example, it does little good to send an abuser home drug-free and presumably "cured" without any prospect of employment. Incarceration can compel abstinence from drugs and address withdrawal symptoms. But it is unlikely that long-term effectiveness will be achieved if the underlying social and psychological causes of physically addictive behavior are not confronted—or if interventions end with the offender's institutional sentence.

 # Learning Goals

Do you know:

1. Why alcohol is in many ways a greater threat than the use of illegal drugs?
2. How the use of alcohol compares to the use of illegal drugs among inmates?

Alcohol Abuse

A long-standing problem that has plagued society well before the current "war" on *illegal* drugs was waged concerns the abuse of a *legal* drug—alcohol. Because it is so widely, inexpensively, and legally available (at least for adults), alcohol in some ways actually may be a greater threat. Certainly, it generates more police activity. When arrests for DUI, drunkenness, and liquor law violations are compiled (almost 2.7 million), they far exceed any other offense category.[99] This does not mean that many people do not consume alcohol in a socially responsible manner. It is when the overuse of this drug begins to damage health, deteriorate family relationships, affect employment, and generate crime that it becomes a problem.

Like illicit drugs, the use of beer, wine, or hard liquor often begins at young ages, even though alcoholic beverages are legally restricted for those under twenty-one in all states. But illegality does not prevent consumption. Alcohol, in fact, is the "drug of choice" among young people. While only 2 to 4 percent of high school seniors report using hard drugs on a monthly basis, more than half (55 percent) admit to monthly use of alcohol.[100] As with illegal drugs, abuse of alcohol does not necessarily result in addiction. But among those who are particularly susceptible, genetically or psychologically, problem drinking can lead to addiction.

Institutional Profile

Within state correctional facilities, a slightly higher percentage of inmates reported being under the influence of alcohol (37 percent) than drugs (33 percent) when they committed their crime.[101] Moreover, alcohol abusers demonstrate criminal behavior patterns similar to their drug-abusing counterparts. For example, the percentage of prisoners who had domestic disputes (40 percent) or prior arrests (29 percent) related to alcohol abuse is almost exactly the same as those reporting such experiences related to drug abuse (42 percent and 30 percent, respectively).[102] The combination of alcohol with other drugs (poly-drug use) is also appearing more frequently among correctional populations.

Of course, being "under the influence" during the commission of a crime does not inherently mean that the person is an alcoholic. It may only indicate that the offender becomes more susceptible to criminal behavior or cannot control impulses when drinking. On the other hand, there are alcoholics who are completely convinced of their ability to "handle" increasingly large amounts of liquor, managing to function without detection in society and not seeking help until alcoholism has begun to destroy their life. As a result, alcoholism is to a great extent a *hidden disease*, with no accurate measures of its prevalence within either corrections or the outside community.

Treatment Programs

As with drug addiction or any other social problem, prevention is a far better remedy than intervention after the fact. Also, like these other maladies, behavior is often symptomatic of deeper underlying problems. Treatment of alcoholism therefore must be based on the realization that drinking may be a *manifestation of other difficulties* (although recently, there is additional evidence that there may be a *genetic link* through which alcoholism is inherited).

In any event, conventional therapy emphasizes strengthening the patient psychologically so that alcohol is no longer a convenient "crutch" for solving problems or relieving emotional tensions. As with drug intervention, treatment approaches range from psychotherapy to special diets designed to counteract vitamin deficiencies, along with self-help groups. In both cases, treatment is more likely to be effective if it is not conducted in isolation, but rather, includes a more comprehensive family-focused approach.

 # Learning Goals

Do you know:
1. How society has responded over the years to those with mental disorders?
2. How the developmentally disabled differ from the mentally ill?
3. Why staff need special training for dealing with the developmentally disabled?

Mentally Disordered Offenders

Throughout history, society has reacted to those who have mental disorders with a mixture of fear, mistrust, and repulsion. In the Middle Ages, it was thought that they were possessed by evil spirits, and if fortunate enough to escape burning at the stake, they faced banishment from society. In later years, ashamed families would hide mentally disordered relatives in basements or attics. When society began to assume more public responsibility for their care, they again were secluded—in large remote institutions closed off from public scrutiny. Eventually, concerns were voiced about both the conditions in which they were being confined and the types of disorders for which they were being held. Mental institutions were criticized as dumping grounds where the elderly, handicapped, and undesirable were virtually imprisoned.[103] Even among those with legitimate mental problems, it was determined that many suffered from conditions that could be treated as effectively on an outpatient basis.

Much of this criticism came to a climax during the civil rights movement of the 1960s—when widespread support was generated for protecting the interests of the disenfranchised, including the mentally ill. As a result, the *deinstitutionalization* of large mental hospitals began with various forms of community mental health legislation in the 1970s. However, somewhere along the way to replacing *institutional confinement* with *community-based treatment*, society ran out of money or interest or both. Earlier, we saw the impact of this transition in terms of how jails have in a sense become a "second-rate mental institution." For chronically homeless mental patients, jails have become "an asylum of last resort."[104]

As with alcoholics and drug addicts, when society cannot or will not effectively care for certain groups, they often become correctional clients. In that respect, public attitudes toward the mentally ill have not changed dramatically over the years—still reflecting a combination of suspicion, fear, and aversion. But the term "mentally disordered" offenders encompasses a wide range of behaviors, from the mildly disoriented or neurotic to those who are severely psychotic and completely out of touch with reality. While this term is used broadly to refer to conditions that differ from what is considered "normal," it is important to make clear distinctions between the developmentally disabled and the mentally ill.

Developmental Disability (Mental Retardation)

Previously known by such terms as "mentally defective" or "feebleminded," and more recently, as *developmentally disabled*, mental retardation is a clinical classification resulting from an abnormally low IQ (70 or below) and a deficiency in two or more adaptive life skills.[105] There is not necessarily any relationship between retardation and criminal behavior. However, the limited intelligence of the developmentally disabled severely restricts their employment opportunities. It also tends to make them susceptible to being led into crime by others. And when they do break the law, they often do not have the mental capacity to do so without being detected. Thus, they often are apprehended quickly—as we see in the next "Close-up On Corrections."

Because of their nominal intelligence, when such persons do engage in crime, they may not be held accountable for their actions in a court of law, just as a small child would not be held criminally responsible due to lack of ability to distinguish right from wrong. As a result, it is not surprising to find that their proportion of the institutional population in corrections is quite small.[106] Because of their limited numbers, programs for them are very scarce—found in less than half of the states.[107] Although there is no "cure" for mental retardation, with special assistance, some can be helped to improve the level of their development toward achieving greater social independence.

But a far greater danger for them than lack of treatment is their potential for being victimized in prison. Not only are they subject to verbal ridicule and

Close-up On Corrections

DEVELOPMENTALLY DISABLED OFFENDERS

Eddie, a fat forty-three-year-old Providence, Rhode Island, man with an IQ of 61, holds up Dunkin' Donuts shops. He walks up to the counter, pretends he has a gun inside the pocket of his tattered green coat, and demands "all your money and a dozen donuts." He has done it at least a half-dozen times. The police catch Eddie every time walking down the sidewalk eating the donuts. Eddie has served at least two prison sentences for such offenses. . . .

Everyone has read about them. They are the hapless, inept criminals who do things like rob a bank and sign the note they give to the teller; who run out of the liquor store they just robbed, jump in their getaway car and discover they have lost the keys; who burglarize the same store or home at the same time every week until the police catch them. Such incidents make humorous fillers for newspaper columns. But if one looks into them more deeply, the facts are not always so funny. Some of these offenders are merely clumsy. Many, however, are mentally retarded. They commit their crimes ineptly because they do not have the mental capacity to plan them. They are easily caught and a disproportionate number of them end up in jails and prisons.

Source: Bruce DeSilva, "The Retarded Offender: A Problem Without a Program," *Corrections Magazine*, Vol. 6, No. 4, August 1980, pp. 24-25.

---

physical abuse by other inmates, but to conceal their deficiencies, they avoid participating in institutional programs.[108] In addition, they are "slower to adjust to routine" and have "more difficulty in learning regulations."[109] Often, they simply do not understand what is expected of them. Staff who are not sensitive to the developmentally disabled, therefore, can mistakenly assume that an inmate is being defiant when actually, the person could not mentally comprehend the officer's instructions, as illustrated in the following "Close-up On Corrections." This is a particular problem for these offenders, since many of them are skillful at hiding their disability in an effort to appear "normal."[110] As a result, they tend to accumulate more disciplinary infractions and are more likely to be denied parole (serving on average two or three years longer than others with the same offense).[111]

To prevent such difficulties, some departments have established procedures for identifying developmentally disabled offenders and placing them in special units where they can receive appropriate care, equitable discipline, and life skills training that will help them become more independent on release.[112] But unfortunately, they are more likely to be either unrecognized or mainstreamed with the general population and supervised by personnel who are not aware of their special condition.

Close-up On Corrections

DEALING WITH THE DEVELOPMENTALLY DISABLED

On one particular hot summer weekend, fifteen minutes before he was to be relieved, Officer Terry . . . asked inmate Ness to assist him [in cleaning up the mess hall]. . . . About twenty minutes later, C.O. Terry returned to the mess hall to check on the work. When he saw what inmate Ness was doing, he first couldn't believe it and then he got angry. Inmate Ness had continued to sweep the garbage back and forth all over the floor, but was not putting it in a pile. In fact, the area that needed cleaning was now larger. Barely able to control his anger, C.O. Terry yelled, "NESS, WHAT THE HELL IS WRONG WITH YOU? WHAT ARE YOU—STUPID? WHAT DO YOU THINK YOU'RE DOING?" Inmate Ness became visibly nervous and stammered, "I, I, I ain't stupid." C.O. Terry disregarded the inmate's remark and stated, "YOU'RE TRYING TO BUST MY CHOPS BECAUSE YOU KNOW I WANT TO GET OUT OF THIS PLACE. LISTEN, NESS, I'M NOT GONNA TELL YA AGAIN, GET THIS MESS PICKED UP NOW!" C.O. Terry then walked out. . . .

Inmate Ness then grabbed a garbage can and began walking around the mess hall picking up a handful here and there, never really making any progress on the scattered mess. After five minutes, Officer Terry returned and once again . . . screams, "O.K., YOU MORON, THAT'S IT, GET OVER HERE." Before the inmate moves, he yells back, "I, I AIN'T NO MORON." C.O. Terry yells, "YOU ARE TOO, NOW GET OVER HERE." Inmate responds, "I AIN'T NO MORON." C.O. Terry yells, "I'M GIVING YOU A DIRECT ORDER TO GET YOUR BUTT OVER HERE RIGHT NOW." Inmate Ness shakes his head violently side to side, indicating that he's not moving. C.O. Terry then calls for officer assistance.

Source: Thomas Tiberia, "Helping Correction Officers Recognize and Interact with Handicapped Offenders," *American Jails*, Vol. 6, No. 2, May/June 1992, pp. 31-32. Used with permission.

Learning Goals

Do you know:

1. How the criminally insane are affected by "guilty but mentally ill" legislation?
2. How the prevalence of mental illness in the general population compares to prisons and jails?
3. Why it is difficult for corrections to provide proper treatment for mentally ill inmates?

Mental Illness in Corrections

Unlike the relative simplicity of identifying mental retardation, the complexities of mental illnesses defy easy classification. In terms of seriousness, mental illness can range from harmless senility to violence-prone psychosis. In this discussion, the term *insanity* will be used to differentiate seriously mentally ill offenders from those with varieties of less-severe disorders. Although it obviously has a medical interpretation, in the criminal justice system, insanity is a legal term—a status that is decided by the court, taking into consideration the opinions of medical experts.

In the past, defendants ruled incompetent to stand trial or declared legally insane during trial could be confined in a *mental health institution* for an indeterminate period of time. In fact, it has been said that "there were places in the 1950s where the mean length of stay was twenty years, and the mean type of discharge was a funeral."[113] But a 1977 Supreme Court ruling (*Jackson v. Indiana*) held that those found incompetent for trial cannot be held indefinitely and established that any such commitment must be justified by treatment progress. However, even if released under criminal law, the patient may be recommitted under civil law.

If at some point, a mentally insane patient is determined by medical staff to be "cured," there may well be nothing to prevent his or her release, since technically, the person was not "convicted" in a court of law. To prevent untimely releases from mental health institutions of those who could otherwise be held in a correctional institution, Michigan passed the first "guilty but mentally ill" legislation in 1972. Several other states have followed suit. Although these statutes vary, the basic intent is to establish factual guilt or innocence in a court of law (regardless of the insanity outcome), which therefore would enable a correctional sentence to be imposed, thus preventing the offender who is declared mentally insane from escaping criminal responsibility.

In addition to mental health institutions, the criminally insane may be confined in a special *forensic hospital* (in other words, a psychiatric hospital that is also a secure correctional institution). In smaller states and localities, a separate *psychiatric ward* may be set up within an existing prison to accommodate them. Contrary to past practices, the legally insane no longer are confined indiscriminately with the general population.

But that certainly does not mean that there are no mentally ill inmates among the general population. An inmate may suffer from any number of mental disturbances without being declared legally insane. There are no valid statistics documenting exactly how many mentally ill offenders are behind bars. Estimates of mental disabilities among the jail population range from 6 percent to 13 percent,[114] which may seem insignificant, but rates of serious mental disorders are two to three times higher among jail inmates than the general public.[115] Moreover, estimates of the mentally ill in prison are even higher (16 percent).[116] In fact, the United States has more mentally ill men and women in prisons and jails than in all state hospitals combined.[117] Regardless of the numbers, whether they get help is another matter.

Treatment for Mental Illness

Treatment is both essential from a compassionate point of view and a practical management necessity—given the fact that "certain types of psychiatric impairment increase the likelihood of . . . violent behavior within the general prison population."[118] But as was discussed in earlier chapters, sophisticated psychiatric and psychological treatment is costly. When available, it may be limited to the most severe cases. Even then, as illustrated by the tragic case in the next "Close-up On Corrections," help may not be forthcoming.

Estimates indicate that less than half of the inmates with severe mental illnesses—and less than one-quarter of those with more moderate mental illnesses—receive treatment for their condition while incarcerated.[119] Responses to mental illness in financially pressed agencies are likely to be limited to simply *containing behavior*. However, as one doctor in charge of mental health services in a correctional system has noted, "[t]reatment programs must include more than separation, close supervision, and administration of medication."[120] And as with addiction, effective treatment cannot end on release—a fact recognized in a class-action lawsuit filed on behalf of mentally ill inmates in New York City jails. The suit charged officials with routinely releasing patients who have received mental health treatment behind bars without making any provision for continuing their care and medication in the community, thus causing many of them to deteriorate and commit new offenses.[121]

 # Close-up On Corrections

MISSED DIAGNOSIS

A man with a known history of schizophrenia and psychiatric hospitalization committed a crime and was sentenced to a maximum-security prison. After he arrived, he would not get out of bed, smeared himself with feces, and was totally uncommunicative. He cut his wrists and attempted to jump from the fourth level of his cellblock. He was referred to the prison psychiatrist who believed that the inmate was being manipulative and that his behavior was caused by a personality defect. He was transferred to a state forensic center for further diagnostic study where he was again diagnosed as being a faker and having a personality disorder.

Following his return to prison, the man was observed sitting on the guard rail outside his cell. He smiled at some nearby inmates and fell over backwards, plunging many feet to the floor. He died of massive brain damage. What is significant about this case is that the correctional staff followed proper procedure and sought the medical and psychiatric consultation that the inmate's behavior required. The psychiatric staff, however, erred.

Source: David Lester and Bruce L. Danto, *Suicide Behind Bars: Prediction and Prevention*, Philadelphia: Charles Press, 1993, p. 11.

It might seem that an obvious solution would be to transfer such cases to a state mental health hospital, which is better equipped for their care. But since the deinstitutionalization movement, that is far more easily said than done. Before accepting an inmate, state mental health laws now often require that in addition to being legitimately mentally ill, "clear objective evidence must also exist that the inmate is a real and immediate danger to himself or herself or to others; or that the inmate is unable to attend to his or her basic needs. . . . This standard, when rigidly applied . . . effectively precludes the transfer of many inmates . . . to mental institutions."[122]

Moreover, without a sufficient psychiatric staff, it is difficult to determine just who is mentally ill. In that regard, it is often the correctional officer who is the first to notice such changes as "poor grooming and hygiene, decreased appetite, or crying spells," along with "talk of suicide."[123] Manipulative inmates, however, may feign symptoms to get attention or a different housing assignment.

 # Close-up On Corrections

MANAGING MALINGERERS

By simply making a vague threat such as "I don't know what I'll do," an inmate will be brought to the institutional psychologist. If the inmate sticks to that line, there is a very good chance he will be sent to the mental health unit. If he continues to threaten suicide when he gets to the unit, we put him on restrictive suicide precautions—we take all his clothing and possessions, give him a paper gown, and place him in a bare cell with nothing to lie on but a paper sheet. We then observe him at fifteen-minute intervals.

While this may sound cruel, it is actually quite useful. If a person is truly depressed and suicidal, he may use any available means to kill himself. I know of inmates who have cut open the bottoms of their mattresses, crawled inside and suffocated. Others have hung themselves with braided toilet paper.

However, the greatest use of these strict precautions may be their diagnostic potential—they separate the truly suicidal from the malinger. Suicidal inmates barely notice the conditions of their confinement; they are withdrawn and continue to brood about whatever it is that is bothering them.

But not so the malingerers. Usually within an hour of being placed in the cell they begin to complain. Many an inmate who absolutely convinced me of his depression and hopelessness will, a day later, let on that he didn't want to do his segregation time or that he was having trouble with another inmate. And since he really isn't suicidal, can't he have a mattress and just stay here for a while? . . . [But] [i]f they're not suicidal, they don't belong in the mental health unit. We encourage them to return to the general population and deal with their problems.

Source: Roy Clymer, "Managing Malingerers: Power Stems from Active Involvement, Not Control," *Corrections Today*, Vol. 54, No. 6, August 1992, pp. 22-24.

For a perceptive illustration of how one mental health worker distinguishes between the truly mentally disturbed and the traditional malingerer, see the previous "Close-up On Corrections."

✳ Learning Goals

Do you know:

1. What is meant by the term "physical impairment"?
2. How those with physical impairments traditionally have been accommodated within correctional facilities?
3. How the Americans with Disabilities Act is affecting corrections?

Physically Challenged Offenders

The needs of *physically challenged offenders* obviously differ substantially from the requirements of those who are psychologically damaged, but in both cases, correctional systems are likely to be ill-equipped to meet them. The physically impaired (or disabled) include those who do not enjoy the benefits of being able to see, hear, speak, walk, or who in some other way face a major restriction as a result of a physical or mental disability. In the past, such persons were referred to as "handicapped," terminology that has changed with greater realization that there is often nothing "handicapping" them more than social attitudes toward their condition.

Previously, disabled offenders had to adjust to correctional facilities as best they could. Now, as a result of the *Americans with Disabilities Act (ADA)*, it is correctional agencies that have to adjust (along with any other public or private establishments in free society that have more than twenty-five employees).

ADA defines the disabled as "anyone with a physical or mental impairment substantially limiting one or more major life activities, [who] has a record of such impairment, or is regarded as having such an impairment."[124] Especially because of the prevalence of mental disabilities among inmates, the ADA raises significant issues for corrections. Under the law, such inmates cannot be excluded from "programs and services available to the rest of the population."[125]

Other far-reaching provisions relate to the requirement that *reasonable accommodations* must be made for the disabled unless it would pose an "undue hardship" on the organization. New buildings must be constructed in a manner that makes them accessible to those with disabilities, and existing buildings must be made accessible.

An additional feature of the law prohibits a public entity from denying program benefits because facilities are inaccessible. It has been pointed out that this provision focuses on "making *programs*, not *buildings*, accessible,"[126] which is obviously a more comprehensive challenge. Recent rulings by the Eighth U.S. Circuit Court of Appeals, however, have cast doubt on whether Congress exceeded its authority in legislating certain program and service requirements of the ADA,[127] giving correctional administrators a legal basis for refusing requests for accommodations that they cannot afford. As is vividly illustrated in the next "Close-up On Corrections," accommodating the needs of the disabled and providing them with equal opportunities can have far-reaching implications within a correctional facility.

 # Close-up On Corrections

MEETING THE NEEDS OF DISABLED OFFENDERS

Custody and Security

Officers should be taught how to properly strip search a wheelchair-bound paraplegic, disassemble wheelchairs and prostheses, and otherwise conduct a proper shakedown. . . . Questions will arise concerning requirements for leg cuffs on paraplegics, waist chains across colostomy bags and even handcuffs for those on crutches. Custody should consult medical personnel when making these decisions. . . .

Personal Safety

First, disabled inmates need to be protected from other inmates. . . . Second, [they] need to be protected in case of fire or natural disaster. Building evacuation planning and emergency response must include special consideration for the disabled. Wheelchairs and crutches can block exits, leading to panic and injury. Plans must include the steps to be taken to safely evacuate this population without slowing the evacuation of the other inmates. . . .

Programs

A major challenge . . . is providing the disabled with meaningful work, study and recreational opportunities. All too often, no attempt has been made to put these inmates to work, and they have been forced to sit back and watch other inmates earn incentive wages and days off their sentences without an opportunity to do likewise.

Medical Service

A major issue is helping with activities of daily living. These include dressing, bathing, feeding, and transporting. . . . Ideally, medical staff such as nurses' aides provide all such required assistance. However, in the real world of limited budgets and insufficient staff, inmates frequently are used for these activities. . . . Any inmate involvement in daily living assistance must be closely monitored by professional staff to ensure inmates are properly trained and that they do not exploit those they are assigned to assist.

Housing

Simply putting up handrails in the showers is no longer adequate. . . . The square footage requirement for handicapped inmates is greater. Lockers must be low enough to be reached from a wheelchair, and writing tables must be high enough for a wheelchair to pull under. . . . While their numbers are few and their needs are great, the system must be prepared to accommodate them.

Source: Herbert A. Rosenfeld, "Enabling the Disabled: Issues to Consider in Meeting Handicapped Offenders' Needs," *Corrections Today*, Vol. 54, No. 7, October 1992, pp. 111-114.

 Learning Goals

Do you know:

1. To what extent the elderly correctional population is increasing?
2. Why there has been such growth in the proportions of older inmates in prison?
3. What special needs are required by elderly prisoners?
4. What alternatives to incarceration have been proposed for geriatric prisoners?

The Elderly in Prison

Just as the population in general is aging, so is that of our correctional institutions. As a result of medical advances and healthier lifestyles, average life expectancy continues to climb. Senior citizens are already a rapidly growing segment of the population, as those in the post-World War II "baby boom" begin to enter retirement. Young people still are far more disproportionately likely to be criminal offenders, although crime among the elderly is no longer as totally unheard of as it was in the past. But in light of trends toward *longer mandatory sentences*, prison populations are getting older.

Moreover, the number of inmates past the age of fifty-five is increasing at twice the rate of the total prison population,[128] generating needs for everything from physical therapy and cardiac medication to wider cell doors for wheelchairs,

As life expectancy increases and sentencing policies confine offenders for longer terms, geriatric inmates are becoming an increasing component of prison populations. Courtesy of the American Correctional Association.

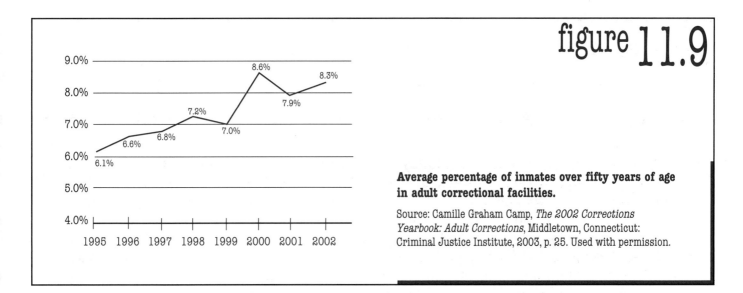

Average percentage of inmates over fifty years of age in adult correctional facilities.

Source: Camille Graham Camp, *The 2002 Corrections Yearbook: Adult Corrections*, Middletown, Connecticut: Criminal Justice Institute, 2003, p. 25. Used with permission.

and even Braille signs on doors.[129] While fifty-five may not seem "elderly" among those in free society, most prisoners have had inadequate (or nonexistent) health care throughout their lives, often combined with years of substance abuse, smoking, and other lifestyle patterns that promote the aging process.

Throughout the 1990s, the percentage of inmates who are fifty or older has been steadily increasing (*see* Figure 11.9). Figures for individual states even more distinctly reflect aging trends. For example, an analysis of the "three-strikes" law in California projects a massive increase in the elderly prison population—from some 20,300 in 1999 to 126,400 by 2020.[130]

As the elderly become a larger percentage of prison inmates, correctional administrators will be faced with unique challenges to address their needs. If aging inmates are simply mainstreamed with the overall population, they will be vulnerable to being preyed on by younger, healthier inmates—as is seen in the plight of one geriatric inmate in the next "Close-up On Corrections." They are also less likely to be able to participate physically in the recreational and vocational programs that traditionally are offered in correctional facilities. Nor can they in many cases eat the same foods as other inmates, since aging is often accompanied by more restrictive diets. Meeting the housing, recreational, rehabilitative, and dietary needs of geriatric inmates presents issues that corrections will be confronting in the years ahead.

But perhaps most significantly in terms of costs, as more and more older offenders are confined behind bars, *long-term health care* will become an increasingly greater concern, just as it is already within the general population in free society. Most geriatric inmates have some long-term chronic condition that requires frequent medical attention,[131] and meeting such needs is expensive. It has been estimated that the average cost of medical care and maintenance for inmates more than fifty-five is about three times the norm,[132] and one study anticipates "enormous hidden costs and consequences" for taxpayers as prisons are "transformed into expensive old-age homes."[133] In fact, one institution spent $200,000 to care for just one geriatric inmate who had open-heart surgery, an angioplasty, and treatment for a stroke (which did not include the cost of physical therapy that he received to regain his speech and

Close-up On Corrections

Growing Old Behind Bars

On a steamy June day in 1973, a fifty-year-old drifter named Quenton Brown robbed a bread store in Morgan City, Louisiana, of $117 and a fifteen-cent cherry pie. He walked across a dusty street, crawled under a house and ate the pie. When the police showed up a few minutes later, he surrendered his .38 pistol and the handful of money without resistance. Brown, whose IQ is 51, told the cops he had bummed his way to the Cajun outback to find work on an oil rig. Unable to find a job, he robbed. The jury gave short shrift to his claim of insanity. The judge gave him thirty years without parole.

Brown has pulled seventeen years in the Louisiana State Prison at Angola, one of the nation's toughest. At sixty-seven, he is feeble, suffering from emphysema, a crushed esophagus, and bleeding ulcers. His prison record is free of all but minor infractions, none involving drugs, sex or violence. . . . Over the years, he has watched former death-row murderers walk to freedom while his bids for release have been repulsed. As he grows older, the worst part of doing time is the younger, bolder prisoners: "They call you names. You go to the prison store, they snatch the bags from your hands as you leave. You're living in a jungle among savages."

Source: Ginny Carroll, "Growing Old Behind Bars," *Newsweek*, November 20, 1989, p. 70.

the use of his right leg, or the daily cost of managing his heart disease, diabetes, and hypertension).[134]

While some states have opened geriatric prisons,[135] others have found creative alternatives. For example, the state of Texas saved $38 million when it shifted medical services for its 135,000 geriatric inmates to a managed care program operated by the state's medical schools.[136] Still others advocate extending *early release* to the elderly, for financial if not humanitarian reasons. In that regard, twenty-two states have implemented a "compassionate release" option for terminally ill inmates who are no longer a risk to society,[137] thereby "giving them an opportunity to live out their remaining days in relative dignity."[138] However, many older prisoners have outlived their relatives and used up their savings. Faced with loneliness and inability to survive on the outside, one ninety-two-year-old offender actually took his own life after release, because he simply "didn't have any other place to go."[139]

For these types of cases, it has been proposed that *secure nursing homes* and *electronic monitoring* would be more suitable alternatives. Options (such as the GRACE project featured in the next "Close-up On Corrections") obviously would be agreeable to the many offenders reflected in the dejection of one aging inmate: "I know I don't have many more years. I'd like to spend a few of them outside prison."[140]

Close-up On Corrections

THE GRACE PROJECT

Lieutenant: You know the real sick inmate you have in the infirmary? Well, if he is able, he goes to court tomorrow morning. We expect he will be released on time served. What is going to happen to him?

RN: Thank goodness. We sure need to get him out of here, and everything is ready for his release.

Lieutenant: What do you mean? We picked him up off the streets. I think he was homeless.

RN: No problem. When we saw how sick he was, we referred him to the GRACE Project nurse. They took him into their program and have everything set. Housing, follow-up medical care, Medicaid support, transportation, whatever . . . Just be sure to coordinate his release with them so they can take him to the nursing home.

Lieutenant: Great! This sure beats just opening the gate and putting him back on the street with nothing.

Source: Herbert A. Rosefield and Margaret Ratcliff, "The GRACE Project in Jails—A Follow-up," *American Jails*, November/December 2003, p. 37. Used with permission.

Summary

Because of their "minority" status among institutional populations, the needs of special offenders often have not been a high priority, despite the fact that their numbers have been growing. For example, as a result of their involvement in drug-related offenses, women are becoming a larger proportion of correctional clientele, although they are still in the distinct minority.

In contrast to male inmates, females are more likely to suffer from the frustration of being unable to care for their children. Separation anxiety can create considerable tension, stress, and reduced self-esteem. Also unlike men, women adapt to the deprivations of confinement by developing quasifamilies, with emotional intimacy among fellow inmates substituted for the loss of family and social ties.

Usually, female institutions are smaller and more remote than male facilities. Thus, they are not generally able to offer the diversity of programs provided within men's prisons. To address this problem economically, some facilities are now coed, with male and female inmates confined within the same compound. They do not share living quarters but may be allowed to interact socially and share the same programs, which involves both advantages and disadvantages.

Like women, those with HIV-infections are appearing more frequently in correctional populations. With the spread of AIDS throughout society, it is not surprising to find that this disease is on the increase among inmates, particularly since those convicted of drug offenses are likely to be sentenced to prison or jail terms. Correctional responses to reducing the transmission of HIV have included offering education programs, issuing condoms, HIV testing, and using separate housing. Legal challenges have focused primarily on mandatory testing and the segregation of HIV-positive inmates. Thus far, the courts have ruled that mandatory testing and/or segregation is neither required under the Eighth Amendment nor prohibited under the Fourth Amendment.

Along with women and AIDS victims, alcohol and drug abusers represent another component of the correctional clientele that is growing at alarming rates. Treatment programs are not reaching everyone in need, and they usually are not followed up by postrelease assistance and monitoring.

Along with those experiencing problems with alcohol or drugs, mentally disordered offenders represent a sizable component of correctional populations, especially since the deinstitutionalization of mental health services. The developmentally disabled differ from the mentally ill in that their mental capacity has been retarded at an early stage of development, which renders them easily susceptible to apprehension. Within correctional institutions, the developmentally disabled represent special problems, since they are slower in adjusting and learning what is expected of them—behavior which can be misinterpreted as defiance.

In contrast, the criminally insane are those so designated by the courts, using legal criteria related to one's capacity to distinguish right from wrong. Those who are legally determined to be insane may be confined in mental health facilities, forensic hospitals, or the separate psychiatric ward of a prison. But there are many others incarcerated who are not legally designated "insane" but who suffer from various forms of mental illnesses. In recent years, it has become more difficult to transfer such inmates to a mental health hospital, but correctional facilities are generally ill-equipped to meet their needs.

In the past, corrections as well as the general public has been slow to respond to the needs of the physically impaired. With implementation of the Americans with Disabilities Act, public agencies are now legally prohibited from discriminating against the disabled. This legislation has generated widespread publicity, calling attention to the special needs of the disabled throughout society.

While the physically impaired are still a small portion of the correctional population, the elderly represent a rapidly expanding group. Along with the overall aging of the population in general, longer prison sentences are resulting in greater numbers of older inmates. As this trend continues, corrections will be faced with meeting their unique needs in terms of everything from housing assignments to health requirements and recreational provisions. Moreover, the long-term health care of geriatric inmates will become increasingly costly. In fact, meeting the special needs of all groups of offenders discussed in this chapter presents a significant challenge for correctional programs and facilities that already are hard-pressed to meet even the basic requirements of more "traditional" offenders.

Endnotes

1. Janie L. Jeffers, "AIDS at Our Door: Preparing for an Unwanted Guest," *Corrections Today*, Vol. 52, No. 1, February 1990, p. 36.

2. Of all arrests for violent crimes in 2002, only 17 percent were women, of arrests for property-related index offenses, 31 percent were women. *Crime in the United States, 2002: Uniform Crime Reports*, Washington, D.C.: Federal Bureau of Investigation, 2003, p. 9.

3. *Ibid.*

4. *Ibid.*

5. Paige M. Harrison and Allen J. Beck, "Prisoners in 2002," *Bureau of Justice Statistics: Bulletin*, Washington, D.C.: U.S. Department of Justice, 2003, p. 9.

6. James J. Stephan and Jennifer C. Karberg, *Census of State and Federal Correctional Facilities, 2000*, Washington, D.C.: U.S. Department of Justice, 2003, p. 6.

7. *Crime in the United States*, p. 9.

8. Paige M. Harrison and Jennifer Karberg, "Prison and Jail Inmates at Midyear 2002," *Bureau of Justice Statistics: Bulletin*, Washington, D.C.: U.S. Department of Justice, 2003, p. 8.

9. *Ibid.*, p. 5.

10. Barbara Owen and Barbara Bloom, "Profiling Women Prisoners: Findings from National Surveys and a California Sample," *Prison Journal*, Vol. 75, No. 2, June 1995, p. 165-186.

11. Key Sun, "Mentally Disordered Offenders in Corrections," in Roslyn Muraskin, ed., *Key Correctional Issues*, Upper Saddle River, New Jersey: Prentice Hall, 2004, p. 125.

12. *Crime in the United States*, p. 9. (The only offense for which female arrest rates have been increasing faster is embezzlement, where the volume is significantly less than for drug violations).

13. Meda Chesney-Lind, "Putting the Brakes on the Building Binge," *Corrections Today*, Vol. 54, No. 6, August 1992, p. 30. For a ten-year comparative profile of female offenders, *see* T. A. Ryan and Kimberly A. McCabe, "A Comparative Analysis of Adult Female Offenders," *Corrections Today*, Vol. 59, No. 4, July 1997, pp. 28-30.

14. Elizabeth A. Klug, "Benefits Ban Impacts Women and Children," *Corrections Today*, Vol. 64, No. 4, July 2002, p. 15.

15. Christopher Mumola, "Incarcerated Parents and Their Children," *Bureau of Justice Statistics: Special Report*, Washington, D.C.: U.S. Department of Justice, 2000, p. 1.

16. *Ibid.*

17. *Ibid.*, p. 10.

18. Sandra Enos, *Mothering from the Inside: Parenting in a Women's Prison*, Albany: State University of New York Press, 2001.

19. "Female Offenders: Survey Summary," *Corrections Compendium*, Vol. 26, No. 1, January 2001, p. 5.

20. *Ibid.*, p. 27.

21. *See*, for example, Gloria Logan, "Family Ties Take Top Priority in Women's Visiting Program," *Corrections Today*, Vol. 54, No. 6, August 1992, pp. 160-161.

22. Jackie Crawford, "Alternative Sentencing Necessary for Female Inmates with Children," *Corrections Today*, Vol. 65, No. 3, June 2003, p. 9, quoting J. Hagan and R. Dinovitzer, "Collateral Consequences of Imprisonment for Children, Communities, and Prisoners," in Michael Tonry and Joan Petersilia, eds., *Prisons, Crime, and Justice*, Chicago: University of Chicago Press, 1999, p. 125-147.

23. Rini Bartlett, "Helping Inmate Moms Keep in Touch," *Corrections Today*, Vol. 63, No. 1, February 2001, p. 102-104.

24. Term coined by Kelsey Kauffman, "Mothers in Prison," *Corrections Today*, Vol. 63, No. 1, February 2001, p.62.

25. Moses, "Girl Scouts Behind Bars," p. 134, and Nicole Carroll, "Girl Scouts Help Inmates, Daughters Bond," *USA Today*, October 19, 1993, p. 8D. *See also* Mary Dallao, "Coping with Incarceration—From the Other Side of the Bars," *Corrections Today*, Vol. 59, No. 6, October 1997, pp. 96-98, and Cynthia Seymour, "Children with Parents in Prison: Child Welfare Policy, Program, and Practice Issues," in Cynthia Seymour and Creasie Hairston, *Child Welfare Journal of Policy, Practice, and Program: Special Issue with Parents in Prison*, Vol. 67, No. 5, 1998, pp. 469-93.

26. Toni Johnson, Katherine Selber, and Michael Lauderdale, "Developing Quality Services for Offenders and Families: An Innovative Partnership," *Child Welfare*, September/October, 1998, pp. 595-615.

27. "Public Correctional Policy on Crime Prevention," unanimously ratified by the American Correctional Association Delegate Assembly, January 17, 1996 and amended January 24, 2001.

28. Crawford, "Alternative Sentencing Necessary," p. 10.

29. Mumola, "Incarcerated Parents and Their Children," p. 5.

30. J. G. Fox, "Women in Prison—A Case Study in the Reality of Stress," in Robert Johnson and Hans Toch, eds., *Pains of Imprisonment*, Beverly Hills, California: Sage Publications, 1982, pp. 205-220.

31. Joycelyn M. Pollock-Byrne, "Women in Prison: Why Are Their Numbers Increasing?" in Peter J. Benekos and Alida V Merlo, eds., *Corrections: Dilemmas and Directions*, Cincinnati, Ohio: Anderson Publishing Company, 1992, p. 91. *See also* Joann Brown Morton, *Working with Women Offenders in Correctional Institutions*, Lanham, Maryland: American Correctional Association, 2004, pp. 148-149.

32. John Gagon and William Simon, "The Social Meaning of Prison Homosexuality," in David M. Petersen and Charles W. Thomas, eds., *Corrections: Problems and Prospects*, Englewood Cliffs, New Jerrsey: Prentice Hall, 1980, p.123.

33. Kathryn Watterson Burkhart, *Women in Prison*, New York: Doubleday, 1973, pp. 365-366.

34. Rose Giallambardo, *Society of Women: A Study of a Women's Prison*, New York: Wiley,1966; Morton, *Working with Women Offenders in Correctional Institutions*, pp. 353-354.

35. *See*, for example, Candance Kruttschnitt and Sharon Krompotich, "Agressive Behavior among Female Inmates: An Exploratory Study," *Justice Quarterly*, Vol. 7, No. 2, June 1990, p. 384, who found that "fewer than one-quarter of the incarcerated females engaged in acts of aggression toward their fellow inmates."

36. Morton, *Working with Women Offenders in Correctional Institutions*, p. 360.

37. Christine E. Rasche, *Special Needs of the Female Offender: Curriculum Guide for Correctional Officers*, Tallahassee, Florida: Florida Department of Education, n.d., p. 68.

See also John DeBell, "The Female Offender, Different...Not Difficult," *Corrections Today*, Vol. 63, No. 1, February 2001, p. 89.

38. Jocelyn M. Pollock, *Women, Prison and Crime*, Belmont, California: Wadsworth, 2002, p. 80.

39. John M. Vanyur and Barbara Owen, "Managing Female Offenders in Mixed-gender Facilities: The Case of a Federal Jail," *American Jails*, May/June 2003, p. 68.

40. Barbara Bloom, Barbara Owen, and Stephanie Covington, *Gender-Responsive Strategies: Research, Practice, and Guiding Principles for Women Offenders*, Washington, D.C.: U.S. Department of Justice, National Institute of Corrections, 2003, p. 58.

41. Merry Morash, Timothy S. Bynum, and Barbara A. Koons, "Women Offenders: Programming Needs and Promising Approaches," *National Institute of Justice: Research in Brief*, Washington, D.C.: U.S. Department of Justice, National Institute of Justice, 1998, p. 4.

42. Human Rights Watch—Women's Rights Project, *All Too Familiar: Sexual Abuse of Women in U.S. State Prisons*, New York: The Ford Foundation, 1996.

43. Bloom, Owen, and Covington, *Gender-Responsive Strategies*, p. 26.

44. Lawrence A. Greenfeld, *Prisons and Prisoners in the United States*, Washington, D.C.: U.S. Department of Justice, 1992, p. 2.

45. Morash, Bynum, and Koons, "Women Offenders: Programming Needs and Promising Approaches," p. 2.

46. Bloom, Owen, and Covington, *Gender-Responsive Strategies*, p. 23. *See also* Merry Morash, Robin N. Haarr, and Lila Rucker, "A Comparison of Programming for Women and Men in U.S. Prisons," *Crime and Delinquency*, Vol. 40, No. 2, 1994, pp. 197-221.

47. James J. Stephan and Jennifer C. Karberg, *Census of State and Federal Correctional Facilities, 2000*, Washington, D.C.: Bureau of Justice Statistics, U.S. Department of Justice, August 2003, p. 13.

48. *Klinger v. Department of Corrections*, 1994, 31 F. 3d. 727 (8th Cir.).

49. Karen Fein, "Women Prisoners," in Roslyn Muraskin, ed., *Key Correctional Issues*, Upper Saddle River, New Jersey: Prentice Hall, 2004, p. 264, citing *Jeldness v. Pearce*, 30 F3d 1220, 1229, 9th Cir. (1994).

50. Pollock, Women, *Prison and Crime*, p. 105. *See also* American Correctional Association, "Policy on Female Offender Services," reviewed and amended, August 2000.

51. Stephan and Karberg, *Census of State and Federal Correctional Facilities*, pp. 6-7.

52. Pollock, Women, *Prison and Crime*, p. 84, citing John Smykla and John Williams, "Co-Corrections in the United States of America, 1970-1999: Two Decades of Disadvantages for Women Prisoners," *Women and Criminal Justice*, Vol. 8, No. 1, 1996, pp. 61-76.

53. *Ibid.*

54. Bloom, Owen, and Covington, *Gender-Responsive Strategies*.

55. Barbara Bloom, Joan Johnson, and Elizabeth Belzer, "Effective Management of Female Offenders: Applying Research on Gender-Responsive Correctional Strategies to Local Jails," *American Jails*, September/October 2003, p. 33.

56. Arena T. Laszlo and Marilyn B. Ayres, *AIDS: Improving the Response of the Correctional System*, 2nd ed., Washington, D.C.: National Sheriffs' Association, 1990, p. 5.

57. Centers for Disease Control and Prevention, "Prevention and Control of Infections with Hepatitis Viruses in Correctional Settings," *Morbidity and Mortality Weekly Report*, Vol. 52, No. RR-1, 2003, p. 57.

58. Laura M. Marushak, "HIV in Prisons, 2001," *Bureau of Justice Statistics: Bulletin*, Washington, D.C.: U.S. Department of Justice, 2004, p. 5.

59. *National Commission on AIDS Report: HIV Disease in Correctional Facilities*, Washington, D.C.: National Commission on Acquired Immune Deficiency Syndrome, 1991, p. 5.

60. There is, however, a vaccine for hepatitis A and B, which the Centers for Disease Control and Prevention strongly recommend for all staff members whose duties involve potential exposure to blood or bodily fluids. *See* the pamphlet (nd) "Viral Hepatitis: Know the Facts," Lanham, Maryland: American Correctional Association.

61. Theodore M. Hammett and Saira Moini, "Update on AIDS in Prisons and Jails," *AIDS Bulletin*, Washington, D.C.: National Institute of Justice, 1998, p. 4.

62. Sherwood E. Zimmerman, Randy Martin, and David Vlahov, "AIDS Knowledge and Risk Perceptions among Pennsylvania Prisoners," *Journal of Criminal Justice*, Vol. 19, No. 3, 1991, pp. 239-256.

63. Kim Marie Thorbum, "Health Programs Do Work to Fight AIDS," *Corrections Today*, Vol. 54, No. 8, December 1992, p. 127.

64. Hammett and Moini, "Update on AIDS in Prisons and Jails," p. 6.

65. Barbara A. Belbot and Rolando V. del Carmen, "AIDS in Prison: Legal Issues," *Crime and Delinquency*, Vol. 37, No. 1, January 1991, p. 137.

66. "Court of Appeals 10th, Rejects Fourth Amendment Challenge to Blood Testing of Prison Inmates for AIDS," *Criminal Law Reporter*, Vol. 45, No. 20, August 23, 1989, p. 2360.

67. "Prisons and Jails—Mandatory AIDS Testing," *Criminal Law Reporter*, Vol. 48, No. 7, November 14,1990, pp. 1150-1151.

68. Belbot and del Carmen, "AIDS in Prison," p. 138.

69. Hammett and Moini, "Update on AIDS in Prisons and Jails," p. 6.

70. "Inmate HIV Testing," *American Jails*, Vol. 6, No. 5, November/December 1992, p. 87.

71. Mark Blumberg and Denny Langston, "Mandatory HIV Testing in Criminal Justice Settings," *Crime and Delinquency*, Vol. 37, No. 1, January 1991, pp. 12-13. *See also* Sherwood E. Zimmerman, Randy Martin, and David Vlahov, "AIDS Knowledge and Risk Perceptions among Pennsylvania Prisoners," *Journal of Criminal Justice*, Vol. 19, No. 3, 1991, pp. 239-256, who indicate that "intraprison transmission rates are less than 1 percent" (p. 249).

72. *National Commission on AIDS*, p. 22.

73. "Rising Number of AIDS Cases May Be Linked to Prison Populations," *Corrections Alert*, Vol. 3, No. 22, February 24,1997, p. 2.

74. A. F. Anderson, "Aids and Prisoners' Rights Law: Deciphering the Administrative Guideposts," *Prison Journal*, Vol. 69, No. 1, Spring/Summer 1989, p. 21.

75. The state's practice is to offer voluntary AIDS tests to all inmates upon entry into the system, along with later testing "if a doctor has reason to think an inmate is infected." *See* "Inmates' Request for Mandatory Testing Denied," *On the Line*, Vol. 15, No. 2, March 1992, p. 2.

76. *National Commission on AIDS*, p. 22, citing *Smith v. Meachum* (1989).

77. M. J. Olivero, "The Treatment of AIDS behind the Walls of Correctional Facilities," *Social Justice*, Vol. 17, No. 1, Spring 1990, p. 114.

78. Belbot and del Carmen, "AIDS in Prison," p. 147.

79. Most cases addressing confidentiality suggest that although disclosure "may be appropriate and even necessary in certain circumstances, the disclosure must be limited in scope." *See* Belbot and del Carmen, "AIDS in Prison," pp. 139-143.

80. Curtis R. Davis, "AIDS and an Officer's Right to Know," *Corrections Today*, Vol. 53, No. 7, December 1991, p. 28.

81. Hammett and Moini, "Update on AIDS," p. 7.

82. *National Commission on AIDS Report*, p. 3.

83. Hammett and Moini, "Update on AIDS," p. 8.

84. James E. Lawrence and Van Zwisohn, "AIDS in Jail," in Joel A. Thompson and G. Larry Mays, eds., *American Jails: Public Policy Issues*, Chicago: Nelson-Hall, 1991, pp. 122-124.

85. Christopher J. Mumola, "Substance Abuse and Treatment," *Bureau of Justice Statistics: Special Report*, Washington, D.C.: U.S. Department of Justice, 1999, pp. 3-5.

86. Howard N. Snyder, "Growth in Minority Detentions Attributed to Drug Law Violators," *Office of Juvenile Justice and Delinquency Prevention: Update on Statistics*, Washington, D.C.: U.S. Department of Justice, 1990, pp. 1-2, 5.

87. Doris James Wilson, "Drug Use, Testing, and Treatment in Jails," *Bureau of Justice Statistics: Special Report*, Washington, D.C.: U.S. Department of Justice, 2000, p. 1.

88. Christopher J. Mumola, "Substance Abuse and Treatment, State and Federal Prisoners, 1997," *Bureau of Justice Statistics: Special Report*, Washington, D.C.: U.S. Department of Justice, 1999, p. 1.

89. Matthew R. Durose and Patrick A. Langan, "Felony Sentences in State Courts, 2000," *Bureau of Justice Statistics: Bulletin*, Washington, D.C.: U.S. Department of Justice, 2003, p. 2.

90. Website of the Office of Justice Programs, Bureau of Justice Statistics, U.S. Department of Justice, http://www.ojp.usdoj.gov/bjs/sent.htm.

91. "When Ex-con's Come Home to the 'Hood, Will Police Be Ready?," *Law Enforcement News*, February 14, 2001, p. 1.

92. "Survey Summary: Drug Treatment Intervention Summary," *Corrections Compendium*, Vol. 63, No. 2, April 2001, p. 8.

93. Michele D. Buisch, "Justice Awards Money for Drug Treatment," *Corrections Today*, Vol. 64, No. 5, August 2002, p. 15.

94. Joey R. Weedon, "The Foundation of Re-entry," *Corrections Today*, Vol. 66, No. 2, April 2004, p. 6.

95. Faye Taxman, "Strategies to Improve Offender Outcomes in Treatment," *Corrections Today*, Vol. 66, No. 2, April 2004, p. 100.

96. Sandra Tunis *et al.*, *Evaluation of Drug Treatment in Local Corrections*, Washington, D.C.: National Institute of Justice, 1996, pp. 11, 18.

97. National Task Force on Correctional Substance Abuse Strategies, *Intervening with Substance-Abusing Offenders: A Framework for Action*, Washington, D.C.: U.S. Department of Justice, National Institute of Corrections, 1991, p. 35.

98. Karen Fein, "Women Prisoners," p. 266, citing a National Institute of Justice study.

99. *Crime in the United States*, p. 234.

100. *Sourcebook of Criminal Justice Statistics, 2001*, Washington, D.C.: U.S. Department of Justice, 2002, p. 248.

101. Mumola, "Substance Abuse and Treatment," p. 1.

102. *Ibid.*, p. 6.

103. Barbara Gordon, *I'm Dancing as Fast as I Can*, New York: Bantam Books, 1979, p. 98.

104. J. R. Belcher, "Are Jails Replacing the Mental Health System for Homeless Mentally Ill?" *Community Mental Health Journal*, Vol. 24, No. 3, 1988, p. 193.

105. Mark Nichols, Lawrence L. Bench, Erica Morlok, and Karen Liston, "Analysis of Mentally Retarded and Lower-functioning Offender Correctional Programs," *Corrections Today*, Vol. 65, No. 2, April 2003, p. 119.

106. *Ibid.* Although early studies found that approximately 9 percent of offenders suffer from mental retardation, more recent research indicates that their prevalence is considerably lower (between 1 percent and 4 percent).

107. *Ibid.*, p. 120.

108. Miles Santamour and Bernadette West, *Sourcebook on the Mentally Disordered Prisoner*, Washington, D.C.: U.S. Department of Justice, 1985, p. 70.

109. *Ibid.*

110. Thomas Tiberia, "Helping Correction Officers Recognize and Interact with Handicapped Offenders," *American Jails*, Vol. 6, No. 2, May/June 1992, p. 32.

111. Santamour and Bernadette West, *Sourcebook*, p. 70.

112. *See*, for example, Mary F. Farkas, "Teamwork in the Social Skills Development Unit Helps Adaptively Impaired Inmates," *Corrections Today*, Vol. 62, No.7, December 2000, pp. 118-120.

113. Daniel Kagen, "Landmark Chicago Study Documents Rate of Mental Illness among Jail Inmates," *Corrections Today*, Vol. 52, No. 7, December 1990, p. 166, quoting John Monahan.

114. Paula N. Rubin and Susan McCampbell, "The Americans with Disabilities Act and Criminal Justice: Mental Disabilities and Corrections," *National Institute of Justice: Research in Action*, Washington, D.C.: U.S. Department of Justice, 1995, p. 1.

115. Kagen, p. 164.

116. Allen J. Beck and Laura M. Maruschak, "Mental Health Treatment in State Prisons, 2000," *Bureau of Justice Statistics: Special Report*, Washington, D.C.: U.S. Department of Justice, 2001, p. 3.

117. Chris Sigurdson, "The Mad, the Bad, and the Abandoned: The Mentally Ill in Prisons and Jails," *Corrections Today*, Vol. 62, No. 7, December 2000, p. 70.

118. Deborah R. Baskin, Ira Sommers, and Henry J. Steadman, "Assessing the Impact of Psychiatric Impairment on Prison Violence," *Journal of Criminal Justice*, Vol. 19, No. 3, 1991, p. 278.

119. Sigurdson, "The Mad, the Bad, and the Abandoned," p. 72.

120. Max J. Mobley "Mental Health Services: Inmates in Need," *Corrections Today*, Vol. 48, No. 3, May 1986, p. 13.

121. "Treatment Plan Sought after Inmates are Released," *Correctional News*, November/ December 1999, p. 22.

122. David Kalinich, Paul Embert, and Jeffrey Senese, "Mental Health Services for Jail Inmates: Imprecise Standards, Traditional Philosophies, and the Need for Change," in Joel A. Thompson and G. Larry Mays, eds., *American Jails: Public Policy Issues*, Chicago: Nelson-Hall, 1991, p. 81.

123. Laura Tahir, "Supervision of Special Needs Inmates by Custody Staff," *Corrections Today*, Vol. 65, No. 6, October 2003, p. 108.

124. "Agencies and Facilities Must Comply with New Federal Law on Disabled," *Corrections Today*, Vol. 54, No. 6, August 1992, p. 143.

125. Rubin and McCampbell, "The Americans with Disabilities Act and Criminal Justice," pp.1-2.

126. Randall Atlas, "Is Accessibility a Disability? The Impact of ADA on Jails," *American Jails*, Vol. 6, No. 5, November/December 1992, p. 55.

127. "8th Circuit Strikes down ADA for State-run Facilities," *Correctional Education Bulletin*, Vol. 3, No. 3, 1999, p. 7.

128. Ericia Kempker, "The Graying of American Prisons: Addressing the Continued Increase in Geriatric Inmates," *Corrections Compendium*, Vol. 28, No. 6, June 2003, p. 1.

129. Mary Cronin, "Gilded Cages," *Time*, May 25, 1992, p. 54.

130. Philip Zimbardo, *Transforming California's Prisons into Expensive Old-Age Homes for Felons: Enormous Hidden Costs and Consequences*, San Francisco: Center on Juvenile and Criminal Justice, 1994. *See also* Ryan S. King and Marc Mauer, "Aging Behind Bars: 'Three Strikes' Seven Years Later," white paper Washington, D.C.: The Sentencing Project, 2001.

131. O. W. Kelsey, "Elderly Inmates: Providing Safe and Humane Care," *Corrections Today*, Vol. 48, No. 3, May 1986, p. 56. *See also* "Elderly Inmates: Survey Summary," *Corrections Compendium*, Vol. 26, No. 5, May 2001, p. 7.

132. Kempker, "The Graying of American Prisons," p. 22.

133. Zimbardo (citation refers to full title of report: *Transforming California's Prisons into Expensive Old-Age Homes for Felons: Enormous Hidden Costs and Consequences for California's Taxpayers*). *See also* "Prison Medical Care: Special Needs Populations and Cost Control," *Special Issues in Corrections*, Longmont, Colorado: National Institute of Corrections, 1997.

134. Kempker, "The Graying of American Prisons," p. 22, citing A. Pelosi, "Age of Innocence," *New Republic*, May 5, 1997, pp. 15-17.

135. Jennifer Reid Holman, "Prison Care," *Modern Maturity*, March/April 1997, p. 34; and Hava Leisner, "Nationwide, More Elderly Inmates are in Prison: States Battle Increasing Health Care Costs by Building Geriatric Prisons," *Correctional News*, July/August 2000, p. 46.

136. Kempker, "The Graying of American Prisons," p. 22, citing D. C. Anderson, "Aging Behind Bars," *New York Times Magazine*, July 13, 1997, p. 28.

137. "Prison Medical Care," p. 2

138. Jeffers, "AIDS at Our Door," p. 38.

139. John M. Glionna, "At 92, Freed Inmate Ends His Life All Alone," *The Herald*, Miami, Florida: July 12, 2002, p. 4A.

140. Ginny Carroll, "Growing Old Behind Bars," *Newsweek*, November 20,1989, p. 70.

CHAPTER  12

JUVENILE CORRECTIONS

> 66 To say that juvenile courts have failed to achieve their goals is to say no more than what is true of criminal courts in the United States. But failure is most striking when hopes are highest.[1] 99
>
> —President's Commission on Law Enforcement and Administration of Justice

Chapter Overview

The future ambitions and far-reaching aspirations of any society depend on its children. The children of today will become tomorrow's leaders, workers, and parents. Unfortunately, some will become its criminals as well. In addressing any social problem, prevention holds far greater promise than intervention after the fact, and crime is certainly no exception. When prevention fails and young offenders confront social authority, they are sending a signal that something has gone wrong. Many will overcome their difficulties simply by maturing and growing up. Others will not. For them, encounters with authority will escalate if that "something" is not corrected. For a certain number of them, confrontations will become increasingly serious and frequent, until any hope for change is all but abandoned.

Before that point of no return is reached, children who come into contact with the justice system present more promise than their adult counterparts. By their very definition, "juveniles" are considered different from adult "criminals." If nothing else, they are younger—and therefore presumably less responsible for their actions—as well as more amenable to change. Involvement in the juvenile justice system, therefore, can offer the potential for addressing their problems and redirecting their behavior at an early stage. On the other hand, it can further alienate and embitter them, fostering the resentment and frustration that propel juvenile offenders toward adult criminality.

In fact, the juvenile court was established in recognition of the unique needs and potential for change among young people. To create an environment where the "best interests" of the child would be served, the juvenile court was meant to be an advocate rather than an adversary of the offender. The intent was to promote the welfare of the child rather than to punish the offender for wrongdoing. But somewhere along the path toward serving their best interests, it became apparent that children were receiving neither the benevolent protection promised by the juvenile court nor the due-process protections afforded to adults.

At the same time, juveniles were engaging in far more serious offenses than the original founders of the juvenile court ever had envisioned. To their victims, it makes little difference whether it was a juvenile or an adult who had raped, assaulted, or robbed them. Thus, demands for greater procedural protections in juvenile court, combined with increasing fear of juvenile crime, have resulted in a juvenile justice system today which more closely resembles its adult counterpart.

The question of whether juveniles should be punished or protected remains a continuing source of debate. Although it is unlikely that this basic issue will be resolved, the manner in which it is addressed will have long-term implications—not only for young offenders themselves, but also for the collective future of our entire society.

 Learning Goals

Do you know:
1. How children were treated historically in comparison to adults?
2. Why reform schools were established?
3. How industrialization, immigration, and urbanization influenced the child-saving movement?

Historical Background

While we are now accustomed to thinking of children as different from adults, that was not always how young people were treated. Throughout medieval society, the idea of childhood simply did not exist. In fact, it has only been within relatively recent history that children have clearly been distinguished from grownups. Previously, young people were considered virtually "miniature adults"—they were dressed like adults, employed in the same backbreaking work, and subject to similar (or in some cases, even more severe) punishments for misbehavior.

In one of the first efforts to separate juveniles from adults, Massachusetts opened a public *reform school* for delinquent boys in the mid-1840s. But at this time, there were no juvenile courts, so youthful offenders were sent to such reformatories to avoid a conviction that would otherwise result in a sentence to be served in an adult prison. This procedure led to litigation on the part of aggrieved parents when children were informally sent to a juvenile institution without having been officially convicted. Although reform schools provided alternatives to incarceration with adults, the treatment of boys and girls confined there was harsh. Children were subjected to strict discipline, long hours of work, and severe punishments. Many of these institutions were actually designed more for industrial production than for nurturing or rehabilitation, and their exploitation of child labor was shameful.[2]

Toward the end of the nineteenth century, conditions cried desperately for improvement. Throughout the Industrial Revolution, sweatshops, mines, and factories had become notorious for their abuse of children. Combined with virtually unrestricted immigration, cities were attracting vast numbers of foreigners to the promise of a better life in urban factories. But the life they found waiting for them was hardly an improvement.

The Child-Saving Movement

As cities expanded, urbanization required accommodating a continuous influx of people, many of whom did not share the same customs or even speak the same language. Crime, poverty, overcrowding, and unemployment escalated dramatically. But perhaps more important, these trends toward industrialization, immigration, and urbanization threatened what had become well-entrenched standards of the "American way of life," firmly rooted in middle-class, rural values.[3]

Under such conditions, it increasingly became apparent that the economic, social, and physical impact of life in crowded ghettos of urban immigrants was creating a negative influence on childhood development. Intervention into the lives of such economically and culturally deprived children, therefore, was justified as essential to "rescue" them from a destiny of doom. This became known as *child-saving*—essentially, a reaffirmation of faith in traditional institutions, including parental authority and home-based education, which had become "contaminated" by urban living.[4]

In retrospect, some have criticized the motives of such social reformers as a hostile reaction against immigration and urbanization that was largely based on self-serving rather than child-saving interests. But at the time, child-savers were cast as righteous campaigners responding to the immorality that was viewed as the cause of delinquency among immigrant children—nor could their timing have been better.

Beyond the social disruptions occurring in America, child-saving emerged when the role of women was expanding. As women began to seek careers outside of the home, intervention into the welfare of children became an acceptable option for them. At the same time, new criminological theories offered hope that behavior might be amenable to change. And who better to begin with than the youngest offenders?

Learning Goals

Do you know:

1. When and where the first juvenile court was created?
2. The definition of "parens patriae" and how it relates to the original intention of the juvenile court?
3. Why procedures are more informal in juvenile than in adult court?

Origin of the Juvenile Court

As a consequence of these widespread social influences supporting a different approach to wayward children, the first *juvenile court* was established in Chicago in 1899. Focusing on *dependency* and *neglect* as well as *delinquency*, reformers envisioned "rescuing" the child from a host of undesirable conditions. To accomplish this, the law provided for:

- The separate hearing of children's cases in a court of chancery rather than one of criminal jurisdiction

- Detention of children apart from adult offenders

- A juvenile probation system[5]

Separate detention and probation already existed in some locations, and the concept of chancery (in other words, civil) jurisdiction also had been established previously.[6] But while the individual elements of the Illinois legislation may not have been so revolutionary, the impact of their combined effect has been felt throughout the country—resulting in the development of a distinct *juvenile justice system* in virtually every state in the United States.

The Power of Parens Patriae. To achieve its wide-ranging mission, the new juvenile courts emphasized an *individualized approach* to justice. A prominent objective of the court was to develop a diagnosis and personalized treatment plan designed to meet each child's specific needs. The priority was to determine the needs of the child rather than to decide "guilt" or "innocence."

To protect rather than prosecute, the court relies on the authority of *parens patriae*—a Latin term that refers to the king as the ultimate parent (*parens*) over all subjects in the country (*patriae*). In the United States, the concept of *parens patriae* derived from the state's power to sever children from their pauper parents under the Poor Laws. With no welfare support available in the nineteenth century, the only alternative for indigents was refuge in the poor houses. Since that was obviously not a healthy atmosphere in which to raise children, the state could remove children from indigent families and place them out as apprentices.

Under *parens patriae*, the juvenile court was invested with responsibility for and authority over the welfare of its clients. Moreover, the jurisdiction of the juvenile court extended well beyond offenses that would be considered criminal if committed by an adult—into such nebulous areas as truancy, begging, and incorrigibility. In many cases, the behaviors targeted were "most directly relevant to the children of lower-class migrant and immigrant families."[7] As a result, the conduct of youths need not be considered particularly serious to justify juvenile court processing. In the name of *parens patriae*, the power of the state assumed priority over the rights of the parents, and the broad but vague authority of the juvenile court far exceeded its adult counterpart.

Procedural Informality. According to this philosophy, the juvenile court did not require an adversarial model of justice, wherein the defense competes against the prosecution. To the contrary, juvenile court was designed to be the defendant's *advocate* rather than *adversary*. Like a reasonable and knowledgeable parent, the court's intent was to serve the "best interests" of the child.

Underlying this concept is the assumption of youthful dependency and vulnerability, which entitles children to certain privileges and protections not afforded to adults. But at the same time, it restricts the child from legal safeguards provided in the adult criminal justice system. According to this view, the state—serving in the parental role—is in the best position to determine what treatment is needed to guide the child back on a proper path. The basic philosophy is that "erring children should be protected and rehabilitated rather than subjected to the harshness of the criminal system."[8]

Much of the justification for this diversion from the adversarial model of justice is based on the desire to *prevent stigmatizing* the child and to *provide flexibility* in prescribing treatment. Removed from a punishment orientation, the court was committed to avoiding the labeling of children as "criminal." In exchange, less formal procedures would be employed to determine the facts of the case. The ultimate outcome was to benefit the child, uninhibited by procedural formalities. In fact, distinctions between the adult and juvenile justice systems extended to the very terminologies used to describe legal procedures, as reflected in Figure 12.1.

Prevention and Treatment

Under this unique approach, it was not the specific offense bringing the child to the court's attention that was of primary concern, but rather, the

---

figure **12.1**

Criminal Justice System	Juvenile Justice System
Crime	Delinquent act
Arrest	Take into custody
Warrant	Summons
Criminal complaint/indictment	Petition
Plea bargain	Adjustment
Trial	Hearing (or adjudication)
Guilty verdict	Adjudicated delinquent
Convicted	Found involved
Sentencing	Disposition
Incarceration	Commitment
Jail	Detention center
Prison	Training school
Inmate	Resident
Parole	Aftercare

Contrasting terminologies of the criminal and juvenile justice systems.

underlying circumstances. Since the individual's behavior was seen as the product of preexisting causes, the court's mission was to discover and address what was actually causing misconduct. But the court's potential to do so was greater the sooner the intervention occurred.

Thus, an important component of the juvenile court related to the ability to identify "predelinquent" children and impose upon them treatment designed to "correct their wayward tendencies."[9] It was for this reason that the court's mandate included a wide variety of deviant behaviors directed toward "children who occupy the debatable ground between criminality and innocence."[10] The rationale for such intervention was largely based on the desire to prevent more serious infractions in the future.

Overall, the court's objective was "not so much to punish as to reform, not to degrade but to uplift, not to crush but to develop. . . ."[11] Equally glowing pictures were painted of the juvenile court's advantages over its adult counterpart: "The old courts relied upon the learning of lawyers; the new courts depend more upon psychiatrists and social workers. . . . Justice in the old courts was based on legal science; in the new courts it is based on social engineering."[12]

With its innovative emphasis on prevention and diagnosis, its noncriminal basis in the doctrine of *parens patriae*, and its ability to deviate from procedural formality, the juvenile court held out promising hope—for personalizing the justice process and making a substantial impact on the delinquency problem. Unfortunately, its promise did not measure up in practice.

Juvenile Justice Transformation

As was observed by the early 1970s, "today's juvenile court personnel have shed the naive expectations of early reformers."[13] After more than half a century of experimentation, the juvenile court had neither curtailed the growth of juvenile crime nor fulfilled its commitment to protect rather than punish its clients. To the contrary, it was becoming apparent that in juvenile court, youths actually receive "the worst of both worlds," getting "neither the protections accorded to adults nor the solicitous care and regenerative treatment postulated for children."[14]

By the 1960s, a newly emerging juvenile justice paradigm was directed toward exactly the opposite—reducing intrusion of the court into children's lives.[15] Spearheaded by the *due-process movement*, the power and intervention of the court were restricted, based on the notion that rights should not be sacrificed in the name of rehabilitation.

 Learning Goals

Do you know:

1. What protections juveniles have during waiver proceedings?
2. What rights were extended to juveniles as a result of the *Gault* and *Winship* decisions?
3. What types of offenses represent most juvenile court cases?

Due-Process Considerations

As a result of growing concerns over the arbitrary manner in which cases were being handled, a number of significant decisions regulating juvenile justice practices have been handed down by the Supreme Court. These changes generally have brought juvenile courts more in line with procedures used in the adult system.

The most significant due-process protections that were extended to juveniles during the 1960s are outlined in the next "Close-up On Corrections." While they have not fully transformed the juvenile justice system into a miniature version of adult criminal courts, they have had a considerable impact. Like the sentencing guidelines, objective classification procedures, and parole decision-making models addressed earlier, they have introduced greater *structure* into what was previously a highly discretionary process.

 # Learning Goals

Do you know:

1. How delinquents differ from status offenders?
2. What the relationship is between age and the commission of violent crimes?
3. For what types of offenses youths are processed in juvenile court?

Juvenile Court Workload

Much of the difficulty experienced by juvenile courts relates to the widespread array of behaviors that can bring a youth into the justice system. In addition to behavior that would be considered "criminal" if committed by an adult—what is today officially termed *delinquency*—youths can be held accountable for *status offenses*—behavior that is illegal only for those under the age of majority. While hundreds of thousands of those under the age of eighteen are arrested each year for running away from home, loitering, or violating curfews, the major status offense that brings youths into the juvenile justice system is truancy. In recent years, truancy has been surpassing everything except liquor law violations in terms of the volume of cases being petitioned to juvenile courts, and it represents the largest increase (92 percent) of any status offense over the previous decade.[16]

That does not, however, mean that juvenile offenders are not frequently engaged in serious criminal activities. Quite the contrary, teenagers and young adults are responsible for a disproportionate share of such offenses. Those under eighteen years of age represented 15 percent of the arrests in 2002 for violent crimes. If the age limit is expanded to those under twenty-one, the figure increases to 28 percent. By age twenty-five, it climbs to 44 percent.[17] In other words, young people under the age of twenty-five account for almost half of the arrests for violent crimes. When arrests for *all* crime index offenses are taken into account, the picture becomes even worse: 26 percent are under eighteen; 41 percent are under twenty-one, and 54 percent are under twenty-five years of age (*see* Figure 12.2).

Close-up On Corrections

LANDMARK DUE PROCESS CASES IN THE JUVENILE JUSTICE SYSTEM

- *Kent v. U.S.* (1966 383 U.S. 541): Prior to this case, juvenile court judges had virtually unlimited discretion when deciding whether to transfer cases to adult court. This was a distressing issue for Morris Kent. His offenses (six counts of housebreaking and robbery) resulted in an adult court sentence of thirty-to-ninety years in prison. Had he been adjudicated in juvenile court, however, he would have faced a maximum of only five years' confinement in a training school. Noting that the juvenile court's duty "to function in a 'parental' relationship is not an invitation to procedural arbitrariness," the Supreme Court ruled that juveniles being considered for transfer to criminal court are entitled to a *hearing* and a *statement of reasons* for the court's decision.

- In *Re Gault* (387 U.S. 1, 1967): In terms of severity of punishment, Gerald Gault's case was quite the opposite. Brought to juvenile court for making lewd phone calls to a neighbor, he was committed to the state industrial school "for the period of his minority," (which at the time was six years). But if he were an adult, the penalty for his offense would have been a $5 to $50 fine or incarceration for no more than two months. In response to his appeal, the Supreme Court held that juveniles are entitled to certain due-process rights—specifically, *notice of charges, the right to remain silent,* and *the right to counsel,* as well as *the right to cross examination* (in proceedings that may result in commitment to an institution).

- In *Re Winship* (397 U.S. 358, 1970): As far reaching as it was, the *Gault* decision did not address the different standard of proof that prevailed in juvenile court (in other words, *preponderance of evidence*). But in 1970, the Supreme Court held that when a twelve-year-old (Samuel Winship) is liable to be confined for as long as six years (for entering a locker and stealing $112), the case must be proven *beyond a reasonable doubt.*

- *McKeiver v. Pennsylvania* (403 U.S. 528, 1971): Despite these expansions of due-process protections, the Supreme Court had not given notice that it intends to make blanket application of constitutional safeguards to delinquency cases. For example, in the *McKeiver* case, the right of juveniles to a jury trial was rejected, with the Supreme Court maintaining that its desire was not to remake juvenile proceedings into a fully adversarial process.

Delinquents in Juvenile Court

Undoubtedly, it is the hard-core, chronic offenders who capture media headlines, creating a distorted perception of the "typical" youthful lawbreaker. But although they are responsible for a disproportionate share of violations, habitual violent juveniles do not by any means represent the bulk of clients coming to the attention of juvenile courts.

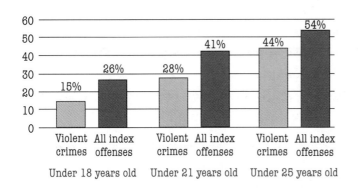

Arrests for violent crimes and crime index offenses by age.

Note: "Violent crimes" include murder, forcible rape, robbery, and aggravated assault. "All index offenses" include violent crimes, as well as burglary, larceny-theft, motor vehicle theft, and arson.

Source: Federal Bureau of Investigation, 2002. *Crime in the United States: Uniform Crime Reports*, Washington, DC: U.S. Government Printing Office, p. 250.

figure 12.2

As Figure 12.3 indicates, most delinquency cases handled by juvenile court are for *property crimes* (primarily larceny). Although violent juvenile crime is a growing concern, these statistics indicate that the bulk of cases appearing in juvenile courts are considerably less serious (especially if status offenses are also taken into account). Perhaps most importantly, it has been estimated that more than 670,000 youths processed in the juvenile justice system each year would meet clinical diagnostic criteria for one or more alcohol, drug, or mental disorders.[18] Such alarming statistics indicate that many juveniles require mental health and/or substance abuse treatment that the justice system is often ill-equipped to provide.

figure 12.3

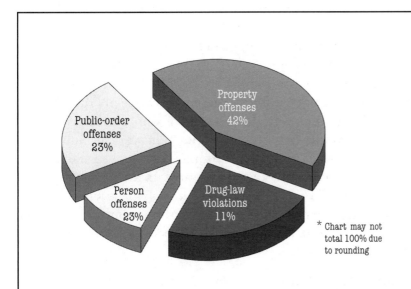

* Chart may not total 100% due to rounding

Delinquency cases handled by juvenile courts.*

Source: Anne L. Stahl, 2003. "Delinquency Cases in Juvenile Courts, 1999," *Office of Juvenile Justice and Delinquency Prevention Fact Sheet*, September, p.1.

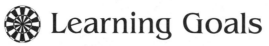 # Learning Goals

Do you know:

1. On what basis a juvenile might be detained prior to court appearance?
2. What the difference is between protective custody and secure detention?
3. The impact of the *Schall v. Martin* case?
4. Why the Juvenile Justice and Delinquency Prevention Act has not been fully successful in removing juveniles from adult jails?

Juvenile Detention

As in the adult system, the seriousness of the offense will be taken into consideration when determining whether to release or detain a youth prior to court appearance. Detention can be either in *protective custody* (such as a foster home or runaway shelter) or in a *secure custodial facility* (what would be termed "pretrial detention" for adults). In general, youths are likely to be detained if they are any of the following:

- A threat to the community
- At risk if returned to the community
- At risk of failing to appear at an upcoming hearing[19]

As shown in Figure 12.4, those involved in property crimes are most likely to face detention, and blacks are disproportionately more likely to be detained than whites. Detaining juveniles prior to their court disposition has been legally challenged. But in the 1984 *Schall v. Martin* case, the Supreme Court upheld the preventive detention of juveniles for their own or society's protection.[20] This does not mean that juveniles can be held indefinitely, and the child is entitled to a subsequent *detention hearing* where a judge determines whether to authorize release or continue with confinement.

Nevertheless, many disturbed young people are confined in juvenile detention without any pending criminal charges, merely because mental health treatment is not available to them. In fact, a 2004 Congressional report revealed that two-thirds of juvenile detention facilities hold youths waiting for community mental health treatment—some as young as seven years of age.[21] The national total of this unnecessary detention represents an estimated price tag of nearly $100 million.[22] Moreover, because many of these children are either suicidal or violently aggressive, they present serious management and safety challenges for facilities that are often ill-equipped to cope with their needs. As one administrator put it:

> We are overwhelmed by the sheer number of mentally challenged youth[s] that we must deal with. We have become the depository of last resort for all acting out, behaviorally challenged, developmentally disabled [youths] when others don't know how to handle them.[23]

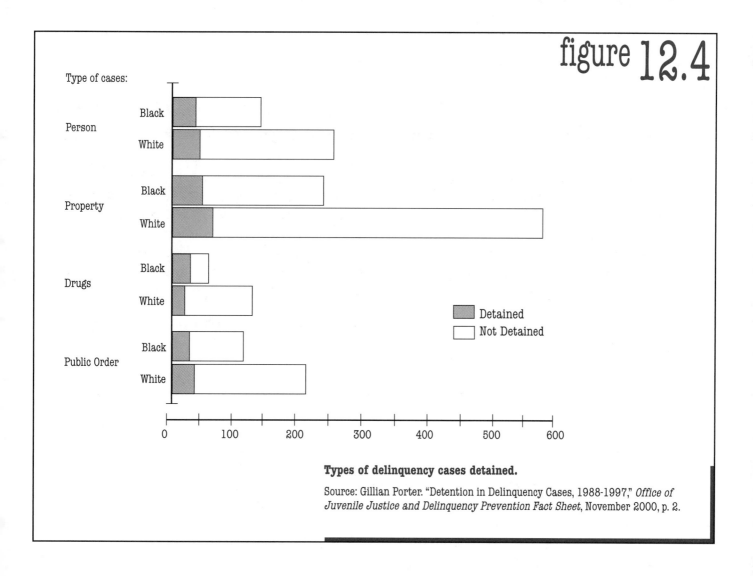

Types of delinquency cases detained.

Source: Gillian Porter. "Detention in Delinquency Cases, 1988-1997," *Office of Juvenile Justice and Delinquency Prevention Fact Sheet*, November 2000, p. 2.

In that regard, it appears that the juvenile justice system is following the same trends toward criminalization of the mentally ill as their adult counterparts in jail. The major difference is that the negative impact is considerably greater when the client is younger.

Juveniles in Adult Jails

A major issue facing the juvenile justice system in recent years has become *where* those held prior to disposition of their case are being confined. Because of the small numbers of offenders requiring custody in the past, many jurisdictions did not provide separate juvenile-detention facilities. Rather, they housed youths in adult jails—where they could face deplorable conditions and even death, as described in the next "Close-up On Corrections."

Given the impact of such an environment, it is not surprising to find that the rate of suicide among juveniles in adult jails has been found to be almost eight times higher than in juvenile detention centers.[24] Yet, there are still thousands of juveniles confined in adult jails.[25] Most of those included in this number (70 percent) are serious offenders being transferred to adult court. There is a valid argument that extremely violent, chronic delinquents can be an intimidating threat to others if they are confined in juvenile facilities. But jails are

Close-up On Corrections

certainly unsuitable for those charged with status offenses or minor delinquencies: "Jails lack adequate physical plant facilities, adequate numbers of appropriately trained staff members, as well as adequate health, recreational, and other programs to meet the minimum standards of juvenile confinement." [26]

Office of Juvenile Justice and Delinquency Prevention Legislation

Recognizing the negative influence that jail confinement can have on juveniles, the federal *Juvenile Justice and Delinquency Prevention Act* of 1974 restricted the confinement of juveniles in adult facilities to limited situations. When the Act was amended in 1980, its provisions went even further—requiring the removal of all juveniles from adult jails and lockups by the end of 1985. But because so many states were not in compliance by the deadline, it was extended three years until 1988, and several exceptions were added—primarily allowing for short-term detention in certain serious juvenile cases, provided that they are separated from adult inmates by "sight and sound." In other words, juveniles and adults must be kept completely separate in terms of all institutional activities (for example, sleeping, eating, engaging in recreation, getting an education, and using health care), and direct-contact staff must be separate from those who service the adult population. Additional modifications in 1996 further clarified the "sight and sound" provisions and permitted exceptions for up to six hours before and after court appearances.[27]

However, responsibility for the juvenile justice system is a state and local function. Although this federal legislation does not carry the weight of law, it does provide funding in exchange for an agreement to comply with its provisions. Compliance is monitored by the U.S. Department of Justice, Office of Juvenile Justice and Delinquency Prevention (OJJDP). States in violation face the possibility of having their federal juvenile justice funds terminated. In addition, lawsuits have been filed challenging state violation of the federal requirements. In one such case (*Hendrickson v. Griggs*), the judge issued an injunction to stop the state from detaining any more delinquent children until a plan was submitted to remove them from adult jails, noting that "it makes little difference . . . that these values were embodied in a funding program rather than a nationwide prohibition. If the state did not share Congress' priorities or did not wish to implement them, it could merely have refused to seek the OJJDP funding."[28]

For many years, reaction was "slow and incomplete," and most states still had not achieved full compliance by 1990.[29] Among the reasons were factors ranging from deliberate defiance to lack of commitment, ignorance of the law, insufficient resources, processing errors, and conflict between state and federal regulations.[30] A decade later, however, the Office of Juvenile Justice and Delinquency Prevention reported forty-six jurisdictions in full compliance with the separation of juvenile and adult offenders in secure institutions,[31] and all participating jurisdictions in complete compliance with jail removal (although forty were categorized as having "minimal exceptions").[32]

 # Learning Goals

Do you know:

1. What percentage of those in short-term detention are being held before adjudication ("pretrial")?
2. What is meant by the "balanced approach" to juvenile justice?

Juvenile Detention Facilities

Short-term *detention facilities* are the juvenile equivalent of adult jails. There are fewer than 500 state and locally administered detention centers

New design strategies balance public safety concerns with the delivery of programs in juvenile detention centers. This is the Crisp County (Georgia) Regional Youth Detention Center. Courtesy of Mark Goldman and Associates, project architect/engineer Rosser International.

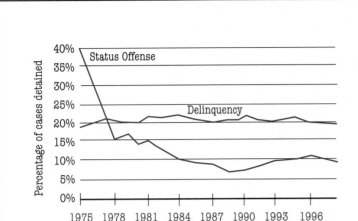

figure 12.5

Use of detention in delinquency and status offense cases.

Source: Howard N. Snyder and Melissa Sickmund. *Juvenile Offenders and Victims: 1999 National Report*, Pittsburgh, Pennsylvania: National Center for Juvenile Justice, 1999, p. 207.

throughout the United States, which house just under 20,000 youths.[33] Like adult jails, some of those in detention are awaiting disposition of their case, while others have already been adjudicated. Only one-third of those being held in public detention facilities have been committed following adjudication in juvenile court. The vast majority are confined while awaiting adjudication (in adult terms, "pretrial").

As might be expected, the bulk of those being temporarily detained are charged with *delinquencies* (offenses that would be considered crimes if committed by an adult). Although 5 percent are status offenders or nonoffenders,[34] this population has been declining in light of the Juvenile Justice and Delinquency Prevention Act's prohibition against the secure confinement of children who are dependent, neglected, or status offenders (*see* Figure 12.5). In that regard, the Office of Juvenile Justice and Delinquency Prevention's 2001 assessment shows almost all jurisdictions in nearly full compliance with this initiative (with minimal exceptions).[35]

While children are in detention, there is an opportunity to learn as much as possible about them. For this reason, progressive facilities employ intelligence, aptitude, and personality testing, along with other diagnostic procedures. Treatment programs are also essential. As is apparent from the profile of their social and emotional problems in Figure 12.6, many detention clients are isolated children, handicapped by feelings of inferiority. In fact, 92 percent of juvenile female offenders in one study reported having been victimized by some form of emotional, physical, and/or sexual abuse.[36] Many enter the system as runaways, seeking to escape abuse at home.[37] Seeking to reach these troubled children, one detention center has found that exposure to the creative arts promotes both treatment and socially acceptable behavior:

> Often from socially and economically impoverished homes . . . this population [in juvenile detention has] never seen a play, . . . played an instrument, . . . been to an art show, . . . learned to draw, . . . written a story. . . . [T]hey have never had the opportunity to put their hands into clay, paint their feelings, draw a portrait, or dance for an audience. By engaging in the communicative, cooperative

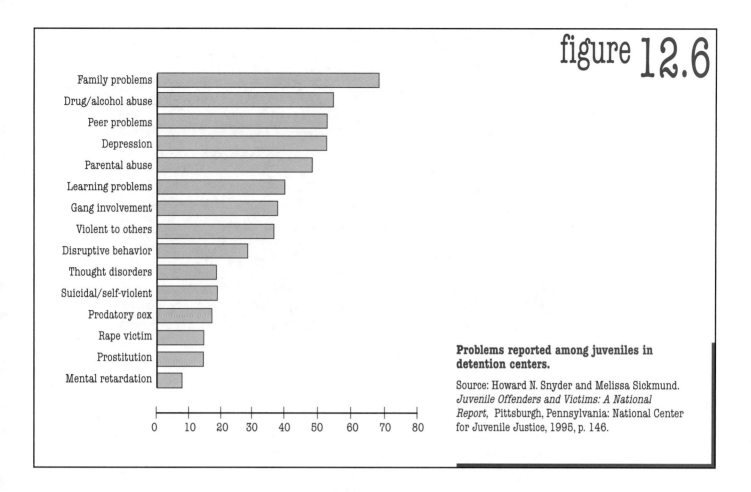

Problems reported among juveniles in detention centers.

Source: Howard N. Snyder and Melissa Sickmund. *Juvenile Offenders and Victims: A National Report,* Pittsburgh, Pennsylvania: National Center for Juvenile Justice, 1995, p. 146.

and playful dimension of the arts, [they] . . . can learn new ways to express themselves. . . . [W]e have seen the fruits of our labors in [their] pride, self-confidence and creativity.[38]

Detention Problems and Alternatives

Secure detention has long been plagued by problems ranging from substandard care to insufficient resources. In fact, as recently as 2003, a juvenile in detention died after suffering for three days in severe pain with the classic symptoms of appendicitis.[39] Moreover, in terms of their ability to satisfy the physical and emotional needs of adolescents, conditions in many detention centers have been described as "not much better than those in adult jails,"[40] and a recent study found that more than half of all detention center residents are confined in crowded facilities.[41]

For these reasons, public or private *shelter care* is often a preferable option to secure confinement for short-term detention. Shelters are a type of residential-home environment for dependent children, those who are neglected, or status offenders. In addition, several states are also using shelter care successfully for cases of minor delinquency pending court disposition. For those with special needs, such options as group homes, mental health facilities, or other programs for juveniles with emotional disturbances often can provide more effective help than detention.

Small facilities, trained staff, case management, and family counseling characterize Missouri's Division of Youth Services. Here, residents of the Northwest Regional Youth Center engage in creative recreation and discussion with administrators. Courtesy of the Northwest Regional Youth Center.

Adjudication

Under the original philosophy of the juvenile court, the intent was to give personalized attention to determining the facts involved and the needs of each offender. That, however, was long before the juvenile justice system was handling well over a million cases each year.[42] Such a workload can severely limit the attention devoted to each case. One study, for example, revealed that most juvenile court cases are heard in approximately fifteen minutes.[43] Obviously, such assembly-line "justice" inhibits the ability to provide the kindly, parental guidance envisioned by early reformers.

Society is concerned that juvenile justice not only serve the needs of the child, but also be in keeping with the public good. As one advocate of the recent trend toward a more *balanced approach* has observed, "We didn't want to assume that 'in the best interest of the child' always meant an adversarial relationship with the best interest of the community. When a crime occurs involving a juvenile, we should try to come up with a penalty that is best for the kid and best for the community."[44]

For a look at how some communities are accomplishing this, *see* the next "Close-up On Corrections." As it demonstrates, the balanced approach maintains a strong emphasis on establishing accountability and responsibility. This does not mean uniformly employing a middle ground between leniency and repression. Rather, it implies providing a more diverse range of options for responding to a similarly wide-ranging array of problems and behaviors. In the absence of a wider assortment of meaningful treatment and programming alternatives, it has been observed that "agencies are caught between naive reformers who believe all juveniles should be handled in the community and reactionary citizens and officials who demand an increase in confinement measures."[45]

Close-up On Corrections

A Balanced Approach to Juvenile Justice

The balanced and restorative justice approach can best be described as a combined emphasis on three priorities:

1. *Accountability.* Restitution, community service, and victim-offender mediation are employed to:

- Create an awareness in offenders of the harmful consequences of their actions for victims

- Require offenders to take action to make amends to victims and the community

- Involve victims directly in the justice process whenever possible

2. *Community protection.* Community-based surveillance and sanctioning systems channel the juvenile's time and energy into productive activities, including:

- A progression of consequences for noncompliance with supervision requirements

- Incentives that reinforce the youth's progress in meeting developmental objectives

3. *Competency development.* Work experience, active learning, and service provide opportunities for offenders to:

- Develop skills and earn money

- Interact positively with conventional adults

- Demonstrate publicly that they are capable of productive, competent behavior

Repairing the Harm—Making Amends

Case Study: After some two hours of heated and emotional dialog, the mediator felt that the offender and victim had heard each other's story and had learned something important about the impact of the crime. . . . They had agreed that the offender, a fourteen-year-old, would pay $200 in restitution to cover the cost of damages to the victim's home resulting from a break-in. In addition, he would be required to reimburse the victim for the cost of a VCR. . . . The offender also had made several apologies to the victim and agreed to complete community service hours working in a food bank sponsored by the victim's church. The victim, a middle-aged neighbor of the offender, said that she felt less angry and fearful after learning more about the offender and the details of the crime and thanked the mediator.

Source: Adapted from Gordon Bazemore and Curt Taylor Griffiths, "Conferences, Circles, Boards, and Mediations: The 'New Wave' of Community Justice Decisionmaking," *Federal Probation*, June 1997, p. 25.

 Learning Goals

Do you know:

1. What general categories of disposition alternatives are available to juvenile courts?

2. The difference between secure and open custodial facilities?

Dispositions

At the *disposition hearing* (or what would be called "sentencing" in adult court), judges have a number of options, ranging in severity from nominal to conditional or custodial:

- *Nominal.* Particularly for first-time delinquents or those involved in less-serious offenses, the judge simply may elect to issue a warning or reprimand, with no further repercussions if the youth avoids future contact with the law.

- *Conditional.* As the term implies, these sanctions require that the offender comply with some type of requirement (for example, paying a fine, providing community service, making restitution to the victim, or completing a training, educational, or treatment program). Among the most frequently used conditional dispositions is formal *probation.* More than half (57 percent) of all delinquency cases and 65 percent of all status offenders receive probation.[46] Like its adult counterpart, juvenile probation sets conditions that the child must abide by—such as attending school, maintaining a curfew, and reporting to a probation officer. Also like the criminal justice system, the judge can suspend formal disposition, dropping the charges if the juvenile complies with the conditions established. But probation's utility is limited by excessively high caseloads, forcing greater reliance on practical requirements than treatment needs. In this respect, it has been observed that probation often becomes "a token effort," which, in terms of its potential, has been underused, but in terms of its funded strength has been badly overused.[47]

- *Custodial.* If custodial commitment is warranted, the court has two choices: *secure* or *nonsecure* facilities. Nonsecure or "open" facilities include foster homes, group homes, camps, ranches, and marine institutes. These are options for those who need some guidance, structure, and supervision, but not as much restraint and limitation as are found in juvenile correctional institutions or training schools. In terms of the length of time that youths committed to confinement must serve, there are at least six different models operating in various states throughout the country—ranging from determinate to indeterminate dispositions (with and without minimums and maximums). Moreover, in some states, correctional agencies are authorized to release youths from confinement, whereas in others, release decisions are reserved for either the judiciary or the parole board.[48]

Success Stories

As the juvenile court has struggled over the years with implementing appropriate dispositions for children accused of everything from truancy to manslaughter, it is tempting to become discouraged by its failures. Research indicates many adult prisoners first came to the attention of the police as juveniles, and in fact, the earlier a youth enters the juvenile justice system, the more likely he or she is to continue to compile an extensive record.[49] To some extent, moreover, the skyrocketing adult prison population could be viewed as evidence of the juvenile justice system's ineffectiveness.

But looking only at the failures obscures the many success stories of troubled youths whose contact with the system points them in the right direction. In commemoration of the juvenile court's 1999 centennial, the Office of Juvenile Justice and Delinquency Prevention profiled case studies of a number of success stories—youths who had been adjudicated for offenses ranging from shoplifting to attempted murder, but who turned their lives around and are now in such occupations as college administrator, journalist, author, professional athlete, district attorney, television broadcaster, corporate tax lawyer, superior court judge, and even retired U.S. senator. The next "Close-up On Corrections" highlights the senator's story.

Vocational programs for at-risk youths are cost effective and provide marketable employment skills. Here YouthBuild offers training in construction to adjudicated youths. Courtesy of YouthBuild.

Close-up On Corrections

SECOND CHANCES—SENATOR ALAN SIMPSON

At the kick-off rally for his 1978 campaign for the U.S. Senate, Alan Simpson spied a familiar face. Simpson waded into the crowd to meet his old friend, J. B. Mosley, and asked him to join his family and campaign workers around the podium. Modestly, he declined the offer. "This is your day," Mosley told the would-be senator. But Simpson could not let the moment pass. After his introductory remarks, he told the crowd there was someone present who had a great influence in his life and had helped him to make it to this moment—his probation officer, J. B. Mosley. The crowd was surprised, but also quite moved. "I tell you, I think I got every vote in that building," Simpson says with a chuckle.

The ex-senator fondly remembers the caring relationship he shared with Mosley during a time when Simpson describes himself as being "on the edge". . . . When he was seventeen, he and four of his friends loaded into his family's old car and drove off to shoot at mailboxes on a dusty rural road. He was a good shot—hitting a number of targets and blasting holes in the mail.

Ultimately, he pled guilty to destroying federal property. Since it was their first known offense, the judge sentenced Simpson and his coconspirators to two years' probation and ordered them to make restitution. For the next two years, J. B. Mosley visited Simpson and his friends at home, in the pool hall, at school, and on the basketball court. Simpson remembers Mosley being a wonderful guy who would sit down with him, asking how he was doing, and keeping tabs on his scholastic work. "He didn't preach . . . he listened". . . .

Many years later, when he went back to practice law, people would see him and say, "I didn't think you had the guts to come back to this town after all you did around here." As Simpson recalls, "I would just smile and say, 'Well, everybody gets a second chance.'"

Source: Adapted from "Second Chances: Giving Kids a Chance to Make a Better Choice," *Juvenile Justice Bulletin*, May, 2000, pp. 19-20.

 # Learning Goals

Do you know:

1. How many youths are being held in custodial confinement?
2. How juvenile custody figures are changing and what demographic groups are most affected?
3. What the greatest predictor is of a male child's likelihood of incarceration?
4. How the populations of public and private juvenile facilities differ?
5. What problems are created by overcrowding in juvenile facilities?

Youths in Custody

The juvenile justice system still in some respects may adhere more to the philosophy of the medical model than that of the justice model. But like their adult counterparts, greater numbers of juveniles are being confined in correctional institutions.

More than 110,000 youth are being held in public and private juvenile facilities throughout the country.[50] This represents a substantial growth in custody rates in recent years, with minorities accounting for much of the increase. In fact, this issue had become such a concern by the mid-1990s that provisions were added to the Juvenile Justice and Delinquency Prevention Act requiring states to determine whether the proportion of minorities in confinement exceeded their proportion in the general population and, if so, to initiate efforts to reduce their overrepresentation.[51]

As shown in Figure 12.7, most of those confined are males, and minorities continue to be overrepresented both in public and in private facilities.[52] Although most are being held for delinquent offenses, some are detained for *nondelinquent* reasons—the most common of which are status offenses and abuse, neglect, or dependency. Many are now also intergenerational offenders. In fact, the single greatest predictor of a male child's likelihood of incarceration is whether his father was incarcerated.[53]

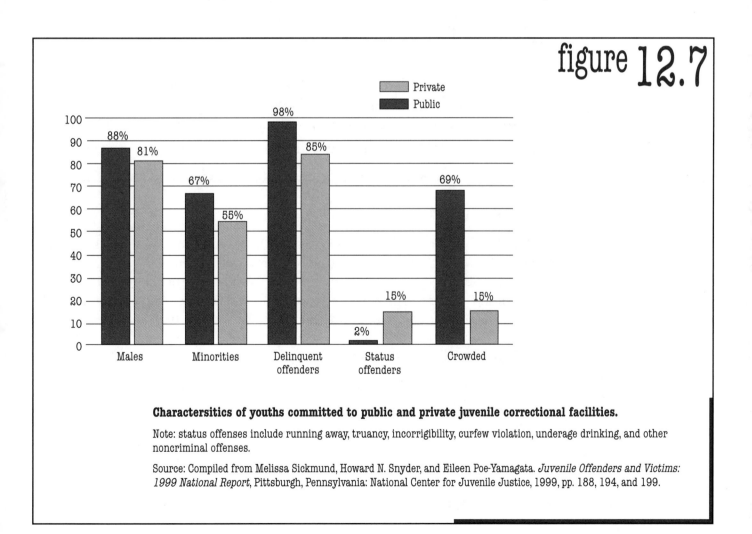

figure 12.7

Characteristics of youths committed to public and private juvenile correctional facilities.

Note: status offenses include running away, truancy, incorrigibility, curfew violation, underage drinking, and other noncriminal offenses.

Source: Compiled from Melissa Sickmund, Howard N. Snyder, and Eileen Poe-Yamagata. *Juvenile Offenders and Victims: 1999 National Report*, Pittsburgh, Pennsylvania: National Center for Juvenile Justice, 1999, pp. 188, 194, and 199.

Perhaps the most striking statistics in the profile of institutionalized youths emerge from the comparison of public and private facility populations in Figure 12.7. It is immediately obvious that males, minorities, and delinquent offenders are more likely to be confined in public than in private facilities. In that regard, research indicates that, in contrast to white youths, minorities are more often placed in public residential facilities with the most-restrictive confinement.[54] Likewise, residents of public facilities are more likely to be confined in crowded conditions (69 percent) than those in private facilities (15 percent).

When juvenile institutions are overcrowded, status offenders may be mingled with delinquents, and overburdened, underpaid staff are expected to meet the needs of those ranging from drug abusers to depressed runaways. Moreover, in crowded facilities, residents spend more time in lockdown, program quality suffers, and staff must focus primarily on safety and security, compromising effective intervention and treatment.[55]

Because youthful offenders are overshadowed by a crowding crisis in adult prisons that has dominated the public agenda, it is difficult to generate concern about their plight. Yet, in terms of the conditions in which they are confined, it is essential to be especially vigilant with juveniles, "because we are dealing with a population that is politically powerless, socially rejected, and easily exploited."[56]

 Learning Goals

Do you know:

1. How the mission and operations of public and private training schools differ?
2. What conditions of confinement are like in juvenile facilities?
3. What types of programs and services are provided in juvenile facilities?
4. Whether juveniles have a right to treatment in correctional institutions?

Juvenile Institutions

Whether public or private, juvenile facilities vary widely—from state and local training schools to detention centers and various types of camps, ranches, and shelters. A national survey assessing the *conditions of confinement* in these diverse facilities reported mixed results. Apparently, juvenile institutions on average may be neither as bad as might be feared nor as good as might be hoped. For example, facilities were assessed as "generally adequate" in several important areas:

- Food, clothing, and hygiene
- Recreation
- Living accommodations

However, "substantial and widespread deficiencies" were found in terms of:

- Crowding
- Security

- Suicide prevention

- Health screenings and appraisal [57]

Just as in the adult system, crowding has become a problem in juvenile confinement. The majority of youths held in long-term confinement are housed in overtaxed facilities, making them more dangerous for both clients and staff.[58] Crowding is also related to security deficiencies, to the extent that it diminishes the ability to "adequately separate predators from victims."[59]

As a result of these findings, it has been concluded that "improving conditions significantly will require broad-scale reforms affecting routine practices in most facilities."[60] That will be a considerable challenge, especially given the varieties of clientele, funding arrangements, and administrative structures that characterize juvenile corrections in both public and privately operated facilities.

Private Facilities

While *private training* schools are supported by contributions, donations, and charitable foundations, they function under state license to assure compliance with minimum standards regarding health, sanitation, residential care, and institutional programming. But because they are private, these schools generally have greater latitude than state schools. Therefore, they can be somewhat selective in terms of the residents admitted so that their resources can be concentrated on specific types of problems.

Although Supreme Court decisions prohibit racial discrimination in the selection process, private institutions do have the flexibility of setting minimum intelligence or educational requirements, prohibiting the admission of serious offenders, or restricting admission to only certain types of cases. As a result of such practices, private facilities confine more non-Hispanic whites, whereas the majority in public facilities are minorities. Private facilities also hold proportionately more females and status offenders, and nonoffenders, (as shown in Figure 12.7). Public facilities do not have the option of specifying what types of cases will be admitted. State training schools must accept everyone committed to them, and, therefore, must be equipped to handle a wider range of behavioral problems.

Accreditation of Juvenile Facilities

As in the adult system, one obvious means for improving the quality of juvenile facilities is through the American Correctional Association's accreditation process. Currently, only about 20 percent of public and private institutions for juveniles are accredited (compared to more than 70 percent of adult facilities),[61] perhaps in part this is because the courts have been less actively involved in litigation related to conditions of confinement for youthful offenders. Yet, accreditation standards address many of the very issues that have plagued juvenile corrections, such as:

- *Administration and management concerns* (personnel training, staff development, records, and information systems)

- *Physical plant operations* (building and safety codes, environmental conditions, programs, and services)

- *Institutional operations* (security and control, safety and emergency procedures, rules, and discipline)
- *Facility services* (food, sanitation, hygiene, and health care)
- *Juvenile services* (classification, academic, vocational, and work programs, library, recreation, religious programming, mail, telephone, visiting, and release) [62]

As we will see in Chapter 15, however, unlike the accreditation of hospitals or schools, accreditation in corrections is a voluntary process for both the adult and juvenile systems. While becoming accredited entails numerous direct and indirect benefits (not the least of which is a reduced potential for litigation), it is also a costly endeavor that generates no additional revenue on successful completion. But whether motivated by the desire for self-improvement or the demands of a lawsuit settlement, accreditation may hold the key to upgrading the conditions, services, and practices of juvenile institutions.

Institutional Operations

Whether public or private, accredited or unaccredited, the operation of juvenile institutions encompasses a wide variety of functions—ranging from security to social services, education, recreation, treatment, food services, maintenance, and administration. In addition to state-mandated education for those of compulsory school attendance age, the counseling, group therapy, and other treatment programs discussed in Chapter 8 are even more important for juveniles. A number of juvenile institutions also operate vocational training programs. This is particularly beneficial for those who are already high school dropouts and need marketable employment skills.

In practice, a combination of education, work, and discipline represents the typical approach of many state training schools, perhaps reflecting their reform school heritage. Unlike adults, however, the courts have recognized that juveniles committed involuntarily for rehabilitative purposes have a statutory and constitutional right to treatment.[63]

> In various jurisdictions, the courts have found that if a juvenile is confined for the purpose of care and rehabilitation, that juvenile must receive the needed psychiatric or other care, and cannot simply be confined with no adequate services provided. These cases have concentrated primarily on status offenders and neglected children, and the courts have required the states to provide the treatment or move the child to a less confining setting. This trend toward the protection of youths who are incarcerated rests on the belief that juvenile correctional programs are primarily rehabilitative and not punitive.[64]

Custodial Treatment

Precisely what is meant by "treatment" is, of course, another issue entirely. We already have seen in Chapter 8 that a wide variety of programs and activities have been loosely defined as treatment in adult prisons and jails.

Moreover, despite the fact that rehabilitation is supposedly the major emphasis of the juvenile justice system, "juvenile corrections professionals speak sparingly these days about correcting the behavior of young offenders and much more about education, skill training, social survival skills, community service and self-discipline. The word 'rehabilitation' is used less and less, and the word 'treatment' is almost extinct." [65]

Some might characterize such trends as reflecting a new approach that is more functional—equipping residents with the social accountability and personal skills that they lack. But to others, they imply an enduring custodial orientation—emphasizing punishment, discipline, and control. Support for the latter view is found in evaluations of juvenile correctional facilities, which reveal "a continuing gap between the rhetoric of rehabilitation and its punitive reality." [66]

 # Learning Goals

Do you know:

1. What is meant by the "adultification" of the juvenile justice system?
2. What factors are taken into account in deciding whether to transfer a juvenile to adult court?
3. How juveniles are dealt with in adult court?

Juveniles in Adult Court

As the public has become increasingly concerned about the growing involvement of teenagers in violent crime, responses have shifted away from treatment toward a more punitive approach. Although proportionately few in number, these hardcore offenders make up a disproportionate share of juvenile crime. Many of them already have been processed through juvenile court for earlier offenses, often at quite young ages, and continue their criminal patterns as adults. In fact, as shown in Figure 12.8, the younger the child was on first being referred to juvenile court, the more likely he or she is to be involved in a violent offense before turning eighteen.

In recent years, public policy has demanded that experienced juvenile offenders, like adult criminals, be held responsible for their actions and pay their "just deserts." While the juvenile justice system has not dismantled the medical model to the same extent as in the adult system, there is little doubt that the justice model has had an impact here as well. Moreover, the extension of due process rights to juveniles has placed youths on a more equal footing with adults in the legal system, generating the implicit assumption that "since children are to be accorded the same rights as adults, then children should be ready to assume adult responsibilities and accept adult-type punishments for their crimes." [67]

An obvious example of what has been termed the "adultification" of the juvenile justice system[68] is the growing trend toward transferring juveniles accused of serious offenses to adult court. In some cases, this is accomplished by discretionary waiver, through which the juvenile court relinquishes its jurisdiction. But a number of states now legislatively exclude certain violent

figure **12.8**

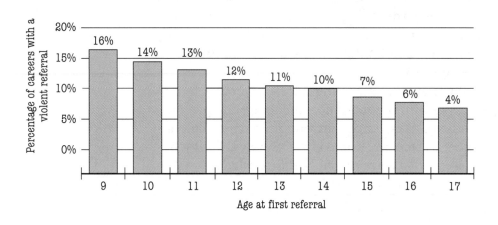

Likelihood of becoming a violent offender relates to age at first referral to the juvenile court.

Source: Melissa Sickmund. "Juveniles in Court," *Juvenile Offenders and Victims: National Report Series*, Washington, DC: Office of Juvenile Justice and Delinquency Prevention, June 2003, p. 29.

offenses from being heard in juvenile court. In others, transfer to adult court is mandated when a young offender already has been adjudicated a specified number of times in juvenile court or has had a prior conviction in adult court. In cases where the waiver is a discretionary decision, the factors generally taken into account include the juvenile's age, seriousness of the offense, previous court history, and considerations related to both rehabilitative prospects and public protection.[69]

The percentage of cases being transferred to criminal courts is still a very small proportion (less than 1 percent) of the total juvenile court workload.[70] But transfers for violent personal offenses have been increasing—partly as a result of judicial waiver, and partly as a result of the fact that more serious cases are being filed directly in criminal court under statutory exclusion legislation.[71]

It may be surprising to those advocating a "tougher" stance against juvenile crime that transferring young offenders to the criminal justice system does not notably increase the severity of sanctions that they are likely to receive, nor does it reduce recidivism:[72]

> While transfer may increase the length of confinement for some of the most serious offenders, the majority of transferred juveniles receive sentences that are comparable to sanctions already available in the juvenile justice system. More importantly, there is no evidence that young offenders handled in criminal court are less likely to recidivate than those remaining in juvenile court.[73]

In fact, research indicates that transferred youths are more likely to reoffend and to reoffend earlier than those who were not transferred.[74] Moreover, as illustrated in the above "Close-up On Corrections," there is wide variation in terms of how such serious juvenile cases are being handled across the country. While the minimum age varies, there are three states (Indiana, South

Close-up On Corrections

Dakota, and Vermont) that "allow the certification [to adult court] of a juvenile as young as ten years old."[75]

 # Learning Goals

Do you know:
1. What is meant by "blended sentencing"?
2. The differences between straight, graduated, and segregated incarceration?
3. The characteristics of youthful offenders in adult prisons?
4. What provisions have been recommended for underage inmates housed in adult prisons?

Juveniles in Adult Prisons

When offenders under the age of eighteen are sentenced in adult court, where will their time be served? The answer depends on where they live. Some states are part of a growing trend toward "*blended sentencing*" options that are explained in Figure 12.9. For those who are sentenced to prison, states, likewise, have varying correctional procedures. Housing options for underage inmates include straight adult incarceration, graduated incarceration, and segregated incarceration, as described in the upcoming "Close-up On Corrections."

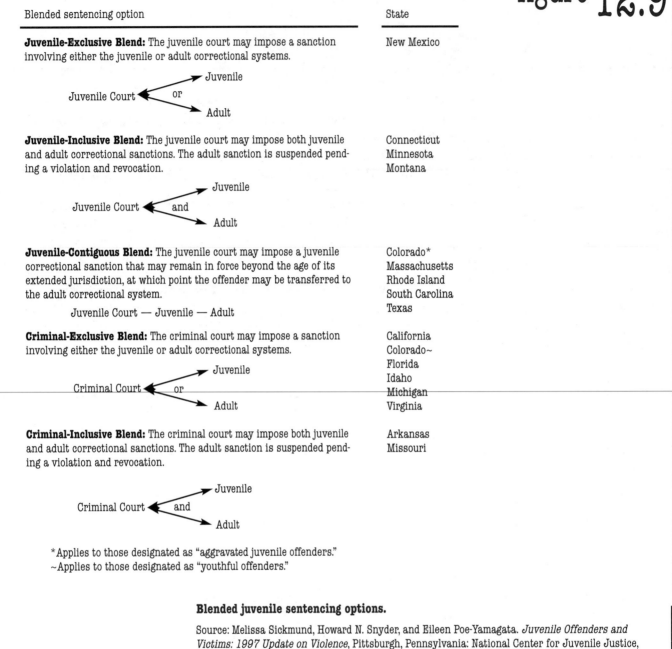

figure 12.9

Blended sentencing option | State

Juvenile-Exclusive Blend: The juvenile court may impose a sanction involving either the juvenile or adult correctional systems.

New Mexico

Juvenile Court ← or → Juvenile / Adult

Juvenile-Inclusive Blend: The juvenile court may impose both juvenile and adult correctional sanctions. The adult sanction is suspended pending a violation and revocation.

Connecticut
Minnesota
Montana

Juvenile Court ← and → Juvenile / Adult

Juvenile-Contiguous Blend: The juvenile court may impose a juvenile correctional sanction that may remain in force beyond the age of its extended jurisdiction, at which point the offender may be transferred to the adult correctional system.

Colorado*
Massachusetts
Rhode Island
South Carolina
Texas

Juvenile Court — Juvenile — Adult

Criminal-Exclusive Blend: The criminal court may impose a sanction involving either the juvenile or adult correctional systems.

California
Colorado~
Florida
Idaho
Michigan
Virginia

Criminal Court ← or → Juvenile / Adult

Criminal-Inclusive Blend: The criminal court may impose both juvenile and adult correctional sanctions. The adult sanction is suspended pending a violation and revocation.

Arkansas
Missouri

Criminal Court ← and → Juvenile / Adult

*Applies to those designated as "aggravated juvenile offenders."
~Applies to those designated as "youthful offenders."

Blended juvenile sentencing options.

Source: Melissa Sickmund, Howard N. Snyder, and Eileen Poe-Yamagata. *Juvenile Offenders and Victims: 1997 Update on Violence*, Pittsburgh, Pennsylvania: National Center for Juvenile Justice, 1997, p. 32, adapted from P. Torbert et al. *State Responses to Serious and Violent Juvenile Crime*, Washington, DC: Office of Juvenile Justice and Delinquency Prevention, 1996.

Those under the age of eighteen who are currently in adult prisons are primarily minority (73 percent) males (92 percent) who are sentenced for a violent crime (69 percent).[76] However, over one-quarter (26 percent) are serving time for either property or drug-related offenses. Regardless of their offense, as shown in Figure 12.10, their numbers have been increasing substantially over the past decade. On average, the increase in new admissions for underage inmates is greater than for offenders of all ages entering prison.[77]

Close-up On Corrections

New Boys on the Block—Juveniles in Adult Prisons

States have differing correctional responses available for persons under eighteen who are sentenced to prison:

- *Straight adult incarceration* enables underage inmates in correctional facilities to be confined with other offenders, with little differentiation in programming. Most states allow straight adult incarceration, although some require separate housing for those under eighteen.

- *Graduated incarceration* is employed in twelve states (Delaware, Georgia, Maryland, Missouri, North Dakota, Ohio, Oregon, Tennessee, Texas, Utah, Washington, and West Virginia). Inmates under eighteen begin their sentences in a juvenile facility until they reach a certain age (usually eighteen). The offender then either can be released or transferred to an adult facility to serve the remainder of the sentence.

- *Segregated incarceration* assigns certain young offenders to specific facilities based on their age and programming needs. Eight states employ this approach (California, Colorado, Florida, Kentucky, New Mexico, New York, South Carolina, and Wisconsin). In some locations, these programs include specialized education, vocational training, and substance abuse treatment.

Source: Adapted from Kevin J. Strom, "Profile of State Prisoners under Age 18, 1985-97," *Bureau of Justice Statistics: Special Report*, February 2000, p. 10.

Because they still represent less than one-half of 1 percent of the state prison population, not much attention has been directed toward targeting programs for young inmates. In fact, they often are forgotten socially and overlooked operationally. In comparison to adult prisoners, they receive fewer visits, and their influx into state prisons "has resulted in few changes in policy or procedures, other than those mandated by law." [78]

Whether or not lack of programming is part of the explanation, young inmates also tend to be involved in more disciplinary incidents than their adult counterparts. In addition, they are five times more likely to be sexually assaulted and twice as likely to be beaten in prison than in a juvenile facility.[79] Such findings have prompted the American Correctional Association to recommend that adult institutions confining youthful offenders should provide for:

- Separate housing

- High school education

- Life management skills

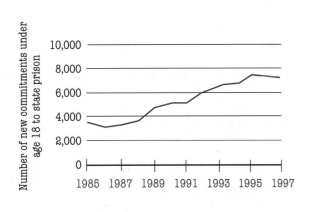

figure 12.10

Growth in state prison commitments of offenders under the age of eighteen.

Source: Kevin J. Strom. "Profile of State Prisoners under Age 18, 1985-97," *Bureau of Justice Statistics: Special Report*, February 2000, p. 3.

- Mandatory counseling and social skills training in such areas as anger management, drug/alcohol guidance, AIDS instruction, and parenting
- An individualized schedule that extends from wake-up to lights-out[80]

Likewise, a national study calls for developing specialized institutional programs for youthful offenders, ensuring that prison classification instruments are valid for juveniles, and enhancing the expertise of security staff in managing this younger, more energetic, and more impulsive prison population.[81] In the rush toward "adultification" of juvenile justice, what has perhaps been overlooked is the fact that changing offenders' legal status does not change their biological or psychological condition. As one prison staff member said of underage prison inmates, "These are still kids!" [82]

 ## Learning Goals

Do you know:

1. What impact institutions have on juvenile residents?
2. Why the negative effects of incarceration are even greater for children than for adults?

Effects of Confinement

Regardless of what types of treatment programs are available or how nonpunitive the facility's orientation is, confinement tends to produce significant negative effects for youth. Even among juvenile facilities, where efforts may be made to deemphasize the institutional atmosphere, training schools are, in fact, *custodial environments*. They are not rehabilitative centers. They are not educational facilities. They are, first and foremost, custodial institutions—where residents are subject to the authority of highly regulated living conditions.

In addition to the negative influence of custodial constraints, training schools have been cited as breeding grounds for abnormal behavior patterns ranging from homosexuality to theft. In this environment are concentrated varieties of delinquents who see life as socially unjust in the first place. Then, these negative values are reinforced by their peers in a setting that too often lacks adequate responses to their problems. Association with other delinquents can intensify hostility. Separation from familiar environments, family members, and other social support promotes feelings of abandonment. Many have been rejected by their home, their school, and now, by their community as well. Such feelings of rejection can lower self-esteem, further underscoring a sense of failure.

Especially for first-time or status offenders, interaction with the institutional population itself can reinforce negative values. And just as in adult prisons, the weak are preyed on by the strong. In fact, even those serving brief stays in short-term detention are vulnerable to abuse: "The weaker juvenile who is sentenced to detention may be subject to violent acts, victimized by extortion, and emotionally scarred. These youths need treatment and services, not a vindictive punishment."[83]

Virtually everyone in confinement is subject to the negative impact of institutionalization discussed in Chapter 10 with regard to adult prisoners—from lack of privacy to resentment of authority. In contrast to adults, however, the intensity of that impact can be considerably greater for children, who are confined in the midst of their emotional and physical development. Even if the programs offered in such settings were implemented as originally intended, they would be hard-pressed to overcome the combined detrimental effects of the repressive institutional atmosphere and the preexisting problems of the clients themselves. Thus, it is not surprising that reports summarizing numerous individual studies "generally come to negative conclusions about the effectiveness of institutional interventions."[84]

 # Learning Goals

Do you know:
1. What correctional boot camps are designed to achieve?
2. The advantages as well as the drawbacks of correctional boot camps?

Shock Incarceration Programs

Because lack of self-discipline and disrespect for authority are common among youthful offenders, a number of states have experimented with an environment structured around a military-style *boot camp*. Also known as "shock incarceration," such programs are generally reserved for older adolescents and young adults, some of whom otherwise would be facing their first term in prison or jail. Like their military counterparts, correctional boot camps emphasize strenuous physical training and strict discipline.

Boot camps have enjoyed considerable emotional appeal. Their supporters range from veterans nostalgically recalling their own military training to policymakers increasingly frustrated by the inability to control youthful offenders. But extensive emotional support is not necessarily based on effective experiential

Pride and discipline are primary products of correctional boot camps. Courtesy of the Broward County (Florida) Sheriff's Office.

outcomes. In fact, "evidence has mounted indicating that boot camps are not the quick-fix, ready-made solution that early supporters had envisioned." [85]

Despite their widespread popularity, evaluation research has not given boot camps high marks. To the contrary, a multisite evaluation of eight programs concluded that their impact on recidivism is "at best negligible." [86] A General Accounting Office review of research findings similarly reported that "graduates have only marginally lower recidivism rates," and "any differences tend to diminish over time." [87] Moreover, another multisite assessment found that reoffending youths from the boot camps actually committed new offenses more quickly than comparison groups,[88] and one official noted that they are not only ineffective, but also potentially harmful to some youths.[89] Even when recidivism rates have been lower, the results appear to be a product of either the types of offenders selected or the intensive supervision they received afterward.[90]

While the reasons for such disappointing results are varied, concerns have been expressed that boot camps do not address long-term solutions to underlying problems.[91] As one therapist describes it, "You can scream at them and have them do as many push-ups as you want, but you are not getting at the pathology [of] their lack of values." [92]

Questions also have been raised about the relationship of boot camps to modern military training. Basic training for new recruits in the military has changed over time, and correctional boot camps may resemble an earlier model that the military has abandoned in its effort to improve an image that sometimes has been tarnished by arbitrary demands and degrading treatment.[93]

Moreover, the discipline instilled in boot camps is only one component of what youthful offenders need to make long-term changes in their behavior on release. In that regard, one boot camp director has noted:

> Within 90 to 120 days, the length of most boot camp programs, we cannot correct all of these young offenders' problems. Nor can we provide them with all the educational and vocational skills they have

missed. . . . Boot camps were never intended to do all that. Consider military boot camps. They are not intended to make a young person into a fully functional soldier. Rather, they provide a foundation of discipline, responsibility and self-esteem [which] the military can build on during the advanced training that follows. Correctional boot camps are designed to do much the same thing. . . . Boot camps are a viable alternative . . . if they are accompanied by appropriate aftercare.[94]

In that regard, it is noteworthy that where graduates did return to confinement at lower rates, the programs were longer, strongly focused on treatment, and followed by postrelease services.[95] Critics suggest that nostalgic legislators recalling their own military service forgot that boot camp was followed by two years in the military with advanced skill-based training, and when they were released, veterans returned to communities where they were welcomed and supported.[96] In contrast, most correctional boot camp graduates return to impoverished communities without supportive aftercare. Thus, any changes that might occur are unlikely to survive the "test of the streets" in the reality of a world "where drill instructors are replaced by drug dealers; . . . where secure confinement is replaced by self-control; . . . where marching in straight lines is replaced by hanging on street corners." [97]

 # Learning Goals

Do you know:
1. What is meant by "aftercare" in the juvenile justice system?
2. Why aftercare is often a low priority?

Juvenile Aftercare

As the critics of boot camps note, it is not just what occurs within confinement that shapes behavior, but equally important, what follow-up services are provided on release. In adult terms, this is what is referred to as "parole" or "mandatory supervised release." In the juvenile justice system, it is called *aftercare*. As the name implies, it is intended to provide continuing care, transitional services, and employment assistance for youths released from a correctional facility.

Unfortunately, aftercare is the function of an already overburdened juvenile justice system. With resources focused on the immediate needs of new cases and younger clients coming before the court, it is a luxury to divert attention to existing cases lingering in the system. Moreover, by the time they are released, some are close to or already have exceeded the age of majority. Thus, any further offenses they commit will be under the jurisdiction of the criminal justice system.

Aftercare is not provided in all jurisdictions, and when available, it is often plagued with administrative and operational difficulties. Additionally, like parole in the adult system, it can be so heavily focused on surveillance that

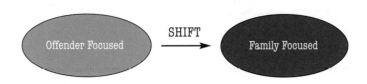

figure 12.11

- Creating a therapeutic alliance with the family
- Reducing negativity and blaming in the family
- Creating new solutions for the family
- Motivating families to participate with their child in treatment
- Helping staff understand the youth's behavior in a family-systems context

Improving the reintegration of youthful offenders through a family-focused approach.

Source: Cheryl Stephani. "Systems Change and Shrinking Budgets: Improving a Juvenile Justice System Despite Declining Resources," *Corrections Today*, February 2004, p. 41.

staff lose sight of its supportive, reintegrative role. To improve the effectiveness of aftercare, a number of jurisdictions are shifting from an exclusive focus on the offender to a more comprehensive focus on the entire family context, as illustrated in Figure 12.11. But even the most progressive, sensitive, holistic, and well-endowed aftercare program cannot erase the effects of confinement. In the end, the negative impact of incarceration is no less severe merely because the institution is called a "training school" or "detention center" rather than a prison or jail.

 ## Learning Goals

Do you know:

1. Why the labeling effects of the juvenile justice system are not limited to those who are incarcerated?
2. What a noninterventionist strategy is?

Alternative Approaches

The detrimental effects of contact with the juvenile justice system are not limited to those who are institutionalized. Simply being officially processed through the system labels the child as a "juvenile delinquent." Under the original philosophy of the juvenile court, of course, this was not supposed to happen. One of the fundamental reasons for establishing a separate juvenile justice system was precisely to *avoid the stigma* that inevitably accompanies involvement in the criminal justice system.

As we saw earlier, the due process movement called attention to the fact that young offenders were not receiving the solicitous care that had been the original philosophy of the juvenile court. To the contrary, it was becoming apparent that for many, formal processing often produces more harm than good. Willingness to make referrals to this benevolent protector of the child's welfare might be greater if, indeed, such action would truly be nonstigmatizing, rehabilitative, and as paternalistic as originally envisioned. That not being the case, there are many who advocate *noninterventionist* strategies—keeping youth out of the system whenever possible, or at least minimizing the extent of penetration into the system. Reducing the court's intrusion into the lives of children has been promoted by efforts directed toward *diversion, decriminalization,* and *deinstitutionalization.*

 # Learning Goals

Do you know:

1. What functions juvenile assessment centers perform?
2. What is meant by the "least restrictive means" of dealing with juvenile offenders?
3. What legal issues are raised by diversion?

Diversion

One of the obvious ways to avoid the negative impact of being processed in the juvenile justice system is to divert troubled children out of it through referral to a nonjudicial agency better equipped to handle their problems. *Diversion* is the disposition of a case without formal adjudication, on condition that the youth fulfill an obligation, such as obtaining counseling.

Today, this concept is seen in the juvenile assessment centers that have been established in a number of cities. But there is evidence that diversion programs often "widen the net" of social control—"drawing clients from youths who previously would have had their cases dismissed or would not even have been referred." [98] Moreover, such strategies traditionally have been *supplements* to the juvenile justice system not *substitutes* for it.[99] Thus "diversion" itself has two meanings: diversion *from* something or diversion *to* something. Simply diverting children from court to some other juvenile justice-affiliated program or service does not remove them from the system. It only directs them into another part of it.

The concept underlying diversion is to employ the *least-restrictive means* of dealing with the case that is in keeping with the welfare of the child and the protection of the community. But in many communities, the range of services available is still quite limited—and weighted heavier on the side of "most" rather than "least"-restrictive alternatives.

Even where energetic attempts have been made to expand community treatment opportunities, invoking diversion raises the question of what legal rights the juvenile is entitled to when informal options are used. Informal adjustment of cases may remove the stigma of court adjudication and the long-lasting negative impact it can produce. At the same time, it can subject the youth to certain restrictions (for example, informal probation) or treatment requirements in the absence of due-process protections that would accompany formal hearings.

On the other hand, some maintain that providing alternative opportunities represents the original mission of serving the child's best interests. Again, as with the juvenile justice system in general, the issue comes down to whether youths are gaining more than they are losing.

✹ Learning Goals

Do you know:

1. What is meant by decriminalization?
2. What arguments can be made for eliminating the court's jurisdiction over status offenders?

Decriminalization

One way to minimize the intrusion of the juvenile justice system would be to restrict the wide range of behaviors over which the court has jurisdiction. Earlier, it was mentioned that one of the original justifications for a separate juvenile court was based on identifying "predelinquent" children to address their difficulties before these preliminary tendencies escalate into more serious violations. That, however, was when considerable optimism still prevailed that official intervention would be more beneficial than harmful. To the contrary, it has been suggested that court intervention actually may increase rather than reduce the future likelihood of engaging in serious criminal activity. As it became increasingly apparent that faith in good intentions was not justified in reality, many began to question whether "borderline" delinquent behavior, such as status offenses, actually should be dealt with in the juvenile justice system at all.

As a result, a number of states have created separate legal categories for status offenders (for example, Children in Need of Supervision—CHINS), designating that such children are in greater need of supervision than prosecution. But using different terms to classify them does not necessarily translate into substantial differences with regard to how they are treated. Moreover, simply attaching new labels to their behavior may be no less stigmatizing.

To address these problems, the National Council on Crime and Delinquency called for complete elimination of court jurisdiction over status offenders some thirty years ago, based on the belief that community-based services are more beneficial than court-mandated supervision in addressing their needs.[100] This is what is known as *decriminalization*—removing noncriminal behaviors (in other words, status offenses) from juvenile court jurisdiction. Decriminalization is based on the belief that there is a need to confine the boundaries of official authority more closely, limiting the system's regulation of moral conduct and minor misbehavior.

Further justification of decriminalization is cited by those who note that eliminating status offenses from juvenile court can reduce racial and economic disparity within the justice system. This does not necessarily mean that the system deliberately discriminates against the poor or minorities. But such groups have fewer options and resources available to them. They are less likely to be able to get decent jobs, afford private treatment, or take advantage of nonjudicial alternatives. As a result, their unaddressed problems are more likely to come to official attention.

Some maintain that in the absence of other choices, something is better than nothing. This argument is based on the premise that if no one else is willing or able to fulfill the needs of status offenders, the juvenile court is obliged to do so. But to others, "doing nothing"—at least judicially—may not be such a bad idea, as one appellate court judge states in no uncertain terms:

> The situation is truly ironic. The argument for retaining beyond-control and truancy jurisdiction is that juvenile courts have to act in such cases because "if we don't act, no one else will." I submit that precisely the opposite is the case: *because* you act, no one else does. Schools and public agencies refer their problem cases to you because you have jurisdiction, because you exercise it, and because you hold out promises that you can provide solutions.[101]

 # Learning Goals

Do you know:

1. What role the Juvenile Justice and Delinquency Prevention Act has played in the deinstitutionalization of status offenders?
2. How much it costs to house a youngster for a year in a juvenile facility?
3. Why Massachusetts closed its large juvenile training schools in the early1970s and whether the public was endangered as a result?
4. What have been some of the unintended consequences of deinstitutionalization?

Deinstitutionalization

Reformers have not been extremely successful in diverting status offenders from the system or decriminalizing their behaviors. But perhaps there is greater hope that they at least can be provided with more appropriate forms of treatment than custodial institutions. Just as decriminalization sought to remove less serious cases from the juvenile court, *deinstitutionalization* (or "decarceration") is directed toward removing low-risk, noncriminal offenders from secure confinement, providing services through community-based resources.

In Chapter 9, we saw how negatively the institutional environment affects adult prisoners. Earlier in this chapter, we saw that these results can be even more devastating for those who are still in their developmental years. In recognition of such disadvantages, the National Advisory Commission on Criminal Justice Standards and Goals recommended that states not only "refrain from building any more state institutions for juveniles" but also "phase-out present institutions over a five-year period."[102] But it was not until passage of the Juvenile Justice and Delinquency Prevention Act of 1974 that there was any real motivation for states to deinstitutionalize.

Like the removal of juveniles from adult jails, federal juvenile justice funding has been used as an incentive to promote the removal of status offenders from secure confinement. Compliance with the act's mandates is monitored annually in all states participating in Juvenile Justice and Delinquency Prevention funding programs, and nearly all are now in compliance fully or with minimal exceptions.[103]

Alternatives to Institutions

However, it is one thing to remove status offenders from secure confinement, and quite another to identify appropriate community-based alternatives for them. Traditional options on the "continuum of care" have included home detention, after-school reporting, restitution, shelter care, and various forms of community-based residential and nonresidential programs.[104] More recently, a number of nontraditional options have emerged—ranging from wilderness excursions to wagon train expeditions and maritime adventures. Through teamwork under difficult situations, such unique experiences are designed to build trust, confidence, and self-esteem.

Just as diversion attempts to provide the *least-restrictive means* of processing a case, deinstitutionalization attempts to offer the *least-restrictive disposition*. This concept recognizes that there is still considerable support for the potential deterrent effect of early intervention, but tries to assure that official intervention is as *nonpunitive* as possible. In fact, it was not actually the detrimental effects of incarceration that prompted Congress to pass the 1974 juvenile justice legislation, but rather, "the argument that deprivation of liberty for persons who have not violated the criminal code is unjust and unwarranted."[105]

Considering the fact that housing *one resident* for a full year in a juvenile facility costs more than $66,817,[106] it is apparent that such sizable expenditures could be directed more productively elsewhere. For that amount of money, a youth could attend any of the most prestigious private schools in the country. And that is only the tip of the iceberg. As shown in the "invoice" featured in Figure 12.12, when everything ranging from victim costs to justice system expenditures, lost productivity, and school dropout costs are totaled, society can end up paying between two and three million dollars for every lost child.

But it is difficult for preventive efforts and incarceration options to co-exist in a society that continues to place so much emphasis on institutional confinement. As recently as the year 2000, "excessive reliance on incarceration" was cited by the Office of Juvenile Justice and Delinquency Prevention as one of the pervasive problems in the current juvenile justice system, "because inadequate resources have been allocated to the development of effective community-based services."[107] Studies, likewise, have reported that juvenile facilities are housing youths who pose no significant threat to community safety and who could be managed as effectively in less-restrictive and less-costly settings.[108] As yet another analysis echoed, "when placement in a secure facility is a jurisdiction's primary—or only—treatment option, it becomes an expensive catchall."[109]

This dilemma was recognized in Massachusetts when, in the early 1970s, the state closed virtually all of its large secure juvenile correctional institutions. Although reserving secure placements in small treatment centers for a relatively

figure 12.12

Invoice

To: **American public**
For: **One lost youth**

Description	Cost
Crime:	
Juvenile career (4 years @ 1-4 crimes/year)	
Victim costs	$62,000-$250,000
Criminal justice costs	$21,000-$84,000
Adult career (6 years @10.6 crimes/year)	
Victim costs	$1,000,000
Criminal justice costs	$335,000
Offender productivity loss	$64,000
Total crime cost	**$1.5-$1.8 million**
Present value*	**$1.3-$1.5 million**
Drug Abuse:	
Resources devoted to drug market	$84,000-$168,000
Reduced productivity loss	$27,600
Drug treatment costs	$10,200
Medical treatment of drug-related illnesses	$11,000
Premature death	$31,800-$223,000
Criminal justice costs associated with drug crimes	$40,500
Total drug abuse cost	**$200,000-$480,000**
Present value*	**$150,000-$360,000**
Costs imposed by high school dropout:	
Lost wage productivity	$300,000
Fringe benefits	$75,000
Nonmarket losses	$95,000-$375,000
Total dropout cost	**$470,000-$750,000**
Present value*	**$243,000-$388,000**
Total loss	**$2.2-$3.0 million**
Present value*	**$1.7-$2.3 million**

*Present value is the amount of money that would need to be invested today to cover the future costs of the youth's behavior.

The costs of one youth leaving high school for a life of crime and drug abuse.

Source: Howard N. Snyder and Melissa Sickmund. *Juvenile Offenders and Victims: 1999 National Report,* Washington, DC: Office of Juvenile Justice and Delinquency Prevention, September 1999, p. 82.

few chronic, violent offenders, the vast majority of the state's juvenile population was deinstitutionalized. By 1975, only 10 percent of those not in aftercare were in secure settings. The remainder were primarily in nonresidential programs, group care, or foster care.[110] Clearly, this change placed young offenders in closer contact with the community. Perhaps more significantly, doing so *did not appear to create any increased danger to the public.* The state's network of community-based alternatives featured intensive supervision and surveillance, and despite concerns to the contrary, "the Massachusetts youth correction reforms did not unleash a juvenile crime wave. In 1985, Massachusetts ranked forty-sixth among the fifty states with respect to their rate of serious juvenile crime. . . . [F]or those who did commit new offenses, there was a tendency to commit less serious crimes. . . . The overall rates of recidivism . . . were as low or lower than any other state."[111]

Unintended Consequences

Although the Massachusetts experiment with deinstitutionalization has influenced other states, it has neither led to widespread implementation nor fully achieved its goals. All decarceration efforts are not equally successful, and overall, findings have been mixed.

Some observers are concerned that, however praiseworthy in theory, deinstitutionalization has produced unintended side effects. As it has become more difficult to institutionalize status offenders in training schools, there is some evidence that parents have become more likely to coerce children into such alternatives as psychiatric hospitalization—in which case "youngsters are merely being shunted to different forms of institutional placement."[112]

Others assert that status offenders are "being cast to the urban streets, where they are exploited and victimized," as reflected in the findings of a task force, which concluded that deinstitutionalization policies were directly contributing to the growing numbers of missing children.[113] From the opposite perspective, still others have found evidence of net-widening and "relabeling" (which refers to cases that previously might have been treated as status offenders being "relabeled" as minor delinquencies).[114]

As with the juvenile justice system in general, it appears that even the best intentions can produce consequences that are contrary to original ambitions. In that regard, "it must be said that at best we have been inefficient, and at worst we have been inhumane, and at all times we have been confused."[115]

Summary

Social policies related to our treatment of children have emerged from a bleak history marked by harsh conditions. By the twentieth century, industrialization, immigration, and urbanization had combined to create problems of growing magnitude in American cities. The resulting poverty, overcrowding, unemployment, and crime obviously did not provide the best environment for raising children. Rather than addressing these underlying conditions, social reform was directed toward intervening in the lives of children to "rescue" them from the contaminating influences of urban life.

Thus, the child-saving movement created the impetus for establishing the first separate juvenile court in 1899, based on the concept of *parens patriae*, which enabled the state to intervene in the place of parents on behalf of the welfare of the child. Serving the "best interests" of youths required that procedures be kept informal and flexible, since the court was designed to be an advocate rather than an adversary. The court's mission included early identification of predelinquent behavior, personalized diagnosis, and prescription of rehabilitative treatment. To further avoid the stigma of criminal processing, it relied on civil procedures and created a vocabulary of tranquilizing terms to distinguish the juvenile justice system from its adult counterpart.

But some sixty years later, serious questions were raised about the court's fulfillment of its commitment to protect rather than punish. Given concerns that juveniles were sacrificing their rights in the name of rehabilitation (and that their "rehabilitation" often amounted to little more than incarceration), the due-process movement sought to reduce the system's power and intrusiveness. During this period, a number of landmark Supreme Court decisions extended due process rights to which juveniles are entitled. These rulings, however, have not fully transformed proceedings into the adversarial nature of the criminal justice system. There is still hope that, ideally, the juvenile court can guarantee legal rights through procedural safeguards without losing its personalized approach.

That potential is difficult to achieve, however, in a system which is empowered to take action in response to wide-ranging behaviors, from delinquent acts to status offenses. As a result, juvenile courts have been accused of being too punitive in their handling of minor cases, while at the same time being too lenient with serious delinquents. With increasing public concern focusing on chronic juvenile offenders engaged in violent crime, many high-risk cases are being transferred to adult court. Moreover, the juvenile court is now coming closer to resembling the justice model in terms of its dispositional practices. As a result, juvenile correctional facilities are witnessing a substantial growth in custody rates, particularly among minorities.

Juvenile institutions include both public and privately operated training schools. Public facilities must accept anyone committed to them, whereas private schools can be more selective, focusing on specific programs for particular types of offenders. If youths are confined for the express purpose of getting treatment, the courts have recognized their legal right to receive it. Unlike adult prisons, the focus of juvenile corrections is still assumed to be primarily rehabilitative rather than punitive. That does not, however, mean that the effects of confinement are not as detrimental for juveniles. Quite the contrary, the negative impact can be even greater for those who are confined in the midst of their emotional and physical development. Moreover, as increasing numbers of serious juvenile offenders are transferred to criminal courts, the adult correctional system is beginning to see considerably more youthful offenders confined in its facilities.

Because official intrusion into the lives of children appears to do more harm than good in many cases, there are those who advocate noninterventionist strategies. Supporters of this approach would keep youths out of the system whenever possible, or at least minimize the extent of their penetration into it. One way to do so is by diverting cases informally into nonjudicial community-based programs and services. Another is to decriminalize status offenses so that juvenile courts do not have jurisdiction over noncriminal conduct. Yet another alternative is to avoid institutionalizing status offenders. All of these approaches involve using the least-restrictive means of dealing with minor indiscretions. But they depend on community resources which are not always available and the use of which can create unanticipated negative consequences.

We undoubtedly have come a long way since the time when the concept of childhood simply did not exist. Yet, in many respects, we still have a long way to go toward creating a juvenile justice system that is characterized as much by concern for kids as contempt for criminals. First, of course, we must distinguish between the two.

Endnotes

1. President's Commission on Law Enforcement and Administration of Justice, *Task Force Report: Juvenile Delinquency and Youth Crime*, Washington, D.C.: U.S. Government Printing Office, 1967, p. 7.

2. *See*, for example, Steven L. Schlossman, *Love and the American Delinquent*, Chicago: University of Chicago Press, 1977, pp. 113-123.

3. Anthony M. Platt, *The Child Savers: The Invention of Delinquency*, Chicago: University of Chicago Press, 1969, pp. 36-43.

4. *Ibid.*

5. Helen Rankin Jeter, *The Chicago Juvenile Court*, Washington, D.C.: U.S. Government Printing Office, 1922, p. 5.

6. In fact, it has been argued that the act itself represented no significant innovations. *See* Sanford J. Fox, "Juvenile Justice Reform: An Historical Perspective," *Stanford Law Review*, Vol. 22, June 1970, p. 1187.

7. Anthony M. Platt, "The Rise of the Child-Saving Movement," in Paul Lerman, ed., *Delinquency and Social Policy*, New York: Praeger, 1970, p. 18.

8. Julian Mack, "The Juvenile Court," *Harvard Law Review*, Vol. 23, 1909, p. 104.

9. Lawrence Schultz, "The Cycle of Juvenile Court History," *Crime and Delinquency*, Vol. 19, No. 4, October 1973, p. 460.

10. Platt, p. 107, quoting from the Illinois Board of Public Charities, *Sixth Biennial Reports*, Springfield, Illinois: H.W Rokker,1880, p. 104.

11. Mack, "The Juvenile Court," p. 104.

12. Bernard Flexner, Reuben Oppenheimer, and Katharine F. Lenroot, *The Child, the Family, and the Court: A Study of the Administration of Justice in the Field of Domestic Relations*, Washington, D.C.: U.S. Government Printing Office, 1939, p. 66, citing the Children's Bureau of the U.S. Department of Labor.

13. National Commission on Criminal Justice Standards and Goals, *Courts*, Washington, D.C.: U.S. Government Printing Office, 1973, p. 289.

14. *Kent v. United States*, 383 U.S. 541, 86 S. Ct. 1045,16 L.Ed.2d 84 (1966).

15. Barry Krisberg, "The Evolution of the Juvenile Justice System," in John J. Sullivan and Joseph L. Victor, *Criminal Justice 92/93*, Guilford, Connecticut: Dushkin Publishing Group, 1992, p. 154.

16. Anne L. Stahl, Offenders in Juvenile Court, 1996: *Juvenile Justice Bulletin*, Washington, D.C.: Office of Juvenile Justice and Delinquency Prevention, 1999, p. 8.

17. Federal Bureau of Investigation, *Crime in the United States: Uniform Crime Reports*, Washington, D.C.: U.S. Government Printing Office, 2002, p. 250.

18. Linda A. Teplin, "Assessing Alcohol, Drug, and Mental Disorders in Juvenile Detainees," *OJJDP Fact Sheet*, January 2001, p. 2.

19. Howard N. Snyder and Melissa Sickmund, *Juvenile Offenders and Victims: A National Report*, Pittsburgh, Pennsylvania: National Center for Juvenile Justice, 1995, p. 141.

20. *Schall v. Martin*, 104 S.Ct. 2403 (1984).

21. *Incarceration of Youth Who are Waiting for Community Mental Health Services in the United States*, Washington, D.C.: U.S. House of Representatives, Committee on Government Reform, July 2004.

22. *Ibid.*, p. 11.

23. *Ibid.*, p. 7.

24. Michael G. Flaherty, "An Assessment of the National Incidence of Juvenile Suicide in Adult Jails, Lockups, and Juvenile Detention Centers," in Ralph A. Weisheit and Robert G. Culbertson, eds., *Juvenile Delinquency: A Justice Perspective*, Prospect Heights, Illinois: Waveland Press, 1985, p. 131.

25. James Austin *et al.*, *Juveniles in Adult Prisons and Jails: A National Assessment*, Washington, D.C.: Institute on Crime, Justice, and Corrections, George Washington University, and National Council on Crime and Delinquency, 1996, p. xi.

26. Ira M. Schwartz, *Justice for Juveniles*, Lexington, Massachusetts: Lexington Books, 1989, p. 82.

27. Melissa Sickmund, Howard N. Snyder, and Eileen Poe-Yamagata, *Juvenile Offenders and Victims: 1997 Update on Violence*, Pittsburgh, Pennsylvania: National Center for Juvenile Justice, 1997, p. 43.

28. Michael J. Dale, "Children in Adult Jails: A Look at Liability Issues," *American Jails*, Vol. 4, No. 5, January/February 1991, p. 31, citing *Hendrickson v. Griggs*, 672 F. Supp. 1126 (N.D. Iowa 1987).

29. Charles E. Frazier and Donna M. Bishop, "Jailing Juveniles in Florida: The Dynamics of Compliance with a Sluggish Federal Reform Initiative," *Crime and Delinquency*, Vol. 36, No. 4, October 1990, pp. 427-428.

30. *Ibid.*, For an account of the specific difficulties encountered by one state in achieving compliance, *see* Ruth B. O'Donnell, "Getting Juveniles Out of Kansas Jails," *American Jails*, Vol. 4, No. 5, January/February 1991, pp.16-22.

31. Eight other states are in full compliance with "exceptional provisions," and two (South Dakota and Wyoming) are not participating. *See OJJDP Annual Report, 2001*, Washington, D.C.: Office of Juvenile Justice and Delinquency Prevention, March 2003, pp. 22-24.

32. *Ibid.*, p. 24.

33. Sickmund, Snyder, and Poe-Yamagata, *Juvenile Offenders and Victims*, pp. 143-144.

34. *Ibid.*, p. 143.

35. *Office of Juvenile Justice and Delinquency Prevention (OJJDP) Annual Report*, p. 24.

36. Leslie Acoca and Kelly Dedel, *No Place to Hide: Understanding and Meeting the Needs of Girls in the California Juvenile Justice System*, San Francisco, California: National Council on Crime and Delinquency, 1998.

37. Meda Chesney-Lind and R. G. Shelden, *Girls, Delinquency, and Juvenile Justice*, Belmont, California: West/Wadsworth, 1998.

38. Robert E. King and Brenda Voshell, "Imagery for Adolescence," *Journal of Correctional Training*, Fall 1992, pp. 8-9.

39. The teenager died at the Miami-Dade Juvenile Detention Center after no response to his pleas for help; *see* "Controversy Follows Death at Detention Center," viewed May 12, 2004 at http://www.local10.com/news/2276210/detail.html.

40. Paul H. Hahn, *The Juvenile Offender and the Law*, Third Edition, Cincinnati, Ohio: Anderson Publishing Company, 1984, p. 3.

41. Sickmund, Snyder, and Poe-Yamagata. *Juvenile Offenders and Victims*, p. 149. For potential remedies, *see* Bart Lubow and Dennis Barron, "Resources for Juvenile Detention Reform," *OJJDP Fact Sheet*, November 2000.

42. Melissa Sickmund, "Juveniles in Court," *Juvenile Offenders and Victims Bulletin*, June 2003, p. 12.

43. James D. Walter and Susan A. Ostrander, "An Observational Study of a Juvenile Court," in Weisheit and Culbertson, *Juvenile Delinquency*, p. 113.

44. Greg Bolt, "Other States Mimicking Juvenile System," *Oregon Corrections Association Reports*, Fall 1991, p. 17, quoting Dennis Maloney.

45. Lloyd W. Mixdorf, "Juvenile Justice: We Need a Variety of Treatment, Programming Options," *Corrections Today*, Vol. 51, No. 4, July 1989, p. 120.

46. Snyder and Sickmund, *Juvenile Offenders and Victims*, pp. 133 and 139.

47. Paul W. Keve, "Some Random Reflections on the Occasion of a Barely Noticed Anniversary," *Crime and Delinquency*, Vol. 24, No. 4, October 1978, p. 456.

48. Larry W. Callicutt, "Placement of State-Committed Juveniles," *Corrections Today*, Vol. 66, No. 1, February 2004, pp. 37-38.

49. Sickmund, "Juveniles in Court," *OJJDP Bulletin*, Washington, D.C.: Office of Juvenile Justice and Delinquency Prevention, October 2000, p. 29.

50. Melissa Sickmund, "Juvenile Residential Facility Census, 2000: Selected Findings," *Juvenile Offenders and Victims Bulletin*, December 2002, p. 2.

51. For a summary of state compliance with this initiative, *see Disproportionate Minority Confinement: 2002 Update*, Washington, D.C.: Office of Juvenile Justice and Delinquency Prevention, 2003.

52. Patricia Devine *et al.*, "Disproportionate Minority Confinement: Lessons Learned from Five States," *Juvenile Justice Bulletin*, December 1998.

53. Anne M. Nurse, "The Structure of the Juvenile Prison," *Youth and Society*, Vol. 23, No. 3, March 2001, p. 360.

54. Randall G. Shelden and Michelle Hussong, "Juvenile Crime, Adult Adjudication, and the Death Penalty: Draconian Policies Revisited," *Justice Policy Journal*, Vol. 1, No. 2, Spring 2003, p. 13.

55. David Roush and Michael McMillen, "Construction, Operations, and Staff Training for Juvenile Confinement Facilities," *JAIBG Bulletin*, January 2000, p. 3.

56. David Shichor and Clemens Bartollas, "Private and Public Juvenile Placements: Is There a Difference?" *Crime and Delinquency*, Vol. 36, No. 2, April 1990, p. 297.

57. Dale G. Parent, "Conditions of Confinement," *Juvenile Justice*, Vol. 1, No. 1, Spring/Summer 1993, pp. 2-7.

58. Sickmund, Snyder, and Poe-Yamagata, *Juvenile Offenders and Victims*, p. 170.

59. Parent, "Conditions of Confinement," p. 5.

60. *Ibid.*, p. 3.

61. Glen E. McKenzie, "ACA Accreditation for Juvenile Corrections," *Corrections Today*, Vol. 66, No. 1, February 2004, p. 53. Camille Graham Camp, ed., *The 2002 Corrections Yearbook: Adult Corrections*, Middletown, Connecticut: Criminal Justice Institute, 2003, p. 90.

62. McKenzie, "ACA Accreditation," p. 53.

63. *See Nelson v. Heyne*, 491 F.2d 352 (7th Cir.1974) and *Morales v. Turman*, 383 E Supp. 53 (Ed. Texas 1974).

64. Robert C. Trojanowicz and Merry Morash, *Juvenile Delinquency: Concepts and Control*, 3rd ed., Englewood Cliffs, New Jersey: Prentice Hall, 1983, p. 391.

65. Hunter Hurst, "Turn of the Century: Rediscovering the Value of Juvenile Treatment," *Corrections Today*, Vol. 52, No. 1, February 1990, p. 49.

66. Barry C. Feld, "The Punitive Juvenile Court and the Quality of Procedural Justice: Disjunctions between Rhetoric and Reality," *Crime and Delinquency*, Vol. 36, No. 4, October 1990, pp. 453.

67. Shelden and Hussong, "Juvenile Crime, Adult Adjudication, and the Death Penalty," p. 6. (It should be noted that the authors are not advocating this approach, but rather, are using metaphorical language here).

68. Cindy S. Lederman, "The Juvenile Court: Putting Research to Work for Prevention," *Juvenile Justice*, Vol. 6, No. 2, December 1999, p. 24.

69. *See* Howard N. Snyder *et al.*, *Juvenile Transfers to Criminal Court in the 1990s*, Washington, D.C.: Office of Juvenile Justice and Delinquency Prevention, August 2000, and Sickmund, "Juveniles in Court."

70. Charles M. Puzzanchera, "Delinquency Cases Waived to Criminal Court, 1989-1998," *OJJDP Fact Sheet*, September 2001, p. 1.

71. Melissa Sickmund, "Offenders in Juvenile Court," *OJJDP Bulletin*, October 2000, p. 11.

72. David L. Myers, *Excluding Violent Youths from Juvenile Court: The Effectiveness of Legislative Waiver*, New York: LFB Scholarly Publishing, 2001.

73. Snyder and Sickmund, *Juvenile Offenders and Victims*, p.156. *See also* Snyder *et al.*, *Juvenile Transfers*, p. xii.

74. D. M. Altschuler, "Trends and Issues in the Adultification of Juvenile Justice," in Patricia Harris, ed., *Research to Results: Effective Community Corrections*, Lanham, Maryland: American Correctional Association and the International Community Corrections Association, 1999; *see also* Donna M. Bishop *et al.*, "The Transfer of Juveniles to Criminal Court: Does It Make A Difference?," *Crime and Delinquency*, Vol. 42, 1996, pp. 171-191, and J. C. Howell, *Juvenile Justice and Youth Violence*, Thousand Oaks, California: Sage, 1997.

75. Shelden and Hussong, "Juvenile Crime, Adult Adjudication, and the Death Penalty," p. 10.

76. Kevin J. Strom, "Profile of State Prisoners under Age 18, 1985-97," *Bureau of Justice Statistics: Special Report*, February 2000, p. 1.

77. *Ibid.*, p. 3.

78. John J. Greene *et al.*, *New "Boys" on the Block: Under-18-year-olds in Adult Prisons—Final Report*, Lanham, Maryland: American Correctional Association, June 1998, p. vi.

79. David W. Roush and Earl L. Dunlap, "Juveniles in Adult Prisons: A Very Bad Idea," *Corrections Today*, Vol. 59, No. 3, June 1997, p. 21.

80. Greene *et al.*, *New "Boys" on the Block*, p. vii.

81. Austin *et al.*, *Juveniles in Adult Prisons and Jails*, p. xi. For a discussion of the pros and cons of sentencing youthful offenders to adult facilities, *see* Lamar Smith, "Sentencing Youths to Adult Correctional Facilities Increases Public Safety," and Shay Bilchik, "Sentencing Juveniles to Adult Facilities Fails Youths and Society," *Corrections Today*, Vol. 65, No. 2, April 2003, pp. 20-21.

82. Quoted in Greene *et al.*, *New 'Boys' on the Block*, p. vi.

83. J. Steven Smith, "Detention Is an Invaluable Part of the System, But It's Not the Solution to All Youths' Problems," *Corrections Today*, Vol. 53, No. 1, February 1991, p. 59.

84. John T. Whitehead and Steven P. Lab, *Juvenile Justice: An Introduction*, Cincinnati, Ohio: Anderson Publishing, 1990, p. 346.

85. Jeanne B. Stinchcomb, "Recovering from the Shocking Reality of Shock Incarceration—What Correctional Administrators Can Learn from Boot Camp Failures," *Corrections Management Quarterly*, Vol. 3, No. 4, 1999, p. 43.

86. Doris Layton MacKenzie and Claire Souryal, *Multisite Evaluation of Shock Incarceration*, Washington, D.C.: U.S. Department of Justice, 1994, p. 28.

87. General Accounting Office, *Prison Boot Camps*, April 1993, cited in *Public Policy Reports: Evaluating Boot Camp Prisons*, Washington, D.C.: Campaign for an Effective Crime Policy, 1994, p. 4.

88. Michael Peters *et al.*, *Boot Camps for Juvenile Offenders: Program Summary*, Washington, D.C.: U.S. Department of Justice, 1997, p. 23.

89. Associated Press, "U.S. Justice Department says Boot Camps Do More Harm than Good," June 1, 1998. Available on-line at http:silcon/ptave/usjd.htm.

90. "Researchers Evaluate Eight Shock Incarceration Programs," *National Institute of Justice: Update*, Washington, D.C.: U.S. Department of Justice, 1994, p.1.

91. For an analysis of where the breakdown has occurred between the intent and reality of boot camps, *see* Jeanne B. Stinchcomb, "From Optimistic Policies to Pessimistic Outcomes: Why Won't Boot Camps either Succeed Pragmatically or Succumb Politically?," *Journal of Offender Rehabilitation*, Spring 2004.

92. "Boot Camp May Not Be Best Method to Help Delinquents," *Corrections Digest*, June 29,1994, p. 8, quoting Kathleen Heidi.

93. Morash, Merry and Lila Rucker, "A Critical Look at the Idea of Boot Camp as a Correctional Reform," *Crime and Delinquency*, Vol. 36, No. 2, April 1990.

94. Donald J. Hengesh, "Think of Boot Camps as a Foundation for Change, Not an Instant Cure," *Corrections Today*, Vol. 53, No. 6, October 1991, pp.106-108.

95. Thomas C. Castellano and Susan M. Plant, "Boot Camp Aftercare Programming: Current Limits and Suggested Remedies," in *Juvenile and Adult Boot Camps*, Lanham, Maryland: American Correctional Association, 1996, pp. 233-256.

96. Eloise Salholz and Frank Washington, "Experiments in Boot Camp," *Newsweek*, May 22, 1989, p. 44, quoting Mark Mauer.

97. Jeanne B. Stinchcomb and W. Clinton Terry, "Predicting the Likelihood of Rearrest among Shock Incarceration Graduates: Moving Beyond Another Nail in the Boot Camp Coffin," *Crime and Delinquency*, Vol. 47, 2001, p. 240.

98. Krisberg, "Evolution of the Juvenile Justice System," p. 158.

99. Bruce Bullington, James Sprowls, Daniel Katkin, and Mark Phillips, "A Critique of Diversionary Juvenile Justice," *Crime and Delinquency*, Vol. 24, No. 1, January 1978, pp. 63-64.

100. National Council on Crime and Delinquency, "Jurisdiction Over Status Offenses Should Be Removed from the Juvenile Court," *Crime and Delinquency*, Vol. 21, No. 2, April 1975, p. 97.

101. *Ibid.*, p. 98, quoting Judge David Bazelon, U.S. District Court of Appeals.

102. National Advisory Commission on Criminal Justice Standards and Goals, *A National Strategy to Reduce Crime*, Washington, D.C.: U.S. Government Printing Office, 1973, p. 121.

103. *OJJDP Annual Report*, 2001, p. 24.

104. Roush and McMillen, "Construction, Operations," p. 3.

105. Anne L. Schneider, *Reports of the National Juvenile Justice Assessment Centers: The Impact of Deinstitutionalization on Recidivism and Secure Confinement of Status Offenders*, Washington, D.C.: U.S. Department of Justice, 1985, p. 1.

106. Compiled from the *2004 Directory: Adult and Juvenile Correctional Departments, Institutions, Agencies, and Probation and Parole Authorities*, Lanham, Maryland: American Correctional Association, 2004. However, this figure includes information from states that have both adult/juvenile systems, such as Indiana and Minnesota, and their average daily cost per offender includes both adults and juveniles.

107. Heidi M. Hsia and Marty Beyer, "System Change through State Challenge Activities: Approaches and Products," *Juvenile Justice Bulletin*, March 2000, pp. 1-2.

108. M. A. Jones and Barry Krisberg, *Images and Reality: Juvenile Crime, Youth Violence, and Public Policy*, San Francisco, California: National Council on Crime and Delinquency, 1994, and C. Boersema, "Strategic Planning as a Means to Address Detention Overcrowding," *Journal for Juvenile Justice and Detention Services*, Spring 1998, pp. 20-31.

109. Roush and McMillen, "Construction, Operations," p. 3.

110. Alden D. Miller, Lloyd E. Ohlin, and Robert B. Coates, "The Aftermath of Extreme Tactics in Juvenile Justice Reform: A Crisis Four Years Later," in David F. Greenberg, ed., *Corrections and Punishment*, Beverly Hills, California, Sage Publications, 1977, p. 230.

111. Ira M. Schwartz, "Correcting Juvenile Corrections," *Criminal Justice 92/93*, Guilford, Connecticut: Dushkin Publishing Group, 1992, p. 179, citing Barry Krisberg, James Austin, and P. A. Steele, *Unlocking Juvenile Corrections: Evaluating the Massachusetts Department of Youth Services*, San Francisco: National Council on Crime and Delinquency, 1989.

112. Whitehead and Lab, *Juvenile Justice*, pp. 348-49, citing a study conducted by Ira M. Schwartz, J. Jackson-Beeck, and R. Anderson, "The Hidden System of Juvenile Control," *Crime and Delinquency*, Vol. 30, 1984, pp. 371-385.

113. Allen F. Breed and Barry Krisberg, "Juvenile Corrections: Is There a Future?" *Corrections Today*, Vol. 48, No. 8, December 1986, p. 17.

114. Schneider, *Reports of the National Juvenile Justice Assessment Centers*, p. vi.

115. Hahn, *The Juvenile Offender and the Law*, p. 220, quoting Don M. Gottfredson.

CHAPTER 13

STAFF—THE KEY INGREDIENT

> **❝** Each success lifts us up a little higher when we are struggling with the daily crises that, over the years of our careers, can start to wear us down.[1] **❞**
>
> —Sharon Johnson Rion

Chapter Overview

Throughout this book, numerous correctional processes, programs, and procedures have been discussed. They have focused on a wide variety of topics from a broad range of perspectives, but however diverse the correctional conglomerate may be, it has one essential ingredient in common.

That crucial component, quite obviously, is people. Those who make the decisions, establish the policies, and administer the correctional system are extremely influential. It is their leadership that shapes future visions and provides direction. Yet, in many respects, those who carry out the policies and deliver the operational services are in the long run even more influential. It is they who have the direct, day-to-day contact with correctional clients. Through them, prevailing theories, public opinions, and political actions are translated into practice. It is their level of professionalism and personal skill that either can help or harden an offender; promote or subvert operational programs; and strengthen or weaken correctional effectiveness: "Correctional administrators can (and do!) manage with crowded conditions, insufficient funding, political setbacks, and conflicting priorities. They cannot, however, manage without qualified, dedicated personnel."[2]

This does not mean that line-level staff are exclusively responsible for the system's successes or failures. Under the best of circumstances, it is difficult to implement policy intentions. But it can be virtually impossible when line personnel are faced with insufficient resources, uncooperative clients, and unsupportive supervisors. Staff members cannot achieve desired results without the fiscal resources necessary to do so. Being constantly short-handed, overworked, underpaid, and inadequately equipped eventually takes its toll on dedication and commitment. Nor can operational personnel be held accountable for offenders who are unwilling to accept help or unmotivated to change their behavior. Dealing with reluctant clients is an acknowledged fact of life for correctional workers.

Confronting these inherent obstacles would be considerably less frustrating, however, within a supportive administrative environment. It is one thing to persevere in the face of an apathetic public and an unappreciative clientele. But line staff cannot be expected to perform competently in an organizational environment that is plagued with contradictory goals, unclear policies, inequitable rules, inconsistent administrative procedures, or autocratic management techniques.

While operational personnel are charged with direct delivery of services, it is the upper-level administrative and managerial staff who set the tone for how well those services will be delivered. It is they who determine how line staff will be selected, trained, and supervised. Because tomorrow's supervisors and managers are recruited primarily from within today's rank and file, these personnel practices will have long-term implications. Thus, it is an important role of administrators to protect that investment in the future. It is they who establish an atmosphere that either will encourage or discourage employees throughout the organization. And that atmosphere will have much to do with the long-term results.

 ## Learning Goals

Do you know:

1. What percentage of the correctional workforce is employed within institutions?
2. What position is held by the vast majority of these employees?
3. In what respects the correctional workforce is changing?

Correctional Personnel

Because it is in the "people business," corrections is a very labor-intensive enterprise. But as the numbers of correctional personnel expand to keep pace with growing client populations, it is also sometimes difficult to keep in mind that every number on every agency's table of organization represents an individual employee—a person with strengths and weaknesses; capabilities and limitations; satisfactions and frustrations. The field of corrections invests tremendous resources in these people. In fact, about two-thirds of all operating costs are spent on employee salaries and benefits.[3] It therefore would

Most correctional personnel hold security-related positions in facilities. Courtesy of the Broward County (Florida) Sheriff's Office.

not seem to make sense to dismiss all of that investment "with the flippant attitude that people are expendable."[4]

Numbers and Characteristics

Although we saw in earlier chapters that the bulk of correctional *clients* are under some form of community supervision, only about 12 percent of correctional *employees* work in probation or parole.[5] The overwhelming majority hold jobs in correctional institutions. During the prime prison-expansion years of the mid-1980s to mid-1990s, employment opportunities virtually doubled.[6] Although the pace has slowed in recent years, corrections remains a growth industry.[7] Secure facilities are not only costly to construct, but also expensive to staff.

Some of these institutional employees are supervisors, managers, or administrators. Some are teachers, counselors, or other professional/technical staff. Some are clerical, maintenance, or other supportive employees. But as shown in Figure 13.1, the vast majority are *correctional officers* who hold custodial/security positions in local, state, and federal correctional facilities.

With the growth of the correctional workforce, there have been a number of changes in the characteristics of these employees. Today, the stereotypical image of a correctional officer as a middle-aged, white male with less than a high school education could hardly be further from reality. That profile was typical of line staff in the past, but today they are younger, better-educated, and more representative of women and minorities. Although males still represent the majority of those on the correctional payroll, female representation has expanded to one-third of the staff working in both jails and prisons,[8] and

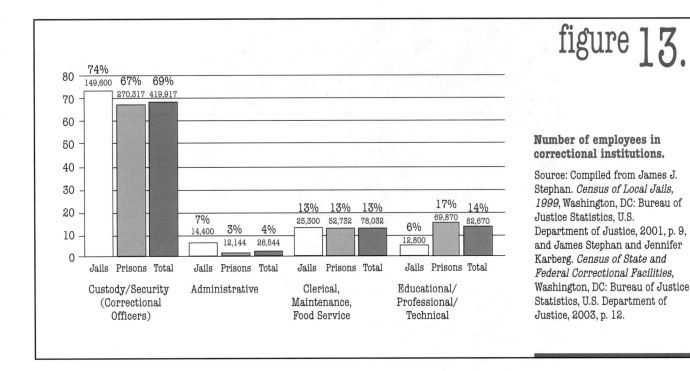

figure 13.1

Number of employees in correctional institutions.

Source: Compiled from James J. Stephan. *Census of Local Jails, 1999*, Washington, DC: Bureau of Justice Statistics, U.S. Department of Justice, 2001, p. 9, and James Stephan and Jennifer Karberg. *Census of State and Federal Correctional Facilities*, Washington, DC: Bureau of Justice Statistics, U.S. Department of Justice, 2003, p. 12.

more than half (55 percent) of those working in probation and parole.[9] Nevertheless, women have been relatively recent additions to the workforce and still represent only about 14 percent of correctional executives.[10]

In terms of race and ethnicity, comparable gains have been made, with minorities representing nearly one-third (30 percent) of correctional personnel [11] (although, again, they are largely concentrated in the lower ranks). While a college degree is not yet required by most departments, over one-third (37 percent) of the agencies responding to a national survey in 2000 indicated that officers are entering correctional service with some college education.[12]

🎯 Learning Goals

Do you know:

1. How Title VII of the Civil Rights Act has affected the correctional workforce?
2. What is meant by a bona fide occupational qualification (BFOQ) and under what circumstances it may be invoked?
3. How the courts have decided the issue of women's right to work versus male-inmate privacy?
4. How the issue of sexual misconduct during cross-gender supervision is being addressed?

Gender Integration

Under equal employment laws, women and minorities cannot be denied correctional positions if they meet the qualification requirements. Particularly with respect to female employees, this has created a major issue in which the male inmate's right to privacy has confronted the female applicant's right to employment.

Women were employed in corrections long before such concern surfaced. But earlier, they were confined to duties within female facilities. Since there are far fewer women's institutions, employment opportunities for female staff were therefore quite limited. Moreover, because of the lack of job variety and promotional opportunities in these facilities, the advancement potential for female employees was further restricted.

All of this changed in 1972 with the passage of amendments to the 1964 Civil Rights Act. Title VII of this act prohibits employment discrimination on the basis of race, religion, sex, or national origin. The amendments added "were crucial to women's advancement in corrections work in two separate ways: First by covering public sector employment, and second by increasing the enforcement power of the Equal Employment Opportunity Commission (EEOC)."[13]

Bona Fide Occupational Qualification (BFOQ) Exception

The law does, however, provide for one exceptional circumstance under which some discriminatory practices might be allowed. That exception occurs when the employing agency can demonstrate that a particular race, religion, sex, or national origin is a *bona fide occupational qualification* (BFOQ) required to perform the job. This does not mean that employers can discriminate on the basis of general assumptions about women's suitability for correctional work. In fact, the law very narrowly defines BFOQ to apply only to certain unique situations, such as a movie role calling for a male actor.

Nor have discrimination suits been limited to females working in male institutions. Comparable questions have been raised by male officers employed in female prisons, and the results have been similar. Overall, the courts "generally have concluded that employees' equal employment opportunity rights and institutional security take priority over inmates' limited privacy rights."[14] In fact, research reveals that in most women's prisons in the United States, men are both employed as correctional officers and routinely assigned to supervise inmate living units.[15]

Cross-Supervision Challenges

Aside from the legal issues involved, prisons never have been the most adaptable environments for accommodating massive change. The integration of women into traditionally male-dominated institutions and job assignments has been especially controversial. In part, resistance has been based on fears that women would jeopardize safety and security, as expressed in the true story told in the next "Close-up On Corrections."

More fundamentally, however, females represent a threat to the pride, homogeneity, and male ego associated with the close-knit world of correctional officers. To the extent that women can perform the job successfully, a serious challenge is posed to conventional beliefs that masculinity is a necessary requirement. As one male supervisor noted: "It really hurts these guys to think that a woman can do their job. They've been walking around town like big

Close-up On Corrections

THE GENDER GAP

[M]en frequently see corrections as a dangerous profession requiring machismo. They believe it is a place where women are especially unsafe. Because men are conditioned to protect women, they may feel that, in addition to working with the inmates, they have an added responsibility to protect the women officers.

These feelings can make men and women uncomfortable with each other. Women may feel patronized, as if they are merely being tolerated rather than appreciated and affirmed for their work. . . . A woman corrections officer recently told me she enjoyed counseling inmates who were close to release or community placement. She said that if she made a difference in the lives of even a few inmates, she felt her efforts were worthwhile.

However, some of her male counterparts thought she was getting too personally involved with the inmates. This baffled her, since she considered much of their contact with the inmates—bantering and favoring some inmates over others, for example—less professional than her counseling. To the male officers, her actions seemed too intimate and were thus inviting danger. . . .

The officer was comfortable with her approach. She was encouraging inmates' participation in an integrated community, a new experience for most of them. The inmates responded to her differently than they did to the men. To her, they expressed fears and confessed weaknesses they did not share with male employees.

Was she protecting the public by her actions or placing lives in jeopardy? The men viewed her activities as unnecessary and in a negative light. She saw her actions as positive. The differences here may be a result of differences in how each gender views the world.

Source: Adria Libolt, "Bridging the Gender Gap," *Corrections Today*, Vol. 53, No. 7, December 1991, pp. 136-138.

shots—like they're doing a job only 'real men' can do. Well, if the woman next door can do your job, then maybe you're not so tough after all. . . . [T]hese men have been going home to their wives for years saying 'you don't know what it's like in there.' Now some of their wives are joining up. The jig is up, so to speak."[16]

Ironically, one of the most unlikely sources of support for greater equality in the assignment of women came from correctional officer labor unions.[17] During the time that women were fighting for equality, union contracts in some states provided that seniority would be the sole criteria for making job assignments. Officers could bid for duty posts, and longevity was to be the only factor considered in selecting those to fill the most preferential assignments. However, when women began to join the corrections department, posts were classified as suitable or unsuitable for females to limit their direct contact with male inmates. The problem was that the noncontact posts designated as appropriate for women also happened to be among those most sought after by men, who were being denied their seniority rights under the contract as more and more women were joining the workforce. Unions therefore demanded an integrated seniority list.

Balancing Inmate and Employee Interests

The outcome is typical of the balance being pursued by many other agencies facing similar issues—that is, attempting to minimize inmate privacy intrusions while balancing the rights of all employees with equal employment opportunities for women. The resulting compromises include such provisions as restricting opposite-sex strip searches and shower duty, teaming female and male officers in housing units, requiring opposite-sex officers to announce their presence, using partial shower and toilet screens, and the like.

Despite widespread initial resistance, female officers today are the beneficiaries of a legacy of more than two decades of employment in a variety of correctional positions. Both federal and state correctional systems (including maximum-security prisons) have adopted "gender-neutral employment policies."[18] As a result, by 1999, three out of four female correctional officers were working in male facilities (*see* Figure 13.2).

Inmate Reaction

Inmate reaction has been mixed but tends to be relatively positive. Some have neutral attitudes about the presence of women, under the theory that the rules are the same no matter who is enforcing them. While in the minority, others remain opposed—degraded by having a female "boss," concerned about lack of privacy, or frustrated by the presence of women in an environment where sex is prohibited. But it appears that the majority favor female officers, feeling that they treat inmates with more respect, professionalism, and compassion.[19] Moreover, research indicates that male inmates are not as prone to attack female officers. A study of female officers working in male maximum-security

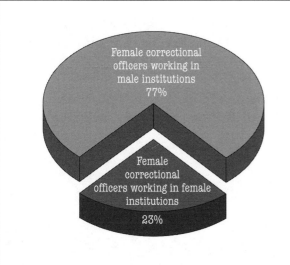

figure 13.2

Average percentage of female correctional officers assigned to male and female institutions in 1999.

Source: Camille Graham Camp, ed. *The 2002 Corrections Yearbook: Adult Corrections*, Middletown, Connecticut: Criminal Justice Institute, 2003, p. 165. Used with permission.

prisons found that they are substantially less likely than male officers to be assaulted on the job.[20]

Staff Sexual Misconduct

That does not, however, mean that cross-gender inmate supervision has been without drawbacks. Correctional practices today commonly involve female officers supervising male inmates as well as male officers supervising female inmates. Within the close confines of a prison, it is not difficult for such working relationships to evolve into inappropriate intimacies, for staff to be manipulated sexually by inmates, or for inmates to be subjected to staff sexual demands. In fact, given the imbalance of power between employees and inmates, there is actually no such thing as "consensual" sexual activities behind bars.

This issue of staff sexual misconduct and undue familiarity with inmates has surfaced in recent years as attention has focused on a number of highly publicized class-action lawsuits. In the past, when the courts were less likely to review such complaints or to decide in favor of the inmates, agencies had little incentive to aggressively investigate and seek remedies for staff sexual misconduct. Today, of course, that has changed, as evidenced by mounting numbers of cases in which plaintiffs have prevailed.

A 1999 survey by the National Institute of Corrections, for example, discovered that within a five-year period, almost half of all state departments of corrections reported that they had faced lawsuits regarding staff sexual misconduct.[21] While some of these allegations eventually are proven to be unfounded, a United Nations study pointed out that sexual misconduct is relatively common in U.S. prisons, especially when compared to other industrialized countries. Moreover, reports by Human Rights Watch have detailed sexual harassment, abuse, and privacy violations in U.S. prisons, along with retaliation by staff against inmates for filing suit.[22]

In response, concerned correctional administrators are doing everything from developing new policies to providing staff training, improving investigatory practices, and even working with the legislature to criminalize sexual contact with inmates. By late 1999, all but seven states had enacted specific laws prohibiting staff sexual misconduct with inmates, thereby making such misbehavior punishable as a criminal offense.[23]

The fact that much more needs to be done, however, was noted in a U.S. Government Accounting Office report, which called for directing more effort toward improved reporting methods, monitoring procedures, tracking investigatory progress, and conducting competent investigations.[24] Nor is this merely a legal or personnel-related issue. In the final analysis, it has been suggested that staff sexual misconduct "should be defined as a security issue," inasmuch as such behavior "damages the safety and security of everyone—staff and inmates alike."[25]

Learning Goals

Do you know:

1. How the changing nature of the workforce is affecting correctional administration?

2. For what reasons employees leave correctional work?

3. To what extent correctional turnover is subject to change?

Implications of a Changing Workforce

Expanding the employment of females and minorities in corrections is beginning to produce a diverse workforce that is more reflective of the people and communities being served. But these changes have not always been easy to adjust to organizationally. In addition to having to accommodate to a "new breed" of employee in terms of race, gender, and ethnicity, those beginning correctional work today are entering at younger ages and bringing with them the values of newer generations.

After the "traditionalists" who shaped early administrative practices came the "baby boomers," who in turn, were followed by "generation x'ers," and now the "millennials" are beginning to enter the workplace. In contrast to these subsequent generations, however, the work-related expectations of traditionalists fit well within highly-structured bureaucracies. Unlike the generations to follow, they were willing to take orders, knew their place in the chain-of-command, respected their superior officers, and were accustomed to "deferring the pursuit of personal autonomy to the power of institutional authority."[26] That is not true of their successors. In essence:

> Traditionalists are classified as coming of age in a "chain of command" environment, whereas for boomers it was "change of command," for x-ers, "self-command," and for millennials "don't command—collaborate!"[27]

This combination of an increasingly younger, better-educated workforce composed of a more diverse population reflecting the often-conflicting values of new generations presents management challenges. Previously, correctional employees were considerably more homogeneous, sharing similar job-related values and attitudes. That was obviously disadvantageous in terms of generating change or meeting the needs of diverse clientele. But it was advantageous in terms of managing, supervising, and accommodating to like-minded employees. Along with the benefits of a more varied workforce, corrections is now faced with the challenge of adapting to the differences they represent.

Today's employees are considerably less likely than their predecessors to quietly endure an autocratic management style or to routinely implement unreasonable policies sent down through the chain of command: "Line employees have become much more sensitive to treatment they receive from supervisors. They are less apt to tolerate the old authoritarian style of command."[28] No longer are operational staff as willing to subserviently accept

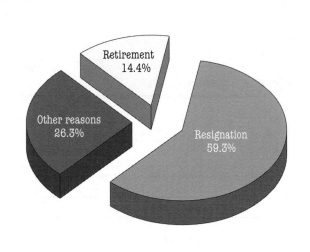

figure 13.3

Reasons for turnover in prison staff.

Source: Camille Graham Camp, ed. *The 2002 Corrections Yearbook: Adult Corrections*, Middletown, Connecticut: Criminal Justice Institute, 2003, p. 173. Used with permission.

managerial practices that do not provide them with some degree of autonomy and recognize their worth as individuals.

Staff Turnover

Although today's correctional employees may more readily leave employment that is not satisfying to them, corrections often has been plagued by high rates of turnover. Depending on the state, separation rates can range up to 37 percent, with annual turnover rates for security staff averaging around 14 percent.[29] As shown in Figure 13.3, more than half of staff departures result from employee resignations.

Needless to say, no stable business could run efficiently with a continuous transition of employees coming and going. Moreover, when staff members leave within the first few years of their employment, turnover is especially costly, in light of the sizable investment made in recruiting, selecting, and training them.

The basic drawbacks of correctional employment are undoubtedly more discouraging to some than others. Yet, considerable research has linked turnover, thoughts about quitting, and decisions to seek employment elsewhere with such administratively controlled factors as:

- Insufficient opportunities for participation in decision making [30]
- Inadequate supervisory support [31]
- Dissatisfaction with supervisors [32]
- A "crisis of faith" in the management ability of ranking staff [33]
- Poor communications between first-line supervisors and line-level employees [34]
- Lack of empowerment—in other words, inability to participate in and contribute to the organization [35]

In one study, the two most important issues separating those who resigned from colleagues who stayed were the quality of the work environment and the opportunity to influence organizational policies. In the work environment, it was neither dangerous conditions nor difficult inmates that led officers to quit. Rather, it was the lack of autonomy, authority, and learning opportunities that most effectively predicted turnover. [36] In that regard, it has been noted that "people do not leave jobs; they leave bosses." [37]

Likewise, it has been found that lack of recognition and problems with administrators are major contributors to correctional officer stress.[38] Other stress-related research further confirms that autonomy on the job and participatory decision making are associated with stronger organizational commitment and less job-related stress.[39] As one study concluded, the more empowered employees perceived themselves to be, the lower their level of occupational stress.[40] Thus, when bureaucratic management oppresses the self-direction, recognition, and organizational participation that employees are seeking on the job, it should not be surprising to find them dissatisfied, burned-out, and resigning. While working with certain inmates may be troublesome, working under certain management practices may be intolerable.

 # Learning Goals

Do you know:

1. The difference between episodic and chronic stress?
2. How agencies traditionally have responded to officer stress and why such responses have been inadequate?
3. What can be done proactively to prevent correctional officer stress?

Officer Stress

Like a chronic cough, certain management practices are among the sources of chronic stress in the day-to-day work environment of corrections. Unlike episodic stress, chronic stress is not the result of a one-time crisis or emergency situation. It is not the adrenalin-pumping reaction to a riot, attack, or hostage-taking situation. Rather, it is the product of a slow, continual process of erosion that occurs over a period of years. Supervising inmates immediately comes to mind as a potential source of chronic stress within correctional institutions. But research reveals that it is actually *other staff* who are more chronically stress provoking: from operational coworkers to supervisors, managers, and administrators. For example, one study reports that officers actually outranked inmates in terms of those creating major, continuing pressures and problems. Furthermore, in terms of how they are treated by supervisors, many indicate that they either are not recognized or are given attention only "when something goes wrong." [41]

Research confirms that the difficulty of work in correctional institutions is related more to problems involving staff relationships than to problems in dealing with inmates.[42] Moreover, even when officer-inmate interaction has been identified as a major stress inducement, the underlying source of the stress often is attributed to administrative problems such as unclear guidelines, inadequate communication, conflicting orders, lack of opportunity to participate in decision making, inappropriate supervision, and the like.[43] In fact, "lack of support from

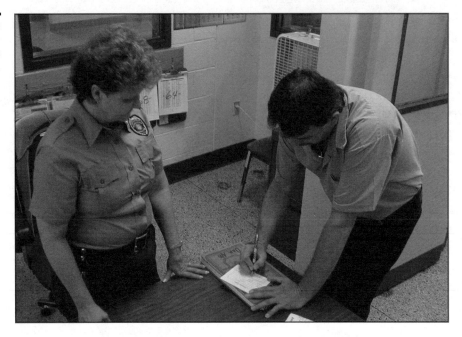

administration" ranked among the highest sources of stress in all three states included in a national study of correctional officer stress.[44]

Organizational Responses to Stress

Correctional administrators have begun to recognize the debilitating impact of stress among their personnel, but that does not mean that they necessarily accept any personal responsibility for it. To the contrary, the primary organizational responses to stress are employee assistance programs and stress-reduction training, both of which have significant limitations:

- *Employee assistance programs (EAPs)*: Designed primarily to offer counseling and similar forms of individual treatment, EAPs assist employees in coping with problems—whether those problems are related to work, home life, substance abuse, or whatever. Such programs can be helpful in dealing with the posttraumatic stress resulting from critical incidents. But we have already seen that episodic incidents are not the most frequent stressors in corrections. Counseling is not likely to resolve chronic job-related stress, because it is treating the *symptoms* rather than dealing with the *causes.*

- *Training programs*: Stress-reduction training typically includes information on nutrition, exercise, meditation, relaxation, and similar techniques for dealing with stress. As with EAPs, however, emphasis is on improving the employee's ability to cope with on-the-job stress by reducing its debilitating *effects* rather than taking steps to eliminate its underlying causes. In that regard, it is "not only foolish but also ineffective to treat correctional officer burnout as an individual pathology best addressed by measures such as relaxation techniques and employee assistance programs." [45]

Close-up On Corrections

When employees return from EAP counseling or stress training, where do they go? The answer is right back into the same work environment that created their stress in the first place! True, they may be better equipped to cope with it (at least in the short term). But long-term chronic stress will not be resolved without a dedicated commitment to *proactive prevention*—that is, eliminating the work-related stressors, rather than treating the stressed-out workers.

The next "Close-up On Corrections" outlines simple techniques designed to address some of the administrative causes of stress. Notice that the emphasis is on keeping employees informed and *involved*. A proactive organizational approach to stress prevention requires the inclusion of all ranks in the agency's problem-solving and decision-making network.

The ironic aspect about focusing on causes as opposed to effects is that it is not likely to be nearly as expensive. EAPs and stress reduction training programs are quite costly. In contrast, it is relatively inexpensive to uncover the supervisory, managerial, and administrative practices that are creating stress and take appropriate actions to change them. Rather than money, what it really costs to proactively address employee stress is the willingness of administrators to confront organizational and managerial shortcomings. But in many agencies, that is considered too high a price to pay.

✸ Learning Goals

Do you know:

1. Why correctional officers have joined labor unions?
2. How economic conditions and membership changes may affect the concerns expressed by unions?
3. What impact unions have had on correctional agencies?

Labor Unions

When an organization is unwilling or unable to respond to the concerns of its employees, it should not be surprising to find frustrated workers either leaving or turning to other avenues to resolve their complaints. One such alternative undoubtedly has been employee unions. As a result, correctional officer unions have been strong for a number of years in some states.

Originally, unions were concerned predominantly with such *extrinsic* matters as salaries and working conditions. These items still remain serious issues on the bargaining table in a number of places. But union interests have begun to expand beyond money and fringe benefits. Unions are now becoming more actively involved in a wide range of issues affecting the health, safety, and well-being of their membership—ranging from equipment and training to disciplinary actions, promotional policies, and other administrative practices.

These more *intrinsic* concerns are likely to become even more significant bargaining issues in the future for two reasons. First, unions are increasingly aware of the fact that in a sluggish economy, demands for higher wages or additional benefits are often simply unrealistic. Second, as union membership becomes increasingly composed of the "new breed" of correctional workers described earlier, it can be expected that their concerns will begin to shift. In place of the extrinsic matters that had been emphasized by their predecessors, today's employees are more likely to fight for issues surrounding work satisfaction, personal autonomy, job enrichment, and self-fulfillment.

From some perspectives, unionization has been viewed as reducing the capacity of administrators to manage the system. For example, nearly half (47.2 percent) of the prison wardens in one survey reported that unions restrict their management style.[46] Labor unions have won such concessions as higher salaries, overtime pay, compensation for being called back to duty, protection against extra-duty requirements, scheduling restrictions, and many other actions that have been perceived as infringements on management prerogatives. Yet, to some degree, it has been management's reluctance to share control and address grievances that has prompted employees to organize collectively. In the long run, however, both have mutual concerns at stake—the employee's best interests are served by working in a progressive organization, and management's best interests are served by organizing a progressive workforce. The more that each can fulfill their complementary roles, the less those roles will conflict.

 # Learning Goals

Do you know:

1. What can be done to improve correctional recruitment?
2. What drawbacks are involved in the use of written tests and oral interviews?
3. Why a job-task analysis is essential to the development of job-related screening tools?

Administrative Practices

It is especially ironic that labor and management are often adversaries, since most of today's administrators were yesterday's line staff. With a few exceptions that occasionally occur at the highest ranks, virtually all correctional managers and supervisors are selected from within the agency. (In fact, most systems have restrictions against lateral entry into all but the uppermost levels). This pattern has long-term implications for how entry personnel are recruited, selected, and trained, since it is largely from the ranks of line-level officers that command staff are chosen.

Recruitment

Historically, the field of corrections has tended to limit its officer recruitment to establishing minimal requirements and accepting anyone who could meet them. The rationale typically given for such rudimentary practices often relates to the pressures induced by lack of public prestige, high turnover, and traditionally low salaries.[47] But each of these justifications is amenable to change.

The Image Issue. Some agencies are locked into the belief that it would be fruitless to set higher entrance standards because the field suffers from an inferior image, and is therefore relegated to taking virtually anyone who is willing to work in it. Restricting standards to the lowest acceptable denominator, however, results in recruiting precisely that. Few of the best suited or most educated will be attracted to a job with requirements that are far below their level of qualification. Thus, a self-fulfilling cycle is created—if only the least qualified are recruited, only the least qualified tend to apply. On the other hand, an agency that expects a high caliber of employee will be considerably more likely to attract better applicants.

Of course, as standards are raised, more candidates naturally will be rejected. That is why organizations concerned about attracting better applicants must be willing to search aggressively for them. Once an agency is recognized as a good place to work where people are proud to be employed and only the best are selected, it will be easier to appeal to suitable candidates. But even under these ideal circumstances, it is essential to put considerable energy into the recruitment process, beyond just distributing posters and brochures. Making personal contacts by attending job fairs, establishing college internships, and the like, are key ingredients of successful recruitment. With high visibility, a respected reputation, and intensive recruitment, the pool of prospective employees is likely to expand, thereby enabling more selectivity.

Vacancy Pressures. Much of the strategy for keeping entrance standards at minimal levels is designed to enable the organization to fill numerous vacancies promptly. Departments that are not at full capacity often will be required to employ officers on overtime, which quickly becomes very costly. Unfortunately, some agencies have come to accept high turnover as the price of doing business in corrections. In many cases, it is not.

Dealing with the turnover problem requires a twofold approach: first, finding out why employees are leaving, and then doing something about it. This does not necessarily mean trying to pry higher salaries from the taxpayers. Although better pay undoubtedly would help, people who enjoy their jobs will be more reluctant to leave, despite the attraction of more money elsewhere. Throughout much of the remainder of this chapter, administrative techniques are addressed that could increase satisfaction without spending any additional money. What is involved in reducing voluntary turnover is not greater cost but greater commitment. And the more that corrections can decrease voluntary resignations, the more it can increase entrance requirements.

Compensation Concerns. In many states, it is readily apparent that few enter corrections for the monetary compensation it offers. While average starting salaries have been increasing (*see* Figure 13.4), given the nature of the job and the qualifications necessary to do it properly, correctional personnel are not generally paid adequately.

This issue likewise has been used as a justification for reducing entrance standards. Yet research indicates that there are other techniques beyond increasing salaries that are both promising and less costly alternatives.[48] Moreover, there are any number of professions—from teaching to nursing or social work—that traditionally have not been well-compensated. Nevertheless, in most states, these occupations have established and maintained relatively rigorous educational and training requirements. Even within corrections, the majority of probation and parole positions require a bachelor's degree, sometimes with additional experience as well.[49] In any event, if the job satisfaction concerns discussed throughout this chapter are addressed, salary may not be as significant a drawback to effective recruitment.

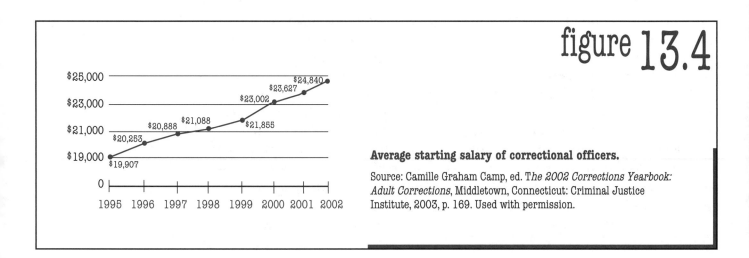

figure 13.4

Average starting salary of correctional officers.

Source: Camille Graham Camp, ed. *The 2002 Corrections Yearbook: Adult Corrections*, Middletown, Connecticut: Criminal Justice Institute, 2003, p. 169. Used with permission.

Selection

Naturally, the purpose of active recruitment is to identify a sufficiently sizable pool of applicants to improve choice in the selection process. Without such choices, an agency may be tempted to fill positions with applicants who would not be considered suitable if there were a larger group from which to draw.

Once the applicant pool is assembled, the selection *screening process* begins. Screening encompasses all of the procedures used to determine who meets the established entrance qualifications and possesses the greatest potential. Ultimately, the screening procedures employed should be designed to accurately predict the candidate's ability to succeed on the job. It is therefore essential that all measurements be *job-related*.

One of the most prevalent screening instruments is a written civil service exam, which is used by almost 80 percent of state agencies in the selection of correctional officers.[50] The next most common procedure is an oral interview. Some agencies also have begun to employ various forms of psychological evaluations, to guard against hiring those with personality disorders. Others also conduct background checks, polygraph tests, medical exams, physical agility tests, and the like. But written exams and oral interviews remain the most widely used screening devices. The usefulness of both largely depends upon how carefully they are structured.

Written Tests. Written exams have the advantage of being easy to administer, relatively inexpensive, and simple to score. Like the Scholastic Aptitude Tests (SATs) and college entrance exams, they are useful for determining a candidate's general level of knowledge and written communication skills. But just because a person is a good "test taker" does not necessarily mean that he or she will work out well on the job. That is especially true if test items are not directly job-related. Moreover, those rejected on the basis of an irrelevant test may well have grounds for legal action.

The question then becomes how to make written tests more reflective of the actual knowledge needed to perform effectively as a correctional officer. Ideally, this is done through a *job-task analysis*, which:

- Identifies the tasks being conducted by those already holding the job

- Determines the knowledge, skills, and abilities necessary to effectively perform job tasks

Then, written test items can be constructed that accurately reflect what a candidate needs to know. But the major disadvantage of even the most carefully constructed, job-related written test is that it is limited to measuring knowledge. Written tests can determine what applicants *know* intellectually, but that may or may not reflect what they are actually able to *do*.

Oral Interviews. Many employing agencies require an oral interview to meet prospective employees face-to-face and get a better feeling for whether they will work out on the job. The primary drawback of oral interviews is exactly that—they are based more on personal *feelings* or subjective judgments than on objective evaluations of capabilities. Like the decision making of parole boards, employment interview panels are open to criticism—and in this case, potentially to legal challenge as well.

Even when interviewers use standardized score sheets and numerical scales to record their ratings, the numbers are subject to individual interpretation. For example, a "3" on a 1-to-5 scale measuring "appearance" presumably reflects an average score. But what is "average appearance" to one interviewer may be below or above average to another.

Another limitation of the oral interview is the tendency of candidates to respond to questions in a manner that they consider socially or organizationally acceptable. It is only natural to tell the interviewers what the applicant thinks they want to hear, regardless of whether such responses are truly accurate reflections of one's personal opinions.

 # Learning Goals

Do you know:

1. How an assessment center can improve selection screening?
2. The difference between historic, traditional, and professional approaches to training?

Innovative Selection Alternatives

To address the shortcomings of traditional selection devices, progressive organizations have implemented more job-related procedures, such as *assessment centers*. Based on a job-task analysis, the assessment center technique is designed to predict more accurately which candidates actually do have the ability needed to perform the job properly. Assessment is based on the concept that the best way to find that out is to place them in the job and see how well they perform. Obviously, that is impossible in corrections—where legal restrictions, certification standards, and liability concerns prohibit such an option. But assessment does the next best thing, through a series of written exercises, videotaped scenarios, and/or live role-playing interactions with the candidate.[51]

For example, information might be provided about a hypothetical problem in a correctional facility, with the candidate instructed to write a memo describing the situation and making a recommendation to correct it. In this way, a number of dimensions can be assessed, such as judgment, decisiveness, and written communication. A similar process could be used to set up a role-playing situation in which, for instance, two "inmates" (actors) wish to speak to the "officer" (job applicant) about their inability to get along together in the cell they share. Trained assessors then would observe and measure the resulting interactions on such dimensions as leadership, verbal communication, judgment, and so on.

This is a very brief description of a rather complex process. Nevertheless, the advantages of using assessment should be apparent. Unlike written exams, they are not limited to testing knowledge. Unlike oral interviews, they are not the product of a subjective process or unstructured opinions. By placing the applicants in simulated, job-related situations and evaluating their reactions, assessment comes as close as possible to reflecting real life, as well as measuring the "common sense" that is so elusive in paper-and-pencil testing.

However, also unlike traditional approaches, assessment centers can be costly to develop and operate. As a result, some agencies are experimenting with modified variations of assessment, such as video-based situational exams and situational interviews.[52] Regardless of the specific techniques used, if the most qualified applicants are not selected, the agency is not only vulnerable to needless and costly litigation, but more importantly, is not accurately predicting who will and will not perform effectively on the job.

Mandated Entry-Level Training

Regardless of how good the selection process is at bringing the most qualified recruits into the agency, they cannot be expected to know what is required of them on the job without proper training. Gone are the days when an officer was given a uniform, a badge, and a set of keys—sent to work with no further instruction than "good luck!" No longer are officers relegated to learning the job through "helpful" inmates. Correctional work is not only more complex today, but is also governed by a multitude of legal restrictions and organizational policies with which staff are expected to comply. When an untrained officer is involved in a situation that results in liability claims, the courts increasingly are holding the employing agency liable for damages, using a "failure to train" rationale.

The American Correctional Association's entry-level officer standards call for a minimum of 160 hours of training within the first year of employment

Since training needs do not end with graduation from the basic academy, in-service classes are necessary to keep updated, prepare for advancement, and learn new skills. Here a staff member learns about hazardous materials. Proper training prevents much stress and lowers burnout. Courtesy of Diane Geiman.

(with at least forty of the 160 hours completed before job assignment), along with an additional forty hours each year thereafter.[53] Given the complex demands and legal liability of correctional work today, these standards are just that—minimal. Moreover, unlike state certification statutes, ACA standards do not carry the weight of law.

Although any correctional facility hoping to achieve ACA accreditation must meet these standards, the minimum required often becomes the maximum provided. A survey by the National Institute of Corrections, for example, found that most states were requiring only the minimum hours established by ACA.[54] However, some jurisdictions voluntarily provide more training than is mandated by ACA standards, or even state law. As a result, a more recent study reported a somewhat higher average of 263 hours of training (although it is uncertain how many of the hours listed reflect actual classroom study rather than less structured on-the-job training).[55]

The Professional Training Model

It is one thing to mandate a certain number of training hours for entry-level preparation, but quite another to assure that the training is provided in a timely manner. With pressures to fill existing vacancies immediately, the *historical approach* to training has been to place new recruits directly on the job, postponing their enrollment in the academy until they could be spared to attend. Needless to say, once employees become a part of the workforce, they tend to become "indispensable," and sparing them at any time creates a hardship.

Many states now prohibit this approach, requiring all preemployment training to be completed before job assignment. But others allow a designated grace period during which the new recruit can legally work prior to being enrolled in the training academy. Among the numerous disadvantages of postponing training, increased liability is the most significant. When training is relegated to on-the-job experience, "Violation of an inmate's rights becomes

Every state now mandates entry-level training for new correctional officers. Courtesy of Capitol Communication Systems, Inc.

almost inevitable, and with the violation comes officer liability. If the officer's actions or inaction can be traced back to a lack of training, higher-ranking officials may also be found liable."[56]

Beyond legal vulnerability, lack of preemployment training puts officers in a very tenuous position. In essence, they are struggling to cope with a job where they are unsure of what rules to enforce, what behaviors are prohibited, and what actions to take. This can promote a dangerous reliance on the inmates for guidance. In addition, untrained officers do not tend to make receptive recruits when they finally do go to the academy, especially if they already have developed inappropriate work habits which must then be "unlearned."

For these and many other reasons, correctional organizations today are more likely to use the *traditional approach* to training. As shown in Figure 13.5, the procedure that is now more widely accepted is to send recruits to training immediately upon employment. Thus, they are not put to work until successful completion of the academy. This is certainly a vast improvement over historical practices. But there are two fundamental drawbacks to the traditional approach: first, what it is costing the organization fiscally, and second, what it is costing the field in terms of recognition as a profession.

Fiscally, the traditional approach is very expensive. Since recruits are hired before training, everyone is on full salary throughout the program, which can become extremely costly. In fact, custody and security expenses represent the largest component of correctional operating budgets,[57] most of which consists of personnel costs. Given the fact that corrections routinely has been underfunded, the potential for reducing such expenditures is appealing.

But perhaps even more important is what the traditional approach is costing in terms of corrections becoming recognized as a *profession*. The professionalization of corrections is a commendable goal that has been supported vigorously by virtually every state and national organization representing correctional personnel throughout the country. Realistically, however, it takes far more than vocal support to make it happen. Among other things, procedures for enacting and enforcing standards, licensing, and certification must be implemented.

One of the consistent hallmarks of any "established" profession is that the education, training, and certification mandated for entrance are required before employment. A person interested in teaching would not apply to the school board and then expect to be sent to college. A person interested in nursing would not apply to a hospital and then expect to be enrolled in nursing school. Occupations with state licensing requirements must meet established provisions before they can obtain their "license to practice."

It is therefore for both fiscal and professional reasons that some agencies are now turning to the *professional (or preservice) approach*. As with the traditional approach, recruits are fully screened to assure that they meet state and agency hiring standards before academy entrance. But that is where the similarity ends. Like existing professions, recruits are not hired under this model until they successfully complete the training necessary to be certified as correctional officers. The major advantage of this form of preservice training is a combination of fiscal savings and the promotion of corrections as an acknowledged profession. As shown in Figure 13.5, the priority of training also increases correspondingly as the field moves from the historical to the traditional, and finally, to the professional/preservice approach.[58]

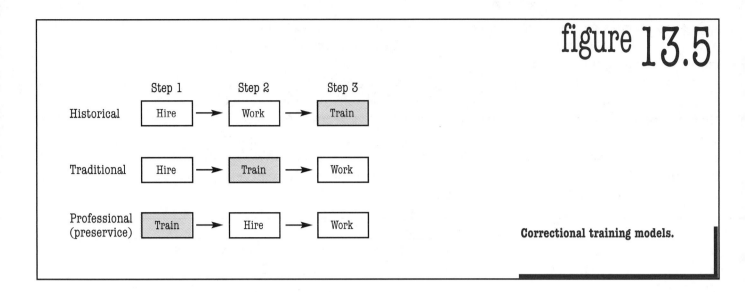

figure 13.5

	Step 1	Step 2	Step 3
Historical	Hire	Work	Train
Traditional	Hire	Train	Work
Professional (preservice)	Train	Hire	Work

Correctional training models.

Professional Certification

An additional step toward professionalization was taken early in the twenty-first century by the American Correctional Association with the development of its national certification program for correctional staff.[59] Designed to promote professionalism, encourage continued learning, and enhance the image of correctional personnel, this program offers employees the option of becoming certified, just as facilities can become accredited. After meeting specific prerequisites and passing a written exam, personnel can be certified at one of four levels (adult and juvenile)—officer, supervisor, manager, or executive. Certification is also available for expertise in security-threat groups and correctional nursing. Just as in established professions, successful candidates subsequently must complete additional training or continuing education requirements to maintain their status and periodically renew their certification. While this process simply represents a "starting point for the arduous journey along the long road toward professional recognition," it is well-known that "a journey of a thousand miles begins with a single step." [60]

Correctional personnel can enhance their professional recognition by becoming certified through a process developed and administered by the American Correctional Association.

Learning Goals

Do you know:

1. The difference between line and staff supervisors?
2. How internal and external motivation differ?
3. Why discipline should be a constructive process?

Line and Staff Supervision

In most jobs, a new employee would have to work for some period of time at the operational level before becoming a supervisor. But unlike entry-level employees in other occupations, beginning correctional, probation, and parole officers are immediately charged with supervisory functions. That is because "every correctional employee who exercises legal authority over offenders . . . is a *supervisor*, even if the person is the lowest-ranking employee in the agency or institution."[61] In that sense, officers are *line* or *field* supervisors—that is, they supervise offenders at the line level of institutional operations or in the field (as in the case of probation or parole). They, in turn, are supervised by personnel at the next level of the organizational hierarchy, who are considered *staff* (or *first-level*) *supervisors*, since they represent the first level in the chain of command that has supervisory authority over other staff members. Within institutional corrections, staff supervisors are generally personnel at the rank of corporal or sergeant.

To supervise inmates, an officer must be able to motivate, discipline, direct, train, and evaluate behavior. To do so, the officer must be skilled in oral and written communication, judgment, sensitivity, leadership, and the like. But what is required of the first-level staff supervisor? The answer is essentially the same. Undoubtedly, staff supervisors have certain additional responsibilities, such as communicating with upper-level management, allocating personnel on a shift, and maintaining payroll records. In terms of their fundamental personnel supervisory functions, however, there is a great deal of similarity.

Staff training is a key ingredient of professionalism in corrections. Courtesy of the Missouri Division of Youth Services. Photo by Rick Lambert.

In essence, both are supervising people—regardless of whether those people are offenders or officers. If a punitive or autocratic approach is learned at the entry level when supervising inmates, it is likely to be passed on to subordinates as one is promoted up the ranks. Thus, officers are likely to reflect the supervisory style of their own supervisor. Improving the *supervision of offenders*, therefore, in many respects, is closely related to improving the *supervision of officers*. Staff members are entitled to be treated with no less equity and respect than would be expected of them in their supervision of offenders. And they are more likely to fulfill those expectations if they, in turn, receive appropriate treatment from their supervisors.

Motivation

One of the most critical elements of good supervision is stimulating subordinates to carry out their jobs in the manner prescribed. This is what is known as *motivation*. People can be motivated either *externally* or *internally*. When personnel are treated in a manner that relies heavily on external controls, they can become just as "institutionalized" as the inmates.

On the other hand, when internal motivations are tapped, personnel are considerably more likely to do a good job simply for the intrinsic benefits of doing so—such as feeling good about themselves, taking pride in their accomplishments, and enjoying a sense of personal satisfaction. In fact, the popular approach known as *total quality management* (or "continuous quality improvement") is based on the belief that "most employees want to perform well but are hindered by systematic issues that interfere with their ability to get the job done."[62]

Within corrections, total quality management (TQM) is especially relevant "because of growing pressures to control costs, which can be accomplished by improving quality. This can only be done when TQM is accepted not as a 'project' or one-time fix, but rather, as a permanent philosophy of operations."[63] Rather than address impediments through organizationwide TQM, however, motivational efforts in corrections often continue to rely on various sources of external incentives.

External motivators are rooted in the theory that behavior is shaped by how the supervisor responds to it. Responses include either *rewards* or *punishments*. Traditionally, rewards have been rather narrowly interpreted as higher salaries, promotions, more benefits, or preferred assignments. What is often overlooked is the simple reward of a "pat on the back" for a job well done—in other words, some indication that the supervisor recognizes and cares about the employee's effort and quality of work.

Maslow's hierarchy of needs demonstrates that people who are beyond basic physiological and safety levels are not inclined to be motivated by money or similar extrinsic rewards. As the correctional workforce increasingly becomes composed of those with higher education and greater career options, the strength of these motivators is diminished. If supervisors are not able to create the type of environment where such employees feel needed, appreciated, and recognized, even the most lucrative benefits are unlikely to be powerful enough to motivate them to do their best.

Discipline

Added to the drawback of external motivators is the fact that from the employee's perspective, it appears that punishments are employed more readily than rewards. It may well take years for even the most competent employee to obtain a salary increase, promotion, or additional benefits. On the other hand, when something inappropriate is done, the disciplinary system is activated much more rapidly. Of course, this is not meant to imply that some form of discipline is not at times warranted and necessary. Even when that is the case, however, the employee is considerably more likely to view disciplinary action as equitable when the supervisor's focus is not limited to punishing what was done wrong on a few occasions, but also includes praising what was done right on far more occasions.

Focusing on fear, threat, or intimidation can become counterproductive. Rather than stimulating proper work-related behavior, such negative conditions are more likely to generate low levels of morale, commitment, and effort. Again, that does not mean that the supervisor should avoid criticizing or correcting the employee. But criticism should be constructive rather than destructive, emphasizing growth and development as opposed to suspicion and mistrust.

Overall, the process of disciplining staff is not unlike that advocated in earlier chapters for inmates—that is, it should be carried out in a manner which is:

- *Firm*: steadfast, dependable, and unambiguous

- *Fair*: proportional to the seriousness and/or frequency of the infraction

- *Consistent*: administered uniformly without personal bias

It is, however, somewhat more difficult to ensure that these criteria are met when disciplining staff. Because supervisors are selected from the rank and file, a co-worker today can become one's boss tomorrow. Under such a situation, it is not always easy for a newly promoted supervisor to maintain neutrality and objectivity. In other words, "to exercise authority fairly, the new supervisor is forced to alter relationships with former peers,"[64] which is not easy to do.

 # Learning Goals

Do you know:
1. The difference between a supervisor's task and relationship behavior?
2. What four supervisory styles are included in situational leadership and when they should be used?
3. What factors should be taken into account in determining one's leadership style?

Direction

With most employees, the need to invoke the disciplinary process occurs relatively infrequently. In contrast, both line and staff supervisors are required to provide ongoing direction for their subordinates on a continual basis. Because

Ongoing in-service training is essential to maintaining certification and developing professionalism in corrections. Photo by Darlene Jones Powell, American Correctional Association.

staff supervisors in particular represent the organizational rank through which *managerial policies* are translated into *operational practices*, their ability to provide appropriate direction will have much to do with how effectively policies are implemented.

But just how much direction is enough—and conversely, how much direction is too much? At one extreme is the micro-managing supervisor who insists on such close scrutiny that the effect is stifling in terms of initiative and motivation. At the other extreme is the *laissez-faire* supervisor, who provides little if any direction, which can result in uncertainty, confusion, and anxiety. But the problem is not simply finding the proper balance between too little and too much direction. Searching for the "one best" supervisory style is a fruitless task. Such all-encompassing perfection simply does not exist. With some staff members and in some circumstances, a more directive approach is needed. With other people and different circumstances, considerably less oversight may produce a better response.

Situational Leadership®

The issue is not identifying the one most appropriate supervisory technique. Rather, the challenge is to select properly from a variety of approaches after determining which is best suited to the situation, particularly with regard to the needs of the employees. This is what is called *Situational Leadership.*® It is not maintaining one constant, unchanging style. Under Situational Leadership®, the supervisory approach varies to meet the demands of the situation.

Situational Leadership® styles range according to how much *task behavior* (guidance) or *relationship behavior* (support) the supervisor provides. As shown in Figure 13.6, they range from high to low emphasis on giving task-related guidance *to* subordinates, and also range from high to low emphasis on developing supportive relationships *with* subordinates.

More specifically, the four Situational Leadership® styles encompass the following approaches:[65]

figure 13.6

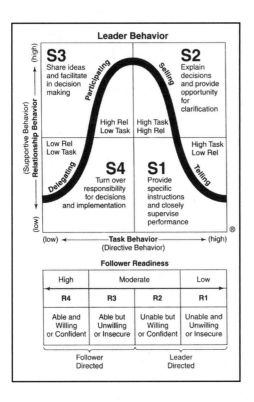

Situational leadership styles.

Source: Paul Hersey, Kenneth H. Blanchard, and Dewey E. Johnson, *Management of Organizational Behavior: Utilizing Human Resources, Seventh Edition.*, Upper Saddle River, New Jersey: Prentice Hall, 2001, p. 182. Used with permission.

1. *Telling* (high task; low relationship). The supervisor provides specific instructions on what is to be done and how it is to be accomplished, and maintains close oversight over job performance.

2. *Selling* (high task; high relationship). The supervisor explains decisions and provides opportunity for clarification. Rather than merely giving instructions on *what* to do, the supervisor describes *why* it should be done, enabling the employee to better understand the merits of the task.

3. *Participating* (high relationship; low task). The supervisor shares decision-making responsibility with subordinates. The main role of the supervisor is communicating and facilitating the process through which subordinates participate in making job-related decisions.

4. *Delegating* (low relationship; low task). The supervisor turns over authority for making and implementing decisions to subordinates. But delegating *does not mean abdicating*. While the authority to make and carry out decisions may be delegated, the supervisor still maintains ultimate responsibility for the end results. Because of the personal maturity of subordinates, neither a high level of relationship nor a high emphasis on task is needed.

Selecting the Right Approach

Needless to say, no single approach is equally suitable for all situations or all employees. During an institutional riot, fire, hostage-taking situation, or other emergency, it is apparent that those with ranking authority must be firmly in command—issuing orders and taking charge in accordance with the "telling" style. In routine, day-to-day circumstances, however, the supervisor may find the need to employ each and every one of these approaches. Selecting the right leadership style for the situation involves determining the employee's level of readiness with regard to the specific task to be done. In other words, the supervisor must assess the employee's:

- *Ability*: the knowledge and skill necessary to be able to do the task
- *Willingness*: the confidence, commitment, and motivation necessary to be *willing* to do the task[66]

New recruits and those being transferred to unfamiliar assignments generally will be relatively low in terms of readiness, at least initially. This is why a more directive, *telling* approach is likely to be appropriate with such employees. The problem is that some supervisors get "locked into" the telling model (or do not know how to implement any other style), despite changes in the subordinate's level of maturity over time. Seniority on the job does not necessarily equate directly with readiness, since even employees who are *able* to do a task may not be *willing*. But as readiness progresses, the supervisor's style should move from telling to selling, then to participating, and ultimately, to delegating.

 # Learning Goals

Do you know:
1. The definition of management?
2. Why planning is needed in correctional agencies?
3. The difference between leaders and managers?
4. What crisis management is and why it is often characteristic of correctional agencies?
5. The relationship between proactively planning and reactively responding?

Correctional Management

It is, of course, at the upper management ranks where overall direction is provided for the entire correctional system. Just as line officers tend to emulate the style of their supervisor, upper-level managers set the tone for the entire organization. However, managers also have much more comprehensive responsibilities than supervisors, since management is the process of *organizing, administering, and coordinating a system that is designed to achieve organizational goals and objectives*. As such, managers are responsible for systematically guiding each phase of the administrative process—from planning to budgeting, staffing, and supervising programs. But it also should be noted that although certain officials carry the title of "managers," management is not the sole responsibility of any particular office. In essence, everyone throughout the organization contributes to the process of managing it.[67]

Planning and Leadership

A considerable part of the manager's job involves planning how to achieve the organization's goals and objectives, since it is planning that "gives us a sense of some control over our own destiny." [68] In fact, it is the visionary foresight involved in long-range planning that largely sets leaders apart from managers, as described in the next "Close-up On Corrections."

Regardless of how many policies are written or how much training is conducted, in the daily administration of a correctional organization, issues are bound to arise that generate conflict or confusion. Effective managers turn controversial issues into opportunities to make progressive change. True leaders proactively anticipate and deal with issues on the horizon before they actually surface and require reactive attention.

Managers focus on keeping the existing system running smoothly, measuring their success by how well goals and objectives are met. But they may get so bogged down in the mundane and immediate matters that their view of the

 # Close-up On Corrections

THE ART OF LEADERSHIP

Component 1. A Leader Knows Where He (or She) is Going

In any organization, people need strong leaders. . . . Often many . . . people feel that they are wandering around in a fog in their organization. They have no sense of vision or direction in their areas of responsibilities. If our top management has no sense of vision or direction, how can we ever expect our people to know where we are going?

Component 2. A Leader Knows How to Get There

For any organization or individual to know where it is going, it is necessary to have a plan. This plan takes the form of goals and objectives. . . . People need to know what to strive for. They desire to know what is expected of them in the performance of their duties. Goals and objectives help an organization stay on target to meet the overall mission and purpose. Without them, we have no path or direction. Without any direction, our purpose becomes clouded . . . [and] motivation is affected.

Component 3. A Leader Knows How to Take People Along

[P]eople want to know and feel that they are needed. . . . An organization that strives to develop that sense of need . . . will see their employee morale grow by leaps and bounds. People will take a stronger interest in their work and a strong bond of unity and cohesiveness will develop between staff members.

Source: Tod Kembel, "Cultivating Our People: The Art of Leadership," *American Jails*, Vol. 5, No. 1, March/April 1991, pp. 87-90. Used with permission.

"big picture" is blocked. Leaders, on the other hand, focus more of their efforts on determining where the organization *should be headed* in the future. That is not meant to imply that they do not oversee the process for achieving goals and objectives. But in contrast to the technical emphasis of managers on controlling what is happening "here and now," leaders are creative visionaries who are already contending with the challenges on the distant horizon. In other words, they direct more of their energies toward *leading* the path to the future than *managing* the process of keeping the organization on its present course.

As in many other fields, however, corrections has traditionally been "over-managed" and "underled."[69] While the mechanics of strategic planning are undertaken at the upper levels of the organization, daily operations are often governed by the old adage, "if it ain't broke, don't fix it," especially in times of fiscal cutbacks—when managers are forced to do more with less. But aside from fiscal limitations, entrenched veteran managers who find change threatening may just want to "keep the lid on." This is understandable in view of external pressures from a turbulent political climate. Political instability contributes to an unwillingness to take risks, and in that type of climate, precedence becomes a good defense. Thus, tradition has a way of becoming ingrained in policy and procedure.

Crisis Management

Moreover, in the short run, it takes much less effort to wait until things fall apart before taking action. It is also more personally stimulating to respond to crisis situations immediately at hand than to plan ahead methodically so that crises can be prevented. For these and many other reasons, there are concerns that corrections is predominantly a "reaction-oriented business."[70] *Proactively planning* is not nearly as enjoyable a task as *reactively responding*. But the less we do of the former, the more we need of the latter.

Management by crisis is not really "managing" anything. It is simply reacting to a situation that is blown out of proportion because of earlier reluctance to be proactive. In other words, the more proactive planning is put off, the more crisis reaction is needed. If nothing was fixed yesterday because it was not yet broken, today and tomorrow will find the manager continually trying to dig out of the resulting "reactive rut."

Decision Making

The manner in which plans are developed will have much to do with how well they can be implemented. Decisions guided by plans that are made by a select few at the top of the organizational hierarchy are likely to encounter resistance—and possibly even active sabotage—as they move down the chain-of-command toward the point of execution. A paramilitary, "telling" approach may be appropriate for jobs that require few discretionary decisions, but work in corrections certainly does not fit that description. Broader representation of more ranks in the planning and decision-making process can promote staff acceptance. That is because people are more likely to be committed to assuring the successful implementation of decisions they were involved in making. Quite simply, "people tend to support what they help to create."[71]

Thus, many agencies have adopted *participatory management* techniques. Often, however, these approaches are modified versions of what is actually meant by participation: "For example, managers may solicit input from employees but not really involve them in the decision-making."[72]

Nor is the need to expand participation limited to those within the agency itself. Correctional administration differs from other types of public administration in terms of the many external stakeholders to which it must respond, each representing varying attitudes, opinions, and beliefs concerning crime and the treatment of criminals. Therefore, a significant part of the correctional leader's job is interacting with that external environment to obtain public support for correctional policies and practices.[73]

Organizational Culture

Perhaps most importantly, correctional managers and leaders set the tone that establishes the agency's cultural environment. It is through their actions, reactions, and inactions that powerful messages are communicated to staff which, in turn, shape the organization's culture. Culture embraces the norms, values, and prevailing beliefs of an organization—in other words, what is considered acceptable or unacceptable, ethical or unethical, appropriate or inappropriate. It is that cultural climate which strongly influences individual behavior throughout the chain of command. Thus, it is essential that organizational culture is properly aligned with the agency's vision and mission.

There is little doubt that the very nature of working in corrections means confronting insufficient resources, uncooperative clients, and an unsupportive public. These drawbacks eventually can take their toll on even the most dedicated personnel. Confronting such inherent obstacles would be considerably less frustrating, however, in a supportive administrative environment. It is one thing to persevere in the face of an apathetic public and an unappreciative clientele. But staff cannot be expected to maintain peak performance within an organizational culture that is plagued with contradiction, ambiguity, inequity, inconsistency, unethical behavior, or autocratic management.[74]

Moreover, in a number of agencies, the leadership challenge is to move from a politically based to a professionally based culture, which represents yet another distinction between leadership and management—in other words, "Leaders create and change cultures, while managers and administrators live within them."[75] It is leaders who establish the cultural foundation that either will uplift and encourage or crush and discourage every employee throughout the organization. That culture will likewise have a decisive effect on long-term results throughout the entire correctional conglomerate.

Summary

The majority of correctional employees in the United States work as officers in prisons and jails. Their stereotypical image is changing as younger, better-educated people and more minorities and women are entering the field. Such trends are both a benefit and a challenge to administrators, who must adjust to greater diversity in the workplace and meet the changing demands of new generations of workers.

Under Title VII of the Civil Rights Act, employers are prohibited from practicing discrimination. As a result, women have been increasingly employed in correctional agencies, creating conflict between equal employment rights and inmate privacy. Initially, this was resolved by restricting female job assignments to noncontact posts. But that practice has been opposed by males who were denied such preferential positions. The outcome has been a compromise involving broader integration of women throughout the workforce while minimizing intrusion on inmate privacy.

The "new breed" of employees with expanded career options may be more likely to join unions or leave unsatisfactory employment. But corrections historically has been plagued by high turnover rates. When management can identify and rectify factors in the work environment that promote dissatisfaction, the organization is likely to experience less attrition.

Because there will always be some turnover, however, there will always be a need for active recruitment. Correctional recruitment traditionally has been hampered by constraints surrounding image, vacancy pressures, and compensation. Although these issues have often been used to justify reduced entrance standards, they are subject to change.

Like selection procedures, basic training should be structured around the knowledge, skills, and abilities reflected in a job-task analysis. In various states, the point at which entry-level training is offered varies—from the historical approach (following time on the job), to the traditional practice (immediately on hire), to the emerging professional model (prior to employment).

Unlike most entry jobs, correctional officers become line supervisors immediately on assignment. Like staff supervisors, they, therefore, must be able to motivate, discipline, and direct subordinates. Both rewards and punishments can be used to shape behavior, although the latter unfortunately tend to be employed more frequently. It is also through supervisors that management policies are translated into operational practices. In that regard, ongoing direction is best provided through situational leadership—that is, adjusting one's style according to the demands of the situation, particularly with regard to the follower's level of readiness in terms of the task at hand.

While supervisors implement policy, upper-level managers are responsible for developing it through the process of planning, decision making, and allocating resources. Proactive planning is essential to avoid the reactive response pattern that creates management by crisis. In fact, it is largely vision and planning foresight that distinguish leaders from managers. Plans and decisions are most effectively made with the active participation of those who will be responsible for their implementation. But it is creating a positive, uplifting organizational culture that is perhaps the greatest challenge for correctional leaders. In that regard, it has been noted that perhaps the most significant difference between leaders and managers is that managers "do things right," whereas leaders "do the right things." [76]

Endnotes

1. Sharon Johnson Rion, "Dinosaurs Don't Make Good Gazelles," *A View from the Trenches: A Manual for Wardens by Wardens*, Lanham, Maryland: American Correctional Association, 1999, p. 7-23.

2. Jeanne B. Stinchcomb, "Introduction," *Correctional Issues: Correctional Management*, Lanham, Maryland: American Correctional Association, 1990, p. vi.

3. James J. Stephan, *State Prison Expenditures, 1996*, Washington, D.C.: U.S. Department of Justice, Bureau of Justice Statistics, 1999, p. 5.

4. Tod Kembel, "Cultivating Our People: The Art of Leadership," *American Jails*, Vol. 5, No. 1, March/April 1991, p. 90.

5. Compiled from Camille Graham Camp, ed., *The 2002 Corrections Yearbook*, Middletown, Connecticut: Criminal Justice Institute, 2003, pp. 154, 219.

6. *Sourcebook of Criminal Justice Statistics, 1998*, Washington, D.C.: U.S. Department of Justice, 1999, p. 24. Data reflect comparisons between 1982 and 1994.

7. James J. Stephan, *Census of State and Federal Correctional Facilities, 2000*, Washington, D.C.: U.S. Department of Justice, Bureau of Justice Statistics, August 2003, p. 12, which reflects employee growth between 1995 and 2000 ranging from 23 to 95 percent.

8. *Ibid.*, p. 14, and James J. Stephan, *Census of Jails, 1999*, Washington, D.C.: U.S. Department of Justice, Bureau of Justice Statistics, 2001, p. 9.

9. Camp, ed., *The 2002 Corrections Yearbook*, p. 219.

10. Timothy J. Flanagan, W. W. Johnson, and K. Bennett, "Job Satisfaction among Correctional Executives: A Contemporary Portrait of Wardens of State Prisons for Adults," *The Prison Journal*, December 1996, p. 386.

11. *Ibid.*, pp. 132 and 200.

12. Jeanne B. Stinchcomb, "Developing Correctional Officer Professionalism: A Work in Progress," *Corrections Compendium*, Vol. 25, No. 5, May 2000, p. 2, citing data gathered by *Corrections Compendium*, May 2000, pp. 10-11.

13. Linda E. Zimmer, *Women Guarding Men*, Chicago: University of Chicago Press, 1986, p. 6. *See also* Joann B. Morton, "The 'Agency of Women': Women and ACA," *Corrections Today*, Vol. 57, No. 5, August 1995, p. 82.

14. Barbara W. Jones, "Relevant Rulings: Examining the Case for Women in Corrections," *Corrections Today*, Vol. 54, No. 6, August 1992, p.104.

15. Linda L. Zupan, "Men Guarding Women: An Analysis of the Employment of Male Correction Officers in Prisons for Women," *Journal of Criminal Justice*, Vol. 20, No. 4, 1992, p. 297.

16. Zimmer, *Women Guarding Men*, p. 57.

17. The following information is summarized from *Ibid.*, pp. 65-69.

18. *Women in Criminal Justice: A Twenty-year Update*, Washington, D.C.: National Institute of Justice, U.S. Department of Justice, 1998.

19. Summarized from Zimmer, *Women Guarding Men*, pp. 60-65.

20. Men were assaulted 3.6 times more often. Joseph R. Rowan, "Who is Safer in Male Maximum Security Prisons?," *Corrections Today*, Vol. 58, No. 2, March 1996, pp. 186-189.

21. *Sexual Misconduct in Prisons: Law, Agency Response, and Prevention*, Longmont, Colorado: National Institute of Corrections, May 2000. For specific examples, *see* Sharon A. Kennedy, "Sex Behind Bars: Court and Corrections Response," *American Jails*, July/August 1996, pp. 33-38.

22. Susan W. McCampbell and Elizabeth P. Layman, *Training Curriculum for Investigating Allegations of Staff Sexual Misconduct with Inmates*, Tamarac, Florida: Center for Innovative Public Policies, October 2000, Section 1, pp. 4-5.

23. *Ibid.*, p. 8.

24. *Women in Prison: Sexual Misconduct by Correctional Staff*, Report to the Honorable Eleanor Holmes Norton, House of Representatives, Washington, D.C.: U.S. Government Accounting Office, June 1999.

25. Barbara Bloom, Barbara Owen, and Stephanie Covington, *Gender-Responsive Strategies: Research, Practice, and Guiding Principles for Women Offenders*, Washington, D.C.: U.S. Department of Justice, National Institute of Corrections, 2003, p. 25.

26. Jeanne B. Stinchcomb, "Police Stress: Could Organizational Culture be the Culprit?," *Law Enforcement Executive Forum*, Spring 2004, p. 155.

27. Lynne C. Lancaster and David Stillman, *When Generations Collide: Who They Are. Why They Clash. How to Solve the Generational Puzzle at Work*, New York:: Harper Collins, 2000, pp. 30-31.

28. David E. Kaup, "Attitude Change," *American Jails*, Vol. 6, No. 5, November/December 1992, p. 36.

29. *2004 Directory of Adult and Juvenile Correctional Departments, Institutions, Agencies, and Probation and Parole Authorities*, Lanham, Maryland: American Correctional Association, 2003. *See also* Eric G. Lambert, "To Stay or Quit: A Review of the Literature on Correctional Staff Turnover," *American Journal of Criminal Justice*, Vol. 26, No. 1, Fall 2001, p. 61, where even higher turnover rates are cited.

30. Barbara Sims, "Surveying the Correctional Environment: A Review of the Literature," *Corrections Management Quarterly*, Vol. 5, No. 2, Spring 2001, p. 4; Risdon N. Slate, Ronald E. Vogel, and W. Wesley Johnson, "To Quit or Not to Quit: Perceptions of Participation in Correctional Decision-making and the Impact of Organizational Stress," *Corrections Management Quarterly*, Vol. 5, No. 2, Spring 2001, p. 74-75; and Mary K. Stohr, Ruth L. Self, and Nicholas P. Lovrich, "Staff Turnover in New Generation Jails: An Investigation of Its Causes and Prevention," *Journal of Criminal Justice*, Vol. 20, 1992, p. 457.

31. Jeff Maahs and Travis Pratt, "Uncovering the Predictors of Correctional Officers' Attitudes and Behaviors: A Meta-Analysis," *Corrections Management Quarterly*, Vol. 5, No. 2, Spring 2001, p. 17.

32. Stohr, Self, and Lovrich, "Staff Turnover in New Generation Jails," p. 457.

33. Allan L. Patenaude, "Analysis of Issues Affecting Correctional Officer Retention within the Arkansas Department of Correction," *Corrections Management Quarterly*, Vol. 5, No. 2, Spring 2001, p. 59.

34. *Ibid.*, p. 64.

35. Gary L. Dennis, "Here Today, Gone Tomorrow: How Management Style Affects Job Satisfaction and, in Turn, Employee Turnover," *Corrections Today*, Vol. 60, No. 3, June 1998, pp. 96-101.

36. Nancy C. Jurik and Russell Winn, "Describing Correctional-Security Dropouts and Rejects—An Individual and Organizational Profile," *Criminal Justice and Behavior*, Vol. 14, March 1987, pp. 5-25.

37. Jane Lommel, "Turning around Turnover," *Corrections Today*, Vol. 66, No. 5, 2004, p. 56.

38. Jeanne B. Stinchcomb "Correctional Officer Stress: Is Training Missing the Target?," *Issues in Correctional Training and Casework*, October 1986, pp. 19-23.

39. Kevin N. Wright, William G. Saylor, Evan Gilman, and Scott Camp, "Job Control and Occupational Outcomes among Prison Workers," *Justice Quarterly*, Vol. 14, No. 3, September 1997, p. 525; and Slate, Vogel, Johnson, "To Quit or Not to Quit," p. 74.

40. Dennis, p. 97.

41. Julie A. Honnold and Jeanne B. Stinchcomb, "Officer Stress: Costs, Causes, and Cures," *Corrections Today*, Vol. 47, No. 7, December 1985, pp. 49-50.

42. Barbara A. Owen, *The Reproduction of Social Control: A Study of Prison Workers at San Quentin*, Westport, Connecticut: Praeger, 1988; Slate, Vogel, and Johnson, "To Quit or Not to Quit: Perceptions of Participation in Correctional Decision-making and the Impact of Organizational Stress," *Corrections Management Quarterly*, Vol. 5, No. 2, 2001, pp. 68-78.

43. Frances E. Cheek and Marie DiStefano Miller, "The Experience of Stress for Correction Officers: A Double-Bind Theory of Correctional Stress," *Journal of Criminal Justice*, Vol. 11, No. 2, 1983, pp. 105-120. *See also* Doris T. Wells, "Reducing Stress for Officers and Their Families," *Corrections Today*, Vol. 65, No. 2, April 2003, pp. 24-25.

44. Gerald W. McEntee and William Lucy, *Prisoners of Life: A Study of Occupational Stress Among State Corrections Officers*, Washington, D.C.: American Federation of State, County and Municipal Employees, n.d., p. 22 and Table 25. (The three states included in this study were Pennsylvania, Illinois, and Washington). For a similar review of the status of stress research, *see* Robert G. Huckabee, "Stress in Corrections: An Overview of the Issues," *Journal of Criminal Justice*, Vol. 20, No. 5, 1992, pp. 479-486.

45. Sarah J. Tracy, "Correctional Contradictions: A Structural Approach to Addressing Officer Burnout," *Corrections Today*, Vol. 65, No. 2, April 2003, p. 94.

46. Marilyn D. McShane, Frank P Williams, and David Shichor, *Correctional Management in the 1990's: A National Survey of Correctional Managers*, Volume II, San Bernardino, California: California State University, Department of Criminal Justice, 1990, p. 10.

47. *See*, for example, Douglas L. Yearwood, "Recruitment and Retention Issues in North Carolina," *American Jails*, September/October 2003, pp. 9-14.

48. *Ibid.*, p. 14.

49. *Vital Statistics in Corrections*, Lanham, Maryland: American Correctional Association, 2000, p. 161.

50. *Ibid.* P. 32.

51. *See* Jeanne B. Stinchcomb, "Why Not the Best? Using Assessment Centers for Officer Selection," *Corrections Today*, Vol. 47, No. 3, June 1985, pp. 120-124.

52. Mary K. Stohr-Gillmore, Michael W. Stohr-Gillmore, and Nicholas P. Lovrich, "Sifting the Gold from the Pebbles: Using Situational Interviews to Select Correctional Officers for Direct Supervision Jails," *American Jails*, Vol. 3, No. 4, Winter 1990, pp. 29-34.

53. *Performance-based Standards for Adult Local Detention Facilities*, 4th ed., Lanham, Maryland: American Correctional Association, 2004, p. 115.

54. Dianne Carter, "The Status of Education and Training in Corrections" (Part II), *Journal of Correctional Training*, Spring 1992, p. 6.

55. "Officer Training Programs: Survey Summary," *Corrections Compendium*, Vol. 25, No. 5, May 2000, p. 9.

56. Jess Maghan and William C. Collins, "What Staff Doesn't Know *Can* Hurt Them: Correctional Law Training," *Corrections Today*, Vol. 50, No. 5, August 1988, p. 164. *See also* Randy Borum and Harley Stock, "Excessive Force Prevention Programs: An Essential Tool to Properly Train Staff and Protect against Litigation," *Corrections Today*, Vol. 54, No. 4, June 1992, pp. 26-30.

57. "Survey Summary: Correctional Budgets," *Corrections Compendium*, Vol. 25, No. 12, December 2000, p. 8.

58. June Damanti and Jeanne B. Stinchcomb, "Moving toward Professionalism: The Preservice Approach to Entry-Level Training," *Journal of Correctional Training*, Summer 1990, pp. 9-10. *See also* Jeanne B. Stinchcomb, "Jails and Academe: A Partnership Made on Wall Street," *American Jails*, May/June 1999, pp. 85-86.

59. Robert B. Levinson, Jeanne B. Stinchcomb, and John J. Greene, "Corrections Certification: First Steps toward Professionalism" *Corrections Today*, Vol. 63, No. 5, August 2001, pp. 125-138.

60. Jeanne B. Stinchcomb, "Correctional Certification: Getting down from the Bandwagon and Leading the Band," *Corrections Now*, February 2004, p. 4.

61. William G. Archambeault and Betty J. Archambeault, *Correctional Supervisory Management*, Englewood Cliffs, New Jersey: Prentice Hall, 1982, p. 5.

62. Peggy Ritchie-Matsumoto, "Using CQI Techniques to Benefit Corrections," *Corrections Today*, Vol. 54, No. 8, December 1992, p. 158. *See also* Clifford E. Simonsen and Douglas Arnold, "Is Corrections Ready for TQM?," *Corrections Today*, Vol. 56, No. 4, July 1994, p. 166.

63. Richard L. Phillips and Charles R. McConnell, *The Effective Corrections Manager: Maximizing Staff Performance in Demanding Times*, Gaithersburg, Maryland: Aspen Publishers, 1996, p. 336.

64. Harry K. Singletary, "The Race for Promotions," in *Correctional Issues: Correctional Management*, Lanham, Maryland: American Correctional Association, 1990, p. 27.

65. Paraphrased from Paul Hersey, Kenneth H. Blanchard, and Dewey E. Johnson, *Management of Organizational Behavior: Utilizing Human Resources*, 7th ed., Upper Saddle River, New Jersey: Prentice Hall, 1996, pp. 201-205.

66. *Ibid.*

67. Stan Stojkovic, David Kalinich, and John Klofas, *Criminal Justice Organizations: Administration and Management*, Belmont, California: Wadsworth, 2003, p. 7.

68. Samuel E Saxton, "A Participatory Approach to Management," in *Correctional Issues: Correctional Management*, Lanham, Maryland: American Correctional Association, 1990, p. 35.

69. John P. Kotter, *What Leaders Really Do*, Boston, Massachusetts: *Harvard Business Review*, 1999, p. 51, (referring to U.S. corporations).

70. Peter Perroncello, "The Role of the Jail Supervisor: Proactive or Reactive?" *American Jails*, Vol. 3, No. 3, Fall 1989, pp. 74-76.

71. Saxton, "A Participatory Approach to Management," p. 31.

72. Frank P. Williams, "An Analysis of Factors Affecting Management Styles in American Prisons and Juvenile Institutions," paper presented at the Academy of Criminal Justice Sciences, Pittsburgh, Pennsylvania, March 1992, p. 4.

73. *See* Jeanne B. Stinchcomb and Susan W. McCampbell, "From Organizational Management to Inspirational Leadership: Changing Roles and Training Implications for Newly Elected Sheriffs," *Sheriff*, January-February 2004, pp. 18-21 and 42-44.

74. Stinchcomb, "Could Organizational Culture be the Culprit?"

75. Edgar Schein, *Organizational Culture and Leadership*, San Francisco, California: Jossey-Bass, 1992, p. 5.

76. Warren Bennis, *On Becoming a Leader*, Reading, Massachusetts: Addison-Wesley, 1989.

CHAPTER 14

LEGAL ISSUES AND LIABILITY

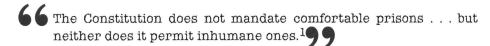

66 The Constitution does not mandate comfortable prisons . . . but neither does it permit inhumane ones.[1] **99**

—Supreme Court Justice David Souter

Chapter Overview

Throughout this chapter, numerous examples are cited of how vigorously the courts have emerged from a long period of reluctance to address correctional operations. In fact, the years of most active intervention generated concern that the judiciary may have been overextending its interference. More recently, the general trend in correctional law has been directed toward achieving an equitable balance between inmate rights and institutional security. Nevertheless, the courts have made it clear that they will respond to valid inmate complaints when administrators are unable or unwilling to do so.

By no means are all of the controversies that result in litigation a reflection of inadequate or uncaring management. There are fundamental differences concerning issues ranging from the morality of the death penalty to methods of inmate discipline that ultimately will be settled in the courts. But it is also important to note that remedies do not need to be strictly dichotomous, "either-or" choices. To acknowledge the interests of both sides, the courts increasingly have attempted to balance the legal rights of inmates with the legitimate needs of correctional institutions. However, that has been a relatively

517

recent development. Earlier rulings tended to benefit one side over the other at differing points in the historical development of correctional law.

✸ Learning Goals

Do you know:

1. The differences between the hands-off, involved-hands, and restrained-hands phases of correctional law?

2. On what basis the courts were initially reluctant to become involved in inmate litigation?

3. How social, political, and public policy trends affect correctional case law?

Legal Issues

Until the 1960s, corrections was largely insulated from legal scrutiny, and the courts were somewhat hesitant to intervene in correctional operations. During this lengthy hands-off period,[2] the inmate's legal status was virtually that of a "slave of the state"—who, upon conviction, no longer enjoyed the rights, privileges, and immunities of law-abiding citizens.[3] Beyond a limited view of inmate rights, the hands-off phase reflected judicial concerns about disrupting the balance of power between the executive and judicial branches of government, and a general acceptance of the presumed expertise of correctional administrators. In other words, during the hands-off phase, correctional managers functioned relatively independently, because it was assumed that:

- While criminal suspects were entitled to constitutional rights at the trial phase, the courts would not respond to their postconviction claims.

- Since corrections was designed to benefit the offender, correctional staff would know what was best for the inmate.

- Whatever was given to an offender was a "privilege"—not a "right"—and, as such, could be subject to conditions or taken away for any reason.[4]

Involved Hands

During the 1960s, however, widespread challenges to traditional authority emerged. Previously disenfranchised groups began to demand equal rights, a voice in government, and protection under the law. It was therefore not surprising to find the courts also directing attention toward those most powerless and unprotected—correctional clients. This expanding recognition of individual rights prompted the *involved-hands phase* of judicial activism, opening corrections to widespread constitutional review.

Under such scrutiny, many of the inmate rights discussed throughout the remainder of this section were enacted. Moreover, the emergence of a receptive audience was not overlooked by the inmates. In the thirty years between 1966 and 1996, as the inmate population has escalated, so has the number of suits they filed in federal courts (*see* Figure 14.1).

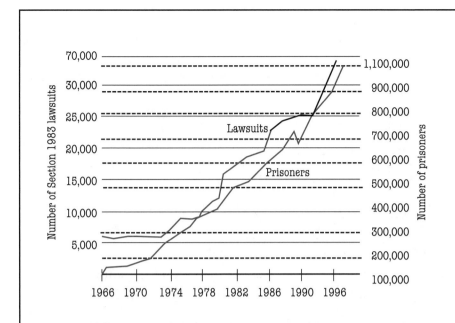

figure 14.1

National trends in the number of state prisoners and liability (Section 1983) lawsuits.

Source: Roger A. Hanson and Henry W. K. Daley, *Challenging the Conditions of Prisons and Jails*, Washington, DC: U.S. Department of Justice, 1995, p. 3, and John Scalia, "Prisoner Petitions Filed in U.S. District Courts, 2000," *Bureau of Justice Statistics: Special Report*, Washington, DC: U.S. Department of Justice, 2002, p.1.

Restrained Hands

As the more conservative social climate of the 1980s replaced the liberalism of the 1960s, judicial intervention began to reflect a compromise between the extremes of the two earlier phases. This does not mean the flagrant violations that prompted the hands-on stage are being tolerated. But neither does it mean that management is as severely curtailed as it was during the involved-hands phase. Rather, the *restrained-hands approach* characteristic of the past two decades has been more likely to attempt to seek a reasonable balance between the rights of inmates and the security interests of correctional administrators.

Using this "balancing test," the Supreme Court has ruled that certain restrictions on an inmate's constitutional rights are allowable if they are reasonably related to legitimate correctional interests, such as promoting institutional safety and security.[5] However, today's courts are not as quick to impose their own solutions. When a violation occurs now, they are somewhat more likely to give correctional administrators an opportunity to correct the problem.

Today's Legal Climate

Ever since the Supreme Court pronounced that "the Constitution does not mandate comfortable prisons,"[6] the stage has been set for turning an unsympathetic judicial ear toward inmate litigation. Fueled in part by media-driven denouncements of frivolous lawsuits, along with more conservative judicial appointments and a less tolerant public that is vocally supportive of "no frills'" prisons, the courts have retreated somewhat from their earlier activist position. In fact, some speculate that the Supreme Court itself is "headed toward a new hands-off doctrine that would require lower courts to defer to the internal actions and decisions of prison officials."[7] In the meantime, it has become more difficult to mount successful constitutional suits challenging prison management.[8] This is largely because "more control over prisons has been given back to the states, and the courts are displaying more tolerance for minor violations of prisoners' constitutional rights."[9] Thus, the case law reported throughout the remainder of this chapter remains subject to ongoing refinement, in keeping with prevailing social, political, and public policy trends.

✸ Learning Goals

Do you know:

1. How court rulings on inmate rights redefine the power, authority, and liability of employees?
2. The difference between civil and criminal liability?
3. What types of damages can result from being held civilly liable?
4. What vicarious liability is and under what conditions it occurs?

Impact of Successful Inmate Litigation

Whenever the courts redefine inmate rights, the outcome produces an accompanying redefinition of the power, authority, and liability of correctional staff. For example, when inmate rights are *expanded*, a substantial impact on personnel results. Their power and authority are subsequently *reduced*, since they no longer have the autonomy to engage in practices that the courts have ruled as unconstitutional. At the same time, employees' liability is *increased*, as those in violation of constitutional provisions find themselves more vulnerable to civil litigation.

Lawsuits filed by offenders are a source of concern to both administrative and operational staff for other reasons as well. Inmates may petition the courts to seek redress for damages or to challenge practices on the basis that constitutional or civil rights have been violated. Thus, both the employing agency and

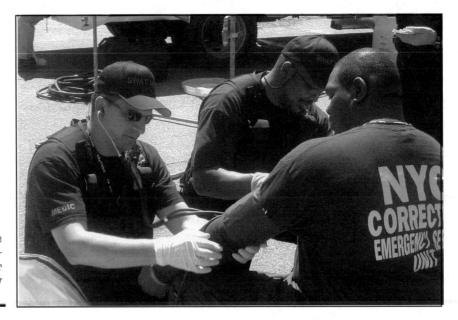

Failure to train is one of the causes of legal action. Here correctional employees practice their skills during a mock riot. Photo by Diane Geiman.

figure 14.2

	Criminal	Civil
Action initiated by	The state	The victim
Invoked as a result of harm caused to	Society overall	A particular person
For the purpose of	Punishment	Compensation

Criminal and civil law comparisons.

its individual employees are subject to being named in lawsuits when their actions or inactions caused harm, injury, or death.

Organizational and Employee Liability

Litigation can take the form of civil or criminal liability (or both), depending on whether a criminal law was violated. *Criminal liability* applies when, in the course of performing one's job, an employee is found to have broken the law and is therefore held accountable in criminal court. For example, an officer who assaults and severely injures an inmate could be held criminally liable if the officer cannot establish that he or she was acting in *self-defense*.

Being prosecuted for a criminal act is not, however, the only form of liability that could result from this situation. Regardless of whether the officer is charged, convicted, and/or punished by the state, the injured inmate can still file a *civil liability* claim. As illustrated in Figure 14.2, there are several fundamental differences between criminal and civil law.

Criminal-law violations are prosecuted by the state for punishment of the disruption of the social order. In contrast, civil action is initiated by the individual victim to obtain compensation for such damages as medical bills, pain, suffering, or lost wages. A conviction of guilt in criminal court may assist in establishing a subsequent civil case, but acquittal in criminal court does not automatically absolve the defendant of possible civil liability.

Damage Awards

If an inmate is successful in pursuing a civil case against a correctional employee or agency, the court can award one of three types of damages:

1. *Nominal*: an insignificant amount of money (such as $1), which may be accompanied by a "cease and desist" injunction prohibiting similar behavior in the future.

2. *Compensatory*: a monetary award that is generally equated with the expenses incurred by the victim to compensate for fiscal losses.

3. *Punitive*: a substantial monetary award that goes beyond mere compensation to punish the offender (or offending agency) "through the pocketbook," under the theory that suffering a major economic setback will prevent the behavior from reoccurring.

Since the ability of individual staff members to pay a large monetary settlement is limited, civil suits often are directed toward the employing governmental agency, which obviously has far greater fiscal resources. Moreover, "most inmates do not file lawsuits directly against line officers; instead, they challenge rules and policies established by administrators or other officials."[10] This raises the question of how an employing agency, a supervisor, or an administrator can be held liable for the actions of a subordinate.

Vicarious Liability

The answer involves another form of civil liability, which encompasses wrongdoing beyond one's own direct actions or inactions. This indirect or *vicarious* liability is created when:

- Someone (such as the employee's supervisor) *knew or should have known* what was occurring or about to occur,[11] but

- *Did nothing* to correct the situation, and

- That lack of action was the *proximate cause* (as opposed to the direct cause) of subsequent harm, injury, or death.

Such vicarious liability can result from a variety of circumstances, including:

- *Failure to train.* If, for example, in the previously cited case, the assaulting officer had recently been employed and had not yet been sent to the training academy, the officer could claim that he or she was not properly prepared for what to expect on the job and how to react appropriately. If successful in doing so, liability could transfer to the employing agency.

- *Negligent supervision.* Again, using the same case, if the employee's supervisor witnessed the assault and did not intervene, the supervisor could incur liability as well. But a supervisor would not necessarily need to observe the incident visually to be held vicariously liable—if, for instance, the supervisor was well aware that this employee engaged in assaultive behavior in the past and had taken no corrective action to stop it.

- *Negligent employment or retention.* Like the supervisory example, this is a form of the "known or should have known" feature of vicarious liability.

Let us say that the employee had a long history of being fired by other correctional institutions for assaulting inmates. The courts could maintain that the pattern of behavior was apparent had any effort been made to look into previous employment, thus holding the organization liable for negligent employment. If, on the other hand, the employee came into the agency with a clean record, but demonstrated a history of assaultive attacks following employment, the agency potentially could be held liable for negligent retention.

These are among the most difficult cases to defend. Research indicates that while correctional officials prevail in most prison litigation, inmates won 53 percent of cases in the category of administrative liability (for example, failure to train, lack of supervision, or deficient policies).[12] Yet, in the daily press of business, organizations and their employees do not always take these possible sources of liability into consideration. For example, look at the scenario

Close-up On Corrections

LIABLE OR NOT?

Officer Johnson arrives on duty for the 11:00 P.M. to 7:00 A.M. shift. Immediately, he realizes that it is not going to be a good night. The sergeant is barking out a constant stream of orders. Phone lines are ringing incessantly. Officers are scurrying off to their posts. Metal is clanging against metal as sallyport gates continually open and close to admit and release coming and going staff. Things look even more chaotic than usual at shift change.

Johnson receives his orders—transporting an inmate from "D" wing to the downtown hospital. The inmate's condition is not exactly an emergency but has been ranked as a high-priority case. Officer Johnson realizes that to do an outside transportation run, he will be required to carry a weapon, and his annual firearms-qualification card expired last month. Momentarily, he debates whether to just do the run without telling the sergeant, but he decides against it.

"Sarge, I hate to say this, but remember last month when they couldn't spare me to go to the range? Well, my firearms qualification is up."

The sergeant is in no mood to hear complaints or excuses: "Yeah, well, this is sure a fine time to tell me that! You know what I have here tonight? Nowhere near enough to run this shift, that's what—three out sick, four on leave, and two more off for some training class."

"But sarge, you know I have to check out a weapon for this run. Can't you give it to someone with a card?"

"Listen, I don't even know where the list is, and does it look like I've got time to hunt for it? Besides, the problem around here is we have too many stupid rules anyway. If that damn phone would just stop. . . ."

"But sarge . . ." The sergeant answers the phone, "Control Desk, hold on." Turning to the officer, "Johnson, that's enough! Get going!" The sergeant goes back to the phone; the officer leaves for the transportation detail.

Officer Johnson pulls up to the hospital admission area. It is close to midnight and only a few people are milling around in the vicinity. They appear to be harmlessly going about their business. He breathes a sigh of relief and begins to remove the inmate from the vehicle. Without warning, two armed men emerge out of the shadows. They hit Johnson, force him to the ground, and take off with the inmate. One turns around briefly, pointing his weapon in the officer's direction. Johnson fires his revolver, and an innocent bystander is shot.

In this case, are there grounds for charging:

- The officer with criminal liability?

- The officer with civil liability?

- Anyone else with criminal or civil liability?

- If so, what type of liability would apply? Why?

(Answers appear at the end of the chapter, page 550.)

presented in the previous "Close-up On Corrections" and see if you can determine what, if any, consequences in terms of civil or criminal liability could result.

Liability Defense

The best protection against liability is a proactive rather than a reactive approach. This means continually being aware of what is going on within the organization, making it clear what is and is not acceptable through written policies and procedures, and taking all reasonable measures to assure that everyone fully recognizes the inmate's constitutional and civil rights. As in sports, the best defense is a good offense. "By addressing identified problems and concerns, the responsible administrator will sharply reduce vulnerability for civil litigation."[13] Managers, supervisors, and operational staff who avoid taking shortcuts, stay abreast of legal issues, and treat inmates with the same respect that they would desire if roles were reversed will achieve far more insulation from liability than any insurance policies could hope to provide.

 # Learning Goals

Do you know:

1. To what extent the freedom to exercise religious rights may be restricted in correctional institutions?
2. What factors the courts have considered in determining whether correctional officials must accommodate religious beliefs in such areas as special diets, worship services, personal grooming regulations, and the wearing or displaying of religious artifacts?

The Changing Nature of Correctional Law

Needless to say, everyone who works in corrections does not abide by such principles of professionalism. And, it is not always clear just how far to extend inmate rights. Often it is only after the courts have decided key issues that correctional personnel actually have clear guidelines to follow. The remainder of this chapter reviews some of the significant areas in which the courts have shaped correctional policies and operational practices.

However, it is important to point out that correctional law is continually changing. New cases are being decided on a regular basis, and thus, their resulting impact is always subject to change. In this dynamic environment, discussions of judicial influence on correctional policy quickly can become dated. Cases cited may have been superseded by more recent rulings, pointing correctional practices in alternate directions. The following material is therefore provided as illustrative demonstrations of how legal decision making has affected correctional policy and practice at one point in time, and not necessarily as definitive statements of the current legal status of correctional practices.

Freedom of Religion

Under the First Amendment of the U.S. Constitution, the right to exercise religious beliefs is protected. Those in free society are readily able to attend whatever religious services they desire, to regulate their diet in accordance with religious practices, to wear or display religious materials, and so on. But enabling inmates to maintain such widespread freedoms would be difficult in a large institution encompassing many different religions, and in some respects, it could jeopardize security as well. Thus, in keeping with the balancing test, inmates' freedom to fully exercise First Amendment rights may be reasonably restricted. In deciding to what extent such restrictions are constitutional, the courts have addressed a number of related questions:

- *To what extent can (or should) government subsidize religious activities?*

Technically, the First Amendment prohibits state establishment of any religion, which could be interpreted as prohibiting the use of government funds for such religious activities as paying the salaries of chaplains. Yet, at the same time, government itself deprives some citizens of the full exercise of their religious rights—when, for example, they are stationed in remote areas on a military base or confined in a correctional facility. To compensate for this state-created deprivation, the Supreme Court has held that provision of compensatory services in the form of prison chaplains is justifiable.[14]

Whether inmates must be provided with state-compensated clergy representative of their *specific faith* is, however, another issue. It has been ruled that corrections is not expected to maintain a "full complement" of religious personnel on the payroll, but rather, that a "representative selection" would suffice. This decision is based on the premise that chaplains "are hired to serve the spiritual needs of all prisoners and are not intended to be merely the emissaries of their particular churches."[15]

- *Exactly what qualifies as an actual religion?*

To be safeguarded under the First Amendment, it is necessary to establish that the protections being sought do represent the practices of a recognized religion. The definition of "religion" is not limited to conventional faiths. For example, the courts have held that witchcraft meets the test of qualifying as a religion. On the other hand, the courts have refused to grant First Amendment protections to an inmate-created group called Church of the New Song (CONS), whose principles require them to be "served steak and wine from time to time."[16]

- *To what extent is the free exercise of religion protected?*

Once it has been established that certain beliefs represent an acknowledged religion, the issue becomes to what degree correctional institutions can interfere with the unrestricted exercise of religious practices. This raises difficult issues, since accommodating religious beliefs essentially means providing special treatment for certain groups.

Some religious principles are relatively uncomplicated and easy to comply with in confinement. When Catholics were prohibited from eating meat on Fridays, for instance, it was not any major imposition to schedule fish to be served. On the other hand, pork is inexpensive and, therefore, frequently used in institutional meals. Both Jewish and Black Muslim religions have challenged this practice, although their claims "have met with mixed success because the dietary requests may pose both logistical and economic problems to prison administrators."[17]

Generally, the courts have favored accommodating pork-free diet restrictions where those holding such religious principles represent a significant portion of the inmate population. However, it has also been held that eliminating pork completely from institutional menus is not required if inmates are provided with a sufficient variety of foods to enable them to "obtain a nutritionally adequate diet without violating their religious beliefs."[18] In deciding these cases, the administrative ease or difficulty of providing special diets will be a significant factor, as vividly portrayed in the next "Close-up On Corrections."

- *Do inmates have a right to attend religious services?*

Given the wide diversity of religions represented within large institutions, it is difficult to provide formal services for every conceivable group. When such services are offered, however, they cannot be confined to traditional faiths. On this issue, the Supreme Court has noted that an inmate is entitled to a "reasonable opportunity of pursuing his faith comparable to the opportunity afforded fellow prisoners who adhere to conventional religious precepts."[19]

Religions that represent sizable numbers of inmates traditionally have been permitted to gather for services, provided that doing so does not represent a risk to institutional order and security. In fact, the practice of religion has been extended to enable Native Americans to participate in sweat lodge ceremonies.[20] Generally, courts have upheld the order-and-security constraint, ruling that

 # Close-up On Corrections

DIET TOO COMPLICATED

A New York federal court refused to order the New York Department of Correctional Services to meet the dietary demands of Rastafarians (. . . a religion with roots in the culture of Jamaica). The demands were quite complex and included such things as no meat, sometimes (depending on the sect) no canned foods or dairy products, no foods treated with nonorganic pesticides or fertilizers, and food only cooked in natural materials, such as clay pots.

It made no difference to the court that the prison system provided Orthodox Jewish inmates with kosher or neutral diets and some special dietary accommodations for Muslims. The complexity of the Rastafarian's dietary requirements and the financial and administrative burdens that those requirements would create justified the differences (*Benjamin v. Coughlin*, 708 F. Supp. 570 (S.D.N.Y 1989)).

Source: William C. Collins, *Correctional Law for the Correctional Officer*, Lanham, Maryland: American Correctional Association, 2004, pp. 72-73.

freedom to exercise religious beliefs is not absolute, but is subject to restraint if prison officials can show that the restriction "is necessary to achieve a compelling government interest." [21]

In other words, while everyone has the right to maintain his or her own personal religious *beliefs*, inmates do not have an unconditional right to *exercise* those beliefs during confinement. On the other hand, using the same reasoning, it has been held that a prison cannot arbitrarily prohibit the practice of an established religion unless it can prove that such practice creates "a clear and present danger to the orderly functioning of the institution." [22]

- *Are there exemptions from hair and beard regulations on religious grounds?*

Those serving time in correctional institutions often are required to maintain short haircuts and a clean-shaven face. Officials have justified such grooming requirements on the basis that they inhibit ready identification of inmates, are unsanitary, and provide potential hiding places for contraband. Some groups, such as Native Americans, have challenged these regulations as a violation of their religious beliefs.

Court decisions have been somewhat diverse on this issue. When it is clearly established that religious beliefs are sincere, it is possible that the inmate's First Amendment argument will prevail. For instance, in one case involving a Cherokee Indian, "[t]he court ruled . . . that even if the justifications themselves were legitimate, they were not warranted in this instance because less restrictive alternatives were available. The inmate could be required to pull his hair back from his face in a ponytail, for example, which would prevent his using it as a mask." [23]

But other rulings have upheld haircut and beard rules. A 1992 appellate court decision in the case of a Rastafarian hairstyle illustrates the greater discretion that is being delegated to correctional administrators. In that case, the court ruled that "it is not for us to impose our own ideas about prison management upon those who attempt the reasonable regulation of that nearly impossible task. . . . [T]he loss of absolute freedom of religious expression is but one sacrifice required by . . . incarceration." [24]

- *Is there a right to wear or use various types of special attire or articles (for example, religious medallions, prayer rugs, shawls, peace pipes)?*

Concern for safety and security also has been used as a rationale for prohibiting the use or display of certain religious artifacts (especially those that could potentially be used as or shaped into weapons). In these areas, courts have tended to uphold reasonable regulations that are justified by the need for prison discipline and order. But again, institutional policies cannot be used to discriminate against a particular religion. When something—such as the wearing of a medal—is permitted for one group, the same consideration must be extended to all denominations under the *equal protection* clause of the Fourteenth Amendment. Nor can the issue be avoided by arbitrarily prohibiting medals for everyone, unless sufficient reason to do so can be demonstrated.

In summary, while inmates are not entitled to freely exercise their religion behind bars, the courts have upheld some religious practices under certain circumstances. Nevertheless, various restrictions on the exercise of religious freedom within correctional facilities have been upheld when they are justified on the basis of:

- The need to maintain *discipline* or *security*
- The proper exercise of *authority* and official *discretion*
- The fact that the regulation is *reasonable*
- The *economic considerations* involved [25]

The extent to which correctional practices are defensible according to such criteria will continue to be defined by the courts. As a result, correctional institutions in various states have made faith-based accommodations ranging from diet and fasting to jewelry and clothing.[26]

Additionally, attempts have been made to influence these issues through legislative action in the form of the 1993 Religious Freedom Restoration Act (RFRA). However, even here the Supreme Court prevailed, nullifying RFRA's applicability to corrections four years later.[27] For a look at the impact of this short-lived law, as well as how its demise has been predicted to reduce frivolous litigation, *see* the next "Close-up On Corrections."

✳ Learning Goals

Do you know:

1. Under what conditions inmate mail can be censored or restricted?
2. What due-process procedures are required when an inmate's mail is rejected?
3. What decision-making standards the courts use today?

Mail Privileges and Censorship

Another First Amendment right enjoyed by those in free society that is subject to modification during confinement is freedom of the press. The nature of incoming mail has been subject to regulation to detect contraband, uncover escape plans, avoid material that would ignite violence, and the like. Because of the labor-intensive and time-consuming process of implementing these constraints, further restrictions often have been placed on the volume of incoming mail that an inmate can receive. In addition, outgoing mail has been subject to such limitations as an approved correspondence list.

However, correctional officials are now being required to more clearly justify such procedures as legitimate reactions to a "clear and present danger." For example, the Supreme Court has held that prison officials "must show that a regulation authorizing mail censorship furthers . . . interests of security, order, and rehabilitation. Second, the limitation . . . must be no greater than is necessary . . . to the protection of the particular government interest involved."[28] Moreover, if an inmate's mail is rejected, case law has established certain due process procedures that must be followed:

- The inmate must be notified of the rejection.
- The letter's author must be allowed to protest the refusal.

Close-up On Corrections

THE RISE AND FALL OF RFRA (RELIGIOUS FREEDOM RESTORATION ACT)

The Supreme Court's nullification [as applied to state corrections] of the Religious Freedom Restoration Act (RFRA), designed to protect religious practice from governmental interference, has raised mixed emotions among the nation's corrections professionals.

On the one hand, the repeal should reduce the number of frivolous lawsuits filed by inmates to justify inappropriate behavior under the guise of religious practice. But on the other hand, the absence of RFRA could mean that correctional administrators will not be as sensitive to the religious practices of those whose religions are not considered "mainstream.". . .

When Congress passed RFRA in 1993, religious leaders hailed the measure as a victory for religious liberty. Following its passage, however, the law was invoked in hundreds of lawsuits, the majority of them filed by inmates. For instance . . . [an inmate] filed suit over a misconduct violation he was given for masturbating in front of an officer, claiming that his religion justified such behavior. Other suits have been filed by inmates whose requests to meet were denied by prison officials as little more than excuses to exchange information or plan gang activity. . . .

Many of these lawsuits were very difficult to defend, as RFRA shifted the burden of proof to correctional administrators, who then had to prove that the inmate did not have a sincerely held religious belief and that the request would seriously threaten the security of the institution. . . .

RFRA's repeal does not necessarily mean that inmates have no recourse to protest legitimate violations of religious freedoms . . . [and does not] preclude an inmate from filing a lawsuit under the First Amendment. However, the courts have not interpreted the latitude of religious freedoms under the First Amendment as broadly as they have those under RFRA. . . . Most correctional administrators also want to encourage the continued practice of [legitimate] religion, since studies have shown that religion can positively impact an inmate's behavior, both inside the facility and upon release.

Source: Gabrielle DeGroot, "Supreme Court Invalidation of RFRA Could Reduce Frivolous Litigation by Inmates," *On the Line*, Vol. 20, No. 4, September 1997, pp. 1-2.

- The complaint must be decided by an official other than the one who made the original decision to refuse delivery.[29]

Of course, such restrictions do not apply to correspondence with the courts, attorneys, or public officials. While these types of "privileged" mail cannot be read or censored, they can be opened and physically inspected for contraband in the presence of the inmate.

What is not so apparent, however, is how to handle sexually explicit publications. The First Amendment does not protect either pornographic material or

Inmates' incoming mail may be opened to inspect it for contraband. Here a drug-sniffing dog aids in the process. Courtesy of the American Correctional Association.

that which "involves a clear and present danger of inciting . . . imminent lawless action." [30] Clearly, materials offering advice on such illegal acts as smuggling contraband, constructing a bomb, or concocting homemade drugs or liquor can be prohibited. Sexually explicit publications also can be banned "on the grounds that the material is detrimental to rehabilitation and leads to deviate sexual behavior." [31]

Current Decision-Making Standards

In deciding inmate cases involving constitutional challenges, courts have fluctuated over the years. Under the "restrained-hands" phase of judicial intervention, decisions have reflected a more balanced approach to the issue of First Amendment rights than inmates had enjoyed just a few decades ago. In fact, some might argue that the "balance" is still off-center—but this time, judicial opinions are more likely to defer to the expertise of correctional administrators. At least in part, that is a result of the four-pronged standard that the courts now use when determining First Amendment claims:

1. Is the regulation being challenged related to a legitimate and neutral governmental objective?

2. Are there alternative means of exercising the right that are available to inmates?

3. What adverse impact will the asserted right have on correctional staff and other inmates?

4. Is the regulation an exaggerated response to the problem—that is, are less restrictive alternatives available? [32]

For the present time at least, this is the lens through which the courts are viewing both First Amendment claims and other constitutionally based challenges described in the remainder of this chapter.

 # Learning Goals

Do you know:

1. When frisk, strip, cell, and body-cavity searches may be conducted without violating constitutional protections?

2. To what extent visitors can be subjected to searches?

3. Under what circumstances employees can be required to undergo drug testing?

Search and Seizure

The right to be free from "unreasonable" search and seizure is guaranteed by the Fourth Amendment. But the necessity to maintain institutional security through the detection of contraband severely limits this right within correctional facilities. Frisks and cell searches can be conducted randomly at any time without cause, unless they are being used for an illegitimate purpose such as abuse or harassment. Inmate pat-downs and cell searches, therefore, do not tend to fall within Fourth Amendment protections. In contrast, there is a far greater degree of protection against body-cavity searches. Because of their intrusiveness, such searches must be based on at least reasonable suspicion and performed only by authorized, medically trained personnel.

Strip searches fall in between these two extremes. The Supreme Court has approved strip searches of inmates "following their exposure to the opportunity to obtain contraband" (for example, after work release or a contact visit).[33] Moreover, at least one appellate court has ruled that "the correctional institution's interest in maintaining security and deterring and discovering contraband permitted it to conduct strip searches without reasonable suspicion or probable cause."[34]

Visitor Searches

Although visitors are entitled to greater protections than inmates, the degree of protection again will depend on the intrusiveness of the search. Visitors can be required to walk through a metal detector, to surrender any articles they are carrying to be searched (for example, briefcases, umbrellas, purses), and to submit to a frisk search. But a strip search cannot be conducted without reasonable suspicion. Moreover, a visitor can refuse to be strip searched even when reasonable suspicion exists. Although the visitor would then be denied admission to the facility, he or she could elect to leave. It is not permissible for an institution to require that visitors consent to a strip search as a condition for being admitted:

> A requirement that every visitor "agree" to a strip search as a condition of being allowed to visit jail inmates resulted in an award of $177,000 [in] damages against a Massachusetts sheriff. The court quickly rejected the argument that the visitor "consented" to the searches, saying that . . . the state cannot condition the granting of

. . . a privilege (such as visiting) on someone giving up a constitutional right (in this case, the right to be free from unreasonable searches).[35]

Employee Searches and Drug Testing

Like visitors, the searching of employees is held to a higher standard than that of inmates. Employees can be frisk-searched for reasonable suspicion. But for a body-cavity search, probable cause is needed, along with a search warrant.

Undoubtedly, the most controversial area of employee searches in recent years has been the analysis of body fluids for detecting drugs. There are no legal prohibitions against *preemployment* urinalysis for job applicants, and the majority of states now test officer applicants.[36]

Once candidates are hired, however, they enjoy greater due-process protections. Although some agencies test on a *random* basis, most restrict testing to those employees who are under *suspicion* of engaging in drug use.[37] But even when drug testing is based on suspicious behavior (such as work performance, physical appearance, or absenteeism), the *reasonableness* of that suspicion under provisions of the Fourth Amendment may be in question.

The primary issues raised in Fourth Amendment challenges to employee drug tests are whether they constitute an actual "search," and if so, to what extent they are "reasonable." The first matter has been clearly settled—courts have established that urinalysis falls within the provisions of being a search (of the person) and seizure (of bodily fluids).[38] Legal decisions have not, however, been quite so unambiguous in terms of the reasonableness measure.

The New York City Department of Corrections, for example, encountered conflicting decisions about its random testing policy. Initially, the state supreme court found that the program did not adequately protect employee's rights.[39] But later, an appellate court upheld the tests, maintaining that the department's compelling interest in employee drug abuse outweighed privacy expectations.[40]

In that regard, other courts have similarly held that the duties of correctional officers in medium- and maximum-security prisons involve a "diminished expectation of privacy," and, therefore, that drug testing is a reasonable intrusion, due to the nature of the job.[41] A summary of these and other cases concludes that the courts appear to be permitting random testing of correctional personnel who have:

- Regular contact with inmates

- Opportunities to smuggle drugs into a facility

- Access to firearms

- Responsibilities that frequently involve driving vehicles that transport passengers [42]

These job functions are so significant that the agency's interest in detecting drug use supersedes the employee's right to privacy. But for all other personnel, testing based on reasonable suspicion is the rule, and future litigation undoubtedly will continue to shape the definition of reasonableness.

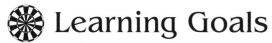 Learning Goals

Do you know:

1. How the courts have ruled on the constitutionality of crowding?

2. What the "totality-of-conditions" test is?

3. How far the right to medical care extends during confinement?

4. The difference between a consent decree and a court injunction?

Cruel and Unusual Punishment

Under the Eighth Amendment, U.S. citizens are protected against the infliction of cruel and unusual punishment. This provision is designed to assure that government's power to punish is "exercised within the limits of civilized standards."[43] Thus, it has been the basis of inmate challenges to a wide variety of correctional practices, including disciplinary procedures, use of force, and various conditions of confinement ranging from crowding to smoking.

Court decisions concerning what does and does not constitute cruel and unusual punishment also have varied over time. During the hands-off period, the judicial definition of "cruel and unusual" was limited primarily to situations involving extreme barbarity, torture, or excessive cruelty. But by the 1980s, legal judgments began to reflect "the evolving standards of decency that mark the progress of a maturing society."[44] But the pendulum seemed to shift again somewhat by the mid-1990s, when the current judicial interpretation of cruel and unusual punishment was illustrated by two similar opinions:

- In the first case, an inmate was placed naked in a strip cell without running water for four days, and yet it was found that this action did not violate the Eighth Amendment.

- The second case involved an inmate who was required to sleep on the floor in a poorly heated jail without a mattress or blanket for more than two months. The court said that this "did not deprive the inmate of the minimal civilized measure of life's necessities."[45]

Decision-Making Guidelines

In making decisions about cases raising Eighth Amendment challenges, courts today are applying guidelines that focus on whether the matter being contested:

- Shocks the conscience of the court

- Violates the evolving standards of decency in a civilized society

- Imposes punishment that is disproportionate to the offense

- Involves the wanton and unnecessary infliction of pain[46]

But while these criteria structure judicial decision making, it is still difficult to predict court rulings in such cases.

Eighth Amendment Rulings

Generally, the use of force has been upheld in situations involving self-defense, defense of others, enforcement of institutional regulations, and prevention of escape or a criminal act.[47] This, of course, is assuming that the amount of force used was not excessive under the particular circumstances involved. The U.S. Supreme Court has made it clear that the standard for using force in a prison setting is governed by the Eighth Amendment ruling that force becomes excessive when it is applied "maliciously and sadistically to cause harm," rather than in a "good faith effort to maintain or restore discipline."

In some situations, an individual action or a particular correctional practice has failed to pass the scrutiny of judicial review. But the U.S. Supreme Court also has taken into account the potential for a combination of conditions to produce "the deprivation of a single, identifiable human need such as food, warmth, or exercise; for example, a low cell temperature at night combined with a failure to issue blankets."[48] On the other hand, overall conditions of confinement do not constitute cruel and unusual punishment when no deprivation of a specific human need can be verified.

Conditions of Confinement

Within the limits of their income, those in free society have the liberty to decide such things as what food they will eat, what clothes they will wear, in what type of residence they will live, with whom they will associate, and when they will visit a doctor or dentist. Needless to say, those incarcerated do not have the freedom to make such choices. As the Supreme Court underscored in one ruling: "An incarcerated person loses more than freedom. The prisoner must depend on the state to make the most basic decisions vital to his or her health and safety."[49]

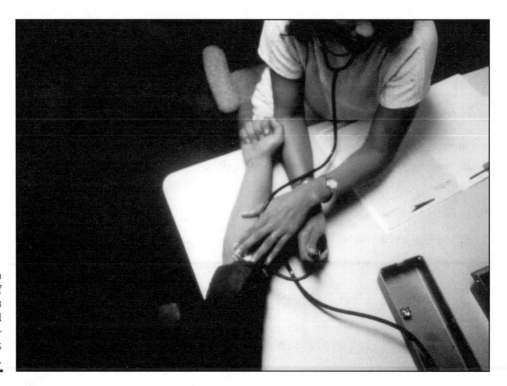

Although inmates have no right to a specified level of care, denial of necessary treatment for serious medical needs is a constitutional violation. Courtesy of the Miami-Dade County (Florida) Department of Corrections and Rehabilitation.

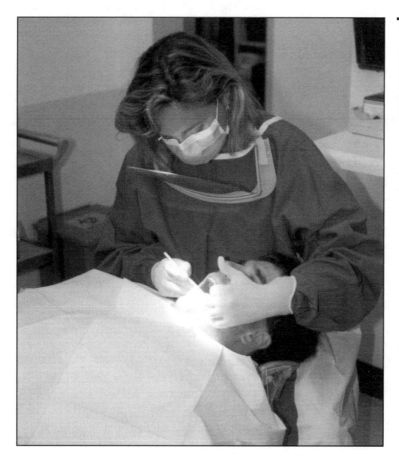

Everyone, of course, does not agree on how adequately government makes such decisions. Consequently, inmates have challenged a host of institutional conditions as being in violation of cruel and unusual punishment—particularly when they are confined in an aging, crowded facility, or subject to inadequate food, clothing, sanitation, or health care. It is obviously beyond the scope of this chapter to consider each of these issues in detail. But when inmates can demonstrate deliberate indifference or intentional mistreatment, it is likely that the courts will afford them a remedy. For example, the next "Close-up On Corrections" illustrates some of the gross inadequacies that have brought medical care to the attention of the courts and examines how the Eighth Amendment has been interpreted in this context.

The inadequacy of specific living conditions is often a result of the overall deterioration of services that accompanies institutional crowding. But in and of itself, crowding has not been found to be an Eighth Amendment violation, as was illustrated in two landmark cases on this subject:

- In *Bell v. Wolfish* [50] the court held that there is no constitutional principle requiring "one man, one cell."

- In *Rhodes v. Chapman* [51] no evidence was found that double-celling either "inflicts unnecessary or wanton pain" or is "grossly disproportionate" to the severity of crimes warranting imprisonment.

Double-bunking has not been considered unconstitutional *unless* "in combination with other factors, it yields a situation that may be intolerable." [52] In

Close-up On Corrections

INADEQUATE MEDICAL CARE

Inmate lawsuits have had a significant effect on the nature of medical care provided in correctional facilities. While truly barbaric issues rarely arise today, consider some of the early cases that "shocked the conscience" of the court:

- An inmate's ear is cut off in a fight. The inmate retrieves the ear, hastens to the prison hospital, and asks the doctor to sew the ear back on. Medical staff, it is alleged, look at the inmate, tell him "you don't need your ear," and toss the ear in the trash. *Williams v. Vincent*, 508 R2d 541 (2d Cir., 1974).

- Medical care for an 1,800-man prison is provided by one doctor and several *inmate* assistants in a substandard hospital. *Gates v. Collier*, 501 A2d 1291 (5th Cir., 1975).

- Medical services are withheld by prison staff as punishment. Treatments, including minor surgery, are performed by unsupervised inmates. Supplies are in short supply and few trained medical staff are available in a prison the court terms "barbarous." Twenty days pass before any action is taken for a maggot-infested wound, festering from an unchanged dressing. *Newman v. Alabama*, 503 A2d 1320 (5th Cir., 1974).

Nevertheless, it is almost impossible for a prisoner to succeed on an Eighth Amendment ground if *some* treatment, no matter how inappropriate or inadequate, was provided. For, to violate the Constitution, the medical care must "shock the conscience," not be "mere negligence." . . .

[T]he Constitution prohibits only the most extreme deprivations; it establishes minimums, a floor. The finding that inadequate care is not cruel and unusual punishment in no way indicates a stamp of approval. A low level of treatment does not necessarily qualify as a reasonable standard of care; it is simply not so extremely horrendous as to fall below the constitutional floor.

Sources [cases]: William C. Collins, *Jail Design and Operation and the Constitution: An Overview*, Longmont, Colorado: National Institute of Corrections, n.d., p. 26; [remainder]: Penelope D. Clute, *The Legal Aspects of Prisons and Jails*, Springfield, Illinois: Charles C. Thomas, 1980, pp. 82-85.

such cases, the primary question is whether the "totality of conditions" resulting from a crowded institution meets the test of being cruel and unusual; for example:

Confinement may be rendered unduly hazardous as security systems and personnel, heating, ventilation, sanitation, and fire protection systems become incapable of meeting the expanded demands made upon them.[53]

It is one thing to be confined in tight living quarters. The courts seem relatively willing to accept that situation. It is a completely different matter, however, when accommodating too many inmates also jeopardizes some other aspect of their well-being—such as health, safety, or sanitation. The courts have been increasingly reluctant to tolerate these additional complications.

Legal and Administrative Remedies

When it appears futile to contest such allegations, correctional officials can enter a *consent decree*, essentially agreeing to take remedial action. If the agency elects to contest the issue and the inmate's claim is ultimately successful, the court can issue an *injunction* requiring that specified deficiencies be corrected within an established time frame.

Moreover, injunctions can declare a whole facility to be unconstitutional. In fact, they can even extend to include all of the institutions within the state's entire department of corrections. As seen in Figure 14.3, many federal and state prisons are affected by some type of court order.

Legal actions challenging conditions of confinement have achieved a significant influence in terms of making improvements in the standard of living within correctional institutions. (*See* the upcoming "Close-up On Corrections" for a list of landmark cases). Perhaps the most significant contribution of legal action, however, has been the efforts it has generated to avoid lawsuits by more proactively addressing legitimate complaints. Without inmate access to the courts, there might never have been as much incentive to employ *administrative remedies* to reduce litigation, such as formal grievance procedures.

Today, many courts will not elect to hear a case until the complainant has exhausted all such internal administrative remedies. For the inmates, this alternative can produce desired results more quickly, without having to go to court. For correctional officials, it can reduce the costly and time-consuming process of becoming entangled in lengthy litigation.

Frivolous Lawsuits

No longer is there any doubt that corrections cannot overlook the legitimate health and safety needs of those entrusted to its care. But not all inmate-initiated litigation has been either fruitful or meaningful. In fact, some maintain that inmate lawsuits have gotten out of control.[54] (In that regard, the next

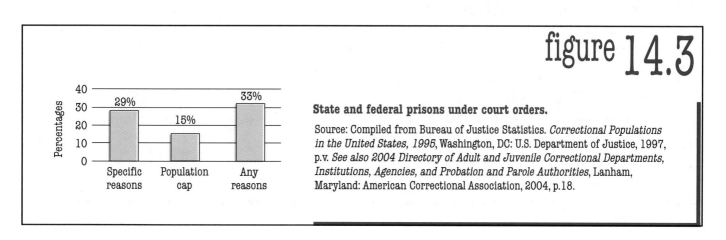

figure 14.3

State and federal prisons under court orders.

Source: Compiled from Bureau of Justice Statistics. *Correctional Populations in the United States, 1995,* Washington, DC: U.S. Department of Justice, 1997, p.v. *See also 2004 Directory of Adult and Juvenile Correctional Departments, Institutions, Agencies, and Probation and Parole Authorities,* Lanham, Maryland: American Correctional Association, 2004, p.18.

Close-up On Corrections

LANDMARK CASES SHAPING CORRECTIONAL LAW

Conditions of Confinement

Rhodes v. Chapman, 452 U.S. 337 (1981): Double celling of prisoners does not, in itself, constitute cruel and unusual punishment.

Wilson v. Seiter, 59 U.S.L.W. 4671 (1991): "Deliberate indifference" is required for liability in conditions of confinement cases under *42 U.S.C. 1983*.

Court Access

Johnson v. Avery, 393 U.S. 483 (1969): Prison authorities cannot prohibit prisoners from helping other prisoners prepare legal writs unless they provide reasonable alternatives whereby inmates can have access to the courts.

Younger v. Gilmore, 404 U.S. 15 (1971): Prison law libraries must have sufficient legal materials to enable prisoners to have reasonable access to the courts.

Disciplinary Hearings

Wolff v. McDonnell, 418 U.S. 539 (1974): Inmates are entitled to due process in prison disciplinary proceedings that can result in the loss of good-time credit or in punitive segregation.

Hughes v. Rowe, 449 U.S. 5 (1980): Placing a prisoner in segregation without a hearing is unconstitutional, unless justified by emergency conditions.

Use of Force

Hudson v. McMillian, 60 U.S.L.W 4151 (1992): Use of excessive physical force against a prisoner may constitute cruel and unusual punishment even though no serious injury results.

Medical Care

Estelle v. Gamble, 429 U.S. 97 (1976): Deliberate indifference to inmate medical needs constitutes cruel and unusual punishment.

Washington v. Harper, 58 U.S.L.W. 4249 (1990): A prisoner with serious mental illness may be treated with antipsychotic drugs against his will and without judicial hearing.

Freedom of Religion

Cruz v. Beto, 405 U.S. 319 (1972): Inmates must be given a reasonable opportunity to exercise their religious beliefs.

(continued)

Close-up On Corrections

"Close-up On Corrections" features some of the frivolous claims that would be humorous were it not for the time and costs that they consumed). In response, action has been taken to stem the tide of inmate lawsuits and curtail court intervention through the Violent Crime Control Act of 1994, which:

- Specifies that federal courts may not find a violation of the Eighth Amendment in a prison or jail crowding case unless the inmate filing the suit demonstrates that he or she has personally been the victim of cruel and unusual punishment

- Requires that when an inmate satisfies this "personal harm" requirement, the remedy awarded "shall extend no further than necessary to remove the conditions that are causing the cruel and unusual punishment"

- Prohibits federal courts from imposing a population ceiling on a prison or jail unless the unconstitutional crowding "is inflicting cruel and unusual punishment on particular identified prisoners"

- Allows review at two-year intervals of federal court orders and consent decrees based on Eighth Amendment violations, if requested by the defendant[56]

Close-up On Corrections

Prison Litigation Reform Act (PLRA)

Additional legislation seeking to reduce frivolous suits, the Prison Litigation Reform Act, was signed into law in 1996. This act, among other things:

- Requires inmates to pay a federal court filing fee and limits the award of attorneys' fees in successful lawsuits

- Encourages conducting court proceedings by telephone or video conference (to discourage those filing cases merely to get a trip outside)

- Requires judges to screen all inmate complaints against the federal government and immediately dismiss those deemed frivolous or without merit (Good-time credits prisoners earn toward early release could be revoked if they file a malicious suit or present false testimony).

- Bars prisoners from suing the federal government for mental or emotional injury unless there also was a physical injury [57]

Overall, this legislation attempts to deter inmate filings, punish those who file frivolous suits, and streamline the litigation process.[58] It also has encouraged states to identify alternatives to litigation through such options as inmate grievance procedures, third-party mediation, and the use of ombudsmen.[59]

Some of the provisions of the PLRA apply only to federal inmates. However, Figure 14.4 indicates that this legislation does seem to have had a restraining effect on the filing of petitions by state prisoners as well. Additionally, the

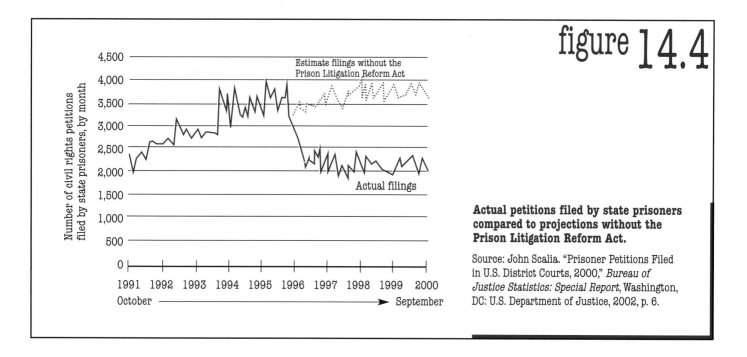

figure 14.4

Actual petitions filed by state prisoners compared to projections without the Prison Litigation Reform Act.

Source: John Scalia. "Prisoner Petitions Filed in U.S. District Courts, 2000," *Bureau of Justice Statistics: Special Report*, Washington, DC: U.S. Department of Justice, 2002, p. 6.

reality is that the vast majority of inmate petitions are actually dismissed. As shown in Figure 14.5, U.S. district courts ruled in favor of inmates in less than 2 percent of their cases. As a result, some inmates complaining about mail service, food quality, and denial of dessert already have lost good-time credits.[60]

National figures also show that even though the number of petitions filed by inmates in federal district courts has been increasing, the rate has declined substantially—from 72.7 cases per 1,000 prisoners in 1980 to 19 cases in 2000.[61] Moreover, in a recent survey, nearly three out of four state departments of corrections indicated that the filing of federal civil rights cases has decreased since passage of the PLRA, with some states citing "dramatic reductions." [62]

Overall Results

The combined impact of such legislation and recent court decisions has been to "set the bar a bit higher for inmates with legitimate complaints and to

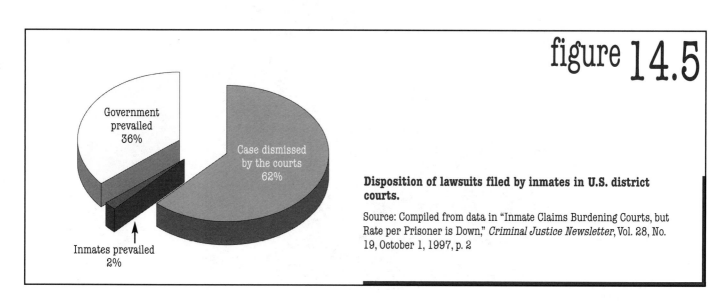

figure 14.5

Disposition of lawsuits filed by inmates in U.S. district courts.

Source: Compiled from data in "Inmate Claims Burdening Courts, but Rate per Prisoner is Down," *Criminal Justice Newsletter*, Vol. 28, No. 19, October 1, 1997, p. 2

reduce the number of frivolous complaints that will survive the process." [63] But not everyone views such declining litigation in a positive light. As some lawyers have cautioned, "the benefits of reduced court intervention may carry a heavy price," costing correctional officials one of their major allies in addressing overcrowding and deteriorating facilities.[64] It also has been ruefully observed that a more proactive approach could have curtailed the problem from the onset: "Much of the federal litigation might have been avoided over the past quarter century if state and local governments had met their responsibilities to correctional institutions in the first place." [65]

Learning Goals

Do you know:

1. To what extent capital punishment is a deterrent to crime?
2. The arguments for and against capital punishment?
3. How the courts have ruled on Eighth Amendment challenges to capital punishment?

Capital Punishment

Thus far, this discussion of inmate litigation has been limited to challenges directed toward some aspect of the restraints or conditions accompanying incarceration. Obviously, inmates also initiate lawsuits to overturn their conviction or alter their sentence. These types of cases do not affect the management or operation of correctional facilities. However, because of its Eighth

Despite the availability of lethal injection, some capital punishment states retain the electric chair. Courtesy of the Florida Department of Corrections.

Amendment implications and the widespread controversy it has generated, one particular focus of such appeals requires further consideration: that is, of course, the death penalty.

The high point of capital punishment occurred during the sixteenth and seventeenth centuries, when tens of thousands of people were put to death—for offenses ranging from murder to failing to remove one's cap in church. Nor were children spared. In 1801, a thirteen-year-old child was hanged in England for stealing a spoon,[66] and by 1810, more than 200 crimes still remained punishable by death.[67] In the United States, the youngest person executed during the twentieth century was fourteen-year-old George Stinney, who was put to death in Texas for murder.[68]

Current Applications

Today, capital punishment is applied much more selectively. Nevertheless, there were some 3,557 inmates under sentence of death by the beginning of 2003, ranging from 18 to 87 years of age.[69] Seventy-four are on death row for crimes they committed as juveniles.[70] Although annual executions have yet to reach pre-1950 levels, (*see* Figure 14.6), California held the largest number of death-row inmates (614), followed by Texas (450), Florida (366), and Pennsylvania (241).[71]

Most of those sentenced to death are white (54 percent) males (99 percent) who have not completed high school (52 percent).[72] Although blacks are disproportionately represented, the Supreme Court has been reluctant to address the potential of racial discrimination in sentencing decisions.[73] However, in 2002, it did overturn the death penalty for those who are mentally retarded.[74]

As a result of the lengthy appellate process involved in capital cases, death row prisoners have been awaiting their fate for an average of about a decade.[75] (Not only do inmates often file appeals on their own behalf, but a sentence of death is subject to automatic review). To better appreciate the long-term

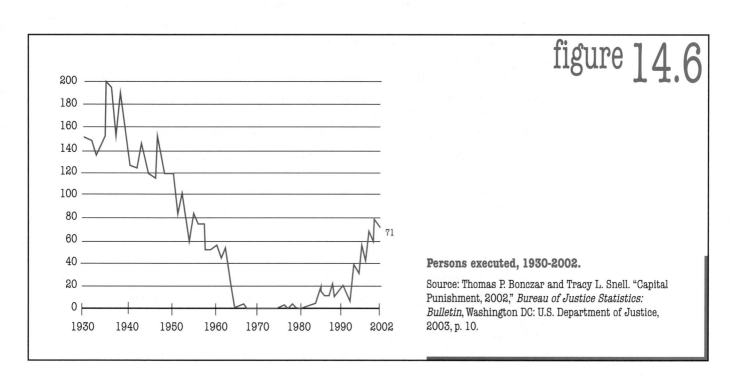

figure 14.6

Persons executed, 1930-2002.

Source: Thomas P. Bonczar and Tracy L. Snell. "Capital Punishment, 2002," *Bureau of Justice Statistics: Bulletin,* Washington DC: U.S. Department of Justice, 2003, p. 10.

Close-up On Corrections

impact of capital punishment, envision spending a decade under the "living death" isolation that is portrayed in the previous "Close-up On Corrections." As one death row inmate put it, "Stay for forty-eight hours and you will have experienced death row—the rest is just a repetition—multiplied by years."[76]

More recently, however, federal legislation has toughened standards for review, set strict time limits, and curbed the repeat petitions that often extended the appellate process year after year [77] (*see* the next "Close-up On Corrections"). Moreover, all states do not authorize the death penalty. As early as 1847, Michigan became the first state to abolish capital punishment, and by 2002, some thirteen states had also done so.[78] Even in those jurisdictions that have death row inmates, years can go by without an execution. But when someone is put to death, particularly a high-profile offender, the heated debate over this issue often resurfaces. For example, Karla Faye Tucker's execution in 1998 ignited renewed controversy over the execution of women.

Death Penalty Debates

Capital punishment is a controversial issue that polarizes people into extreme positions. In fact, research over the past twenty years indicates that most of our death penalty attitudes (both pro and con) are based on emotion rather than information or rational argument: "People feel strongly about the death penalty, know little about it, and feel no need to know more. . . ."[79] As

Close-up On Corrections

shown in the next two "Close-up On Corrections" boxes, there are staunch advocates for retaining as well as abolishing the death penalty,[80] and evidence does not always support the common myths surrounding this issue.

No one has yet argued conclusively that the death penalty—on the basis of empirical evidence—is a deterrent to crime. It is apparent that capital punishment—at least in the manner in which it is presently administered—does not appear to accomplish the purpose of protecting society through general deterrence: "When studies have compared the homicide rates for the past fifty years in states that employ the death penalty and in adjoining states that have abolished it, the numbers have in every case been quite similar; the death penalty has had no discernible effect on homicide rates."[81] In that regard, a former correctional administrator who observed the perpetrators of this act for over

Close-up On Corrections

half a century concluded that murderers are "often chronic misfits with years of failure behind them," who are "driven by the towering impulse of the moment and incapable of making any fine distinction between [the] consequences of imprisonment versus death."[82]

Constitutional Challenges

Regardless of the public's views supporting or opposing the death penalty, the Supreme Court is ultimately the arbitrator of its constitutionality. Numerous challenges have been filed by death row inmates claiming violation of the cruel and unusual punishment protections of the Eighth Amendment. For many years, these appeals had been largely unsuccessful, until the 1972 *Furman v. Georgia* case. In that ruling, the Supreme Court found that the arbitrary, capricious, and unfair manner in which capital punishment was being applied did represent a constitutional violation.

As illustrated in Figure 14.7, this decision had a significant impact on the death row population throughout the country as unconstitutionally imposed death sentences were commuted. Since the Court's action did not ban the death penalty outright, however, a number of states made efforts to rewrite

Close-up On Corrections

THE DEATH PENALY DEBATE

	SUPPORTERS ARGUE THAT THE DEATH PENALTY:	OPPONENTS COUNTER THAT:
Deterrence	Has a deterrent effect (or would be a deterrent, if it were carried out with greater speed and certainty).	Studies tend to indicate there is little significant difference in murder rates between states with and without the death penalty.[a] Moreover, this argument raises the question of whether executions can be justified "by the good which their deaths may do the rest of us."[b]
Protection	Is needed to protect society from the most serious and feared offenders.	The public could be adequately protected by life without parole and in any event, murder is a crime with relatively low rates of recidivism.[c]
Retribution	Is fitting retribution or "just deserts"—that is, the most (perhaps the only) appropriate punishment for murder.	Human life is sacred and society does not have the moral right to take it—especially given the potential that an innocent person could be wrongfully executed, or that the death penalty may be applied in a discriminatory manner.[d]
Social Utility	Is not completely useless—even if it cannot be defended on other grounds, it may be a legitimate expression of vengeance or aggression by collective society.	If so, the issue becomes one concerning how many people are expendable for this purpose, along with the extent to which such a violent response may be reinforcing further violence rather than strengthening respect for life.

[a] See, for example, William J. Bowers and Glenn Pierce, "Deterrence or Brutalization: What Is the Effect of Executions?," *Crime and Delinquency*, Vol. 26, 1980, pp. 453-84; and Brian Forst, "Capital Punishment and Deterrence: Conflicting Evidence?," *Journal of Criminal Law and Criminology*, Vol. 74, 1983, pp. 927-12.

[b] David Hoekema, "Capital Punishment: The Question of Justification," in John B. Williamson, Linda Evans, and Anne Munley, eds., *Social Problems: The Contemporary Debates*, 3rd ed., Boston: Little, Brown, 1981, p. 318.

[c] Gennaro F. Vito and Deborah G. Wilson, "Back from the Dead: Tracking the Progress of Kentucky's Furman-Commuted Death Row Population," *Justice Quarterly*, Vol. 5, No. 1, 1988, pp. 101-111.

[d] Although it is difficult to document the extent of racism in capital punishment, research indicates that those who murder whites are more likely to receive the death penalty than the killers of blacks. Among the many studies in this area, *see*, for instance, U.S. General Accounting Office, *Death Penalty Sentencing: Research Indicates Pattern of Racial Disparities*, Gaithersburg, Maryland: U.S. General Accounting Office, 1990.

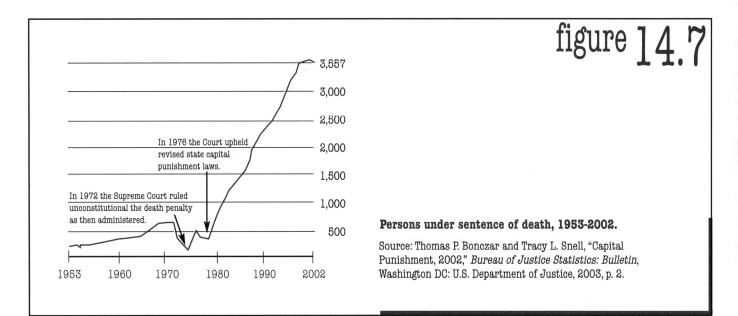

figure 14.7

In 1976 the Court upheld revised state capital punishment laws.

In 1972 the Supreme Court ruled unconstitutional the death penalty as then administered.

Persons under sentence of death, 1953-2002.

Source: Thomas P. Bonczar and Tracy L. Snell, "Capital Punishment, 2002," *Bureau of Justice Statistics: Bulletin*, Washington DC: U.S. Department of Justice, 2003, p. 2.

their statutes governing capital punishment in a manner that would be constitutionally acceptable. As a result, in the case of *Gregg v. Georgia*, the Supreme Court subsequently reinstated death penalty statutes that contain sufficient safeguards against arbitrary and capricious application.[83] As reflected in

 Close-up On Corrections

RIGHTING WRONGFUL CONVICTIONS

In 1994, a congressional judiciary committee researched the possibility of innocent people being executed in this country. Their findings were published in a report titled *Innocence and the Death Penalty: Assessing the Danger of Mistaken Executions*. It lists fifty-two death-penalty prisoners from 1975 to 1994 who were released from death row after authorities determined they were innocent. Those were the lucky ones, fortunate enough to have had competent legal counsel and to have been allowed back into court with newly discovered evidence of their innocence. One must wonder how many of the nearly 350 executed since 1975 were innocent and unlucky. . . .

The average length of time between conviction and release was almost seven years for the fifty-two death row inmates released. Had the Effective Death Penalty Act been passed prior to those fifty-two people prevailing on their claims of innocence, the majority would have been executed.

Source: Lane Nelson, "The Great Writ—Re: The Condemned," in Lane Nelson and Burk Foster, eds., *Death Watch: A Death Penalty Anthology*, Upper Saddle River, New Jersey: Prentice Hall, 2001, p. 126.

figure 14.8

Country	Estimated annual rate per 1 million population
Singapore	13.57
Saudi Arabia	4.73
Sierra Leone	2.37
Jordan	2.15
China	1.85
Iran	1.76
Taiwan	1.12
United States	.23

Per capita rate of executions in selected nations.

Source: Gary Hill. "Capital Punishment—A World Update," *Corrections Compendium*, Vol. 26, No.7, July 2001, p.16.

Figure 14.7, many of these revised statutes have withstood legal scrutiny, and consequently, the death row population has now climbed to an all-time high.

Support for Capital Punishment

But at the same time, public support for the death penalty appears to be waning.[84] At least in part, this may be a result of the high-profile publicity that has accompanied the exoneration of some death-row inmates on the basis of DNA analysis. As the previous "Close-up On Corrections" explains, such erroneous convictions may occur considerably more often than we realize. The Effective Death Penalty Act is anticipated to have a chilling impact in that regard.

Aside from attitudes in the United States, however, it has been predicted that international pressure to abolish capital punishment someday may become strong enough to threaten death-penalty states with economic isolation, thus providing a substantial fiscal incentive for abolishment.[85] As shown in Figure 14.8, death penalty countries are concentrated in the Middle East, North Africa, and Asia. The United States and English-speaking countries of the Caribbean are the only jurisdictions in the Western Hemisphere that retain the death penalty. In fact, the European Union has made the abolition of capital punishment a precondition for membership, and the United Nations Commission on Human Rights has called on all members who have not yet abolished the death penalty to consider suspending executions.[86]

But the U.S. Supreme Court has yet to find capital punishment an Eighth Amendment violation. In that regard, inmates have been more successful challenging the conditions in which they are confined during life than the constitutional issues that constrain their death.

Summary

One of the most prevalent forces shaping correctional policies and procedures in recent years has been the impact of court decisions. Although properly enforced standards may help to protect against litigation, correctional agencies and their employees are subject to civil liability when their actions or inactions result in harm, injury, or death. Beyond direct liability, vicarious liability can occur for failure to train, negligent supervision, or negligent employment/retention.

It is, of course, court rulings that have increased the potential for correctional liability. As the Supreme Court began to intervene more actively after a long "hands-off" period, constitutional rights during incarceration were redefined and expanded. Among the First Amendment rights now recognized by the courts are various freedoms related to the practice of religion. However, such protections can be restricted when justified on the basis of institutional order, safety, discipline, or security. Additionally, the freedom to communicate through the mails can be limited. Nor do Fourth Amendment protections against unreasonable search and seizure generally encompass frisk or cell searches. But searches of any kind cannot be employed to abuse or harass inmates. The courts also have recognized personnel drug testing as falling within the definition of "search and seizure." Although job applicants routinely can be tested, employees enjoy greater safeguards.

Numerous legal challenges have been raised under the Eighth Amendment's prohibition against cruel and unusual punishment. Many of these cases involve institutional crowding. The courts have held that crowding in and of itself does not constitute an Eighth Amendment violation, unless it produces a "totality of conditions" that jeopardizes the inmates' health, safety, or well-being. Some such cases have been settled by voluntary consent decrees. In others, the courts have issued injunctions ordering correctional officials to remedy deficiencies within a given period of time. To reduce inmate litigation, correctional institutions are initiating more proactive administrative remedies, and Congress has passed legislation restricting frivolous suits.

In addition to challenging the conditions of confinement, inmate litigation also has sought to overturn the death penalty. Although some states have abolished capital punishment, more than 3,500 prisoners remain on death row today. Because of the extreme emotion on both sides of this issue, the death penalty continues to generate considerable controversy. Although the Supreme Court overturned a number of death sentences in 1972 as a result of the manner in which they were implemented, the Court has yet to find capital punishment itself an Eighth Amendment violation. In that regard, inmates have been more successful challenging the conditions in which they are confined during life than the constitutional issues that constrain their death.

Answers to Liability Close-Up

- *Criminal liability.* Since the officer did not intentionally shoot the bystander, it is unlikely that it could be proven that a crime was committed.

- *Direct civil liability.* Since Johnson raised objections to completing the transportation detail and made it very clear that he was not currently firearms qualified, it is unlikely that he could be held civilly liable. Even if the sergeant later denies remembering Johnson's verbal objection, the courts could maintain that it is the supervisor's duty to make assignments in a manner consistent with the requisite qualifications (in other words, the supervisor "should have known").

- *Vicarious liability.* Because the sergeant persisted with assigning Johnson inappropriately despite his protests, grounds potentially exist for holding the sergeant vicariously liable. In other words, the sergeant *knew* what the situation was, *did nothing* about it, and that inaction potentially could be construed as the *proximate cause* of the resulting injury. It is also possible that the agency or other upper-level administrators could be held vicariously liable for "failure to train," since the officer indicated that he had been unable to go to the firearms range when scheduled because the shift was also short-handed at that time. Here, however, it gets somewhat more complicated. If, for instance, the organization had a clear-cut written policy requiring annual firearms requalification and strictly prohibiting the issuance of weapons to anyone without it, liability could be limited to those who actually violated the policy.

Endnotes

1. *Farmer v. Brennan*, 511 U.S. 825, 114 S.Ct. 1970 (1994).

2. Terms used to describe these three phases of correctional law development are from William G. Archambeault and Betty J. Archambeault, *Correctional Supervisory Management: Principles of Organization, Policy, and Law*, Englewood Cliffs, New Jersey: Prentice Hall, 1982, p. 195; *see also* Kate King, "Prisoners' Constitutional Rights," in Roslyn Muraskin, ed., *Key Correctional Issues*, Upper Saddle River, New Jersey: Prentice Hall, 2004, pp. 151-152.

3. *Ruffin v. Virginia*, 62 Va. 790 (1871). However, it also has been argued that "the *Ruffin* case itself does not particularly support the restrictive view attributed to it," and that other cases decided in the same time period "do not indicate that the judiciary had no interest in the welfare of prisoners." *See* Donald H. Wallace "*Ruffin v. Virginia* and Slaves of the State: A Nonexistent Baseline of Prisoners' Rights Jurisprudence," *Journal of Criminal Justice*, Vol. 20, No. 4, 1992, pp. 334, 340.

4. Paraphrased from William C. Collins, *Legal Responsibility and Authority of Correctional Officers*, Lanham, Maryland: American Correctional Association, 1982, p. 5.

5. Chadwick L. Shook and Robert T. Sigler, *Constitutional Issues in Correctional Administration*, Durham, North Carolina: Carolina Academic Press, 2000, p. 40, citing *Turner v. Safley*, 482 U.S. 78 (1987).

6. *Rhodes v. Chapman*, 452 U.S. 337 (1981), p. 349.

7. "The Prisoners' Mailbox and the Evolution of Federal Inmate Rights," *Federal Rules Decisions*, Vol. 114, 1993, p. 169.

8. Linda Greenhouse, "High Court Makes It Harder for Prisoners to Sue," *New York Times*, June 20, 1995, p. A11.

9. W. Wesley Johnson, Katherine Bennett, and Timothy J. Flanagan, "Getting Tough on Prisoners: Results from the National Corrections Executive Survey, 1995," *Crime and Delinquency*, Vol. 43, No. 1, January 1997, p. 26.

10. *Correctional Officer Resource Guide*, 2nd ed., Lanham, Maryland: American Correctional Association, 1989, p. 13.

11. However, in a recent case, it should be noted that the Supreme Court held that what an official "should have known" cannot be used to prove "deliberate indifference." *See* William C. Collins and John Hagar, "Jails and the Courts . . . Issues for Today,

Issues for Tomorrow," *American Jails*, May/June 1995, p. 22, citing *Farmer v. Brennan*, 114 S.Ct. 1970 (1994).

12. Darrell L. Ross, "A 20-year Analysis of Section 1983 Litigation in Corrections," *American Jails*, May/June 1995, p. 14.

13. Alvin W. Cohn, "Reducing Opportunities for Litigation," *American Jails*, May/June 1998, p. 36.

14. Barbara B. Knight and Stephen T. Early, Jr., *Prisoners' Rights in America*, Chicago: Nelson-Hall, 1986, p. 188.

15. *Ibid.*, pp. 188-189.

16. William C. Collins, *Correctional Law for the Correctional Officer*, 4th ed., Lanham, Maryland: American Correctional Association, 2004, p. 70.

17. Knight and Early, *Prisoners' Rights in America*, p. 188.

18. Collins, *Correctional Law for the Correctional Officer*, p. 72.

19. Collins, *Legal Responsibility*, p. 19, citing *Cruz v. Beto*, 405 U.S. 319 (1972).

20. "Handling Problems in the Face of Ambiguous RFRA," *The Corrections Professional*, Vol. 1, No. 1, August 25,1995, p. 8.

21. King, "Prisoners' Constitutional Rights," p. 155.

22. *Ibid.*, citing *Banks v. Havener*, 234 F. Supp. 27 (E.D. Va. 1964).

23. Knight and Early, p. 207, citing *Gallahan v. Hollyfield*, 670 F.2d 1345 (C.A.8 1982).

24 Daniel Pollack, "Legal Briefs," *Corrections Today*, Vol. 54, No. 8, December 1992, p. 156, citing *Scott v. Mississippi Department of Corrections*, U.S. App. (5th Cir. 1992).

25. Palmer, *Constitutional Rights*, p. 73. For a summary of related court cases, *see* Michael J. Dale, "Religion in Jails and Prisons: Defining the Inmate's Legal Rights," *American Jails*, Vol. 5, No. 3, July/August 1991, pp. 30-34, and John McLaren, "Prisoners' Rights: The Pendulum Swings," in Joycelyn M. Pollock, ed., *Prisons: Today and Tomorrow*, Gaithersburg, Maryland: Aspen Publishers, 1997, p. 357.

26. "Faith-based Programming–Table 3: Accommodations," *Corrections Compendium*, Vol. 28, No. 8, August 2003, pp. 16-18.

27. "Court's Invalidation of RFRA Should Ease, But Not Remove, Burden on Correctional Facilities," *Corrections Alert*, Vol. 4, No. 8, July 28, 1997, pp. 1-5.

28. Palmer, *Constitutional Rights*, p. 41, citing *Procunier v. Martinez*, 94 S. Ct. 1800 (1974).

29. Collins, *Correctional Law for the Correctional Officer*, p. 77, citing *Procunier v. Martinez*, 94 S. Ct. 1800 (1974).

30. Palmer, *Constitutional Rights*, p. 50, citing *Brandenburg v. Ohio*, 395 U.S. 444, 48 Ohio Op.2d 320 (1969).

31. *Ibid.*, p. 52, citing *Carpenter v. South Dakota*, 536 F.2d 759 (8th Cir. 1976).

32. McLaren, "Prisoners' Rights: The Pendulum Swings," in Pollock, *Prisons: Today and Tomorrow*, p. 357.

33. Collins, *Correctional Law for the Correctional Officer*, p. 92.

34. Daniel Pollack, "Legal Briefs," *Corrections Today*, Vol. 54, No. 2, April 1992, p. 28.

35. *Ibid.,* p. 76 citing *Blackburn v. Snow,* 771 F.2d 556 (1st Cir. 1985). *See also Spear v. Sowders,* 33F.3d 576 (Kentucky, 1994).

36. Camille Graham Camp, ed., *The 2002 Corrections Yearbook: Adult Corrections,* Middletown, Connecticut: Criminal Justice Institute, 2003, p. 175.

37. "Drug Testing: Survey Summary," *Corrections Compendium,* Vol. 25, No. 9, September 2000, p. 12.

38. *Allen v. City of Marietta,* 601 F. Supp. 482 (N.D. Ga. 1985).

39. "NY Judge Bans Drug Tests for Corrections Officers," *Corrections Digest,* July 13, 1988, p. 2.

40. "NY Appeals Court Upholds Drug Testing for Jail Officers," *Corrections Digest,* November 15, 1988, p. 9.

41. Randall Guynes and Osa Coffey, "Employee Drug-Testing Policies in Prison Systems," *National Institute of Justice: Research in Action,* Washington, DC: U.S. Department of Justice, 1988, p.6.

42. J. Devereux Weeks, "Jail Employee Drug Testing under Fourth Amendment Limitations," *American Jails,* Vol. 4, No. 3, September/October 1990, p. 30.

43. Alvin J. Bronstein, "Prisoners' Rights: A History," in Geoffrey P. Alpert, ed., *Legal Rights of Prisoners,* Beverly Hills, California: Sage Publications, 1980, p. 26.

44. *Rhodes v. Chapman,* 452 U.S. 337 (1981).

45. Allen F. Breed, "Corrections: A Victim of Situational Ethics," *Crime and Delinquency,* Vol. 44, No. 1, January 1998, p. 14., citing respectively, *Williams v. Delo,* 49 F. 3d. 442, 8th Cir. (1995) and *Summers v. Sheahan,* 883 F. Supp. 1163, Northern District, Illinois (1995).

46. Collins, *Correctional Law for the Correctional Officer,* p. 106.

47. Palmer, *Constitutional Rights,* p. 25.

48. *Wilson v. Seiter,* 111 S. Ct. 2321 (1991). For a full interpretation of this case, *see* Rolando del Carmen, Susan E. Ritter, and Betsy A. Witt, *Briefs of Leading Cases in Corrections,* Cincinnati: Anderson Publishing, 1993, pp. 6-8.

49. Daniel Pollack, "Legal Briefs," *Corrections Today,* Vol. 53, No. 4, July 1991, p. 27, citing *Hutto v. Finney* (1978).

50. *Bell v. Wolfish,* 441 U.S. 520, 542 (1979).

51. *Rhodes v. Chapman,* 452 U.S. 337, 348 (1981).

52. Dale K. Sechrest and William C. Collins, *Jail Management and Liability Issues,* Coral Gables, Florida: Coral Gables Publishing Company, 1989, p.109.

53. Knight and Early, *Prisoners' Rights,* p. 131.

54. *See,* for example, Rick M. Steinmann, "Are Inmate Lawsuits Out of Control?," in Charles B. Fields, ed., *Controversial Issues in Corrections,* Needham Heights, Massachusetts: Allyn and Bacon, 1999, pp. 239-246.

55. Note: More recently, the Supreme Court also upheld visitation restrictions limiting the number of visits an inmate may receive and prohibiting visits (except from attorneys or clergy) for a minimum of two years for inmates who commit two or more substance abuse disciplinary infractions. *See* Stanley E. Adelman, "Supreme Court Rules Restrictions on Prison Visitation are Constitutional," *Corrections Today,* Vol. 66, No. 2, April 2004, p. 26, citing *Overton v. Bazzetta,* 123 S.Ct. 2162 (2003).

56. Jack E. Cole, "Assessing the Possible Impact of the Violent Crime Control Act of 1994 on Prison and Jail Overcrowding Suits," *Prison Journal*, Vol. 76, No. 1, March 1996, p. 92.

57. "New Law Curbs Lawsuits," *Corrections Digest*, Vol. 27, No. 22, May 31, 1996, pp. 1-2.

58. Jeffery R. Maahs and Craig Hemmens, "The Prison Litigation Reform Act and Frivolous Section 1983 Suits," *Corrections Management Quarterly*, Vol. 2, No. 3, Summer 1998, p. 93.

59. Chadwick L. Shook and Robert T. Sigler, *Constitutional Issues in Correctional Administration*, Durham, North Carolina: Carolina Academic Press, 2000, p. 51.

60. "Texas Prisoners Penalized for Frivolous Lawsuits," *Corrections Digest*, November 8, 1996, p. 6.

61. John Scalia, "Prisoner Petitions in U.S. District Courts, 2000," *Bureau of Justice Statistics: Special Report*, Washington, D.C.: U.S. Department of Justice, 2002, p. 1.

62. "The Prison Litigation Reform Act: Survey Summary," *Corrections Compendium*, Vo. 25, No. 7, July 2000, pp. 7-15. A follow-up study in 2003 likewise found a 69 percent decrease. *See* "Inmate Lawsuits and Grievances: Survey Summary," *Corrections Compendium*, Vol. 28, No. 6, June 2003, p. 8.

63. Chadwick L. Shook and Robert T. Sigler, *Constitutional Issues in Correctional Administration*, Durham, North Carolina: Carolina Academic Press, 2000, p. 42.

64. Collins and Hagar, "Jails and the Courts," p. 19.

65. Ken Kerle, "Editorial: *Jones v. Wittenburg*," *American Jails*, May-June 1995, p. 5.

66. L. Kay Gillespie, *Inside the Death Chamber: Exploring Execution*, Boston: Pearson Education, 2003, p. 111.

67. *The Handbook Guide to Murder*, London: Handbook Publishing, 1998, p. 17.

68. Gillespie, *Inside the Death Chamber*, p. 112.

69. Thomas P. Bonczar and Tracy L. Snell, "Capital Punishment, 2002," *Bureau of Justice Statistics: Bulletin*, Washington, D.C.: U.S. Department of Justice, November 2003, p.1.

70. Lynn Cothern, *Juveniles and the Death Penalty*, Washington, D.C.: OJJDP Coordinating Council on Juvenile Justice and Delinquency Prevention, November 2000, p. 1.

71. Bonczar and Snell, "Capital Punishment, 2002,"p.1.

72. *Ibid.*, p. 6.

73. Michael J. Sniffen, "No Reversal of Fortune for Blacks on Death Row," in John J. Sullivan and Joseph L. Victor, eds., *Criminal Justice 92/93*, 16th ed., Guilford, Connecticut: Dushkin Publishing Group, 1992, p. 227. *See also* Paige H. Ralph, Jonathan R. Sorensen, and James W. Marquart, "A Comparison of Death-Sentenced and Incarcerated Murderers in Pre-Furman Texas," *Justice Quarterly*, Vol. 9, No. 2, June 1992, p.185, whose study concludes that it was not the defendant's race but the victim's race that was the primary extralegal variable affecting sentencing decisions.

74. Joan Biskupic, "Door Open to Death Penalty Limits," *USA Today*, June 21, 2002, p. 3A.

75. Bonczar and Snell, "Capital Punishment, 2002,"p.11.

76. Gillespie, *Inside the Death Chamber*, p. 36.

77. *See*, for example, "Death Penalty Appeals Centers Winding Down as Federal Funding Ends Nationwide," *Corrections Digest*, February 23, 1996, p. 8.

78. Bonczar and Snell, "Capital Punishment, 2002,"p.1.

79. Phoebe C. Ellsworth and Samuel L. Gross, "Hardening of the Attitudes: Americans' Views on the Death Penalty," *Journal of Social Issues*, Vol.1, 1994, pp. 19-52.

80. For a more complete discussion of both sides of this issue, *see* Ernest van den Haag and John P. Conrad, *The Death Penalty: A Debate*, New York: Plenum Press, 1983, along with Alan S. Bruce and Theresa A. Severance, "The Death Penalty," in Roslyn Muraskin, ed., *Key Correctional Issues*, Upper Saddle River, New Jersey: Prentice Hall, 2004, pp. 322-324

81. David Hoekema, "Capital Punishment: The Question of Justification," in John B. Williamson, Linda Evans, and Anne Munley, eds., *Social Problems: The Contemporary Debates*, 3rd ed., Boston: Little, Brown, 1981, p. 318.

82. Paul W. Keve, "The Costliest Punishment—A Corrections Administrator Contemplates the Death Penalty," *Federal Probation*, Vol. 56, No. 1, March 1992, p. 13.

83. *Gregg v. Georgia*, 428 U.S. 153 (1976).

84. Robert M. Bohm, "The Future of Capital Punishment in the U.S.," *ACJS Today*, November/December 2000, p. 1.

85. *Ibid.*, p. 5.

86. Gary Hill, "Capital Punishment—A World Update," *Corrections Compendium*, Vol. 26, No. 7, July 2001, p. 16.

CHAPTER 15

CURRENT TRENDS AND FUTURE ISSUES

66 There is a Latin proverb that says: "If there is no wind, row." And row we will, and we will make it upstream, because we have . . . vision, vigor and values.[1] **99**

—Helen G. Corrothers

Chapter Overview

With the rapid pace of change in terms of everything from technology to social policy, there never has been in the history of corrections such a need for farsighted, creative, and proactive leadership. The challenges that are accompanying the twenty-first century demand visionary leaders with farsighted plans for change—leaders who are determined but adaptable. As one correctional official phrased it, "flexibility is the best hedge against the future."[2]

To address current challenges, correctional agencies have employed various strategies. Some have turned to greater involvement of the private sector, on the theory that the competitiveness and cost-efficiency characteristic of private industry can be used productively in corrections. Others have sought to reduce litigation by adhering to the administrative and operational standards required for accreditation. Still others have made efforts to enhance the training, education, and compensation of personnel; to improve physical facilities, work conditions, and administrative practices; to devote more attention to experimentation, research, and evaluation.

Some are beginning to take proactive measures to address potential problems before they become pressing crises. But many others are still reacting. When buffeted and confused by the winds of change, it is often tempting to respond with an overreliance on high-tech equipment, short-term fads, or quick-fix solutions. Yet, the fundamental issues facing corrections are not amenable to short-cut solutions. They have not developed, nor will they be resolved, overnight. To the extent that corrections is reluctant to anticipate the future or unwilling to seriously address what can be anticipated, the legacy that is passed on will be of limited improvement over the one that was inherited. Whatever actions are taken or postponed today will shape both the problems and prospects passed on to our successors. In essence, how we respond to today's difficulties will shape tomorrow's destinies.

Current Trends

Court decisions will continue to influence correctional policies and practices as long as differences remain between the rights of free citizens and convicted offenders. However, there are also a number of trends beyond changes produced by legal procedures that are shaping the nature of corrections. Some of these have been described in previous chapters—such as trends involving structured sentencing, intermediate sanctions, restorative justice, unit management, objective classification, direct supervision jailing, and mandatory supervised release.

Beyond the changes and emerging issues discussed previously, corrections is heading in new directions as a result of such catalysts as accreditation and privatization. Of course, these are not by any means the only current trends that have been unaddressed thus far. But they have been singled out for special attention here as a result of a combination of factors, largely related to either the substantial contribution or significant controversy that they have generated.

Learning Goals

Do you know:

1. What types of standards must be met to achieve correctional accreditation?
2. Whether accreditation is voluntary or mandatory in corrections?
3. Why so many agencies have initiated the accreditation process?
4. To what extent accreditation may be a defense in liability lawsuits?

Accreditation

Every year, an increasing number of correctional institutions and programs undertake the lengthy process of seeking *accreditation* by the American Correctional Association (ACA) Commission on Accreditation for Corrections. These efforts represent a voluntary desire to upgrade the field of corrections and a proactive means of seeking some protection against litigation. Accreditation is

An ACA accreditation audit team examines every aspect of an institution and decides whether the facility meets the requirements to become accredited. The pictures on this and the following page show several aspects of an audit at various Ohio prisons. Photo courtesy of Julie Riley.

Auditors talk to staff and inmates to gauge the atmosphere of the institution apart from the records. Photo courtesy of Julie Riley.

Here, Southeastern Correctional Institution staff are being interviewed. Photo courtesy of Julie Riley.

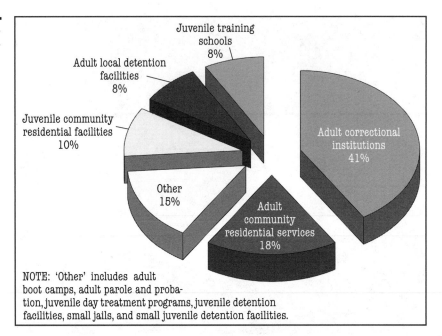

Juvenile training schools
8%

Adult local detention facilities
8%

Juvenile community residential facilities
10%

Other
15%

Adult correctional institutions
41%

Adult community residential services
18%

NOTE: 'Other' includes adult boot camps, adult parole and probation, juvenile day treatment programs, juvenile detention facilities, small jails, and small juvenile detention facilities.

Since tools can be forms of contraband, it is important that they be inventoried and accounted for at all time. Here is the tool inventory at the Chillicothe Correctional Institution. Photo courtesy of Julie Riley, Ohio Department of Rehabilitation and Correction.

important in corrections, just as it is in hospitals, universities, and other services interested in maintaining appropriate standards and levels of performance.

The American Correctional Association has developed more than sixteen manuals that provide *standards and guidelines* governing correctional administration and operations—for everything from food services to health care, correctional industries, juvenile facilities, adult institutions, small jails, probation, and parole. These guidelines represent minimum requirements that must be met for a facility or program to become accredited. Thus, they provide a measure of the quality of service being provided.

Standards regarding correctional administration include such areas as staffing, training, fiscal management, record keeping, and legal rights of offenders. With regard to the direct delivery of services, the guidelines govern basic living conditions, health care, and safety concerns. As such, they cover a wide variety of topics, including:

- The physical plant

- Classification

- Custody and security

- Inmate discipline

- Counseling, education, and recreation

- Health and medical care

- Food services

- Property control

- Library services

- Inmate activities and privileges

In each of these areas, ACA has established minimum standards, and those pursuing accreditation must be in compliance with them. The intent is to define fundamental levels of service and operation below which accredited agencies, facilities, or programs must not fall. Because standards are applicable uniformly throughout the country, they are set at a level that is within reason to achieve, rather than a higher level that ideally might be more desirable. There is nothing to prevent organizations from exceeding the standards, but neither is there any fiscal incentive to do so.

Although seeking ACA accreditation is voluntary, 73 percent of adult correctional facilities at the state and federal level are now accredited.[3] Yet, there are no legislative or legal mandates requiring accreditation nor is any additional funding necessarily forthcoming for accredited agencies. The question then becomes why so many have elected to undertake this rather costly and time-consuming process. There are any number of answers, among them:

- *Self-improvement.* By examining its existing practices against nationally accepted minimum standards, an agency can better determine in what areas it is lacking and take appropriate steps to make improvements. Of those involved in accreditation, the vast majority (93 percent) report an improvement in the overall quality of their facilities and programs as a result of this process.[4] As correctional managers themselves have stated:

    "Accreditation's major benefit to top administration comes from the knowledge that every aspect of operations and administration are now routinely and regularly reviewed. It confirms the organization's strengths, identifies its weaknesses, and enables the organization to develop a systematic resolution to those weaknesses."[5]

- *Pride and morale.* Working toward accreditation is a lengthy process that requires commitment and teamwork on the part of everyone from top management to line staff and even inmates. In an agency that suffers from divisiveness or lack of cooperation, pulling together toward this common goal can generate a "team spirit" that enhances pride and morale when it is successfully accomplished.

- *Legal defensibility.* By meeting ACA standards, correctional agencies can proactively reduce some of the expensive litigation that otherwise could result from unsafe, unsanitary, or unacceptable conditions. While accreditation will not fully protect an organization from liability, having achieved accredited status can be a strong asset in defending against certain types of claims. For example, a research project that reviewed thousands of pages of court decisions concluded that:

> Courts often consult ACA standards when attempting to determine appropriate expectations in a correctional setting. . . . [However], while there is no doubt ACA standards are a primary reference source for courts, they are not considered the only source, nor are they always adopted as the measure of adequacy. . . . [C]ompliance with ACA standards does not automatically ensure acceptance in court.[6]

In summary, although accreditation is a costly and time-consuming process, it is pursued for a variety of reasons that largely relate to the desire of correctional managers to improve their facilities, services, and administration. Accreditation demonstrates that the agency has accepted a basic set of national standards and that it is moving in the direction of developing the types of policies and procedures that are beneficial not only to the inmates, but ultimately, to staff and the public as well.

At the national level, the American Correctional Association has been instrumental in promoting correctional advancements in such areas as accreditation and certification. Other nationwide membership groups also working to stimulate progress include the American Jail Association, the National Sheriffs' Association, and the American Probation and Parole Association. Similarly, the National Council on Crime and Delinquency and the National Institute of Corrections are instrumental in disseminating information and conducting research to advance the field of corrections.

✸ Learning Goals

Do you know:

1. How the private sector has influenced corrections historically?
2. What correctional services are provided today by religious groups and private organizations?
3. What change the concept of privatization has undergone in recent years?
4. The arguments in support of and in opposition to the privatization of corrections?

Privatization in Correctional History

Not everyone would agree that accreditation is being implemented properly or setting standards high enough. Nevertheless, it is difficult to find fault with the basic concept. The same cannot, however, be said of privatization. Although

Close-up On Corrections

INFLUENCE OF THE PRIVATE SECTOR IN CORRECTIONAL HISTORY

- Victims and their families were the early forerunners of the justice system, performing functions now reserved for police and judicial officials.

- The first permanent home for wandering children was built by the Society of St. Vincent de Paul in 1648.

- John Howard used his own resources to travel throughout Europe examining jail conditions, which resulted in reform of the English penal system.

- The American penitentiary, established in 1790, was based on the philosophy and reform efforts of a private Quaker-affiliated group.

- John Augustus took it upon himself to provide bail, supervise, and redeem petty criminals assigned to him by the courts.

- Today's juvenile court was initiated as a result of pressure on the part of the Chicago Women's Clubs.

privatization is emerging as both a trend and a source of controversy today, private individuals and groups always have played a major role in the field of corrections. *See* the above "Close-up On Corrections" for a few of the influential efforts that the private sector has exerted throughout history in the field of corrections. Then, compare past efforts to some examples of private organizations working on behalf of corrections today, as highlighted in the subsequent "Close-up On Corrections."

Current Developments in Privatization

In addition to the many religious and secular groups that traditionally have been involved in some aspect of correctional work, the *privatization of corrections* has taken on new meaning today. Publicly funded correctional enterprises are turning with increasing frequency to the private sector in a wide variety of ways.

When government either does not have the specialized expertise necessary to accomplish a particular project, or finds that certain services can be provided at less cost by the private sector, it is not uncommon to *contract* with private industry. In corrections, for example, the preparation of meals and provision of health care typically are contracted out when it is determined that private enterprise is better equipped to offer the service more economically. Particularly for small institutions, it may be cost-prohibitive to hire the personnel and invest in the sophisticated equipment necessary to sustain such services independently.

Treatment Services. Likewise, private sector contracts increasingly have been filling gaps in correctional treatment services. From boot camps to group therapy programs, there are hundreds of privately operated noncustodial initiatives operating throughout the country under contract to state and local governments. As long as the demand for drug and alcohol programs continues to outpace supply, it can be expected that such private-sector involvement in correctional treatment will expand.

Community-based Corrections. Another area where privatization undoubtedly will have further impact is in the operation of community-based sanctions. Earlier, it was noted that as attention has been riveted on skyrocketing institutional populations, corresponding caseload increases in community corrections largely have gone unheeded. As a result, private firms are now involved in drug-testing probationers and parolees, administering electronically monitored home confinement, and in some places, even supervising community-based offenders. Additionally, as tightened restrictions and closer supervision increase the number of probation and parole violators, needs are expanding for community-based residential facilities.[7] Again, entrepreneurs are offering privatized services to fill gaps in public services.

Technical Assistance. Beyond operational contracts, the private sector often is engaged in short-term technical assistance when corrections is faced with

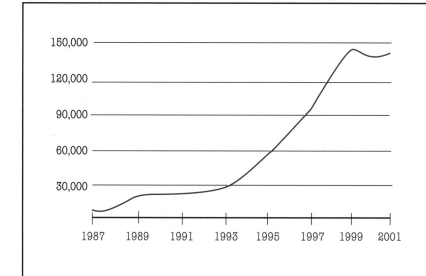

Growth of inmates in privately operated adult prisons.

Source: Peter Wagner. *The Prison Index: Taking the Pulse of the Crime Control Industry*, Northampton, Massachusetts: Prison Policy Initiative, 2003, p. 8. Used with permission.

figure 15.1

undertaking something highly specialized or beyond its existing capabilities. A typical example is the design, construction, or expansion of a facility. From a cost-benefit point of view, the correctional payroll cannot be expected to maintain a permanent staff of the architects, engineers, and other personnel needed for these major, one-time projects.

Secure Facility Operation. But specific service contracts, short-term consulting, and facility construction represent the privatization of only selected components of the correctional system, much of which has been commonplace for some time. What has changed—and created controversy—in recent years is the movement toward contracting the full operation of secure facilities to the private sector.[8]

As shown in Figure 15.1, the capacity of privately operated correctional institutions has been increasing steadily over the past decade. In fact, the state legislature in Tennessee seriously considered a proposal that would have privatized nearly the entire prison system.[9] By the end of 1996, the two companies most actively involved in privatization, Corrections Corporation of America (CCA) and Wackenhut Corrections Corporation, had reported record levels of business and profits.[10]

But then profits took a nosedive. For example, Wackenhut Corrections' stock dropped from an all-time high of $45 in June, 1996, to less than $8 by mid-April, 2000,[11] and CCA's shares likewise plunged from a high of $44 in 1998 to 96 cents by April, 2001.[12] Some of the reasons for this decline are highlighted in the dilemmas experienced by these two leaders of prison privatization in the following "Close-up On Corrections." (By 2004, however, their performance had rebounded somewhat, as reflected in stock prices that were once again on the rise).[13]

Speculative Prisons. By the turn of the twenty-first century, privatization had taken on yet another dimension—*speculative prisons.* Constructed by private, for-profit companies without a contract with any agency, bed space in "spec" prisons is marketed to departments of corrections across the country. They have been referred to as a "Field of Dreams approach—in other words, if you build it, they will come." [14]

Close-up On Corrections

PRISONS, PROFITS, AND PROBLEMS

Six prisoners had escaped in broad daylight from the Northeast Ohio Correctional Center and were still at large. The inmates had cut a four-foot hole in the prison's fence during outdoor recreation, then maneuvered through three rolls of razor ribbon without being detected. No alarm went off, and the officers patrolling the perimeter didn't notice anything amiss. . . .

The company staffed the facility with guards who had little or no experience in corrections—and then imported 1,700 of the most violent inmates from Washington, D.C., to fill what was supposed to be a medium-security prison. CCA left metal equipment everywhere, which the prisoners quickly stripped and fashioned into weapons. During the first year alone, twenty prisoners were stabbed and two were murdered.

Source: Michael Wilson, "Steel Town Lockdown," *Mother Jones*, May/June, 2000, pp. 39-40.

A series of scandals in at least four states has hurt Wackenhut where it hurts the most—its bottom line. . . . :

- After an August 1999 riot [in New Mexico] that left an inmate and a guard dead, Wackenhut was faulted for having inadequate and ill-prepared staff earning Wal-Mart wages.

- In Texas, Wackenhut was stripped of a $12 million-a-year contract and fined $625,000. . . . Twelve former officers were indicted for having sex with female inmates. . . .

- In Ft. Lauderdale, five guards at a Wackenhut work-release facility were fired or punished for having sex with inmates. . . .

- In April, 2000, Wackenhut agreed to surrender control of its fifteen-month-old juvenile prison in Jena, Louisiana. That came a week after the U.S. Justice Department named Wackenhut in a lawsuit seeking to protect imprisoned boys from harm at the hands of guards and fellow inmates.

Source: James McNair, "Wackenhut Corrections: Prisons, Profits, and Problems," *The Herald*, Miami, Florida: April 16, 2000, E-1.

Much like the residents of hotels and motels who live out-of-town, inmates in these facilities might come from any number of states, depending on which agencies buy beds there. And much like the Internet connects travelers with hotel vacancies, there is now a web site (jailbedspace.com) for correctional administrators looking for beds available for rent.[15] It could be entirely possible that no inmates housed in a spec prison come from the state in which the facility is located. (In fact, the state of Hawaii's third largest prison in recent years has been in Newton, Texas).[16] Nor does the host state's department of corrections have any inherent oversight power over it.

Needless to say, this has raised a number of controversial issues in the ongoing debate over the advantages and disadvantages of privatization—as a result of which, at least two spec prisons in one state are standing empty because there is no interest in using them.[17] Some of the unique concerns regarding speculative prisons are highlighted in the next "Close-up On Corrections."

The Prison-Industrial Complex

Communities that once shunned the construction of a prison in "their back yard" are today actively courting speculative brokers and site planners. As the United States has shifted from manufacturing to a service economy, rural areas in particular have felt the brunt of agricultural setbacks, plant closures, layoffs, and unemployment. Many localities therefore not only present no objection to prison construction, but often actively solicit it:

> Prisons are labor-intensive institutions, offering year-round employment. They are recession-proof, usually expanding in size during hard times. And they are nonpolluting—an important consideration in rural areas where other forms of development are often blocked by environmentalists. Prisons have brought a stable, steady income to regions long accustomed to a highly seasonal, uncertain economy.[18]

As a result, some towns now have more inmates than inhabitants. But a recessionary rural economy is not the only driving force that is fueling the momentum of private interests in corrections.

Each new prison or jail creates a corresponding need for everything from miles of concertina wire to years of telephone services. Just as legislators have determined that being tough on crime is politically popular, private enterprise has discovered that corrections is big business. This combination of political,

Correctional facilities are becoming more electronically sophisticated, and new architecture and management styles are reflecting the principles of direct supervision jailing as seen here at the Arlington County, Virginia, Detention Facility. Courtesy of Arlington County, Virginia.

Close-up On Corrections

SPECULATIVE PRISON CHECKLIST

For-profit speculative prisons raise several troubling issues concerning the three governmental entities involved—the local community, the host state, and the sending state. For example, how would you answer the following questions?

From the perspective of the local community . . .

- What are the economic benefits and costs?

- Should the private provider be required to reimburse the county and/or municipality for governmental costs associated with the prison's development (for example, new roads, water and sewer systems, and so forth)?

- What regulatory control and oversight will local government exercise (for example, types of inmates admitted, staffing patterns, perimeter security, release procedures)?

- Will such regulation (or lack thereof) increase local government's liability exposure?

From the perspective of the host state . . .

- If the prison is to be regulated, should it be the function of state or local government?

- Will the private company be charged for regulation costs and oversight?

- Who mobilizes and pays for emergency support-response services?

- Should there be restrictions on where out-of-state offenders can be released?

- What is the response of organized labor to private prisons in the state?

From the perspective of the sending state . . .

- Does the department have statutory authority to place inmates out-of-state?

- Are there minimum qualifications that the private provider must meet?

- Is there a mechanism to monitor the contract to ensure that requirements are being met?

- What is the sending state's liability exposure?

- How will inmates be transported to the private facility?

- How will the effectiveness of privatization be assessed?

Source: Compiled from William C. Collins, *Privately Operated Speculative Prisons and Public Safety: A Discussion of Issues*, Washington, D.C.: U.S. Department of Justice, n.d., Appendix A.

economic, and entrepreneurial interests supporting increased spending on imprisonment has been termed the *prison-industrial complex*.

In psychology, a "complex" is "an overreaction to some perceived threat."[19] In corrections, that threat perception now advances the self-interests of prominent architecture and construction firms, along with major Wall Street banks

The Cook County Department of Corrections is the American Correctional Association's largest accredited detention facility. Located on ninety-seven acres in southwest Chicago, this public facility annually processes more than 100,000 inmates. Courtesy of Cook County Department of Corrections.

financing prison bonds, not to mention the thousands of private enterprises providing the locking devices, transportation vehicles, security equipment, office furniture, facility plumbing, electrical wiring, health care, food services, and other items that every correctional institution needs to operate. In this entrepreneurial atmosphere, "the higher the occupancy rate, the higher the profit margin," which has led to concern that choices about the denial of personal freedom may be made with an eye toward the bottom line. [20]

Benefits of Privatization

On the one hand, privatization of correctional facilities has been supported on the grounds of efficiency and cost effectiveness. This rationale maintains that the private sector has a number of advantages over government, including:

- *Reduced costs.* Because of the competitive nature of private industry and its profit motive, there is more incentive to reduce waste, eliminate duplication, and otherwise streamline activities in a more cost-effective manner: "Since private sector companies function in a competitive environment, they must offer high-quality services at minimum cost." [21] Thus, it is maintained that government can obtain more service for less money by opening the management of correctional facilities to a competitive bidding process.

- *Flexibility and creativity.* Bureaucracies are traditionally slow to experiment with new approaches or even respond to immediate needs. In contrast, "[w]hen a need is identified for audiovisual monitors or two-way, portable radios, for example, a corporate decision can be made in minutes and the equipment can be immediately forthcoming." [22] Advocates of privatization therefore cite additional advantages in terms of greater flexibility, creativity, and responsiveness. As one executive has noted, "when you are looking for innovation, you don't look to government, you look to business." [23]

- *Competitive choice.* When there is dissatisfaction with the manner in which corrections is performing, it may not be easy to do anything about it through the existing system. By bringing in a "clean slate" through privatization, corrections is no longer burdened with "positions remaining from old, out-dated programs . . . or particular management preferences from a long-gone administrator." [24] Moreover, if the performance of a private company is unacceptable, government has the choice of resuming operation of the facility itself or contracting with a competitor. Knowing this presumably generates further incentive to provide high-quality service.

Concerns about Privatization

In short, proponents of privatization maintain that economy, flexibility, and competition enable private companies to be more innovative and efficient at less cost. Not everyone would agree with that glowing assessment, however. Opponents of the full privatization of correctional facilities cite such concerns as:

- *Quality assurance.* Given the fact that the profit motive is such a strong incentive in the private sector, fear has been expressed that "private operators may be tempted to take shortcuts that could compromise safety" or "reduce the quality and quantity of staff and services." [25] When government contracts with private industry to operate a prison or jail, it is obviously important to specify clearly what minimum standards the contractor must adhere to, as well as to establish procedures for monitoring and enforcing compliance. But even if care is taken in that regard, there is always the danger that the *minimum required will* become the *maximum provided* to lower costs while raising profits. Advocates of privatization counter that "good services and competitive prices are not mutually exclusive." [26] Opponents warn that "the best policy is, buyer beware." [27]

- *Selectivity.* A related argument concerns the types of clients and facilities with which the private sector is willing to become involved. To the extent that low-risk populations and minimum-security institutions are more appealing to private companies, government may find itself in a position of being left with the least desirable correctional workload. As the "last resort," public corrections could ultimately be limited to dealing with the most hardcore clients and managing the highest-security institutions. Earlier, trends in this direction were noted in the juvenile justice system, and Figure 15.2 points to a similar pattern in the adult system.

- *Liability.* Initially, it might appear that an enticing feature of privatization would be reduced liability for government. However, that attractive potential may occur only to the extent that a privately managed facility is subject to fewer lawsuits than those under public management. In other words, government cannot simply transfer liability to a private corporation through a contractual arrangement. In fact, the Supreme Court dealt with this issue in 1997, holding that the state "cannot transfer its sovereign immunity to a contractor in response to a Section 1983 lawsuit." [28]

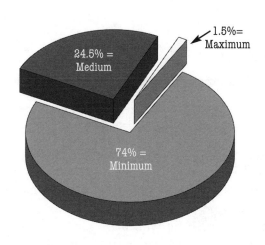

figure 15.2

Security levels of privately operated prisons.

Source: Calculated from James J. Stephan and Jennifer C. Karberg. *Census of State and Federal Correctional Facilities, 2000.* Washington, D.C.: Bureau of Justice Statistics, 2001, p. 16.

Government is ultimately responsible for its actions, whether they are carried out directly or indirectly through a private company. Nor are private sector employees immune from liability, as established by the Supreme Court in 1997.[29] However, several more recent cases have muddied the legal waters, with results sometimes differing on the basis of such factors as what jurisdiction the lawsuit is brought against and whether it targets the correctional agency or employees personally.[30] But it has been noted that government liability "can be reduced by wise contracting," specifying that it be reimbursed for the cost of litigation and indemnified against damage awards.[31]

The bottom line is that the state is responsible for every institution operated under its authority—whether private or public. That same protection, however, does not appear to extend to privately employed staff, as seen in the next "Close-up On Corrections."

- *Appropriate roles.* Few would question the involvement of private industry in providing selected services or short-term technical assistance. But whether the entire operation of a correctional facility should be turned over to private enterprise is another issue entirely. Some contend that corrections is essentially a government obligation that should not be divorced from the democratic process in which society formulates public policy through elected officials. In that regard, it has been noted that privatization involves the potential for ethical and legal problems that may "erode the sovereignty" of governmental jurisdictions.[32] As a result of such considerations, an opinion from the attorney general's office in the state of Washington maintains that cities cannot contract with a private company to operate local jail facilities because jails by definition "are to be operated by government."[33]

Using this line of reasoning, questions also have been raised about the appropriateness of private-sector decision making in such sensitive matters as

Close-up On Corrections

"[inmate] discipline, use of force, good time forfeiture, and parole recommendations."[34] Especially if compensation is based on a per inmate fee, there is concern that private-sector involvement in such decisions could encourage the overuse of institutions. For example, policies may be adopted that are designed to maintain full occupancy by increasing the frequency of disciplinary actions that, in turn, can lead to less good time and longer sentences. As the John Howard Association has argued, "[s]hort of the death penalty, incarceration is the state's most intrusive control over a citizen's life. It is inappropriate to relinquish this authority to an organization operating with profit as its primary goal."[35]

In response to this concern, many privatization contracts have been written in a manner prohibiting the contractor from making final decisions that "could have an adverse effect on the liberty interests of prisoners."[36] Under such contractual provisions, "private firms have no power to determine who will or who will not be committed to their facilities, to shape determinations of when those who are committed to their facilities will be released, or to control disciplinary processes whose outcome could alter significantly the conditions of confinement."[37]

Research Findings

As these wide-ranging positions on both sides demonstrate, privatization is neither good nor bad; right nor wrong. Nor is it even clear whether privately operated facilities are less expensive. As one correctional administrator has observed: "A well-run correctional facility is a well-run correctional facility—no matter who runs it. A good administrator, whether in the private or public sector, should—and must—be conscious of cost. It is taxpayer money, whether it's being spent by a private contractor or a public sector manager." [38]

Some studies indicate that going private has resulted in "more and better prison services for less money." [39] One review of the research in this area, for example, concludes that private management is not only significantly less expensive, but that the cost savings can be achieved without any sacrifice in terms of the quality of correctional services. [40] But a General Accounting Office review of several studies was unable to document clear evidence of savings and noted that findings in terms of cost and of quality of service in any given year may not hold true for other years. [41]

In that regard, some suspect that private companies may engage in "low-balling" (in other words, purposely underestimating actual costs to win a contract); that they have "hidden costs" which are being subsidized by the public sector (for example, routinely sending serious medical cases to state-operated facilities); and that they may use a smaller and/or less qualified workforce to cut labor costs. [42]

Related Issues

While there is no firm evidence that institutional stability is a direct product of the quality or quantity of staff, questions have been raised about the role that staffing shortcuts may have played in recent disturbances at privately run facilities. In some cases, these concerns are jeopardizing the expansion or renewal of private contracts. For instance, one of the reasons that the Federal Bureau of Prisons decided against further privatization was the outbreak of riots at two facilities operated under private contract. [43] Moreover, the state with the largest number of private prisons—Texas—expressed serious concerns about the need for greater regulation after a "rash of escapes and disturbances." [44]

These high-profile problems have drawn attention to some of the unresolved issues surrounding the obligations of each party—such as whether government or the private contractor is responsible for paying the costs of recapturing escaped inmates. They also have generated objections to bringing out-of-state inmates into private facilities—a practice that could potentially make the recipient state a "dumping ground" for problem inmates from other jurisdictions.

These and other issues will continue to be debated as more research is conducted, experience is gained, and opinions are voiced. [45] In the meantime, privatization continues to generate contradictory evidence and widely varying points of view, making it somewhat premature to come to definitive conclusions about supporting or opposing it, since neither side has definitively proven its case. While the evidence is mounting, on privatization, "the jury is still out." [46]

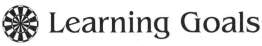

Do you know:

1. How drug-related crime can be expected to influence the future of corrections?

2. What mistakes were made during implementation of the justice model that can be avoided when making future social policy changes?

3. What impact the events of 9/11 and national economic conditions are having on corrections?

4. What is meant by "evidence-based" decision making?

Future Issues

Future correctional administrators no doubt will continue to face issues that are as challenging as accreditation and as controversial as privatization. But beyond some of these obvious ongoing concerns, predicting the future is quite speculative. It is difficult enough to guess what the weather will be tomorrow, much less what the horizon holds for such a vast and varied enterprise as corrections. Even today, the multiple goals, diverse practices, and emerging issues in the correctional conglomerate are neither clearly defined nor easily resolved. But simply because the future cannot be anticipated with complete accuracy does not mean that we cannot be alert to the implications of current trends for shaping future issues.

Unfortunately, crisis is frequently the major catalytic agent in stimulating social progress. But changes rarely occur overnight in a revolutionary manner. To the contrary, they tend to come about over time through a slower, evolutionary process. Nor are changes in the field of corrections generally extreme diversions from the present. Rather, they tend to be gradual modifications of what currently exists. To the extent that the past is prolog to the future, there is much that we can anticipate about tomorrow from what is occurring today.

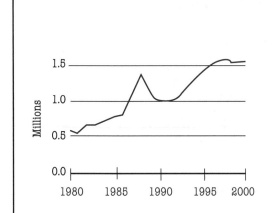

figure 15.3

Drug offenses represent a steadily increasing number of arrests in the past two decades.

Source: *http://www.ojp.usdoj.gov/bjs/dcf/arrtot/gif, July 6, 2004.*

Drugs, Crime, and Crowding

One of the harshest realities that Americans have had to face in recent years has been the drug epidemic. The prevalence of drugs throughout all socioeconomic classes is undoubtedly among the major explanations for why high crime rates have persisted. As drugs have begun to affect a broader segment of society, attitudes concerning appropriate responses to the problem are beginning to shift. But there remains a heavy emphasis on enforcement, as reflected in Figure 15.3, which indicates that the number of drug-related arrests has continued at a steady pace for the past two decades, as has its fiscal impact. By the turn of the twenty-first century, it was estimated that the economic damage of drug use on the American economy had reached a staggering $160 billion.[47]

Despite the "war on drugs" (or more accurately, because of it), drug-related cases have fueled rising probation and parole caseloads and continue to contribute to jail and prison crowding. Moreover, this dilemma has created a vicious cycle. The burden of accommodating ever-increasing numbers of drug-related offenders has forced corrections into a regressive "back to the basics"—often limiting probation and parole services to "monitoring and reporting," and concentrating institutional resources on security and space allocations at the expense of program initiatives. With increasingly crowded correctional facilities, emphasis during the 1990s shifted from treatment to containment, with resources normally allocated to programs being diverted to security.[48]

Economics and Fiscal Priorities

Finally, early in the twenty-first century, the ongoing growth of institutional populations began to level-off somewhat. But that encouraging development was more than offset by the discouraging fallout of a declining economy. The national economic slowdown following the terrorist attacks of September 11, 2001 (along with the reallocation of fiscal priorities to homeland security), combined to create budgetary shortfalls throughout the correctional conglomerate. Even worse, at the same time that revenues began decreasing, expenses further increased as a result of the escalating populations with chronic illnesses, infectious diseases, and geriatric disabilities.

Correctional administrators, therefore, have faced making painful fiscal choices between institutional security, health care, and inmate programming. Given the fundamental necessity of security and health care, many have reduced programming as their only realistic alternative:

> Thus, federal, state, and local correctional systems have seen a sharp reduction in programs that provide offenders with the education, vocational, and life skills necessary to prepare for reintegration into society.[49]

But at the same time, increasing numbers of inmates are entering the correctional system with serious therapeutic needs—ranging from drug treatment to anger management. Likewise, increasing numbers of inmates are preparing for release, many without benefit of institutional or post-release programming. As one critic has put it, "Building more prisons to address crime is like building more graveyards to address a fatal disease." [50] Yet, fiscally shortsighted public policies continue to respond to the consequences without addressing the underlying causes:

> Many Americans still believe that the answer to the failures of punitive prohibition is more punitive prohibition. This is close to believing that when a medicine is found to fail and have nasty side effects, the patient should be made to take a double dose of it. . . . When arresting half a million Americans . . . did not stop illicit drug use, the fundamentalist response was to arrest a million. [51]

Changing Public Opinion and Policy Implications

As reflected in the drug issue, it is not crime alone that determines the size of correctional caseloads and institutional populations, but rather, prevailing public policy—which reflects the manner in which society responds to criminal behavior. In that regard, we have watched social trends shift from the medical model to the justice model, along with the accompanying fluctuations in prison populations. In fact, it has been observed that "the failure of the medical model, in turn, fueled the fears and discontent of those who saw drug use as a moral problem rather than a medical one," [52] thus justifying harsher penalties.

Yet, many of the same conditions that promoted the justice model are equally prevalent today—for example, continuing concern over crime rates and a widespread belief that current practices are not working. One major study, for example, concluded that while California's "get-tough-on-crime" policies have fueled a massive influx of inmates, putting more people behind bars has had little effect on the state's crime rate. [53] Reactions to such findings have been emphatic: "Never has there been a better experimental demonstration that there is no real relationship between increasing the prison population and decreasing the crime rate." [54]

In other states, it has been found that "three-strikes" provisions are rarely being invoked. Despite the political rhetoric surrounding the passage of such legislation, in many states it appears to be having a greater impact on the courts (as a plea bargaining tool) than on crime rates. [55] In that regard, if left unchecked, such prosecutorial discretion has the potential to regenerate "the very disparities that sentencing reform was intended to alleviate." [56] Overall, it has been noted that:

> Criminal justice policies may be thought of as irrational when their benefits in terms of crime are outweighed by the harms they cause. By most accounts, three-strikes laws meet this definition. [57]

Whether the public will continue to support increasingly punitive legislation in the absence of research demonstrating its effectiveness will depend on politics and social attitudes. In terms of such attitudes, it is becoming increasingly apparent that the public may not actually be as punitive as policymakers would have us believe. For example, various studies in recent years have revealed that:

- There is a "strong dissatisfaction" with the current state of criminal justice. While not showing leniency toward crime, polls do indicate support for providing inmates with skills and nonviolent offenders with noninstitutional alternatives such as education, job training, victim compensation, and community service.[58]

- Six out of ten Americans believe that prisons are largely failing in their rehabilitative mandate.[59]

- Although punitive toward criminals, the public is "more lenient toward inmates because they are no longer seen as an immediate threat . . . which lends support to current correctional practices that seek to integrate programs for inmates with the more general concerns of correctional management." [60]

- Overall, citizens advocate "a more balanced approach to crime—one that extracts an appropriate measure of just deserts and protects the public from the truly dangerous but that also makes a concerted effort to rehabilitate and restore to the community those who need not be ensnared in a life of crime." [61]

- Even community leaders who are justice policymakers express views that are "most supportive of rehabilitation and serving the needs of those with mental health and substance abuse problems." [62]

These results suggest an emerging foundation for social policy revisions. To the extent that they are truly indicative of prevailing trends, today's politicians are "woefully and persistently misperceiving public views." [63] And to the extent that the public is becoming increasingly disenchanted with the existing process, the time is ripe for more creative and uplifting alternatives. In fact, by 2001, a number of jurisdictions had already taken some initial actions:

- Four states had revised mandatory sentencing laws.

- Five states had expanded drug treatment as a sentencing option.

- Seven states had passed legislation to ease prison crowding.[64]

If nothing else, the era of "doing more with less" under the justice model has created the opportunity to consider alternative approaches. Moreover, corrections has been confronted with the reality that public perceptions cannot be ignored.[65] But embarking on new, more uplifting ventures is not likely to occur on a widespread basis unless correctional administrators are willing to pursue a more proactive role in influencing public policy choices.

In that regard, calls to action have advocated greater correctional involvement in public policy development,[66] encouraging leaders to "be proactive in educating and shaping public opinion." [67] A united front has yet to emerge in the form of a determined effort to influence public mandates that guide management practices. Nevertheless, it is clear that correctional administrators no longer can seek refuge in the isolated existence they once enjoyed behind literal and figurative walls.

Learning from Past Mistakes

If there is one lesson that has been learned from the self-defeating impact of the justice model, it is the necessity to plan properly in advance of making

A new approach to helping offenders make it in the free world is the transitional living units or halfway houses. Here is the Fort Peck Transitional Living Unit in Polar, Montana on the Fort Peck Assiniboine-Sioux Reservation. Its purpose is post-adjudicatory treatment and holding of tribally enrolled youths ages twelve through eighteen who are conducive to reintegration back into the community. Courtesy Mark Goldman and Associates, Project Architect/Engineer: EKM&P.

significant policy changes. In fact, it is actually impossible to determine whether the justice model might have been more effective if it had not been confronted with the massive institutional crowding that resulted in such widespread early release that its original intent was severely compromised. Moreover, that same argument could be made with respect to the medical model. Without funding for treatment programs, its intent was likewise compromised.

As these breakdowns between ambition and actuality illustrate, public policy cannot be fulfilled effectively in the absence of advance planning and resource allocation. It is insufficient simply to change policy to appease political constituents. Public opinion and political leadership too often have reacted emotionally to crime, calling for severe and simplistic solutions that have overloaded the correctional conglomerate without commensurate funding. Even the best intentions are doomed to failure in the absence of informed decisions based on projections of expected impact, including the resources required for policy implementation.

Policymaking Based on Evaluation Research

Prior to establishing a new policy, serious consideration of fiscal and operational repercussions is critical to achieving success. But even with careful foresight, plans do not always materialize in practice as they were anticipated in theory. Thus, the need for ongoing study and empirical evaluation cannot be overlooked.

Before conclusions can be drawn about any program, evaluation must be integrated into program planning and practice. Few employers would advocate keeping staff on the payroll without periodic standardized performance evaluations. Yet, major criminal justice policies are commonly implemented without giving thought to how their effectiveness will be measured.

Even when outcome assessments have been conducted, the research in this field generally has been haphazard—conducted on an *ad hoc* basis, often as an afterthought or to meet a funding requirement. Attempts at evaluation in the past often have suffered from unscientific methodology, focused on small populations, and provided disconnected bits of information rather than cumulative knowledge. But that uninspiring legacy is beginning to change as more correctional administrators are recognizing the value of rigorous empirical research.

Establishing Evidence-Based Practices

Contemporary correctional policy largely has been driven by factors ranging from public opinion to political grandstanding. As a result, policy shifts and programmatic changes often have occurred with little regard for their effectiveness in reducing recidivism. In the past, this was compounded by the absence of well-designed evaluation studies. As sound research has emerged in more recent years, however, the capability now exists to use a more objective, evidence-based decision-making process in program and policy development.

Whether corrections will move forward in this direction or remain trapped in the shifting sands of politically based policymaking remains to be seen. In that regard, it has been observed that "the use of evaluation results has been a missing link in correctional decision-making."[68] But in the meantime, solid research is accumulating that identifies what does and does not work, which progressively can be used to shape future policy and practice.

As the next "Close-up On Corrections" reveals, the perception that "nothing works" is now woefully outdated. While "nothing works" may be a catchy political sound bite, it reflects uninformed thinking and obsolete policy. On the other hand, as the "Close-up On Corrections" also reveals, some of the most popular and prevalent correctional initiatives have earned a rather dismal report card on the basis of empirical findings.[69]

Corrections cannot expect to get the funding it deserves without proving its value, which depends on measuring results.[70] Evaluation research therefore must become an essential component in the process of planning policy changes—if for no other reason, than because people who are paying the bills have a right to know what is and is not working.

 Learning Goals

Do you know:

1. What the most significant drawback of intermediate options is?
2. How restorative justice differs from retributive justice?
3. How correctional treatment is changing?
4. What types of treatment programs are most effective?
5. Why greater efficiency and cost-saving measures will continue to be high correctional priorities?

Close-up On Corrections

What Works?

- Rehabilitation programs that are structured and focused, use multiple treatment components, focus on developing skills, and use behavioral methods
- Prison-based therapeutic communities for drug-involved offenders
- Cognitive-behavioral therapy that focuses on changing thoughts and attitudes either through moral development or problem-solving
- Non-prison-based sex-offender treatment programs using cognitive-behavioral methods
- Vocational education programs in prison or residential settings
- Multicomponent correctional industry programs

What Does Not Work? [71]

- Programs emphasizing specific deterrence, such as shock probation and "Scared Straight"
- Vague, nondirective, unstructured counseling
- Programs emphasizing structure, discipline, and challenge, such as old-style military boot camps and juvenile wilderness excursions
- Initiatives that focus exclusively on increased control and surveillance in the community without accompanying treatment, such as intensive supervised probation or parole, home confinement, and urine testing

Source: Adapted from Doris Layton MacKenzie, "Evidence-based Corrections: Identifying What Works," *Crime and Delinquency*, Vol. 46, No. 4, October 2000, pp. 457-471.

Projecting Correctional Trends

Beyond the issues discussed above, a number of emerging trends have been addressed throughout earlier chapters of this book. It is useful at this point to recap briefly some of these transitions and consider their implications for the future direction of corrections.

Intermediate-Sentencing Alternatives. Initially developed as a "front-door" option for reducing jail and prison crowding, such alternatives as electronic monitoring/home confinement and intensive supervision probation have become recognized as legitimate approaches in their own right. As a compromise between the lesser restrictions of traditional probation and the severity of incarceration, they provide a reasonable middle ground—addressing the concerns of those who advocate more punitive practices, as well as those who object to the futility of imprisonment.

On a practical level, both crowded facilities and the exorbitant cost of new construction are inspiring a growing interest in intermediate sanctions.[72] Of course, to say that such sanctions are less expensive is not to say that they are cost free—or, as we have seen earlier, that they are necessarily effective. One of the significant drawbacks of many intermediate sanctions is that they often are implemented "without creating the organizational capacity to ensure compliance with court-ordered conditions."[73] For example, it does no good whatsoever to order a client to get help for a drug problem if there is a minimum two-year waiting list for local drug treatment programs.

Without the accompanying resources, research shows that intensive supervision is unlikely to be any more effective than its traditional predecessor. (*See* the previous "Close-up On Corrections"). In the words of one concerned probation administrator, "We need to convince a conflicted public—torn between fear of crime and fear of taxes—that we merit the increased funding needed to make us more effective on their behalf."[74] With appropriate resources, intermediate options also provide an opportunity to fulfill two correctional objectives that have been gaining popularity in recent years: *restitution and restoration*.

Restorative Justice Concepts. In contemporary society, government assumes full responsibility for apprehending, prosecuting, and punishing criminal behavior. As a result, crime is viewed by the state in almost an abstract manner—as a violation against the interests of society. Such an approach does little to reinforce any sense of either personal responsibility on the part of the offender or personal involvement in the justice process on the part of the victim.

To address these issues, the concept of *restorative justice* has been gaining momentum. Using various forms of victim-offender mediation and dispute resolution, the restorative focus is centered on bringing together all parties with a stake in a particular offense to deal with the aftermath of the crime, along with its implications for the future.[75] As such, it emphasizes both:

- Restoring at least some of the tangible losses experienced by the victim through negotiated restitution arrangements

Successful offender reentry is crucial. One way to enhance success is through Citizens Circles, as shown here in Marion, Ohio. These groups form plans in concert with parole supervision guidelines to aid offenders with job-seeking, education, family issues, mental health, substance abuse, and many other areas. Photo by John R. Matthews. Courtesy of *Corrections Today* magazine.

- Restoring the offender's sense of personal accountability for the harm caused by his or her actions (and ultimately, the community's trust in the offender)

For a closer look at how restorative justice differs from the more conventional concept of retributive justice, *see* the next "Close-up On Corrections." As that comparison shows, sentencing based on restorative justice offers "something for everyone":

- *For victims*: Success is measured by the degree to which damages have been repaired and victims have been involved in, as well as satisfied with, the justice process.

 # Close-up On Corrections

CHANGING CONCEPTS OF JUSTICE

RETRIBUTIVE JUSTICE	RESTORATIVE JUSTICE
Crime defined as violation of the state	Crime defined as violation of one person by another
Focus on establishing blame, on guilt, on past behavior	Focus on problem solving, liabilities, obligations, and the future
Relationships are adversarial	Relationships involve dialog and negotiation
Suffering is imposed to punish, deter, and prevent	Reconciliation/restoration is the goal
Interpersonal nature of crime is obscured; conflict seen as individual versus state	Crime recognized as interpersonal conflict
Victim is ignored; offender is passive	Victim rights/needs recognized
Offender accountability defined as taking punishment	Offender accountability defined as understanding impact of action, taking responsibility, and making things right
Response focused on offender's past behavior	Response focused on harmful consequences of offender's behavior

Source: Adapted from Howard Zehr, "Restorative Justice," *IARCA (International Association of Residential and Community Alternatives) Journal*, March 1991, p. 7.

- *For offenders*: Objectives emphasize gaining an understanding of the consequences of crime for victims, feelings of remorse, recognition that they have been sanctioned, and (ideally) development of empathy with victims. Positive behavioral outcomes include prompt repayment to victims, completion of community service, and other reparative requirements (for example, facing the victim in mediation).

- *For the community*: The most important objectives are overall satisfaction that justice has been served, a sense that offenders have been held accountable, and a feeling of community well-being.[76]

Programs based on restorative-justice principles can be expected to become increasingly attractive to the extent that social attitudes and values move in a more moderate direction, while still expressing discomfort with absolving offenders of individual responsibility for their conduct.

Changing Nature of Treatment. Even with considerably diminished support for the medical model over past decades, belief in the potential benefits of treatment has not been demolished. The difference today is that it is more likely to be offered on a *voluntary basis* rather than as an inducement for early release. Like restorative justice, this reflects a trend toward placing more individual responsibility on the offender, recognizing that rehabilitation is unlikely to be successful in the absence of personal motivation. In that regard, it may be as inappropriate to hold corrections accountable for the behavior of its clients as it would be to hold a hospital accountable for the postrelease behavior of its patients:

> When people . . . are treated successfully [in hospitals] but are known to be returning to poor diets or to smoking, drinking, or taking drugs that will endanger their well-being, is it said that hospitals "don't work." In reality, their treatment may or may not "work.". . . It would be strange to think of a hospital where staff disregard the welfare of patients because they are likely to remain ill.[77]

Today, the nature of "treatment" is taking on a more *pragmatic orientation*. In contrast to counseling, group therapy, and other forms of psychological treatment, emphasis now is being placed on developing productive employment skills.

Society's continuing expression of concern over adult illiteracy, likewise, can be expected to further strengthen a more pragmatic approach to treatment, with additional emphasis on basic education programs. Beyond expanded vocational training and educational opportunities, more specifically targeted treatment programs also can be anticipated in the future—but only to the extent that treatment becomes a greater fiscal priority.

As opposed to the counseling-for-everyone approach, treatment that survives in this era of fiscal austerity increasingly will be tailored to the particular needs of alcoholics, drug addicts, sex offenders, and other high-profile disorders. In fact, it has been suggested that we "rethink our use of the term "treatment," and cast it aside, replacing it with "risk reduction," a more realistic objective of correctional programs"[78]—and also one that is more likely to generate public support and accompanying funds.

In many respects, correctional treatment is still coping with fallout from the widely held premise that "nothing works." Yet, as noted earlier, new evidence is emerging that carefully constructed programs *can* work. For a more detailed look at the concepts on which effective programming is based, see the following "Close-up On Corrections." [79]

Changing Features of Institutions. In addition to the nature of programs offered, indications are already on the horizon that the physical features of correctional institutions are beginning to change as well. These modifications are

---

 # Close-up On Corrections

What Works?

Programs that have reduced recidivism by 25 percent to 60 percent have several common characteristics—specifically, the services that they provide:

- Are intensive, lasting three to nine months

- Are based on cognitive and social learning theories

- Target the specific needs of high-risk offenders, such as antisocial attitudes and values

- Match the style and mode of treatment to the offender

- Use positive reinforcement much more frequently—by a ratio of four-to-one—than punishment

- Disrupt the criminal network by placing offenders in situations where pro-social activities predominate

Source: Paul Gendreau and Mario A. Paparozzi, "Examining What Works in Community Corrections," *Corrections Today*, Vol. 57, No. 1, February 1995, p. 29.

Why Does It Work?

The core dimensions of effective correctional practices include:

- *Relationships*: Relating in open, enthusiastic, caring ways

- *Authority*: Using a "firm but fair" style for monitoring and reinforcing compliance (not interpersonal domination or abuse)

- *Anticriminal modeling and reinforcement*: Demonstrating and reinforcing vivid alternatives to procriminal styles of thinking, feeling, and acting

Source: Roger J. Lauen, *Positive Approaches to Corrections: Research, Policy, and Practice*, Lanham, Maryland: American Correctional Association, 1997, p. 168, citing Donald A. Andrews and James Bonta, *The Psychology of Criminal Conduct*, Cincinnati, Ohio: Anderson Publishing, 1994.

---

perhaps most apparent among local jails—where some of the most antiquated facilities are being abolished or modernized, small jails are being consolidated through *regionalization*, and new architecture and management styles are reflecting the principles of *direct supervision* (new generation) jailing.

Both jails and prisons are also becoming more electronically sophisticated—as keys, locks, and staff monitors are giving way to computers, video cameras, "smart cards," and even satellite surveillance. In fact, as described in the upcoming "Close-up On Corrections," such technology is already available. One of the dangers of extensive reliance on high-tech hardware, of course, is that it further promotes the dehumanizing effect of incarceration. Direct supervision and unit management strategies work toward overcoming this drawback, since officers are stationed directly inside housing units, interacting with the inmates on a continual basis.

Economic Shortfalls and Cost-Saving Measures. Just as in other components of government, corrections is being expected to do more with less. As noted earlier, this has become even more pronounced since the devastating economic impact of the attacks of 9/11. By the fall of 2002, it was estimated that states throughout the country faced a $40 billion shortfall. (Ironically, that is also precisely what it was costing in 2002 to incarcerate the nearly two million inmates confined in correctional facilities).[80]

In the wake of such massive fiscal shortages, it has become necessary to use personnel and resources more efficiently. Examples of creative means of doing so exist in both institutional and community-based corrections. Within correctional facilities, for instance, labor-intensive methods of tracking inmate movements and purchases through passes, checklists, and cumbersome paperwork are giving way to the use of *electronic scanning devices*. In community-based corrections, *electronic monitoring* has reduced the need for numerous field visits and home checks, while *caseload classification* is enabling officers to concentrate their efforts on clients most in need of careful supervision. And everywhere costs are being offset by charging user fees—for services ranging from health care to community supervision, transportation, and even food and lodging.

Despite such efforts, however, corrections continues to struggle with the effects of a declining economy, which creates both an increasing burden and a decreasing ability to pay for it. As a result, some states are even closing prisons and laying off correctional staff. As one distraught worker wearily summarized the situation, "We have to do so much with so little for so many."[81]

 # Learning Goals

Do you know:

1. How privatization will influence future correctional practices?
2. In what ways computers and other technological advancements will shape the future of corrections?
3. What new trends in juvenile justice, correctional populations, and employment practices will have an impact?
4. Why leadership and professionalism are essential to meet future challenges?

Close-up On Corrections

HOT NEW TECHNOLOGIES

Ground-Penetrating Radar

Prison administrators in California heard rumors of an impending inmate outbreak. The word was out that a handful of inmates had built a tunnel underneath the . . . institution and were planning to make a break for freedom. Special Technologies Laboratories (STL) was called in to investigate. A team . . . using a new technology called Ground Penetrating Radar (GPR) was able to locate the elusive tunnel.

Heartbeat Monitoring

The weakest security link in any prison has always been the sallyport, where trucks unload their supplies and trash and laundry are taken out of the facility. Over the years, inmates have hidden in loads of trash, old produce, laundry, any possible container that might be exiting the facility. Today . . . a new technology can detect the heartbeat of a person hidden in a vehicle. The Advanced Vehicle Notification System (AVIAN) . . . works by identifying the shock wave generated by the beating heart, which couples to any surface the body touches.

Smart Cards

Every time an inmate receives an aspirin for a headache, or buys toothpaste from the commissary, a prison clerk must record and file the transaction. Now comes the smart card, a plastic card embedded with a computer chip that will store all types of information about an inmate—movements, medical care, commissary purchases, treatment needs, meals eaten—any information at all.

Drug-Detection Devices

Time-consuming physical searches for drugs may become a thing of the past with ion mobility spectrometry. This noninvasive device detects trace amounts of narcotics in people, on clothing, or concealed in packages.

Body Alarms

This electronic alarm enables staff to summon assistance quickly to a particular area. It relies on a pager-sized pendant worn by the employee that, when activated by depressing a button, sends a radio signal to a locator. The central control computer then automatically broadcasts a radio message that an officer in a certain location needs assistance. The time lapse between alarm initiation and broadcast is no more than a few seconds.

Supervision and Management Automated Record Tracking (SMART)

A hand-held version of SMART will soon accompany community corrections officers into the field to allow real-time data entry and immediate access to case records. In addition to maintaining an offender's drug test results, treatment referrals, and violation reports, SMART can do anything from tracking offenders' community service to keeping tabs on their participation in vocational, educational, and employment programs.

(continued)

Close-up On Corrections

(CONTINUED)

Law Library Terminal

Gone are the days when inmates had to be transported to rooms full of thick legal books to meet the requirement of access to a law library. Now, in less than the size of a bulletin board, there is a new wall-mounted computer terminal that delivers required state and federal law data for inmate research at the touch of a finger. Best of all, the system works without need to connect with the Internet, and correctional staff can electronically track each inmate's use, in defense against allegations of restricted access.

Sources: Compiled from Gabrielle deGroot, "Hot New Technologies," *Corrections Today*, Vol. 59, No. 4, July 1997, pp. 60-61; "Ionscan Drug Detection Devices Will Be Installed in New California Prison," *Corrections Digest*, Vol. 26, No. 7, February 17,1995, Vol. 66, No. 4, p. 7; Jay Lowe, "Technology Enhances Public Safety in Texas," *Corrections Today*, July 2004, p. 71; Frank Lu and Lawrence Wolfe, "Technology that Works: An Overview of the Supervision and Management Automated Record Tracking (SMART) Application," *Corrections Today*, July 2004, p. 80; and *Correctional News*, "Product of the Month," July/August, 2004, p. 50.

Privatization. One of the ways that government may well be looking to save money is through privatization. As described previously in this chapter, it is not at all clear that "for-profit" prisons actually operate at a substantial cost savings—especially when the quality of services and hidden costs are taken into account. But regardless of the evidence supporting or refuting their costs or capabilities, private providers now have established a firm foothold in corrections. The momentum that they have sparked is expected to continue to grow, and pressure on government agencies to operate more efficiently and engage in more public/private partnerships can be expected to further enhance the prospects for greater private involvement in corrections.

In fact, it is perhaps the "threat" more than the reality of privatization that will influence the future of correctional practices. To the extent that public employees believe that their job security is endangered by the potential of privatization, the stimulus may be provided for better services at lower cost in the public sector. As in business and industry, competition can provide a strong incentive for improved performance.

Objectivity in Decision Making. The expanded use of computers has made a substantial impact throughout the field, both directly and indirectly. In a wide variety of capacities, computers are now performing what previously had been very time-consuming and labor-intensive efforts. What is somewhat less apparent is how reliance on computers and other technological innovations has shaped decision making in a more quantifiable direction. No longer is the system as willing to accept individual judgments or personal opinions.

Rather, we have limited judicial discretion through *sentencing guidelines*, streamlined parole decision making through *prediction tables*, and in many jurisdictions, replaced discretionary parole with *mandatory supervised release*, based on the figures generated by good/gain time schedules. "Hard numbers" are more and more often replacing human judgments in the decision-making process at various points in the justice system. This transition not only has reduced the potential for abuse, disparity, and favoritism, but also has contributed to a false sense of security—a belief that data alone can direct human effort, while overlooking the fact that the figures themselves are inherently a product of human values.

Juvenile Justice Transitions. If there is one aspect of the system that still makes an attempt to cling to more personalized, discretionary decision making, it is juvenile justice. Despite the greater *due process protections* now afforded young offenders, the juvenile field has yet to abandon its emphasis on *parens patriae* and the medical model. That does not, however, mean that serious juvenile offenders are escaping the wrath of public consternation. Indeed, it appears that responses to juvenile law violators are splitting in opposite directions. On the one hand, hard-core, violent juvenile offenders increasingly can expect to be dealt with in a manner commensurate with the seriousness of their offenses— that is, through adult courts and more punitive sentencing.

At the same time, responses to the least-serious status offenders include options ranging from *removing* them from secure institutions, to *diverting* them out of the system, to *decriminalizing* their behavior completely. Again, as in the adult system, it is not simply benevolence that is driving such changes, but also the necessity for efficiency and cost-effectiveness in the face of increasing workloads without accompanying resource allocations. Dealing with status offenders outside the official juvenile justice system meets such objectives; however, it will be essential to assure that appropriate services are provided to them through alternative avenues. Otherwise, they risk becoming the youthful equivalent of the deinstitutionalization of mental health—in which case the egalitarian objectives of reformers were never fulfilled in practice or provided for in terms of funding.

Regardless of the nature of their offenses, there is little doubt that the most optimistic approaches for juveniles are those that target early intervention. In that regard, a national panel of experts stated emphatically that in responding to youthful offenders:

- *It is never too early*. Preventive interventions for young children at risk of becoming serious or violent juvenile offenders are effective and should be implemented at an early age.

- *It is never too late*. Interventions and sanctions for known serious or violent juvenile offenders can reduce their risk of reoffending.[82]

Changing Correctional Populations. Society's reaction to the needs of special groups within the larger population can be expected to continue to shape responsiveness to the changing nature of correctional populations. Corrections will be especially challenged to meet the needs of increasing numbers of female offenders, along with those who have AIDS or are physically impaired or elderly. In fact, the geriatric inmates described in the next "Close-up On Corrections" will become increasingly prevalent, and costly, in the future.

Close-up On Corrections

GERIATRIC INMATES

- Richard McGuire, sixty-six, shuffles slowly among the throng of younger inmates. . . . Unlike them, he's a frail old man who lacks the stamina to stand in line at the commissary . . . his head hangs low, and his breathing is labored. . . . [He] spends most of his day lying on the narrow cot in his cell or waiting for his turn on the dialysis unit in the prison infirmary.

- Sixty-five-year-old Herbert Miller also spends most of the day huddled in his cell, a small radio pressed to his ear . . . blind, he [is confined to] a wheelchair. Sometimes younger inmates wheel him out to the exercise yard and park him in the sun.

Like the first wrinkles in an aging face, signs that our nation's prison population is growing older are beginning to appear . . . in a correctional system that is not equipped to be a nursing home.

Source: Jennifer Reid Holman, "Prison Care," *Modern Maturity*, March/April 1997, pp. 31-32.

Nor is there expected to be any decline in the already sizable numbers of correctional clients suffering from alcohol/drug addictions or mental disorders. To what extent these populations will receive treatment consideration will depend on overall economic conditions, as well as the willingness of taxpayers to support such efforts.

Personnel Transitions. It is not, however, only those on the inside of the bars who have been undergoing change. In recent years, the correctional labor force itself has experienced a significant transition. The white-male-dominated tradition of correctional employment is being dismantled by a *more diverse and better-educated* workforce that represents *new generations* of employees—whose values, priorities, attitudes, and work habits differ substantially from their predecessors. This "new breed" of workers is both introducing new perspectives on the job and creating new challenges. Today's workers are demanding a voice in making decisions and establishing policies that affect them.

Moreover, it is today's operational personnel who represent tomorrow's managers and administrators. Line employees who never have experienced anything but passively responding to orders coming down the chain-of-command do not make very likely candidates for displaying the creative leadership skills that will be essential to guide corrections into the twenty-first century.

Professionalism. From the agency director to the entry-level officer, it is the dedication and commitment of qualified employees that enables corrections to function in the face of inadequate resources, insufficient public support, and involuntary clientele. The ability of corrections to recruit and retain the quality of personnel needed to continue to do so in the upcoming century largely will depend on how well it encompasses higher education, encourages broad-based participation, decentralizes decision making, empowers employees, and promotes ongoing career development—in other words, how much emphasis is placed on professionalizing its most valuable asset.[83]

Additionally, if corrections begins to embark on the pre-service approach to entry-level training, a significant step will be taken toward obtaining recognition as a profession (as well as achieving substantial cost reductions). However, the wrong person trained is still the wrong person for the job. Serious attention to valid, reliable, and job-related selection screening, therefore, will become of even greater importance.

Further strides toward professionalism also can be expected from the *national certification* initiative undertaken by the American Correctional Association. In terms of its emphasis on testing, ethics, and continuing education, ACA's correctional certification standards in many ways emulate the credentialing procedures of traditional professions.[84] But it is also essential to note that professionalism is not a "quick fix" for organizational problems, personnel shortcomings, or political impediments:

> Professionalism is not a commodity that can be issued like a uniform, provided like a training program, awarded like a promotion, or decreed like a policy. It is not a weapon to be wielded defensively in response to public apprehensions. It cannot be mandated, forced, or shouted into practice. To the contrary, it is a calling rather than a job. . . . not something with which to comply, but rather, to be committed to.[85]

Visionary Leadership. It is difficult to imagine a point in time when there has been a greater need for farsighted, visionary leadership within the correctional conglomerate. Late in the twentieth century, national surveys already had begun to identify *institutional crowding, staff and funding shortages*, and resulting *workload increases* as the key problems that corrections was anticipated to face in the "near future."[86] Well, the "near future" is now upon us, and overcrowding and understaffing continue to plague the correctional conglomerate, to the point that they have been cited as "underlying virtually every departmental problem in corrections today."[87] Moreover, while the pressure of institutional numbers may ease somewhat in the coming years, the same is not as likely to be true for probation and parole caseloads.

Maximizing the quality of personnel cannot be expected to miraculously resolve these difficult challenges. But it can contribute considerably toward minimizing their negative impact. Notice that each of these issues represents a *quantifiable* aspect of correctional work. As focus shifts more and more in that direction, it is easy to lose sight of the fact that people are changed by other people. They are not changed for the better by a "program" or a "system," although they can be changed for the worse by being regimented and dehumanized. Overall, the system is much less important than the people who breathe life into it.

As the issue of grooming future leadership illustrates, before it is feasible to deal effectively with the future, it is essential to address the here-and-now.

Yet, focusing exclusively on the present also perpetuates a continuously reactive cycle. To use an analogy, the first priority for a drowning person obviously is being rescued. Only by learning how to swim, however, will the potential for further near misses be avoided. The field of corrections may not yet be "drowning." But as noted at the beginning of this chapter, it is rowing upstream amid strong currents. In such a situation, there are three choices: give up, row harder, or reduce the strength of the currents.

Shaping the Future. Most of today's correctional administrators are undoubtedly rowing harder. For the most part they are making vigorous efforts to cope with limited resources and a dynamic legal, social, and political environment. But as at least one self-critic of correctional leadership has observed, too much time is still spent complaining about how little control we have over our own destiny and not enough time actively planning to shape that destiny: "It is time for us not merely to respond to issues which others put before us, but rather, to identify those issues and be persuasive as to how they should be addressed and resolved." [88]

Only to the extent that vigorous efforts today are combined with a far-reaching vision of tomorrow can we hope to reduce the strength and impact of changing currents for our successors. As reflected throughout this text, in many respects, efforts are being made by forward-thinking leaders to plant the seeds of change, but:

> Whether they will continue to thrive and grow in the shifting sands of personal emotion, outspoken opinion, and politically driven policies that have tended to influence the correctional environment remains to be seen. What is not so uncertain is the impact that the correctional conglomerate will continue to exercise on the lives of millions of clients under its care, custody, and control.[89]

In the long run, future generations will judge us not by what obstacles we have or have not faced today, but rather, by what opportunities we have or have not seized today to shape tomorrow's destiny. For destiny is not a result of chance, but a reflection of choice.

Summary

Among the forces that have affected corrections in recent years, accreditation and privatization have been among the most influential. In an effort directed toward voluntarily improvement, agencies increasingly are pursuing accreditation by meeting national standards. Privatization is a much more controversial issue. While private enterprises have long been involved in corrections, the nature of their involvement has been changing dramatically in recent years, particularly in terms of contracting the full operation of entire correctional facilities. Strong sentiments exist on both sides, and reservations have been expressed about whether the administration of correctional institutions is an appropriate role for private industry.

In the future, corrections will be continue to be affected by everything from the national economy and prevailing public opinion to drug-related crime and the aging of prison populations. Resulting burdens on both correctional facilities and community caseloads necessitate doing more with less.

Today's "new breed" of correctional officers reflects more cultural diversity, demands more organizational participation, and represents tomorrow's managers. Courtesy of the Miami-Dade County Department of Corrections and Rehabilitation, Miami, Florida.

In many respects, the justice model does not appear to be functioning much more effectively than its predecessors. However, it also must be acknowledged that like earlier models, its implementation was hampered by lack of proper foresight, evaluation research, and resource allocation. With more sophisticated empirical studies being conducted today, the potential exists to convert to evidence-based decision making. However, it remains to be seen whether such objectivity will prevail in the politically driven environment which historically has characterized corrections.

Among the trends that are expected to continue to exert an impact on the correctional conglomerate are intermediate-sentencing alternatives, restorative justice, more pragmatic treatment, regionalization of jails, and direct supervision/unit management strategies. Increasingly sophisticated electronic devices, workload classification, and objectivity also can be expected to characterize the future—particularly as pressures continue to mount for greater efficiency, productivity, and cost savings.

The most significant key to the quality of future correctional services, however, will be the quality of future personnel. Much of the capability of tomorrow's leaders will depend on the extent to which today's personnel pursue professionalization through greater involvement with higher education, correctional certification, employee empowerment, and similar advancements toward professional identity.

As in all endeavors, effectively accommodating the future requires both a current commitment toward immediate improvements and the visionary leadership necessary to proactively influence forces on the distant horizon. Shaping the future destiny of the correctional conglomerate is a hefty challenge. It is a lot to expect. It is why corrections is at the same time both fascinating and frustrating.

Endnotes

1.   Helen G. Corrothers, "Facing Future Challenges," *Corrections Today*, Vol. 54, No. 7, October 1992, p. 62.

2.   Reginald A. Wilkinson, testimony provided to the National Council on Crime and Delinquency's Conference on "Reducing Crime in America: The Agenda for the 21st Century," December 5, 1997, quoting Dr. Kenneth Moritsugu.

3.   Camille Graham Camp, ed., *The 2002 Corrections Yearbook: Adult Corrections*, Middletown, Connecticut: Criminal Justice Institute, 2003, p. 90.

4.   *1989 Directory of Adult and Juvenile Correctional Departments, Institutions, Agencies, and Probation and Parole Authorities*, Lanham, Maryland: American Correctional Association, 1990, p. 596.

5.   M. Wayne Huggins and Charles J. Kehoe, "Accreditation Benefits Nation's Jails, Juvenile Detention Centers," *Corrections Today*, Vol. 54, No. 3, May 1992, p. 42.

6.   Rod Miller, "Standards and the Courts: An Evolving Relationship," *Corrections Today*, Vol. 54, No. 3, May 1992, p. 60.

7.   Kenneth McGinnis, "Impact of 'Get Tough' Policies on Community Corrections," *Corrections Management Quarterly*, Vol. 2, No. 3, Summer 1998, pp. 70-78.

8.   For a thorough examination of both sides of this issue, *see* Kenneth A. Ray and Kathy O'Meara-Wyman, "Privatizing and Regionalizing Local Corrections: Some Issues for Local Jurisdictions to Consider," *Corrections Today*, Vol. 62, No. 6, October 2000, pp. 116-120.

9.   However, the measure was defeated in 1998. James Turpin and Donna Lyons, "Criminal Justice Legislation," *Corrections Compendium*, Vol. 24, No. 2, February 1999, p. 3.

10. "Top Two's Revenues Grow," *Prison Privatisation [sic] Report International*, November 1996, p. 3.

11. James McNair, "Wackenhut Corrections: Prisons, Profits, and Problems," *The Herald*, Miami, Florida: April 16, 2000, E-1.

12. "Private Prisons Feel the Financial Crunch," *American Police Beat*, May 2001, p. 53.

13. For example, Corrections Corporation of America was trading for $39.13 on July 13, 2004. (After reaching a high of $142 in 1999, it dropped 66 percent in the subsequent five years). Wackenhut Corrections was bought out at $33 a share in May, 2002 by GEO Corporation Group.

14. William C. Collins, *Privately Operated Speculative Prisons and Public Safety: A Discussion of Issues*, Washington, D.C.: U.S. Department of Justice, n.d., p. 3.

15. "Web Site Connects Jail-bed Renters with Sellers," *Correctional News*, July/August 2004, p. 45.

16. Eric Schlosser, "The Prison-Industrial Complex," *The Atlantic Monthly*, December 1998, p. 61.

17. "Private Prisons Feel the Financial Crunch," *American Police Beat*, May 2001, p. 53.

18. Schlosser, "The Prison-Industrial Complex," p. 57.

19. *Ibid.*, p. 54.

20. *Ibid.*, p. 60; *see also* "CCA Wants More People in Prison," *Correctional News*, March/April 2001, p. 8.

21. T. Don Hutto, "Corrections Partnership: The Public and Private Sectors Work Together," *Corrections Today*, Vol. 50, No. 6, October 1988, p. 20.

22. *Ibid.*

23. Michael A. Kroll "Prisons Cannot Rehabilitate," in Bonnie Szumski, ed., *America's Prisons*, 4th ed., St. Paul, Minnesota: Greenhaven Press, 1985, p. 26.

24. James D. Henderson, "Private Sector Management: Promoting Efficiency and Cost-Effectiveness," *Corrections Today*, Vol. 50, No. 6, October 1988, p. 100.

25. Allen L. Patrick, "Private Sector: Profit Motive vs. Quality," *Corrections Today*, Vol. 48, No. 2, April 1986, p. 68.

26. Hutto, "Corrections Partnership," p. 22.

27. Patrick, "Private Sector," p. 74.

28. James Turpin, "1997 Supreme Court Decisions," *Corrections Today*, Vol. 59, No. 6, October 1997, p. 19.

29. Chadwick L. Shook and Robert T. Sigler, *Constitutional Issues in Correctional Administration*, Durham, North Carolina: Carolina Academic Press, 2000, p. 102, citing *Richardson v. McKnight*, 521 U.S. 399 (1997).

30. Stanley E. Adelman, "Supreme Court Rules on Potential Liabilities of Private Corrections," *Corrections Today*, Vol. 64, No. 4, July 2002, p. 28. *See also* Alexander M. Holsinger and Tom "Tad" Hughes, "*Correctional Services Corporation v. Malesko*: Boss, 'They Can't Hurt You Now,'" *Criminal Justice Police Review*, Vol. 14, No. 4, December 2003, pp. 451-463.

31. Samuel F. Saxton, "Contracting for Services: Different Facilities, Different Needs," *Corrections Today*, Vol. 50, No. 6, October 1988, p.18.

32. Michael Gilbert, "Ethical Considerations About Privatization, Correctional Practice, and the Role of Government," Paper presented at the Academy of Criminal Justice Sciences, Pittsburgh, Pennsylvania, March 1992, p. 112.

33. "Private Jail Controversy in Washington State Causes Problems," *Correctional News*, March/April 2001, p. 1.

34. Michael J. Mahoney, "Prisons for Profit: Should Corrections Make a Buck?," *Corrections Today*, Vol. 50, No. 6, October 1988, p. 107.

35. *Ibid.*, p. 107.

36. Charles W. Thomas and Charles H. Logan, "The Development, Present Status, and Future Potential of Correctional Privatization in America," in Gary W. Bowman, Simon Hakim, and Paul Seidenstat, eds., *Privatizing Correctional Institutions*, New Brunswick, New Jersey: Transaction Publishers, 1993, p. 223.

37. *Ibid.*

38. Saxton, "Contracting for Services," p. 17.

39. Charles H. Logan and Bill W. McGriff, *Comparing Costs of Public and Private Prisons: A Case Study*, Washington, D.C.: U.S. Department of Justice, 1989, p. 7. *See also* Robert W. Poole, Jr., "Privately Operated Prisons Are Economical," in Szumski, *America's Prisons*, pp. 123-126.

40. Thomas and Logan, "The Development, Present Status, and Future Potential of Correctional Privatization in America," p. 231.

41. U.S. General Accounting Office. *Private and Public Prisons: Studies Comparing Operational Costs and/or Quality of Service*, Washington, D.C.: U.S. General Accounting Office, 1996, p. 13.

42. Dale K. Sechrest and David Shichor, "Private Jails: Locking Down the Issues," *American Jails*, March/April 1997, p.12.

43. *Ibid.*, p. 14.

44. "TDCJ Board Chairman Says He's Fed Up with Private Prisons after Escapes, Riots," *Corrections Digest*, Vol. 27, No. 36, September 6,1996, p.1. *See also* "Laws Lag Behind Booming Private Prison Industry," *Corrections Digest*, Vol. 27, No. 46, November 15, 1996, pp. 1-2.

45. *See*, for example, Scott Camp and Gerald Gaes, *Private Prisons in the U.S., 1999: An Assessment of Growth, Performance, Custody Standards, and Training Requirements*, Washington, D.C.: U.S. Bureau of Prisons, 2000.

46. Robert B. Levinson, "Privatization: The Jury Is Still Out," *Corrections Today*, Vol. 50, No. 6, October 1988, p. 6.

47. Office of National Drug Control Policy, *The Economic Costs of Drug Abuse in the U.S.*, Washington, D.C.: U.S. Department of Justice, Office of National Drug Control Policy, 2001.

48. "NIJ Survey of Wardens and State Commissioners of Corrections," *National Institute of Justice: Update*, Washington, D.C.: U.S. Department of Justice, 1995, p. 2.

49. Joey R. Weedon, "The Foundation of Re-entry," *Corrections Today*, Vol. 66, No. 2, April 2004, p. 6.

50. Robert Gangi, Jr., cited in "The Crime of Black Imprisonment," *Los Angeles Times*, April 22, 1990.

51. Craig Reinarman and Harry G. Levine, *Crack in America: Demon Drugs in America*, Berkeley, California, University of California Press, 1997, p. 334.

52. Andrew D. Leipold, "The War on Drugs and the Puzzle of Deterrence," *Journal of Gender, Race, and Justice*, Spring/Summer 2002, retrieved from http://web.lexis-nexis, p. 12.

53. Leonard A. Marowitz, *Why Did the Crime Rate Decrease through 1999? (And Why Might It Decrease or Increase in 2000 and Beyond?)*: A Literature Review and Critical Analysis, Sacramento, California: California Department of Justice, 2000. *See also* Lisa Stoltzenberg and Stewart J. D'Alessio, "Three Strikes and You're Out: The Impact of California's New Mandatory Sentencing Law on Serious Crime Rates," *Crime and Delinquency*, Vol. 43, No. 4, 1997, pp. 457-469.

54. "A Crowding Case Study," *Corrections Alert*, August 21, 1995, p. 2, quoting Vincent Schiraldi.

55. *The Impact of Three Strikes and You're Out Laws: What Have We Learned?*, Washington, D.C.: The Campaign for an Effective Crime Policy, 1996. *See also* John Clark, James Austin, and D. Alan Henry, "'Three Strikes and You're Out': A Review of State Legislation," *NIJ Research In Brief*, September 1997.

56. Kirby D. Behre and A. Jeff Ifrah, "You Be the Judge: The Success of Fifteen Years of Sentencing under the United States Sentencing Guidelines," *American Criminal Law Review*, Vol. 40, No. 1, Winter 2003, p. 6.

57. Matthew B. Robinson, "The Mouse Who Would Rule the World: How American Criminal Justice Reflects the Themes of Disneyization," *Journal of Criminal Justice and Popular Culture*, Vol. 10, No. 1, 2003, p. 70.

58. "New Poll Shows Surprisingly Forgiving Attitude toward Crime and Punishment: Most Americans Don't Want to Throw Away the Key," July 19, 2001, available at www.aclu.org/features/f071901a.html.

59. *Ibid.*

60. Christopher A. Innes, "Recent Public Opinion in the U.S. toward Punishment and Corrections," *The Prison Journal*, Vol. 73, No. 2, June 1993, pp. 220.

61. Francis T. Cullen, *et al.*, "Public Support for Correctional Rehabilitation in America: Change or Consistency?," in Julian V. Roberts and Mike Hough, eds., *Changing Attitudes to Punishment: Public Opinion, Crime and Justice*, Devon, England: Willan Publishing, 2002, p. 143.

62. Brandon K. Applegate *et al.*, "The Multifunction Jail: Policy Makers' Views of the Goals of Local Incarceration," *Criminal Justice Policy Review*, Vol. 14, No. 2, June 2003, p. 155.

63. Francis T. Cullen *et al.*, "Public Support for Correctional Rehabilitation in America," p. 143.

64. Ryan S. King and Marc Mauer, *State Sentencing and Corrections Policy in an Era of Fiscal Restraint*, Washington, D.C., 2002, p. 3.

65. Barry J. Nidorf, "Surviving in a 'Lock Them Up' Era," *Federal Probation*, Vol. 60, No. 3, March 1996, p. 4.

66. Richard P. Seiter, "Managing Within Political Comfort Zones: An Interview with Allen Ault," *Corrections Management Quarterly*, Vol. 1, No. 1, Winter 1997, p. 74.

67. Mike DeWine, "Public Opinion and Corrections: A Need to Be Proactive," *Corrections Management Quarterly*, Vol. 1, No. 3, Summer 1997, p. 6.

68. Doris Layton MacKenzie, "Evidence-based Corrections: Identifying What Works," *Crime and Delinquency*, Vol. 46, No. 4, October 2000, p. 463.

69. Merely because a program does not appear on the "what works" list does not necessarily mean that it is ineffective. Nor does absence from the "what does not work" list necessarily indicate the reverse, since the researcher who compiled these lists used relatively high standards of methodological rigor before incorporating individual studies into the overall assessment.

70. Nidorf, "Surviving in a 'Lock Them Up' Era," p. 10.

71. It should be noted that these results reflect only the specific initiatives listed, and do not, for instance, reflect whether they might be more effective when combined with various other forms of treatment.

72. Charles B. DeWitt, "Assessing Criminal Justice Needs," *National Institute of Justice: Research in Brief*, Washington, D.C.: U.S. Department of Justice, 1992, p. 3.

73. Joan Petersilia, "Probation in the United States: Practices and Challenges," *NIJ Journal*, September 1997, p. 5.

74. Nidorf, "Surviving in a 'Lock Them Up' Era," p. 8.

75. Paul McCold, "Restorative Justice Handbook," *Corrections Compendium*, Vol. 23, No. 12, December 1998, p. 1.

76. Gordon Bazemore and Mark Umbreit, "Rethinking the Sanctioning Function in Juvenile Court: Retributive or Restorative Responses to Youth Crime," *Crime and Delinquency*, Vol. 41, No. 3, July 1995, p. 305. *See also* Gordon Bazemore and Jeanne B. Stinchcomb, "Promoting Successful Re-entry through Service and Restorative Justice: Theory and Practice for a Civic Engagement Model of Community Reintegration," *Federal Probation*, Vol. 68, No. 2, 2004, pp. 14-24.

77. Tessa West, "Prisons of Promise," *Journal of Correctional Training*, Winter 1996, p. 25.

78. Orville B. Pung, "Let's Abolish 'Probation' and 'Treatment,'" *Overcrowded Times*, April 1993, p. 3.

79. *See also* "A Directory of Programs that Work," *Corrections Today*, August 1996, pp. 124-136, and *Ideas that Work: Crime and Public Safety*, Annapolis, Maryland: NGA Publications, 1996.

80. Vincent Schiraldi and Judith Greene, "Public Opinion Shifts as States Re-examine Prison Policies in Face of Tightening Budgets," *On the Line*, May 2002, p. 1.

81. "Soaring Probation Caseloads Leave Agents, Experts Fearing a Breakdown," *Crime Control Digest*, March 28, 1997, p. 1, quoting Diego Cruz.

82. "Expert Panel Issues Report on Serious and Violent Juvenile Offenders," *OJJDP Fact Sheet*, Washington, D.C.: U.S. Department of Justice, 1997, p. 2.

83. *See* Jeanne B. Stinchcomb, "Making the Grade: Professionalizing the 21st Century Workforce through Higher Education Partnerships," *Corrections Today*, Vol. 66, No. 5, August 2004.

84. Jeanne B. Stinchcomb, "Correctional Certification: Getting down from the Bandwagon and Leading the Band," *Corrections Now*, February 2004, p. 4.

85. Jeanne B. Stinchcomb, "Developing Correctional Officer Professionalism: A Work in Progress," *Corrections Compendium*, Vol. 25, No. 5, May 2000, pp. 4, 18.

86. "NIJ Survey of Police Chiefs and Sheriffs," *NIJ Update*, Washington, D.C.: U.S. Department of Justice, 1995, pp. 1-2, and DeWitt, "Assessing Criminal Justice Needs," p. 8.

87. "Assaults against Corrections Officers Rise in Illinois, Texas," *Corrections Digest*, August 16, 1996, p. 4, citing Steve Trossman.

88. Richard G. Kiekbusch, "Leadership Roles: How Are We Doing?" *American Jails*, Vol. 6, No. 5, November/December 1992, p. 6. *See also* "Gaining Influence: How Corrections Leaders Can Create Strong Roles in State Legislation," *The Corrections Professional*, Vol. 2, No. 14, April 4, 1997.

89. Stinchcomb, "Correctional Certification," p. 4.

ABOUT THE AUTHOR

Dr. Jeanne Stinchcomb is an associate professor of criminal justice at Florida Atlantic University. Previously, she has taught at Barry University, Florida International University, and Virginia Commonwealth University. Beyond academic appointments, her career embraces two decades of administrative experience on the staffs of federal, state, and local criminal justice agencies—ranging from the FBI in Washington, D.C., to the Miami-Dade Department of Corrections and Rehabilitation. Currently, she chairs the national Commission on Correctional Certification.

Over the past twenty-five years, she has also served as a consultant for numerous agencies, including the National Institute of Corrections, the American Correctional Association, and the Center for Innovative Public Policies. She is the 2002 recipient of the Peter Lejins Research Award, an award for nationally competitive research that has contributed significantly to the field of corrections. In addition to her two-volume publication on *Stress Management: Performing under Pressure*, Dr. Stinchcomb's research articles appear in such publications as *Justice Quarterly*, *Crime and Delinquency*, *Journal of Offender Rehabilitation*, *Criminal Justice Policy Review*, *American Journal of Criminal Justice*, *Corrections Today*, *Corrections Compendium*, and *American Jails*. She invites you to send any inquiries, comments, or feedback to her e-mail address: stinchco@fau.edu.

INDEX

Note: p = picture; f = figure.